Empirical Macroeconomics for Interdependent Economies

Supplemental Volume

Empirical Macroeconomics for Interdependent Economies

Supplemental Volume

RALPH C. BRYANT * DALE W. HENDERSON
GERALD HOLTHAM * PETER HOOPER
STEVEN A. SYMANSKY
EDITORS

THE BROOKINGS INSTITUTION
Washington, D.C.

1775 Massachusetts Avenue, N.W., Washington, D.C. 20036

Library of Congress Cataloging-in-Publication Data
Empirical macroeconomics for interdependent economies / Ralph C. Bryant . . . [et al.] editors.
p. cm.
Vol. 2: Supplemental volume.
Includes bibliographies and indexes.
ISBN 0-8157-1140-9 (v. 1).
ISBN 0-8157-1139-5 (pbk. : v. 2)
1. Economic policy—Mathematical models.
2. International economic relations—Mathematical models.
I. Bryant, Ralph C., 1938– . II. Brookings Institution.
HD75.5.E5 1988
339.5′0724—dc19 87-34156
CIP

9 8 7 6 5 4 3 2 1

THE BROOKINGS INSTITUTION is an independent organization devoted to nonpartisan research, education, and publication in economics, government, foreign policy, and the social sciences generally. Its principal purposes are to aid in the development of sound public policies and to promote public understanding of issues of national importance.

The Institution was founded on December 8, 1927, to merge the activities of the Institute for Government Research, founded in 1916, the Institute of Economics, founded in 1922, and the Robert Brookings Graduate School of Economics and Government, founded in 1924.

The Board of Trustees is responsible for the general administration of the Institution, while the immediate direction of the policies, program, and staff is vested in the President, assisted by an advisory committee of the officers and staff. The by-laws of the Institution state: "It is the function of the Trustees to make possible the conduct of scientific research, and publication, under the most favorable conditions, and to safeguard the independence of the research staff in the pursuit of their studies and in the publication of the results of such studies. It is not a part of their function to determine, control, or influence the conduct of particular investigations or the conclusions reached."

The President bears final responsibility for the decision to publish a manuscript as a Brookings book. In reaching his judgment on the competence, accuracy, and objectivity of each study, the President is advised by the director of the appropriate research program and weighs the views of a panel of expert outside readers who report to him in confidence on the quality of the work. Publication of a work signifies that it is deemed a competent treatment worthy of public consideration but does not imply endorsement of conclusions or recommendations.

The Institution maintains its position of neutrality on issues of public policy in order to safeguard the intellectual freedom of the staff. Hence interpretations or conclusions in Brookings publications should be understood to be solely those of the authors and should not be attributed to the Institution, to its trustees, officers, or other staff members, or to the organizations that support its research.

Contents

PART ONE

Design and Description of the Model Simulations

This supplemental volume contains background and reference materials to accompany the papers in the main volume. It has been designed with a spiral binding, enabling it to remain flat on a surface when opened, so that readers can readily consult its charts and tables simultaneously with their reading of the main volume.

The information here is more detailed than that in the main volume. Points of analysis and interpretation made in the main volume, however, are not repeated. It is assumed that users of this volume will read the chapters in the main volume.

After outlining the contents of this volume, these initial pages describe the research project and the participating models, discuss some important design issues that arose during the project, and summarize the instructions followed by model groups when preparing the simulations.

Part 2 of this volume then presents reference charts that compare the simulation results across models. A sequence of charts is provided for each simulation, beginning with the baseline (simulation A). Each chart plots the time paths of individual variables as generated by all twelve models (or by as many models as reported the variable in question). The initial letter of a chart's label indicates the simulation in which the results were generated; the number refers to the chart's position in the sequence of charts for that simulation. For example, chart D-5 shows the models' time paths for the short-term interest rate in the United States, the fifth chart in the series comparing the results for simulation D; chart F-10 shows the current account balance for all OECD countries other than the United States (the ROECD region), the tenth chart in the series for simulation F.

In addition to comparative charts, part 2 includes a table of summary statistics for each of the simulations B through H. For nine key variables and for each of the six years of the simulations, these tables show the mean values, standard deviations, and ranges (difference between the maximum and minimum) of the responses across the participating models. Each table for a simulation—for example, table B for simulation B—follows the charts for that simulation.

Part 3 of this volume presents standardized, detailed tables of the simulation results, presented model by model (and, for each model, simulation by simulation). These tables give the fullest account of the simulation results in the two volumes.[1]

Part 4 of this volume provides a listing of bibliographical references. After a few general references on empirical modeling in a multicountry context, the remaining references are organized by model group. Within the references for a given model group, the ordering is alphabetical.

Description of the Project and Participating Models

The editors held the first planning sessions for the project in the fall of 1984. As explained in chapter 1 of the main volume, our discussions were motivated by two goals. The dominant goal was to initiate an examination and discussion of the current state of empirical modeling of cross-border macroeconomic interactions among the major industrial economies. The second goal was to shed light on some issues of current policy concern. We sought to explore the implications of the mix of macroeconomic policies in the United States—an expansionary fiscal policy and a relatively tight monetary policy—for the U.S. economy itself, for the exchange value of the U.S. dollar, and for economic activity and inflation in the rest of the world.

Initial telephone calls were made and letters of inquiry were sent to prospective model groups and conference participants in January and February 1985. In mid-March, a first draft of "instructions" describing the prospective simulations was circulated to the model groups. Detailed reactions from these groups were then incorporated in the instructions. A revised set of instructions was mailed to the groups in mid-April.

Preliminary simulation results, written on computer magnetic tape, were sent to the editors in the months of July through September 1985. Computer processing of the results was carried out on the World Bank computer system by Solomon Goldfarb, under the supervision of Steven Symansky. For some model groups, several iterations of the results took place.

On October 4, 1985, a workshop was held at Brookings to discuss the preliminary simulation results. The main focus of the workshop was on materials that summarized and compared those results. Discussions at the workshop and immediately thereafter led to significant modifications in the design of the simulations. Accordingly, revised instructions were sent to the model groups in mid-October. A deadline of early December was specified for receipt of the revised simulation results.

1. As noted in chapter 1 of the main volume, the editors are prepared to supply, at cost, copies of a magnetic computer tape containing the simulation results shown in the tables of part 3. Unlike the tables, the tape contains unrounded data; it also contains the full quarterly and semiannual series for the models that have a quarterly or semiannual periodicity.

In early December the organizers sent the model groups preliminary versions of standardized tables, together with queries about aspects of the results that seemed problematic. Subsequent telephone conversations led to the correction of errors and eliminated misinterpretations. Before the Christmas holidays, the organizers mailed out, to model groups and authors of papers, a revised set of tables and a package of preliminary charts. Authors submitted first drafts of their papers by early February 1986. The conference itself was held on March 10–11, 1986.

Further corrections to the simulation results were made in April–May 1986. Revised papers from most authors were received in the summer and fall. The manuscript entered the copy-editing and production process in the fall of 1986.

A summary description of the twelve macroeconometric models that participated in the project is given in the following alphabetical listing. The models are identified in terms of their geographic coverage, their size, and other key features—for example, the treatment of expectations, the form of the linkage mechanism used in modeling trade flows, and the nature of the treatment of exchange rate determination.

Models with fewer than 25 equations per country or region are characterized here as "small." "Large" pertains to models with 200 or more (in one or two cases as many as 1,000) equations per country or region. The mnemonics on the left-hand side are used for summary reference to the models throughout this volume. Full references to the publications and documents about the models cited in the following footnotes appear in the bibliography in part 4 of this volume.

DRI: The DRI international model consists of three large country models for the United States, Japan, and Canada, plus a separate regional model for Europe that contains submodels for Germany, France, the United Kingdom, and Italy. Expectations are modeled adaptively.[2]

EEC: The COMPACT model, developed by the staff of the EC Commission, includes three small models of the United States, Japan, and the EC region, plus an abbreviated rest-of-world sector. The models for the United States and Japan are simplified versions of country sectors taken from the Japanese EPA model. Expectations are modeled adaptively. The model's trade linkage equations allocate a region's imports among the other regions in the model and computes its import prices as a weighted average of the export prices of the other regions. Capital flows and net external-asset positions are modeled in a modified portfolio adjustment framework.[3]

EPA: The World Econometric Model of the Japanese Economic Planning Agency, built and maintained in its Economic Research Institute, consists of nine medium-to-large country models for Japan, the United States, Germany, France, the United Kingdom, Italy, Canada, Australia, and South Korea, plus six smaller regional models covering the rest of the world. Expectations are modeled adaptively. Trade linkages are modeled along the lines developed by Samuelson and Kurihara.[4] Exchange rates can be treated as fixed or alternatively as floating under official management (with exchange rate bands and reserve-flow targets).[5]

LINK: Project LINK contains seventy-nine large individual-country and regional models covering in principle the entire world economy. The U.S. model is an earlier version of the U.S. model developed by Wharton Econometric Associates. Models for most of the other industrial countries and a number of developing countries were developed and are maintained separately by various organizations in the individual countries. Trade-matrix and exchange rate linkages are superimposed on the system at the Project LINK headquarters at the University of Pennsylvania.[6] The LINK system was originally developed for the Bretton Woods adjustable-peg system of exchange rates; subsequent modifications, using purchasing-power-parity assumptions or official reaction functions, allow

2. An introduction to the DRI model may be found in R. Brinner, "The 1985 DRI Model: Overview." A memorandum by Nigel Gault, "Notes on the DRI Simulations," was prepared for the March 1986 conference.

3. The model is discussed in A. Dramais, "COMPACT—Prototype of a Macro Model for the European Community in the World Economy." The modeling of capital flows and net external assets follows the approach suggested by L. Klein and K. Marwah, "A Model of Foreign Exchange Markets: Endogenizing Capital Flows and Exchange Rates."

4. See L. Samuelson and E. Kurihara, "OECD Trade Linkage Methods Applied to the EPA World Econometric Model"; and A. Amano and others, "Trade Linkage Sub-Models in the EPA World Economic Model."

5. The EPA model is unusually well documented. For an introduction, see Economic Planning Agency, World Economic Model Group, "The EPA World Economic Model: An Overview."

6. For a description of the trade-linkage system, see L. R. Klein and A. van Peetersson, "Forecasting World Trade within Project LINK."

for floating exchange rates.[7] In each of the individual models of LINK, expectations are treated adaptively.

LIVERPOOL: The Liverpool model, built and maintained by Patrick Minford and his associates at the University of Liverpool, includes seven small models for the United States, Japan, Germany, France, the United Kingdom, Italy, and Canada, plus trade linkages with several other countries and regions. The model assumes that markets clear continuously. It includes equations specified for the current account balance (rather than imports and exports separately); imports are thus determined indirectly, as a residual between total expenditures and expenditures on home-produced goods. Expectations are forward-looking and model-consistent ("rational expectations"). In determining exchange rates, the model imposes a real interest parity condition on real exchange rates.[8]

MCM: The Multicountry Model developed and maintained by the staff of the U.S. Federal Reserve Board consists of five large single-country models for the United States, Canada, Japan, Germany, and the United Kingdom, plus an abbreviated rest-of-world sector. Imports are determined bilaterally, as a function of income and relative prices (including competitors' prices). Exchange rates can be modeled exogenously or endogenously (in the latter case through an inverted capital-account portfolio-balance equation). Expectations are modeled adaptively.[9]

MINIMOD: The MINIMOD model, constructed and maintained by Richard Haas and Paul Masson at the International Monetary Fund, is a small two-region model, with its regions the United States and an aggregation of other OECD countries (representative of Japan, Canada, Germany, and the United Kingdom). Many of the model's parameters were obtained from partial-equilibrium simulations using a version of the Federal Reserve MCM.[10] Exchange rates are determined using an open interest-parity condition. A rational expectations version of the model (with forward-looking, model-consistent expectations of exchange rates, inflation rates, and long-term interest rates) was used for the simulations produced for this conference.[11]

MSG: The MSG (McKibbin-Sachs Global) model—also sometimes identified with the acronym MCKIBB—was developed by Warwick McKibbin and Jeffrey Sachs at Harvard University. It includes five small country and regional models of the United States, Japan, other OECD countries as a single region, OPEC countries, and other developing countries. The model, rather than being estimated independently, takes most of its parameters from other models or from the research literature; the model is calibrated to 1983 trade shares and asset stocks. Imports are determined bilaterally by income and relative prices. Expectations in asset markets are forward-looking and model-consistent, so that long-term interest rates and expected exchange rates are conditioned on the model's solution for the future paths of interest rates and exchange rates. The model specifies asset demand functions in a general portfolio-balance fashion, but the parameter values imposed on the functions make the model behave almost as if assets denominated in different currencies were perfect substitutes.[12]

OECD: The INTERLINK model system, constructed and maintained by the Economics and Statistics Department of the OECD, consists of models for each of twenty-three OECD countries, plus abbreviated trade sectors for each of six non-OECD regions. The models for major OECD countries are large, while those for smaller countries are medium in scale (roughly 100 equations). Trade linkages are modeled with a modified version of the Samuelson-Kurihara method. Exchange rates are determined by a

7. P. Pauly and C. Petersen, "Exchange Rate Responses in the LINK System."

8. For an initial reference, see P. Minford and others, "The Liverpool Macroeconomic Model of the United Kingdom."

9. The basic volume describing the MCM model is G. Stevens and others, *The U.S. Economy in an International World: A Multicountry Model.* An updated description is given in H. J. Edison, J. R. Marquez, and R. W. Tryon, "The Structure and Properties of the FRB Multicountry Model."

10. The technique is described in P. R. Masson, "Deriving Small Models from Large Models," annex B in volume 1 of this publication.

11. Haas and Masson have presented results for MINIMOD with and without a treatment of expectations that is forward-looking and model-consistent. For a comparison of the results from both versions, see R. D. Haas and P. R. Masson, "MINIMOD: Specification and Simulation Results." The results reported in this publication always pertain to the version with rational expectations (MINIMODR).

12. For an initial reference on the model, see W. McKibbin and J. Sachs, "Comparing the Global Performance of Alternative Exchange Arrangements."

closed system of equations (FINLINK) based on a portfolio-balance theory of net capital flows. Expectations are modeled adaptively; they depend not only on the current value and past values of the variable in question but also on current and past values of other variables.[13]

TAYLOR: This model, developed and maintained by John Taylor and associates at Stanford University, contains small models for each of six countries: the United States, Japan, Germany, France, the United Kingdom, Canada, and Italy. Imports are determined as functions of home income and relative prices; exports are determined as functions of relative prices and trade-weighted averages of foreign outputs. The model enforces an open interest-parity condition that assumes perfect substitutability between assets denominated in different currencies. Expectations about long-term interest rates and exchange rates are forward-looking and model-consistent.[14]

VAR: The Minneapolis World VAR model is the work of Robert Litterman and Christopher Sims at the University of Minnesota and the Federal Reserve Bank of Minneapolis. It is a vector autoregression of three small regional blocks (fifteen endogenous variables each) for the United States, Japan, and Europe; Europe is represented by an aggregation of Germany, France, and the United Kingdom. The full model also includes several endogenous rest-of-world variables.[15]

WHARTON: The world model of Wharton Econometrics Forecasting Associates includes twenty-four medium-to-large models for each of twenty-three OECD countries plus South Africa, together with six regional models for developing countries and centrally planned economies. It uses a modified version of the Samuelson-Kurihara approach to trade linkages. Exchange rates are determined by long-run purchasing-power-parity relationships modified by current account imbalances. Capital flows and interactions between interest rates and exchange rates are not modeled in the version of the model used for the simulations reported here. Expectations are modeled adaptively.[16]

Six of the models—DRI, EPA, MCM, MINIMOD, VAR, and TAYLOR—have a quarterly periodicity. The OECD model is based on semiannual data. The remaining models—EEC, LINK, MSG, LIVERPOOL, and WHARTON—are annual.[17]

Most of the structural models have been more or less freely estimated. The exceptions are MINIMOD, MSG, and two of the countries in the EEC's COMPACT model; in those cases, most of the parameters were imposed, either having been derived from other estimated models or having been extracted from empirical results reported in the research literature.

Several of the models—DRI, EPA, LINK, MCM, OECD, and WHARTON—have been operating in some form for a long time. The EPA, MCM, and OECD models, however, have undergone major reestimation in recent years. Linked multicountry simulation with the DRI system is a fairly recent development. The EEC, LIVERPOOL, MSG, MINIMOD, TAYLOR, and Minneapolis VAR models are all relatively new, having been constructed in the early or middle 1980s.

As discussed by John Helliwell in chapter 6 of volume 1, the models can be usefully classified into four groups: the linkage of available national models (LINK and DRI), multicountry structural models that were constructed with cross-border trade or financial linkages explicitly in mind (EPA, MCM, OECD, EEC, and WHARTON), the linking of small national models with special attention to expectations and monetary linkages (LIVERPOOL, MINIMOD, MSG, and TAYLOR), and a nonstructural model-free approach to the estimation of international linkages (VAR).

13. For an overview of the INTERLINK system, see OECD, "The OECD International Linkage Model"; and G. E. Llewellyn, L. W. Samuelson, and S. J. Potter, *Economic Forecasting and Policy*. For the FINLINK modeling of exchange rates and net capital flows, see G. Holtham, "Multinational Modelling of Financial Linkages and Exchange Rates."

14. For an initial reference, see the appendix to chapter 7 of volume 1 of this publication. Taylor intends to publish a book about the model and its policy implications (tentative title: *International Monetary Rules: A Rational Expectations Econometric Evaluation*).

15. An abbreviated description of the model is given in the "Model Notes" section of C. A. Sims, "Identifying Policy Effects," annex A in volume 1 of this publication. Sims plans to make available a separate discussion paper documenting the model in greater detail.

16. This model is an extension of research carried out by Project LINK at the University of Pennsylvania. An earlier version of the model is described in K. Johnson, "Balance of Payments Disequilibrium and Equilibrating Exchange Rates in a World Econometric Model." The 1987 version (including some modifications made to the model subsequent to the version used for the simulations reported here) is discussed in J. Green and H. Howe, "Results from the WEFA World Model."

17. Readers requiring detailed information about the models should turn to publications or working documents prepared by the model groups themselves; part 4 of this volume contains numerous additional bibliographical references, organized by model group.

Issues of Project Design

Many issues about the design of the commonly specified simulations had to be resolved during the planning and implementation stages of the project. The most important of these issues are briefly identified here.

The draft suggestions initially sent to model groups in March 1985 proposed that the baseline simulation be forward-looking, covering the period 1985–90, rather than historical, covering, say, the period 1978–85. A forward-looking baseline lends itself better to experiments of topical policy concern. A significant advantage of a historical baseline, however, is that it can be founded on observed data.

The responses to the initial proposal varied. Two modeling groups strongly preferred to run the simulation experiments off a historical baseline. For one of those groups, the construction of a forward-looking baseline would have required a great deal of additional work. Three other groups strongly preferred a baseline projected into the future. For at least one of those groups, great effort would have been required to construct a historical baseline. Most of the remaining groups consulted did not express strong preferences one way or the other.

No choice of baseline was capable of reconciling all the competing criteria. In the event, a forward-looking baseline was adopted (further described below). Because of difficulties that would have been encountered in conforming to the commonly specified baseline, three of the model groups (EEC, LINK, and WHARTON) used forward-looking projections of their own as the baseline for their simulation results.

Many detailed choices had to be made about the specification of the baseline. Controversial choices were made in consultation with the model groups. Considerable discussion occurred about the importance of model groups conforming to all aspects of the common baseline. We have included some discussion of this comparability issue in chapter 3 of the main volume, and will therefore not repeat those points here.

With the wisdom of hindsight, a majority of the project organizers wish they had made stronger efforts to urge the model groups to conform to the common baseline—perhaps by specifying margins of tolerance for a wide range of key variables and then engaging in iterative consultations with individual model groups until each group's baseline paths fell within the specified margins. The organizers also wish that the specification of the common baseline had included certain additional variables, in particular current account balances and government budget deficits.

Specification of the monetary policy reaction functions of governments was another difficult issue of project design. The problematic question is, what variable should be treated as the "exogenous" instrument of monetary policy? Since individual nations tend to conduct monetary policy with different operating procedures, in principle one's answers should vary from country to country. Given the simulation experiments carried out for this project, the issue was thought to be especially pertinent for ROECD countries.

Views about the most appropriate assumption to use when specifying ROECD monetary policies evolved during the life of the research project. In the initial draft of the simulation instructions, it was proposed that an interest rate reaction function for ROECD monetary policies be used for most of the experiments. In other words, it was suggested that model groups identify a key short-term interest rate as the monetary policy instrument for each ROECD country and determine movements in that instrument in a policy reaction function. Deviations of the interest rate instrument from its baseline path would be tied to deviations of U.S. short-term interest rates from their baseline paths. ROECD monetary aggregates would be determined endogenously.[18] Two rationales underpinned this suggestion: it was felt that more comparable results could be obtained by standardizing the ROECD monetary reaction functions across the various model groups, and the proposed reaction function roughly approximated the "halfway-house" operating procedures actually used by a number of ROECD central banks.

Extensive discussions during the summer of 1985 and at the October 1985 workshop led to the abandonment of any variant of a "realistic" reaction function for ROECD monetary policies. A majority of project participants came to believe that, given the limited resources available to the project and the model groups, it would be preferable to focus only on the conventional polar assumptions of "constant monetary aggregate" or "constant short-term interest rate" (details are given below). Such polar assumptions were acknowledged to be less realistic;

18. Specifically, the interest rate instrument for Canada was to be tied, basis point for basis point, to the full deviation of the U.S. short-term interest rate from its baseline. For the other ROECD countries, it was suggested that deviations in the interest rate instrument from baseline should be set equal to one half of the deviation of the U.S. short-term interest rate from baseline.

but simulations conducted under those assumptions lend themselves better to clear interpretation and comparison across the models.

Definition of monetary policy shocks was a related design issue. It was eventually decided to specify monetary shocks as deviations of a key monetary aggregate from its baseline path (rather than, say, deviations of the central bank's discount rate or a key market interest rate from baseline). Even with this decision, a question remained whether the policy action should be phased in gradually over the course of several periods or, alternatively, whether the increment in the monetary aggregate should occur all at once as a lump sum. The initial draft instructions suggested that monetary policy actions take the form of a gradual raising of the key monetary aggregate above baseline over a period of *two* years, remaining thereafter at the same constant percentage increment above baseline. After the October 1985 workshop, this period was shortened to *one* year. No simulations were run in which the monetary action takes the form of an instantaneous lump-sum increase.[19]

Unfortunately, as explained in chapter 3 of the main volume, implementation of the phased-in monetary shocks was not fully uniform across the models, and this fact was not discovered until it was too late for corrections to be made. The discrepancies in implementation are discussed below in conjunction with the detailed descriptions of the monetary simulations.

One other major design issue was debated extensively during the life of the project. Was it desirable to specify certain simulation experiments in the form of "combination shocks"; for example, a reduction of U.S. government expenditures occurring simultaneously with an expansion of U.S. monetary policy? Alternatively, were combination shocks unnecessary because one could accurately infer the combination effects merely by adding or appropriately varying the separate effects of the individual shocks? The underlying issue here, as with the question whether all model groups should be required to conform closely to the baseline, is whether the behavior of the models is approximately linear.

At the outset of the project, the organizers suggested several shocks that represented combination policy packages. The preliminary results of several such experiments were reported at the October 1985 workshop. Those results, and most opinions voiced during the workshop, suggested that the behavior of most of the models is approximately linear, at least for the initial conditions and types of shocks under study in this project. That presumption was therefore accepted for the time being, and combination shocks were omitted from the list of "mandatory" simulations to be prepared for the March 1986 conference. See chapter 4 of the main volume for a further discussion of combination shocks.

19. As discussed in chapter 4 of the main volume, simulations in which the shock is phased in gradually over several periods pose greater difficulties than instantaneous lump-sum simulations if analysts use the simulation results to recover estimates of final-form coefficients.

Instructions to Modeling Groups and Detailed Description of Simulations

We now present an abridged account of the instructions followed by model groups in preparing the baselines and simulation results reported in this publication. This material will give the interested researcher full details of the guidelines under which the simulations were run.

Rationale for Common Simulations

From the outset of the project it was recognized that some prospective participants might not be able to run precisely identical simulations. To achieve the objectives of the project, however, it was essential that each modeling group conform as closely as possible to a common set of specifications. The basic goal was to compare simulations generated with a common set of assumptions, thereby facilitating the comparison and evaluation of the different models. It was therefore a condition of participating in the project that each model group make an effort in good faith to conform to the specifications in the agreed instructions.

Mandatory and Supplementary Simulations

The October 1985 workshop, as noted already, resulted in agreed modifications to the list of "mandatory" simulations, the outcome being seven simulations labeled B through H (with the baseline, simulation A, representing in effect an eighth).

The October workshop had revealed significant differences across the models in the baseline paths of many variables.[20] But in view of the difficulties of making agreed changes and given the tight deadlines that would have to be met to hold the March 1986 conference, it was decided not to require "mandatory" adjustments in the model groups' baselines. Model groups were urged, if feasible within the

20. Charts summarizing the differences in baselines across the models were distributed and discussed at the October 1985 workshop.

deadlines, to make adjustments to their baselines that would bring them closer to the central tendencies for all the participating models. Most model groups were unable to make any further adjustments.

Even though the October workshop resulted in the abandonment of "combination shocks" and some simulation experiments that had earlier been planned, modeling groups were still invited to supplement the mandatory simulations with additional simulations of their own choosing. For example, it was suggested that supplementary experiments might be designed to illustrate features of an individual model that were not well captured in the commonly specified simulations. It was also suggested that, if feasible, model groups might want to conduct their own "combination" simulations or otherwise try to test the linearity presumption for their particular model. With few exceptions, model groups did not have the time and resources to conduct supplementary experiments.

Time Period for Baseline Path and Simulations

The fourth quarter of 1984 (the second half of 1984 for models using semiannual data, and the year 1984 for annual models) was selected as the starting point for the baseline path. The fourth quarter of 1990 (second half of 1990, or year 1990) was chosen as the terminal period for the baseline and the simulation experiments. All "shocks"—defined as deviations from the baseline—were to begin in the first quarter of 1985 (first half of 1985, or year 1985).

Definition of Baseline Path

The proposed baseline paths for key variables were initially provided to model groups in a memorandum of April 17, 1985. The baseline for 1984 through the first half of 1986 was to be identical with the values for key variables (1984 estimated data and forecasts for 1985 and the first half of 1986) contained in the *OECD Economic Outlook* published in December 1984. For periods after the second half of 1986, model groups were asked to extrapolate growth paths through 1990, for the same key variables, at the growth rates forecasted by the OECD for the first half of 1986. The list of constant-price key variables was as follows:

Private consumption
Government consumption
Gross fixed investment
  Public
  Private residential
  Private nonresidential
Final domestic demand
Change in stockbuilding from previous period
Total domestic demand
Real GNP (or GDP)
Industrial production
Exports of goods and services
Imports of goods and services
Net exports of goods and services

In addition, the key variables included:

GNP (or GDP) at current market prices
GNP (or GDP) implicit price deflator
Consumer price index

All these key variables were specified for each of the seven largest OECD countries. Comparable figures were given for the smaller OECD countries to the extent that such figures were published in the December 1984 *Economic Outlook*.[21]

When the Economics and Statistics Department of the OECD published its projections, it assumed that exchange rates and interest rates would remain unchanged over the projection period. Accordingly, model groups were asked to hold baseline interest rates and exchange rates unchanged at the average values prevailing during the first quarter of 1985.

Commodity prices and energy prices other than oil, expressed in U.S. dollars, were to increase along the baseline at the same rate as U.S. consumer prices. Oil prices, expressed in U.S. dollars, were to be held constant in nominal terms until the end of 1986 and were then to be increased in line with U.S. consumer prices.

Model groups were given some latitude in how to define monetary aggregates for the baseline (since the different models incorporate a variety of definitions and treatments). The project organizers presumed that the key monetary aggregates in a model would grow roughly in line with the path for nominal GNP specified in the baseline instructions. For models in which changes in money growth had significant direct effects operating through channels other than interest rates, model groups were asked to constrain the baseline paths of key monetary aggregates (for example, by endogenizing residuals in money demand equations) to grow at the same rate as baseline nominal GNP.

The instructions asked model groups to constrain all the key variables identified above to the common baseline assumptions. They also requested, for instances in which a model required especially large add factors or other adjustments to track the baseline

21. The instructions memorandum of April 17, 1985, included duplicated copies of a number of tables from the December 1984 *Economic Outlook*; those tables are not reproduced here.

paths, that the model groups report the steps that had to be taken to force the model onto the baseline.

The instructions did not try to specify growth paths for every variable appearing in the various models. But model groups were asked to develop the remainder of the baseline for their model in a way that would be consistent with the common assumptions. For example, in the case of import and export prices and of other such nominal variables, model groups were asked to specify paths that would be consistent with the assumptions for domestic consumer prices and GNP deflators (such as growth in a country's export prices at the same rate as its GNP deflator).

When the instructions for preparing the baseline were issued in April 1985, it was recognized that some unanticipated problems might arise. Model groups were asked to construct their baselines and report any difficulties to the project organizers as promptly as possible.

An illustration of such problems occurred with the baseline assumptions for constant-price exports and imports of goods and services. For some countries, in particular Japan and the United States, an extrapolation for these variables of the OECD's forecast growth rates for the first half of 1986 implied trade and current account imbalances by the end of the baseline period that seemed implausibly large to some of the model groups. Accordingly, a revision in the instructions was made: model groups were asked to extrapolate the growth of real exports (goods and services) and real imports (goods and services), over the period from the third quarter of 1986 (or second half of 1986, or year 1986) through 1990, at the *average* annual growth rate for real exports and imports *combined* in the OECD's projection for the first half of 1986.

By the time of the October 1985 workshop, it had become clear that significant differences existed in the model groups' baselines. There was particular concern about the differences for the levels of interest rates and exchange rates, for government budget deficits, and for current account imbalances. It had also become clear, however, that the differences could not be reduced or eliminated without major further efforts on the part of the model groups. As noted above, the decision was made to encourage, but not require, adjustments—provided they could be made in time to meet the deadline for submitting material for the March 1986 conference—that would bring individual model baselines closer to the central tendencies summarized in the comparative charts passed out at the October 1985 workshop.

Prevailing Policy Stances for Simulations

To provide a meaningful comparison of simulation results across the participating models, it was important that model groups conform to common assumptions about prevailing policies or policy reaction functions. As noted above, significant differences of view existed among the model groups about which assumptions were most appropriate—in particular, which assumptions to make about monetary policies in the ROECD region. The guidelines reported here are those that were agreed to after the extensive discussion of the subject at the October 1985 workshop.

For fiscal policies, both in the United States and the ROECD, model groups held government purchases exogenous in real (not nominal) terms for all levels of government (for example, in the United States for federal, state, and local combined). Tax rates were also held exogenous. Tax revenues and transfer payments, however, were determined endogenously. In simulations B and C, the path for real U.S. government purchases falls below its baseline path; in simulation G, the paths for real government purchases in all ROECD countries simultaneously rise by comparable amounts above their baseline paths. Apart from those exceptions, real government purchases and tax rates, in both the United States and the ROECD, remained fixed on their baseline paths.

In the United States, monetary policy was defined in terms of an exogenous path for the M1 money stock (taken as a proxy for the policy decisions of the Federal Reserve). For simulations B, C, F, G, and H, the path for M1 in the United States was kept identical to its baseline path. In simulations D and E, the postulated shock produces a path for M1 that rises above its baseline path.

For each of the ROECD countries, monetary policies were to follow the polar case of an "unchanged money" path (for simulations B, D, F, and G) or alternatively the opposite polar case of an "unchanged interest rate" path (simulations C and E). In simulation H, it was to be assumed that the central banks of all ROECD countries simultaneously execute comparable expansionary actions causing the paths of key monetary aggregates in those countries to rise above their baseline paths.[22]

22. Insufficient time existed after the October 1985 workshop to try to standardize across models which monetary aggregate in particular countries should be taken as the "key" aggregate in simulation H proxying for monetary policy decisions. Model groups were asked, when submitting their results, to provide specific

Details of Simulation Experiments

Each of the simulations labeled B through G represents a "shock" assumed to be announced on January 1, 1985. Model groups were told to assume that before January 1985 the shock was unanticipated. After announcement, the shock was assumed to be regarded as credible; agents were thus assumed to expect the subsequent path of the shocked variable to follow the announced path. (See below for further discussion of the instructions for models with forward-looking expectations.)

Simulation B studies a reduction in U.S. government purchases with ROECD monetary aggregates unchanged from baseline. Model groups were asked to reduce real federal government purchases—proportionately in defense and nondefense spending—by an amount equal to 1 percent of baseline real GNP in the first quarter of 1985. This 1-percent-of-real-GNP reduction was then maintained during all subsequent periods through 1990 (the amount measured in constant dollars gradually increasing through the simulation period). The cut was hypothesized to be "permanent," that is, persisting beyond 1990 indefinitely. The M1 money stock in the United States and the "policy-proxy" monetary aggregate in all ROECD countries were assumed to remain unchanged from their baseline paths.

Simulation C studies a reduction in U.S. government purchases with ROECD short-term interest rates unchanged from baseline. The simulation assumed a path for U.S. federal government purchases identical to that in simulation B. For ROECD monetary policies, however, model groups were asked to assume that each ROECD central bank holds the short-term interest rate in its country unchanged from its baseline path. Therefore, the ROECD monetary aggregate treated as an exogenous policy proxy in simulation B was to be determined endogenously in this simulation. (In the United States, as for simulation B, model groups assumed that the Federal Reserve policy was quantity oriented, keeping U.S. M1 on its baseline path.)

Simulation D studies a U.S. monetary expansion with ROECD monetary aggregates unchanged from baseline. Model groups were asked to assume a temporary one-year raising of the growth rate, by 4 percentage points, of the U.S. M1 money stock during calendar 1985. After the end of 1985, the M1 growth rate was assumed to fall back to the rate along the baseline path.[23] To define the shock path, groups with quarterly models were asked to increase the level of U.S. M1 to be 0.5 percent higher than baseline during the first quarter of 1985, 1.5 percent higher during the second quarter, 2.5 percent higher during the third quarter, 3.5 percent higher during the fourth quarter, and 4.0 percent higher during the first quarter of 1986 and all subsequent quarters. Groups with semiannual models were asked to make the level of M1 1 percent higher than baseline during the first half of 1985, 3 percent higher during the second half of 1985, and 4 percent higher in the first half of 1986 and all subsequent periods. Groups with annual models were to make M1 2 percent higher than baseline during 1985 and 4 percent higher during 1986 and subsequent years.[24] For all countries other than the United States, model groups were to make the same "money unchanged" assumptions as used for simulation B.

Simulation E studies a U.S. monetary expansion with ROECD short-term interest rates unchanged. Model groups were asked to impose a path for the U.S. M1 money stock identical to that defined for simulation D. For ROECD monetary policies, however, model groups were asked to assume that ROECD short-term interest rates remain unchanged from baseline (assumptions identical to those used in simulation C).

Simulation F studies a nonpolicy, exogenous depreciation of the U.S. dollar. Unlike the shocks in all the other simulations, the shock in this case is postulated to occur because of a change in private-sector rather than government behavior. For those models containing capital-flow or exchange rate equations with imperfect substitutability among assets denominated in different currencies, simulation F presumes an unexpected, exogenous shift in asset preferences from dollar-denominated interest-bearing securities to a weighted average of interest-bearing securities denominated in the currencies of ROECD countries. For those models imposing the perfect-substitutes assumption through an interest-parity relationship, simulation F presumes an exog-

information about which aggregates in individual countries they had chosen as their policy proxies.

23. The preliminary monetary expansion simulations discussed at the October 1985 workshop assumed a raising of money growth rates by 2 percentage points during a period of two years. The definition of the monetary expansion shocks was changed to the version in the text in response to suggestions made at the workshop.

24. These percentages assumed that model groups measure their monetary aggregates as *average values* of the stock outstanding *during the period*. If model groups used a different form of measurement (for example, the stock outstanding at the end of a period), they were asked to make corresponding adjustments. As far as the project organizers know, all model groups measure monetary aggregates as average values during the period.

enous change in long-run expected equilibrium exchange rates (an expected long-run depreciation of the dollar against a weighted average of ROECD currencies). The shock is hypothesized to take place gradually and to cumulate over the course of the three years 1985–87.

For simulation F, model groups were asked to keep government budget policies and monetary policies (defined in terms of key monetary aggregates) unchanged from baseline paths, for both the United States and ROECD countries. These assumptions about policies were not meant to be likely policy responses to the posited shock; rather, the assumptions were made to facilitate diagnosis of the shock's consequences.

To make the simulation F experiment as comparable as possible across models, model groups were asked first to exogenize the dollar's exchange rates against ROECD currencies in a manner that left the baseline paths of variables unchanged. Having made that transformation, model groups were then asked to set exchange rates on new exogenous paths as follows. For all currencies other than the Canadian dollar, exchange rates against the U.S. dollar, expressed as units of foreign currency per dollar, were to be reduced relative to baseline rates at a 10 percent annual rate over the three years from the end of 1984 to the end of 1987; after 1987 the rates were to be held relative to baseline at the resulting lower levels. Model groups were asked to make the depreciation occur smoothly during the three-year period. For example, for quarterly models the exchange rates between the U.S. dollar and the deutsche mark, yen, French franc, and so on—expressed as foreign currency per U.S. dollar—were to decline from the fourth quarter of 1984 values by 2.60 percent per quarter to a level roughly 27 percent below baseline by the fourth quarter of 1987 (thereafter remaining below baseline by that percentage).[25] For the Canadian dollar, model groups were asked to reduce the exchange rate (Canadian dollars per U.S. dollar) by a 5 percent annual rate (1.27 percent per quarter), resulting in a level a little more than 14 percent below baseline by the fourth quarter of 1987.

As explained in chapter 3 of the main volume, the implementation of this simulation was not fully uniform across the models. The discrepancies, however, were not discovered early enough to be corrected.

25. Expressed the other way around (U.S. dollars per unit of foreign currency), these exchange rates were to increase from the fourth quarter of 1984 at an annual rate of 11.1 percent (2.67 percent per quarter) to a level roughly 37 percent above baseline by the fourth quarter of 1987.

Simulation G studies an increase in government purchases in ROECD countries with U.S. policies unchanged from baseline. Model groups were asked to assume an across-the-board, simultaneous expansion of government expenditures in each of the OECD countries except the United States. Analogous to the experiment in simulations B and C, real government purchases in each ROECD country were to be raised by amounts equivalent to 1 percent of real GNP (or GDP) beginning in the first quarter of 1985 and continuing through 1990, with the change in policy expected to continue "permanently." Baseline computations and shock paths for composite variables for the ROECD as a whole, as elsewhere, were to follow specified instructions for weighting (see below). U.S. budgetary policies were to remain unchanged from baseline. Similarly, U.S. M1 and key monetary aggregates in all ROECD countries were to remain unchanged from baseline (that is, the same assumptions about monetary policies used in simulations B, C, and F).

Simulation H studies a monetary expansion in ROECD countries with U.S. policies unchanged from baseline. Model groups were asked to assume a temporary one-year increase in the growth rate of the "policy-proxy" monetary aggregate in each ROECD country analogous to the monetary expansion assumed for the United States in simulations D and E. The monetary aggregate shocked in each ROECD country was to be the same aggregate kept unchanged from baseline in simulations B, D, F, and G. Models with quarterly frequencies were to make the level of each ROECD aggregate be 0.5 percent higher than the baseline during the first quarter of 1985, 1.5 percent higher during the second quarter, 2.5 percent higher during the third quarter, 3.5 percent higher during the fourth quarter, and 4.0 percent higher during the first quarter of 1986 and all subsequent quarters. Corresponding shock paths were to be defined for models with semiannual and annual frequencies (analogous to the instructions for simulation D). Model groups were asked to check that their baseline and simulation computations for the composite monetary aggregate and other variables for the ROECD matched the weighting instructions specified elsewhere in the instructions (see below). In simulation H budgetary policies in all countries and monetary policy in the United States (defined in terms of M1) were to be held unchanged from baseline.

Implementation of Monetary Simulations

As already noted, some model groups did not correctly implement the first-year phasing-in of the monetary shocks in simulations D, E, and H. Table 1-1 reports the figures for the exogenous monetary aggregates that model groups actually incorporated in their simulations. Chapter 3 in the main volume discusses the implications of these discrepancies for the simulation results.

Instructions for Models with Forward-Looking Expectations

In the preliminary simulations conducted before the October 1985 workshop, model groups whose models imposed forward-looking, model-consistent expectations—the LIVERPOOL, MINIMOD, MSG, and TAYLOR models—found that they could not make their models conform to a straightforward extrapolation of the prescribed baseline beyond 1990. (The resulting constellation of interest rates, exchange rates, and budget deficits proved to be incompatible with steady-state equilibrium.) Each of those modeling groups adjusted its baseline to obtain a solution, but each group made a different adjustment.

It was infeasible to achieve a complete harmonization of baselines for these model groups before the deadline for submitting revised results for the March 1986 conference. As best could be judged from the discussions at the October 1985 workshop, however, the effect on simulation results of differences in post-1990 baselines was small.

The four model groups with rational expectations models were therefore asked simply to observe the following guidelines with respect to their baselines: (1) follow as closely as possible the baseline specified for all models for the years 1985–90; (2) confine any additional adjustments necessary to achieve a baseline solution to the years after 1990; and (3) force the budget deficit of the U.S. government on to a "sustainable" path by progressive increases in direct taxation occurring after 1990.[26]

26. Policy measures tending to reduce the U.S. budget deficit seemed necessary in all these models to make the government budget position compatible with interest rate and exchange rate extrapolations. Further precision in the instructions about the timing

Table 1-1. Implementation of Monetary Shocks in Simulations D, E, and H
Percent deviations of shocked monetary aggregate from baseline

	Quarterly pattern during initial year				*Annual average data*	
Simulation and model	*Q1*	*Q2*	*Q3*	*Q4*	*Year 1 (1985)*	*Year 2 (1986)*
Simulations D and E						
DRI	1.0	2.1	3.0	4.0	2.5	4.0
EEC	a	a	a	a	2.0	4.0
EPA	0.6	2.2	3.8	4.9	2.9	4.8
LINK	a	a	a	a	2.0	4.0
LIVERPOOL	a	a	a	a	2.0	4.1
MCM	0.5	1.5	3.5	4.0	2.4	4.0
MINIMOD	0.5	1.5	2.5	3.5	2.0	4.0
MSG	a	a	a	a	4.1	4.1
OECD	b	b	b	b	2.0	4.0
TAYLOR	0.5	1.5	2.5	3.5	2.0	4.0
VAR[c]	0.2	0.8	1.5	2.4	1.2	4.0
WHARTON	a	a	a	a	4.0	4.0
Simulation H						
DRI	d	d	d	d	d	d
EEC	a	a	a	a	e	e
EPA	d	d	d	d	d	d
LINK	a	a	a	a	2.0	4.0
LIVERPOOL	a	a	a	a	2.0	4.0
MCM	0.5	1.5	3.5	4.0	2.4	4.0
MINIMOD	0.5	1.5	2.5	3.5	2.0	4.0
MSG	a	a	a	a	4.1	4.1
OECD	b	b	b	b	1.9	3.7
TAYLOR	0.5	1.5	2.5	3.5	2.0	4.0
VAR	1.3	2.6	3.8	4.5	3.0	4.0
WHARTON	a	a	a	a	4.2	4.2
Correct specification	**0.5**	**1.5**	**2.5**	**3.5**	**2.0**	**4.0**

Source: Computer tapes from model groups. See also tables in part 3 of this volume.
a. Model uses annual data.
b. Model uses semiannual data.
c. These figures pertain to simulation D. Simulation E results were slightly larger numbers in the first year (averaging 1.4 percent).
d. Simulation H results not available for this model.
e. Information not on computer tape.

Because the post-1990 baselines would differ somewhat across these four models, these groups were asked to report by memorandum the interest rates, exchange rates, real government purchases, monetary aggregates, and assumed changes in tax rates that characterized their baselines for the years 1990–2000.

In the preliminary work done by the four rational expectations models for the October 1985 workshop, not only the baselines but also the fiscal-shock simulations had caused difficulties. In particular, when the model groups had adjusted their baseline to satisfy conditions for reaching a steady-state equilibrium, an assumed "permanent" change in government purchases then proved inconsistent with the assumptions of unchanged (from baseline) tax rates and money supply growth. Accordingly, model groups made assumptions to complete the specification of the fiscal shock in a way that was consistent with reaching a new steady state. But the assumptions differed across models.

Following the October 1985 workshop, the model groups with forward-looking expectations were asked to treat the change in government purchases in simulations B, C, and G as permanent (consistent with the assumptions used by all the other models) and, as necessary, to use progressive changes in direct real taxation to achieve a U.S. government budget deficit consistent with a steady-state solution. They were asked to begin such changes in taxation in 1991 and to complete them by 2001. As with their baselines, the model groups were asked to report by memorandum exactly what taxation policy changes had been assumed to complete these simulations.[27]

Weighting Procedures for Composite Variables

Model groups were asked to use a uniform set of country weights to construct all ROECD composite variables. The weights were based on 1982 shares of countries in total OECD gross product (with the data taken from the December 1984 issue of the *OECD Economic Outlook*). The figures in the first column of table 1-2 are the percentage shares of the countries in 1982 total OECD output. The weights in the second column for percentage shares in the ROECD, derived from the figures in the first column, were the figures given to model groups for use in their computations.

Table 1-2. Country Shares in OECD Gross Product
Percent

Country	*Share in total OECD*	*Share in ROECD*
Japan	14.0	23.5
Germany	8.7	14.6
France	7.1	11.9
United Kingdom	6.4	10.7
Italy	4.6	7.7
Canada	3.8	6.4
Netherlands	1.8	3.0
Belgium	1.1	1.8
Spain	2.4	4.0
Sweden	1.3	2.2
Switzerland	1.3	2.2
Other OECD Europe	4.8	8.0
Australia	2.1	3.5
New Zealand	0.3	0.5
Total ROECD	59.7	100.0
United States	40.3	...
Total OECD	100.0	...

Model groups were asked to use weights for individual countries based on the second column, but to adjust the weights for the country coverage of their models. The weights for individual ROECD countries were to be scaled to sum to unity to allow for the behavior of nonmodeled countries. The assumption implicit in this procedure is that nonmodeled countries move in line with countries that are modeled. For example, suppose a model contained separate country submodels only for Japan, Canada, Germany, and the United Kingdom in the ROECD. The group operating that model was in effect asked to treat those four countries as if their behavior proxied the behavior of the whole ROECD region. The weights for the four countries were to be chosen to sum to unity. The individual weight for Japan would be 0.426, calculated as 23.5 divided by the sum (23.5 + 14.6 + 10.7 + 6.4). The weights for Germany, the United Kingdom, and Canada would be, respectively, 0.264, 0.194, and 0.116.

Weights for calculating the weighted-average exchange value of the U.S. dollar were also to be derived from table 1-2. All weighted averages were to be calculated geometrically, using the formula

$$WAX = \prod_i (X_i)^{w_i},$$

where WAX is the weighted average of variable X for the included countries, X_i is X's value for country i, w_i is country i's weight (GNP share), and the w_i

of increases in direct taxation was not offered, because the definition of a sustainable deficit path appeared to differ from model to model.

27. These model groups were urged to carry out, if feasible, some optional simulations—for example, a repetition of the fiscal shocks in simulations B, C, and G with different post-1990 dates for the implementation of offsetting tax changes or with alternative post-1990 policy changes (such as a change in the growth of the policy-proxy monetary aggregate as a counterpart to the change in government purchases). Such additional simulations would have demonstrated the degree of sensitivity of the fiscal simulations to alternative long-run terminal steady states. In the event, the model groups were unable to carry out these additional simulations.

sum to unity. For prices, wages, and exchange rates, all X_i were to be indexed to 1972 = 100. For variables measured in local currency units, such as monetary aggregates, the X_i were to be the product of the local currency value and the bilateral exchange rate with the numeraire currency (the U.S. dollar).

Variables to Be Reported

Model groups were asked to report variables for the following countries or regions (to the extent that the details existed in their model): United States (mnemonic U), Japan (J), Germany (G), Canada (C), United Kingdom (E), France (F), Italy (I), total ROECD (O), and the rest of the world outside the OECD (R).[28] The country mnemonic was to precede the variable mnemonic in the variable name (for example, JEXCH for the exchange rate index for U.S. dollars per Japanese yen).

For the ROECD countries and region, model groups were asked to report current account balances and government budget deficits in billions of U.S. dollars, with local currency values converted to dollars *at baseline exchange rates* rather than the exchange rates generated in the simulations. Use of baseline exchange rates for conversion abstracts from valuation changes due to exchange rate movements.

Tables 1-3 and 1-4 show the variables that model groups were asked to report (to the extent that model coverage permitted). Variables marked with two asterisks (**) were to be reported as both a level change (absolute difference between shock path and baseline path) and as a percentage change (percent deviation of shock path from baseline path). Variables indicated with the number symbol (#) were to be reported as an absolute change from the baseline rather than as a percentage change. All other variables were to be reported as percent deviation of the shock path from the baseline path.

Model groups were given precise specifications for how to write the variables on magnetic tape for processing by the project organizers. The comparative charts and tables generated for the project were prepared by Steven Symansky and Solomon Goldfarb on the computer system of the World Bank.

28. France and Italy were added to this list after the October 1985 workshop.

Table 1-3. Variables to Be Reported for the United States

Variable[a]	*Units*
Real GNP (UGNP)**	Billions of 1972 dollars, annual rate
Nominal GNP (UGNPV)	Billions of current dollars, annual rate
Real private consumption (UC)#	Billions of 1972 dollars, annual rate
Real private fixed investment (UIFP)#	Billions of 1972 dollars, annual rate
Change in real inventories (UII)#	Billions of 1972 dollars, annual rate
Real government expenditures, goods and services (UG)#	Billions of 1972 dollars, annual rate
Real exports, goods and services, national income and product accounts basis (UXGS)#	Billions of 1972 dollars, annual rate
Real imports, goods and services, national income and product accounts basis (UMGS)#	Billions of 1972 dollars, annual rate
GNP deflator (UPGNP)	Index, 1972 = 100
Consumer price index (UCPI)	Index, 1972 = 100
Nominal wage rate or index (UW)	Index, 1972 = 100
Nominal disposable income (UYDV)	Billions of current dollars, annual rate
Unemployment rate (UUN)#	Percent
Employment (total) (ULE)	Millions
Money stock M1 (UM1)	Billions of dollars
Short-term interest rate (URS)#	Percentage points (for example, 9.2%)
Long-term interest rate (URL)#	Percentage points
Total government budget receipts (nominal) (UGR)	Billions of current dollars, annual rate
Total government budget expenditures (nominal) (UGE)	Billions of current dollars, annual rate
Government budget deficit (UGDEF)#	Billions of current dollars, annual rate
Price deflator for exports, goods and services (UPXGS)	Index, 1972 = 100
Price deflator for imports, goods and services (UPMGS)	Index, 1972 = 100
Balance on current account in the balance of payments (UCURBAL)#	Billions of current dollars, annual rate
Weighted average exchange rate, foreign currency per U.S. dollar (UEXCH)[b]	Index, 1972 = 100

a. See text for explanation of ** and #.
b. See table 1-2 for weights to use in calculating this variable.

Table 1-4. Variables to Be Reported for Other Countries and Regions

Variable[a]	*Units*
Nominal GNP or GDP (iGNPV)	Billions of local currency units[b]
Real GNP or GDP (iGNP)**	Billions of 1972 local currency units[c]
Real exports, goods and services (iXGS)#	Billions of 1972 local currency units[c]
Real imports, goods and services (iMGS)#	Billions of 1972 local currency units[c]
Real private investment (iIFP)#	Billions of 1972 local currency units[c]
Real private consumption (iC)#	Billions of 1972 local currency units[c]
Real government expenditures, goods and services (iG)#	Billions of 1972 local currency units[c]
Consumer price index (iPCPI)	Index, 1972 = 100
GNP deflator (iPGNP)	Index, 1972 = 100
Nominal wage rate or index (iW)	Index, 1972 = 100
Unemployment rate (iUN)#	Percent
Key monetary aggregate (iMON)[d]	Billions of local currency units[b]
Short-term interest rate (iRS)#	Percentage points (for example, 9.2%)
Long-term interest rate (iRL)#	Percentage points
Government budget deficit (iGDEF)#	Billions of local currency units or billions of U.S. dollars at baseline exchange rates[b]
Export price deflator, goods and services (iPXGS)	Index, 1972 = 100
Import price deflator, goods and services (iPMGS)	Index, 1972 = 100
Bilateral dollar exchange rate, U.S. dollars per local currency unit (iEXCH)	Index, 1972 = 100[e]
Balance on current account in the balance of payments (iCURBAL)	Billions of U.S. dollars, annual rate[f]

a. In the symbols in this table, "i" represents a country mnemonic: J (Japan), G (Federal Republic of Germany), C (Canada), E (United Kingdom), F (France), I (Italy), O (all countries of the ROECD), or R (the rest of the world outside the OECD). See text for explanation of ** and #.

b. The units for the composite ROECD region should be billions of U.S. dollars, with conversion from local currency units at baseline exchange rates.

c. The units for the composite ROECD region should be billions of constant 1972 U.S. dollars, with conversion from local currency units at baseline exchange rates.

d. Please specify which aggregate is selected.

e. For the composite ROECD region, this index should be a weighted-average rate against the U.S. dollar (with weights based on table 1-2).

f. Conversion from local currency units should be at baseline exchange rates.

PART TWO

Reference Charts and Tables

SIMULATION A

Baseline

Chart A-1. U.S. Nominal GNP (UGNPV)—Baseline

Year-to-year percent changes for level of baseline path

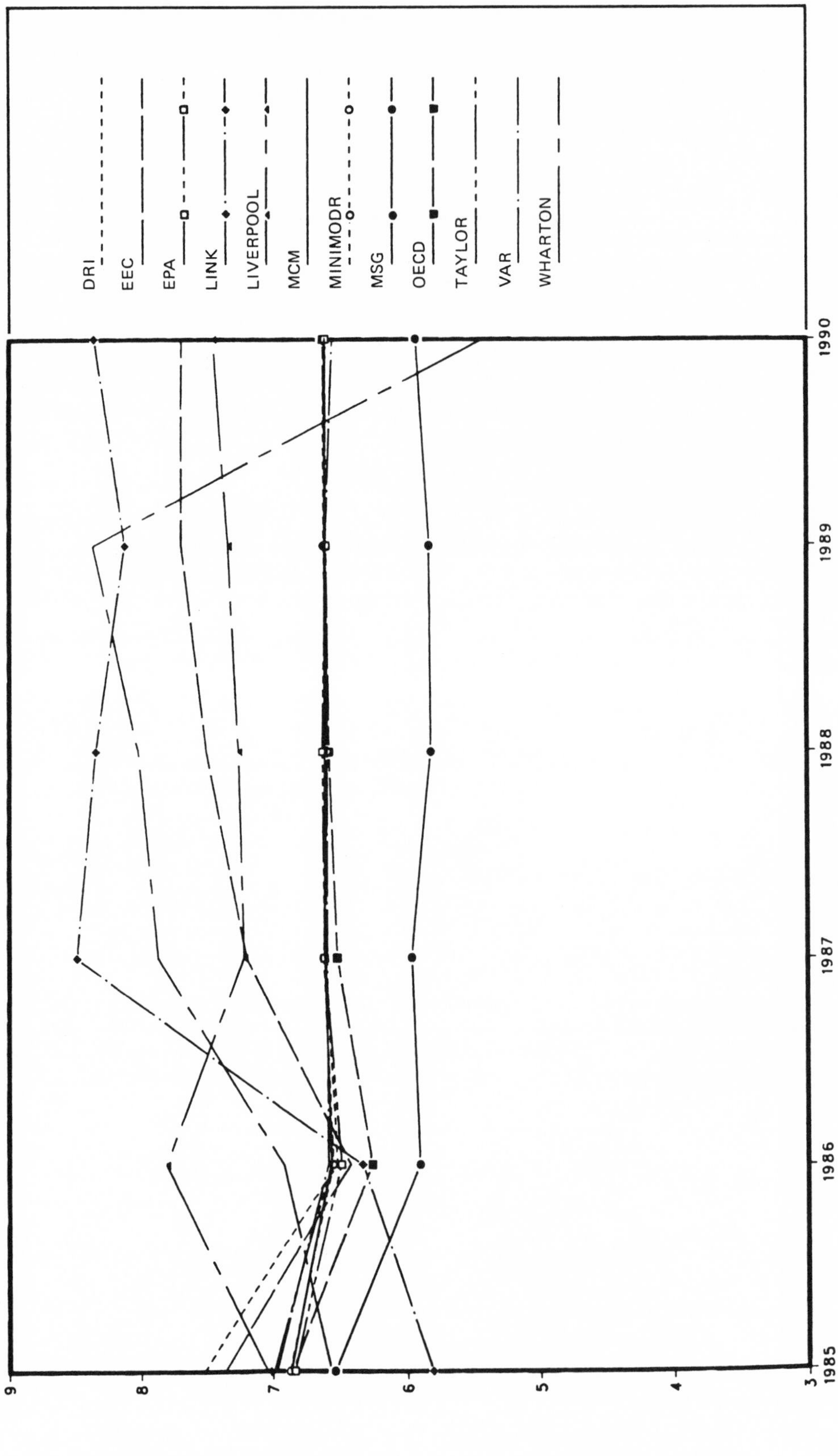

DRI
EEC
EPA
LINK
LIVERPOOL
MCM
MINIMODR
MSG
OECD
TAYLOR
VAR
WHARTON

9
8
7
6
5
4
3

1985
1986
1987
1988
1989
1990

Chart A-2. ROECD Nominal GNP (OGNPV)—Baseline

Year-to-year percent changes for level of baseline path

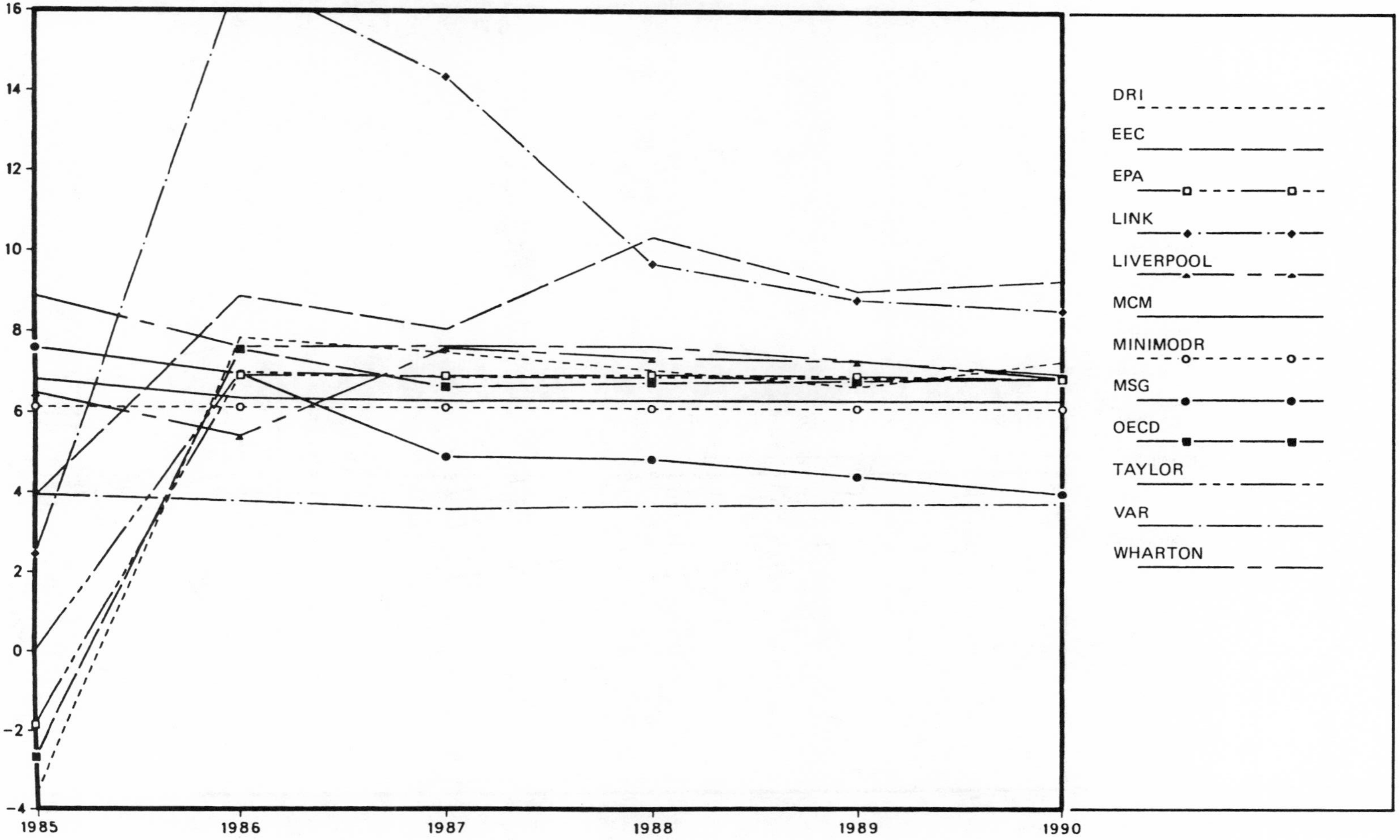

Chart A-3. U.S. Real GNP (UGNP)—Baseline

Year-to-year percent changes for level of baseline path

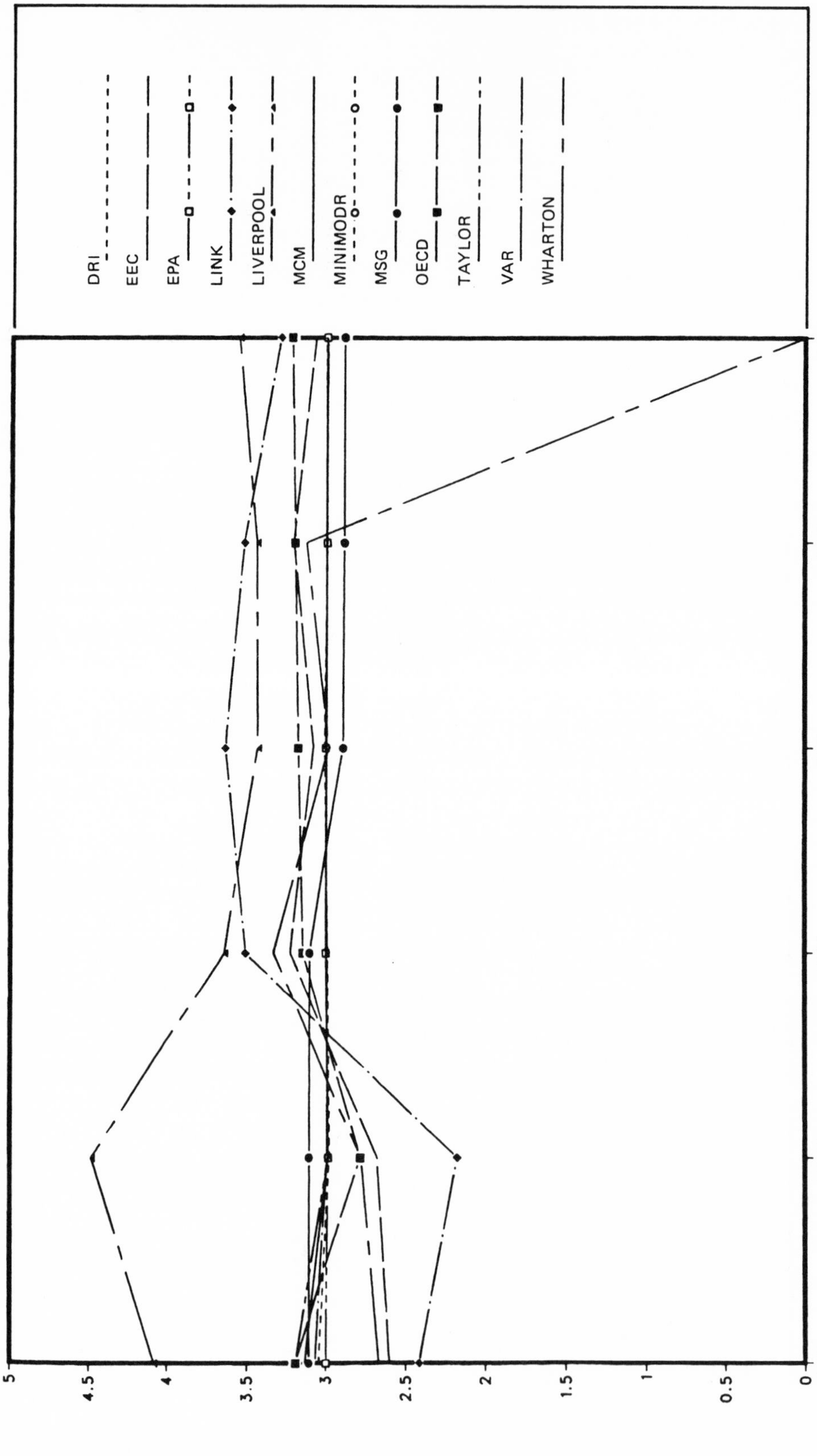

Chart A-4. ROECD Real GNP (OGNP)—Baseline

Year-to-year percent changes for level of baseline path

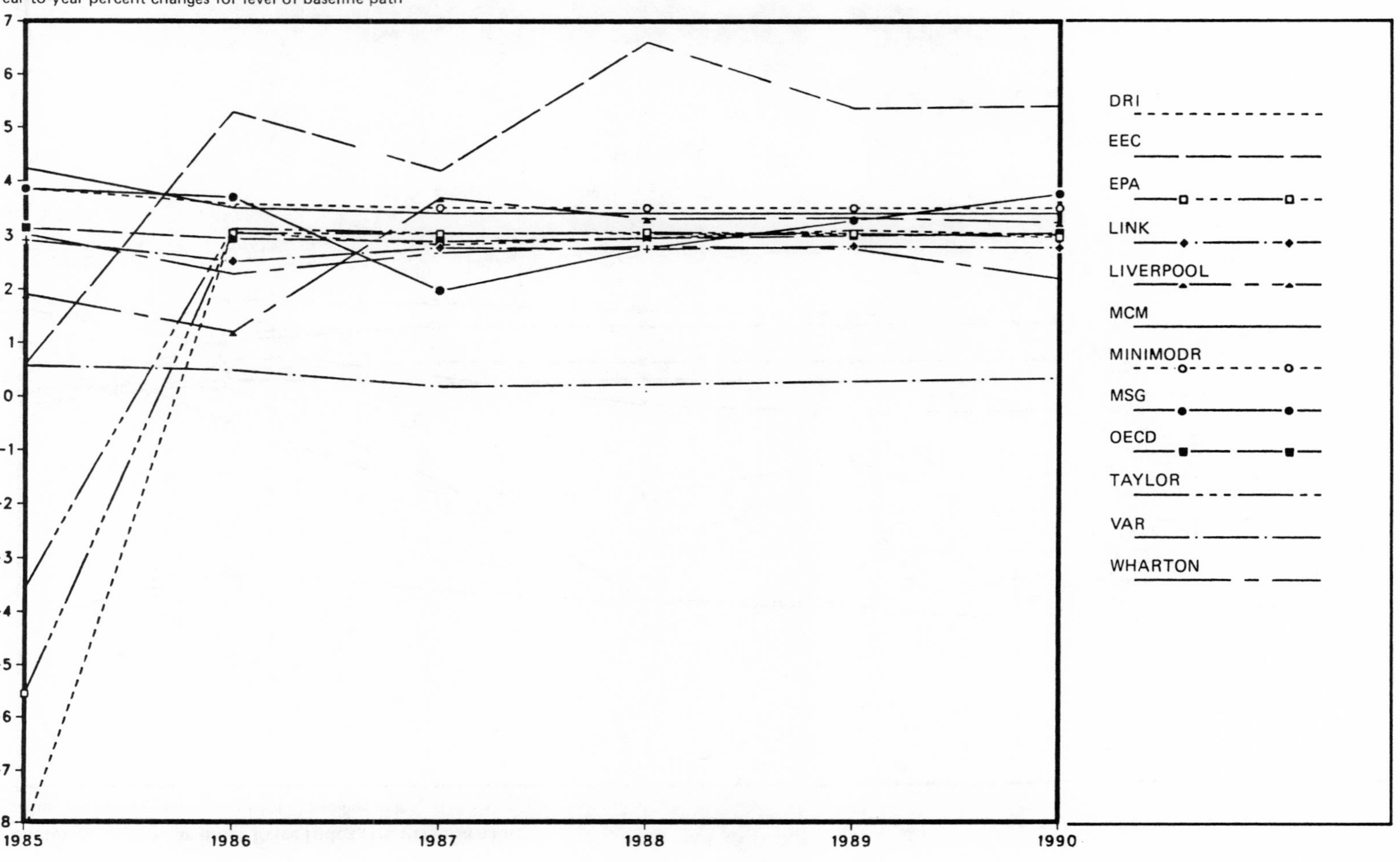

Chart A-5. U.S. Consumer Price Index (UCPI)—Baseline

Year-to-year percent changes for level of baseline path

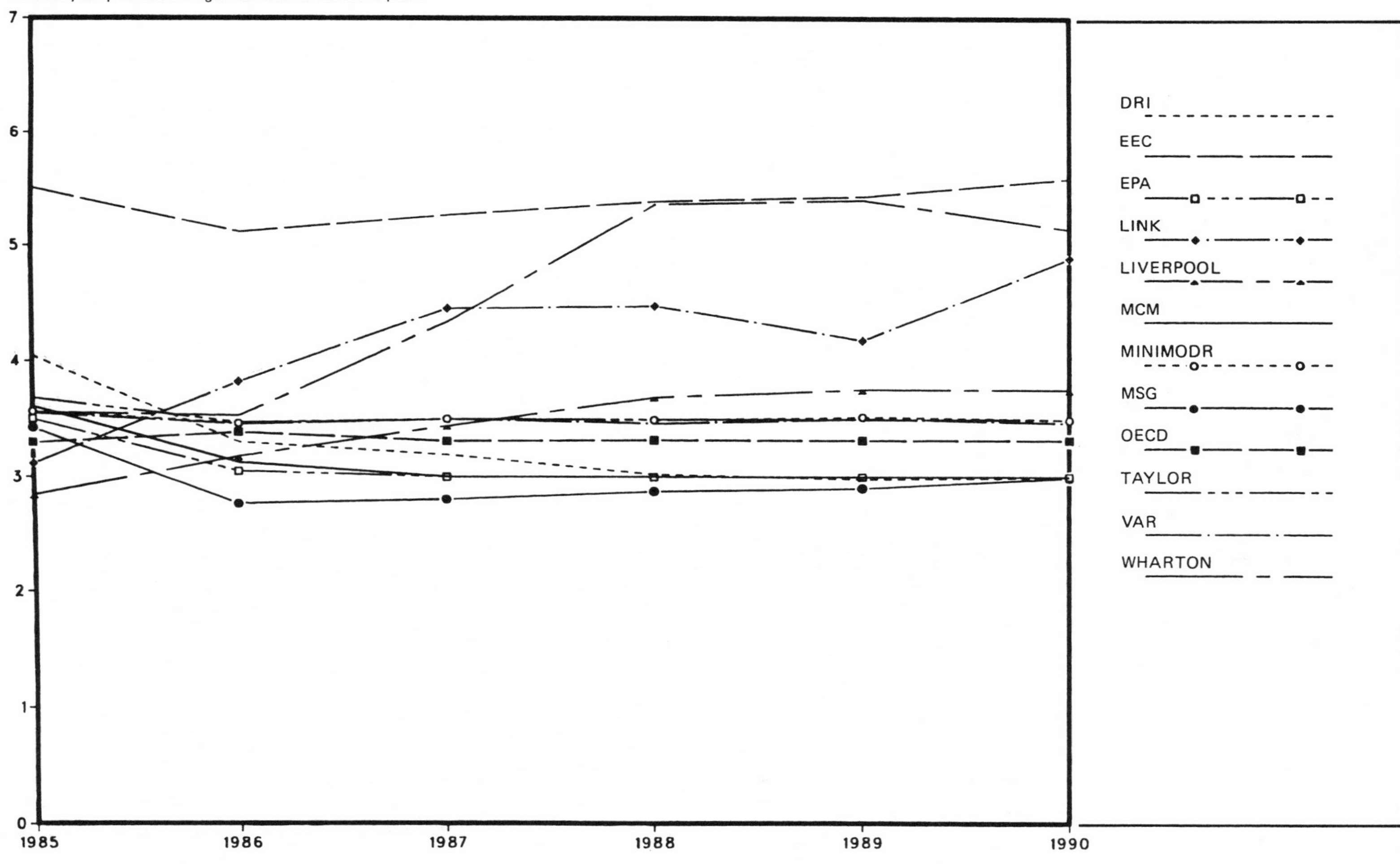

Chart A-6. ROECD Consumer Price Index (OPCPI)—Baseline

Year-to-year percent changes for level of baseline path

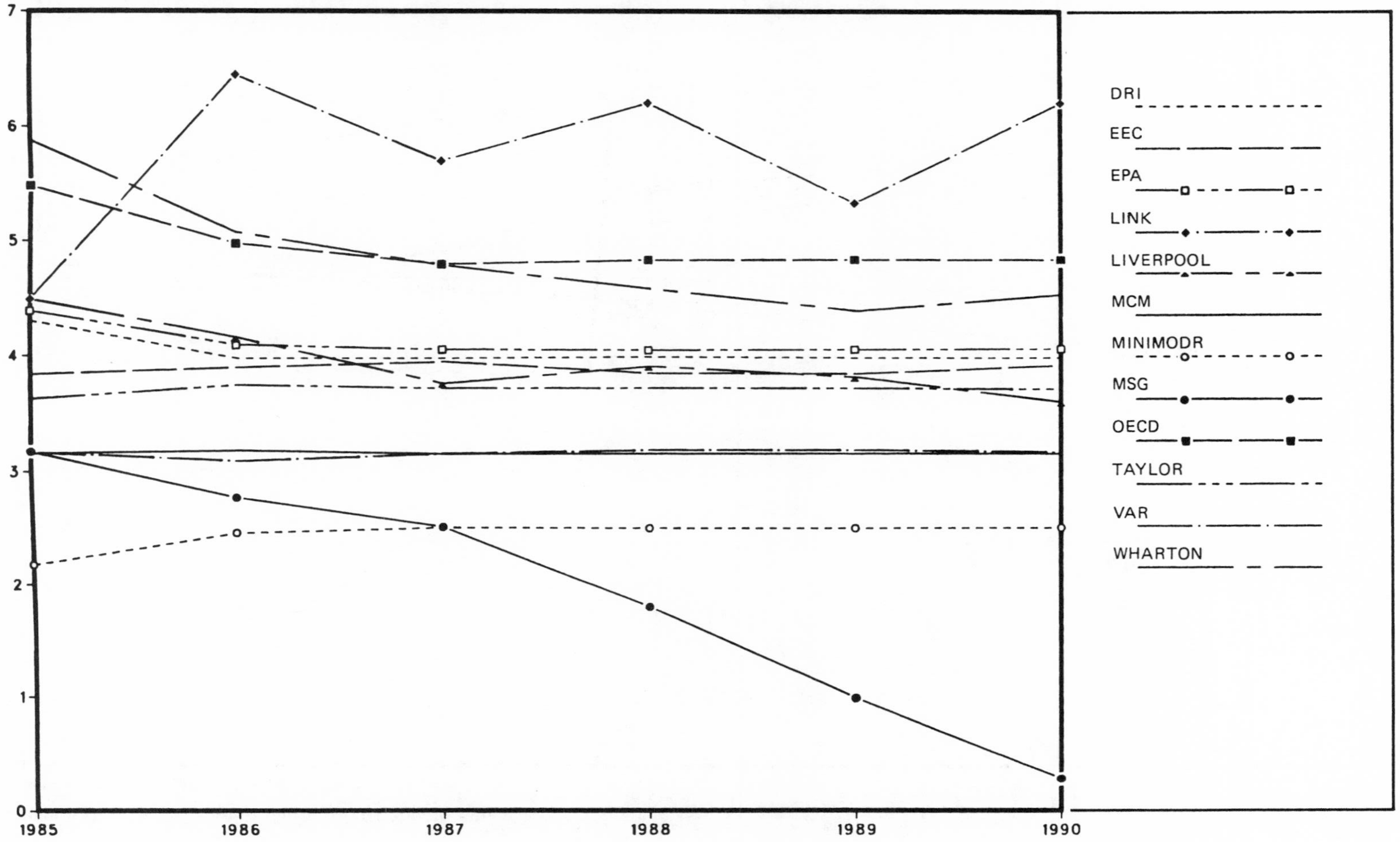

Chart A-7. U.S. Unemployment Rate (UUN)—Baseline

Level of baseline path, percentage points

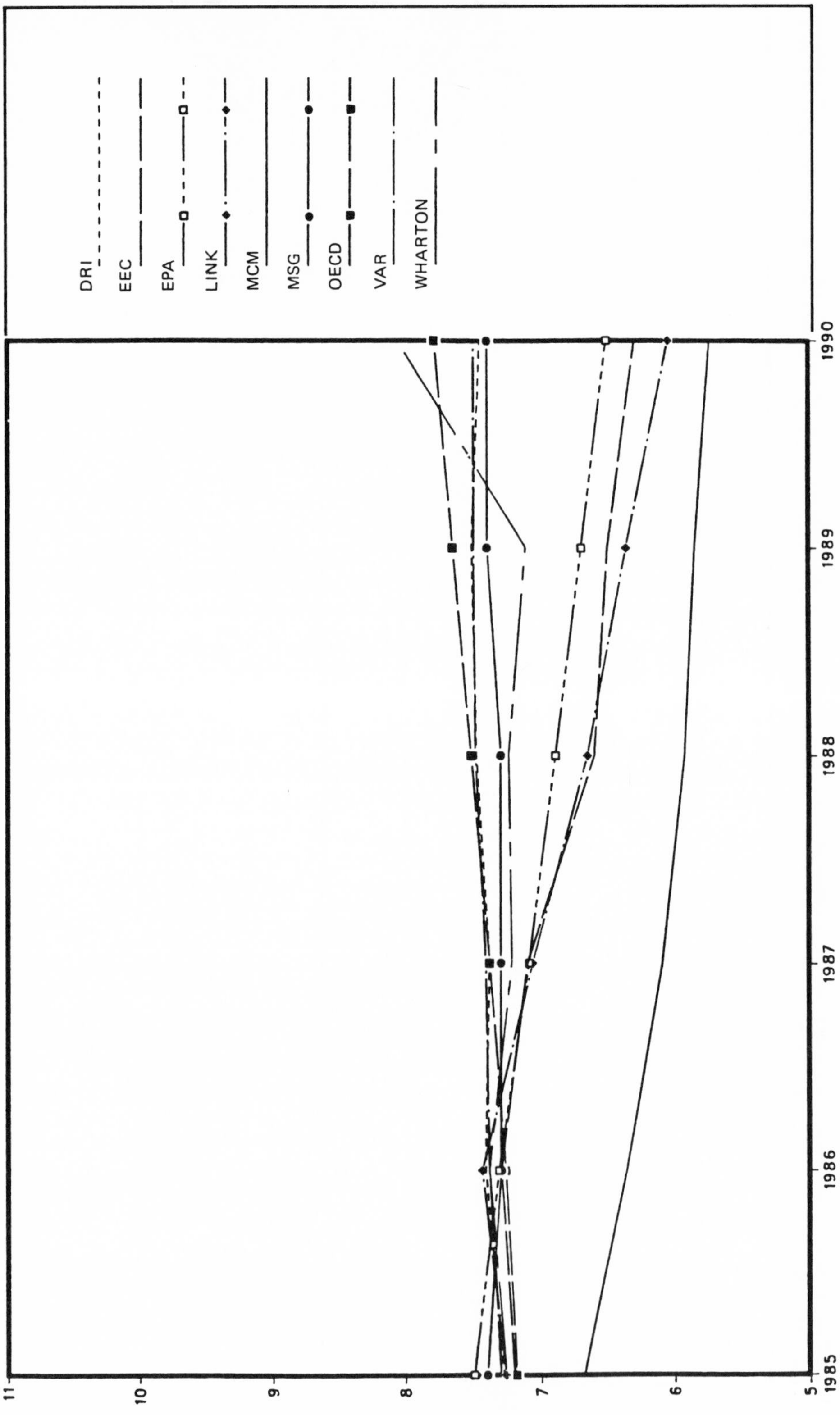

DRI
EEC
EPA
LINK
MCM
MSG
OECD
VAR
WHARTON

11
10
9
8
7
6
5

1985
1986
1987
1988
1989
1990

Chart A-8. ROECD Unemployment Rate (OUN)—Baseline

Level of baseline path, percentage points

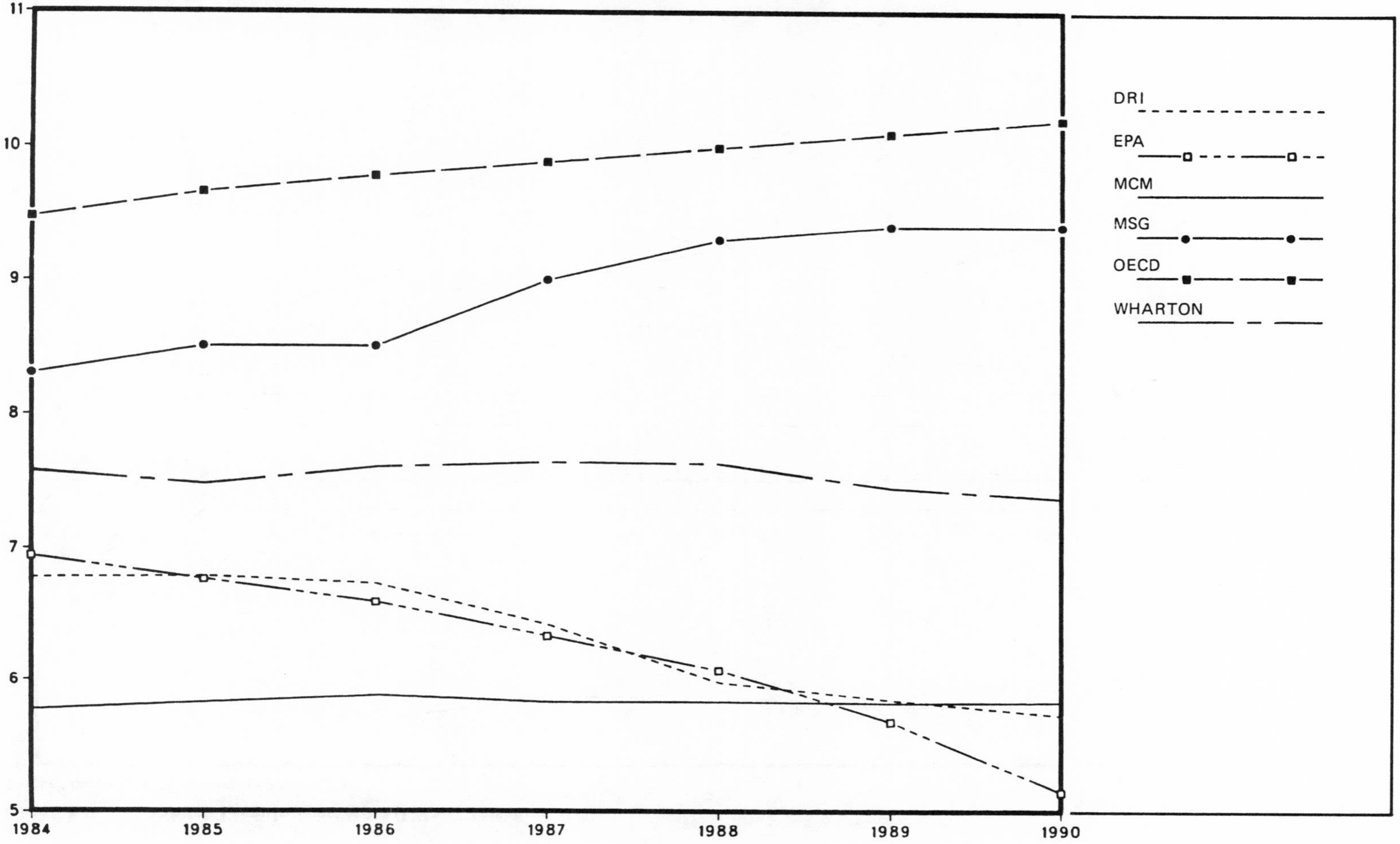

Chart A-9. U.S. Short-Term Interest Rate (URS)—Baseline

Level of baseline path, percentage points

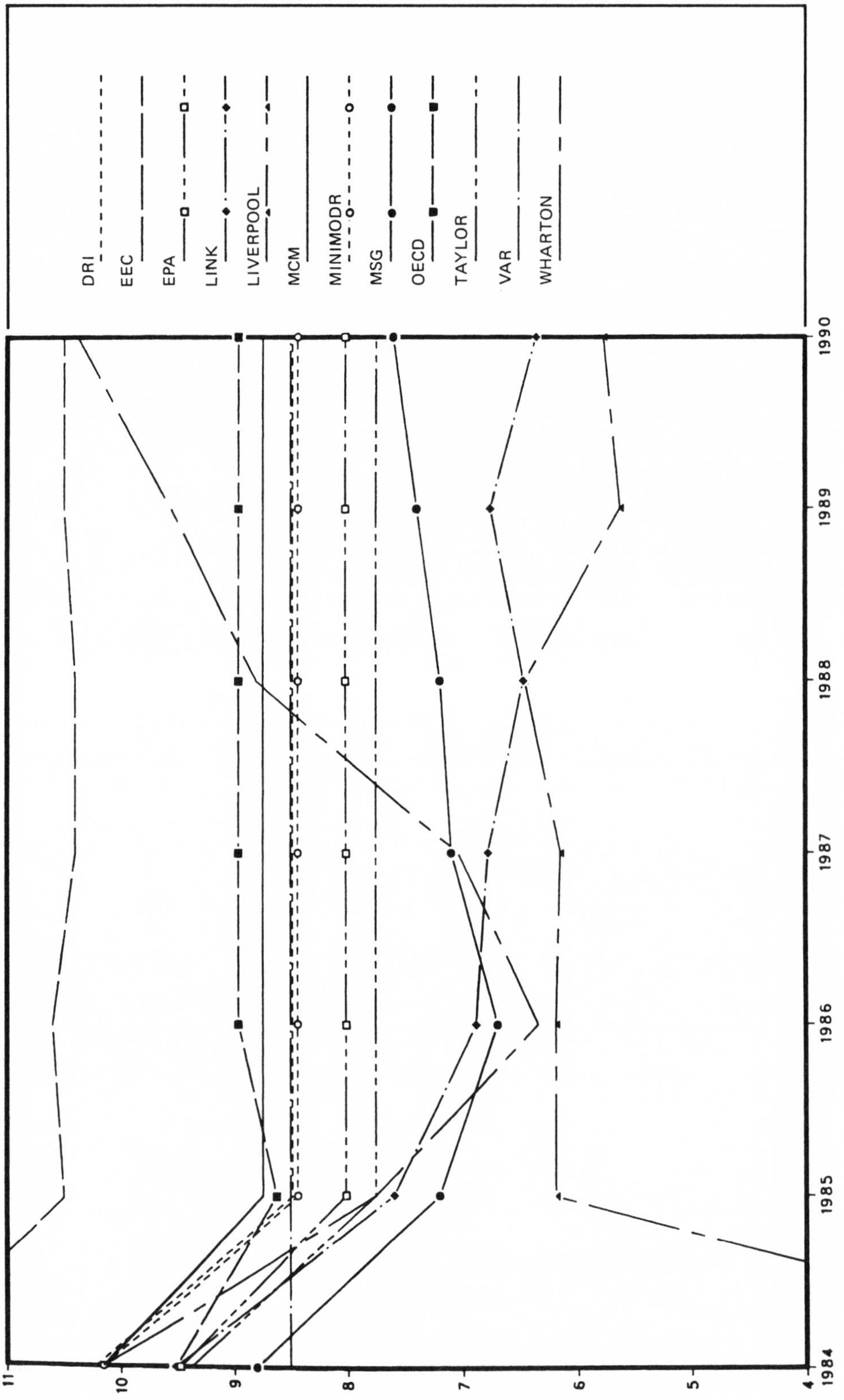

Chart A-10. ROECD Short-Term Interest Rate (ORS)—Baseline

Level of baseline path, percentage points

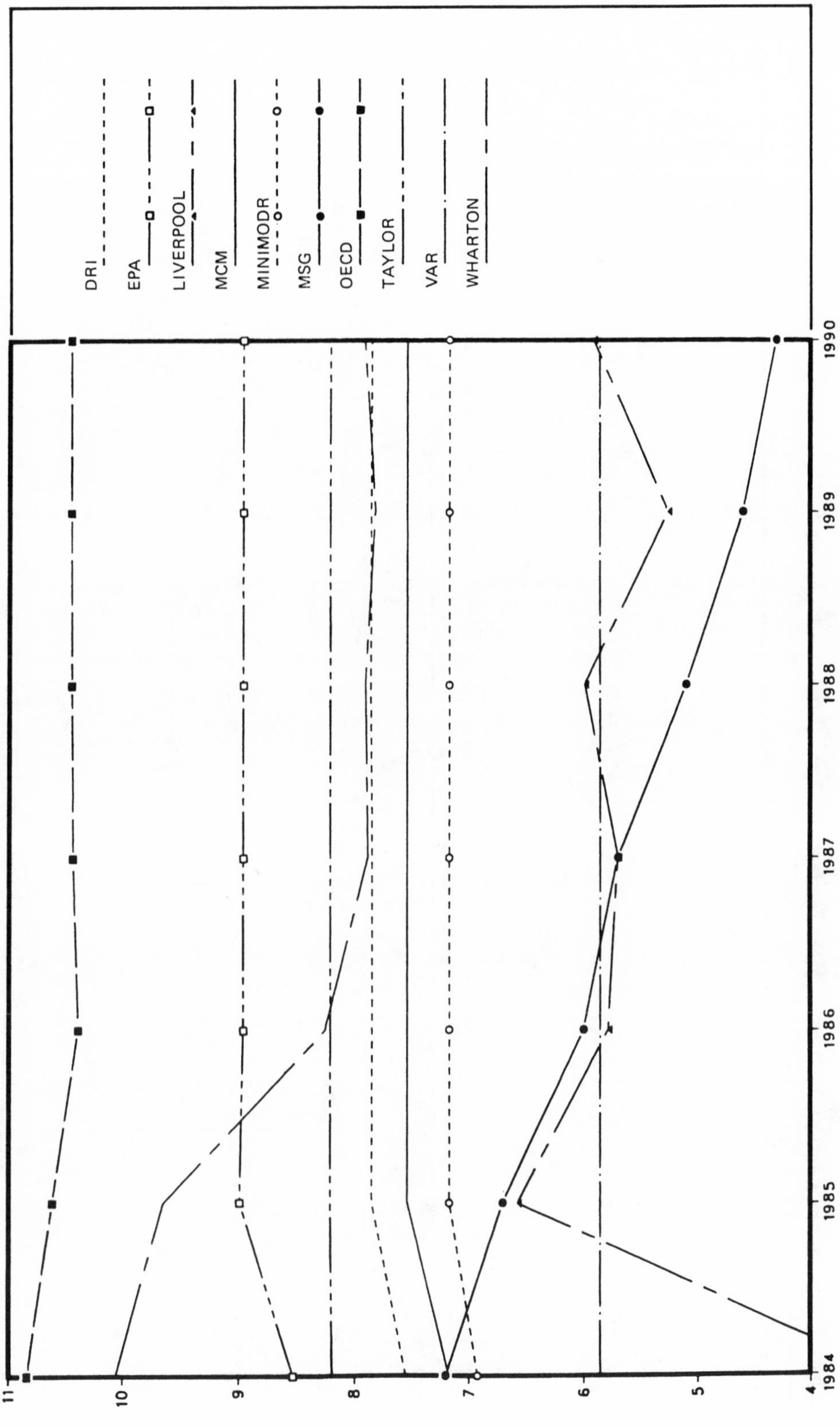

Chart A-11. U.S. Key Monetary Aggregate (UM1)—Baseline

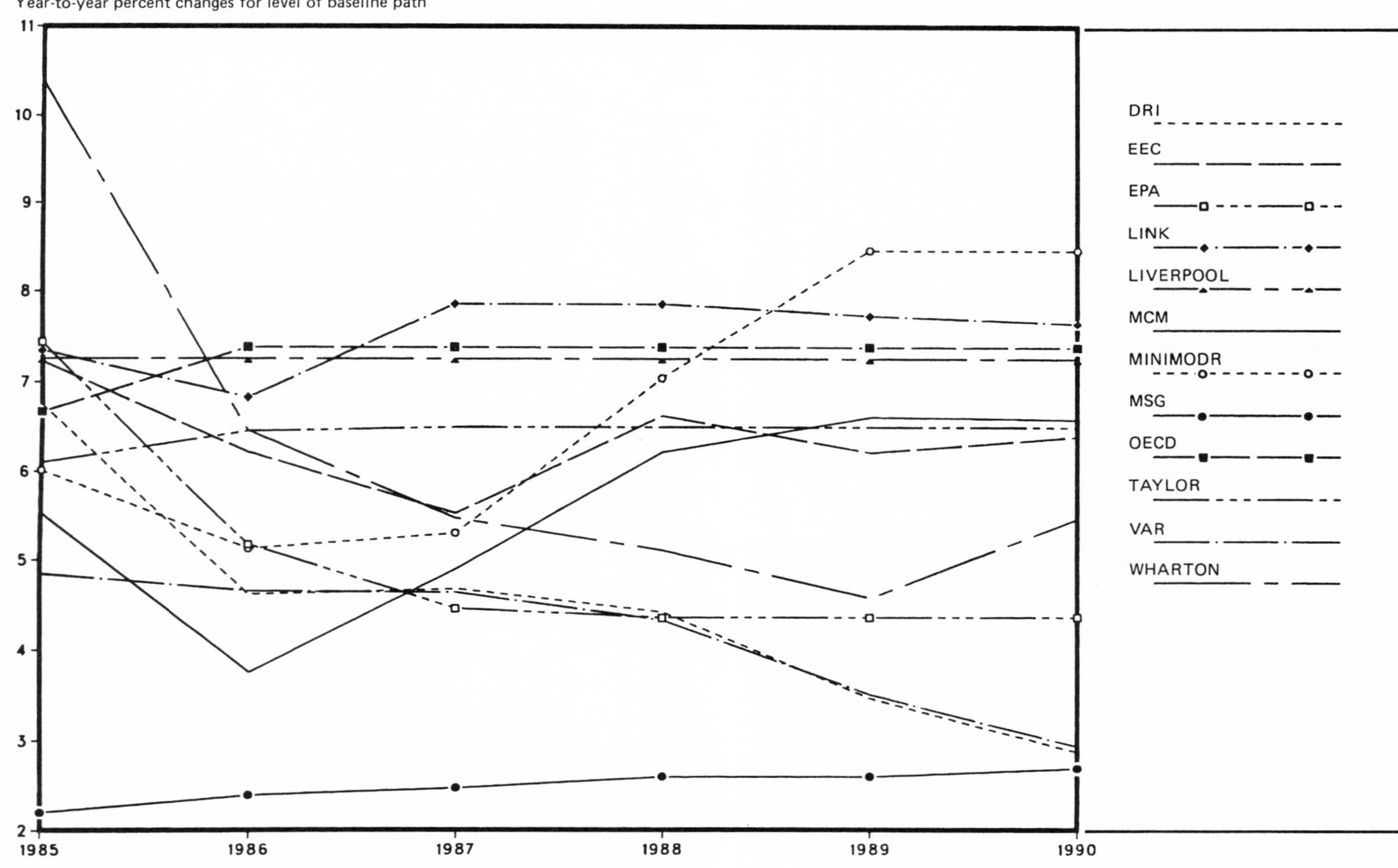

Chart A-12. ROECD Key Monetary Aggregate (Composite) (OMON)—Baseline

Year-to-year percent changes for level of baseline path

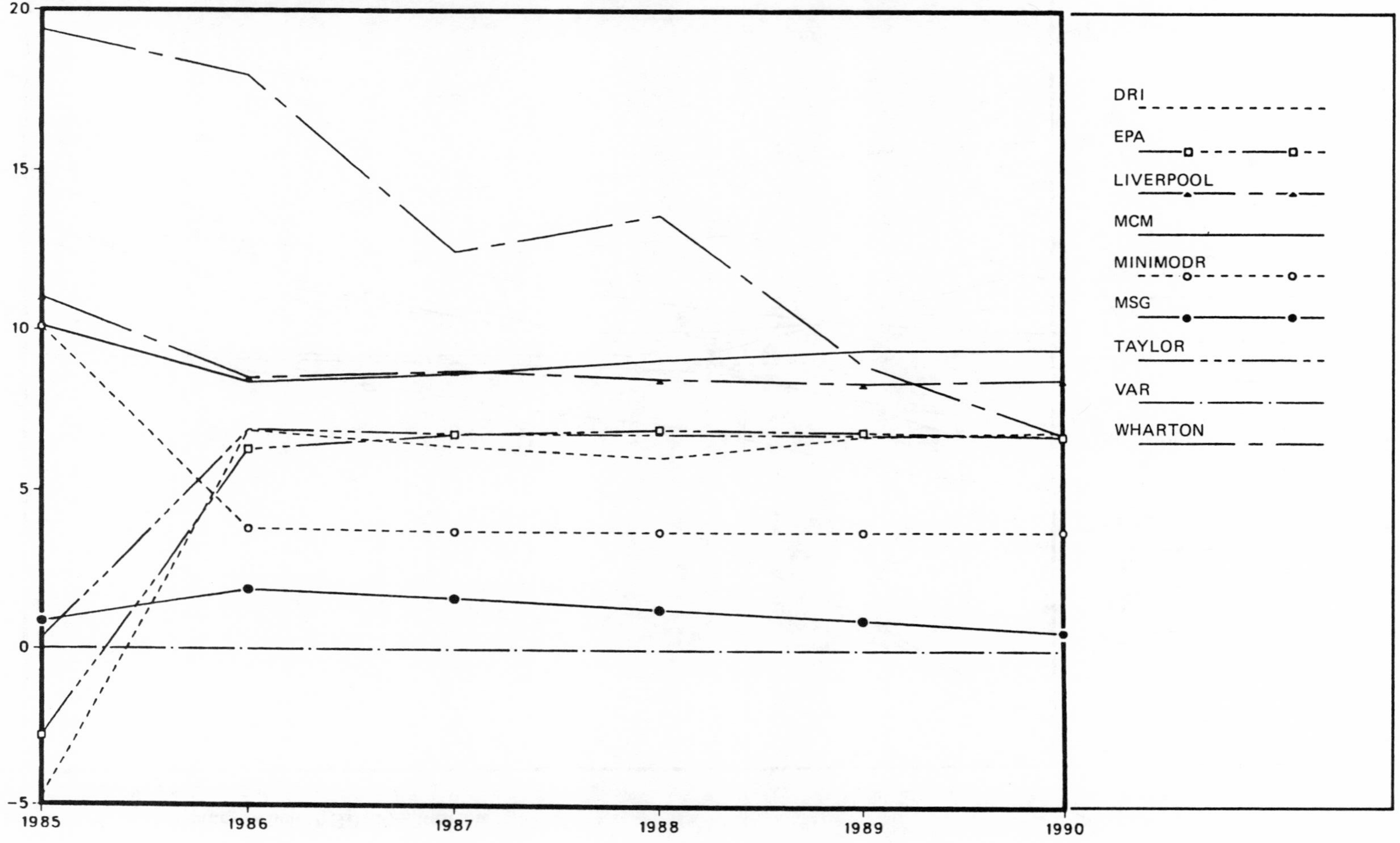

Chart A-13. U.S. Budgetary Deficit (UGDEF)—Baseline

Level of baseline path, U.S. billion $

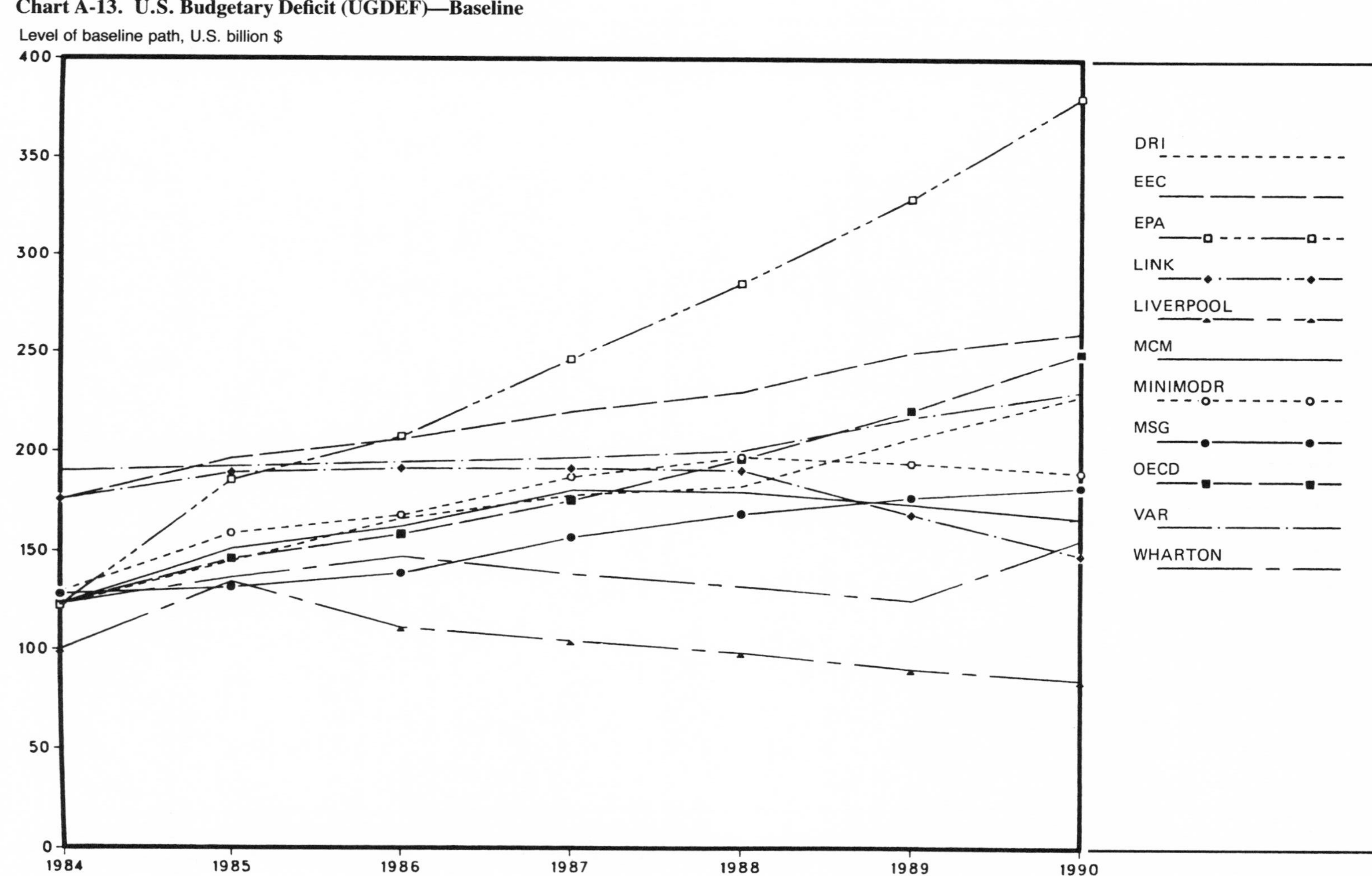

Chart A-14. ROECD Budgetary Deficit (OGDEF)—Baseline

Level of baseline path, U.S. billion $ at baseline exchange rates

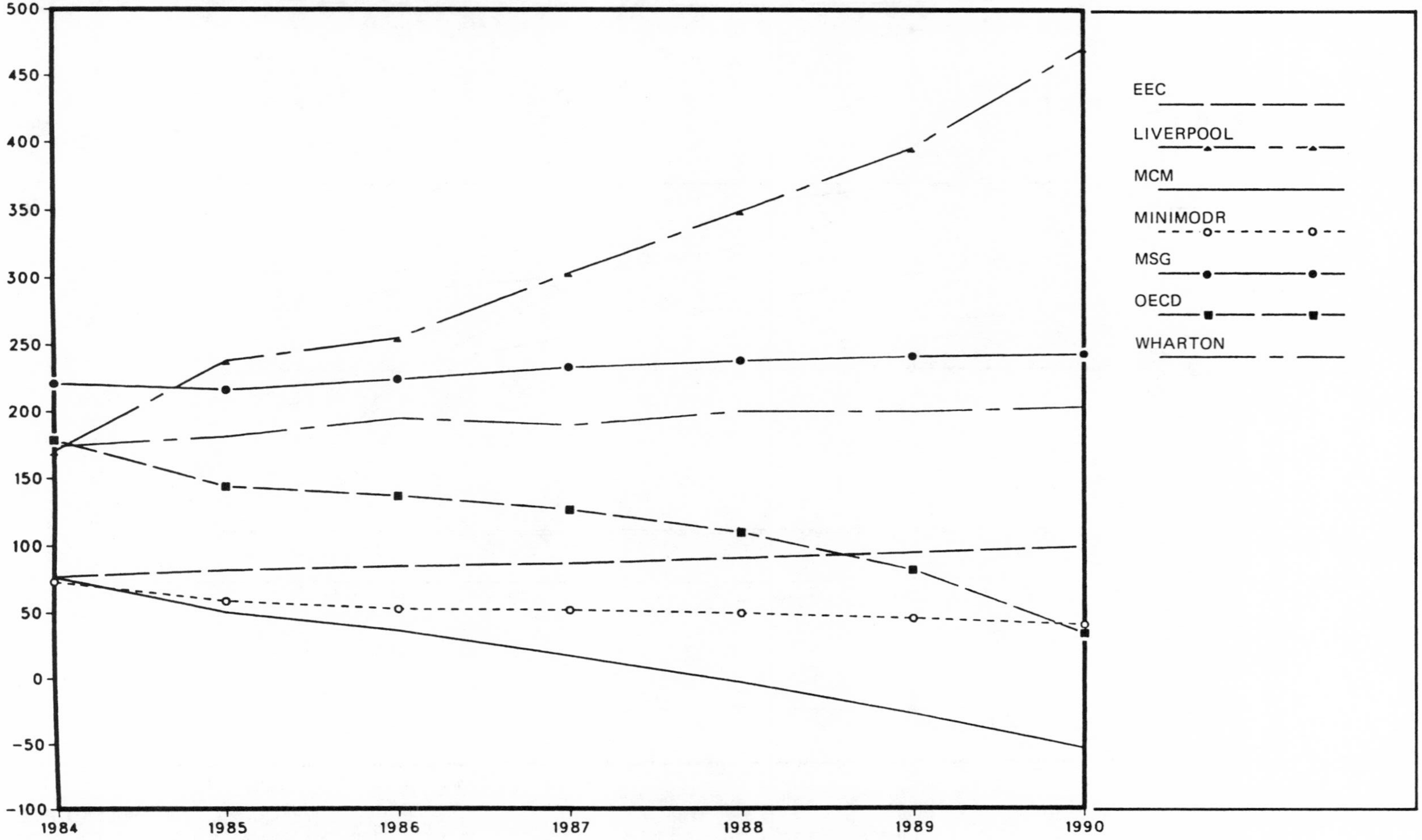

500
450
400
350
300
250
200
150
100
50
0
−50
−100

1984
1985
1986
1987
1988
1989
1990

EEC
LIVERPOOL
MCM
MINIMODR
MSG
OECD
WHARTON

Chart A-15. Weighted Average Exchange Value of U.S. Dollar (Foreign Currencies per U.S. Dollar) (EXCH)—Baseline

Level of baseline path, 1972 = 100 (increase is dollar appreciation)

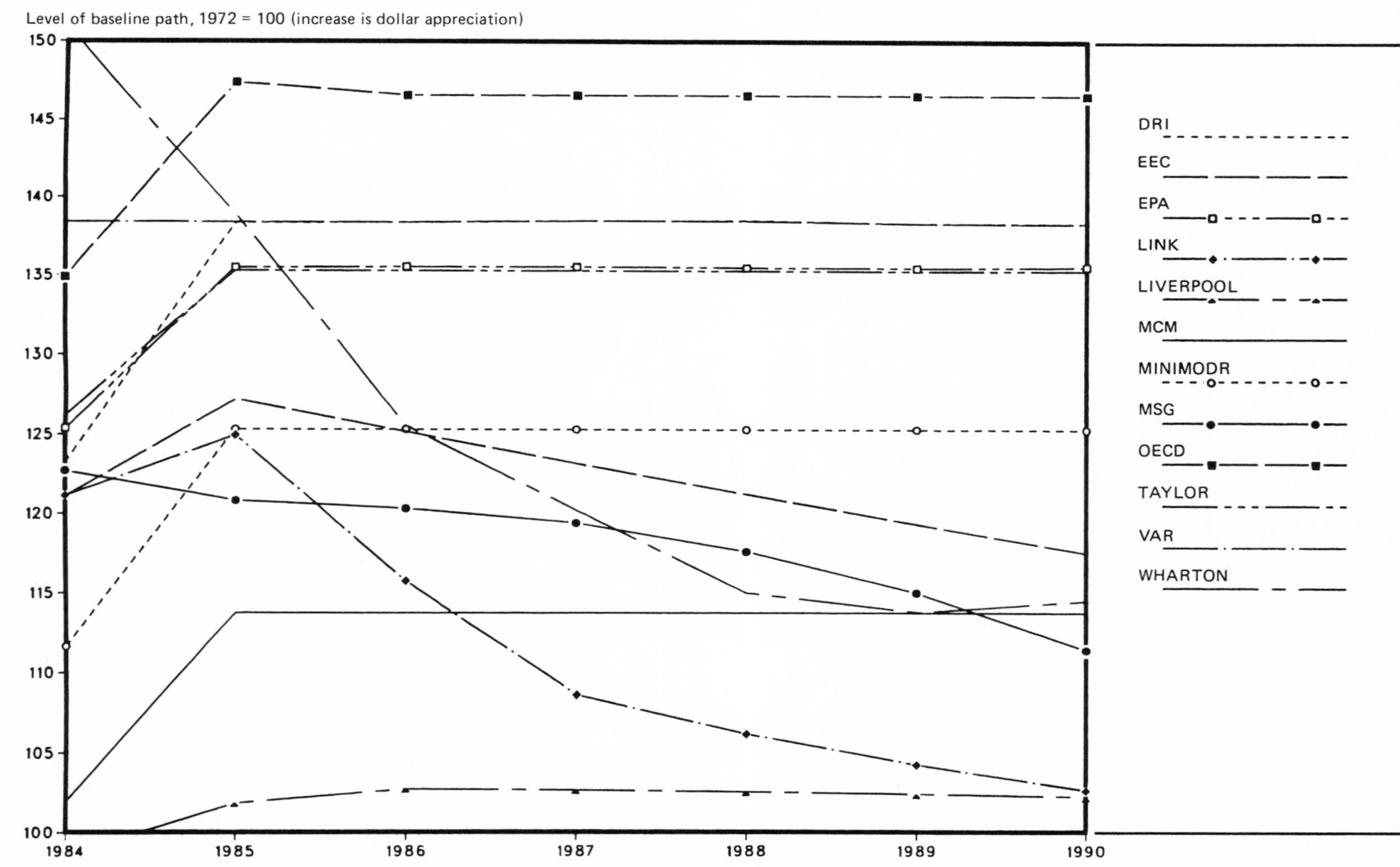

Chart A-16. Weighted Average Exchange Value of ROECD Currencies against U.S. Dollar (U.S. Dollars per ROECD Currency Basket) (OEXCH)—Baseline

Level of baseline path, 1972 = 100 (increase is appreciation of ROECD currencies)

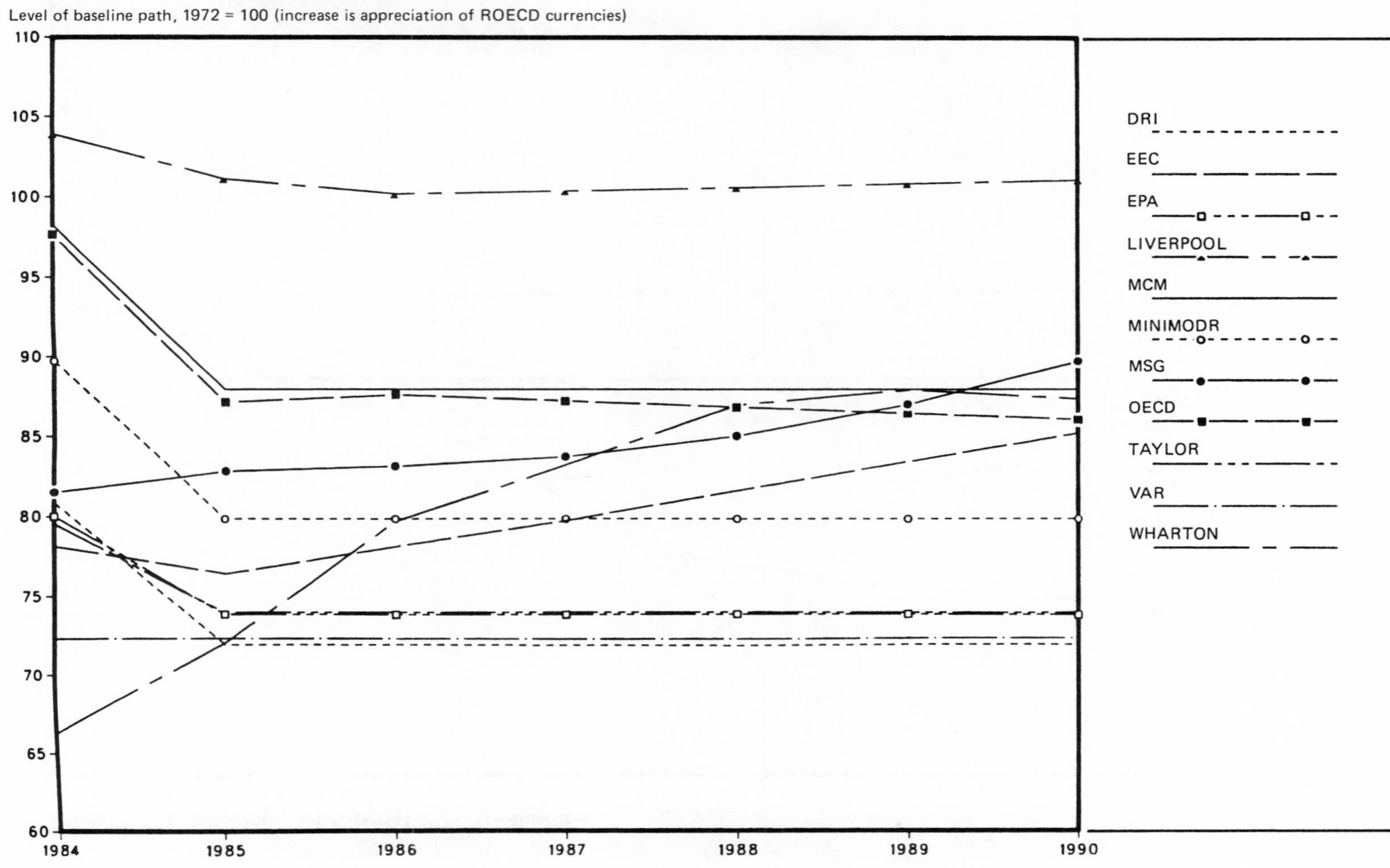

Chart A-17. U.S. Price Index for Exports (UPXGS)—Baseline

Year-to-year percent changes for level of baseline path

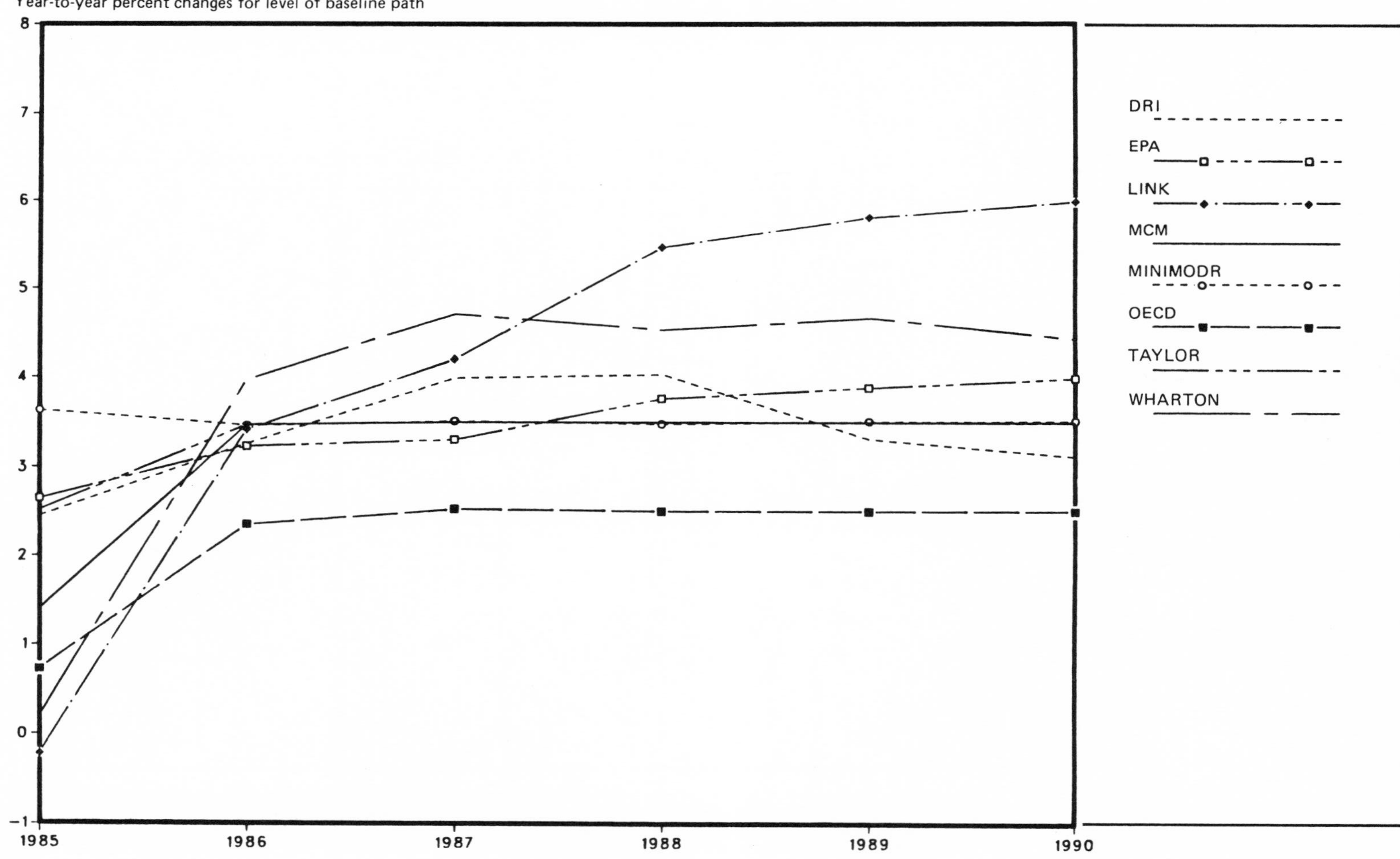

Chart A-18. ROECD Price Index for Exports (OPXGS)—Baseline

Year-to-year percent changes for level of baseline path

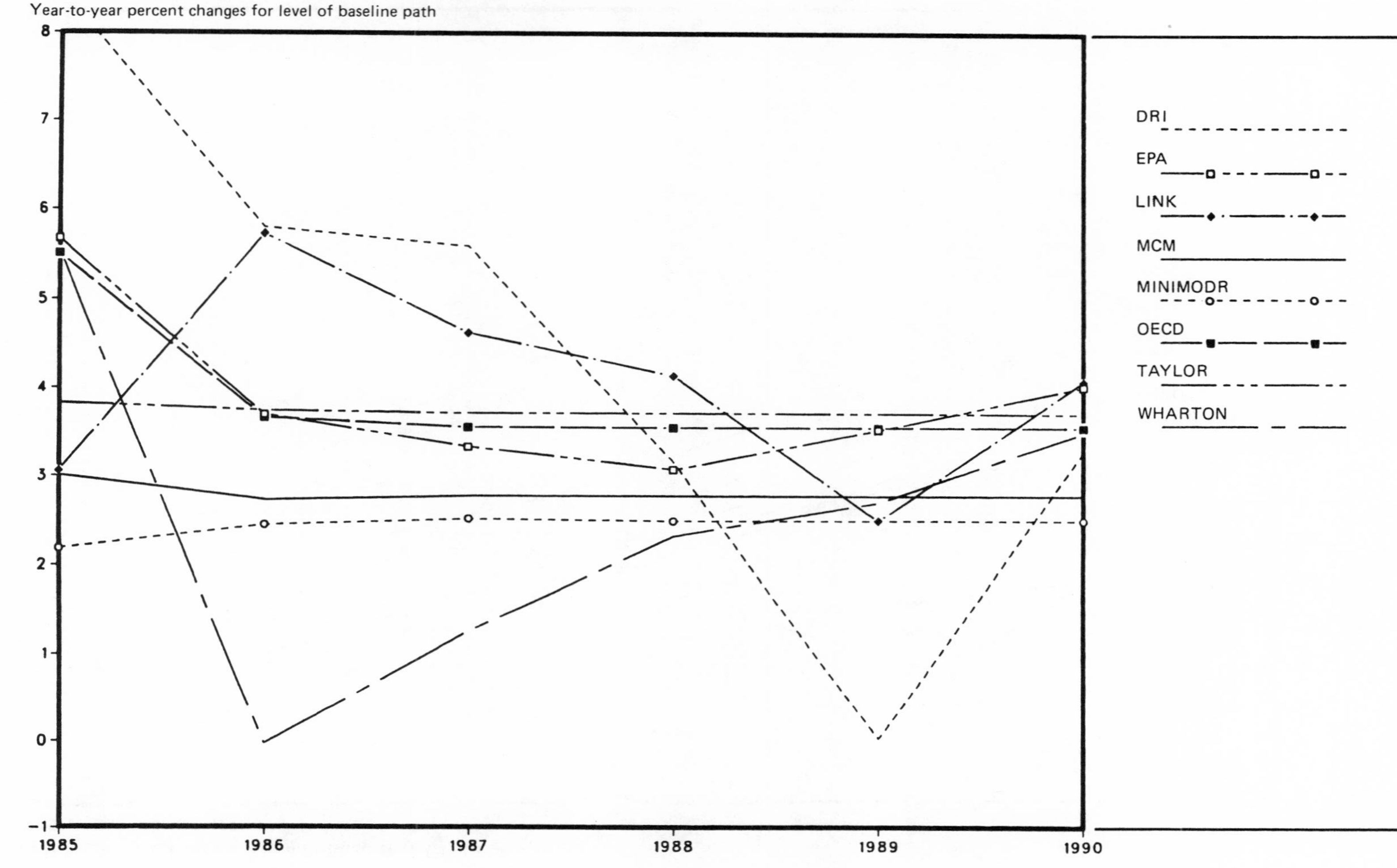

Chart A-19. U.S. Current Account Balance (UCURBAL)—Baseline

Level of baseline path, U.S. billion $

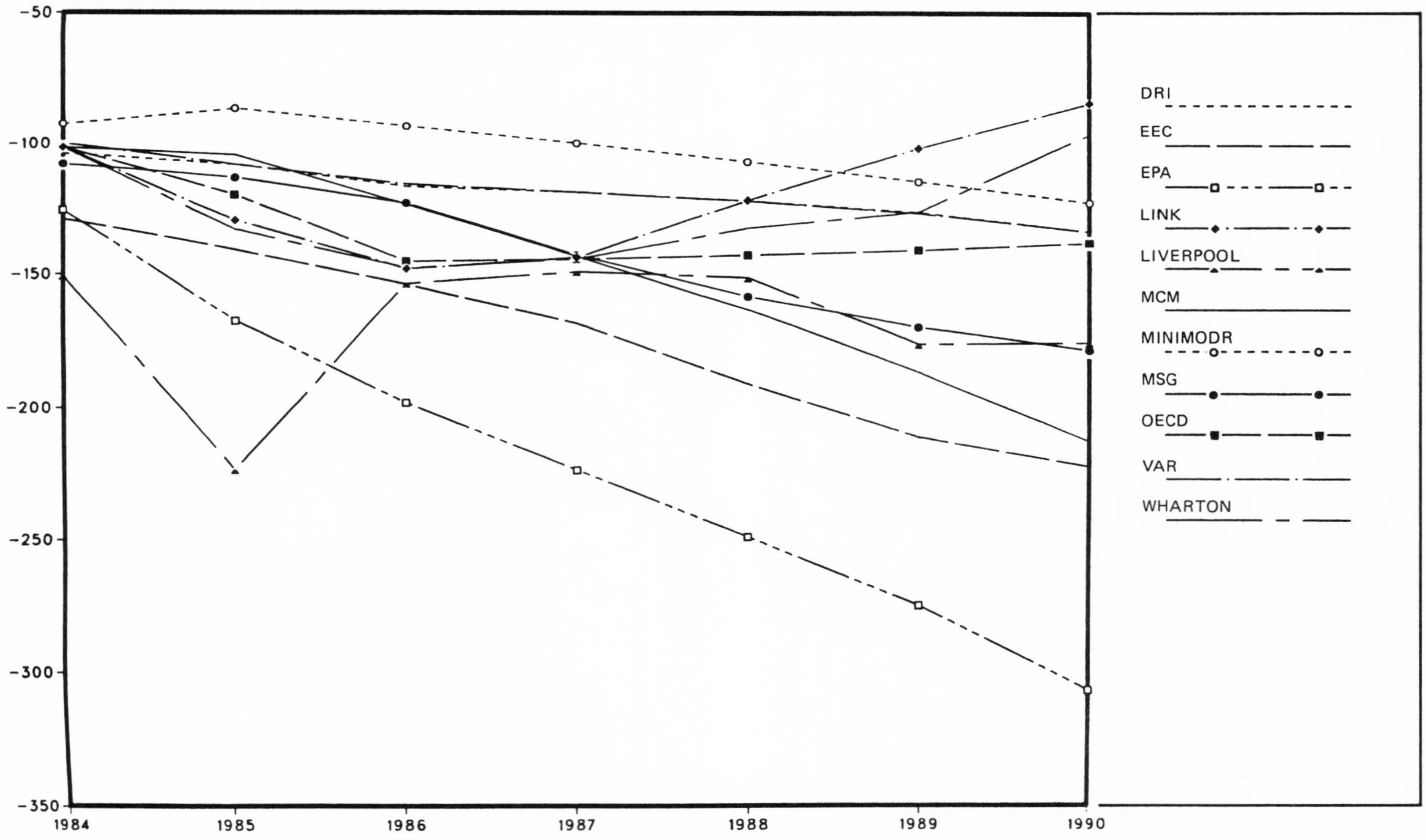

-50
-100
-150
-200
-250
-300
-350

1984
1985
1986
1987
1988
1989
1990

DRI
EEC
EPA
LINK
LIVERPOOL
MCM
MINIMODR
MSG
OECD
VAR
WHARTON

Chart A-20. ROECD Current Account Balance (OCURBAL)—Baseline

Level of baseline path, U.S. billion $ at baseline exchange rates

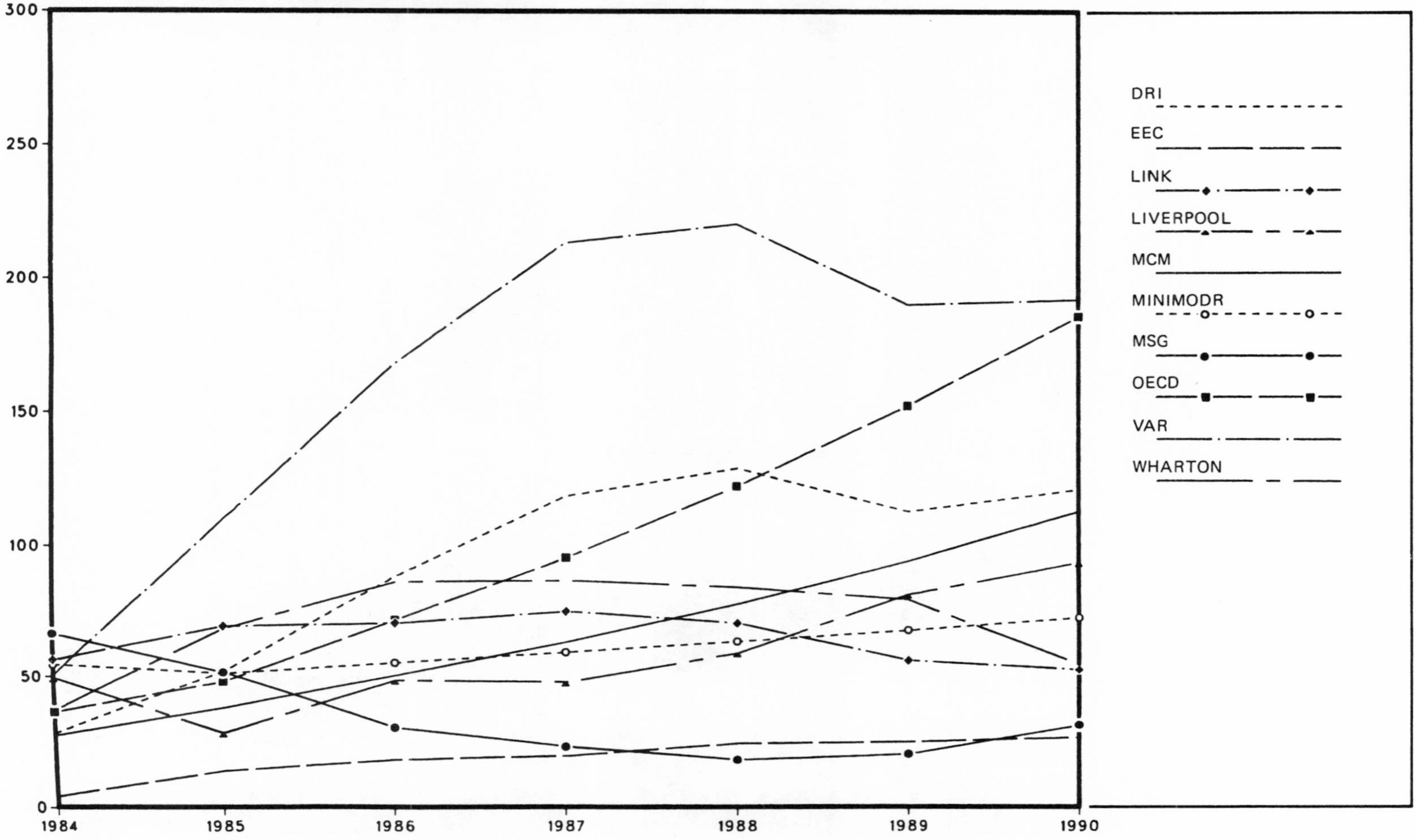

300
250
200
150
100
50
0

1984 1985 1986 1987 1988 1989 1990

DRI
EEC
LINK
LIVERPOOL
MCM
MINIMODR
MSG
OECD
VAR
WHARTON

SIMULATION B

U.S. Fiscal Contraction, Foreign Monetary Aggregates Unchanged

Chart B-1. Effects on U.S. Real GNP (UGNP) of Reduction in U.S. Government Purchases (Foreign Monetary Aggregates Unchanged from Baseline)

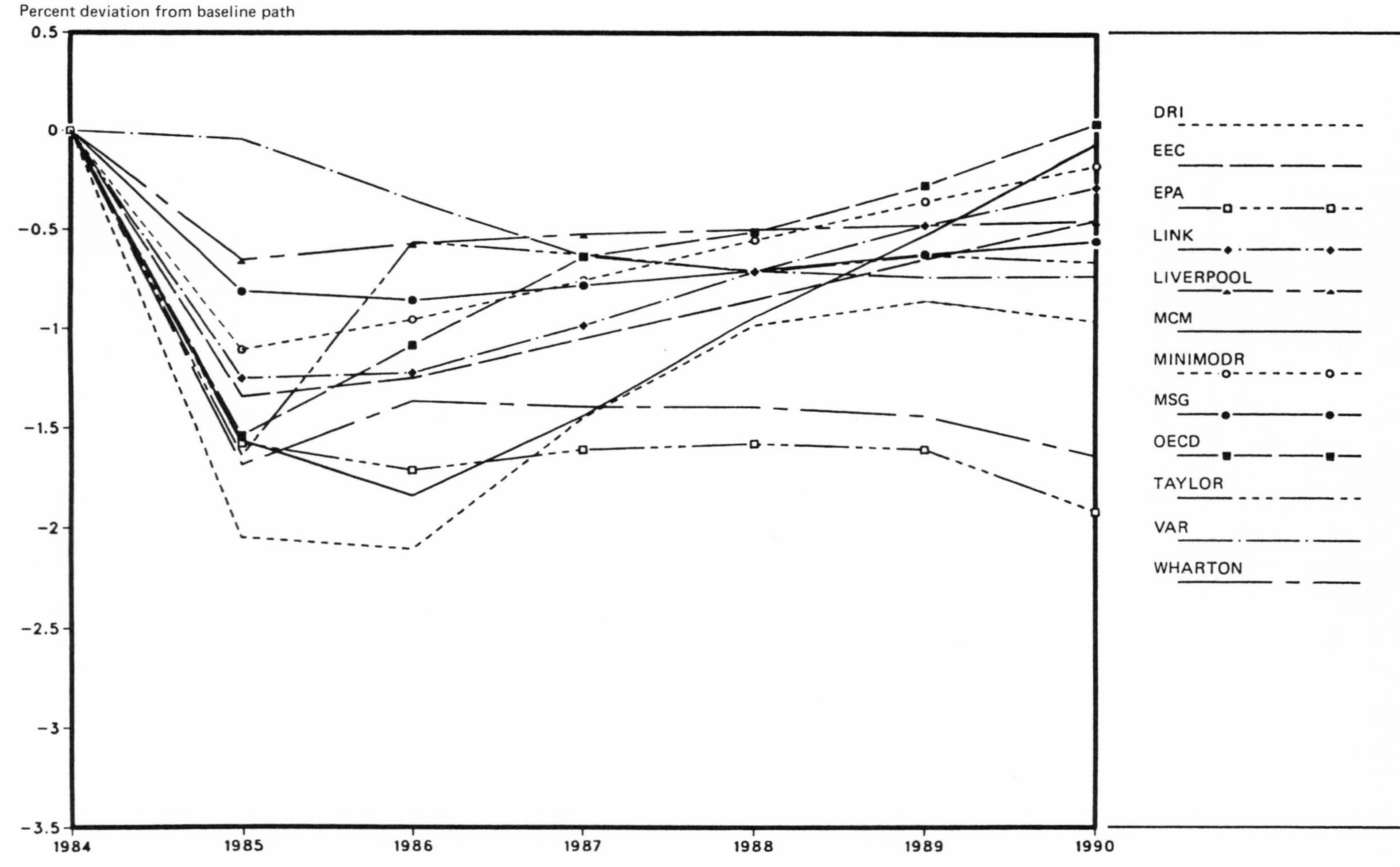

Chart B-2. Effects on ROECD Real GNP (OGNP) of Reduction in U.S. Government Purchases (Foreign Monetary Aggregates Unchanged from Baseline)

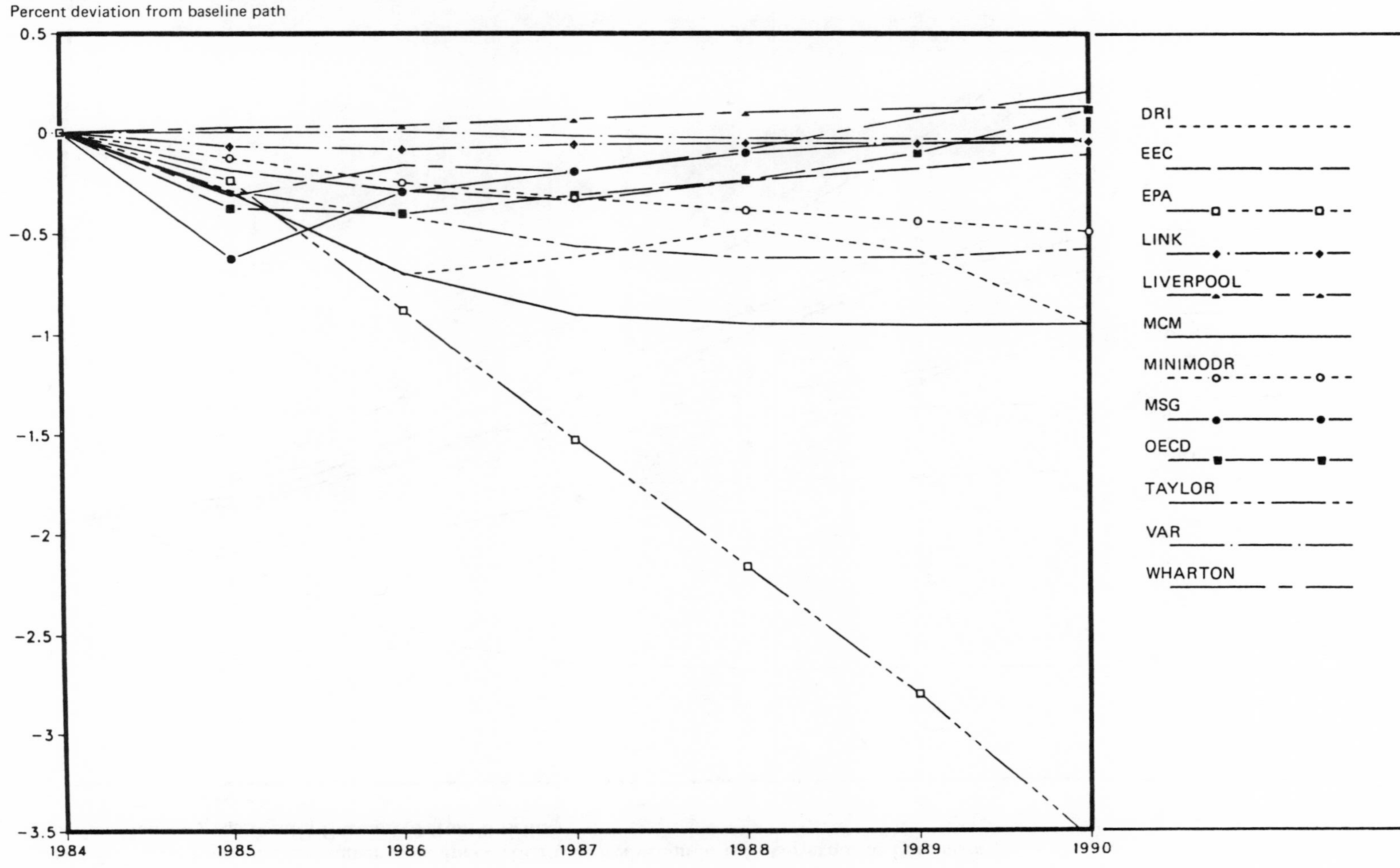

Chart B-3. Effects on U.S. Consumer Price Index (UCPI) of Reduction in U.S. Government Purchases (Foreign Monetary Aggregates Unchanged from Baseline)

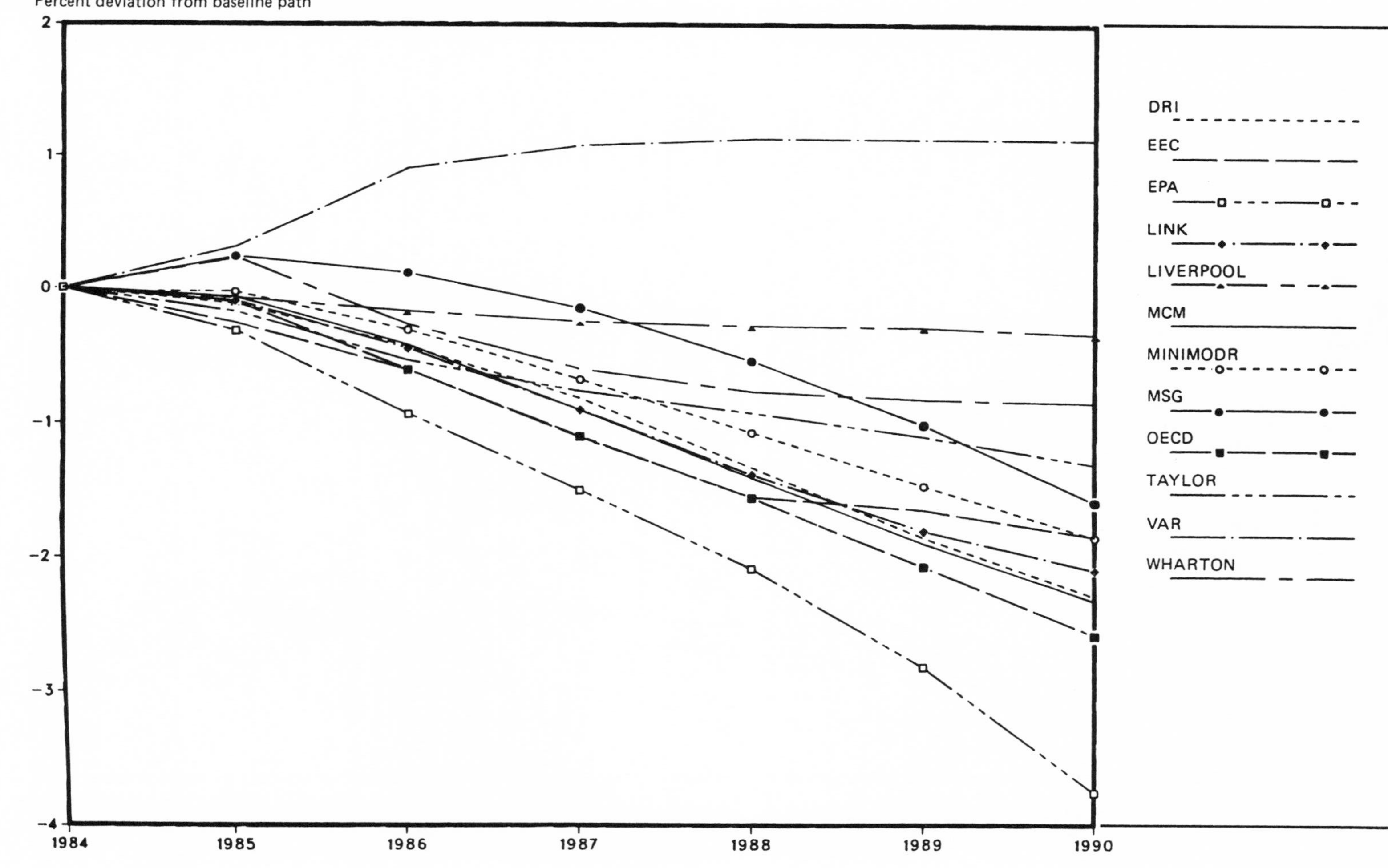

Chart B-4. Effects on ROECD Consumer Price Index (OPCPI) of Reduction in U.S. Government Purchases (Foreign Monetary Aggregates Unchanged from Baseline)

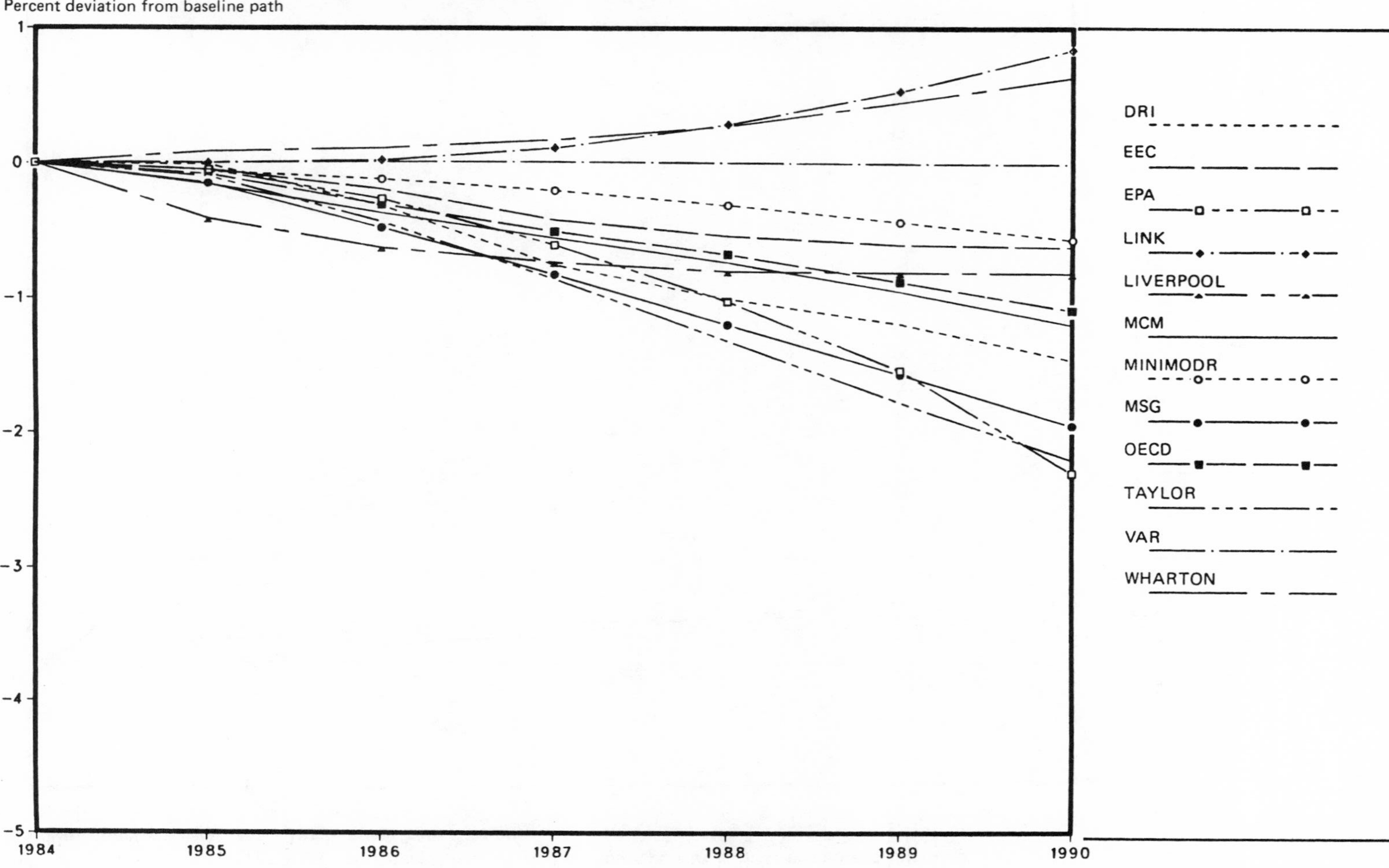

Chart B-5. Effects on U.S. Short-Term Interest Rate (URS) of Reduction in U.S. Government Purchases (Foreign Monetary Aggregates Unchanged from Baseline)

Deviation from baseline path, percentage points

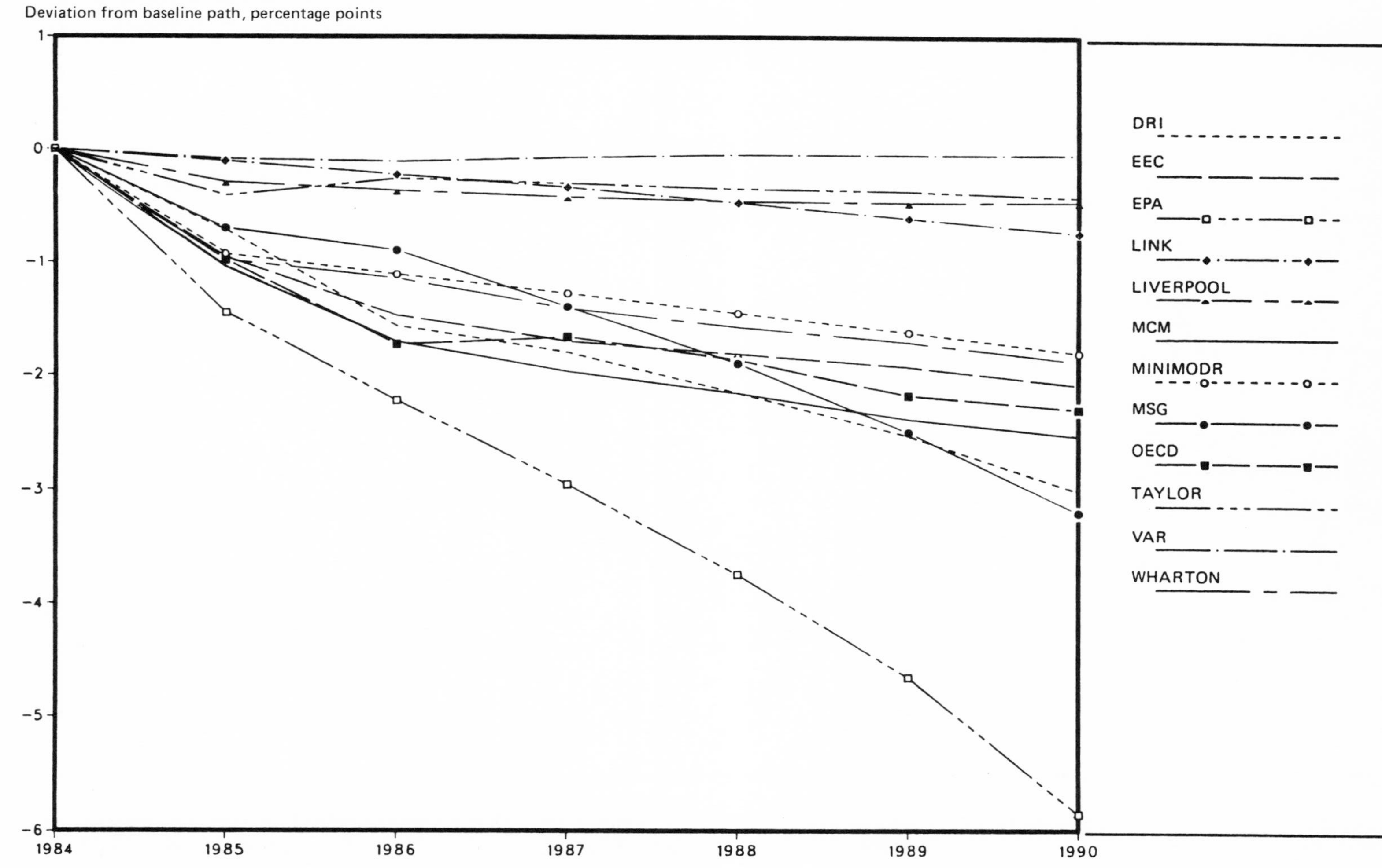

Chart B-6. Effects on ROECD Short-Term Interest Rate (ORS) of Reduction in U.S. Government Purchases (Foreign Monetary Aggregates Unchanged from Baseline)

Deviation from baseline path, percentage points

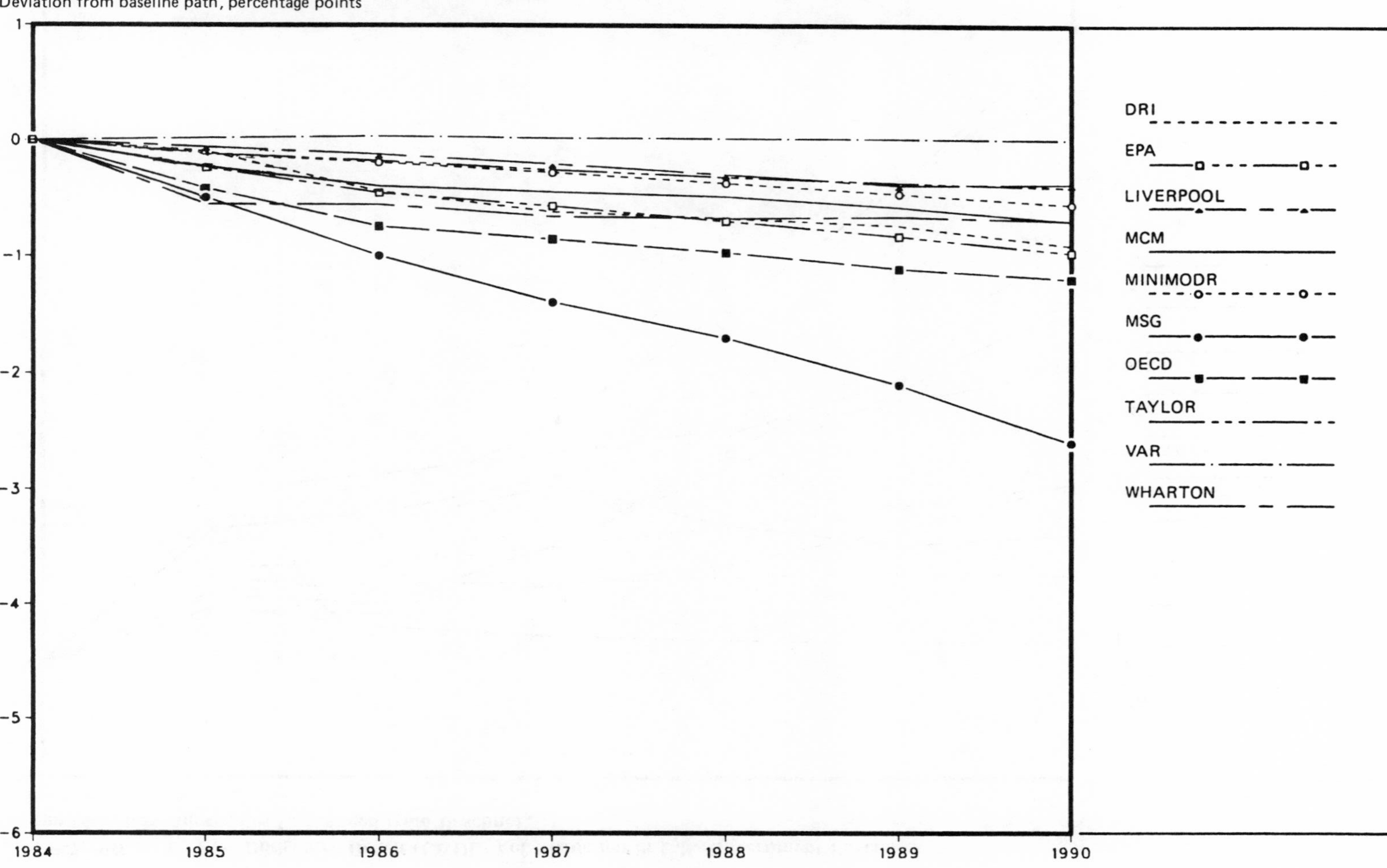

Chart B-7. Effects on U.S. Budgetary Deficit (UGDEF) of Reduction in U.S. Government Purchases (Foreign Monetary Aggregates Unchanged from Baseline)

Deviation from baseline path, U.S. billion $

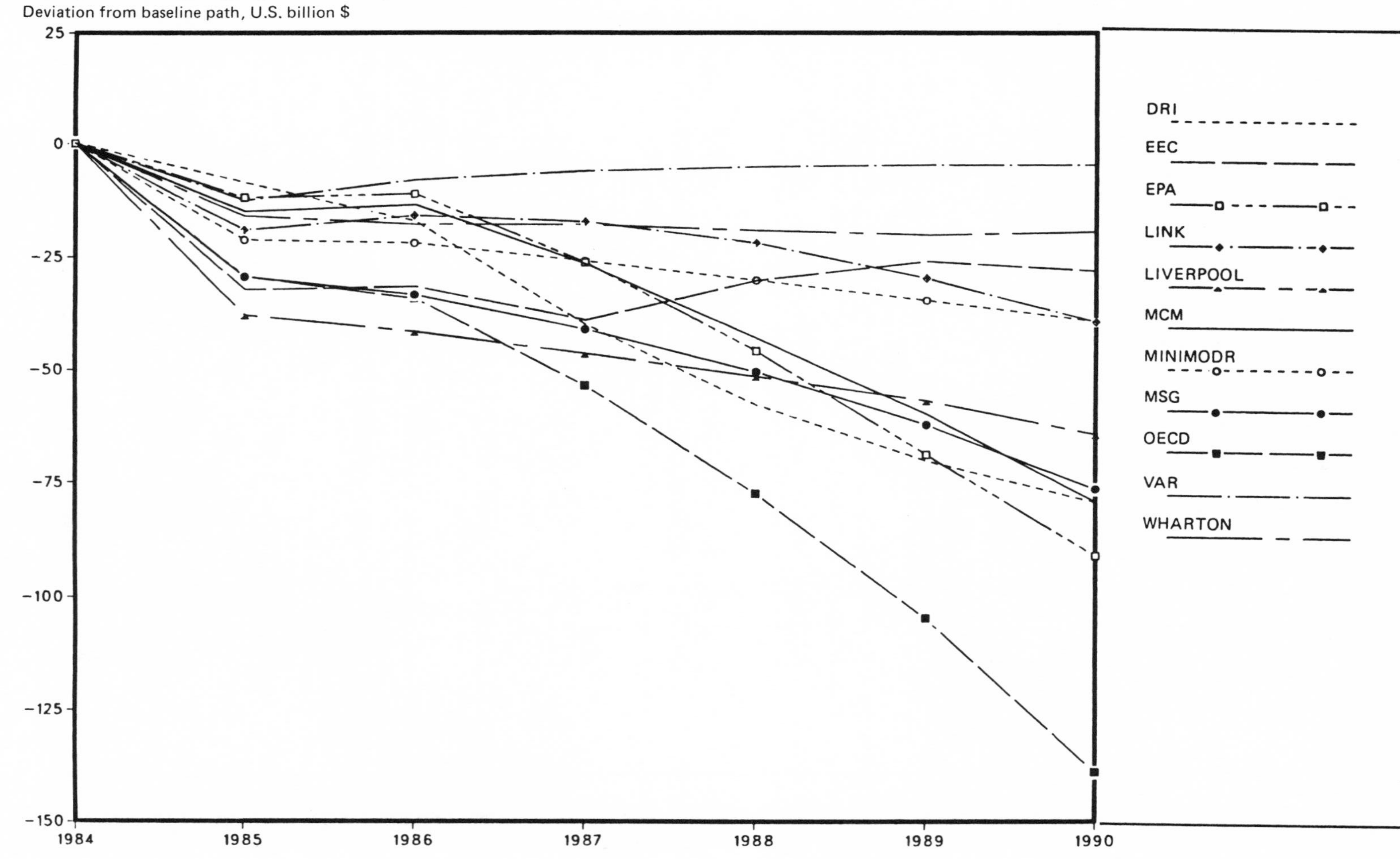

Chart B-8. Effects on Weighted Average Exchange Value of U.S. Dollar (Foreign Currencies per U.S. Dollar) (UEXCH) of Reduction in U.S. Government Purchases (Foreign Monetary Aggregates Unchanged from Baseline)

Percent deviation from baseline (+ = dollar appreciation)

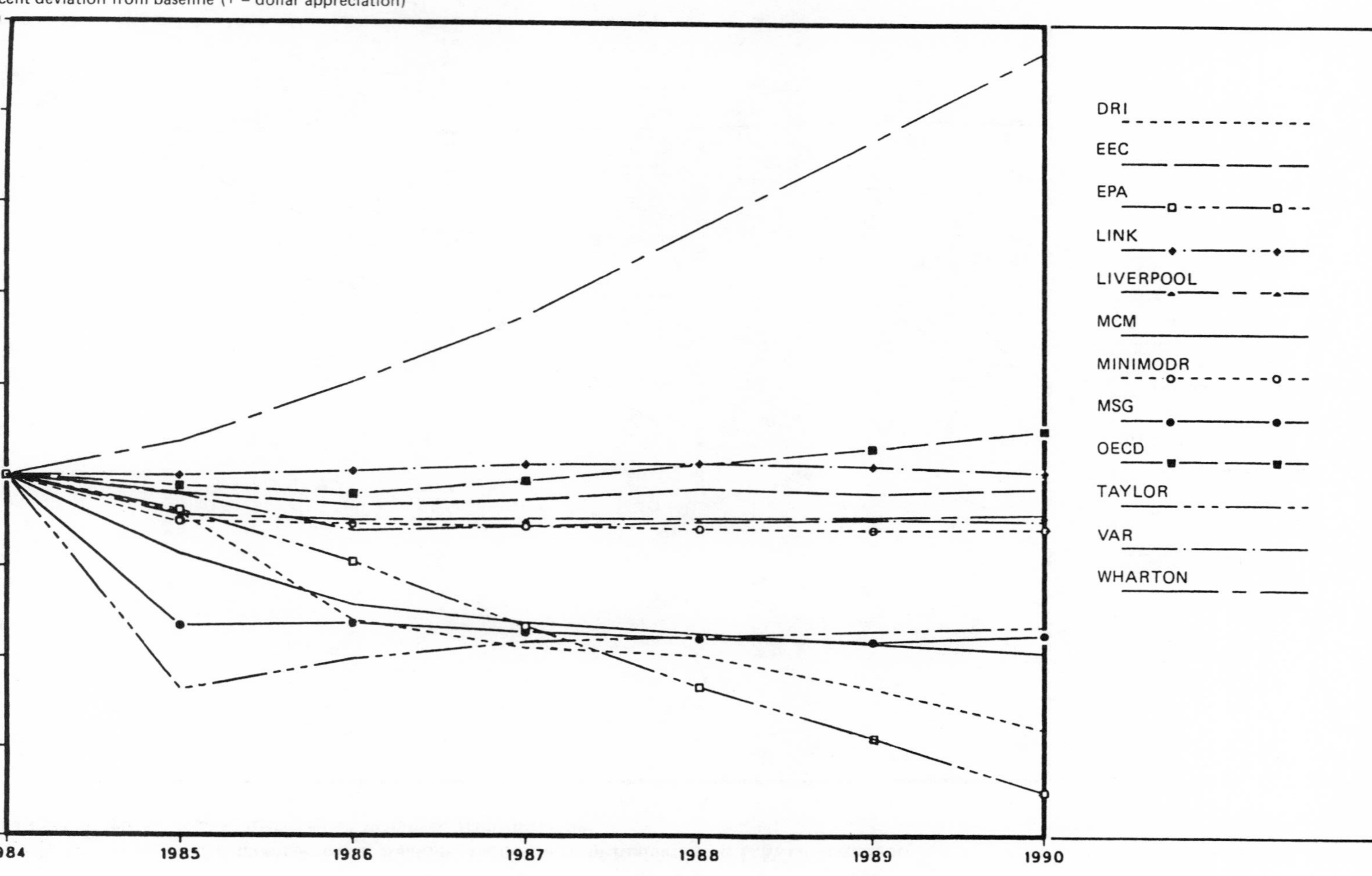

Chart B-9. Effects on U.S. Current Account Balance (UCURBAL) of Reduction in U.S. Government Purchases (Foreign Monetary Aggregates Unchanged from Baseline)

Deviation from baseline path, U.S. billion $

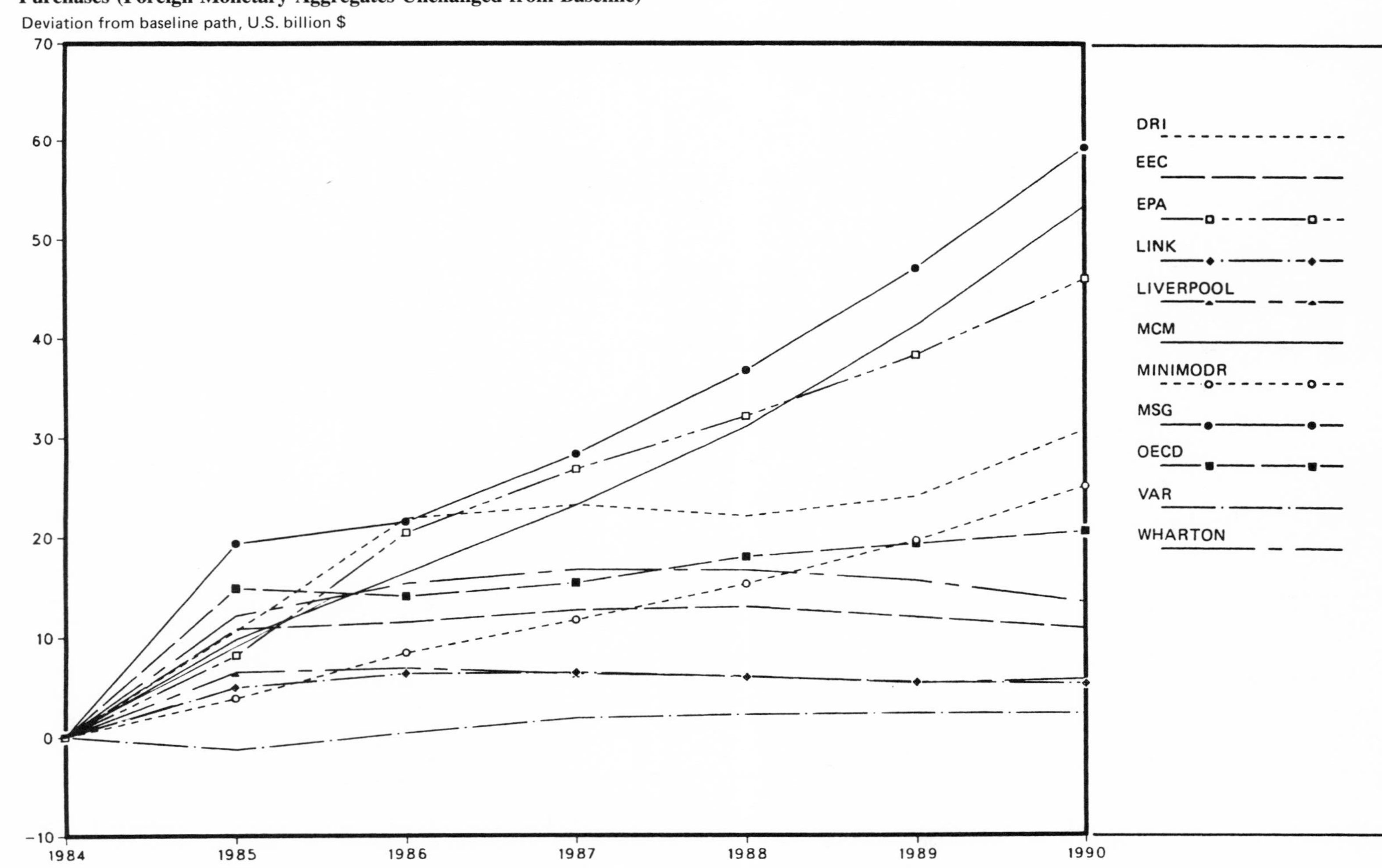

Chart B-10. Effects on ROECD Current Account Balance (OCURBAL) of Reduction in U.S. Government Purchases (Foreign Monetary Aggregates Unchanged from Baseline)

Deviation from baseline, U.S. billion $ at baseline exchange rates

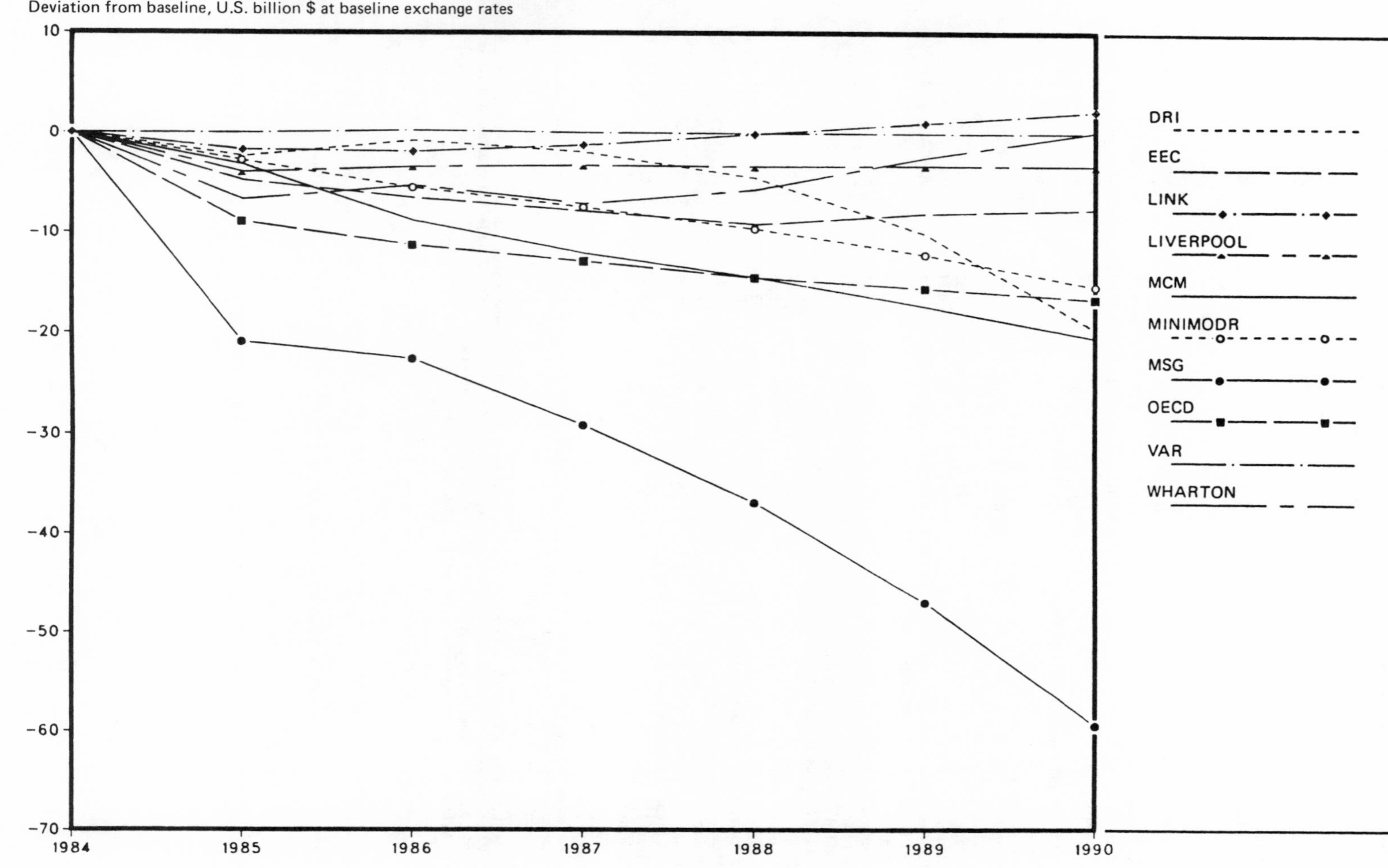

Table B. Average Responses, Standard Deviations, and Ranges for Simulated Effects of U.S. Fiscal Contraction with Foreign Monetary Aggregates Unchanged

(Simulation B—12 Models)

Variable	*Year 1 (1985)*	*Year 2 (1986)*	*Year 3 (1987)*	*Year 4 (1988)*	*Year 5 (1989)*	*Year 6 (1990)*
U.S. real GNP (UGNP)[a]						
Mean	−1.27	−1.16	−0.99	−0.84	−0.72	−0.65
Standard deviation	0.52	0.52	0.37	0.32	0.39	0.57
Range	2.00	1.75	1.08	1.08	1.33	1.96
ROECD real GNP (OGNP)[a]						
Mean	−0.23	−0.35	−0.42	−0.44	−0.47	−0.53
Standard deviation	0.17	0.28	0.43	0.59	0.77	0.99
Range	0.65	0.92	1.60	2.26	2.93	3.76
U.S. consumer price index (UCPI)[a,e]						
Mean	−0.04	−0.31	−0.64	−0.98	−1.30	−1.64
Standard deviation	0.19	0.44	0.63	0.79	0.97	1.18
Range	0.64	1.84	2.58	3.22	3.95	4.88
ROECD consumer price index (OPCPI)[a,f]						
Mean	−0.09	−0.25	−0.43	−0.59	−0.73	−0.90
Standard deviation	0.12	0.21	0.35	0.53	0.73	0.99
Range	0.50	0.74	1.04	1.61	2.32	3.15
U.S. short-term interest rate (URS)[b]						
Mean	−0.72	−1.07	−1.25	−1.50	−1.75	−2.03
Standard deviation	0.40	0.67	0.81	1.00	1.22	1.53
Range	1.37	2.12	2.88	3.70	4.60	5.82
ROECD short-term interest rate (ORS)[b,g]						
Mean	−0.23	−0.41	−0.53	−0.62	−0.72	−0.84
Standard deviation	0.18	0.30	0.38	0.45	0.54	0.67
Range	0.58	1.04	1.42	1.71	2.12	2.61
Weighted average exchange value of U.S. dollar (UEXCH)[a]						
Mean	−1.12	−1.43	−1.44	−1.36	−1.36	−1.33
Standard deviation	1.45	1.64	2.08	2.67	3.30	3.98
Range	5.50	6.12	7.32	10.13	13.18	16.40
U.S. current account balance (UCAB)[c,h]						
Mean	9.15	13.11	15.77	18.16	21.02	24.84
Standard deviation	5.34	6.66	8.46	10.91	14.63	19.28
Range	20.66	21.49	26.48	34.54	44.73	57.00
ROECD current account balance (OCAB)[d,i]						
Mean	−5.57	−6.63	−8.34	−9.87	−11.56	−14.11
Standard deviation	5.68	6.34	8.12	10.27	13.27	17.21
Range	21.00	22.92	29.19	36.84	48.01	61.65

Source: Detailed tables in part 3.
a. Percent deviation from baseline path.
b. Deviation from baseline path in percentage points.
c. Deviation from baseline path in U.S. $ billion.
d. Deviation from baseline path in U.S. $ billion at baseline exchange rates.
e. TAYLOR and VAR models did not report results for U.S. consumer prices; results for the U.S. GNP deflator for those models are used as a substitute.
f. VAR model did not report results for ROECD consumer prices; results for the ROECD GNP deflator for that model are used as a substitute.
g. EEC and LINK models did not report results for the ROECD short-term interest rate.
h. TAYLOR model did not report results for the U.S. current account balance.
i. EPA and TAYLOR models did not report results for the ROECD current account balance.

SIMULATION C

U.S. Fiscal Contraction, Foreign Interest Rates Unchanged

Chart C-1. Effects on U.S. Real GNP (UGNP) of Reduction in U.S. Government Purchases (Foreign Short-Term Interest Rates Unchanged from Baseline)

Percent deviation from baseline path

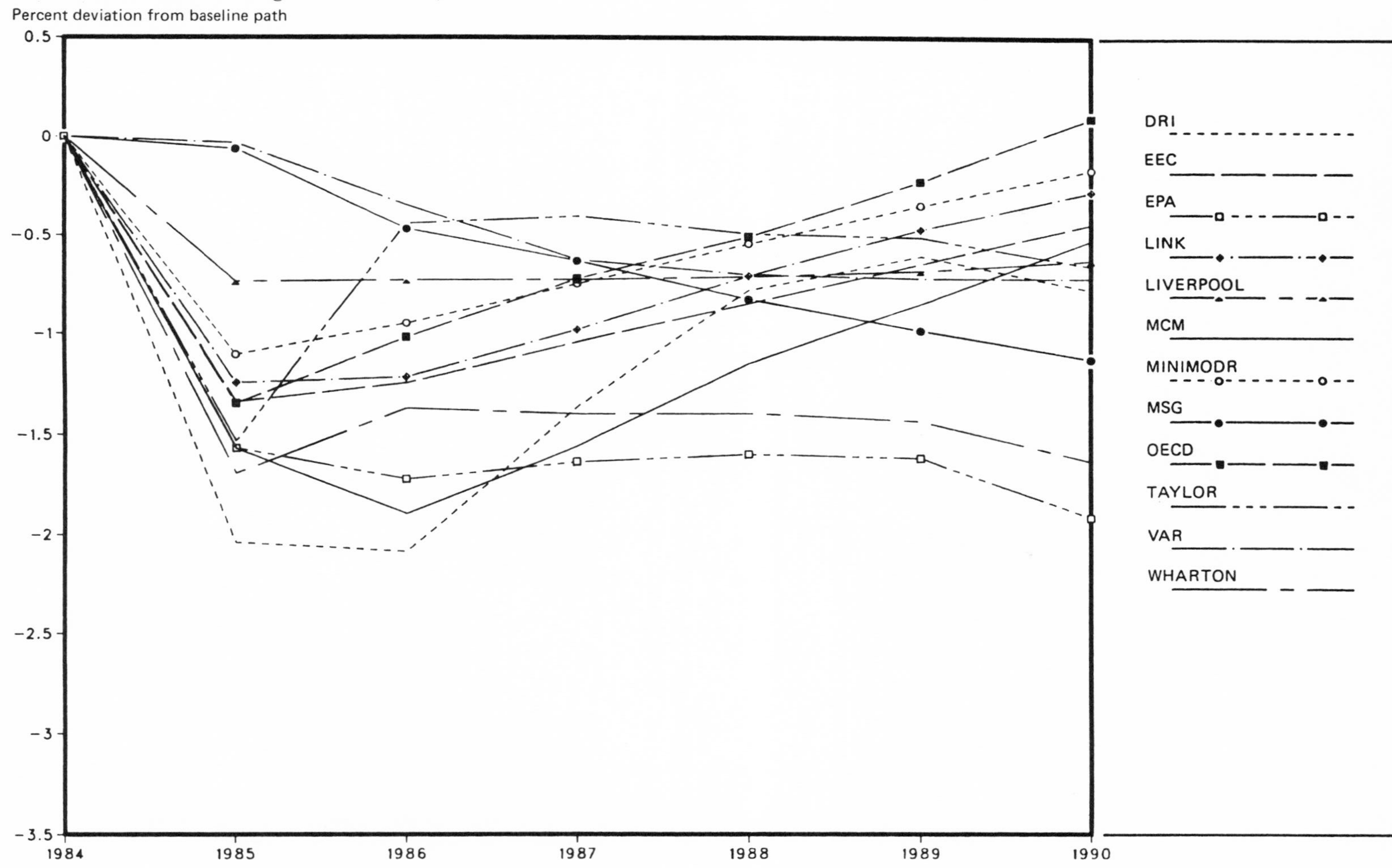

Chart C-2. Effects on ROECD Real GNP (OGNP) of Reduction in U.S. Government Purchases (Foreign Short-Term Interest Rates Unchanged from Baseline)

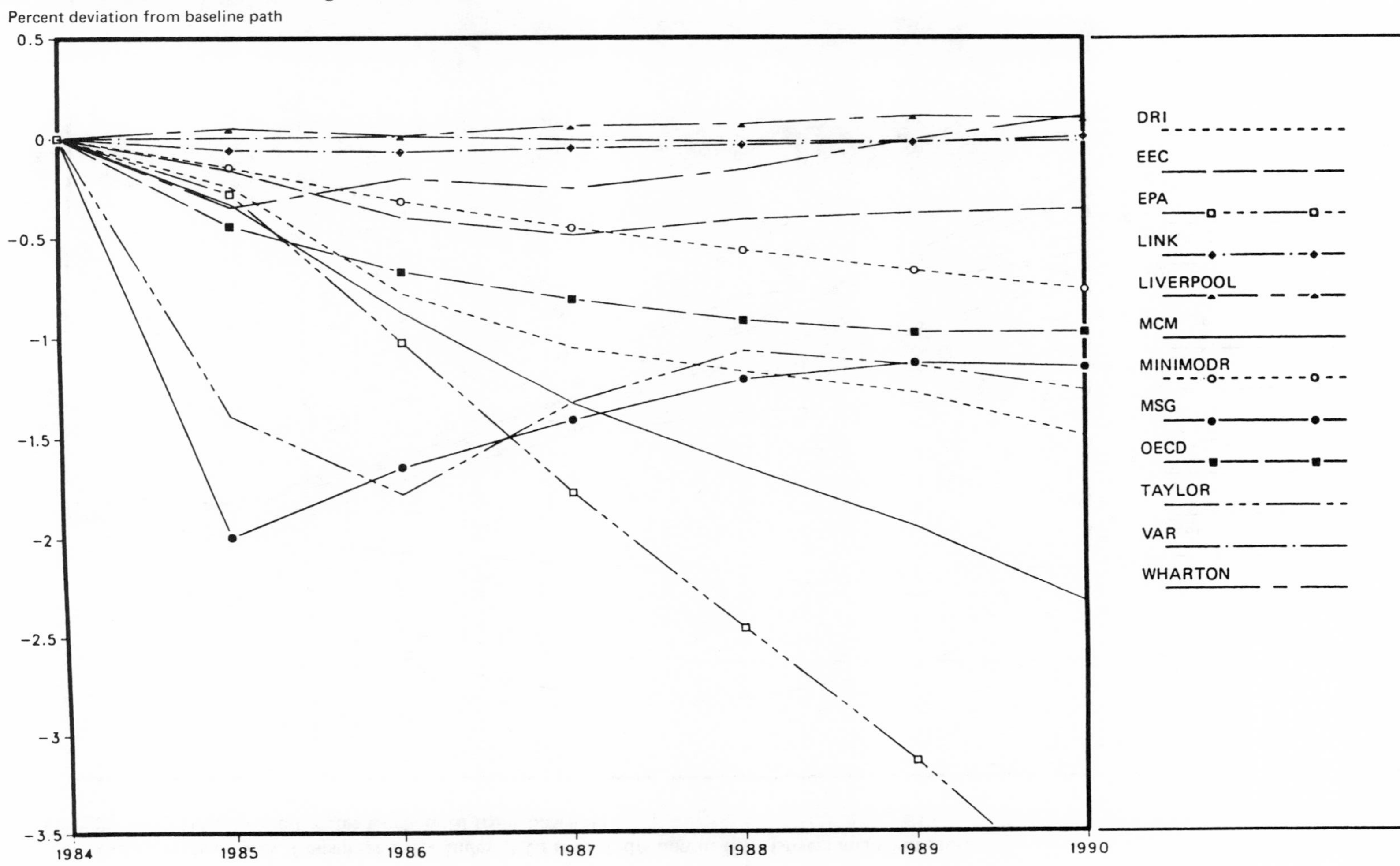

Chart C-3. Effects on U.S. Consumer Price Index (UCPI) of Reduction in U.S. Government Purchases (Foreign Short-Term Interest Rates Unchanged from Baseline)

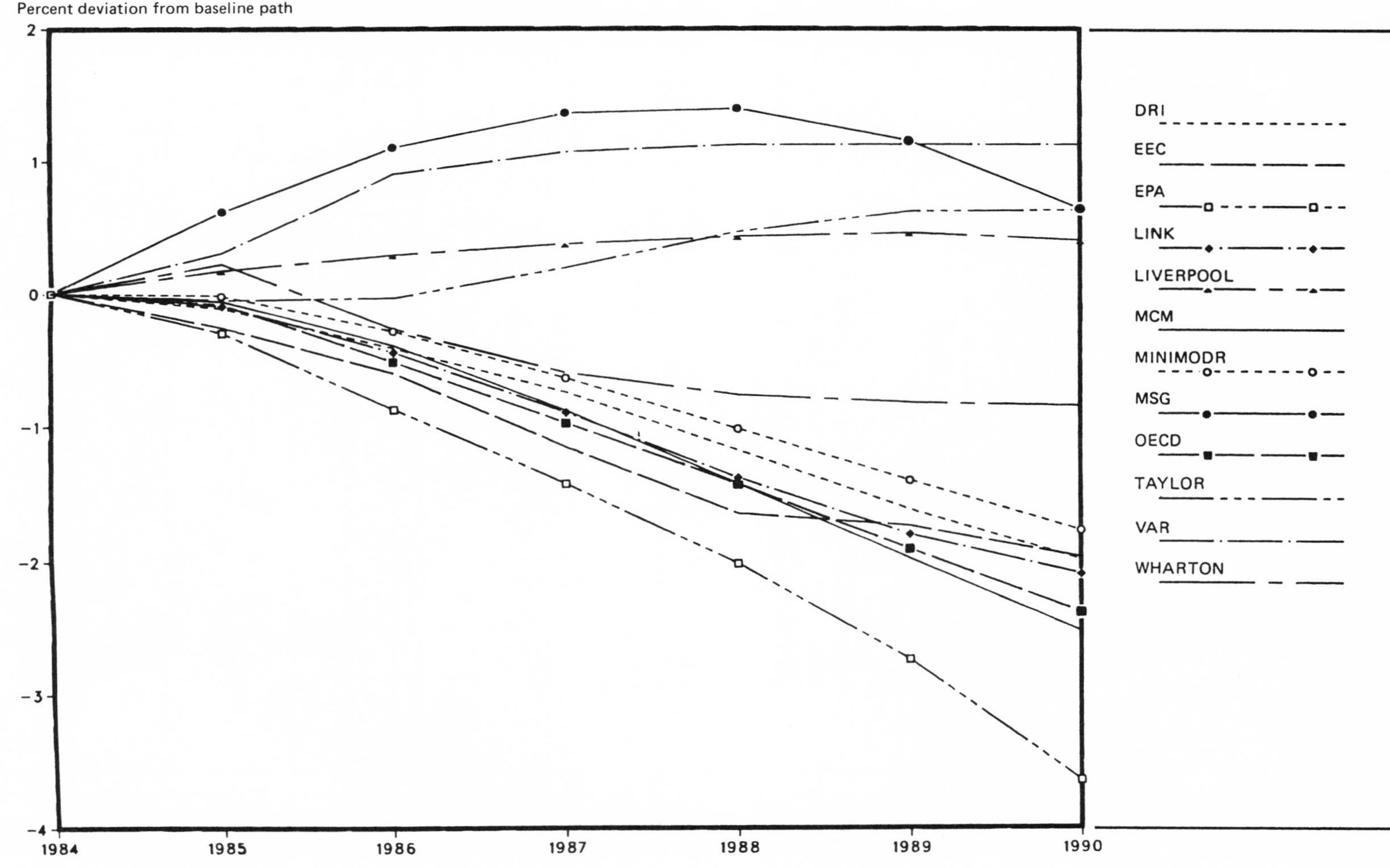

Chart C-4. Effects on ROECD Consumer Price Index (OPCPI) of Reduction in U.S. Government Purchases (Foreign Short-Term Interest Rates Unchanged from Baseline)

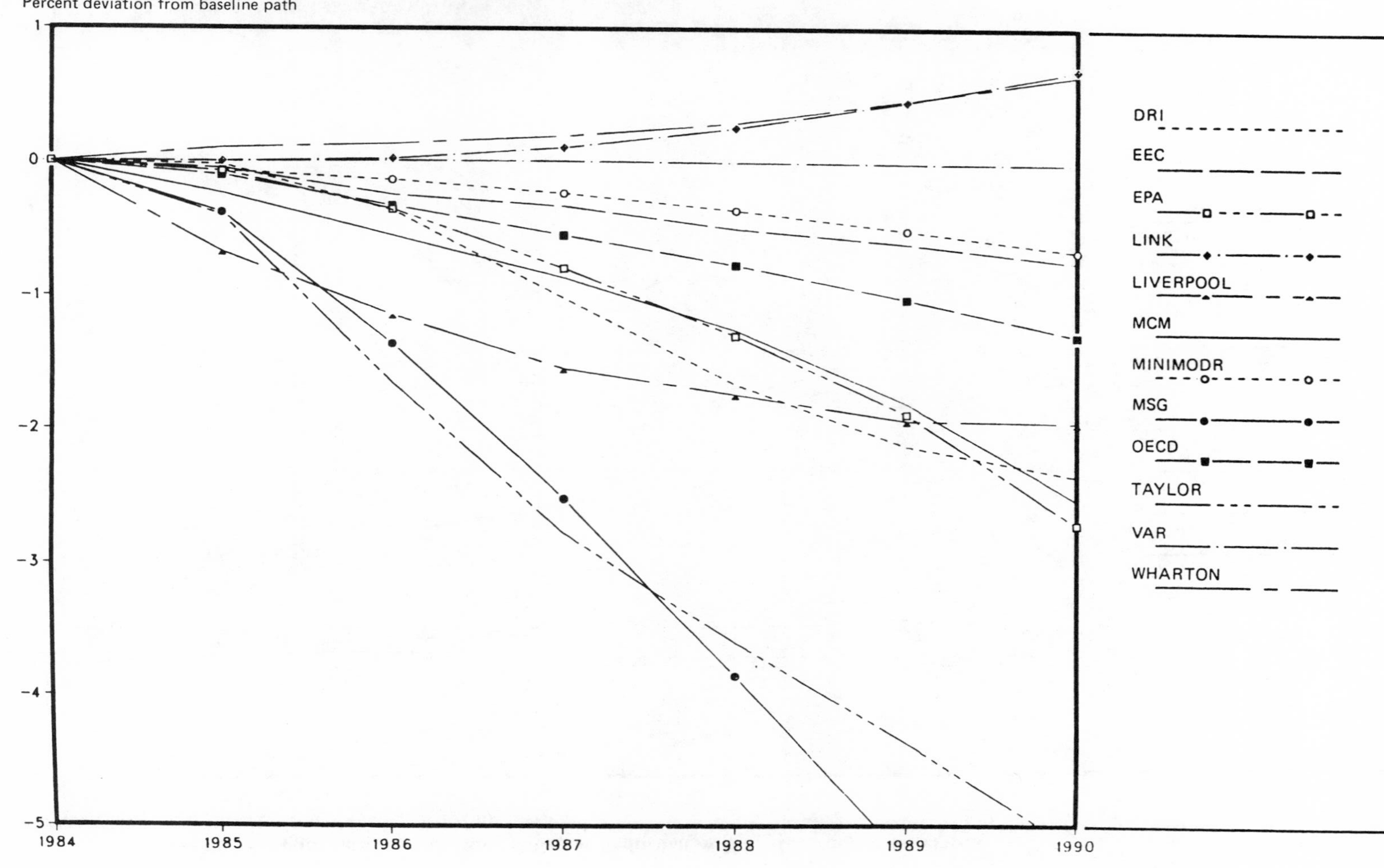

Chart C-5. Effects on U.S. Short-Term Interest Rate (URS) of Reduction in U.S. Government Purchases (Foreign Short-Term Interest Rates Unchanged from Baseline)

Deviation from baseline path, percentage points

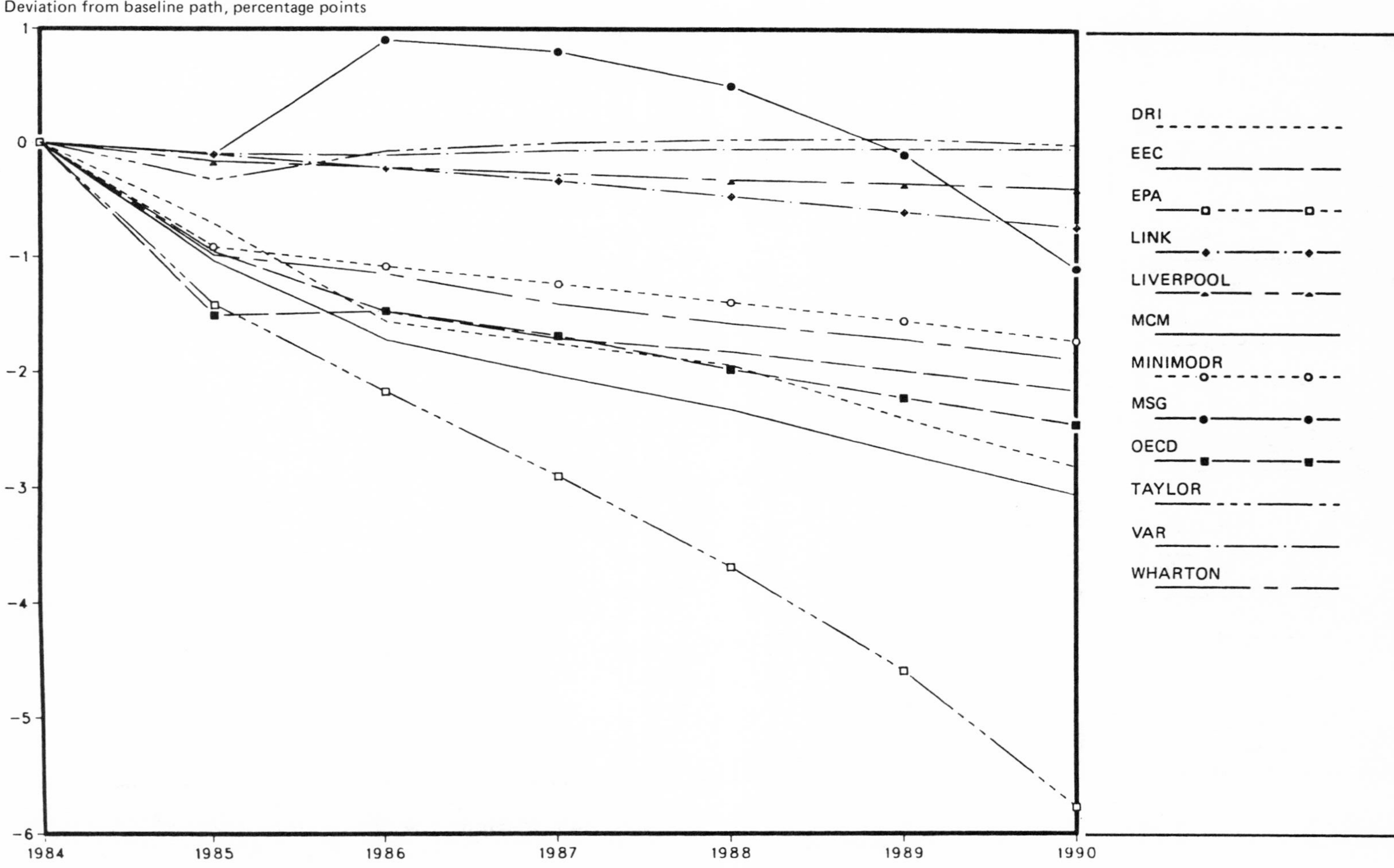

Chart C-7. Effects on U.S. Budgetary Deficit (UGDEF) of Reduction in U.S. Government Purchases (Foreign Short-Term Interest Rates Unchanged from Baseline)

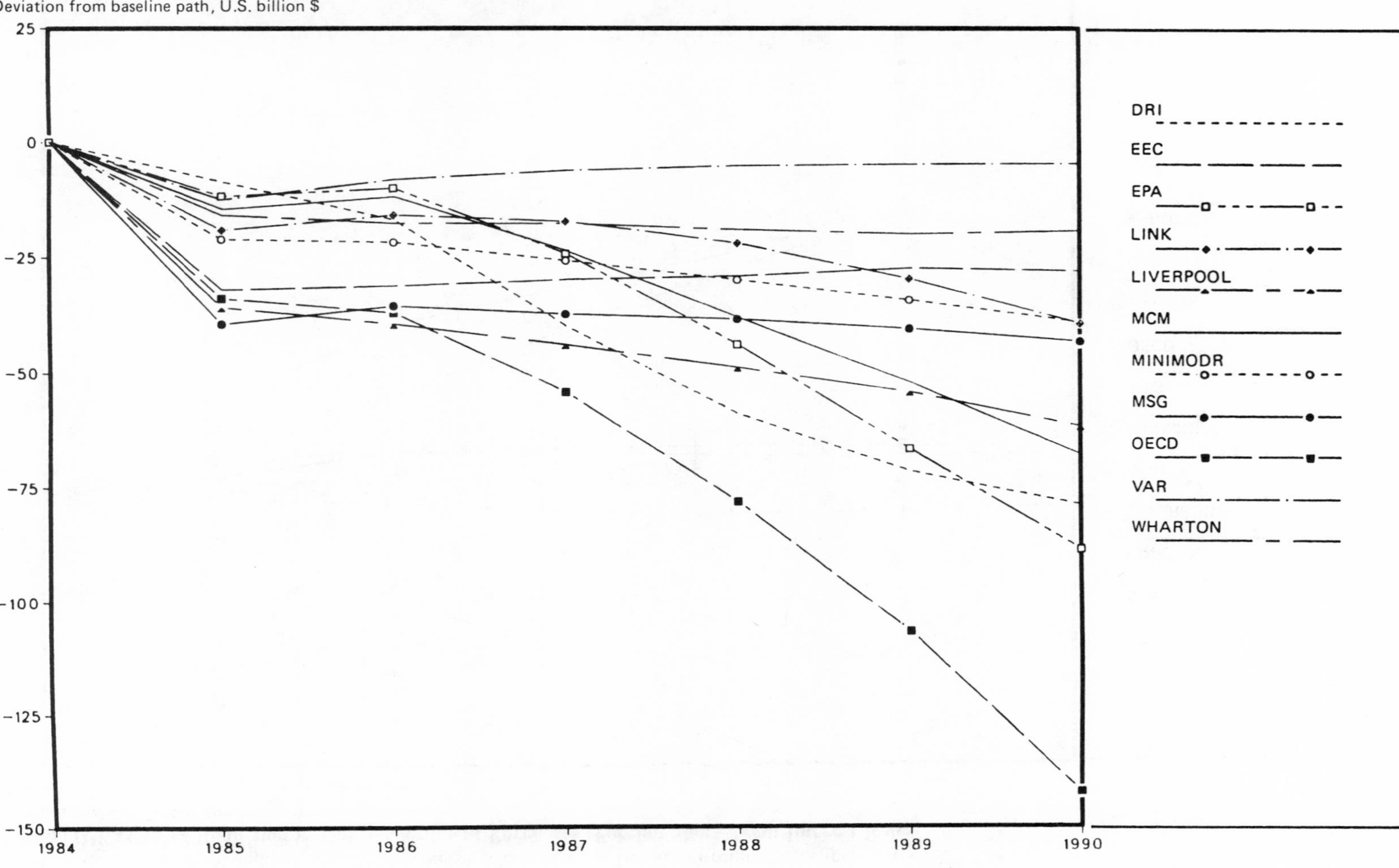

Chart C-8. Effects on Weighted Average Exchange Value of U.S. Dollar (Foreign Currencies per U.S. Dollar) (UEXCH) of Reduction in U.S. Government Purchases (Foreign Short-Term Interest Rates Unchanged from Baseline)

Percent deviation from baseline (+ = dollar appreciation)

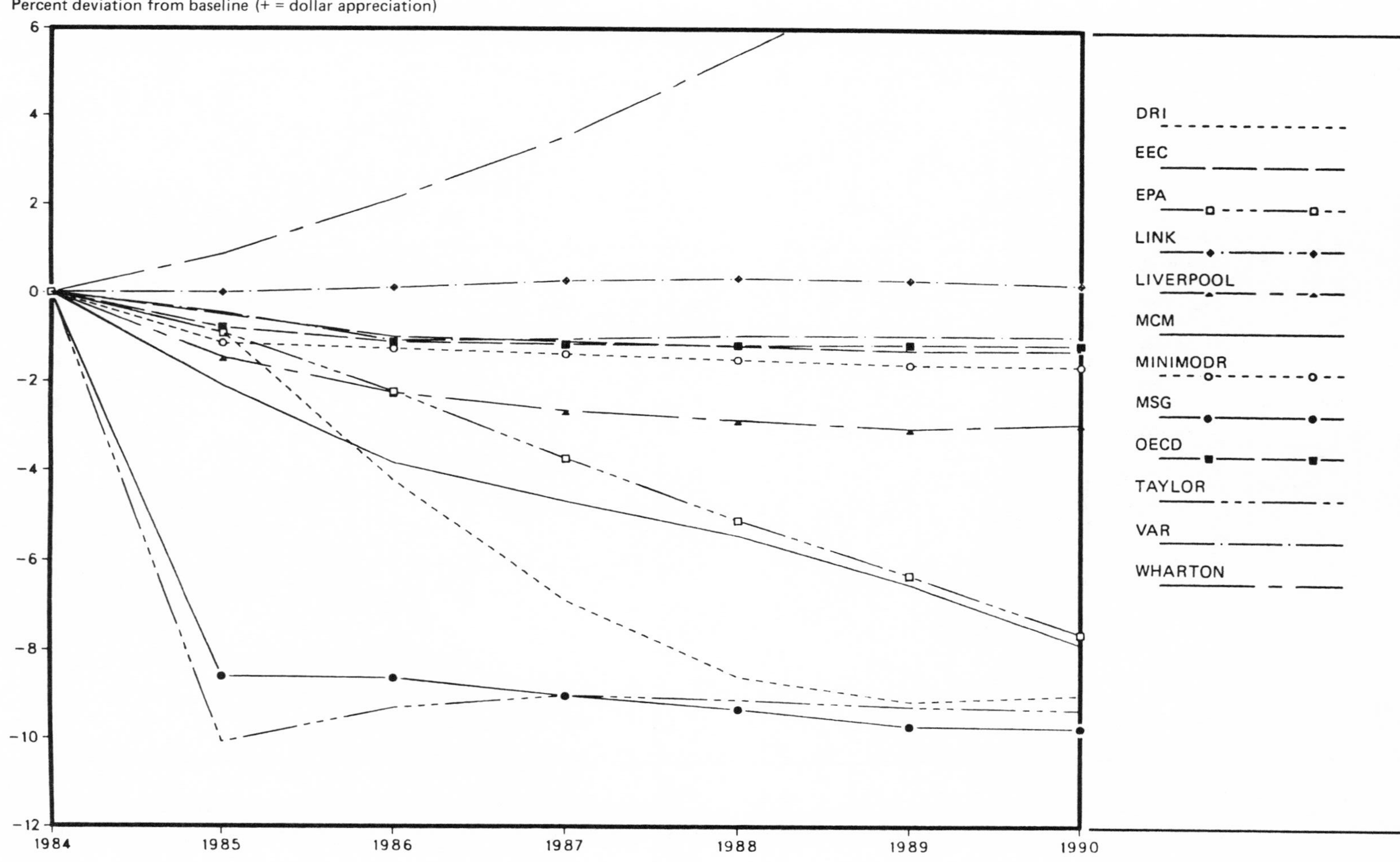

Chart C-9. Effects on U.S. Current Account Balance (UCURBAL) of Reduction in U.S. Government Purchases (Foreign Short-Term Interest Rates Unchanged from Baseline)

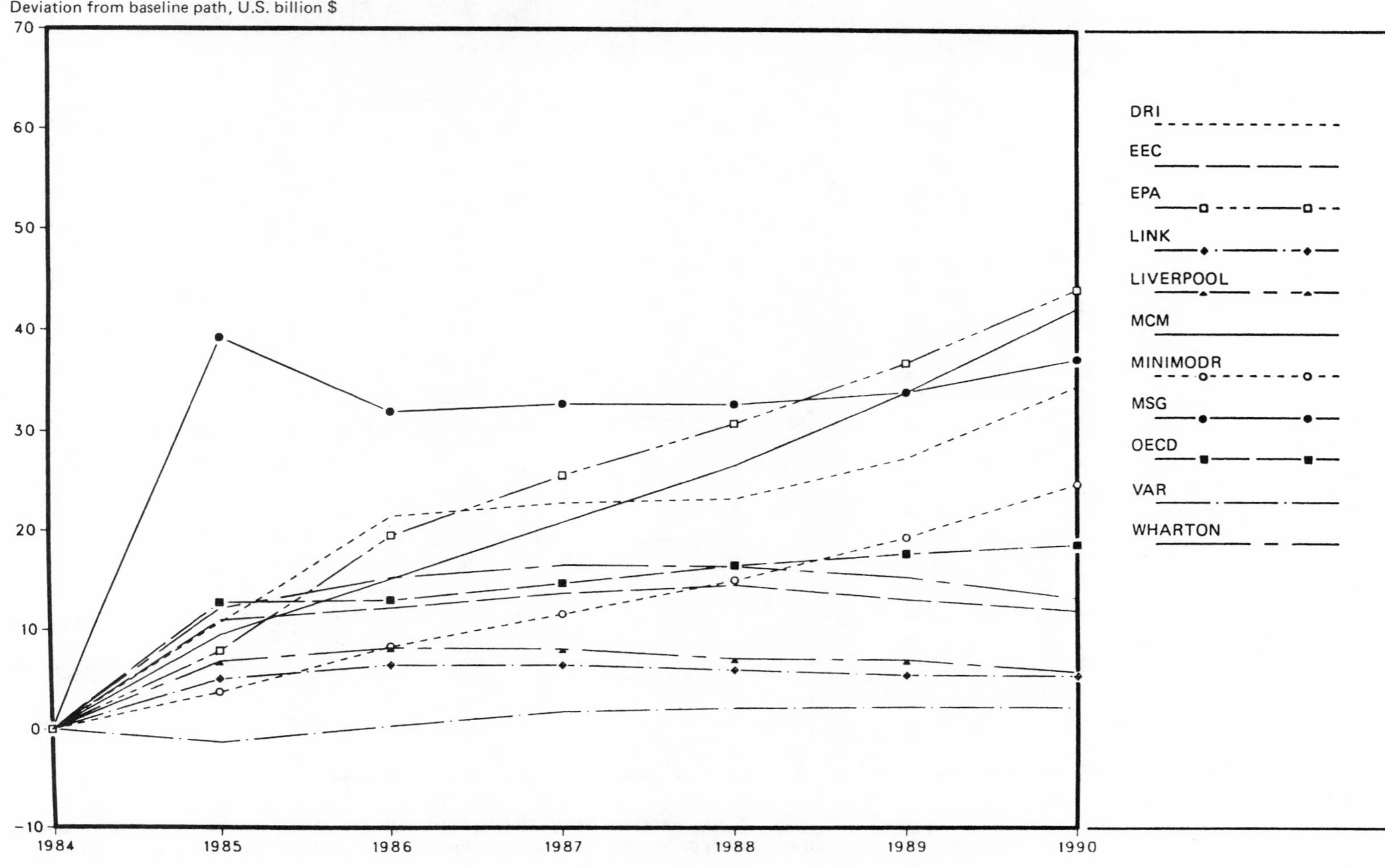

Chart C-10. Effects on ROECD Current Account Balance (OCURBAL) of Reduction in U.S. Government Purchases (Foreign Short-Term Interest Rates Unchanged from Baseline)

Deviation from baseline, U.S. billion $ at baseline exchange rates

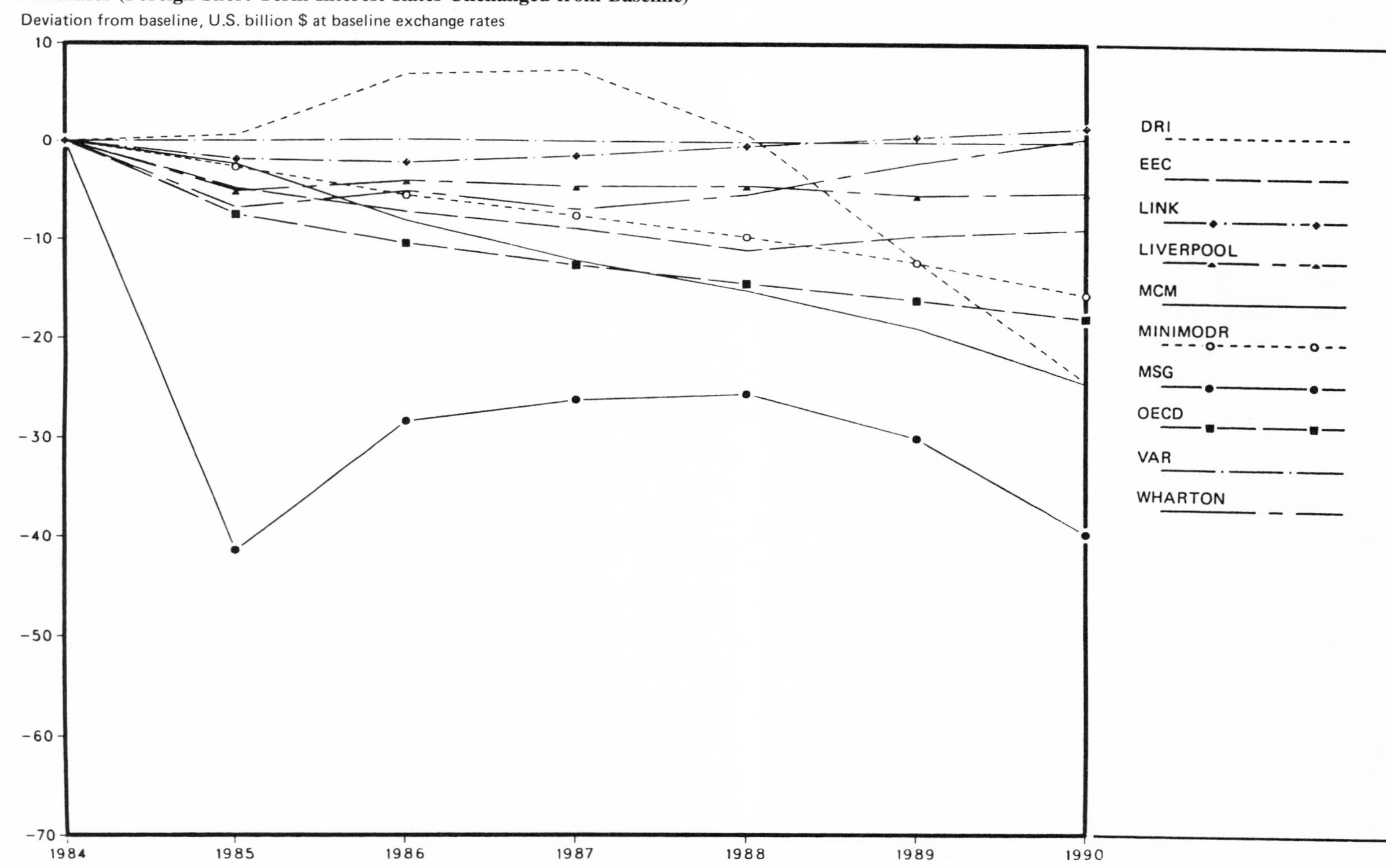

Table C. Average Responses, Standard Deviations, and Ranges for Simulated Effects of U.S. Fiscal Contraction with Foreign Short-Term Interest Rates Unchanged

(Simulation C—12 Models)

Variable	*Year 1 (1985)*	*Year 2 (1986)*	*Year 3 (1987)*	*Year 4 (1988)*	*Year 5 (1989)*	*Year 6 (1990)*
U.S. real GNP (UGNP)[a]						
Mean	−1.19	−1.12	−0.99	−0.86	−0.76	−0.73
Standard deviation	0.60	0.55	0.39	0.33	0.40	0.56
Range	2.01	1.74	1.23	1.10	1.39	2.01
ROECD real GNP (OGNP)[a]						
Mean	−0.45	−0.65	−0.74	−0.80	−0.89	−1.01
Standard deviation	0.59	0.58	0.60	0.73	0.92	1.13
Range	2.05	1.79	1.84	2.53	3.25	4.01
U.S. consumer price index (UCPI)[a,e]						
Mean	0.03	−0.13	−0.36	−0.62	−0.89	−1.20
Standard deviation	0.25	0.58	0.86	1.11	1.30	1.98
Range	0.93	1.98	2.79	3.41	3.89	4.77
ROECD consumer price index (OPCPI)[a,f]						
Mean	−0.16	−0.49	−0.86	−1.21	−1.55	−1.91
Standard deviation	0.21	0.56	0.94	1.31	1.71	2.15
Range	0.78	1.80	2.98	4.15	5.72	7.46
U.S. short-term interest rate (URS)[b]						
Mean	−0.70	−0.87	−1.05	−1.25	−1.52	−1.85
Standard deviation	0.50	0.87	1.02	1.16	1.33	1.55
Range	1.42	3.07	3.70	4.19	4.63	5.76
Weighted average exchange value of U.S. dollar (UEXCH)[a]						
Mean	−2.18	−2.73	−3.08	−3.30	−3.46	−3.51
Standard deviation	3.30	3.22	3.63	4.23	4.78	5.33
Range	10.98	11.45	12.57	14.79	17.07	19.14
U.S. current account balance (UCAB)[c,g]						
Mean	10.69	13.83	15.92	17.41	19.31	21.83
Standard deviation	9.85	8.09	8.62	9.58	11.60	14.79
Range	40.48	31.52	30.88	30.50	34.50	41.82
ROECD current account balance (OCAB)[d,h]						
Mean	−7.22	−6.39	−7.31	−8.57	−10.64	−13.45
Standard deviation	11.68	8.64	8.46	7.89	9.02	12.79
Range	42.09	35.24	33.46	26.29	30.52	41.19

Source: Detailed tables in part 3.
a. Percent deviation from baseline path.
b. Deviation from baseline path in percentage points.
c. Deviation from baseline path in U.S. $ billion.
d. Deviation from baseline path in U.S. $ billion at baseline exchange rates.
e. TAYLOR and VAR models did not report results for U.S. consumer prices; results for the U.S. GNP deflator for those models are used as a substitute.
f. VAR model did not report results for ROECD consumer prices; results for the ROECD GNP deflator for that model are used as a substitute.
g. TAYLOR model did not report results for the U.S. current account balance.
h. EPA and TAYLOR models did not report results for the ROECD current account balance.

SIMULATION D

U.S. Monetary Expansion, Foreign Monetary Aggregates Unchanged

Chart D-1. Effects on U.S. Real GNP (UGNP) of U.S. Monetary Expansion (Foreign Monetary Aggregates Unchanged from Baseline)

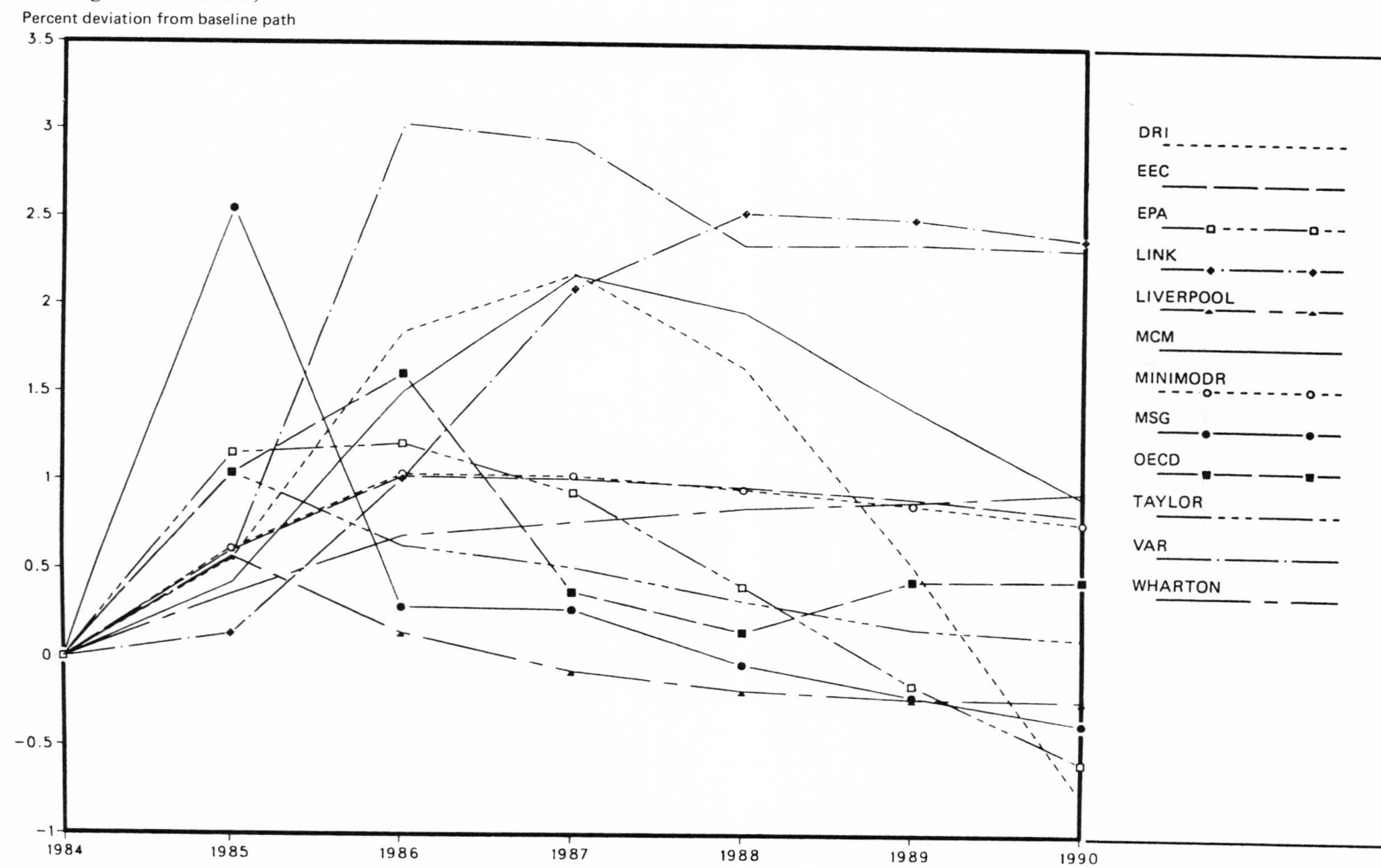

Chart D-2. Effects on ROECD Real GNP (OGNP) of U.S. Monetary Expansion (Foreign Monetary Aggregates Unchanged from Baseline)

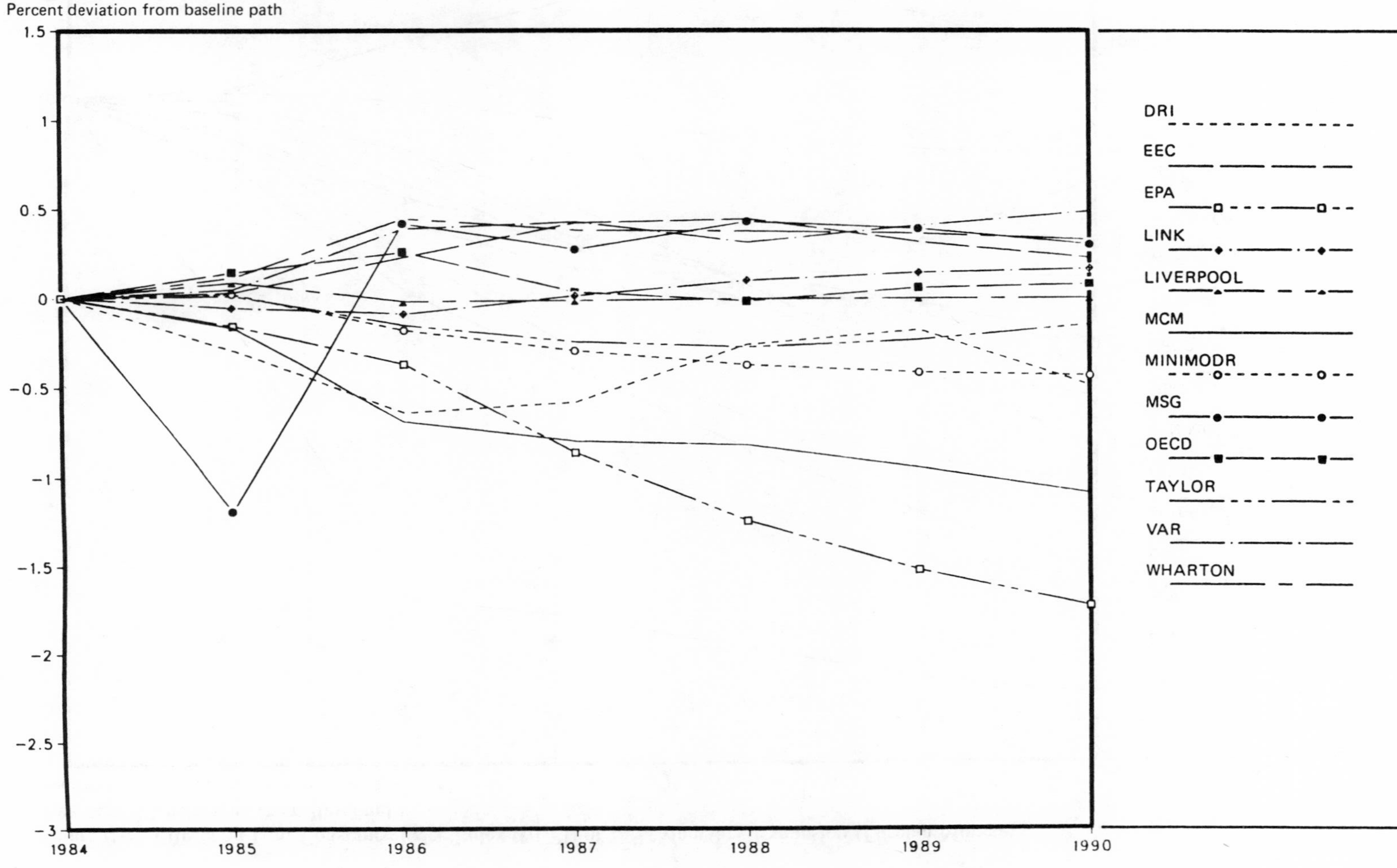

Chart D-3. Effects on U.S. Consumer Price Index (UCPI) of U.S. Monetary Expansion (Foreign Monetary Aggregates Unchanged from Baseline)

Percent deviation from baseline path

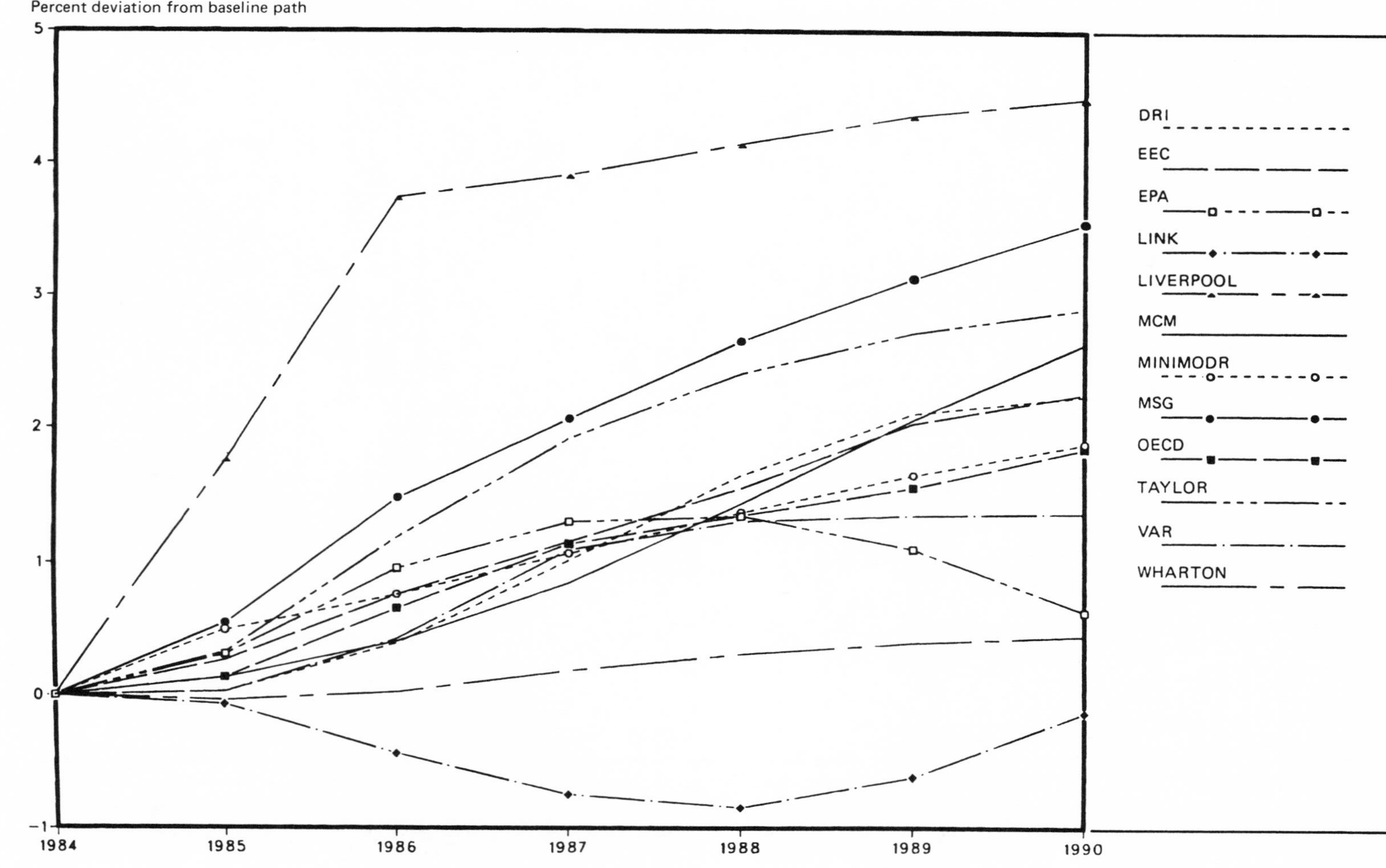

Chart D-4. Effects on ROECD Consumer Price Index (OPCPI) of U.S. Monetary Expansion (Foreign Monetary Aggregates Unchanged from Baseline)

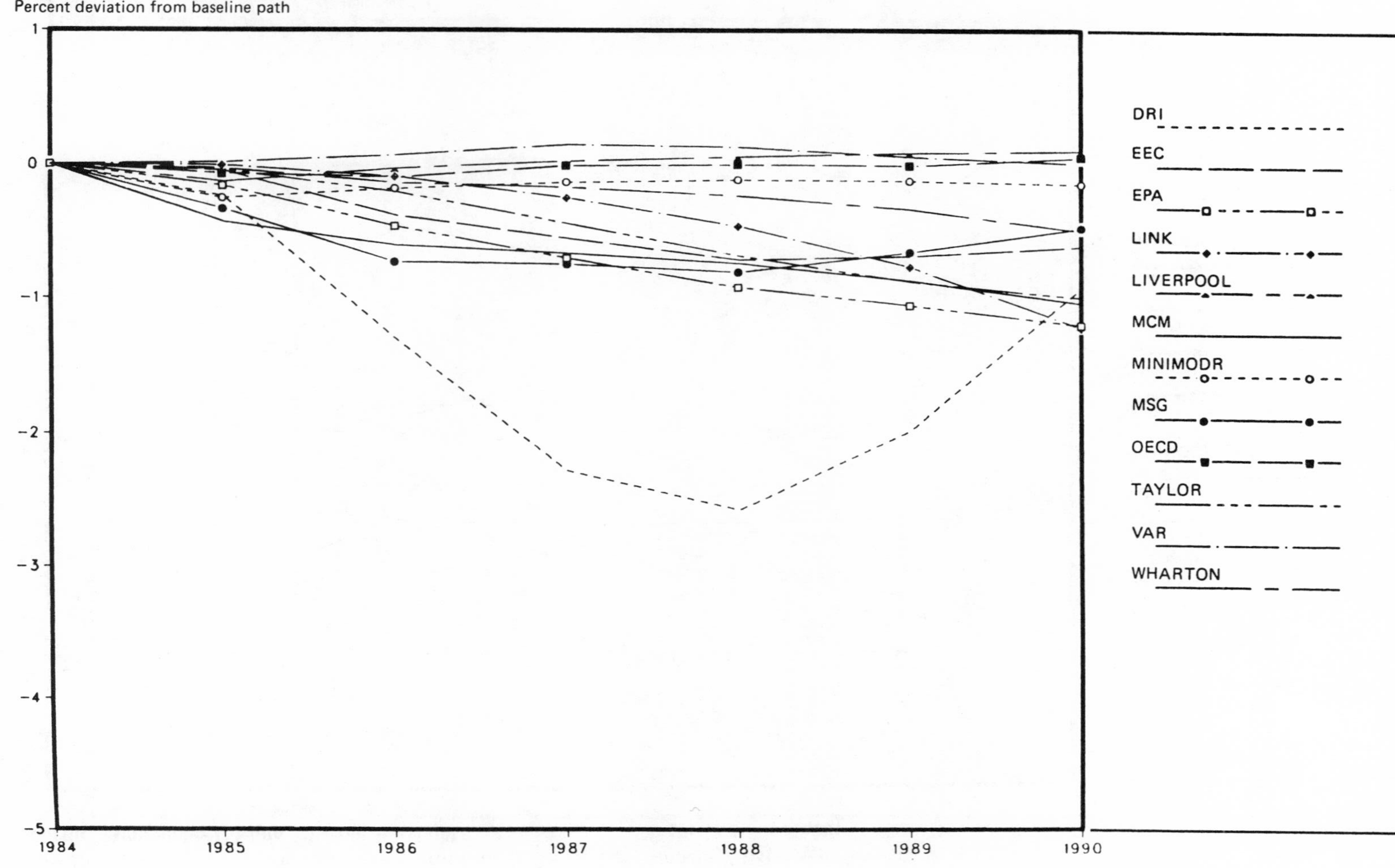

Chart D-5. Effects on U.S. Short-Term Interest Rate (URS) of U.S. Monetary Expansion (Foreign Monetary Aggregates Unchanged from Baseline)

Deviation from baseline path, percentage points

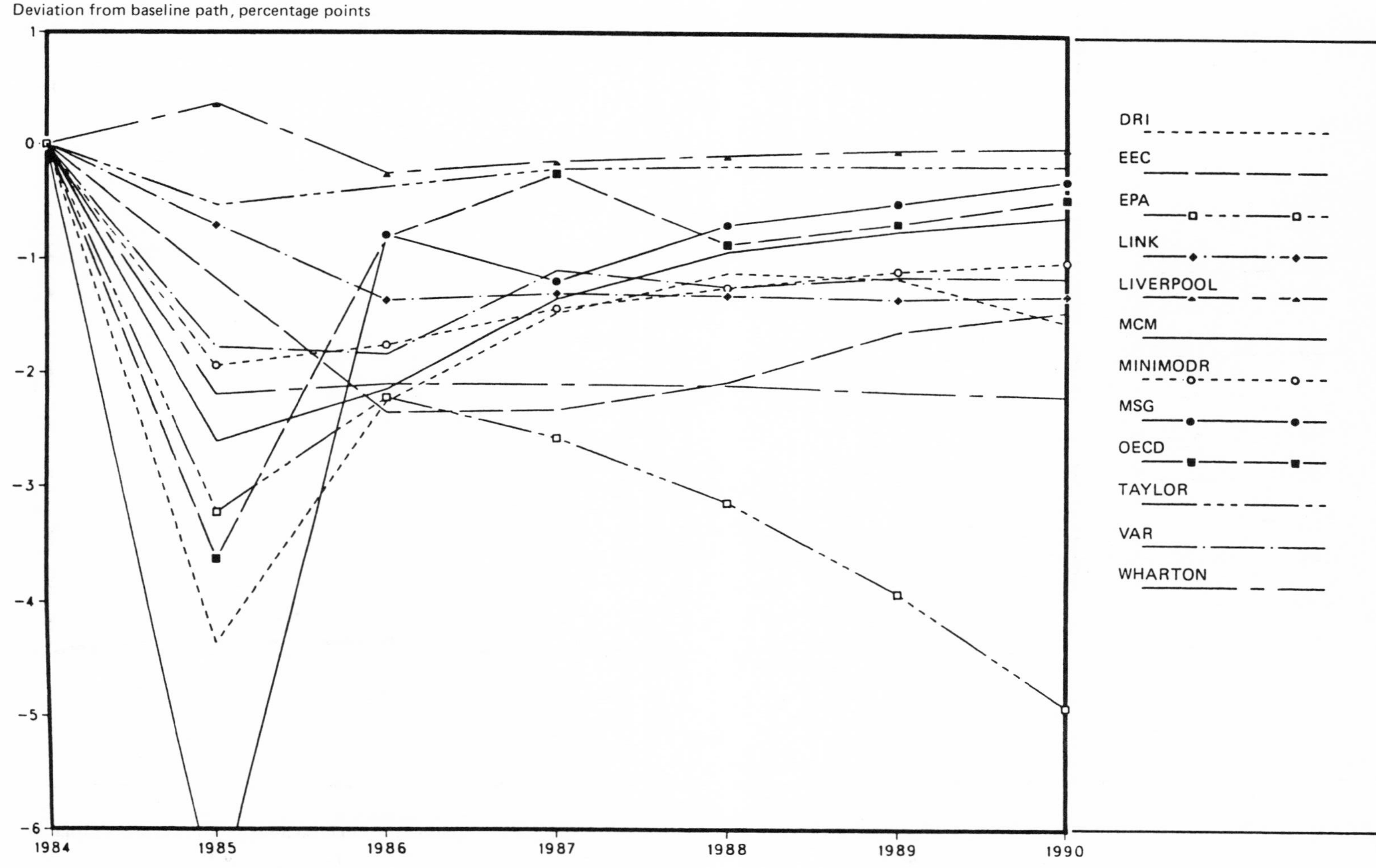

Chart D-6. Effects on ROECD Short-Term Interest Rate (ORS) of U.S. Monetary Expansion (Foreign Monetary Aggregates Unchanged from Baseline)

Deviation from baseline path, percentage points

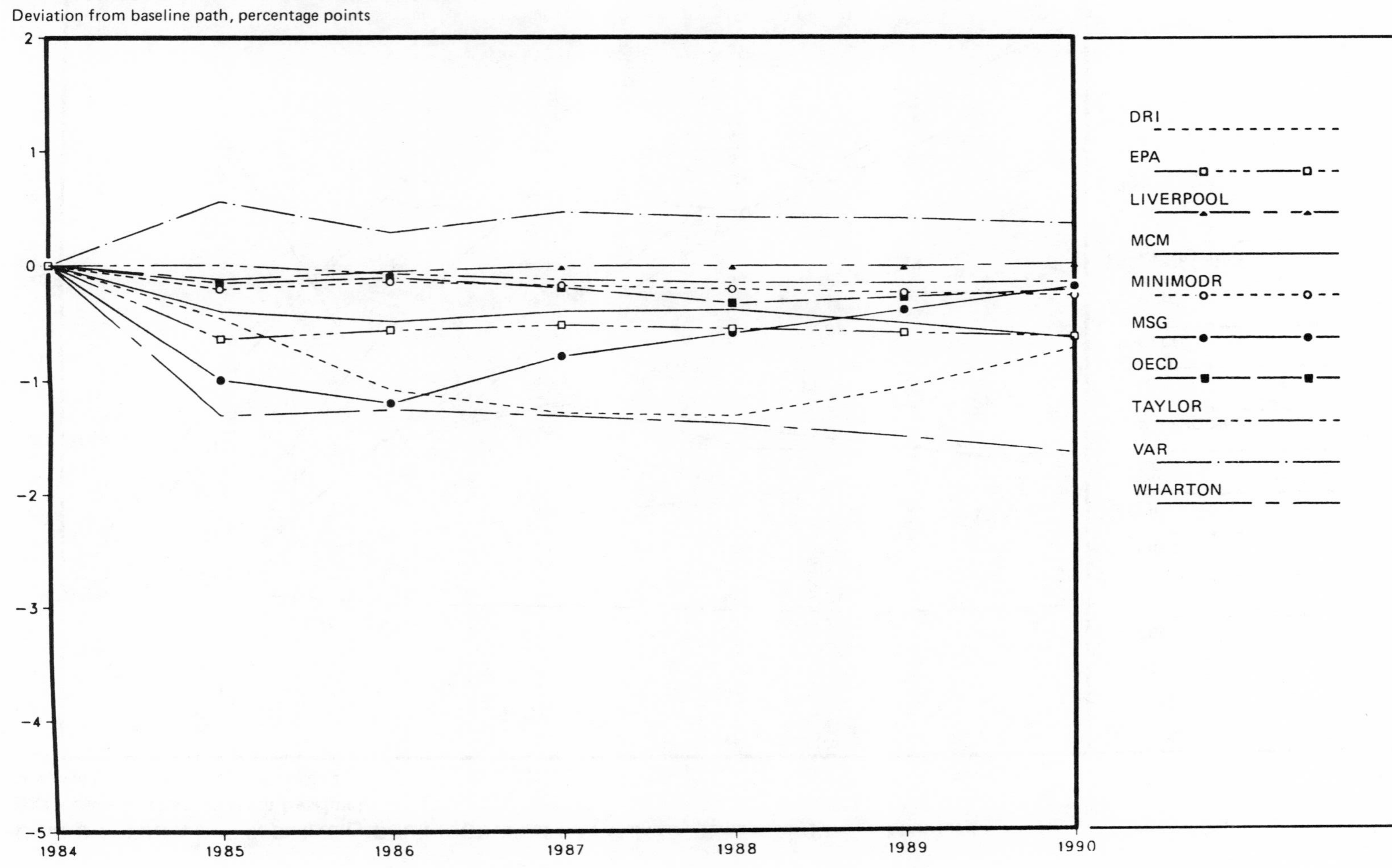

Chart D-7. Effects on U.S. Budgetary Deficit (UGDEF) of U.S. Monetary Expansion (Foreign Monetary Aggregates Unchanged from Baseline)

Deviation from baseline path, U.S. billion $

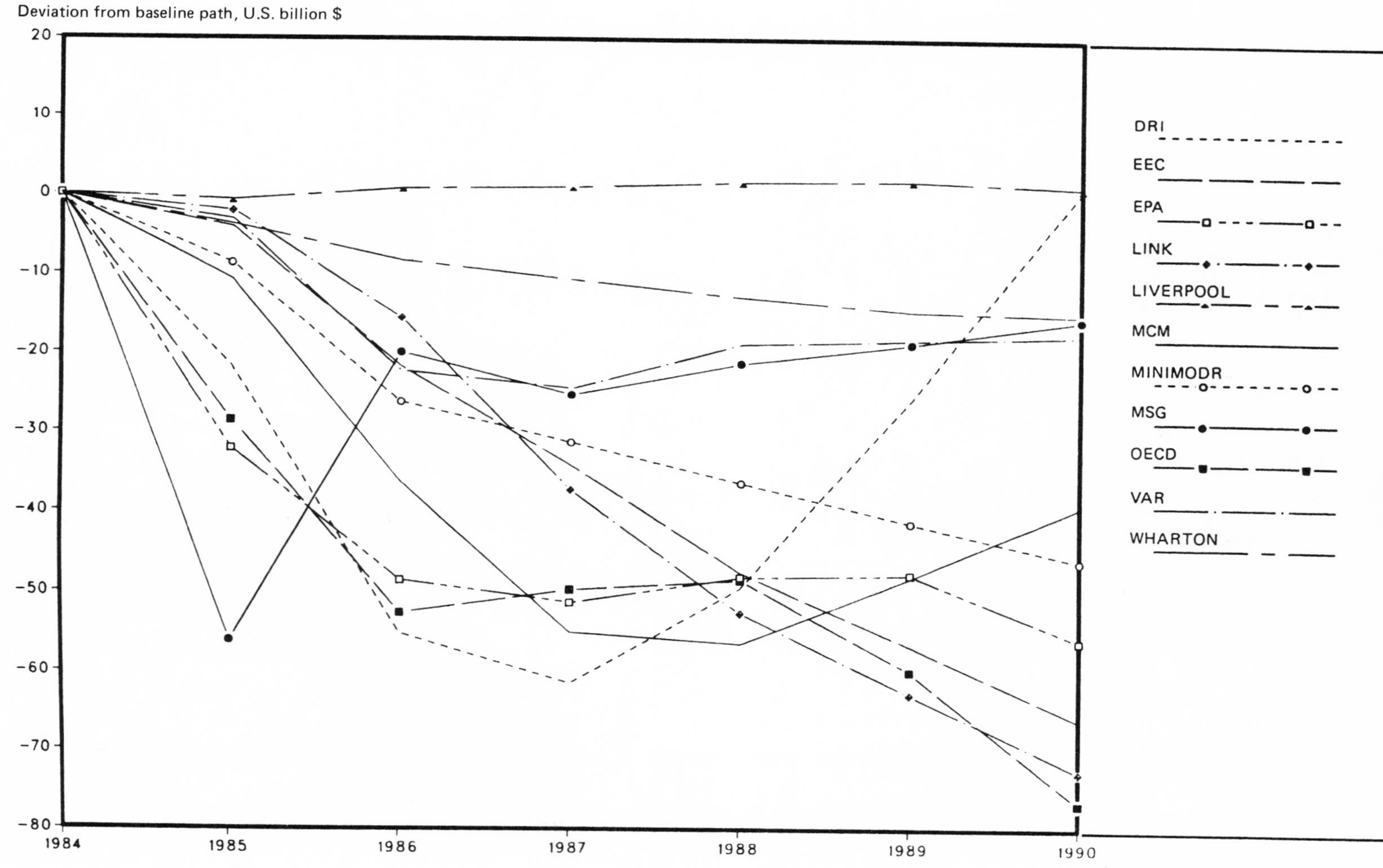

Chart D-8. Effects on Weighted Average Exchange Value of U.S. Dollar (Foreign Currencies per U.S. Dollar) (UEXCH) of U.S. Monetary Expansion (Foreign Monetary Aggregates Unchanged from Baseline)

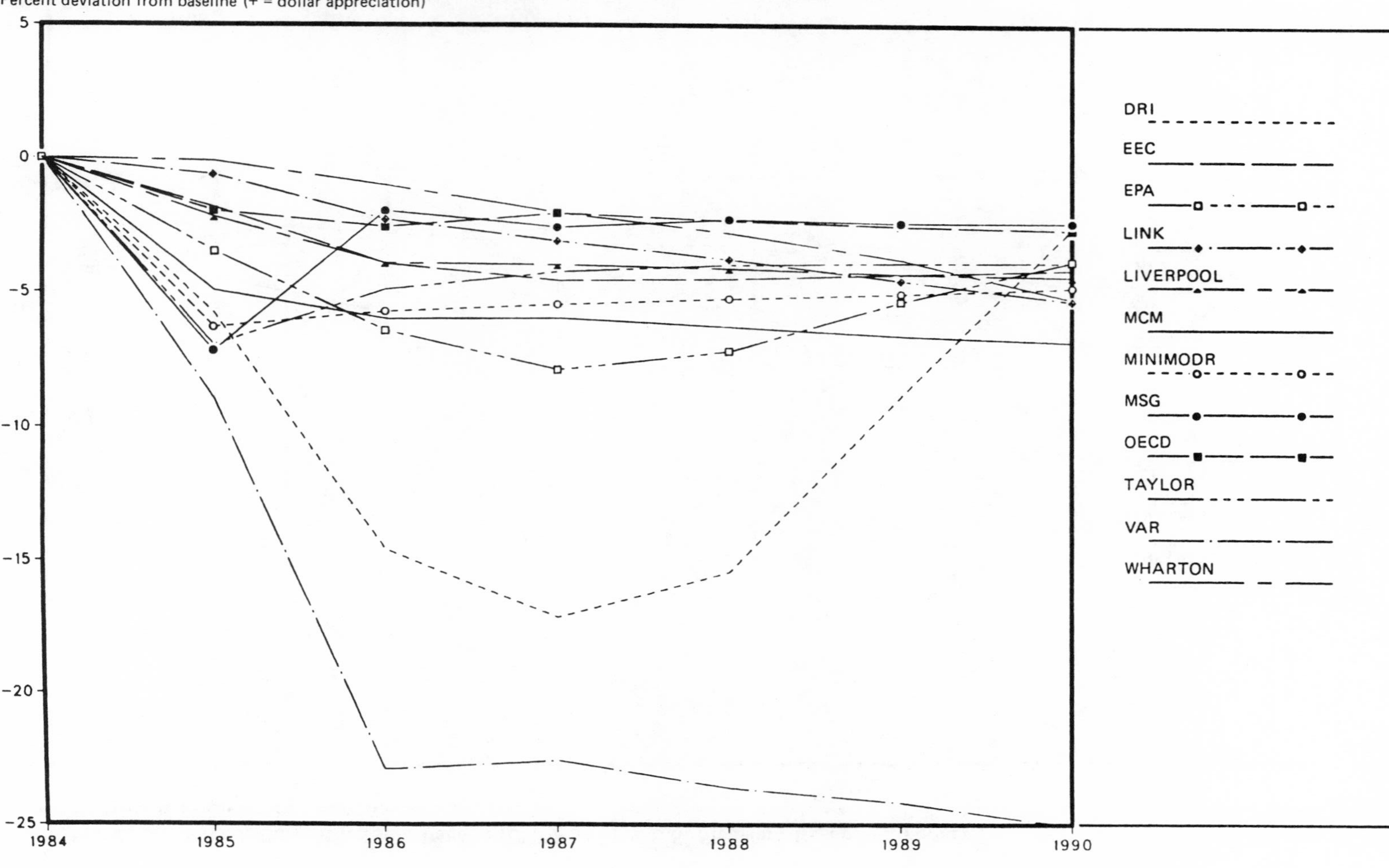

Chart D-9. Effects on U.S. Current Account Balance (UCURBAL) of U.S. Monetary Expansion (Foreign Monetary Aggregates Unchanged from Baseline)

Deviation from baseline path, U.S. billion $

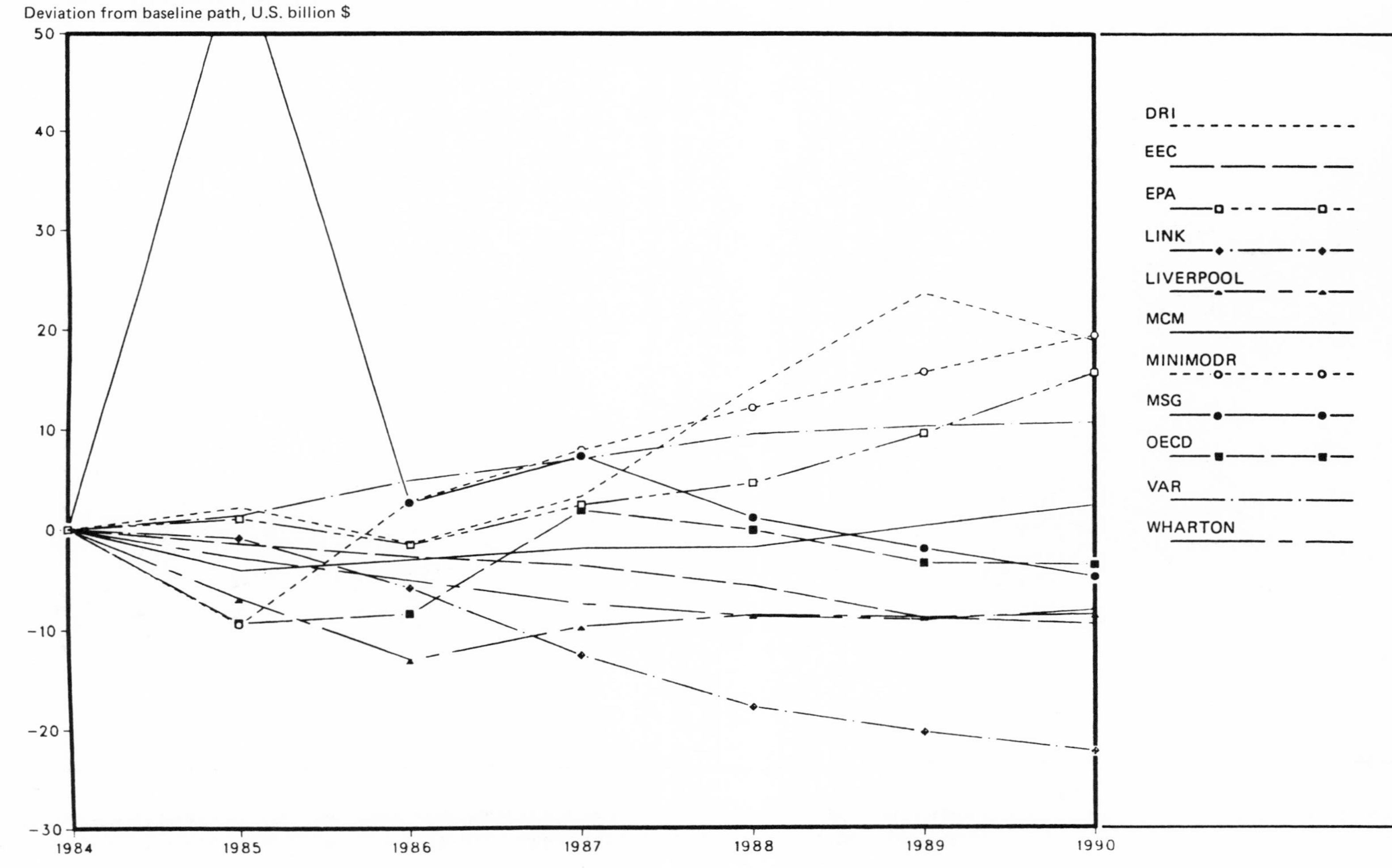

Chart D-10. Effects on ROECD Current Account Balance (OCURBAL) of U.S. Monetary Expansion (Foreign Monetary Aggregates Unchanged from Baseline)

Deviation from baseline, U.S. billion $ at baseline exchange rates

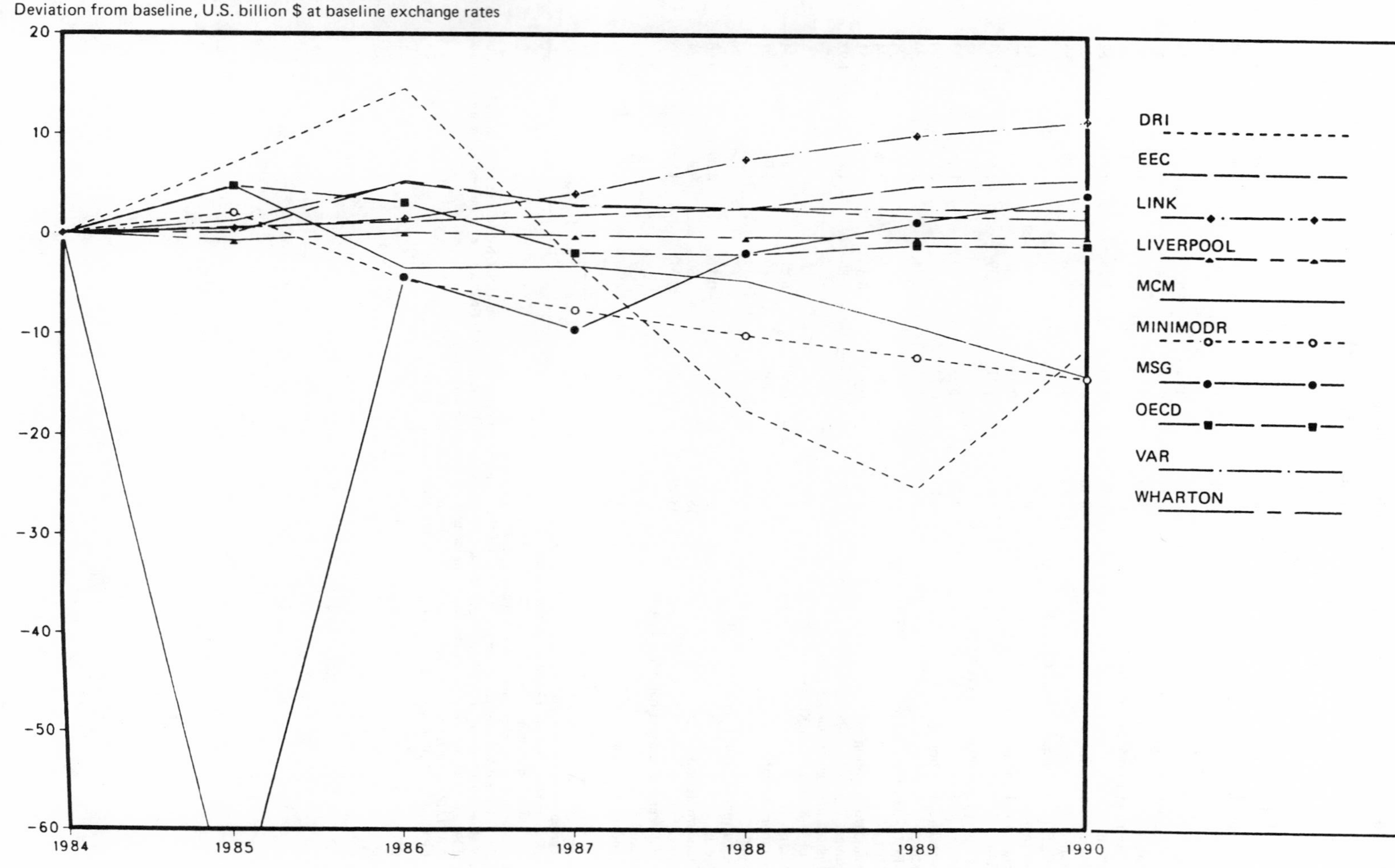

Table D. Average Responses, Standard Deviations, and Ranges for Simulated Effects of U.S. Monetary Expansion with Foreign Monetary Aggregates Unchanged

(Simulation D—12 Models)

Variable	*Year 1 (1985)*	*Year 2 (1986)*	*Year 3 (1987)*	*Year 4 (1988)*	*Year 5 (1989)*	*Year 6 (1990)*
U.S. real GNP (UGNP)[a]						
Mean	0.80	1.16	1.18	1.00	0.80	0.57
Standard deviation	0.60	0.74	0.89	0.89	0.88	0.99
Range	2.41	2.89	2.99	2.71	2.72	3.17
ROECD real GNP (OGNP)[a]						
Mean	−0.12	−0.04	−0.11	−0.12	−0.14	−0.20
Standard deviation	0.35	0.38	0.44	0.50	0.56	0.63
Range	1.34	1.14	1.29	1.69	1.93	2.21
U.S. consumer price index (UCPI)[a,e]						
Mean	0.33	0.86	1.25	1.56	1.82	2.01
Standard deviation	0.48	0.99	1.06	1.16	1.22	1.27
Range	1.85	4.18	4.66	4.99	4.98	4.63
ROECD consumer price index (OPCPI)[a,f]						
Mean	−0.15	−0.35	−0.50	−0.59	−0.61	−0.59
Standard deviation	0.13	0.37	0.61	0.69	0.56	0.48
Range	0.44	1.41	2.39	2.68	2.07	1.33
U.S. short-term interest rate (URS)[b]						
Mean	−2.38	−1.53	−1.29	−1.25	−1.22	−1.26
Standard deviation	1.84	0.74	0.77	0.82	1.00	1.27
Range	7.07	2.11	2.44	3.05	3.90	4.91
ROECD short-term interest rate (ORS)[b,g]						
Mean	−0.37	−0.47	−0.44	−0.46	−0.44	−0.42
Standard deviation	0.50	0.52	0.54	0.53	0.51	0.52
Range	1.88	1.56	1.80	1.82	1.92	2.01
Weighted average exchange value of U.S. dollar (UEXCH)[a]						
Mean	−4.22	−6.38	−6.81	−6.81	−6.34	−5.96
Standard deviation	2.75	6.01	6.16	6.09	5.63	5.89
Range	8.80	21.85	20.50	21.33	21.75	22.66
U.S. current account balance (UCAB)[c,h]						
Mean	2.55	−2.83	−0.51	−0.09	0.66	0.95
Standard deviation	18.18	4.99	6.80	9.37	12.34	12.98
Range	68.19	17.87	20.51	31.99	44.05	41.74
ROECD current account balance (OCAB)[d,i]						
Mean	−5.02	1.81	−1.37	−2.13	−2.74	−1.59
Standard deviation	21.89	5.46	4.34	6.88	9.70	8.38
Range	77.39	19.23	13.62	25.15	35.36	25.88

Source: Detailed tables in part 3.
a. Percent deviation from baseline path.
b. Deviation from baseline path in percentage points.
c. Deviation from baseline path in U.S. $ billion.
d. Deviation from baseline path in U.S. $ billion at baseline exchange rates.
e. TAYLOR and VAR models did not report results for U.S. consumer prices; results for the U.S. GNP deflator for those models are used as a substitute.
f. VAR model did not report results for ROECD consumer prices; results for the ROECD GNP deflator for that model are used as a substitute.
g. EEC and LINK models did not report results for the ROECD short-term interest rate.
h. TAYLOR model did not report results for the U.S. current account balance.
i. EPA and TAYLOR models did not report results for the ROECD current account balance.

SIMULATION E

U.S. Monetary Expansion, Foreign Interest Rates Unchanged

Chart E-1. Effects on U.S. Real GNP (UGNP) of U.S. Monetary Expansion (Foreign Short-Term Interest Rates Unchanged from Baseline)

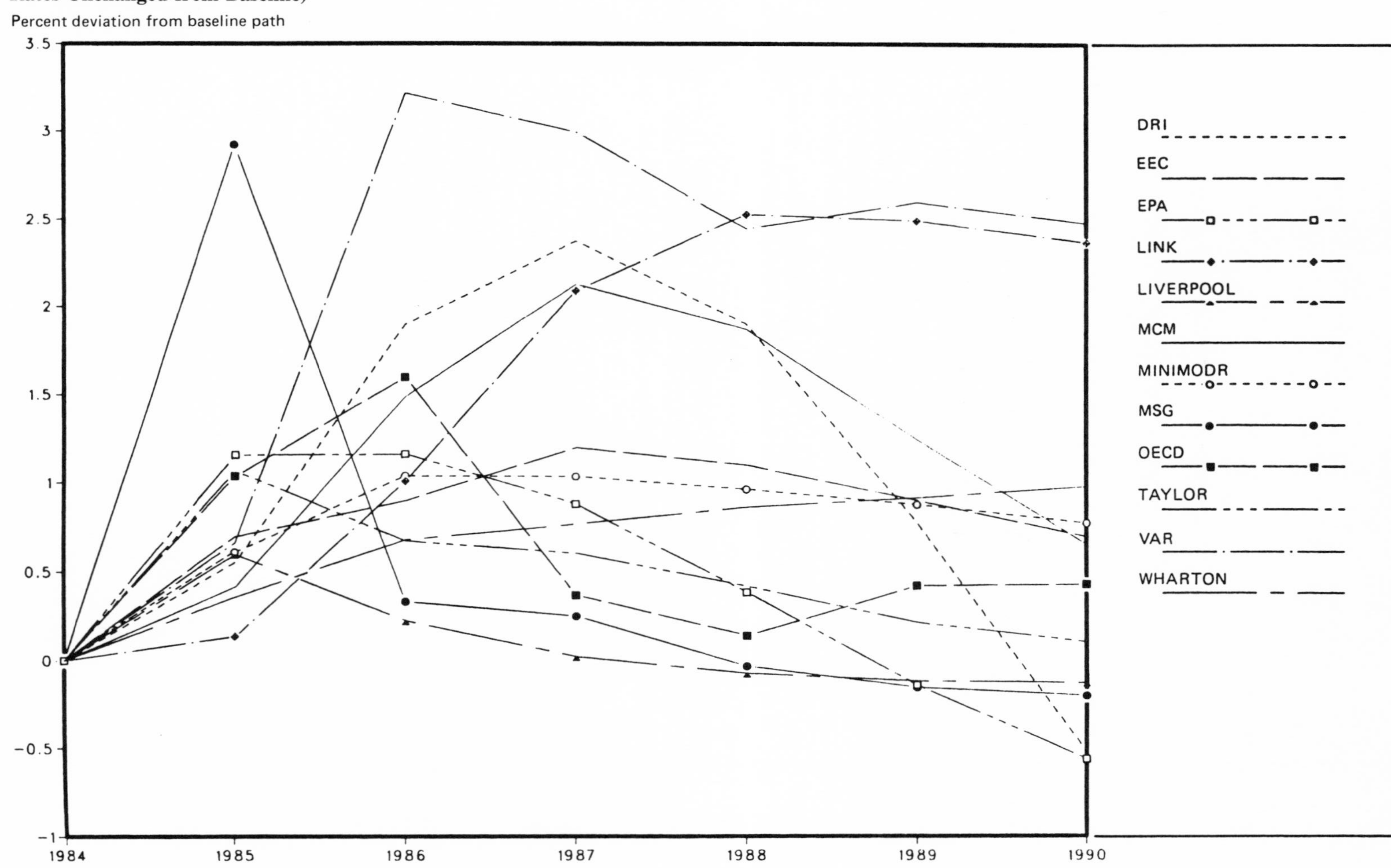

Chart E-2. Effects on ROECD GNP (OGNP) of U.S. Monetary Expansion (Foreign Short-Term Interest Rates Unchanged from Baseline)

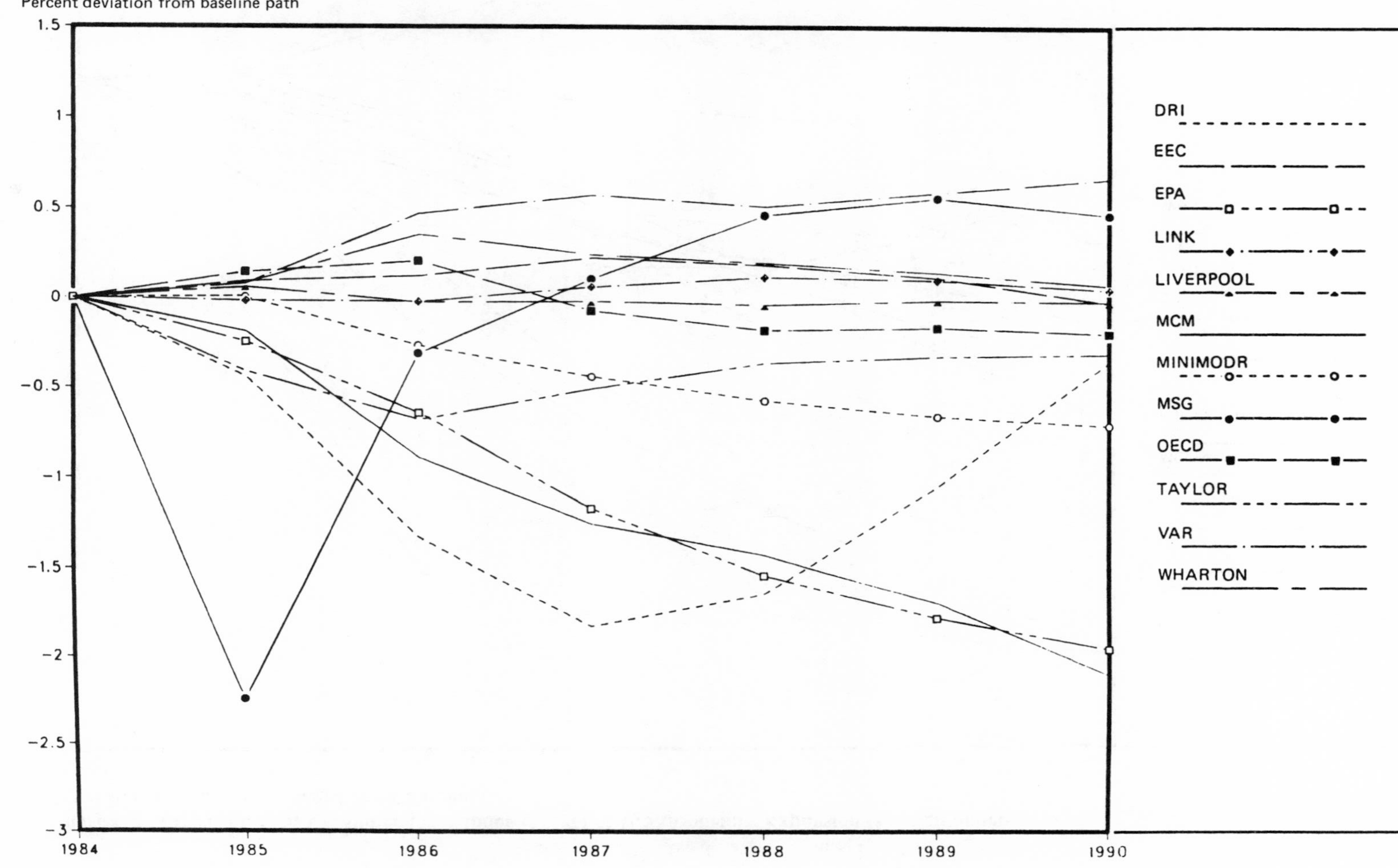

Chart E-3. Effects on U.S. Consumer Price Index (UCPI) of U.S. Monetary Expansion (Foreign Short-Term Interest Rates Unchanged from Baseline)

Percent deviation from baseline path

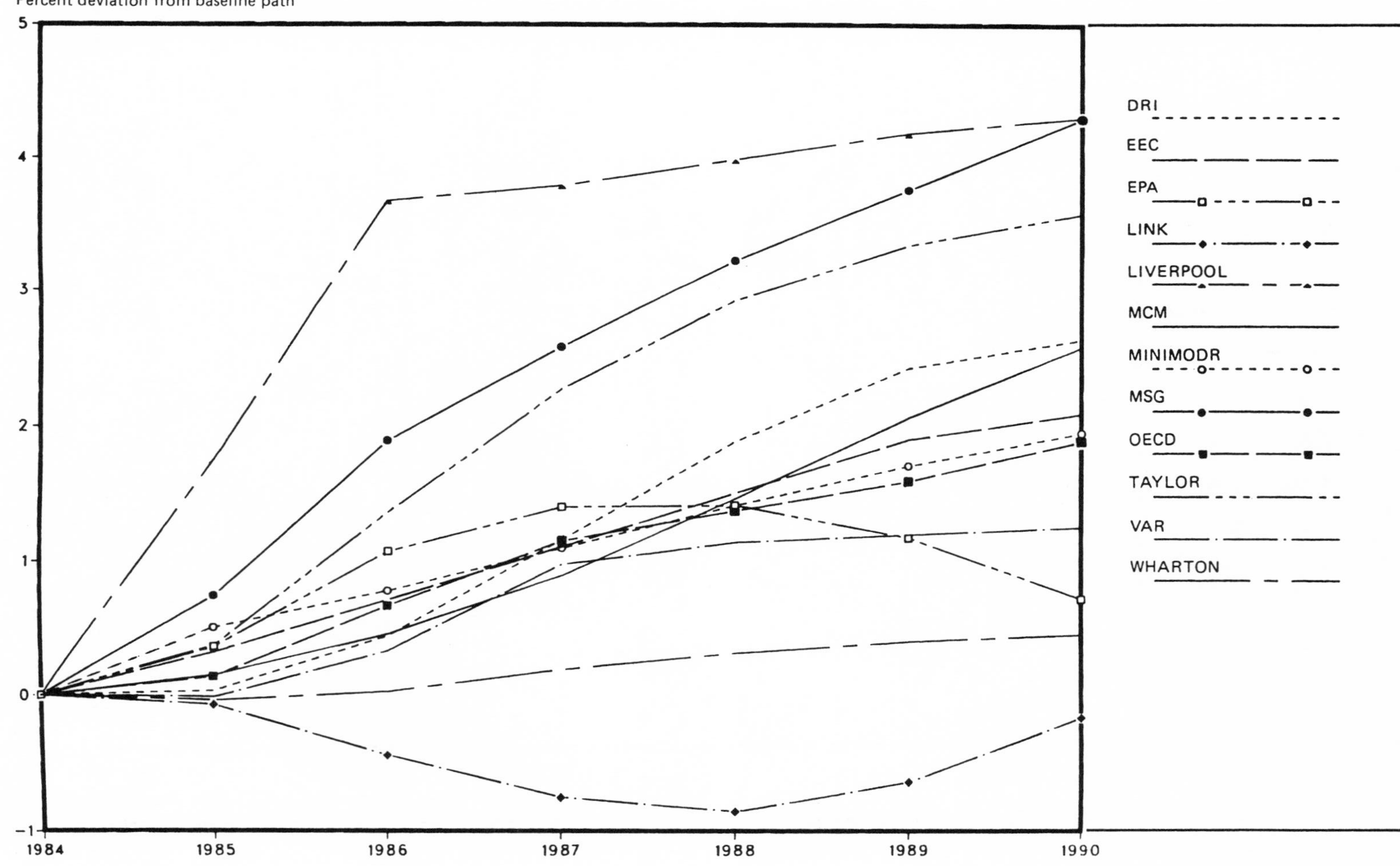

Chart E-4. Effects on ROECD Consumer Price Index (OPCPI) of U.S. Monetary Expansion (Foreign Short-Term Interest Rates Unchanged from Baseline)

Percent deviation from baseline path

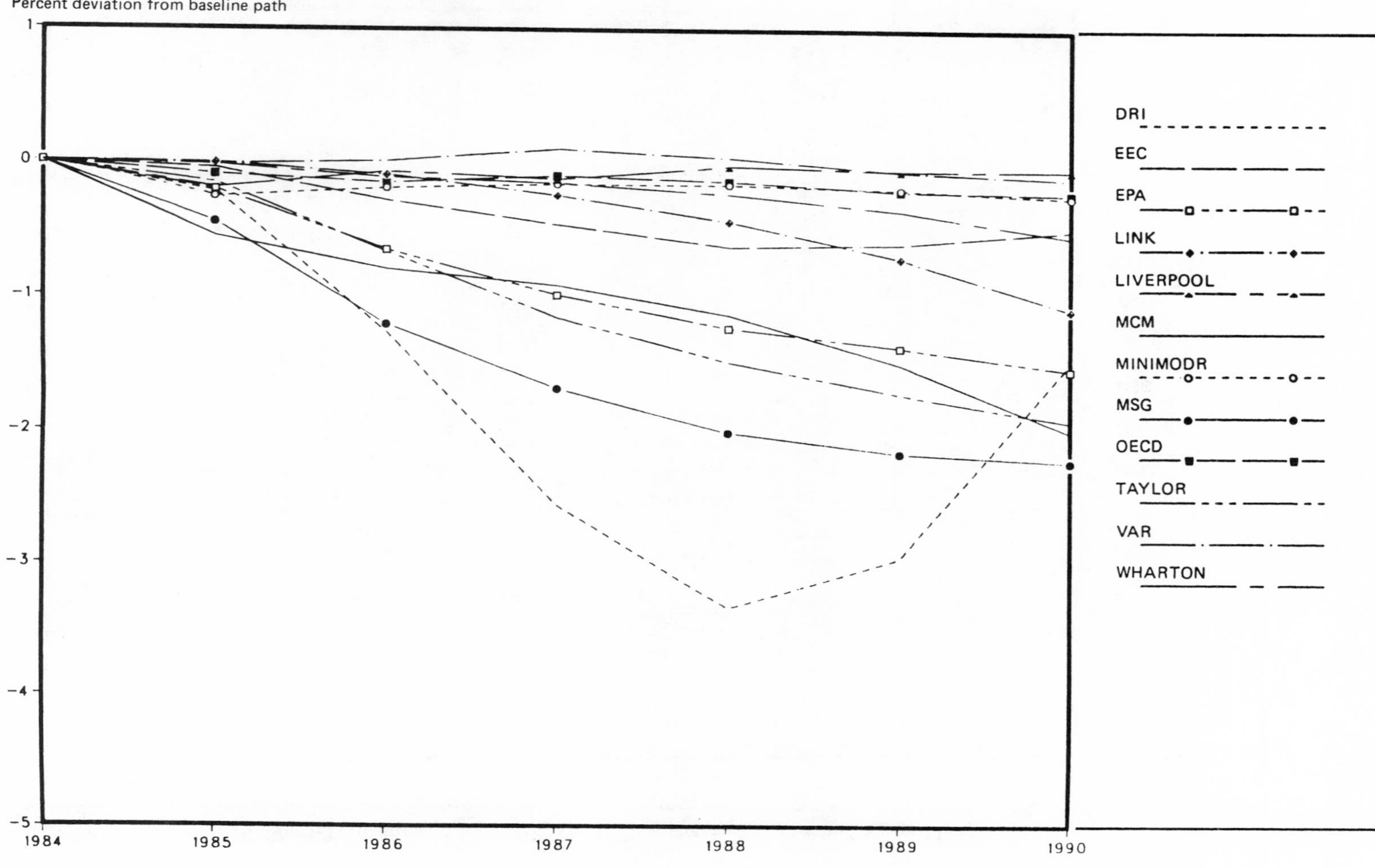

Chart E-5. Effects on U.S. Short-Term Interest Rate (URS) of U.S. Monetary Expansion (Foreign Short-Term Interest Rates Unchanged from Baseline)

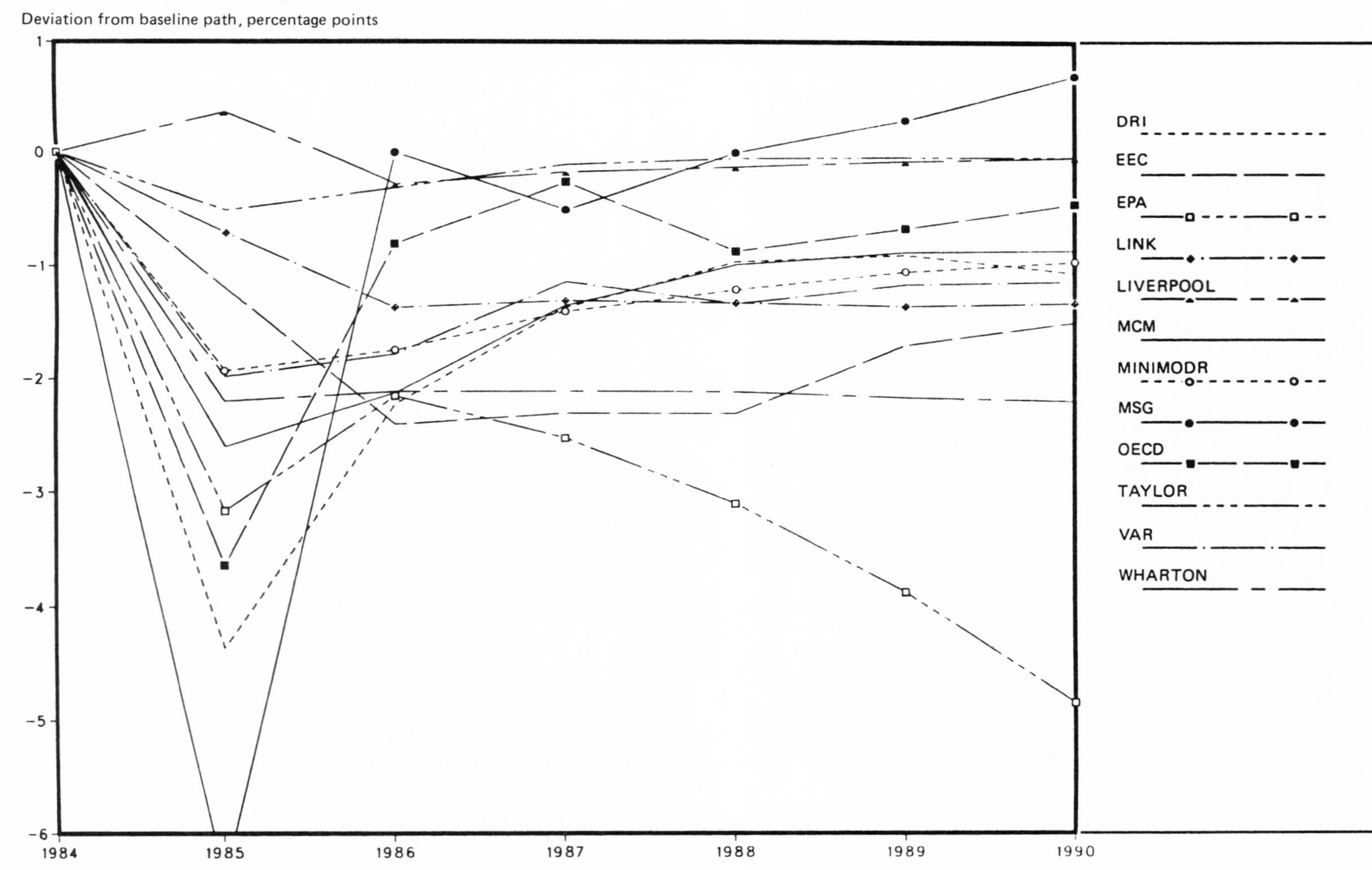

Chart E-7. Effects on U.S. Budgetary Deficit (UGDEF) of U.S. Monetary Expansion (Foreign Short-Term Interest Rates Unchanged from Baseline)

Deviation from baseline path, U.S. billion $

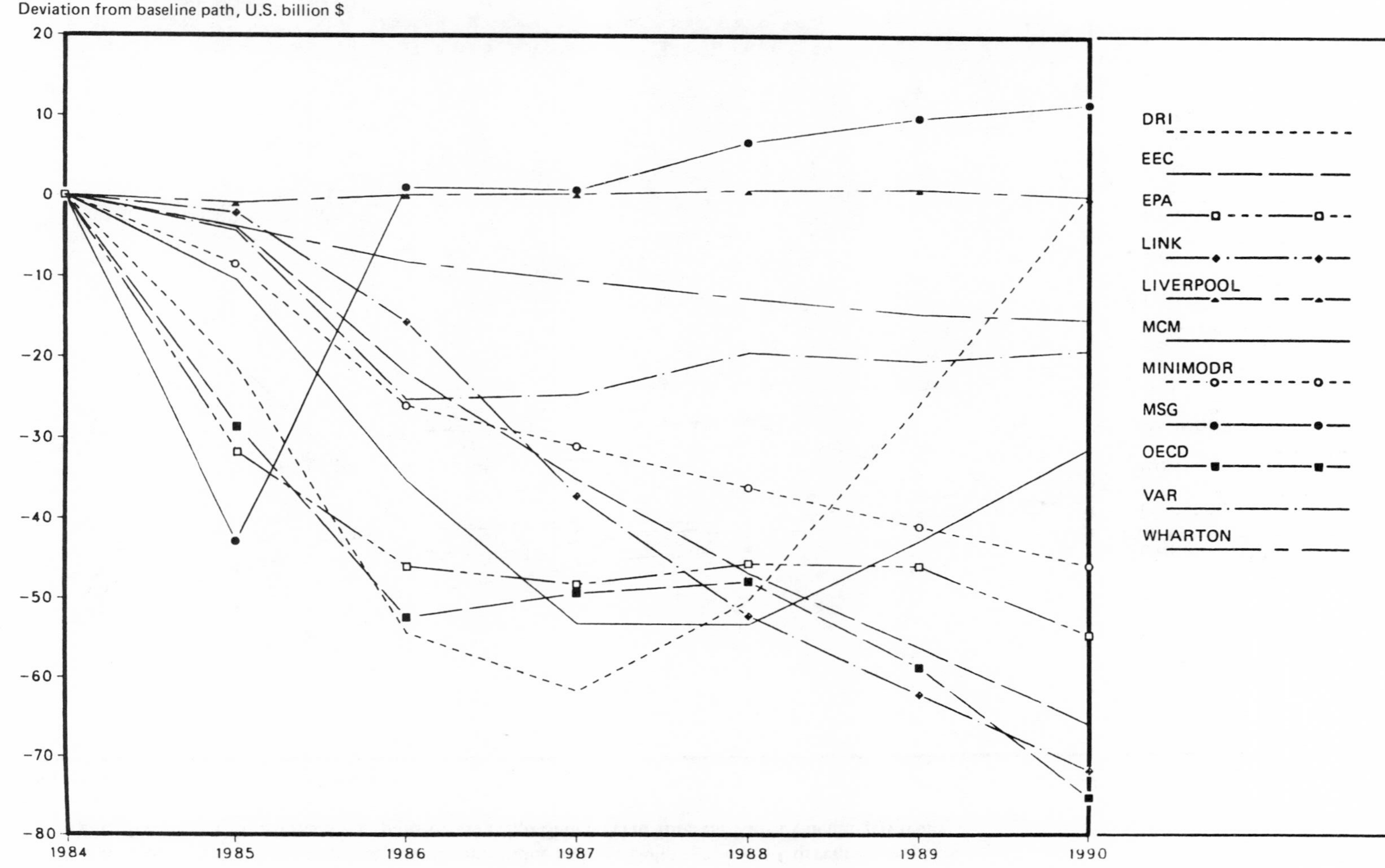

Chart E-8. Effects on Weighted Average Exchange Value of U.S. Dollar (Foreign Currencies per U.S. Dollar) (UEXCH) of U.S. Monetary Expansion (Foreign Short-Term Interest Rates Unchanged from Baseline)

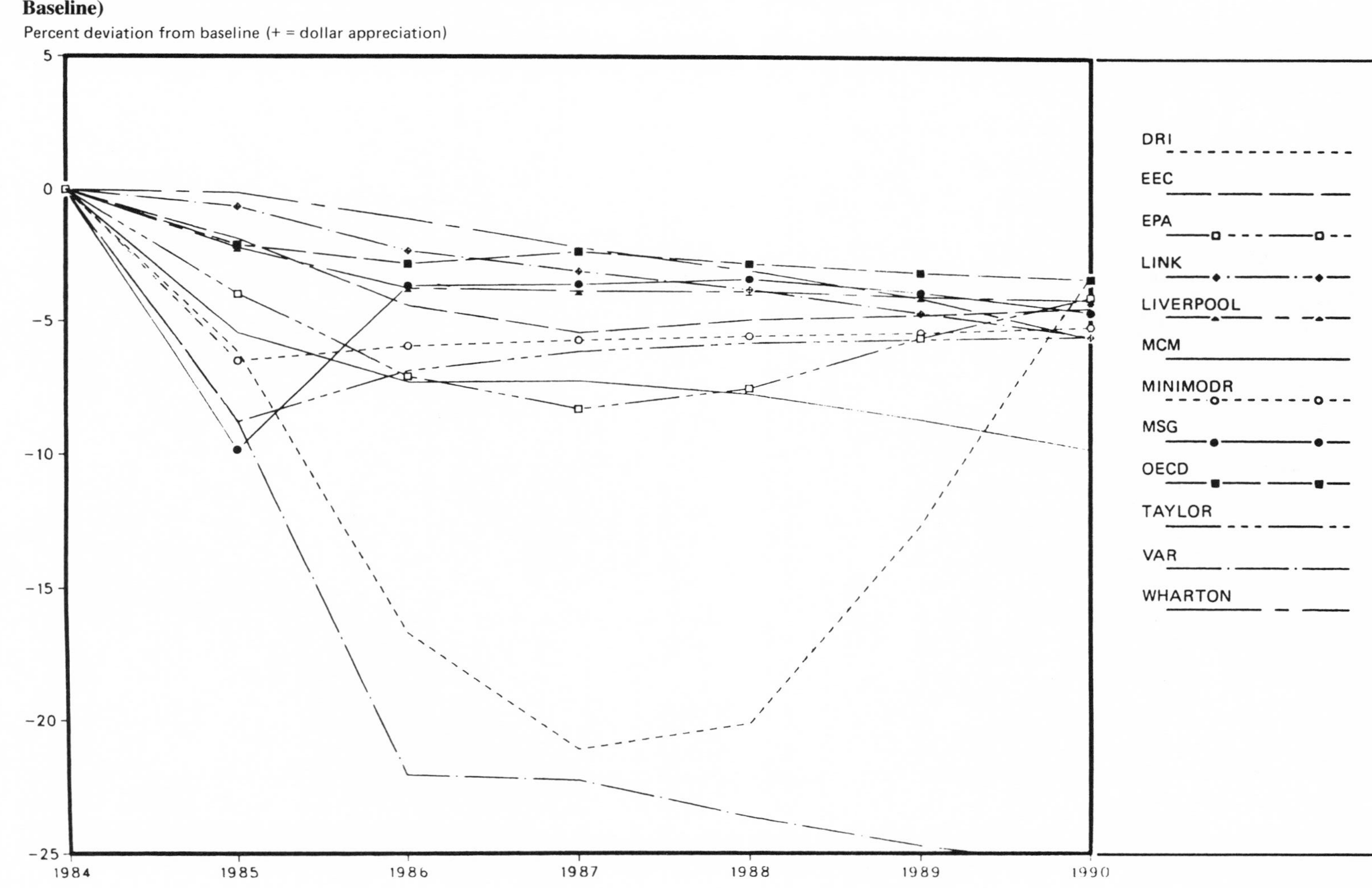

Chart E-9. Effects on U.S. Current Account Balance (UCURBAL) of U.S. Monetary Expansion (Foreign Short-Term Interest Rates Unchanged from Baseline)

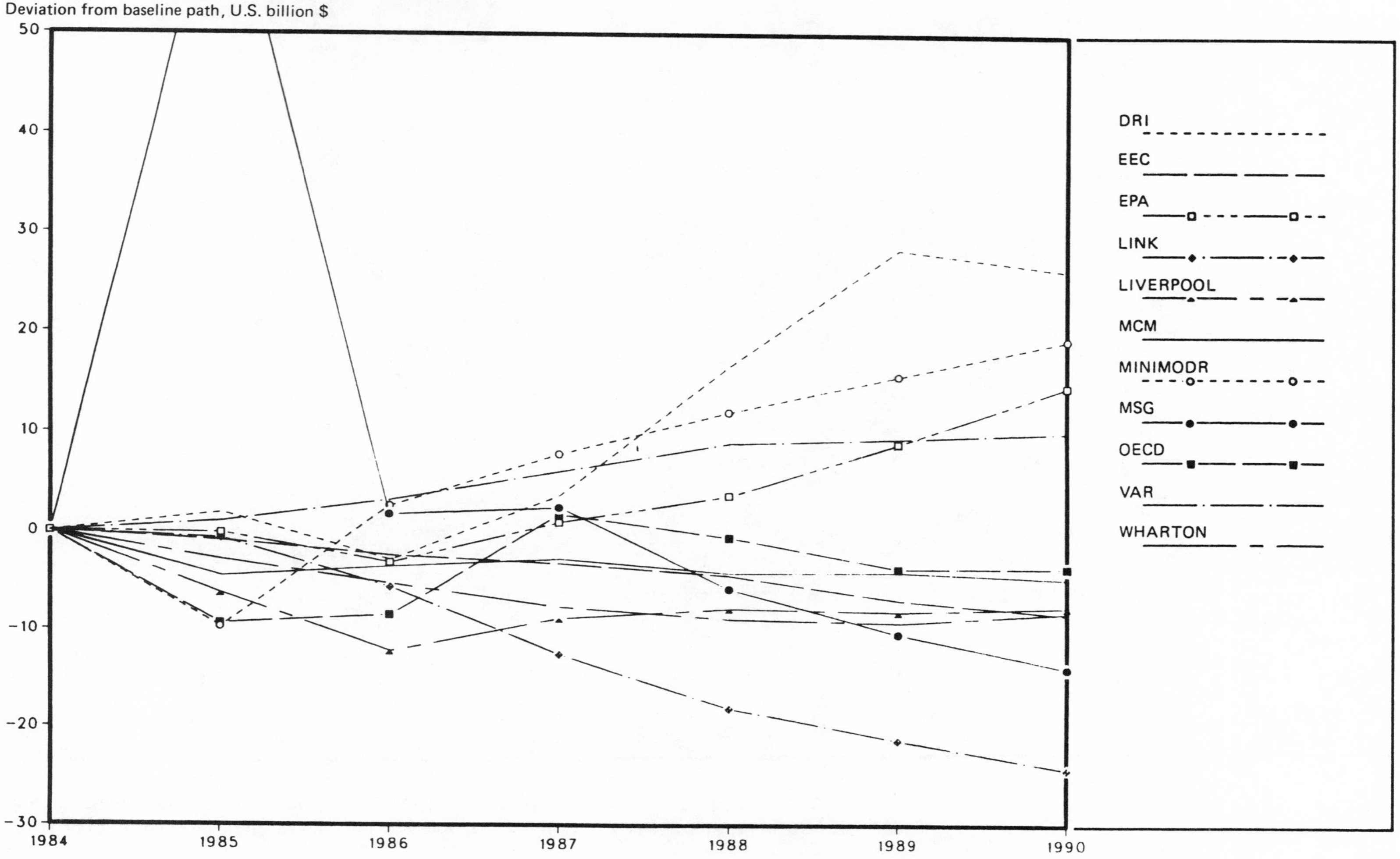

Chart E-10. Effects on ROECD Current Account Balance (OCURBAL) of U.S. Monetary Expansion (Foreign Short-Term Interest Rates Unchanged from Baseline)

Deviation from baseline, U.S. billion $ at baseline exchange rates

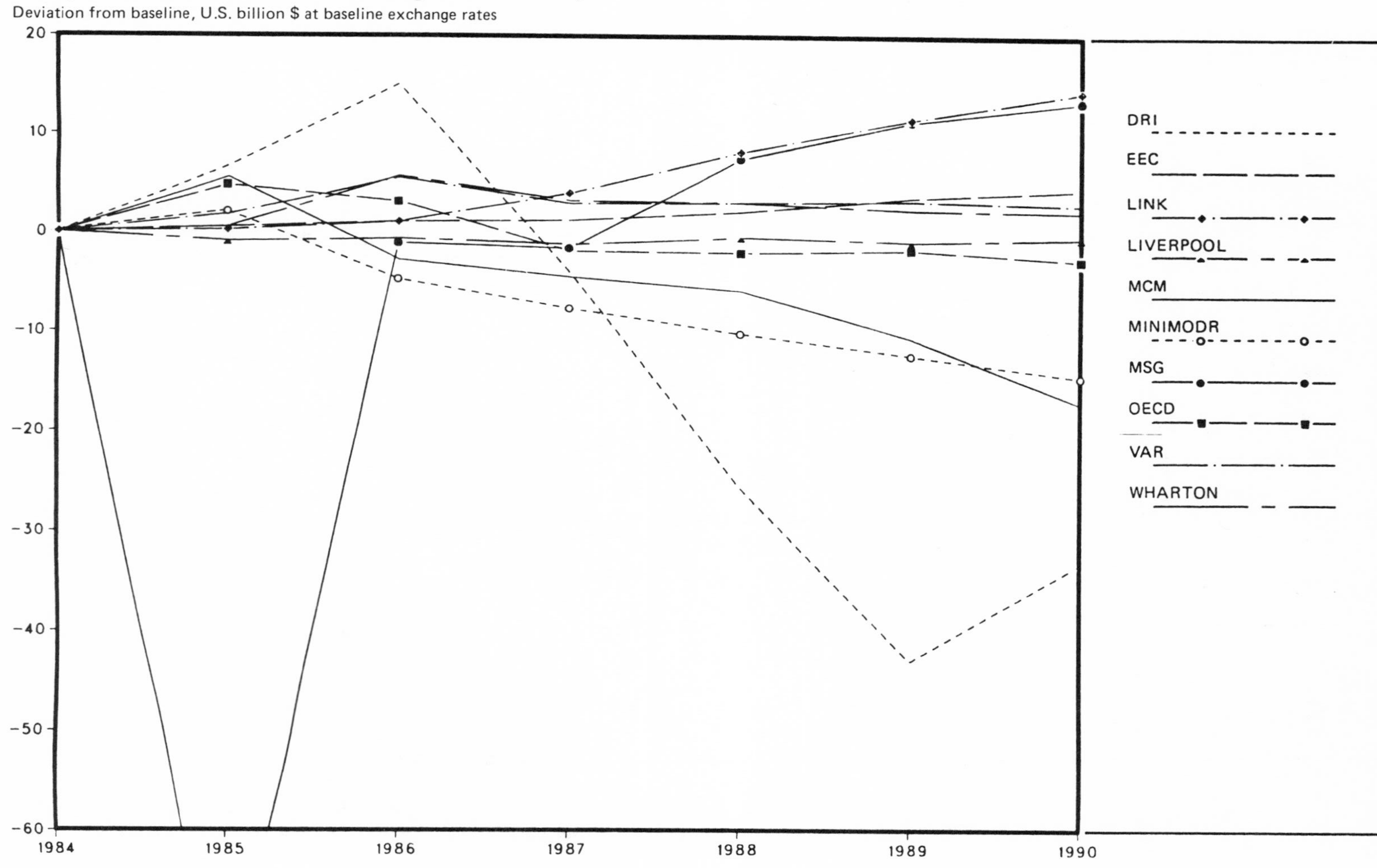

Table E. Average Responses, Standard Deviations, and Ranges for Simulated Effects of U.S. Monetary Expansion with Foreign Short-Term Interest Rates Unchanged

(Simulation E—12 Models)

Variable	*Year 1 (1985)*	*Year 2 (1986)*	*Year 3 (1987)*	*Year 4 (1988)*	*Year 5 (1989)*	*Year 6 (1990)*
U.S. real GNP (UGNP)[a]						
Mean	0.85	1.19	1.23	1.04	0.84	0.59
Standard deviation	0.69	0.78	0.91	0.90	0.89	0.95
Range	2.78	3.00	2.95	2.60	2.75	3.04
ROECD real GNP (OGNP)[a]						
Mean	−0.26	−0.26	−0.35	−0.36	−0.35	−0.37
Standard deviation	0.63	0.52	0.70	0.74	0.76	0.82
Range	2.39	1.80	2.40	2.14	2.37	2.77
U.S. consumer price index (UCPI)[a,e]						
Mean	0.35	0.91	1.32	1.65	1.93	2.13
Standard deviation	0.48	1.01	1.11	1.23	1.32	1.38
Range	1.83	4.11	4.55	4.85	4.82	4.47
ROECD consumer price index (OPCPI)[a,f]						
Mean	−0.19	−0.47	−0.71	−0.90	−0.99	−0.99
Standard deviation	0.17	0.42	0.76	0.96	0.91	0.79
Range	0.56	1.21	2.67	3.34	2.95	2.23
U.S. short-term interest rate (URS)[b]						
Mean	−2.36	−1.44	−1.21	−1.19	−1.13	−1.14
Standard deviation	1.78	0.83	0.79	0.90	1.07	1.33
Range	6.78	2.40	2.42	3.10	4.17	5.54
Weighted average exchange value of U.S. dollar (UEXCH)[a]						
Mean	−4.72	−7.01	−7.63	−7.70	−7.31	−6.79
Standard deviation	3.23	5.94	6.54	6.56	5.81	5.88
Range	9.72	20.94	20.03	20.82	21.55	22.26
U.S. current account balance (UCAB)[c,g]						
Mean	3.28	−3.32	−1.18	−0.83	−0.20	−0.12
Standard deviation	20.84	4.48	6.19	9.74	13.53	14.74
Range	77.87	15.48	20.37	34.66	49.71	50.50
ROECD current account balance (OCAB)[d,h]						
Mean	−5.86	2.24	−0.92	−2.01	−3.63	−3.07
Standard deviation	24.80	5.34	3.63	9.51	15.08	13.94
Range	86.57	19.77	11.77	33.78	54.49	47.64

Source: Detailed tables in part 3.

a. Percent deviation from baseline path.

b. Deviation from baseline path in percentage points.

c. Deviation from baseline path in U.S. $ billion.

d. Deviation from baseline path in U.S. $ billion at baseline exchange rates.

e. TAYLOR and VAR models did not report results for U.S. consumer prices; results for the U.S. GNP deflator for those models are used as a substitute.

f. VAR model did not report results for ROECD consumer prices; results for the ROECD GNP deflator for that model are used as a substitute.

g. TAYLOR model did not report results for the U.S. current account balance.

h. EPA and TAYLOR models did not report results for the ROECD current account balance.

SIMULATION F

Nonpolicy Exogenous Depreciation of U.S. Dollar

Chart F-1. Effects on U.S. Real GNP (UGNP) of Nonpolicy Exogenous Depreciation of U.S. Dollar (U.S. and ROECD Policies Unchanged from Baseline)

Percent deviation from baseline path

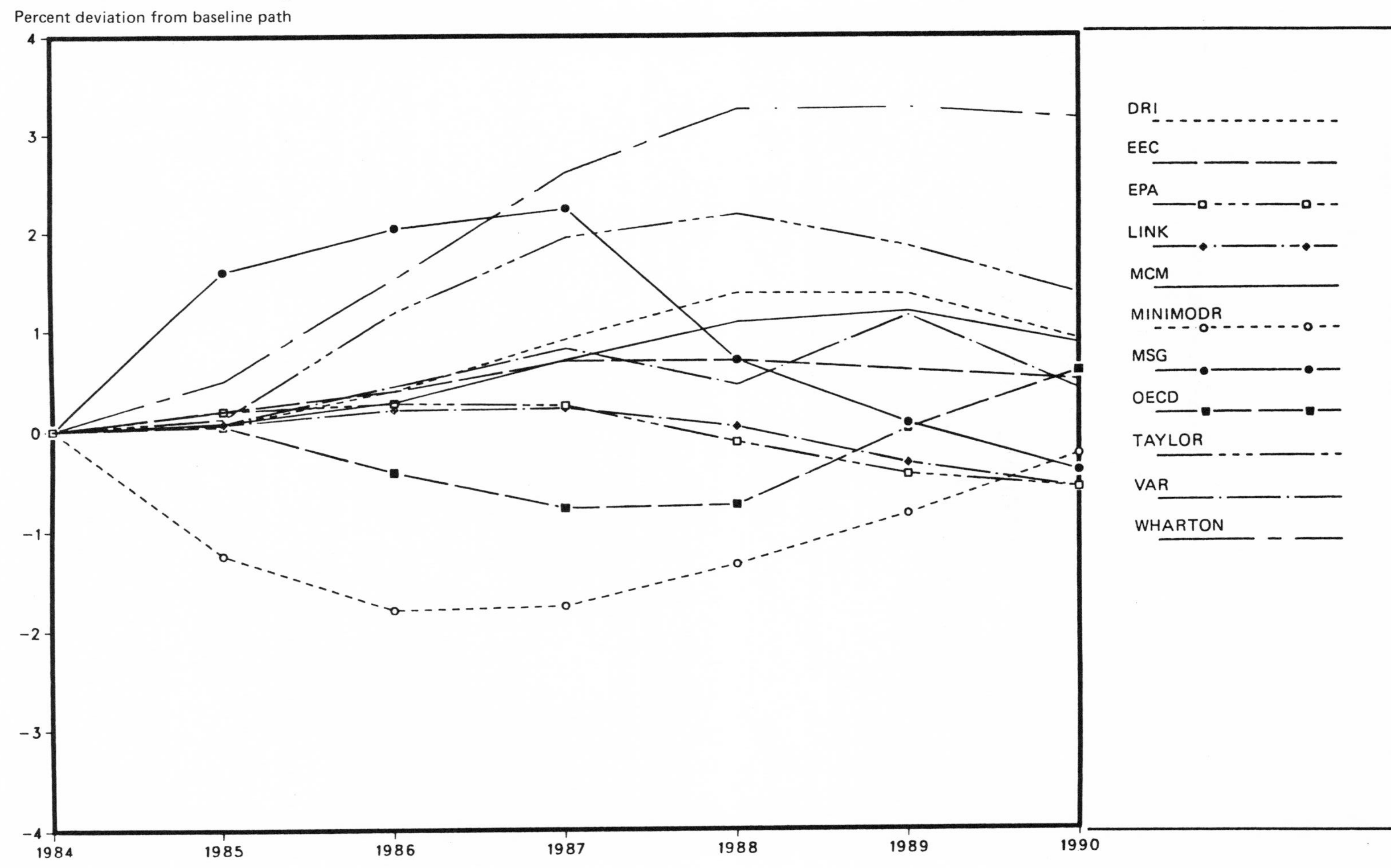

Chart F-2. Effects on ROECD Real GNP (OGNP) of Nonpolicy Exogenous Depreciation of U.S. Dollar (U.S. and ROECD Policies Unchanged from Baseline)

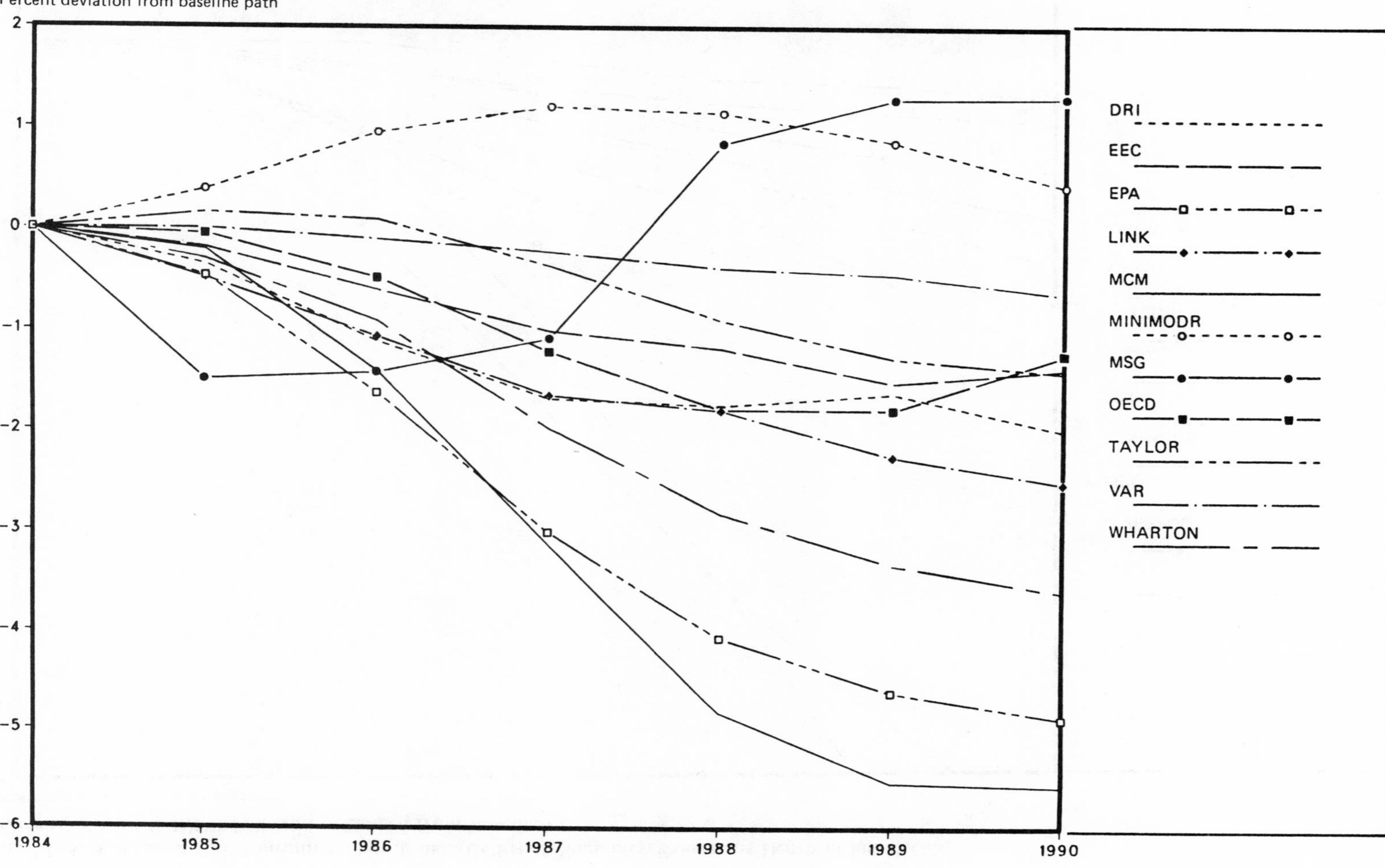

Chart F-3. Effects on U.S. Consumer Price Index (UCPI) of Nonpolicy Exogenous Depreciation of U.S. Dollar (U.S. and ROECD Policies Unchanged from Baseline)

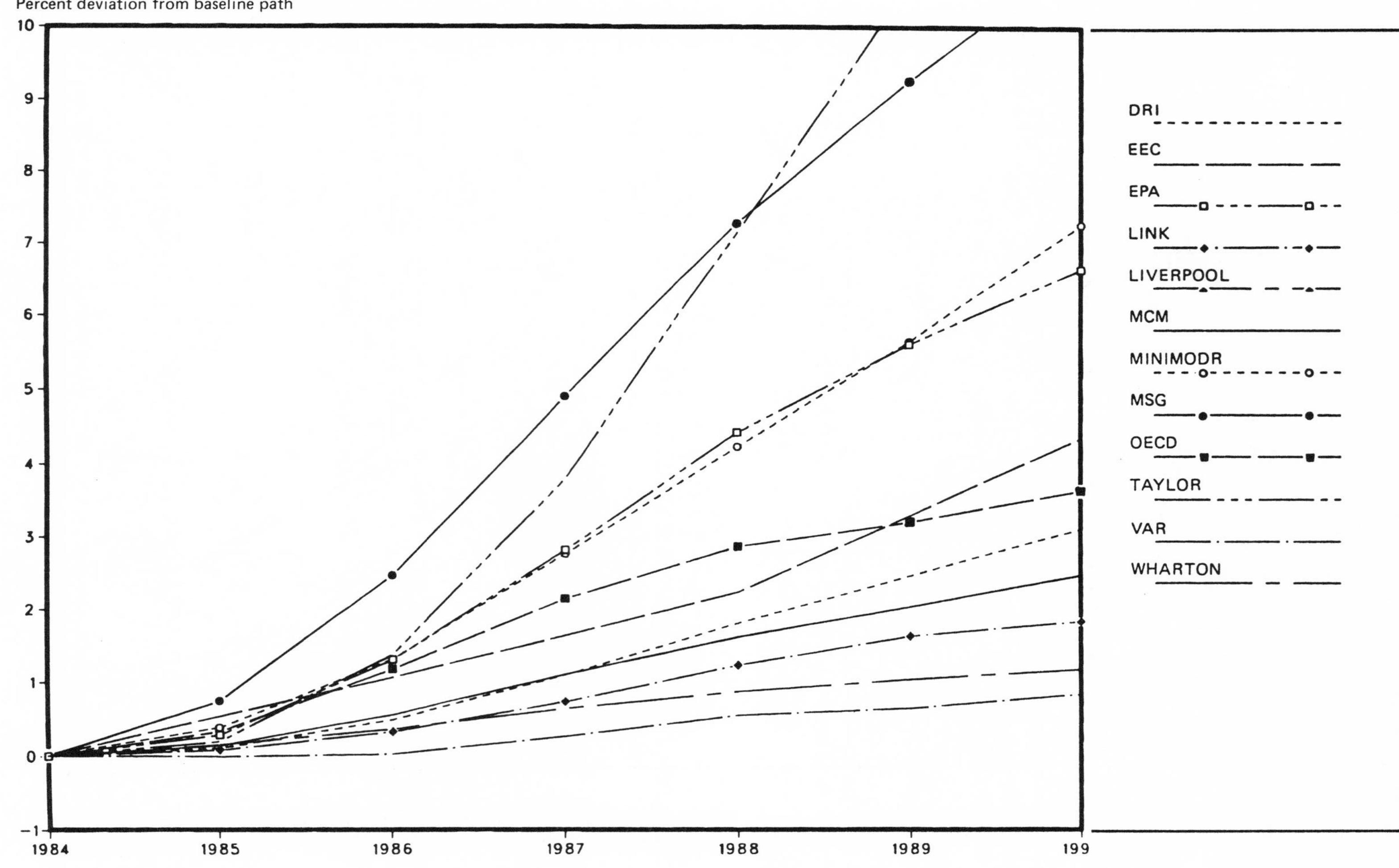

Chart F-4. Effects on ROECD Consumer Price Index (OPCPI) of Nonpolicy Exogenous Depreciation of U.S. Dollar (U.S. and ROECD Policies Unchanged from Baseline)

Percent deviation from baseline path

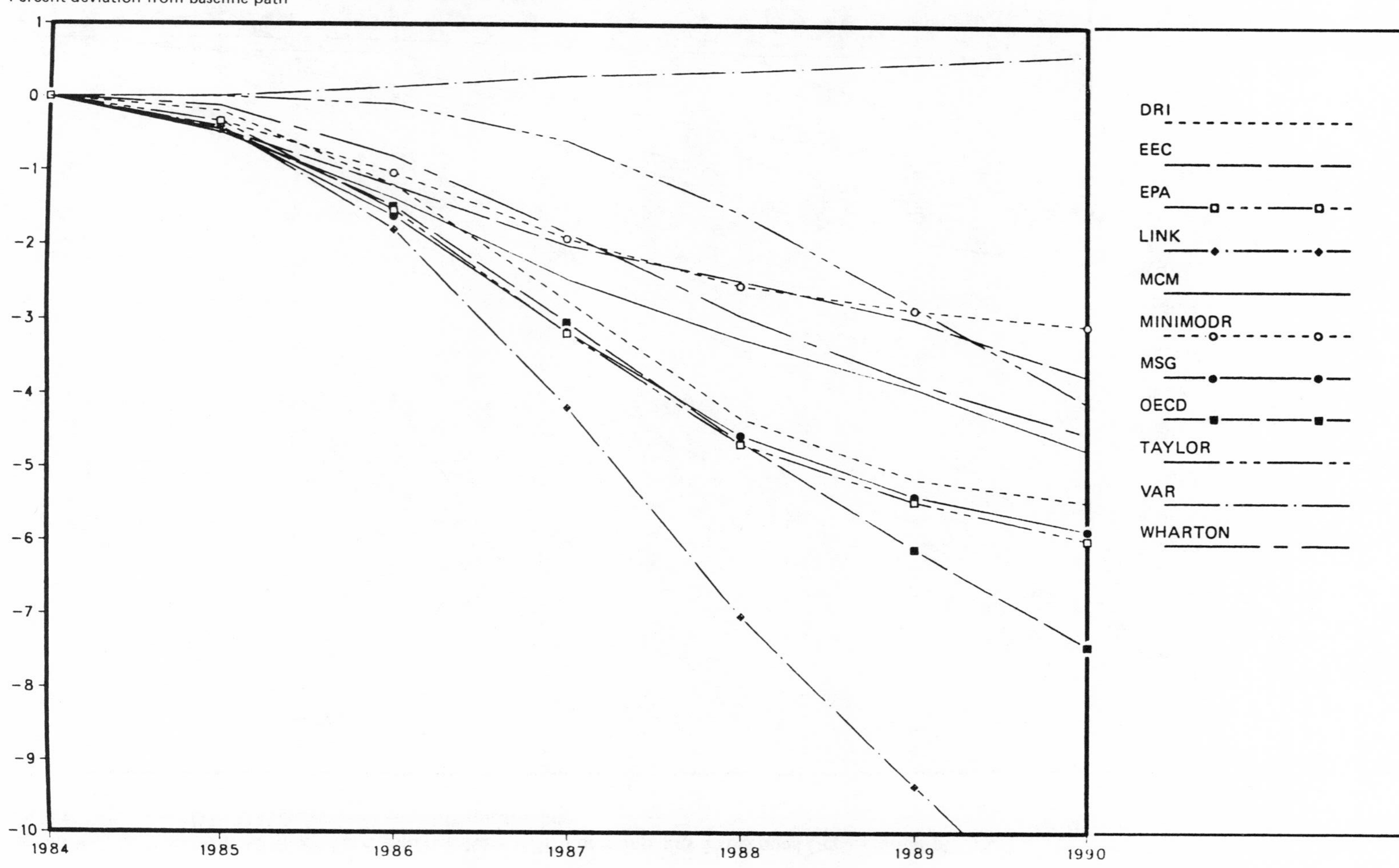

Chart F-5. Effects on U.S. Short-Term Interest Rate (URS) of Nonpolicy Exogenous Depreciation of U.S. Dollar (U.S. and ROECD Policies Unchanged from Baseline)

Deviation from baseline path, percentage points

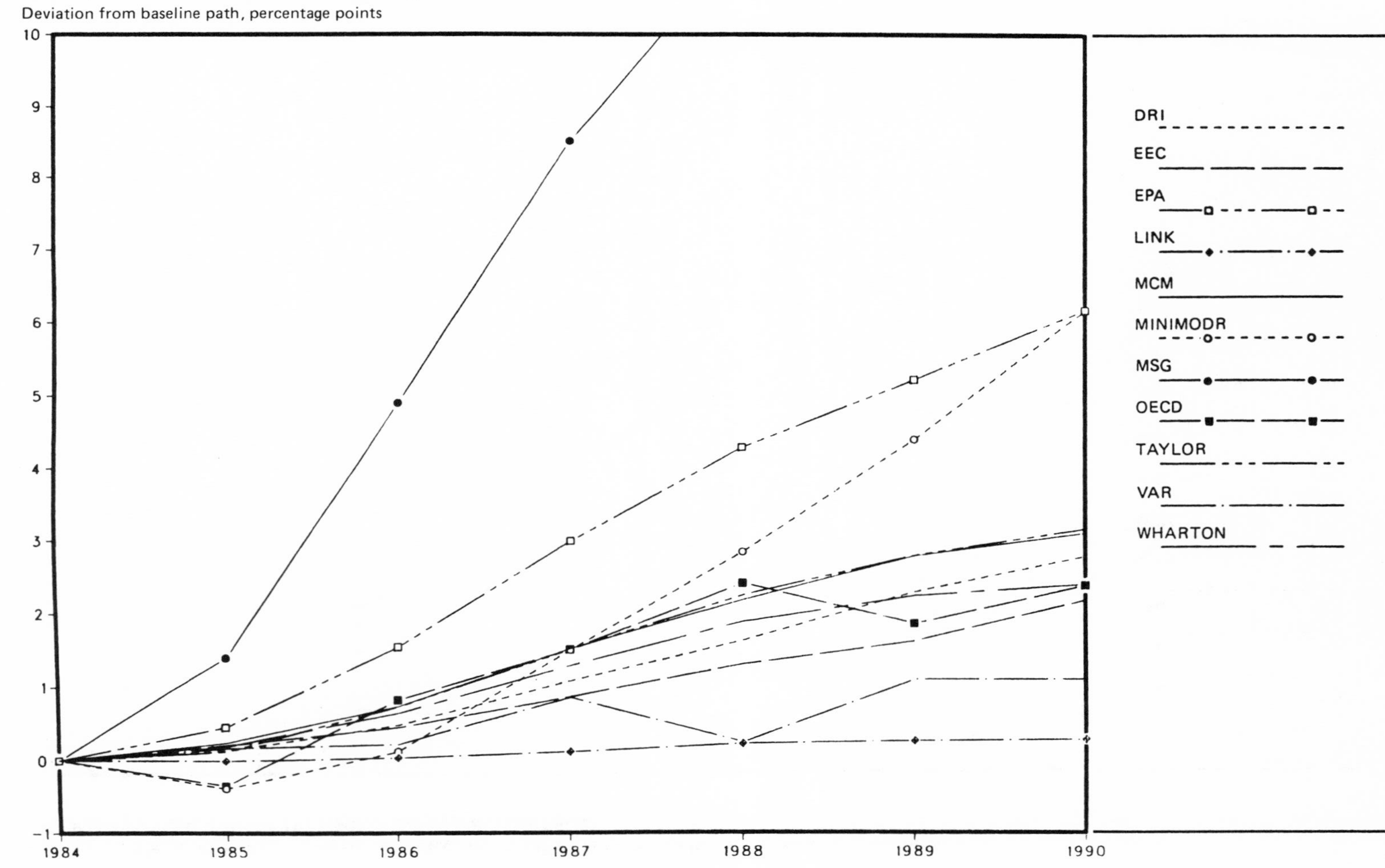

Chart F-6. Effects on ROECD Short-Term Interest Rate (ORS) of Nonpolicy Exogenous Depreciation of U.S. Dollar (U.S. and ROECD Policies Unchanged from Baseline)

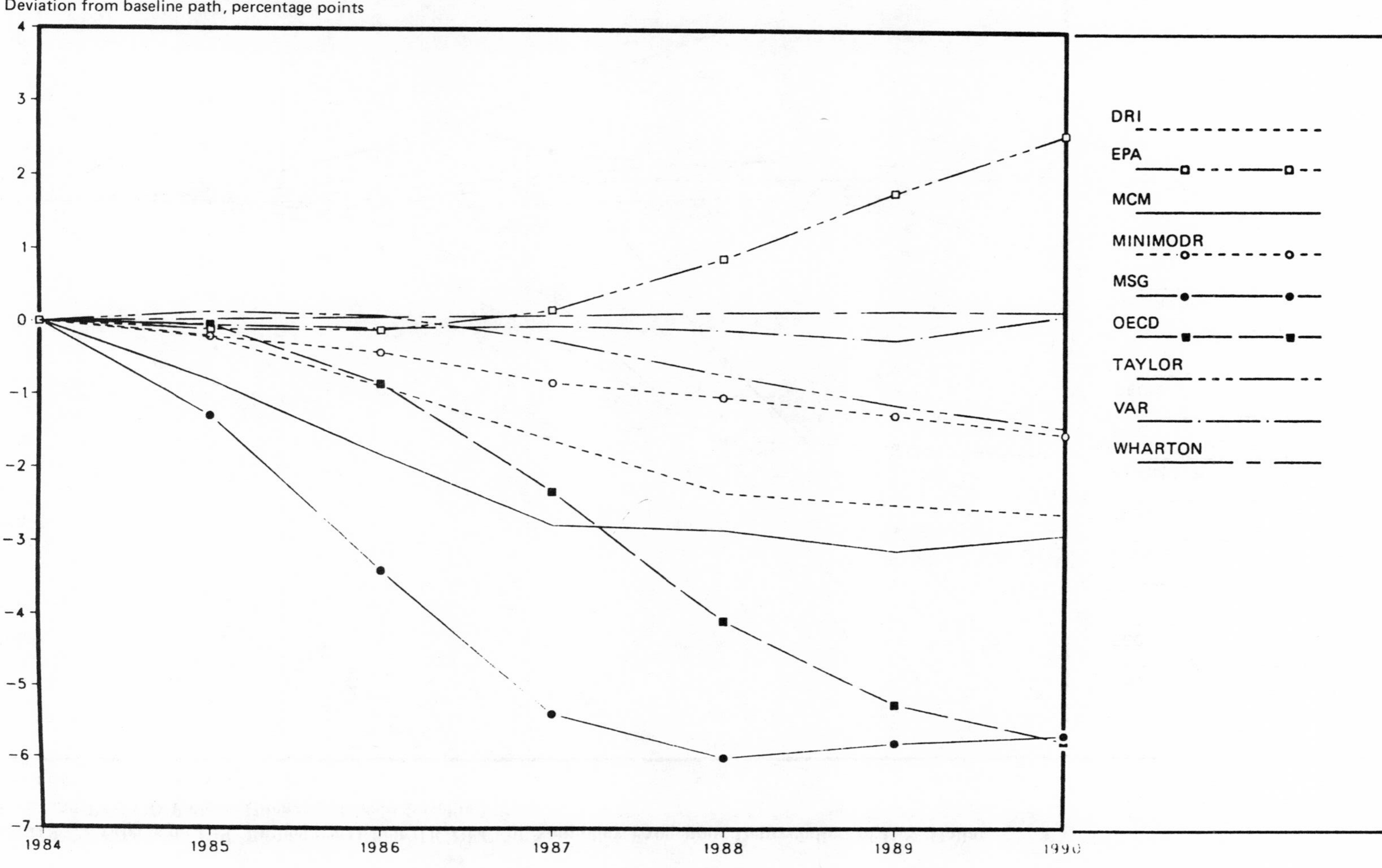

Chart F-7. Effects on U.S. Budgetary Deficit (UGDEF) of Nonpolicy Exogenous Depreciation of U.S. Dollar (U.S. and ROECD Policies Unchanged from Baseline)

Deviation from baseline path, U.S. billion $

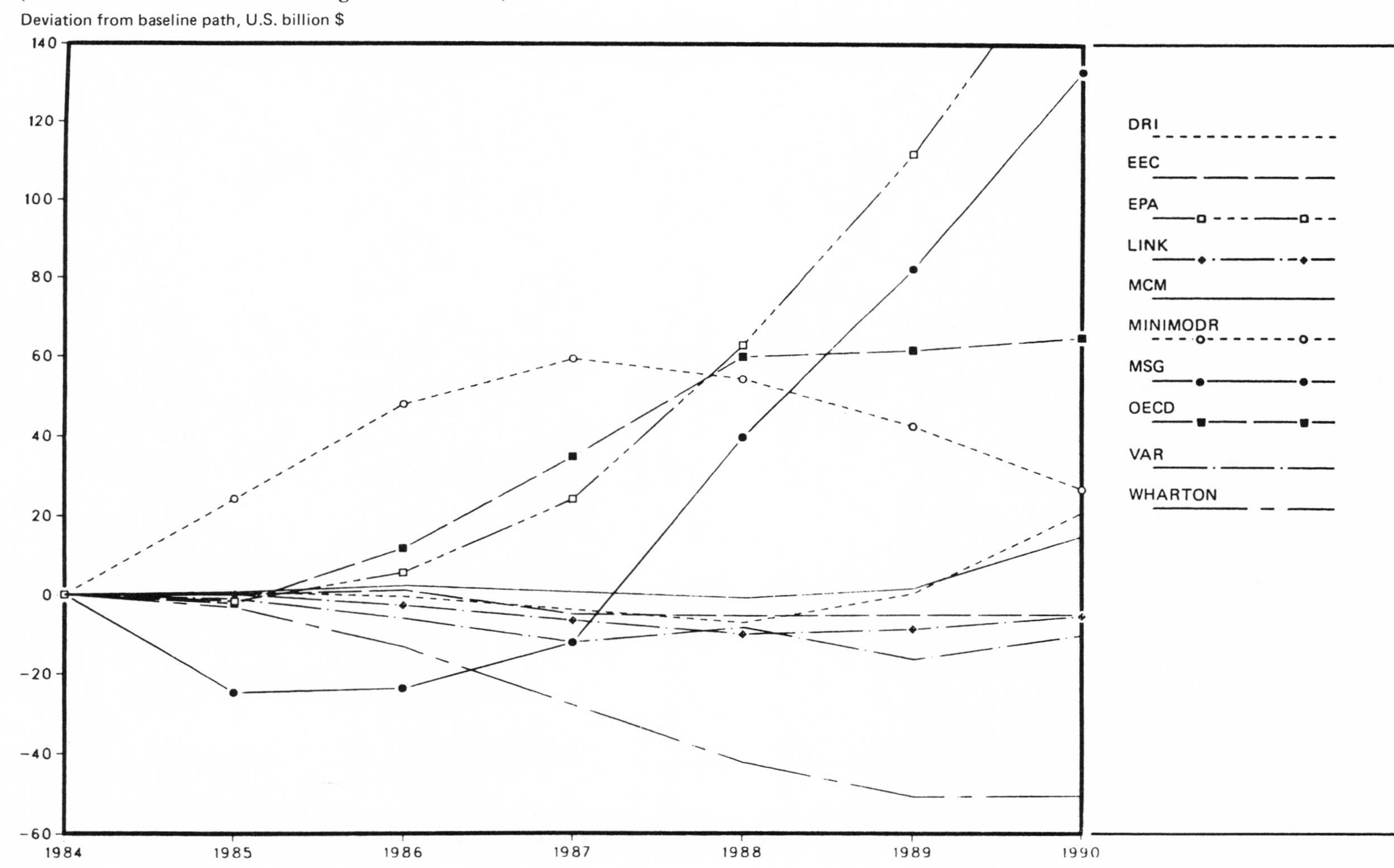

Chart F-8. Effects on Weighted Average Exchange Value of U.S. Dollar (Foreign Currencies per U.S. Dollar) (UEXCH) of Nonpolicy Exogenous Depreciation of U.S. Dollar (U.S. and ROECD Policies Unchanged from Baseline)

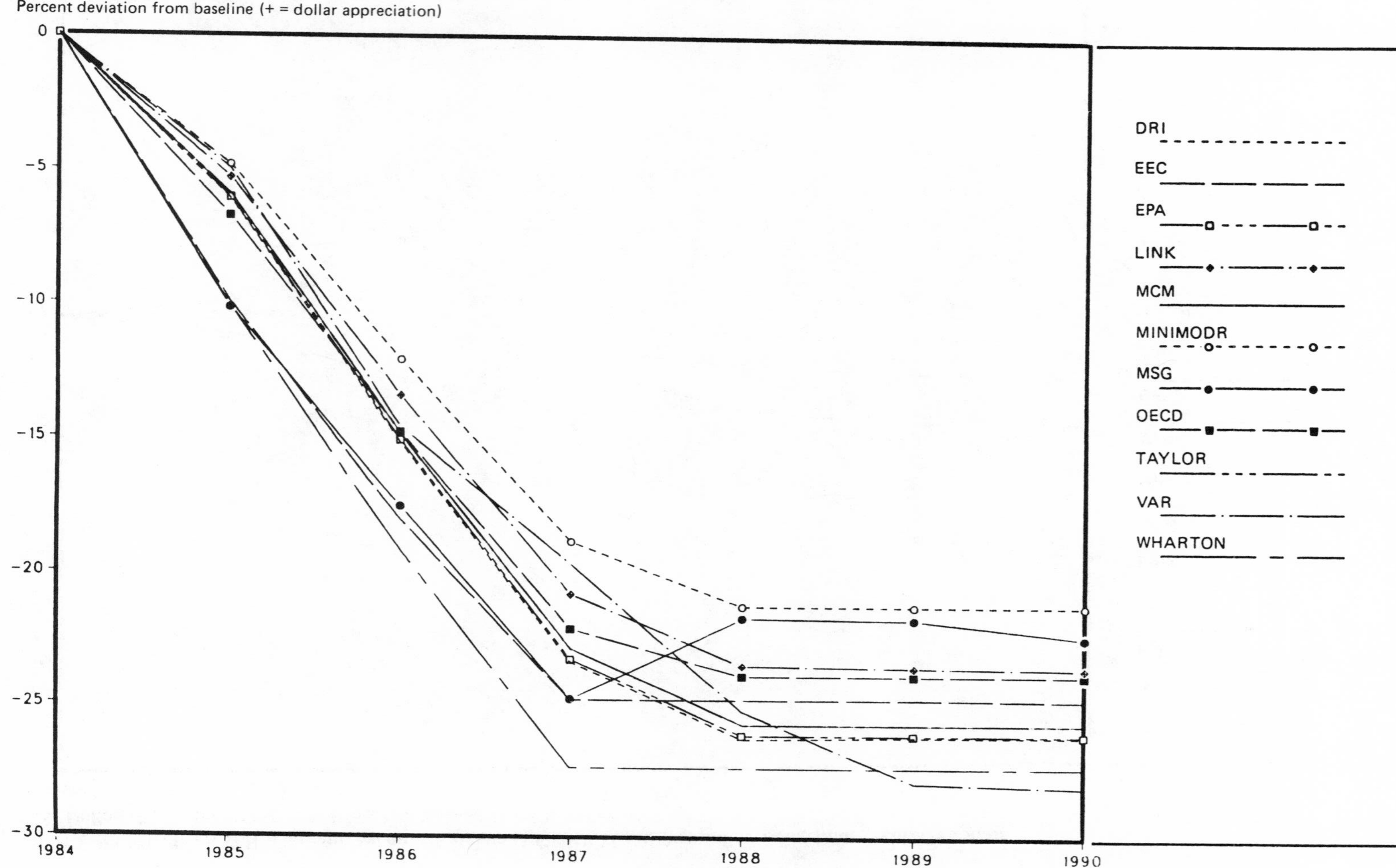

Chart F-9. Effects on U.S. Current Account Balance (UCURBAL) of Nonpolicy Exogenous Depreciation of U.S. Dollar (U.S. and ROECD Policies Unchanged from Baseline)

Deviation from baseline path, U.S. billion $

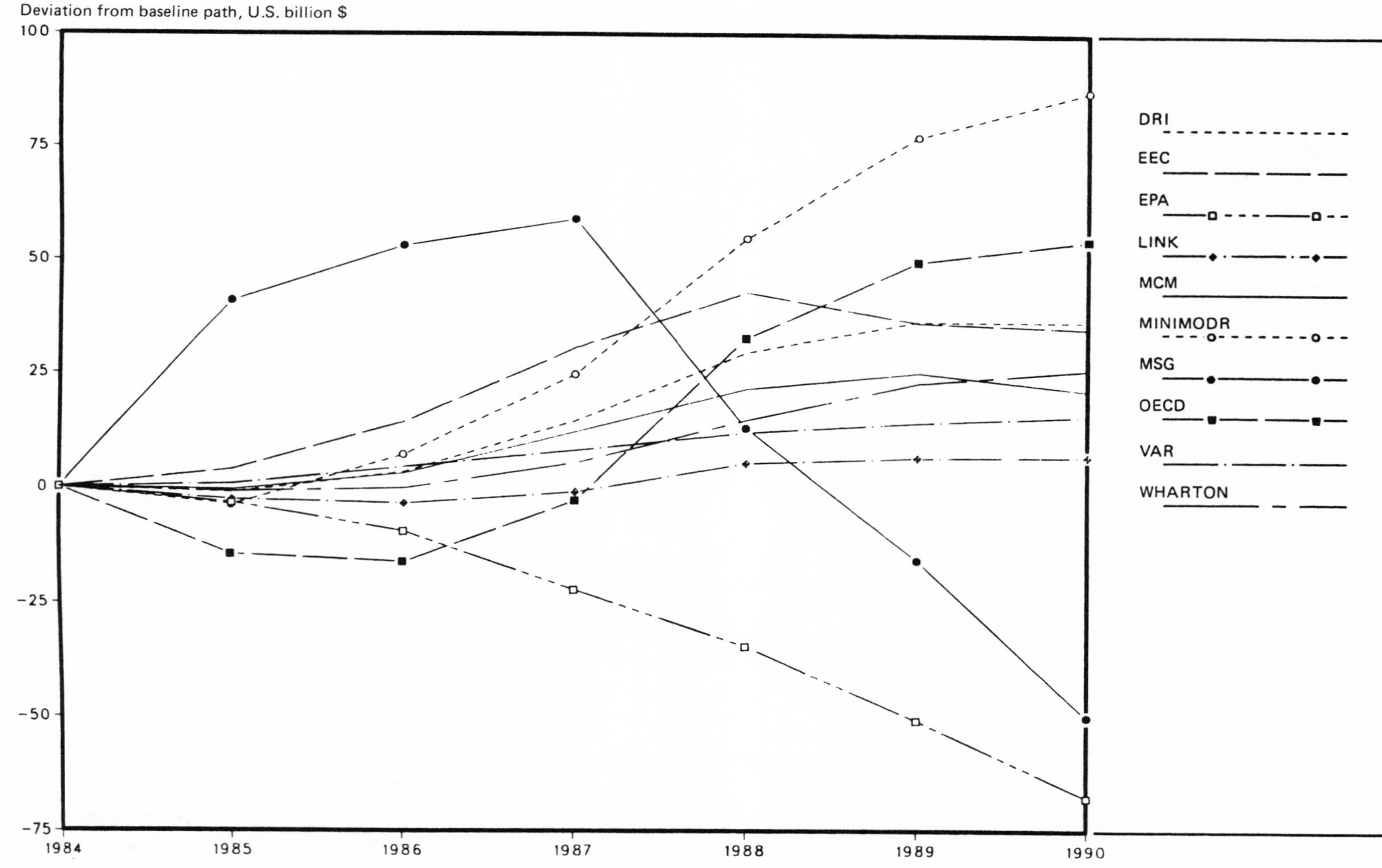

Chart F-10. Effects on ROECD Current Account Balance (OCURBAL) of Nonpolicy Exogenous Depreciation of U.S. Dollar (U.S. and ROECD Policies Unchanged from Baseline)

Deviation from baseline, U.S. billion $ at baseline exchange rates

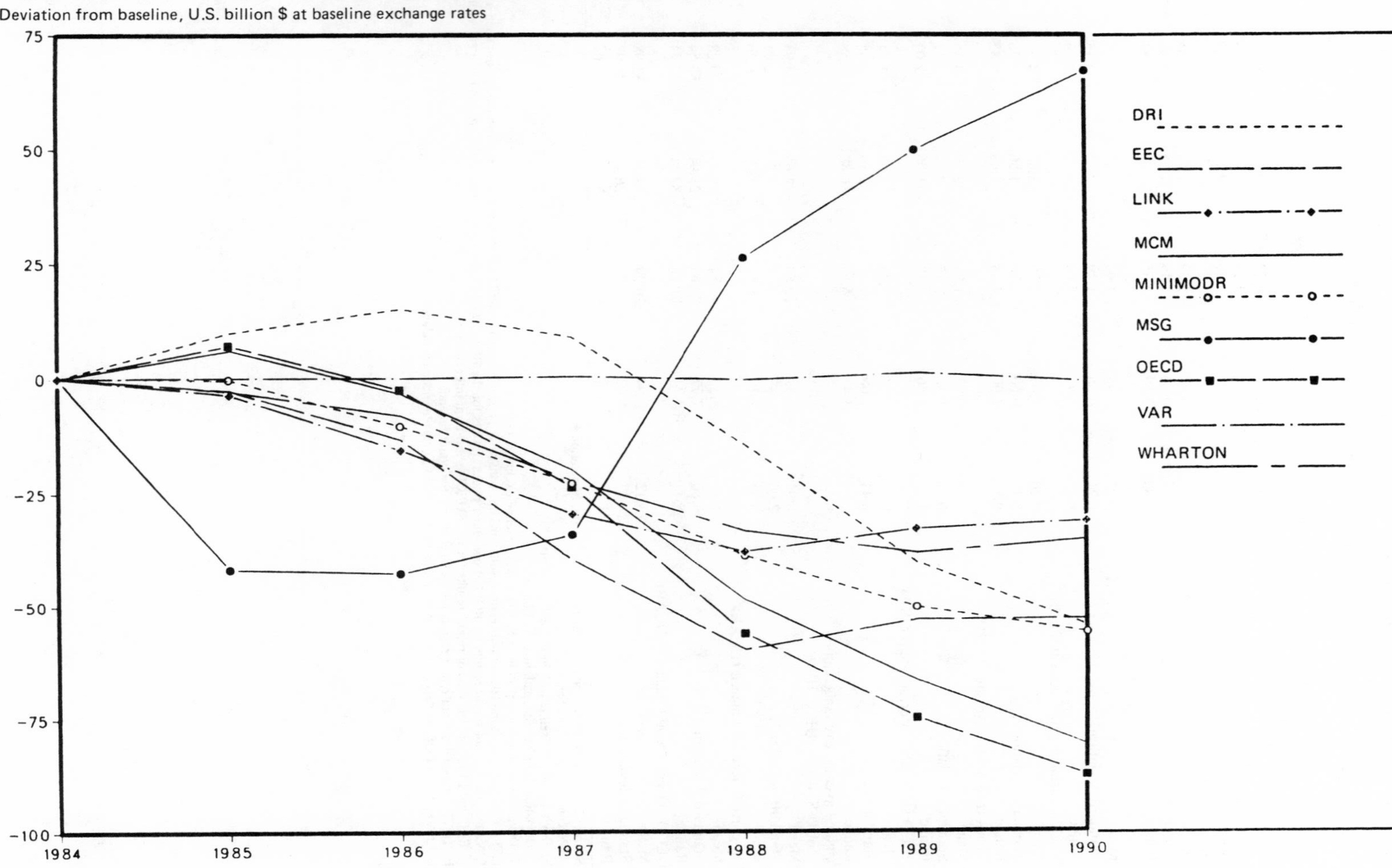

Table F. Average Responses, Standard Deviations, and Ranges for Simulated Effects of Nonpolicy Exogenous Depreciation of the Dollar

(Simulation F—11 Models)

Variable	*Year 1 (1985)*	*Year 2 (1986)*	*Year 3 (1987)*	*Year 4 (1988)*	*Year 5 (1989)*	*Year 6 (1990)*
U.S. real GNP (UGNP)[a]						
Mean	0.16	0.42	0.72	0.69	0.72	0.55
Standard deviation	0.62	0.96	1.21	1.23	1.14	1.03
Range	2.85	3.83	4.36	4.58	4.09	3.72
ROECD real GNP (OGNP)[a]						
Mean	−0.28	−0.71	−1.29	−1.60	−1.85	−1.96
Standard deviation	0.46	0.74	1.19	1.75	1.98	2.00
Range	1.89	2.59	4.35	5.98	6.81	6.88
U.S. consumer price index (UCPI)[a,e]						
Mean	0.27	0.95	1.99	3.12	4.13	5.09
Standard deviation	0.21	0.66	1.39	2.27	3.15	3.96
Range	0.75	2.44	4.64	6.72	9.96	12.79
ROECD consumer price index (OPCPI)[a,f]						
Mean	−0.30	−1.09	−2.26	−3.42	−4.31	−5.09
Standard deviation	0.18	0.60	1.20	1.86	2.36	2.86
Range	0.50	2.00	4.48	7.43	9.85	12.31
U.S. short-term interest rate (URS)[b]						
Mean	0.20	0.92	1.98	2.79	3.36	3.94
Standard deviation	0.45	1.30	2.17	2.90	3.12	3.50
Range	1.78	4.86	8.38	11.06	12.03	13.31
ROECD short-term interest rate (ORS)[b,g]						
Mean	−0.29	−0.84	−1.46	−1.80	−1.94	−1.91
Standard deviation	0.44	1.08	1.73	2.10	2.35	2.57
Range	1.43	3.48	5.57	6.88	7.58	8.36
Weighted average exchange value of U.S. dollar (UEXCH)[a]						
Mean	−6.94	−15.42	−22.80	−24.65	−24.93	−25.02
Standard deviation	2.00	1.97	2.33	1.84	2.05	1.98
Range	5.35	7.10	8.54	6.13	6.70	6.88
U.S. current account balance (UCAB)[c,h]						
Mean	1.83	5.55	12.84	19.23	20.28	16.53
Standard deviation	13.80	17.77	20.83	23.04	33.54	43.52
Range	55.47	69.24	81.35	89.31	128.24	155.14
ROECD current account balance (OCAB)[d,i]						
Mean	−3.12	−8.94	−20.39	−29.31	−33.98	−36.89
Standard deviation	14.42	14.62	14.73	26.49	35.97	44.18
Range	51.67	57.61	48.55	85.70	124.62	154.66

Source: Detailed tables in part 3; LIVERPOOL did not run Simulation F.
a. Percent deviation from baseline path.
b. Deviation from baseline path in percentage points.
c. Deviation from baseline path in U.S. $ billion.
d. Deviation from baseline path in U.S. $ billion at baseline exchange rates.
e. TAYLOR and VAR models did not report results for U.S. consumer prices; results for the U.S. GNP deflator for those models are used as a substitute.
f. VAR model did not report results for ROECD consumer prices; results for the ROECD GNP deflator for that model are used as a substitute.
g. EEC and LINK models did not report results for the ROECD short-term interest rate.
h. TAYLOR model did not report results for the U.S. current account balance.
i. EPA and TAYLOR models did not report results for the ROECD current account balance.

SIMULATION G

ROECD Fiscal Expansion

Chart G-1. Effects on U.S. Real GNP (UGNP) of Increase in ROECD Government Purchases (U.S. Policies Unchanged from Baseline)

Percent deviation from baseline path

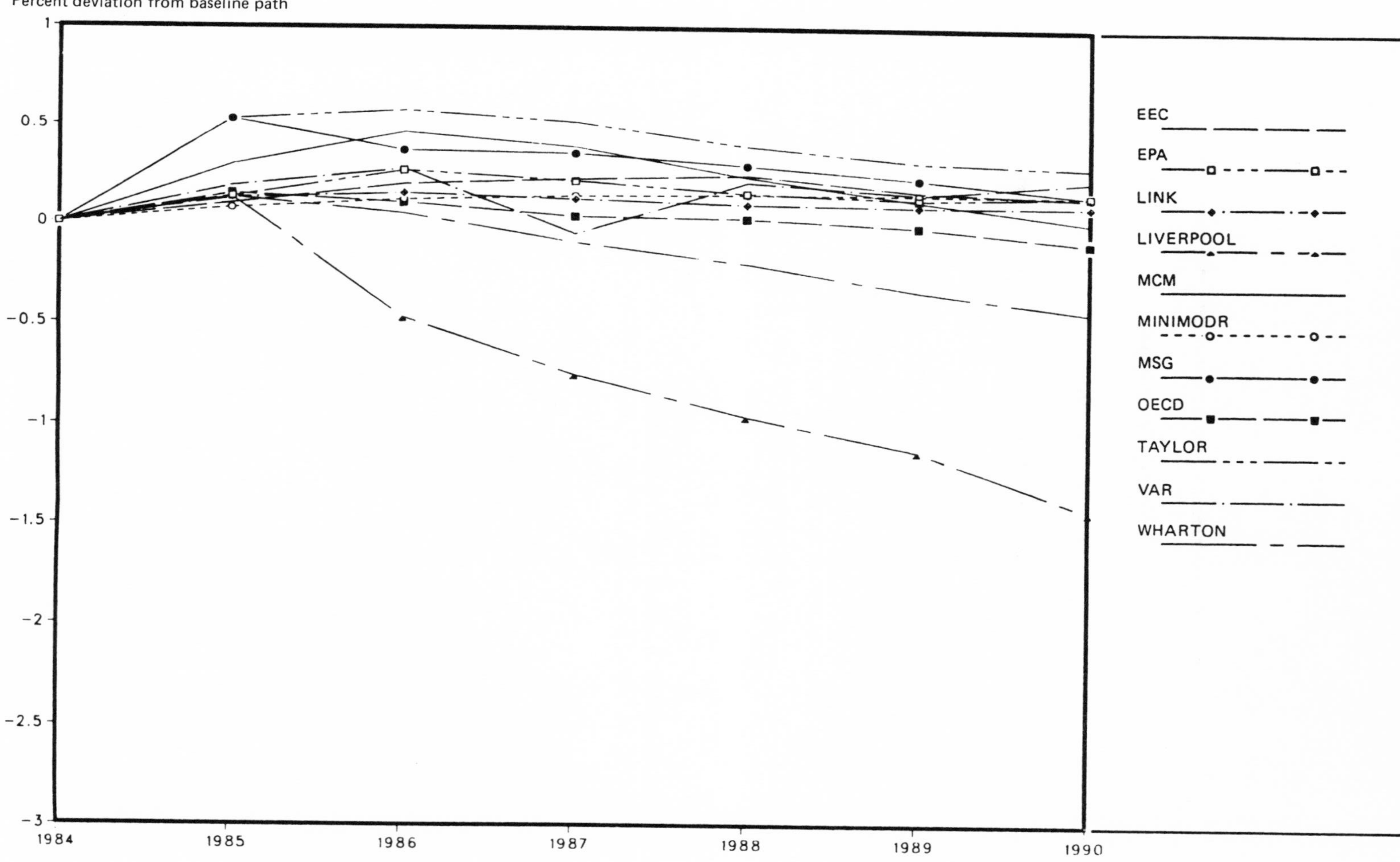

Chart G-2. Effects on ROECD Real GNP (OGNP) of Increase in ROECD Government Purchases (U.S. Policies Unchanged from Baseline)

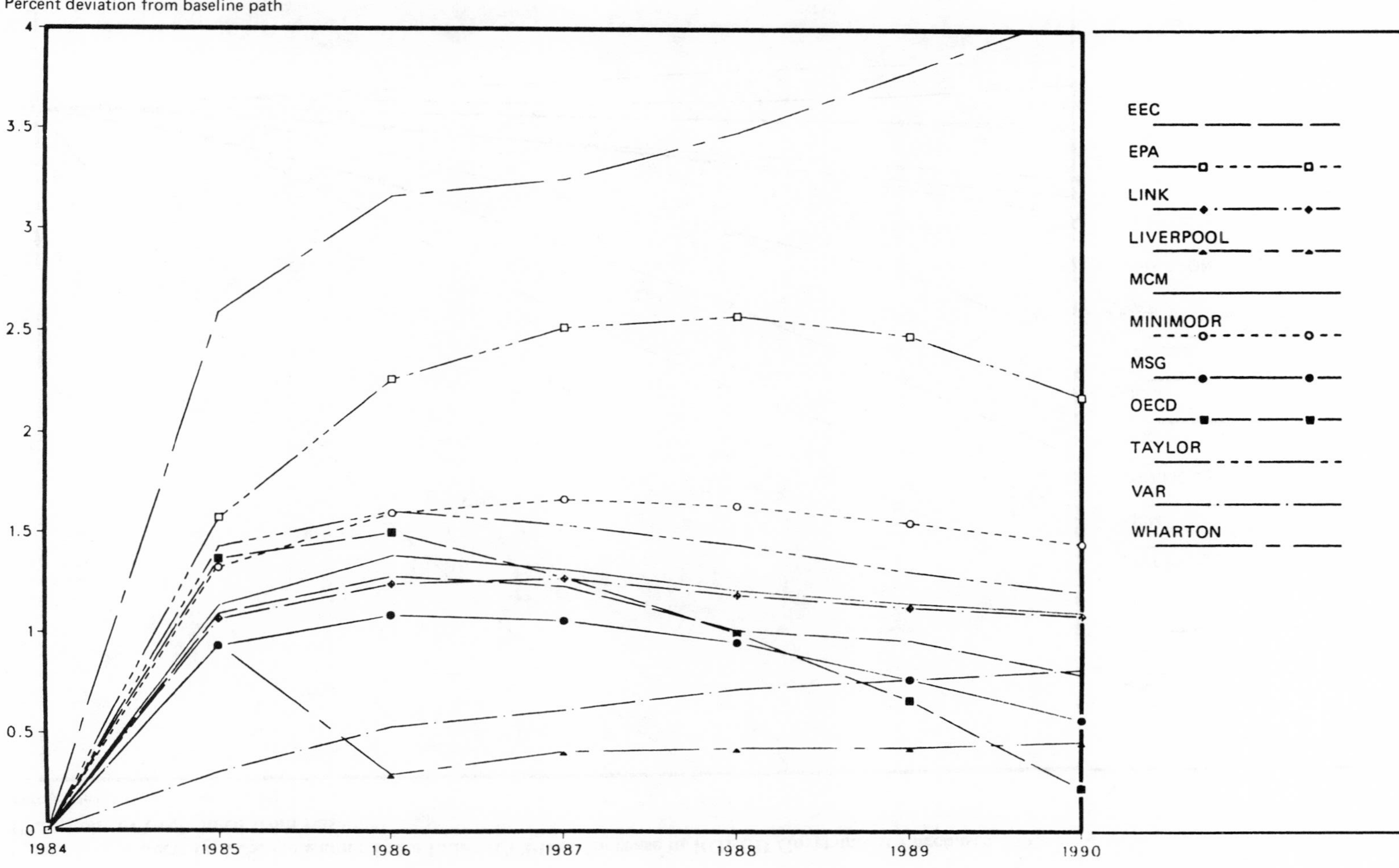

Chart G-3. Effects on U.S. Consumer Price Index (UCPI) of Increase in ROECD Government Purchases (U.S. Policies Unchanged from Baseline)

Percent deviation from baseline path

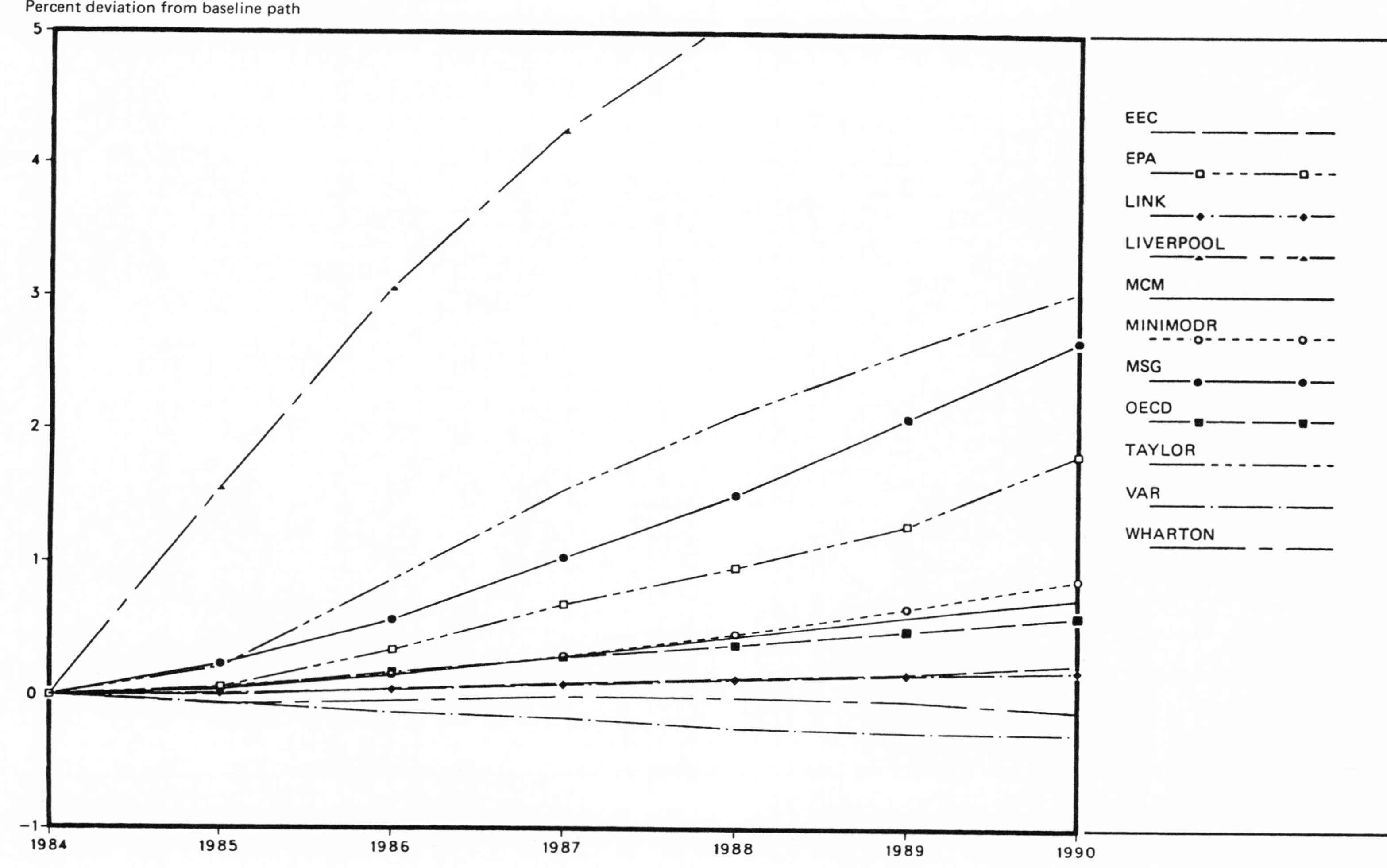

Chart G-4. Effects on ROECD Consumer Price Index (OPCPI) of Increase in ROECD Government Purchases (U.S. Policies Unchanged from Baseline)

Percent deviation from baseline path

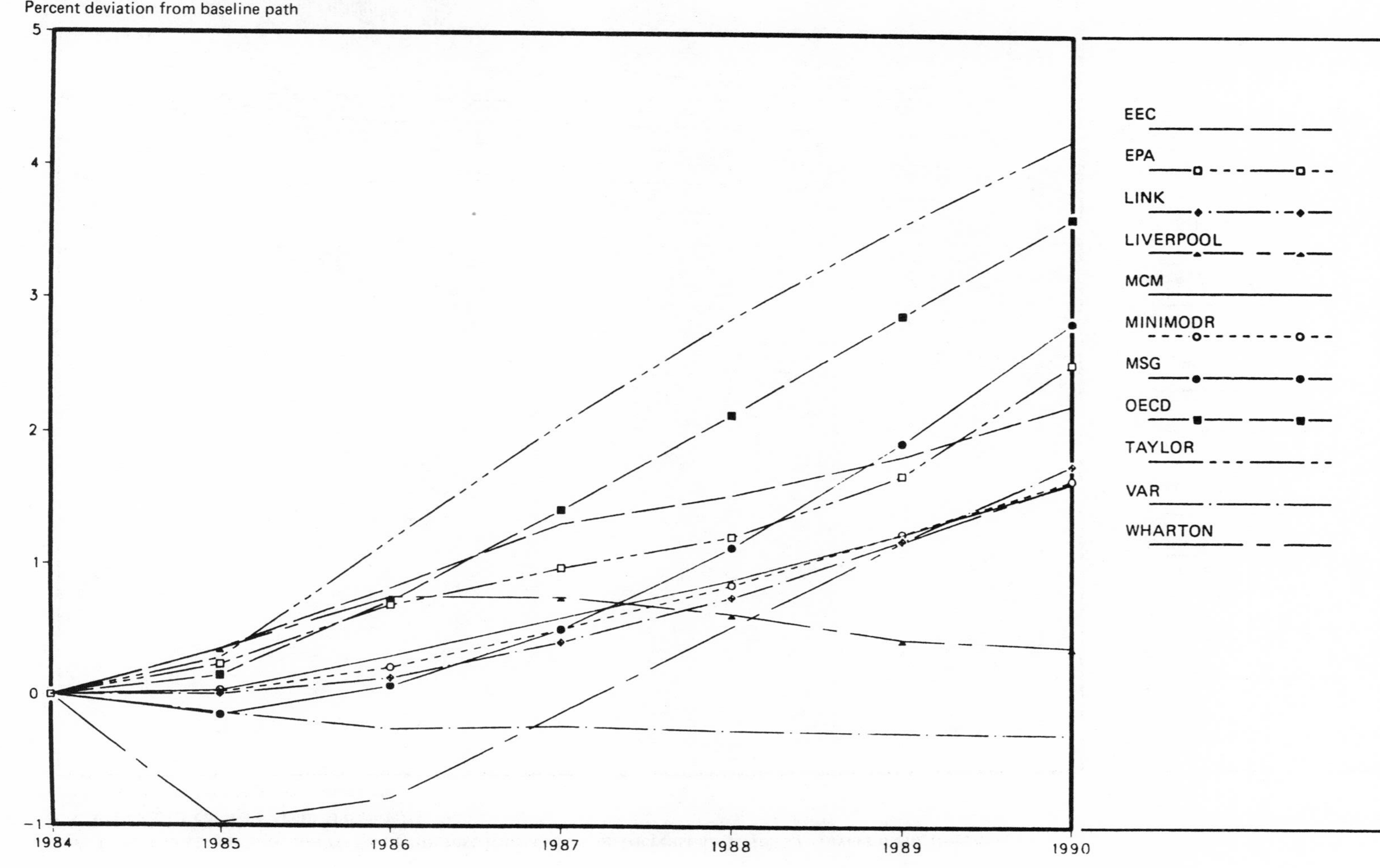

Chart G-5. Effects on U.S. Short-Term Interest Rate (URS) of Increase in ROECD Government Purchases (U.S. Policies Unchanged from Baseline)

Deviation from baseline path, percentage points

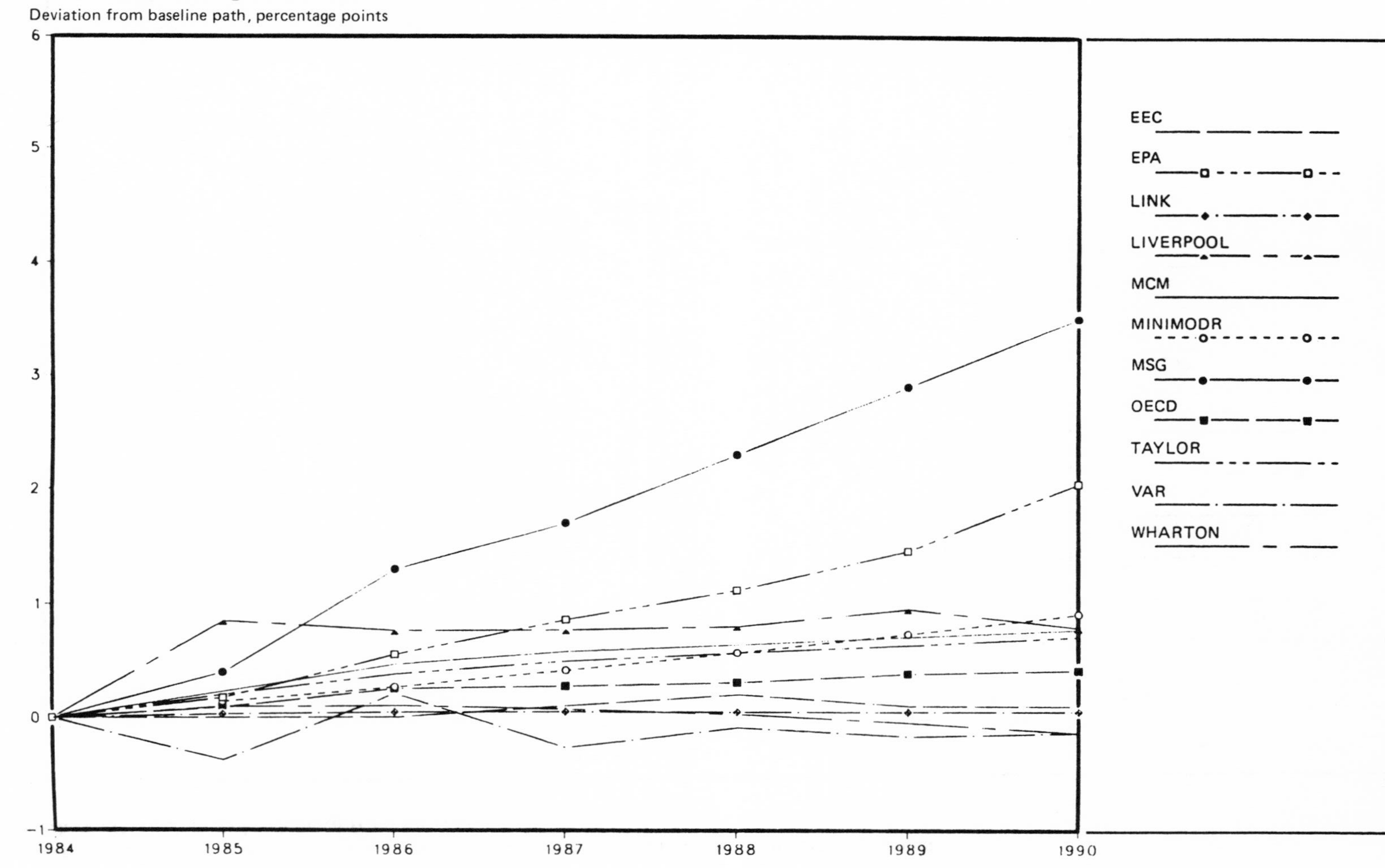

Chart G-6. Effects on ROECD Short-Term Interest Rate (ORS) of Increase in ROECD Government Purchases (U.S. Policies Unchanged from Baseline)

Deviation from baseline path, percentage points

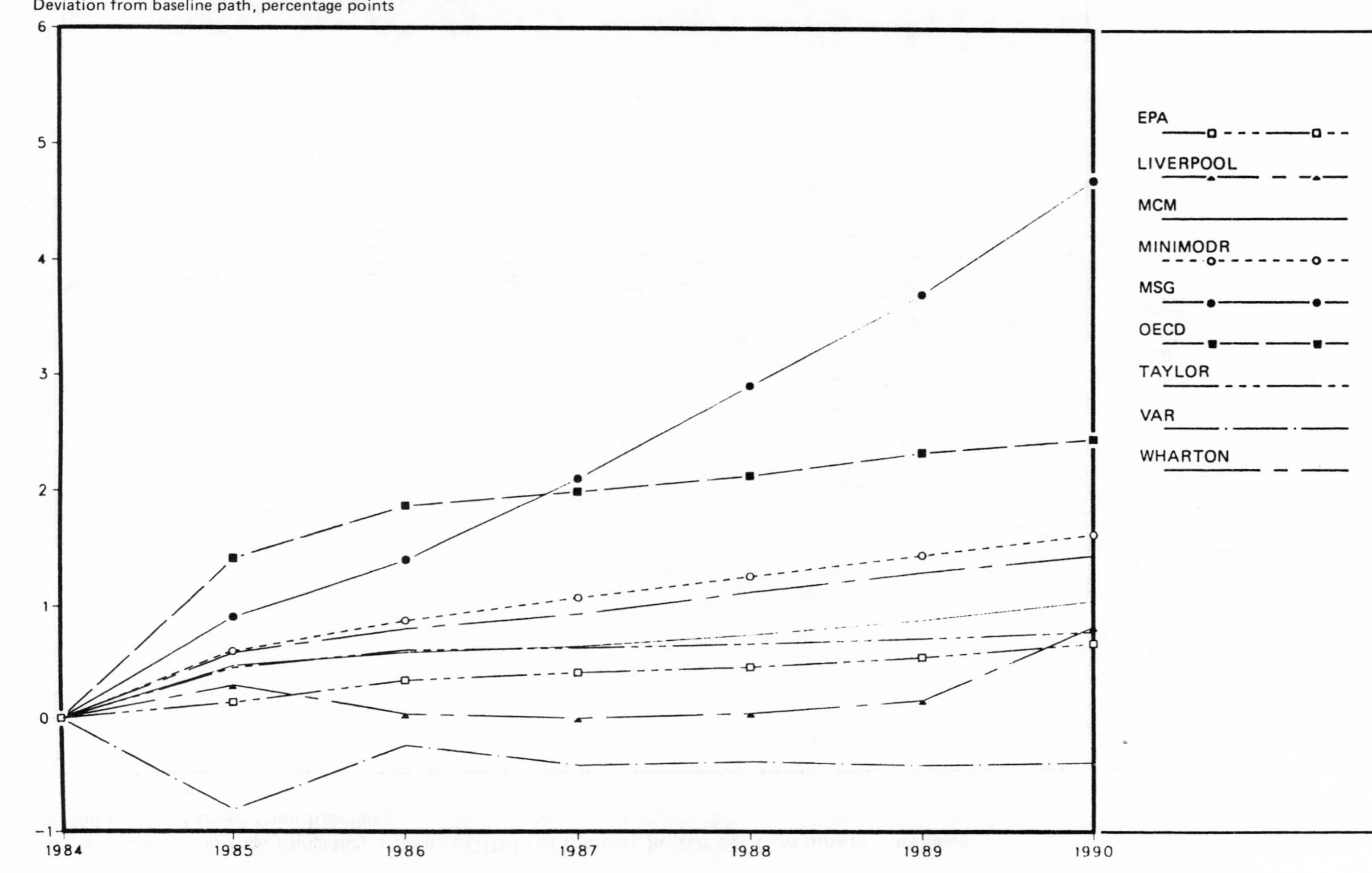

Chart G-7. Effects on U.S. Budgetary Deficit (UGDEF) of Increase in ROECD Government Purchases (U.S. Policies Unchanged from Baseline)

Deviation from baseline path, U.S. billion $

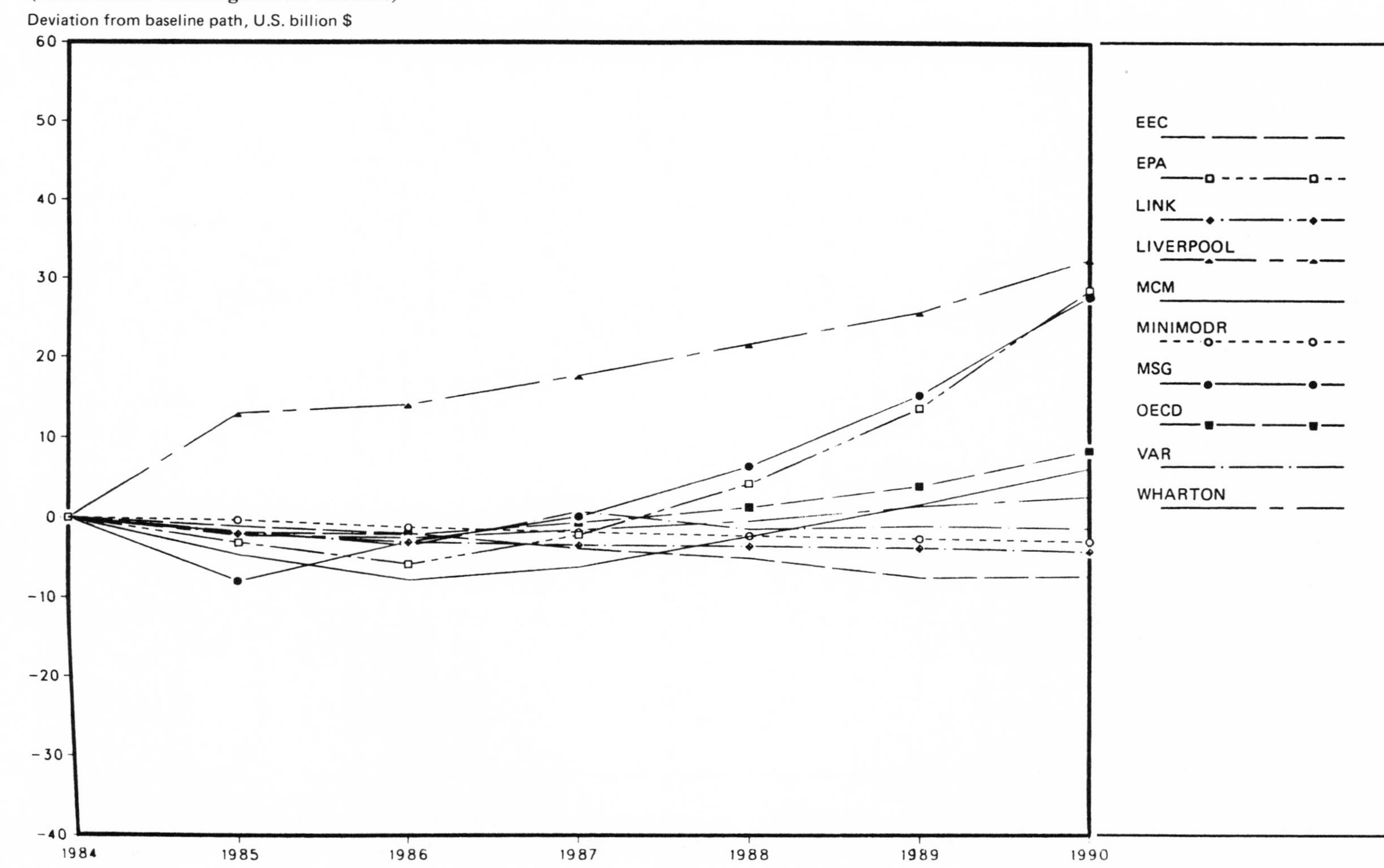

Chart G-7A. Effects on ROECD Budgetary Deficit (OGDEF) of Increase in ROECD Government Purchases (U.S. Policies Unchanged from Baseline)

Deviation from baseline path, U.S. billion $ at baseline exchange rates

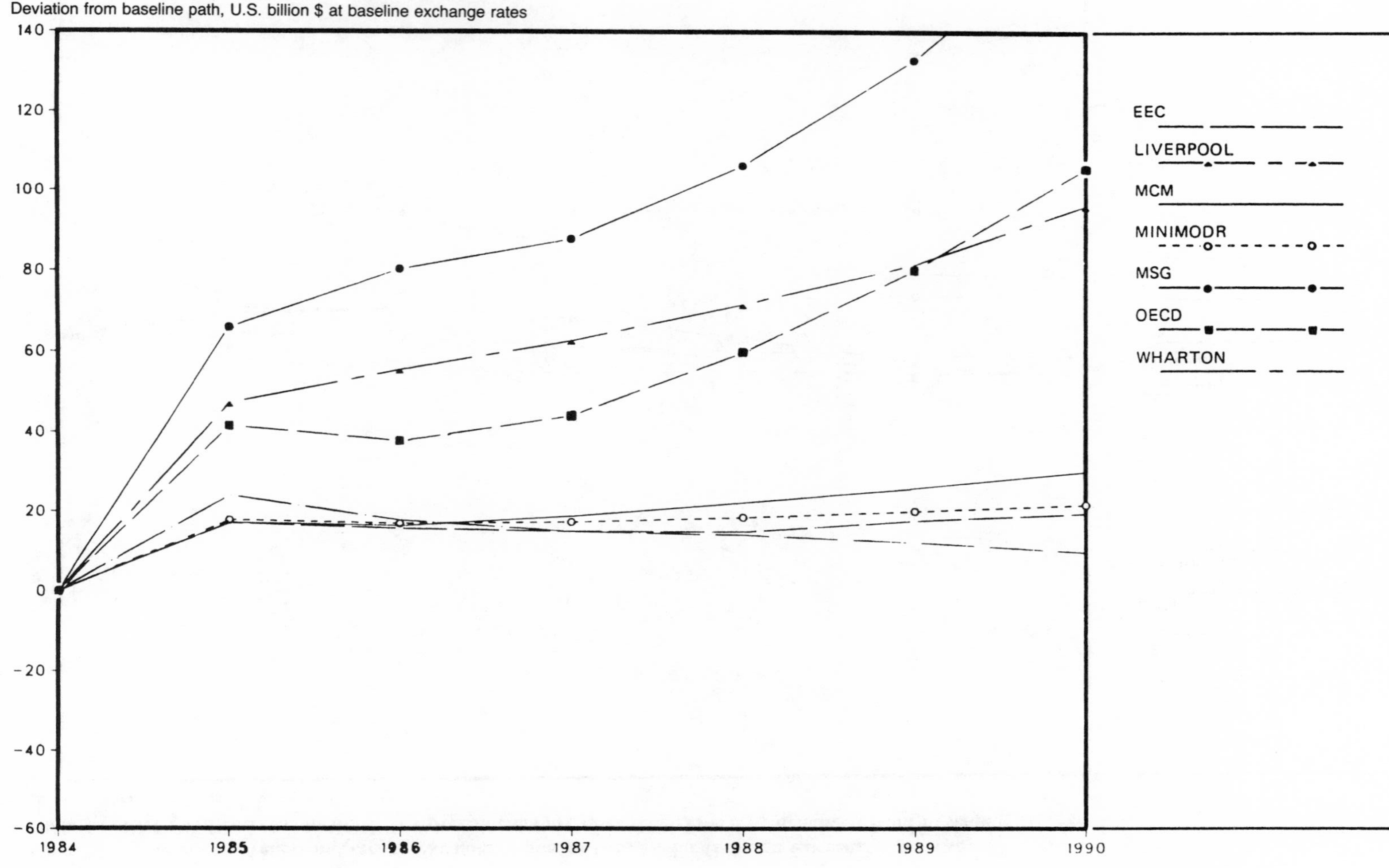

Chart G-8. Effects on Weighted Average Exchange Value of U.S. Dollar (Foreign Currencies per U.S. Dollar) (UEXCH) of Increase in ROECD Government Purchases (U.S. Policies Unchanged from Baseline)

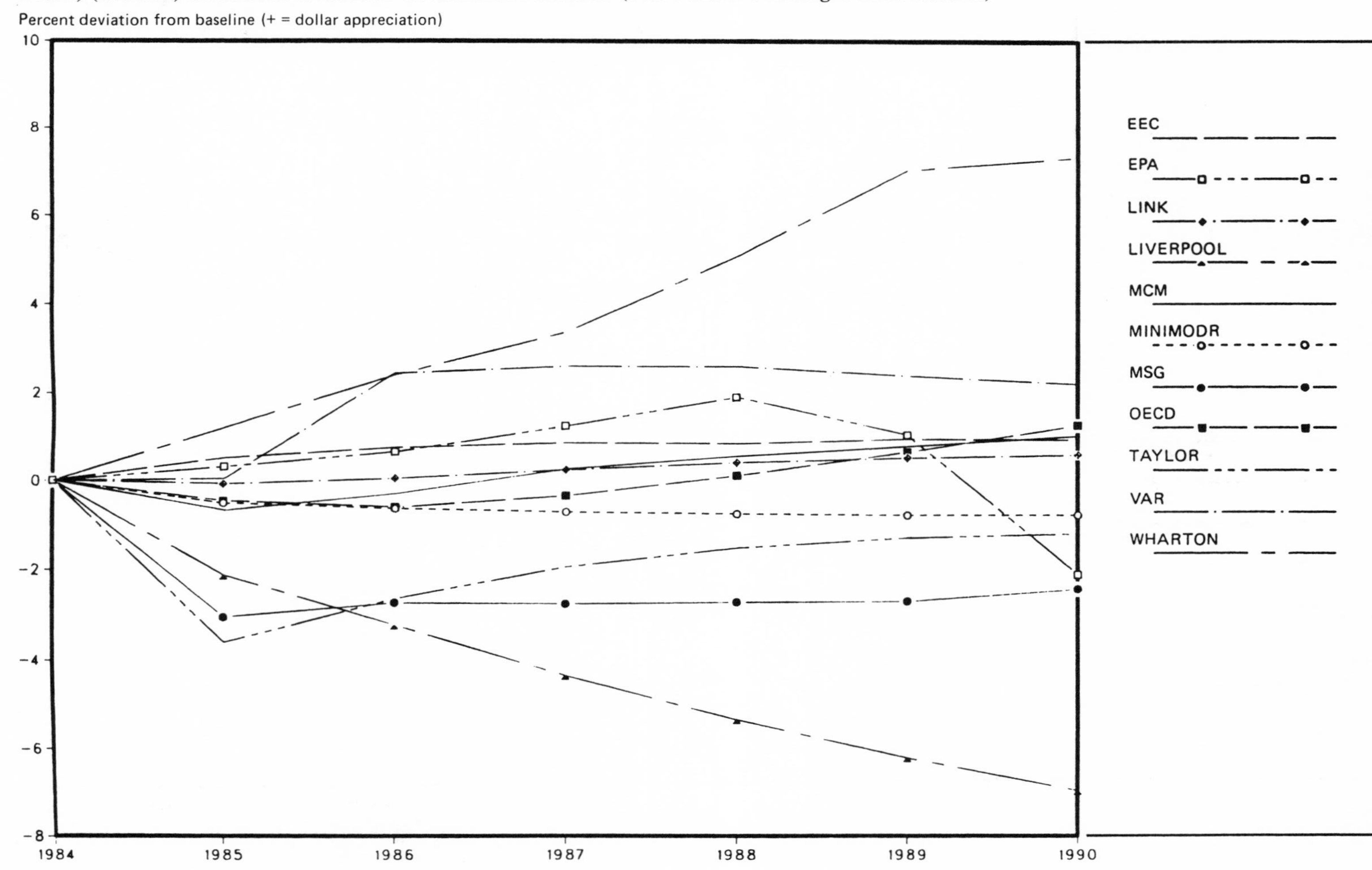

Chart G-9. Effects on U.S. Current Account Balance (UCURBAL) of Increase in ROECD Government Purchases (U.S. Policies Unchanged from Baseline)

Deviation from baseline path, U.S. billion $

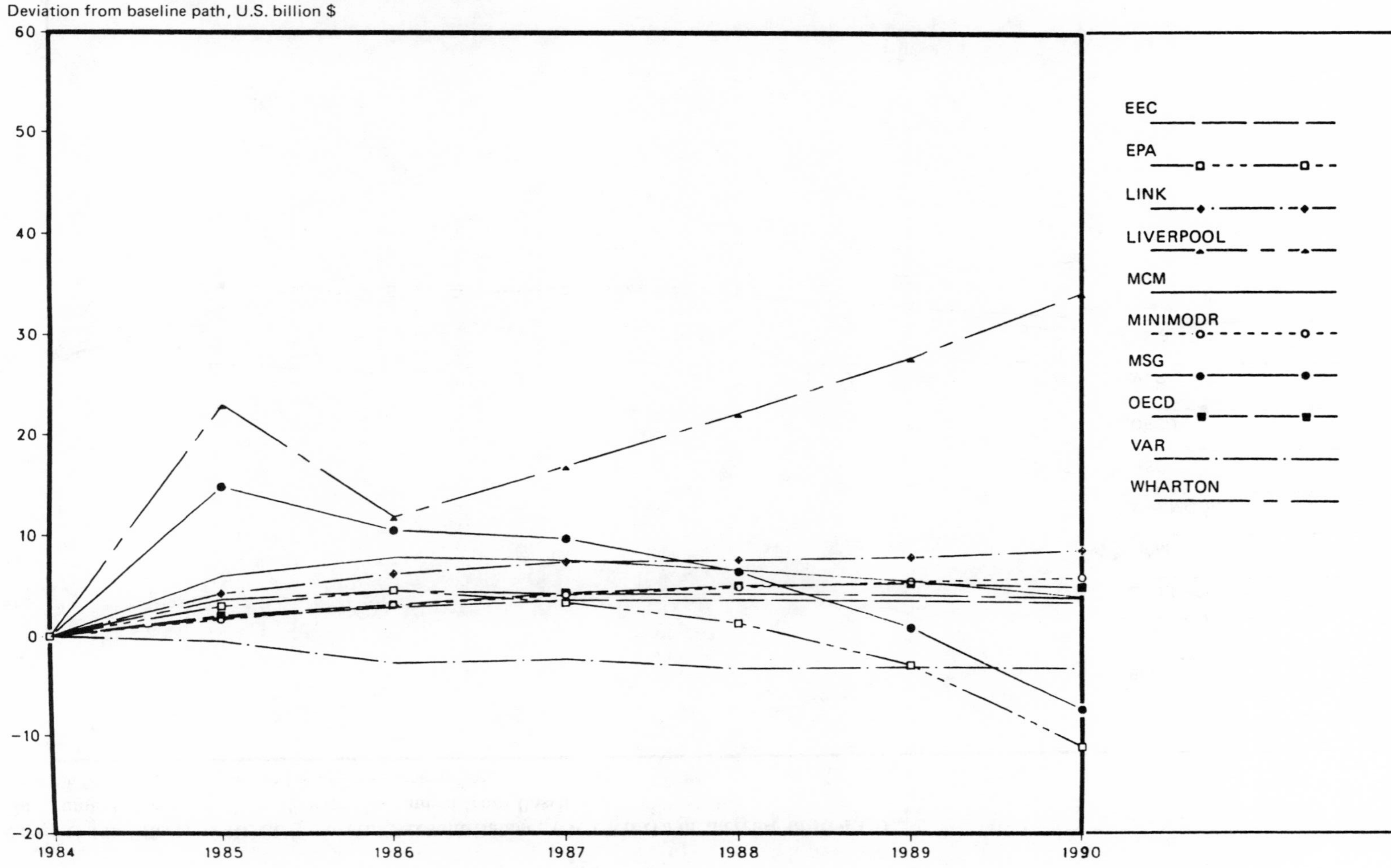

Chart G-10. Effects on ROECD Current Account Balance (OCURBAL) of Increase in ROECD Government Purchases (U.S. Policies Unchanged from Baseline)

Deviation from baseline, U.S. billion $ at baseline exchange rates

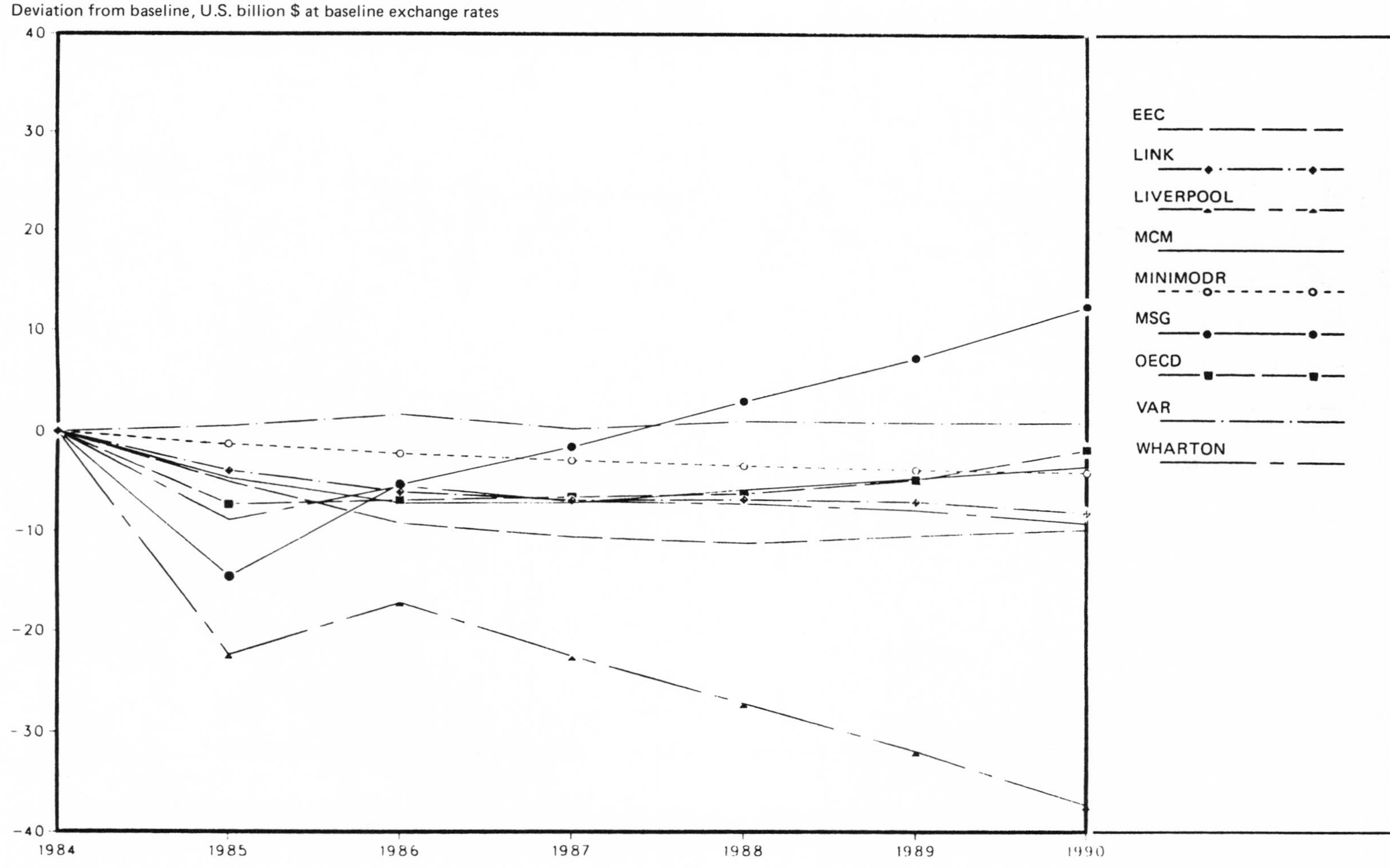

Table G. Average Responses, Standard Deviations, and Ranges for Simulated Effects of ROECD Fiscal Expansion with U.S. Policies Unchanged

(Simulation G—11 Models)

Variable	*Year 1 (1985)*	*Year 2 (1986)*	*Year 3 (1987)*	*Year 4 (1988)*	*Year 5 (1989)*	*Year 6 (1990)*
U.S. real GNP (UGNP)[a]						
Mean	0.22	0.19	0.10	0.06	−0.01	−0.07
Standard deviation	0.16	0.26	0.32	0.35	0.39	0.47
Range	0.46	1.05	1.27	1.35	1.45	1.72
ROECD real GNP (OGNP)[a]						
Mean	1.25	1.45	1.47	1.42	1.36	1.27
Standard deviation	0.53	0.74	0.77	0.84	0.93	1.03
Range	2.29	2.87	2.84	3.06	3.36	3.89
U.S. consumer price index (UCPI)[a,e]						
Mean	0.19	0.48	0.76	1.01	1.23	1.47
Standard deviation	0.44	0.86	1.20	1.47	1.68	1.86
Range	1.63	3.20	4.43	5.40	6.09	6.60
ROECD consumer price index (OPCPI)[a,f]						
Mean	0.03	0.35	0.74	1.11	1.53	2.01
Standard deviation	0.36	0.54	0.65	0.80	1.01	1.24
Range	1.37	1.97	2.37	3.16	3.86	4.51
U.S. short-term interest rate (URS)[b]						
Mean	0.17	0.40	0.46	0.59	0.70	0.82
Standard deviation	0.29	0.36	0.51	0.64	0.84	1.04
Range	1.24	1.30	1.97	2.39	3.07	3.63
ROECD short-term interest rate (ORS)[b,g]						
Mean	0.44	0.68	0.81	0.98	1.17	1.44
Standard deviation	0.58	0.63	0.80	0.98	1.17	1.38
Range	2.28	2.21	2.62	3.40	4.23	5.21
Weighted average exchange value of U.S. dollar (UEXCH)[a]						
Mean	−0.78	−0.35	−0.14	0.11	0.22	−0.01
Standard deviation	1.45	1.84	2.16	2.63	3.10	3.34
Range	4.83	5.68	7.72	10.44	13.23	14.27
U.S. current account balance (UCAB)[c,h]						
Mean	6.01	5.28	5.95	5.95	5.53	4.35
Standard deviation	6.90	3.94	4.75	6.18	8.19	11.61
Range	23.52	14.50	19.17	25.39	30.79	45.33
ROECD current account balance (OCAB)[d,i]						
Mean	−7.54	−6.44	−7.22	−7.09	−6.92	−6.69
Standard deviation	6.71	4.84	6.29	8.22	10.12	12.58
Range	22.98	18.89	22.87	30.24	39.22	49.76

Source: Detailed tables in part 3; DRI did not run simulation G.
a. Percent deviation from baseline path.
b. Deviation from baseline path in percentage points.
c. Deviation from baseline path in U.S. $ billion.
d. Deviation from baseline path in U.S. $ billion at baseline exchange rates.
e. TAYLOR and VAR models did not report results for U.S. consumer prices; results for the U.S. GNP deflator for those models are used as a substitute.
f. VAR model did not report results for ROECD consumer prices; results for the ROECD GNP deflator for that model are used as a substitute.
g. EEC and LINK models did not report results for the ROECD short-term interest rate.
h. TAYLOR model did not report results for the U.S. current account balance.
i. EPA and TAYLOR models did not report results for the ROECD current account balance.

SIMULATION H

ROECD Monetary Expansion

Chart H-1. Effects on U.S. Real GNP (UGNP) of ROECD Monetary Expansion (U.S. Policies Unchanged from Baseline)

Percent deviation from baseline path

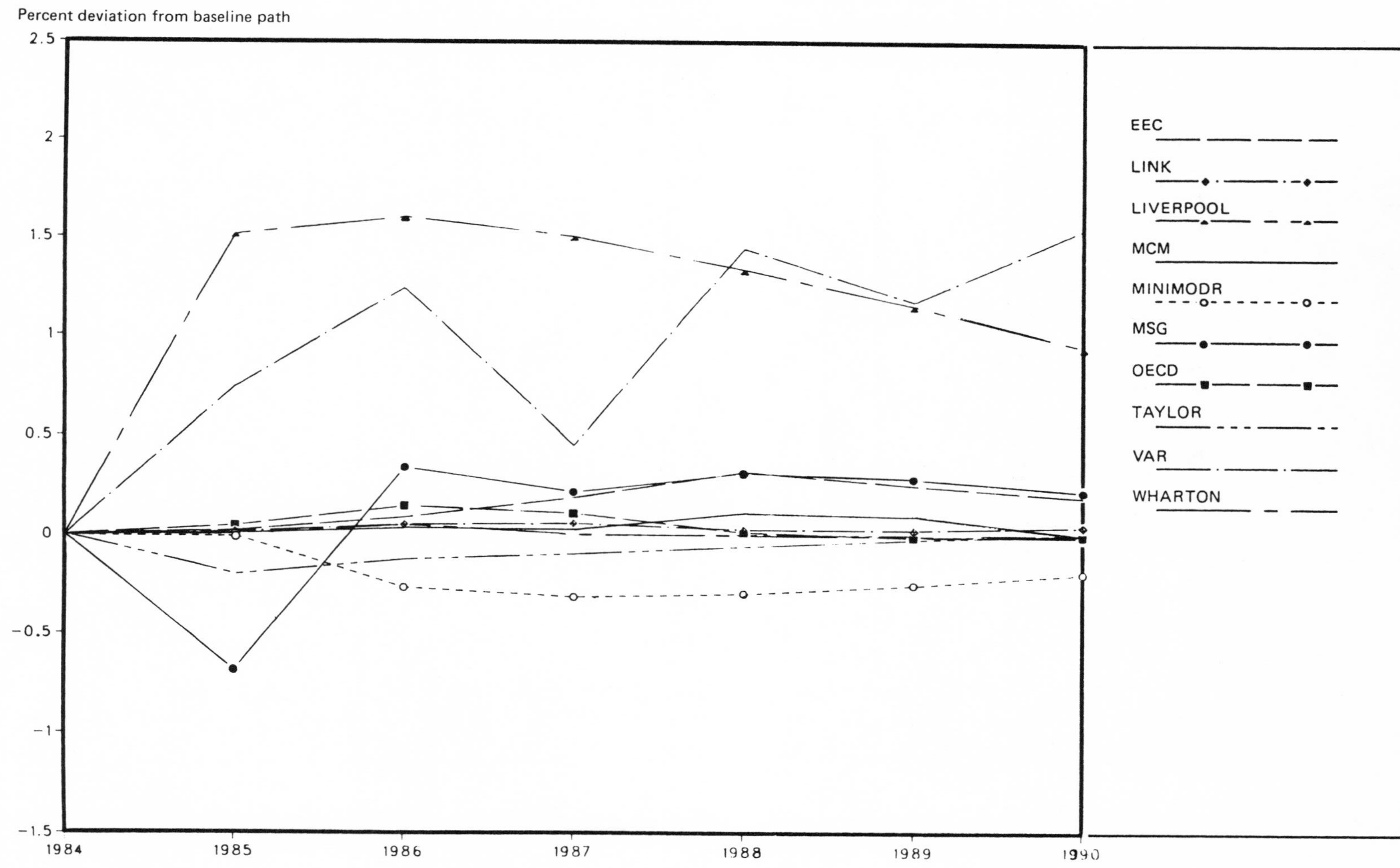

Chart H-2. Effects on ROECD Real GNP (OGNP) of ROECD Monetary Expansion (U.S. Policies Unchanged from Baseline)

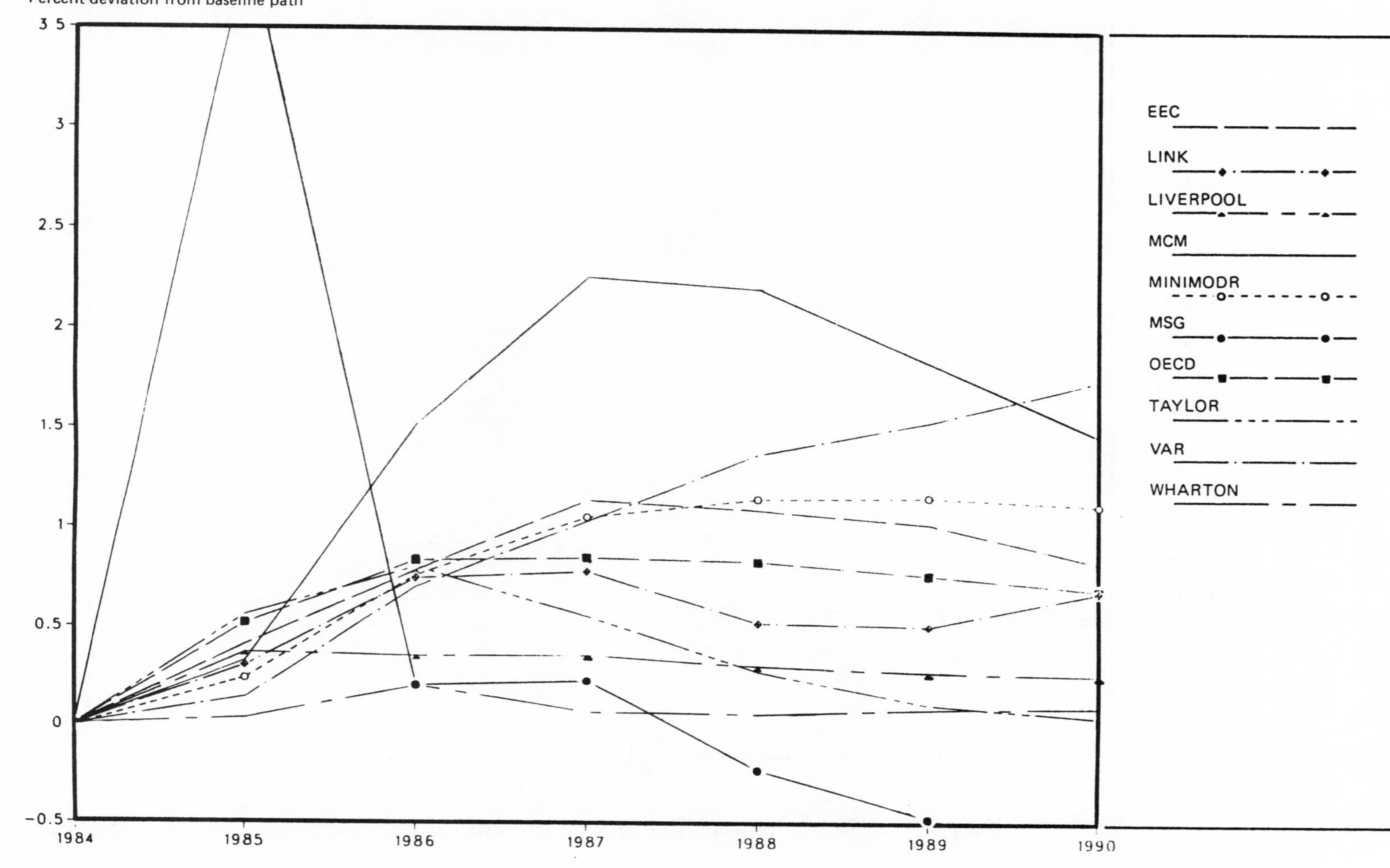

Chart H-3. Effects on U.S. Consumer Price Index (UCPI) of ROECD Monetary Expansion (U.S. Policies Unchanged from Baseline)

Percent deviation from baseline path

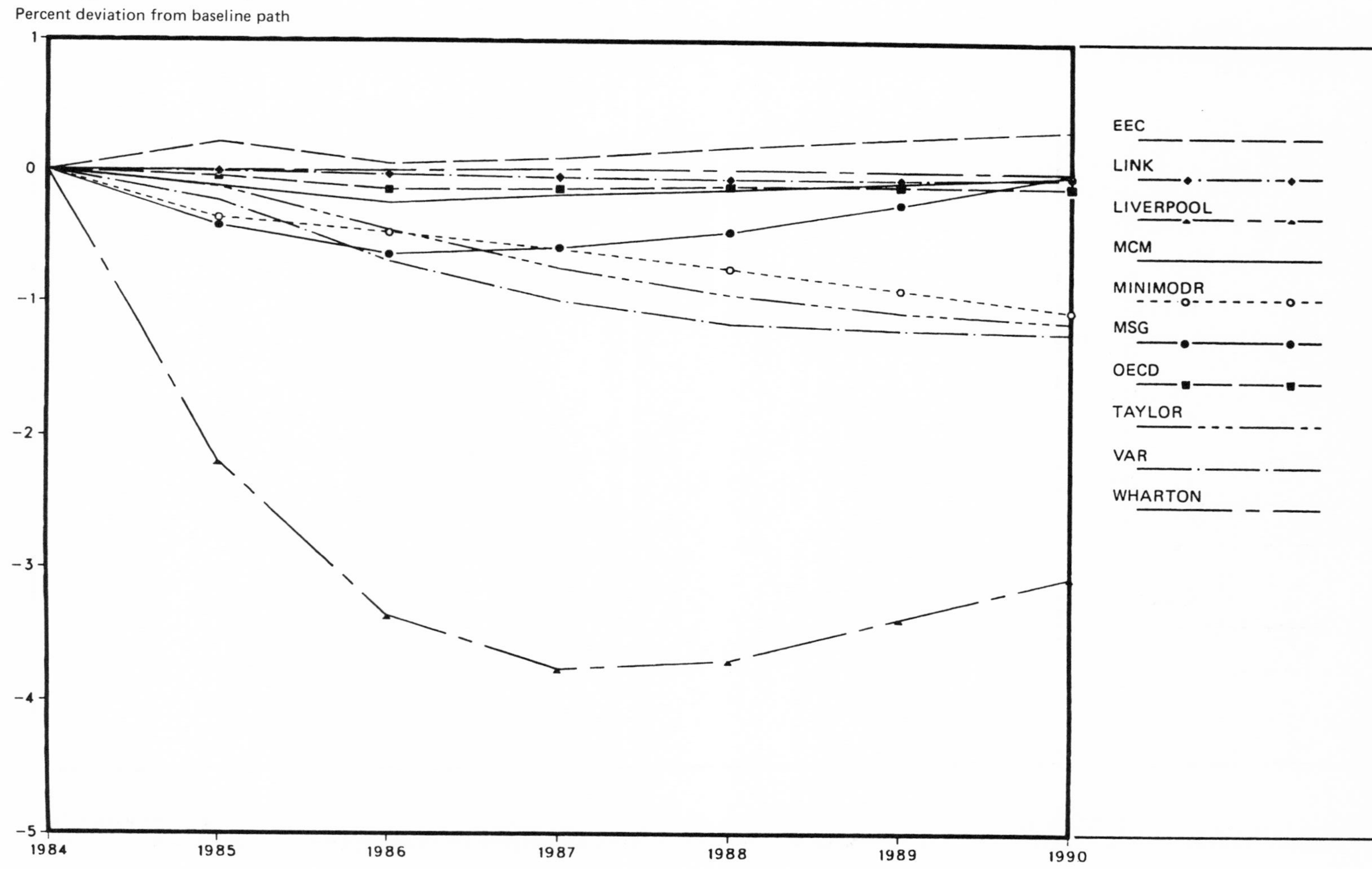

Chart H-4. Effects on ROECD Consumer Price Index (OPCPI) of ROECD Monetary Expansion (U.S. Policies Unchanged from Baseline)

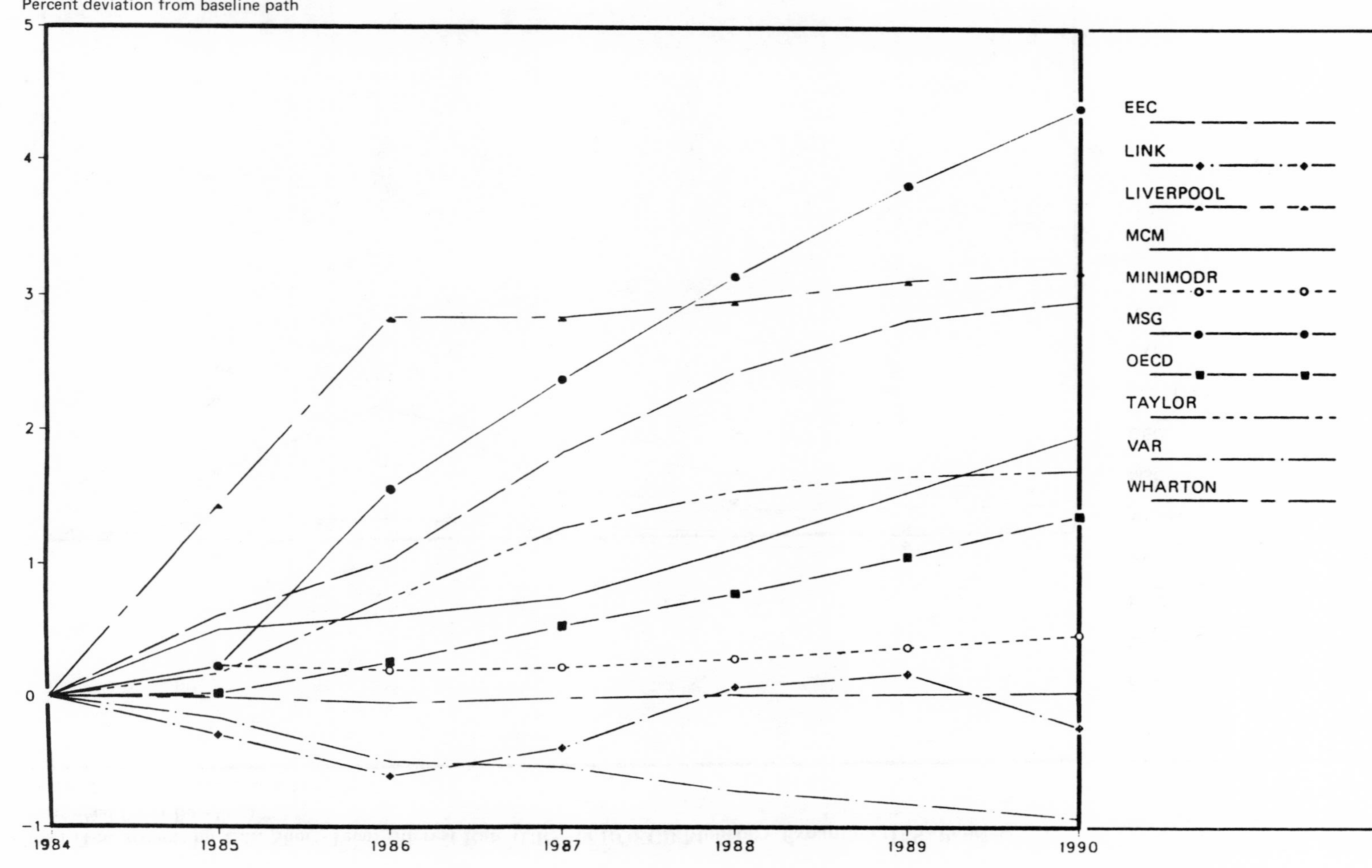

Chart H-5. Effects on U.S. Short-Term Interest Rate (URS) of ROECD Monetary Expansion (U.S. Policies Unchanged from Baseline)

Deviation from baseline path, percentage points

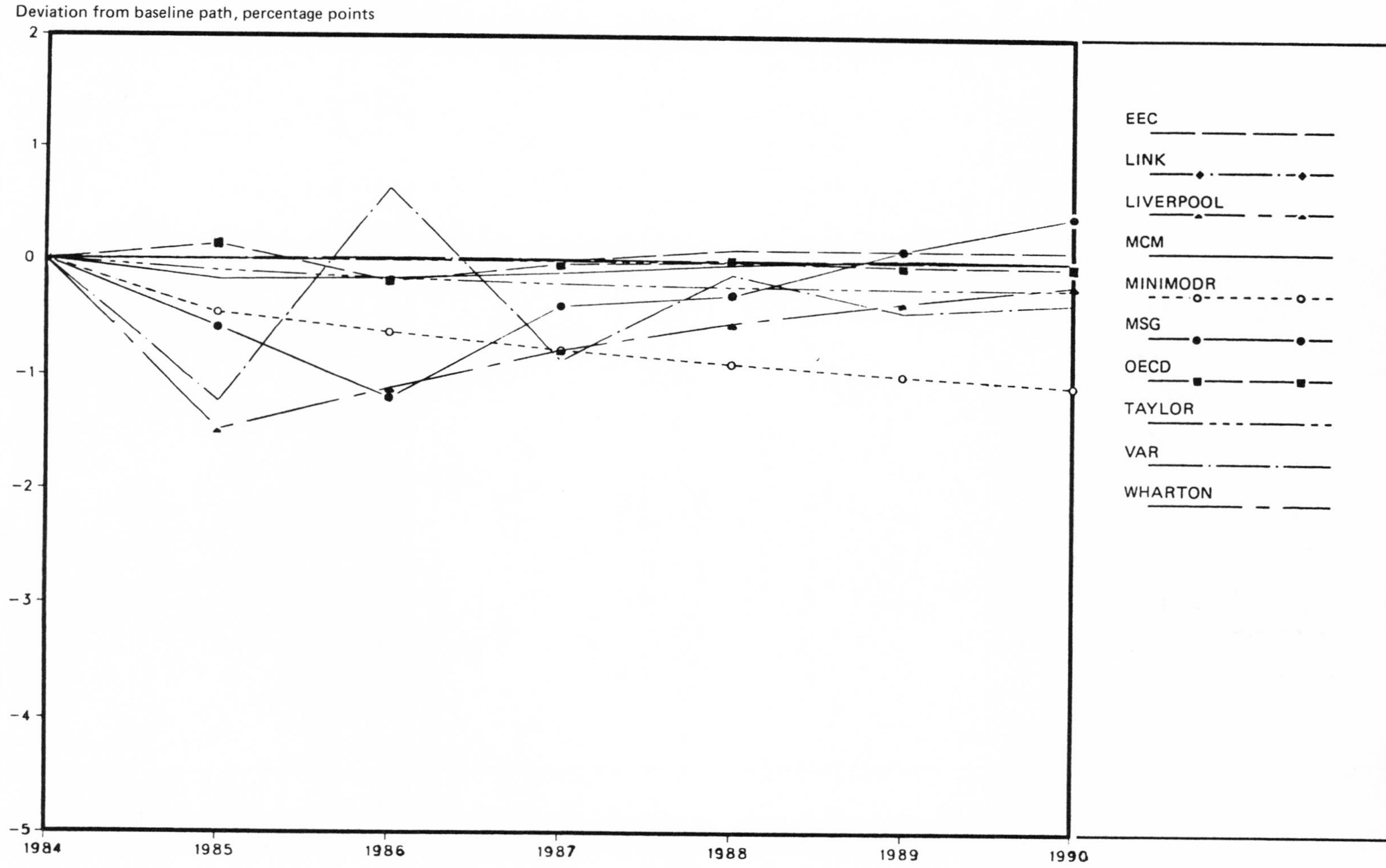

Chart H-6. Effects on ROECD Short-Term Interest Rate (ORS) of ROECD Monetary Expansion (U.S. Policies Unchanged from Baseline)

Deviation from baseline path, percentage points

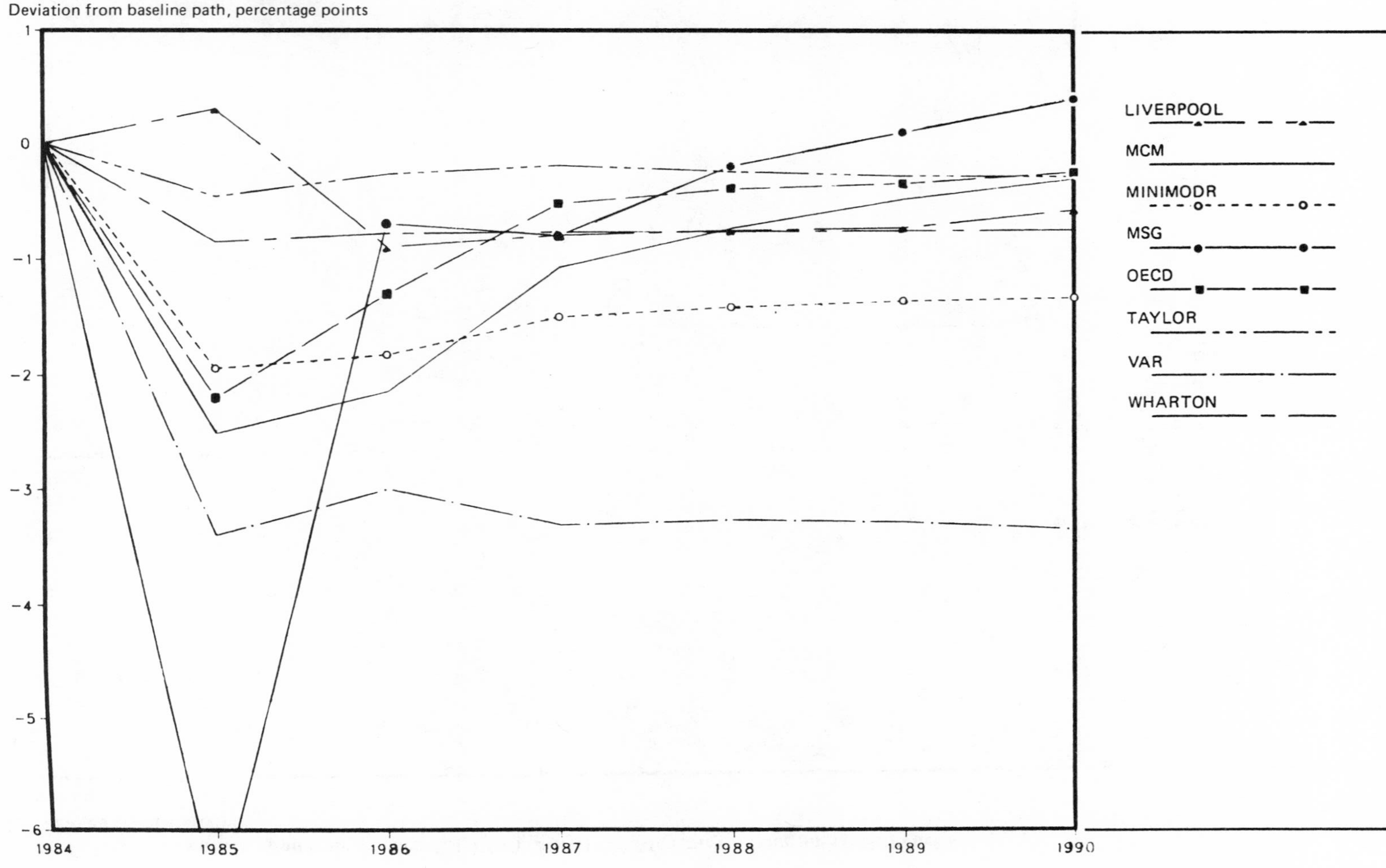

Chart H-7. Effects on U.S. Budgetary Deficit (UGDEF) of ROECD Monetary Expansion (U.S. Policies Unchanged from Baseline)

Deviation from baseline path, U.S. billion $

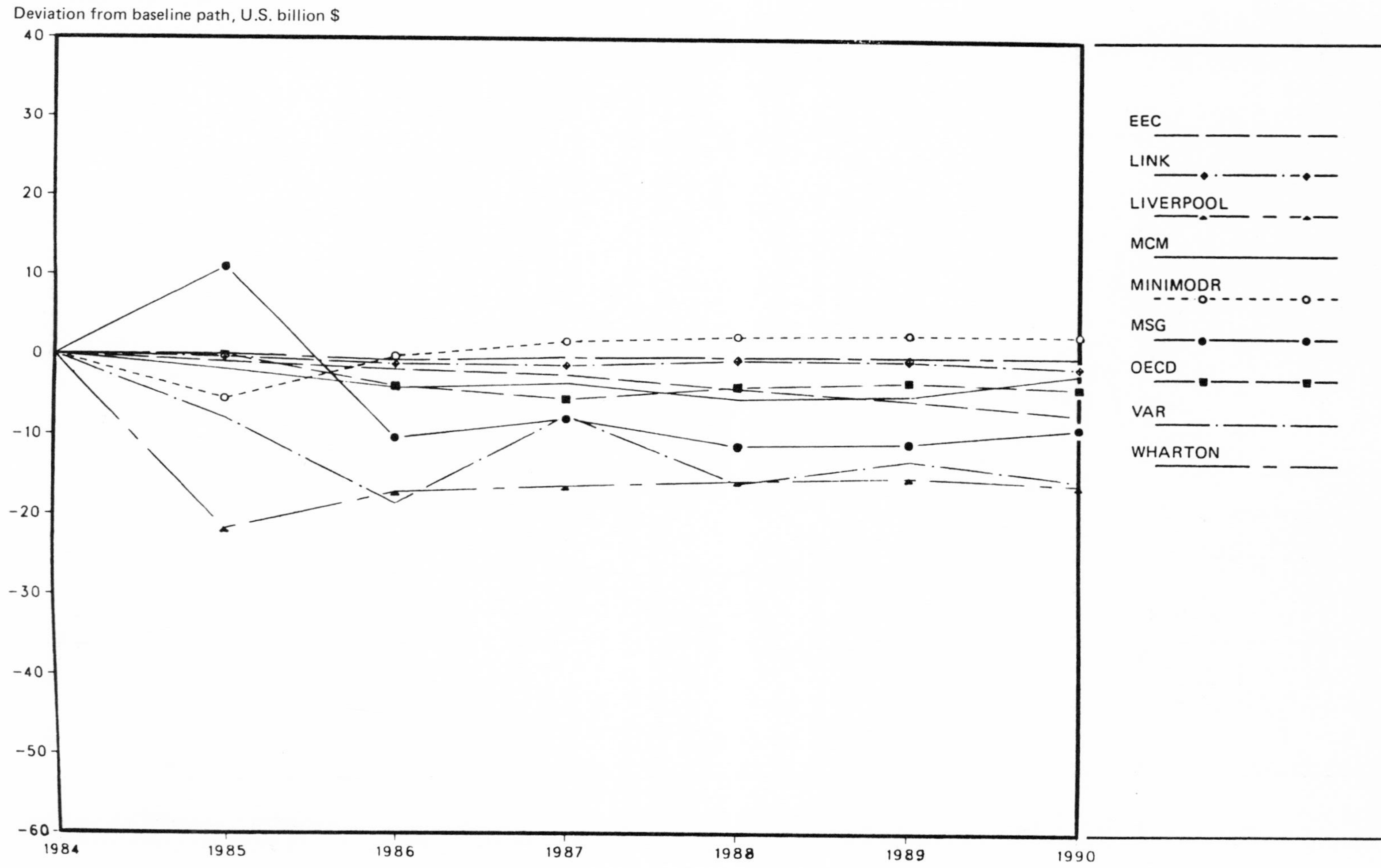

Chart H-7A. Effects on ROECD Budgetary Deficit (OGDEF) of ROECD Monetary Expansion (U.S. Policies Unchanged from Baseline)

Deviation from baseline path, U.S. billion $ at baseline exchange rates

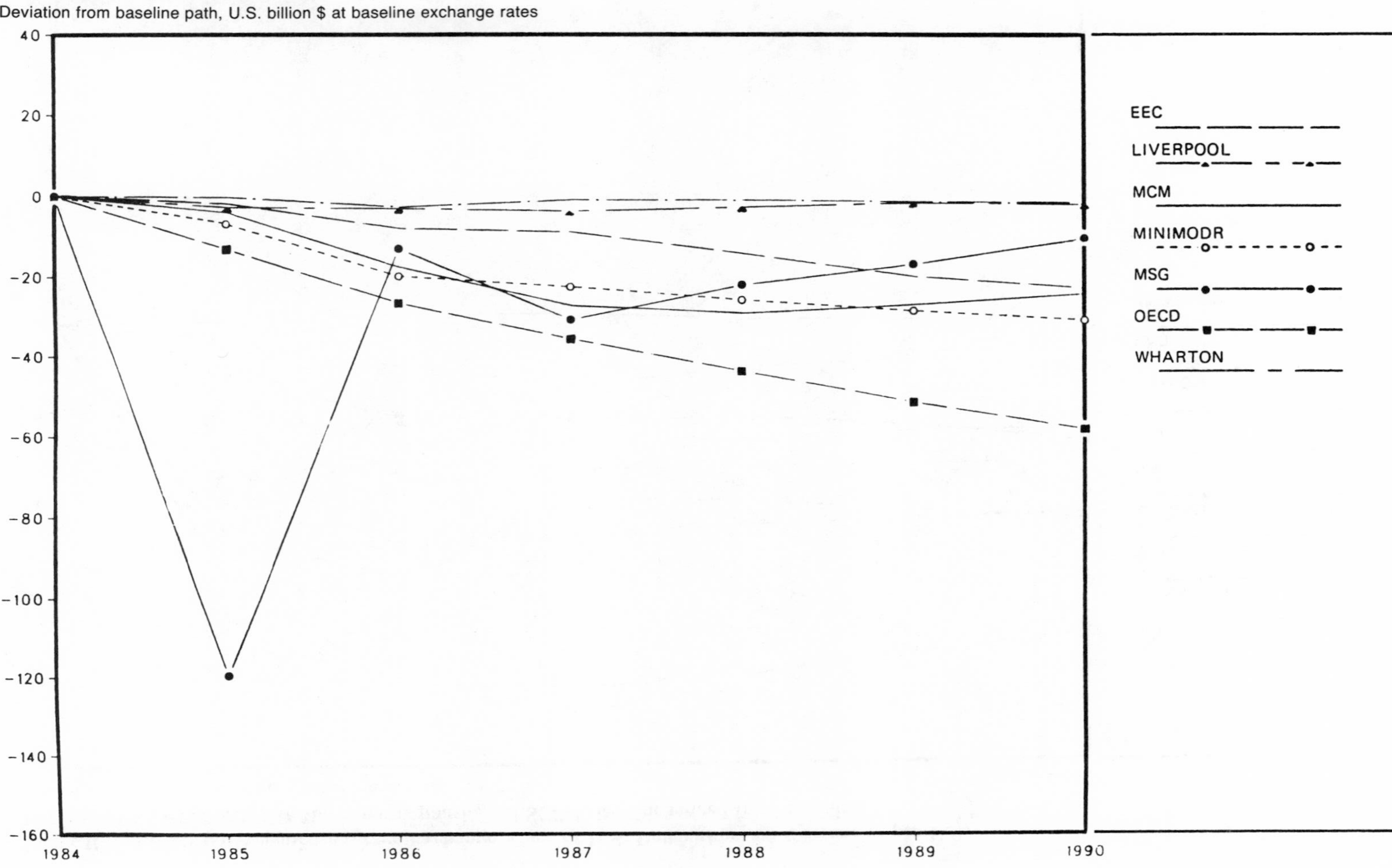

Chart H-8. Effects on Weighted Average Exchange Value of U.S. Dollar (Foreign Currencies per U.S. Dollar) (UEXCH) of ROECD Monetary Expansion (U.S. Policies Unchanged from Baseline)

Percent deviation from baseline (+ = dollar appreciation)

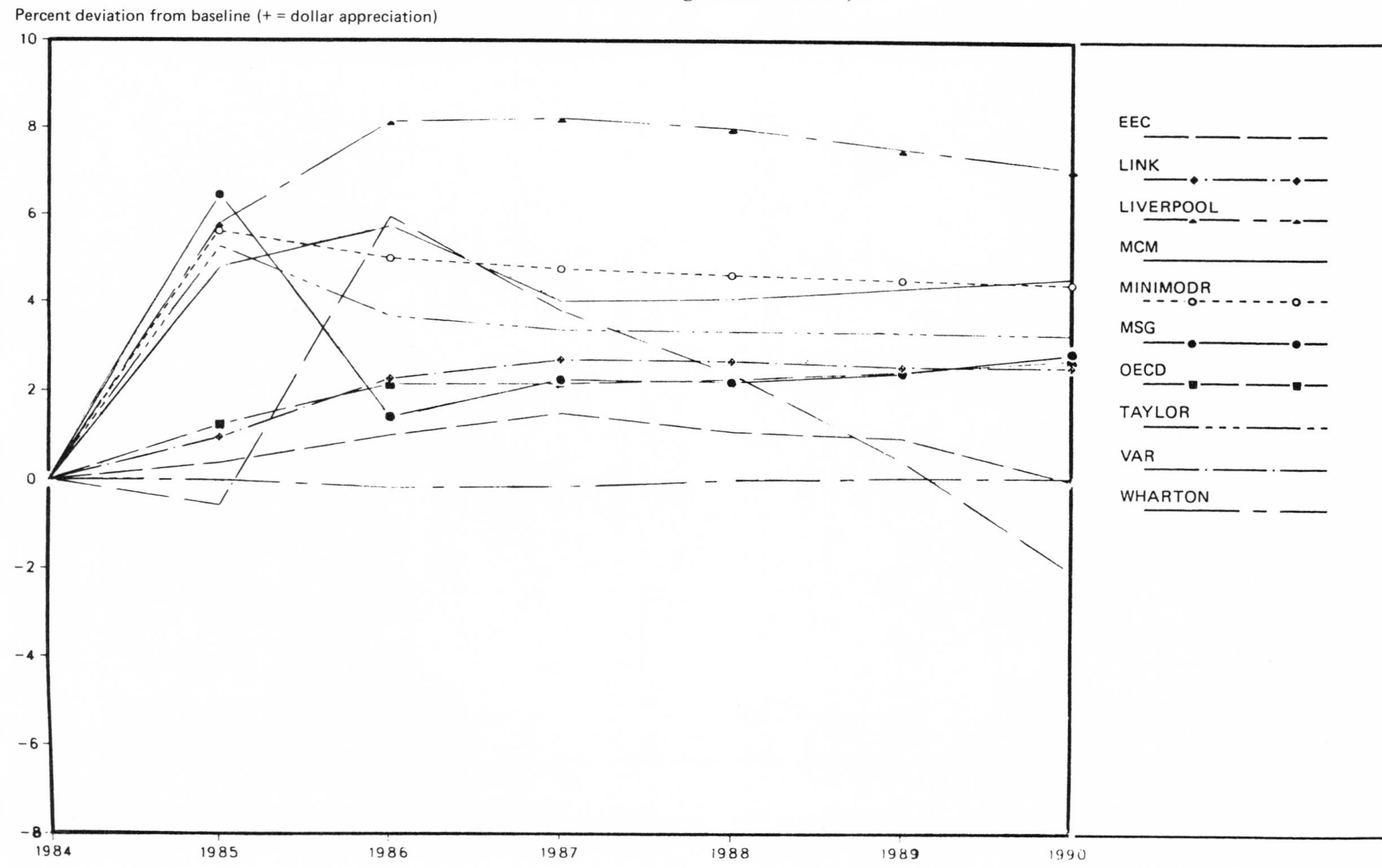

Chart H-9. Effects on U.S. Current Account Balance (UCURBAL) of ROECD Monetary Expansion (U.S. Policies Unchanged from Baseline)

Deviation from baseline path, U.S. billion $

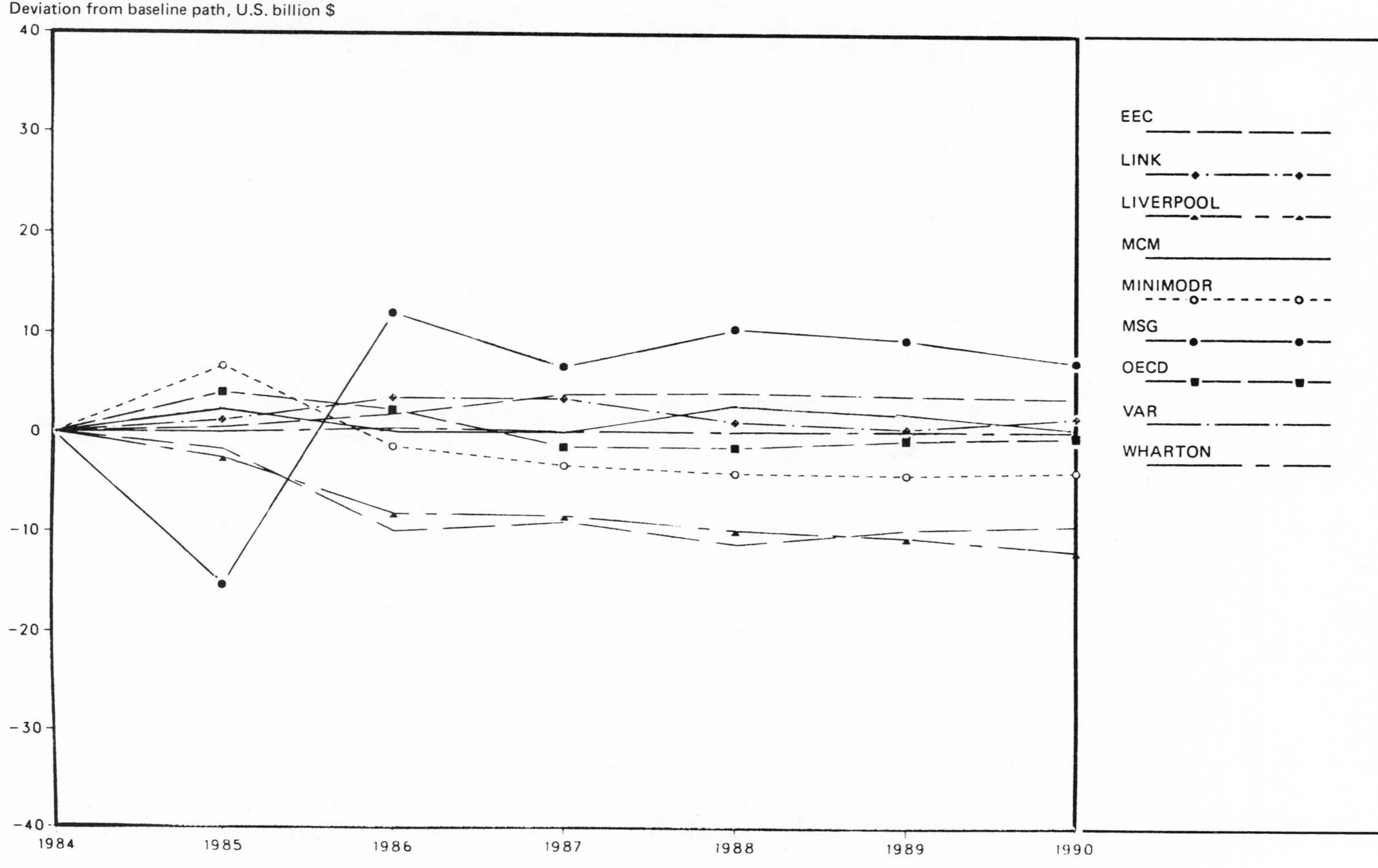

Chart H-10. Effects on ROECD Current Account Balance (OCURBAL) of ROECD Monetary Expansion (U.S. Policies Unchanged from Baseline)

Deviation from baseline, U.S. billion $ at baseline exchange rates

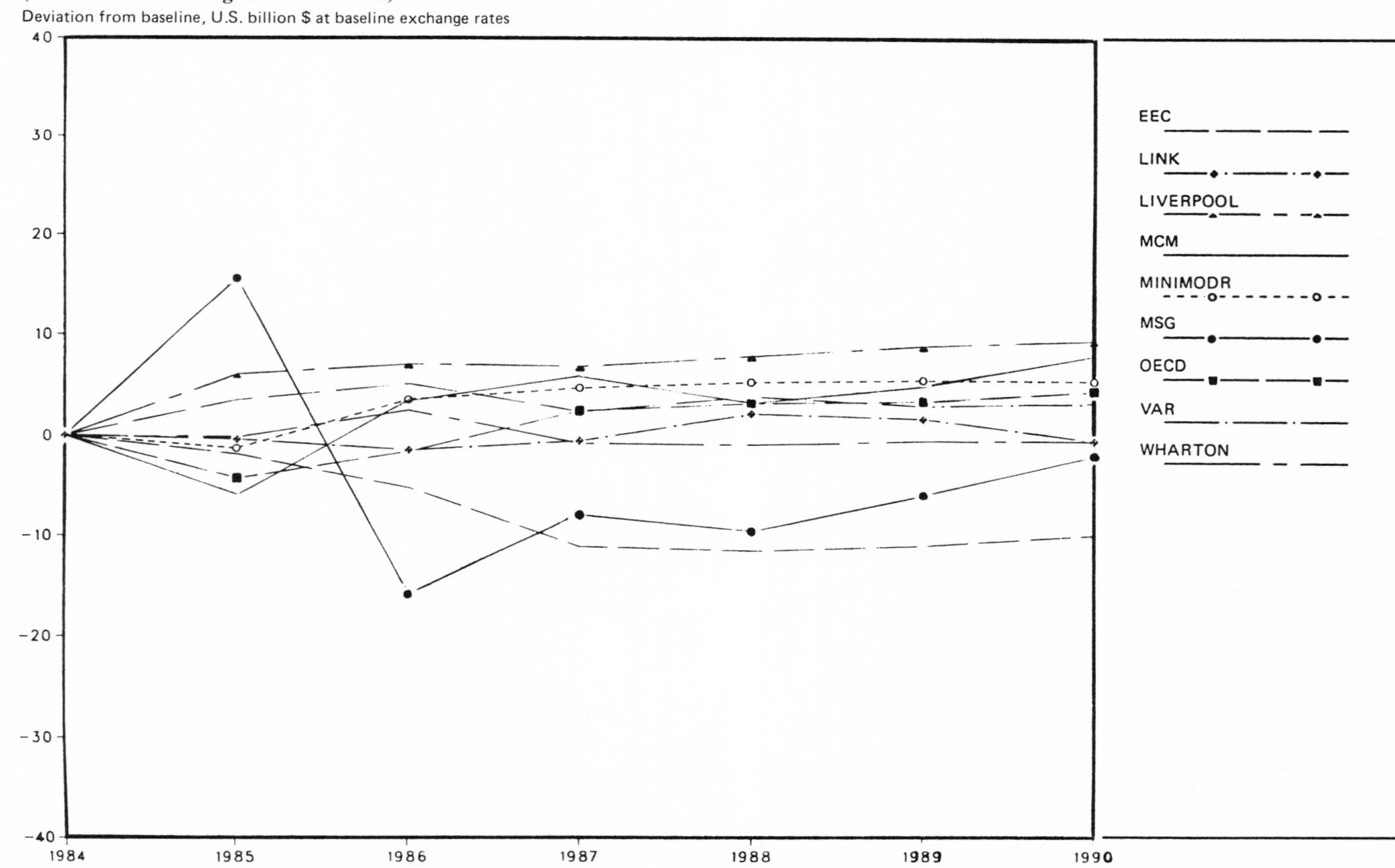

Table H. Average Responses, Standard Deviations, and Ranges for Simulated Effects of ROECD Monetary Expansion with U.S. Policies Unchanged

(Simulation H—10 Models)

Variable	*Year 1 (1985)*	*Year 2 (1986)*	*Year 3 (1987)*	*Year 4 (1988)*	*Year 5 (1989)*	*Year 6 (1990)*
U.S. real GNP (UGNP)[a]						
Mean	0.14	0.31	0.22	0.32	0.27	0.27
Standard deviation	0.56	0.58	0.47	0.56	0.47	0.52
Range	2.20	1.87	1.82	1.74	1.42	1.74
ROECD real GNP (OGNP)[a]						
Mean	0.68	0.70	0.83	0.76	0.68	0.63
Standard deviation	1.09	0.37	0.59	0.68	0.68	0.68
Range	3.88	1.32	2.19	2.42	2.31	2.41
U.S. consumer price index (UCPI)[a,e]						
Mean	−0.33	−0.60	−0.70	−0.71	−0.68	−0.63
Standard deviation	0.65	0.96	1.08	1.08	1.02	0.97
Range	2.41	3.42	3.86	3.88	3.64	3.39
ROECD consumer price index (OPCPI)[a,f]						
Mean	0.27	0.60	0.89	1.16	1.38	1.49
Standard deviation	0.47	0.97	1.09	1.25	1.42	1.62
Range	1.73	3.44	3.34	3.85	4.62	5.40
U.S. short-term interest rate (URS)[b]						
Mean	−0.39	−0.28	−0.32	−0.20	−0.19	−0.14
Standard deviation	0.53	0.53	0.35	0.29	0.32	0.37
Range	1.61	1.84	0.88	0.99	1.09	1.48
ROECD short-term interest rate (ORS)[b,g]						
Mean	−2.24	−1.39	−1.15	−1.00	−0.92	−0.84
Standard deviation	2.04	0.90	0.97	1.01	1.06	1.14
Range	7.01	2.94	3.33	3.31	3.63	4.01
Weighted average exchange value of U.S. dollar (UEXCH)[a]						
Mean	2.99	3.51	3.26	3.07	2.86	2.55
Standard deviation	2.67	2.49	2.12	2.07	2.11	2.50
Range	7.04	8.33	8.38	7.95	7.44	9.13
U.S. current account balance (UCAB)[c,h]						
Mean	−0.55	0.08	−0.85	−0.85	−1.02	−1.34
Standard deviation	5.86	6.09	5.05	6.41	5.96	5.69
Range	21.93	21.96	15.69	21.66	19.89	18.99
ROECD current account balance (OCAB)[d,i]						
Mean	1.24	−0.23	0.28	0.49	1.20	2.06
Standard deviation	6.14	6.62	5.82	6.30	5.83	5.60
Range	21.59	23.03	18.02	19.46	19.94	19.40

Source: Detailed tables in part 3; DRI and EPA did not run simulation H.
a. Percent deviation from baseline path.
b. Deviation from baseline path in percentage points.
c. Deviation from baseline path in U.S. $ billion.
d. Deviation from baseline path in U.S. $ billion at baseline exchange rates.
e. TAYLOR and VAR models did not report results for U.S. consumer prices; results for the U.S. GNP deflator for those models are used as a substitute.
f. VAR model did not report results for ROECD consumer prices; results for the ROECD GNP deflator for that model are used as a substitute.
g. EEC and LINK models did not report results for the ROECD short-term interest rate.
h. TAYLOR model did not report results for the U.S. current account balance.
i. TAYLOR did not report results for the ROECD current account balance.

PART THREE

Detailed Tables for Simulation Results

DRI International Model

See part 1 of this volume for design and detailed description of the simulations. See part 4 for bibliographical references. Simulations G and H are not available for this model.

Model: DRI
Simulation A: Baseline Path

	1985	1986	1987	1988	1989	1990
UNITED STATES						
GNPV(B.$)	3944.5	4201.5	4478.7	4773.5	5088.6	5424.5
GNP(B.72$)	1689.8	1740.1	1792.2	1846.1	1901.4	1958.6
PGNP(72=100)	233.4	241.4	249.9	258.5	267.6	276.9
CPI(72=100)	258.7	267.2	275.7	284.0	292.5	301.3
WAGES(72=100)	238.3	245.1	253.2	262.2	272.6	283.6
UN(%)	7.3	7.4	7.4	7.5	7.5	7.5
G(B.72$)	318.2	331.1	344.3	358.1	372.4	387.3
C(B.72$)	1091.8	1126.3	1159.8	1194.7	1230.5	1267.5
IFP(B.72$)	280.8	289.5	298.6	308.3	318.4	329.3
II(B.72$)	26.3	23.9	21.9	19.3	16.2	12.6
XGS(B.72$)	157.7	166.9	176.6	186.9	197.7	209.1
MGS(B.72$)	184.9	197.6	209.1	221.1	233.8	247.1
M1(B.$)	582.4	609.3	637.8	666.0	689.1	708.9
RS(%)	8.5	8.5	8.5	8.5	8.5	8.5
RL(%)	11.6	11.6	11.6	11.6	11.6	11.6
GDEF(B.$)	144.8	166.3	178.1	182.8	207.0	228.2
PXGS(72=100)	255.8	264.1	274.7	285.8	295.2	304.4
PMGS(72=100)	258.3	265.4	271.7	278.9	285.5	293.2
EXCH(72=100) *	138.4	138.4	138.5	138.5	138.3	138.3
CAB(B.$)	-108.3	-116.5	-118.6	-121.9	-126.3	-133.9
NON-US OECD						
GNPV(B.$) **	602.0	649.1	697.5	746.6	796.0	853.9
GNP(B.72$) **	216.5	223.2	229.5	236.3	243.6	251.0
PGNP(72=100)	277.9	290.7	303.9	315.9	326.7	340.2
CPI(72=100)	297.4	309.2	321.5	334.3	347.5	361.3
WAGES(72=100)	415.2	440.8	467.7	494.8	523.9	555.7
UN(%)	6.8	6.7	6.4	6.0	5.8	5.7
C(B.72$) **	122.4	125.6	128.9	132.3	136.1	140.0
IFP(B.72$) **	40.2	41.9	43.5	45.3	47.3	49.2
RS(%)	7.8	7.8	7.8	7.9	7.9	7.8
RL(%)	9.8	9.7	9.7	9.8	9.8	9.7
GDEF(B.US$) **	-	-	-	-	-	-
PXGS(72=100)	268.9	284.5	300.5	310.0	310.1	320.2
PMGS(72=100)	353.3	362.0	372.8	383.9	393.1	405.5
EXCH(72=100) ***	71.9	71.9	71.8	71.8	71.9	71.9
CAB(B.US$)	51.6	88.2	118.4	128.8	112.4	120.8

* Exchange rate : (Weighted average of foreign currencies)/U.S. $.
** Local currency units translated into U.S. $ at baseline exchange rates.
*** Exchange rate : U.S. $/(weighted average of non-US OECD currencies).

Model: DRI
Simulation A: Baseline Path

	1985	1986	1987	1988	1989	1990
JAPAN						
GNP(B.72Y)	158923.3	166028.9	173425.2	181477.7	189799.4	198476.4
CPI(72=100)	247.3	254.4	261.8	269.5	277.4	285.6
RS(%)	5.0	5.0	5.0	5.0	5.0	5.0
GDEF(%GNPV) *	-0.4	-0.6	-0.8	-0.9	-0.9	-1.0
EXCH(72=100) **	118.0	118.0	118.0	118.0	118.0	118.0
CAB(B.US$) ***	54.0	82.7	107.1	111.0	88.9	92.7
GERMANY						
GNP(B.72DM)	1066.2	1097.3	1120.5	1145.3	1172.0	1201.3
CPI(72=100)	177.8	181.7	185.7	189.9	194.2	198.5
RS(%)	5.8	5.8	5.8	5.8	5.8	5.8
GDEF(%GNPV) *	1.5	1.0	-0.2	-0.4	-0.5	-0.6
EXCH(72=100) **	98.1	98.1	98.0	98.0	98.2	98.2
CAB(B.US$) ***	6.0	12.0	14.1	16.0	18.8	21.4
FRANCE						
GNP(B.72F)	1338.2	1365.7	1393.0	1421.0	1449.2	1478.1
CPI(72=100)	356.3	376.0	396.8	418.7	441.6	465.8
GDEF(%GNPV) *	3.2	3.7	3.7	3.9	4.0	4.1
EXCH(72=100) **	50.8	50.7	50.7	50.7	50.8	50.8
CAB(B.US$) ***	-1.1	-0.5	0.2	1.4	3.5	4.3
UNITED KINGDOM						
GNP(B.72LB)	80.4	82.6	84.9	87.2	89.6	92.1
CPI(72=100)	432.1	452.2	472.6	494.0	516.3	539.7
GDEF(%GNPV) *	2.0	1.8	1.3	0.8	0.4	-0.4
EXCH(72=100) **	44.5	44.4	44.4	44.4	44.4	44.4
CAB(B.US$) ***	-2.5	-2.8	-2.5	-2.3	-3.2	-5.0
ITALY						
GNP(B.72L)	101176.9	103254.4	105286.8	107344.2	109446.3	111630.2
CPI(72=100)	636.9	686.8	740.4	798.1	859.9	926.1
GDEF(%GNPV) *	15.0	13.7	12.6	12.1	11.1	10.4
EXCH(72=100) **	29.0	29.0	28.9	28.9	29.0	29.0
CAB(B.US$) ***	-1.7	1.2	4.0	8.2	11.8	13.4
CANADA						
GNP(B.72C$)	151.3	154.5	157.6	160.8	164.0	167.2
CPI(72=100)	287.8	298.1	308.8	319.9	331.4	343.3
GDEF(%GNPV) *	6.4	6.4	6.5	6.8	7.3	7.9
EXCH(72=100) **	73.4	73.4	73.4	73.4	73.4	73.4
CAB(B.US$) ***	-3.1	-4.3	-4.6	-5.4	-7.4	-6.0
REST OF WORLD						
CAB(B.US$) ***	-	-	-	-	-	-

* Government deficit as a percentage of baseline nominal GNP.
** Exchange rate: Bilateral rate against U.S. $ ($/local currency).
*** Local currency units translated into U.S. $ at baseline exchange rates.

Model: DRI
Simulation B: Reduction in U.S. Government Purchases with Foreign Monetary Aggregates Unchanged from Baseline
(Deviation of Shock Path from Baseline Path)

	1985									
	Q1	Q2	Q3	Q4	1985	1986	1987	1988	1989	1990
UNITED STATES										
GNPV(%)	-1.6	-2.2	-2.6	-2.8	-2.3	-2.8	-2.6	-2.7	-3.1	-3.7
GNP(%)	-1.5	-2.0	-2.3	-2.4	-2.0	-2.1	-1.4	-1.0	-0.9	-1.0
PGNP(%)	-0.1	-0.2	-0.3	-0.5	-0.3	-0.7	-1.2	-1.7	-2.3	-2.7
CPI(%)	0.0	-0.1	-0.2	-0.2	-0.1	-0.4	-0.8	-1.3	-1.9	-2.3
WAGES(%)	-0.1	-0.2	-0.3	-0.5	-0.3	-0.8	-1.3	-1.8	-2.4	-2.9
UN(% PTS)	0.2	0.5	0.7	0.8	0.6	0.8	0.5	0.2	0.1	0.2
GNP(B.72$)	-25.5	-34.1	-38.4	-40.5	-34.6	-36.6	-25.9	-18.1	-16.2	-18.8
G(B.72$)	-16.7	-16.8	-17.0	-17.1	-16.9	-17.4	-17.9	-18.5	-19.0	-19.6
C(B.72$)	-6.0	-12.4	-16.6	-19.5	-13.6	-22.2	-21.8	-19.9	-20.8	-25.2
IFP(B.72$)	-3.8	-5.8	-6.8	-7.2	-5.9	-4.9	1.3	6.3	7.8	7.2
II(B.72$)	-0.3	-3.9	-5.3	-5.9	-3.8	-4.1	-0.4	1.3	1.0	0.5
XGS(B.72$)	0.0	-0.3	-0.8	-1.2	-0.6	-1.4	-0.2	0.9	1.5	1.2
MGS(B.72$)	-1.5	-5.0	-8.2	-10.3	-6.2	-13.4	-13.1	-11.7	-13.3	-17.2
M1(%)	0.0	0.0	-0.0	-0.1	-0.0	0.0	-0.0	-0.0	-0.0	-0.0
RS(% PTS)	-0.1	-0.8	-0.9	-1.0	-0.7	-1.6	-1.8	-2.2	-2.5	-3.0
RL(% PTS)	-0.0	-0.5	-0.7	-0.8	-0.5	-1.1	-1.4	-1.7	-1.9	-2.2
GDEF(B$)	-13.9	-8.6	-5.9	-6.0	-8.6	-17.1	-40.1	-58.0	-70.3	-79.5
PXGS(%)	-0.1	-0.2	-0.4	-0.7	-0.4	-1.0	-1.5	-2.0	-2.6	-3.0
PMGS(%)	0.5	0.5	0.7	0.7	0.6	1.1	0.9	0.4	0.5	0.6
EXCH(%) *	-0.1	-0.7	-1.0	-1.5	-0.8	-3.2	-3.8	-4.0	-4.7	-5.6
CAB(B$)	1.5	8.9	14.4	18.1	10.7	22.0	23.2	22.1	24.1	30.8
NON-US OECD										
GNPV(%) **	-0.0	-0.1	-0.2	-0.2	-0.1	-0.5	-0.8	-1.0	-1.2	-1.7
GNP(%) **	-0.1	-0.2	-0.4	-0.5	-0.3	-0.7	-0.6	-0.5	-0.6	-1.0
PGNP(%)	0.1	0.2	0.2	0.3	0.2	0.2	-0.2	-0.5	-0.6	-0.8
CPI(%)	0.0	0.0	-0.0	-0.1	-0.0	-0.3	-0.8	-1.0	-1.2	-1.5
WAGES(%)	0.0	0.0	-0.0	-0.0	-0.0	-0.3	-0.8	-1.1	-1.2	-1.4
UN(% PTS)	0.0	0.0	0.0	0.0	0.0	0.1	0.0	0.0	0.0	0.1
C(%) **	-0.0	-0.0	-0.0	-0.0	-0.0	-0.1	0.0	0.1	0.1	0.0
IFP(%) **	0.0	0.0	0.0	0.0	0.0	0.1	0.3	0.5	0.7	0.6
RS(% PTS)	-0.0	-0.1	-0.1	-0.2	-0.1	-0.4	-0.6	-0.7	-0.7	-0.9
RL(% PTS)	-0.0	-0.1	-0.1	-0.1	-0.1	-0.3	-0.5	-0.6	-0.6	-0.7
GDEF (B.US$) **	-	-	-	-	-	-	-	-	-	-
PXGS(%)	0.3	0.3	0.4	0.5	0.4	0.6	0.1	-0.5	-1.4	-1.9
PMGS(%)	-0.0	-0.4	-0.6	-1.1	-0.5	-2.0	-2.6	-3.1	-3.9	-4.8
EXCH(%) ***	0.0	0.6	1.0	1.6	0.8	3.3	3.9	4.1	4.9	5.9
CAB(B.US$) **	-0.4	-2.6	-3.7	-2.9	-2.4	-0.8	-2.0	-4.5	-10.2	-19.8

* Exchange rate : (Weighted average of foreign currencies)/U.S. $.
** Local currency units translated into U.S. $ at baseline exchange rates.
*** Exchange rate : U.S. $/(weighted average of non-US OECD currencies).

Model: DRI
Simulation B: Reduction in U.S. Government Purchases with Foreign Monetary Aggregates Unchanged from Baseline
(Deviation of Shock Path from Baseline Path)

	1985									
	Q1	Q2	Q3	Q4	1985	1986	1987	1988	1989	1990
JAPAN										
GNP(%)	-0.2	-0.5	-0.7	-0.9	-0.6	-1.3	-1.3	-1.2	-1.5	-2.3
CPI(%)	0.0	0.1	0.1	0.1	0.1	0.1	-0.1	-0.2	-0.1	0.1
RS(% PTS)	-0.0	-0.1	-0.2	-0.3	-0.2	-0.5	-0.7	-0.7	-0.7	-0.8
GDEF(%GNPV) *	0.0	0.0	0.0	0.0	0.0	-0.0	-0.0	-0.1	-0.1	-0.1
EXCH(%) **	0.1	0.7	1.1	1.8	0.9	3.7	4.6	4.8	5.6	6.6
CAB(B.US$) ***	0.5	-0.7	-0.6	-0.1	-0.2	3.8	4.1	1.2	-3.9	-10.1
GERMANY										
GNP(%)	-0.0	-0.0	-0.1	-0.1	-0.1	-0.2	-0.4	-0.6	-0.7	-0.8
CPI(%)	0.0	0.0	-0.0	-0.1	-0.0	-0.4	-1.0	-1.5	-2.0	-2.3
RS(% PTS)	-0.0	-0.1	0.3	0.1	0.1	-0.0	-0.3	-0.6	-0.8	-0.8
GDEF(%GNPV) *	0.0	0.0	0.0	0.0	0.0	0.1	0.2	0.3	0.3	0.4
EXCH(%) **	0.1	0.7	1.1	1.9	0.9	4.0	5.2	5.6	6.6	7.6
CAB(B.US$) ***	-0.1	-0.1	0.0	0.1	0.0	-0.1	-1.3	-1.3	-1.6	-2.7
FRANCE										
GNP(%)	-0.0	-0.1	-0.2	-0.0	-0.1	-0.4	-0.3	-0.1	-0.0	-0.2
CPI(%)	-0.0	-0.0	-0.1	-0.1	-0.0	-0.3	-0.6	-0.4	-0.1	-0.1
GDEF(%GNPV) *	0.0	0.0	0.0	0.0	0.0	0.1	0.2	0.1	0.0	0.0
EXCH(%) **	0.1	0.7	1.1	1.7	0.9	3.5	3.6	2.9	2.9	3.6
CAB(B.US$) ***	-0.0	-0.0	-0.4	0.5	0.0	-0.8	-1.8	-1.7	-0.9	-0.8
UNITED KINGDOM										
GNP(%)	-0.0	-0.1	-0.1	-0.2	-0.1	-0.3	-0.2	-0.2	-0.1	-0.1
CPI(%)	0.0	0.0	-0.0	-0.1	-0.0	-0.2	-0.5	-1.1	-1.9	-3.0
GDEF(%GNPV) *	0.0	0.0	0.1	0.1	0.0	0.2	0.2	0.2	0.2	0.2
EXCH(%) **	0.1	0.7	1.0	1.5	0.8	3.0	3.9	4.6	5.8	7.2
CAB(B.US$) ***	-0.1	-0.2	-0.3	-0.4	-0.3	-0.7	-0.7	-0.9	-1.4	-2.2
ITALY										
GNP(%)	-0.0	-0.0	-0.1	-0.2	-0.1	-0.3	-0.0	0.4	0.6	0.7
CPI(%)	-0.0	-0.0	-0.1	-0.3	-0.1	-0.8	-1.6	-2.1	-2.3	-2.6
GDEF(%GNPV) *	0.0	0.0	0.0	0.1	0.0	0.1	0.1	-0.0	-0.1	-0.1
EXCH(%) **	0.1	0.7	1.1	1.8	0.9	3.8	4.8	4.9	5.6	6.6
CAB(B.US$) ***	-0.0	0.0	0.1	0.1	0.0	-0.1	-1.2	-2.2	-2.6	-2.9
CANADA										
GNP(%)	-0.3	-0.8	-1.2	-1.4	-0.9	-1.3	-0.2	0.2	-0.4	-1.1
CPI(%)	0.0	0.0	-0.1	-0.4	-0.1	-1.3	-2.1	-2.5	-3.0	-3.8
GDEF(%GNPV) *	0.1	0.2	0.4	0.5	0.3	0.4	-0.4	-1.0	-1.3	-1.3
EXCH(%) **	0.0	0.2	0.1	-0.2	0.0	-0.9	-1.7	-1.1	0.2	0.9
CAB(B.US$) ***	-0.7	-1.6	-2.4	-3.1	-2.0	-3.0	-1.1	0.4	0.2	-1.1
REST OF WORLD										
CAB(B.US$) ***	-	-	-	-	-	-	-	-	-	-

* Government deficit as a percentage of baseline nominal GNP.
** Exchange rate : Bilateral rate against U.S. $ ($/local currency).
*** Local currency units translated into U.S. $ at baseline exchange rates.

Model: DRI
Simulation C: Reduction in U.S. Government Purchases with Foreign Short-Term Interest Rates Unchanged from Baseline
(Deviation of Shock Path from Baseline Path)

	1985									
	Q1	Q2	Q3	Q4	1985	1986	1987	1988	1989	1990
UNITED STATES										
GNPV(%)	-1.6	-2.2	-2.6	-2.8	-2.3	-2.8	-2.6	-2.5	-2.8	-3.3
GNP(%)	-1.5	-2.0	-2.3	-2.4	-2.0	-2.1	-1.4	-0.8	-0.6	-0.8
PGNP(%)	-0.1	-0.2	-0.3	-0.5	-0.3	-0.8	-1.2	-1.7	-2.2	-2.5
CPI(%)	0.0	-0.1	-0.2	-0.2	-0.1	-0.4	-0.7	-1.2	-1.6	-2.0
WAGES(%)	-0.1	-0.2	-0.3	-0.5	-0.3	-0.8	-1.3	-1.8	-2.2	-2.6
UN(% PTS)	0.2	0.5	0.7	0.8	0.6	0.8	0.4	0.1	0.0	0.1
GNP(B.72$)	-25.5	-34.1	-38.3	-40.4	-34.6	-36.3	-24.5	-14.4	-11.6	-15.3
G(B.72$)	-16.7	-16.8	-17.0	-17.1	-16.9	-17.4	-17.9	-18.5	-19.0	-19.6
C(B.72$)	-6.0	-12.4	-16.5	-19.4	-13.6	-22.3	-22.3	-20.5	-21.4	-25.7
IFP(B.72$)	-3.8	-5.8	-6.8	-7.1	-5.9	-4.9	1.4	6.4	7.7	6.7
II(B.72$)	-0.3	-3.9	-5.4	-6.1	-3.9	-4.4	-0.9	1.2	1.4	0.7
XGS(B.72$)	0.0	-0.3	-0.7	-1.1	-0.5	-1.1	0.7	2.6	3.4	2.8
MGS(B.72$)	-1.5	-5.0	-8.1	-10.3	-6.2	-13.8	-14.6	-14.3	-16.3	-19.8
M1(%)	0.0	0.0	-0.0	-0.1	-0.0	0.0	0.0	-0.0	0.0	0.1
RS(% PTS)	-0.1	-0.8	-0.9	-1.0	-0.7	-1.6	-1.8	-1.9	-2.4	-2.8
RL(% PTS)	-0.0	-0.5	-0.7	-0.8	-0.5	-1.1	-1.4	-1.6	-1.8	-2.1
GDEF(B$)	-13.9	-8.6	-5.9	-6.0	-8.6	-17.0	-40.0	-58.9	-71.6	-79.0
PXGS(%)	-0.1	-0.2	-0.4	-0.7	-0.4	-1.0	-1.5	-1.9	-2.3	-2.6
PMGS(%)	0.5	0.5	0.7	0.8	0.6	1.6	2.2	2.4	2.5	2.2
EXCH(%) *	-0.1	-0.7	-1.1	-1.7	-0.9	-4.2	-6.9	-8.6	-9.2	-9.0
CAB(B$)	1.5	8.9	14.4	18.1	10.7	21.5	22.8	23.3	27.3	34.5
NON-US OECD										
GNPV(%) **	0.0	-0.0	-0.1	-0.1	-0.1	-0.5	-1.3	-2.1	-2.7	-3.1
GNP(%) **	-0.1	-0.2	-0.3	-0.4	-0.2	-0.8	-1.1	-1.2	-1.3	-1.5
PGNP(%)	0.1	0.2	0.2	0.3	0.2	0.3	-0.3	-0.9	-1.4	-1.6
CPI(%)	0.0	0.0	-0.0	-0.1	-0.0	-0.4	-1.0	-1.7	-2.1	-2.4
WAGES(%)	-0.0	-0.0	-0.0	-0.1	-0.0	-0.4	-1.1	-1.8	-2.4	-2.7
UN(% PTS)	0.0	0.0	0.0	0.0	0.0	0.1	0.1	0.1	0.1	0.2
C(%) **	-0.0	-0.0	-0.0	-0.1	-0.0	-0.1	0.0	0.1	0.1	-0.0
IFP(%) **	0.0	-0.0	-0.0	-0.1	-0.0	-0.3	-0.7	-0.8	-0.8	-0.7
RS(% PTS)	-0.0	0.0	0.0	0.0	-0.0	0.0	-0.0	-0.0	-0.0	-0.0
RL(% PTS)	-0.0	-0.0	-0.0	-0.0	-0.0	-0.1	-0.2	-0.3	-0.3	-0.3
GDEF (B.US$) **	-	-	-	-	-	-	-	-	-	-
PXGS(%)	0.3	0.3	0.5	0.6	0.4	0.6	-0.5	-1.8	-2.9	-3.2
PMGS(%)	-0.0	-0.4	-0.7	-1.1	-0.5	-2.7	-4.6	-6.1	-6.8	-7.0
EXCH(%) ***	0.1	0.7	1.1	1.8	0.9	4.4	7.4	9.4	10.1	9.9
CAB(B.US$) **	0.3	0.0	0.3	2.1	0.7	6.9	7.4	0.8	-12.1	-24.3

* Exchange rate : (Weighted average of foreign currencies)/U.S. $.
** Local currency units translated into U.S. $ at baseline exchange rates.
*** Exchange rate : U.S. $/(weighted average of non-US OECD currencies).

Model: DRI
Simulation C: Reduction in U.S. Government Purchases with Foreign Short-Term Interest Rates Unchanged from Baseline
(Deviation of Shock Path from Baseline Path)

	1985									
	Q1	Q2	Q3	Q4	1985	1986	1987	1988	1989	1990
JAPAN										
GNP(%)	-0.1	-0.3	-0.4	-0.6	-0.4	-1.4	-2.2	-2.6	-2.9	-3.4
CPI(%)	0.0	0.0	0.0	0.1	0.0	0.0	-0.2	-0.4	-0.5	-0.4
RS(% PTS)	0.0	0.0	0.0	0.0	0.0	0.0	0.0	0.0	0.0	0.0
GDEF(%GNPV) *	-0.0	0.0	0.0	0.0	0.0	0.0	0.0	0.0	0.0	0.0
EXCH(%) **	0.1	0.7	1.2	2.0	1.0	4.8	8.1	10.4	11.2	11.0
CAB(B.US$) ***	1.2	1.9	3.2	4.5	2.7	10.4	11.1	5.1	-5.1	-13.0
GERMANY										
GNP(%)	-0.0	-0.1	-0.1	-0.1	-0.1	-0.2	-0.5	-0.9	-1.3	-1.7
CPI(%)	0.0	0.0	-0.0	-0.1	-0.0	-0.4	-1.4	-2.4	-3.4	-4.2
RS(% PTS)	0.0	0.0	0.0	0.0	0.0	0.0	0.0	-0.0	0.0	0.0
GDEF(%GNPV) *	0.0	0.0	0.0	0.0	0.0	0.1	0.2	0.4	0.7	0.9
EXCH(%) **	0.1	0.7	1.2	2.1	1.0	5.2	8.9	11.7	13.1	13.2
CAB(B.US$) ***	-0.1	-0.0	0.1	0.2	0.0	0.2	-0.5	-0.5	-0.9	-1.6
FRANCE										
GNP(%)	-0.0	-0.1	-0.2	-0.0	-0.1	-0.4	-0.4	-0.1	0.1	-0.0
CPI(%)	-0.0	-0.0	-0.1	-0.1	-0.0	-0.4	-1.0	-1.3	-1.2	-0.5
GDEF(%GNPV) *	0.0	0.0	0.0	0.0	0.0	0.1	0.2	0.3	0.2	0.1
EXCH(%) **	0.1	0.7	1.3	2.0	1.0	4.8	7.7	9.0	8.1	6.3
CAB(B.US$) ***	-0.0	-0.0	-0.3	0.7	0.1	-0.3	-0.8	-1.5	-2.4	-2.9
UNITED KINGDOM										
GNP(%)	-0.0	-0.1	-0.1	-0.2	-0.1	-0.3	-0.2	-0.2	-0.1	-0.1
CPI(%)	0.0	0.0	-0.0	-0.1	-0.0	-0.2	-0.5	-1.0	-1.7	-2.6
GDEF(%GNPV) *	0.0	0.0	0.1	0.1	0.1	0.2	0.3	0.3	0.3	0.3
EXCH(%) **	0.1	0.7	1.0	1.7	0.9	3.7	5.9	7.4	8.3	9.1
CAB(B.US$) ***	-0.1	-0.2	-0.3	-0.4	-0.3	-0.8	-1.0	-1.2	-1.6	-2.2
ITALY										
GNP(%)	-0.0	-0.0	-0.1	-0.2	-0.1	-0.4	-0.7	-0.6	-0.2	0.4
CPI(%)	-0.0	-0.0	-0.1	-0.3	-0.1	-0.9	-2.3	-3.8	-4.9	-5.3
GDEF(%GNPV) *	0.0	0.0	0.0	0.1	0.0	0.2	0.4	0.6	0.7	0.7
EXCH(%) **	0.1	0.7	1.2	2.0	1.0	4.9	8.5	11.0	11.9	11.8
CAB(B.US$) ***	-0.0	0.0	0.1	0.2	0.1	0.4	0.5	-0.0	-0.9	-2.2
CANADA										
GNP(%)	-0.3	-0.8	-1.2	-1.5	-0.9	-1.8	-1.2	-0.8	-1.0	-1.5
CPI(%)	0.0	0.0	-0.1	-0.3	-0.1	-1.3	-2.7	-3.7	-4.4	-4.8
GDEF(%GNPV) *	0.1	0.2	0.4	0.5	0.3	0.6	0.1	-0.4	-0.7	-0.7
EXCH(%) **	-0.0	0.1	0.2	0.3	0.2	0.9	1.8	2.9	3.7	4.1
CAB(B.US$) ***	-0.7	-1.6	-2.4	-3.0	-1.9	-3.0	-1.9	-1.1	-1.2	-2.4
REST OF WORLD										
CAB(B.US$) ***	-	-	-	-	-	-	-	-	-	-

* Government deficit as a percentage of baseline nominal GNP.
** Exchange rate : Bilateral rate against U.S. $ ($/local currency).
*** Local currency units translated into U.S. $ at baseline exchange rates.

Model: DRI
Simulation D: U.S. Monetary Expansion with foreign Monetary Aggregates Unchanged from Baseline
(Deviation of Shock Path from Baseline Path)

	1985									
	Q1	Q2	Q3	Q4	1985	1986	1987	1988	1989	1990
UNITED STATES										
GNPV(%)	-0.0	0.3	0.7	1.0	0.5	2.1	3.1	3.3	2.9	2.0
GNP(%)	0.0	0.4	0.7	1.0	0.6	1.8	2.2	1.6	0.5	-0.8
PGNP(%)	-0.0	-0.1	-0.1	-0.0	-0.1	0.2	0.9	1.6	2.4	2.8
CPI(%)	0.0	0.0	0.0	0.1	0.0	0.4	1.0	1.6	2.1	2.2
WAGES(%)	-0.0	0.0	0.1	0.2	0.1	0.5	1.3	2.1	2.7	3.0
UN(% PTS)	0.0	-0.1	-0.1	-0.3	-0.1	-0.6	-0.7	-0.5	0.0	0.5
GNP(B.72$)	0.4	6.8	12.5	17.8	9.4	32.1	39.0	30.4	10.2	-15.2
G(B.72$)	0.0	0.0	0.0	0.0	0.0	0.0	0.0	0.0	0.0	0.0
C(B.72$)	-1.1	-1.2	-0.8	-1.3	-1.1	4.4	7.1	3.0	-4.9	-13.8
IFP(B.72$)	0.3	2.3	6.0	9.7	4.6	15.7	16.2	10.6	2.4	-3.6
II(B.72$)	-0.6	2.2	3.0	3.4	2.0	4.3	4.1	1.6	-0.6	-2.5
XGS(B.72$)	-0.5	-0.6	-0.4	0.3	-0.3	4.8	9.8	11.0	6.3	-1.8
MGS(B.72$)	-2.5	-4.1	-4.8	-5.6	-4.3	-2.9	-2.0	-4.1	-6.9	-6.6
M1(%)	1.0	2.1	3.0	4.0	2.5	4.0	4.0	4.0	4.0	4.0
RS(% PTS)	-3.5	-4.3	-4.5	-5.2	-4.4	-2.3	-1.5	-1.1	-1.2	-1.6
RL(% PTS)	-1.0	-1.7	-2.1	-2.4	-1.8	-1.6	-1.2	-0.9	-0.9	-1.0
GDEF(B$)	-4.4	-16.6	-27.3	-39.0	-21.8	-55.3	-61.4	-49.4	-25.8	0.8
PXGS(%)	0.1	0.2	0.3	0.5	0.3	1.2	2.4	3.4	4.0	4.0
PMGS(%)	0.6	1.5	2.4	3.3	1.9	5.3	7.3	7.9	6.0	2.8
EXCH(%) *	-2.3	-4.4	-6.7	-9.9	-5.8	-14.6	-17.2	-15.4	-8.9	-2.6
CAB(B$)	2.5	2.6	1.4	2.1	2.2	-1.4	3.2	14.2	23.7	18.9
NON-US OECD										
GNPV(%) **	0.1	0.0	-0.1	-0.1	-0.0	-0.7	-1.5	-1.8	-1.6	-1.2
GNP(%) **	-0.2	-0.3	-0.3	-0.4	-0.3	-0.6	-0.6	-0.3	-0.2	-0.5
PGNP(%)	0.2	0.3	0.3	0.3	0.3	-0.0	-0.9	-1.5	-1.4	-0.7
CPI(%)	-0.0	-0.1	-0.3	-0.5	-0.2	-1.3	-2.3	-2.6	-2.0	-0.9
WAGES(%)	0.0	-0.0	-0.1	-0.3	-0.1	-1.0	-2.1	-2.6	-2.1	-1.0
UN(% PTS)	0.0	0.0	-0.0	-0.0	0.0	-0.1	-0.1	-0.1	-0.1	0.1
C(%) **	0.0	0.1	0.1	0.2	0.1	0.5	1.1	1.2	0.9	-0.0
IFP(%) **	0.1	0.3	0.4	0.7	0.4	1.2	1.9	2.3	1.5	-0.1
RS(% PTS)	-0.1	-0.3	-0.6	-0.8	-0.5	-1.1	-1.3	-1.3	-1.1	-0.7
RL(% PTS)	-0.2	-0.3	-0.5	-0.6	-0.4	-0.8	-1.1	-1.0	-0.6	-0.1
GDEF (B.US$) **	-	-	-	-	-	-	-	-	-	-
PXGS(%)	0.0	-0.3	-0.6	-1.2	-0.5	-2.0	-3.5	-3.9	-2.3	-0.0
PMGS(%)	-1.1	-2.3	-3.6	-5.6	-3.2	-8.3	-9.7	-8.2	-4.1	-0.4
EXCH(%) ***	2.3	4.5	7.2	11.1	6.3	17.4	20.8	18.2	10.0	3.0
CAB(B.US$) **	2.7	4.8	8.7	12.1	7.1	14.5	-2.7	-17.6	-25.3	-11.3

* Exchange rate : (Weighted average of foreign currencies)/U.S. $.
** Local currency units translated into U.S. $ at baseline exchange rates.
*** Exchange rate : U.S. $/(weighted average of non-US OECD currencies).

Model: DRI
Simulation D: U.S. Monetary Expansion with Foreign Monetary Aggregates Unchanged from Baseline
(Deviation of Shock Path from Baseline Path)

	1985 Q1	1985 Q2	1985 Q3	1985 Q4	1985	1986	1987	1988	1989	1990
JAPAN										
GNP(%)	-0.5	-0.8	-1.1	-1.6	-1.0	-2.6	-2.9	-2.2	-1.7	-1.7
CPI(%)	0.0	0.1	0.1	0.0	0.1	-0.2	-0.5	-0.3	0.1	0.5
RS(% PTS)	-0.5	-0.9	-1.1	-1.5	-1.0	-1.5	-1.5	-1.1	-0.5	-0.1
GDEF(%GNPV) *	-0.0	-0.0	-0.0	-0.0	-0.0	-0.0	-0.1	-0.1	-0.1	-0.1
EXCH(%) **	2.4	4.7	7.6	11.9	6.6	19.0	23.0	20.2	11.1	3.4
CAB(B.US$) ***	0.6	0.8	2.6	3.0	1.7	7.7	-1.3	-8.4	-8.4	2.7
GERMANY										
GNP(%)	0.1	0.1	0.2	0.4	0.2	0.4	-0.2	-0.9	-1.4	-1.6
CPI(%)	-0.0	-0.1	-0.3	-0.5	-0.2	-1.5	-3.2	-4.6	-5.1	-4.2
RS(% PTS)	0.4	0.4	0.4	0.5	0.4	-0.1	-0.9	-1.9	-2.4	-2.1
GDEF(%GNPV) *	-0.0	-0.1	-0.1	-0.2	-0.1	-0.3	-0.2	0.1	0.3	0.4
EXCH(%) **	2.3	4.9	7.9	12.5	6.9	20.2	24.8	23.2	14.5	6.1
CAB(B.US$) ***	0.7	1.5	2.3	3.0	1.9	1.4	-2.1	-2.6	-4.8	-4.1
FRANCE										
GNP(%)	0.0	0.0	0.1	0.4	0.1	0.4	1.0	1.7	1.6	0.6
CPI(%)	-0.0	-0.1	-0.3	-0.5	-0.3	-1.7	-3.4	-3.3	-0.8	2.3
GDEF(%GNPV) *	-0.0	-0.0	-0.0	-0.0	-0.0	0.1	0.3	0.2	-0.2	-0.7
EXCH(%) **	2.4	4.9	7.9	12.2	6.8	19.9	23.4	17.5	5.2	-2.7
CAB(B.US$) ***	0.7	1.4	2.1	4.1	2.1	3.1	-0.1	-4.1	-5.9	-2.1
UNITED KINGDOM										
GNP(%)	-0.0	-0.0	-0.0	-0.0	-0.0	0.0	0.2	0.2	0.1	0.0
CPI(%)	-0.0	-0.1	-0.1	-0.2	-0.1	-0.4	-0.7	-1.0	-1.2	-1.3
GDEF(%GNPV) *	0.0	0.2	0.2	0.3	0.2	0.4	0.4	0.4	0.2	0.1
EXCH(%) **	2.4	4.1	6.3	9.6	5.6	13.6	15.3	13.6	7.5	2.6
CAB(B.US$) ***	-0.1	-0.4	-0.6	-0.9	-0.5	-1.4	-1.9	-2.1	-2.0	-1.8
ITALY										
GNP(%)	0.0	-0.0	-0.0	-0.1	-0.0	0.0	1.2	3.0	4.2	4.1
CPI(%)	-0.1	-0.4	-0.8	-1.5	-0.7	-3.5	-6.4	-7.4	-6.1	-3.3
GDEF(%GNPV) *	-0.0	-0.0	-0.0	0.0	-0.0	0.1	-0.0	-0.6	-1.3	-1.6
EXCH(%) **	2.3	4.8	7.7	12.0	6.7	19.6	24.2	21.3	12.0	3.9
CAB(B.US$) ***	0.5	1.1	1.7	2.3	1.4	2.2	-0.1	-2.5	-3.8	-2.7
CANADA										
GNP(%)	-0.2	-0.4	-0.5	-0.5	-0.4	0.3	0.9	0.4	-0.9	-1.6
CPI(%)	-0.1	-0.6	-1.3	-2.1	-1.1	-3.0	-2.5	-1.4	-0.5	-0.8
GDEF(%GNPV) *	-0.0	-0.0	-0.0	-0.1	-0.0	-0.6	-1.4	-1.3	-0.6	0.0
EXCH(%) **	1.3	2.7	3.9	5.0	3.2	5.1	5.6	6.0	6.6	4.8
CAB(B.US$) ***	0.3	0.5	0.6	0.7	0.5	1.6	2.8	2.1	-0.4	-3.4
REST OF WORLD										
CAB(B.US$) ***	-	-	-	-	-	-	-	-	-	-

* Government deficit as a percentage of baseline nominal GNP.
** Exchange rate : Bilateral rate against U.S. $ ($/local currency).
*** Local currency units translated into U.S. $ at baseline exchange rates.

Model: DRI
Simulation E: U.S. Monetary Expansion with Foreign Short-Term Interest Rates Unchanged from Baseline
(Deviation of Shock Path from Baseline Path)

	1985									
	Q1	Q2	Q3	Q4	1985	1986	1987	1988	1989	1990
UNITED STATES										
GNPV(%)	-0.0	0.3	0.6	1.0	0.5	2.1	3.2	3.6	3.3	2.6
GNP(%)	0.0	0.4	0.7	1.0	0.6	1.9	2.4	1.9	0.8	-0.5
PGNP(%)	-0.0	-0.1	-0.1	-0.1	-0.1	0.2	0.8	1.7	2.5	3.1
CPI(%)	0.0	0.0	0.0	0.1	0.0	0.4	1.2	1.9	2.4	2.6
WAGES(%)	-0.0	0.0	0.1	0.1	0.1	0.5	1.3	2.3	3.0	3.4
UN(% PTS)	0.0	-0.1	-0.1	-0.3	-0.1	-0.6	-0.8	-0.6	-0.1	0.4
GNP(B.72$)	0.4	6.8	12.5	17.9	9.4	33.1	42.5	35.0	14.8	-10.2
G(B.72$)	0.0	0.0	0.0	0.0	0.0	0.0	0.0	0.0	0.0	0.0
C(B.72$)	-1.1	-1.2	-0.8	-1.3	-1.1	3.9	6.0	2.3	-5.1	-13.3
IFP(B.72$)	0.3	2.3	6.0	9.7	4.6	15.8	16.3	10.5	2.0	-4.1
II(B.72$)	-0.6	2.2	2.7	3.1	1.9	3.6	3.8	2.0	-0.2	-2.0
XGS(B.72$)	-0.5	-0.6	-0.3	0.6	-0.2	5.7	11.4	12.6	8.5	1.1
MGS(B.72$)	-2.5	-4.1	-4.8	-5.7	-4.3	-4.1	-5.1	-7.5	-9.6	-8.0
M1(%)	1.0	2.1	3.0	4.0	2.5	4.0	4.0	4.0	4.0	4.0
RS(% PTS)	-3.5	-4.3	-4.5	-5.2	-4.4	-2.2	-1.4	-1.0	-0.9	-1.1
RL(% PTS)	-1.0	-1.7	-2.1	-2.4	-1.8	-1.6	-1.1	-0.8	-0.7	-0.8
GDEF(B$)	-4.5	-16.5	-27.1	-38.5	-21.7	-54.5	-61.9	-50.3	-25.9	0.4
PXGS(%)	0.1	0.2	0.3	0.5	0.3	1.2	2.5	3.6	4.4	4.5
PMGS(%)	0.6	1.5	2.5	3.7	2.1	6.7	9.8	10.3	8.0	4.2
EXCH(%) *	-2.3	-4.6	-7.2	-10.7	-6.2	-16.7	-21.1	-20.1	-12.6	-3.3
CAB(B$)	2.5	2.5	1.1	1.4	1.9	-2.9	3.6	16.5	28.3	26.2
NON-US OECD										
GNPV(%) **	0.0	-0.0	-0.2	-0.3	-0.1	-1.1	-2.7	-3.7	-3.4	-2.0
GNP(%) **	-0.2	-0.4	-0.5	-0.7	-0.5	-1.3	-1.8	-1.6	-1.0	-0.4
PGNP(%)	0.2	0.3	0.4	0.4	0.3	0.2	-0.9	-2.0	-2.4	-1.6
CPI(%)	-0.0	-0.1	-0.3	-0.5	-0.2	-1.3	-2.6	-3.3	-3.0	-1.5
WAGES(%)	0.0	0.0	-0.0	-0.2	-0.0	-0.9	-2.4	-3.6	-3.6	-2.1
UN(% PTS)	0.0	0.0	0.0	0.0	0.0	0.0	0.0	0.0	0.1	0.2
C(%) **	0.0	0.1	0.1	0.2	0.1	0.4	0.8	0.9	0.6	-0.2
IFP(%) **	0.0	0.1	0.1	0.1	0.1	-0.1	-0.3	-0.3	-0.1	0.2
RS(% PTS)	0.0	0.0	0.0	-0.0	-0.0	-0.0	-0.0	-0.0	0.0	0.0
RL(% PTS)	-0.1	-0.2	-0.2	-0.3	-0.2	-0.4	-0.5	-0.6	-0.5	-0.1
GDEF (B.US$) **	-	-	-	-	-	-	-	-	-	-
PXGS(%)	0.0	-0.2	-0.6	-1.2	-0.5	-2.1	-4.3	-5.4	-4.1	-1.5
PMGS(%)	-1.1	-2.3	-3.8	-6.0	-3.3	-9.4	-12.1	-11.2	-6.2	-0.5
EXCH(%) ***	2.3	4.7	7.7	12.1	6.7	20.1	26.6	25.1	14.5	3.4
CAB(B.US$) **	2.4	4.3	8.2	11.8	6.7	15.1	-3.9	-25.6	-42.9	-33.2

* Exchange rate : (Weighted average of foreign currencies)/U.S. $.
** Local currency units translated into U.S. $ at baseline exchange rates.
*** Exchange rate : U.S. $/(weighted average of non-US OECD currencies).

Model: DRI
Simulation E: U.S. Monetary Expansion with Foreign Short-Term Interest Rates Unchanged from Baseline
(Deviation of Shock Path from Baseline Path)

	1985									
	Q1	Q2	Q3	Q4	1985	1986	1987	1988	1989	1990
JAPAN										
GNP(%)	-0.6	-1.2	-1.7	-2.4	-1.5	-4.4	-5.8	-5.3	-3.4	-1.0
CPI(%)	0.1	0.1	0.2	0.2	0.1	0.2	-0.1	-0.4	-0.3	0.2
RS(% PTS)	0.0	0.0	0.0	0.0	0.0	0.0	0.0	0.0	0.0	0.0
GDEF(%GNPV) *	0.0	0.0	0.0	0.0	0.0	0.1	0.1	0.1	0.0	-0.0
EXCH(%) **	2.4	5.0	8.2	12.9	7.1	21.8	29.4	28.2	16.8	4.5
CAB(B.US$) ***	0.3	0.1	1.6	1.6	0.9	5.9	-6.7	-20.7	-27.7	-16.2
GERMANY										
GNP(%)	0.1	0.1	0.2	0.4	0.2	0.3	-0.4	-1.5	-2.6	-3.0
CPI(%)	0.0	-0.1	-0.3	-0.5	-0.2	-1.6	-3.8	-5.9	-7.1	-6.3
RS(% PTS)	0.0	0.0	0.0	0.0	0.0	0.0	0.0	0.0	0.0	0.0
GDEF(%GNPV) *	-0.0	-0.1	-0.1	-0.2	-0.1	-0.2	-0.1	0.4	1.0	1.4
EXCH(%) **	2.4	5.1	8.5	13.5	7.4	23.3	31.8	32.1	21.4	8.5
CAB(B.US$) ***	0.8	1.5	2.5	3.3	2.0	1.8	-1.3	-1.5	-3.1	-1.6
FRANCE										
GNP(%)	0.0	0.0	0.1	0.4	0.1	0.3	0.8	1.5	1.7	0.9
CPI(%)	-0.0	-0.1	-0.3	-0.6	-0.3	-1.9	-4.1	-4.6	-2.1	2.3
GDEF(%GNPV) *	-0.0	-0.0	-0.0	-0.0	-0.0	0.1	0.4	0.5	0.1	-0.7
EXCH(%) **	2.4	5.1	8.5	13.4	7.3	23.2	31.1	26.6	10.3	-4.1
CAB(B.US$) ***	0.7	1.5	2.2	4.3	2.2	3.9	1.0	-3.9	-8.3	-6.5
UNITED KINGDOM										
GNP(%)	-0.0	-0.0	-0.0	-0.0	-0.0	0.0	0.1	0.2	0.2	0.1
CPI(%)	-0.0	-0.1	-0.1	-0.2	-0.1	-0.3	-0.4	-0.5	-0.3	0.1
GDEF(%GNPV) *	0.0	0.2	0.2	0.3	0.2	0.5	0.5	0.5	0.3	0.1
EXCH(%) **	2.4	4.3	6.8	10.3	5.9	15.2	18.0	15.9	8.1	1.0
CAB(B.US$) ***	-0.1	-0.4	-0.6	-1.0	-0.5	-1.7	-2.3	-2.3	-1.8	-0.9
ITALY										
GNP(%)	0.0	-0.0	-0.1	-0.2	-0.1	-0.6	-0.5	0.7	2.8	5.0
CPI(%)	-0.1	-0.4	-0.9	-1.6	-0.8	-3.9	-7.7	-10.1	-9.7	-6.5
GDEF(%GNPV) *	-0.0	-0.0	0.0	0.1	0.0	0.3	0.8	1.0	0.6	-0.4
EXCH(%) **	2.4	5.0	8.3	13.1	7.2	22.5	31.1	30.2	18.9	6.1
CAB(B.US$) ***	0.6	1.2	1.9	2.8	1.6	3.7	3.4	1.5	-1.7	-5.3
CANADA										
GNP(%)	-0.2	-0.3	-0.4	-0.5	-0.3	-0.2	0.2	0.2	-0.2	-1.0
CPI(%)	-0.2	-0.6	-1.3	-2.0	-1.0	-2.9	-2.9	-2.0	-0.5	0.4
GDEF(%GNPV) *	-0.0	-0.0	-0.1	-0.1	-0.1	-0.5	-1.0	-1.1	-0.7	-0.1
EXCH(%) **	1.0	2.3	3.6	5.2	3.0	6.6	7.8	7.2	5.5	3.8
CAB(B.US$) ***	0.2	0.4	0.6	0.8	0.5	1.4	1.9	1.3	-0.3	-2.7
REST OF WORLD										
CAB(B.US$) ***	-	-	-	-	-	-	-	-	-	-

* Government deficit as a percentage of baseline nominal GNP.
** Exchange rate : Bilateral rate against U.S. $ ($/local currency).
*** Local currency units translated into U.S. $ at baseline exchange rates.

Model: DRI
Simulation F: Nonpolicy Exogenous Depreciation of the Dollar
(Deviation of Shock Path from Baseline Path)

	1985									
	Q1	Q2	Q3	Q4	1985	1986	1987	1988	1989	1990
UNITED STATES										
GNPV(%)	-0.1	-0.1	-0.0	0.0	-0.0	0.3	1.0	2.1	2.8	3.0
GNP(%)	-0.0	0.0	0.1	0.2	0.1	0.4	0.9	1.4	1.4	0.9
PGNP(%)	-0.0	-0.1	-0.1	-0.1	-0.1	-0.1	0.1	0.7	1.4	2.1
CPI(%)	0.0	0.1	0.1	0.2	0.1	0.5	1.1	1.8	2.5	3.1
WAGES(%)	-0.0	-0.0	-0.0	0.0	-0.0	0.1	0.5	1.2	2.0	2.7
UN(% PTS)	0.0	0.0	-0.0	-0.0	-0.0	-0.1	-0.3	-0.4	-0.4	-0.3
GNP(B.72$)	-0.6	0.4	1.4	3.0	1.1	7.0	16.4	25.5	26.0	17.7
G(B.72$)	0.0	0.0	0.0	0.0	0.0	0.0	0.0	0.0	0.0	0.0
C(B.72$)	0.1	-0.4	-0.9	-1.1	-0.6	-3.0	-5.2	-5.6	-4.3	-5.7
IFP(B.72$)	0.1	0.0	0.1	0.3	0.1	0.1	-0.3	-1.2	-3.6	-7.5
II(B.72$)	-1.4	-1.3	-1.6	-2.0	-1.6	-2.4	-2.1	-0.3	0.2	-1.5
XGS(B.72$)	0.6	1.5	2.4	3.5	2.0	6.6	12.7	17.2	18.4	17.1
MGS(B.72$)	-0.1	-0.5	-1.4	-2.2	-1.1	-5.9	-11.4	-15.5	-15.2	-15.3
M1(%)	0.0	0.1	0.1	-0.0	0.0	-0.0	-0.0	-0.0	-0.0	-0.1
RS(% PTS)	0.0	0.0	0.0	0.6	0.1	0.5	1.1	1.6	2.3	2.8
RL(% PTS)	0.0	0.0	0.0	0.2	0.0	0.3	0.5	0.9	1.2	1.6
GDEF(B$)	1.3	0.6	0.2	0.2	0.6	-0.4	-3.6	-6.9	0.5	21.1
PXGS(%)	-0.0	0.0	0.1	0.1	0.1	0.4	1.1	2.0	3.0	3.7
PMGS(%)	0.6	1.4	2.4	3.3	1.9	6.2	10.6	13.0	12.8	12.7
EXCH(%) *	-2.6	-5.0	-7.3	-9.6	-6.1	-15.2	-23.4	-26.3	-26.2	-26.2
CAB(B$)	-0.7	-1.5	-1.6	-0.7	-1.1	3.3	14.5	29.5	36.5	36.5
NON-US OECD										
GNPV(%) **	0.1	0.1	-0.0	-0.1	0.0	-0.9	-2.3	-3.8	-4.4	-5.0
GNP(%) **	-0.1	-0.3	-0.4	-0.6	-0.4	-1.1	-1.7	-1.8	-1.6	-2.0
PGNP(%)	0.2	0.4	0.4	0.4	0.4	0.2	-0.6	-2.0	-2.9	-3.0
CPI(%)	-0.0	-0.1	-0.2	-0.4	-0.2	-1.2	-2.8	-4.3	-5.2	-5.5
WAGES(%)	-0.0	-0.0	-0.1	-0.3	-0.1	-1.0	-2.5	-4.2	-5.2	-5.6
UN(% PTS)	0.0	0.0	0.0	0.0	0.0	0.0	0.0	-0.1	-0.1	-0.0
C(%) **	0.0	0.1	0.1	0.2	0.1	0.5	1.1	1.7	1.9	1.7
IFP(%) **	0.0	0.0	0.1	0.1	0.1	0.4	1.1	2.0	2.5	2.4
RS(% PTS)	-0.0	-0.1	-0.3	-0.4	-0.2	-0.9	-1.6	-2.3	-2.5	-2.6
RL(% PTS)	-0.0	-0.1	-0.2	-0.2	-0.1	-0.6	-1.1	-1.5	-1.4	-1.2
GDEF (B.US$) **	-	-	-	-	-	-	-	-	-	-
PXGS(%)	-0.0	-0.3	-0.7	-0.9	-0.5	-2.0	-4.8	-7.2	-8.2	-8.2
PMGS(%)	-1.3	-2.6	-4.0	-5.6	-3.4	-9.2	-15.1	-17.7	-17.8	-17.6
EXCH(%) ***	2.6	5.2	7.9	10.7	6.6	17.9	30.5	35.5	35.3	35.3
CAB(B.US$) **	5.0	8.1	11.7	14.6	9.9	15.0	8.8	-14.4	-40.3	-54.5

* Exchange rate : (Weighted average of foreign currencies)/U.S. $.
** Local currency units translated into U.S. $ at baseline exchange rates.
*** Exchange rate : U.S. $/(weighted average of non-US OECD currencies).

Model: DRI
Simulation F: Nonpolicy Exogenous Depreciation of the Dollar
(Deviation of Shock Path from Baseline Path)

	1985 Q1	1985 Q2	1985 Q3	1985 Q4	1985	1986	1987	1988	1989	1990
JAPAN										
GNP(%)	-0.4	-0.8	-1.3	-1.7	-1.1	-3.2	-5.0	-5.6	-5.9	-7.3
CPI(%)	0.0	0.1	0.1	0.0	0.0	-0.1	-0.5	-0.7	-0.6	-0.2
RS(% PTS)	-0.1	-0.2	-0.4	-0.6	-0.3	-1.0	-1.5	-1.7	-1.5	-1.3
GDEF(%GNPV) *	0.0	0.0	0.0	0.0	0.0	0.0	0.0	-0.1	-0.1	-0.1
EXCH(%) **	2.7	5.4	8.2	11.1	6.9	18.7	31.9	37.2	37.2	37.2
CAB(B.US$) ***	2.6	4.1	6.4	8.1	5.3	12.6	13.0	0.9	-17.4	-27.3
GERMANY										
GNP(%)	0.1	0.2	0.3	0.4	0.2	0.4	0.1	-0.5	-1.3	-1.7
CPI(%)	-0.0	-0.1	-0.3	-0.5	-0.2	-1.4	-3.2	-5.3	-6.7	-7.4
RS(% PTS)	0.0	-0.1	-0.2	-0.2	-0.1	-0.4	-1.1	-2.3	-3.1	-3.7
GDEF(%GNPV) *	-0.0	-0.1	-0.1	-0.2	-0.1	-0.3	-0.3	-0.2	-0.0	0.2
EXCH(%) **	2.7	5.5	8.3	11.2	6.9	18.9	32.2	37.5	37.2	37.2
CAB(B.US$) ***	0.9	1.7	2.5	2.6	1.9	1.5	0.2	-2.4	-3.9	-4.0
FRANCE										
GNP(%)	0.0	0.0	0.1	0.3	0.1	0.3	0.8	1.6	2.0	1.7
CPI(%)	-0.0	-0.1	-0.3	-0.6	-0.3	-1.6	-3.5	-4.9	-4.9	-4.2
GDEF(%GNPV) *	-0.0	-0.0	-0.0	-0.0	-0.0	0.1	0.3	0.4	0.3	0.1
EXCH(%) **	2.7	5.5	8.3	11.2	6.9	18.9	32.2	37.5	37.2	37.2
CAB(B.US$) ***	0.8	1.5	2.0	3.5	1.9	2.6	1.4	-2.2	-5.8	-7.5
UNITED KINGDOM										
GNP(%)	-0.0	-0.1	-0.1	-0.2	-0.1	-0.3	-0.6	-0.6	-0.2	0.4
CPI(%)	-0.0	-0.1	-0.3	-0.5	-0.2	-1.1	-2.7	-5.1	-7.9	-11.1
GDEF(%GNPV) *	0.0	0.2	0.3	0.4	0.2	0.6	0.9	1.0	0.8	0.7
EXCH(%) **	2.7	5.5	8.3	11.2	6.9	18.9	32.2	37.5	37.2	37.2
CAB(B.US$) ***	-0.2	-0.4	-0.7	-1.0	-0.6	-1.9	-3.6	-5.2	-6.9	-9.0
ITALY										
GNP(%)	0.0	-0.0	-0.0	-0.1	-0.0	0.1	1.1	3.0	5.2	6.5
CPI(%)	-0.1	-0.5	-0.9	-1.5	-0.8	-3.4	-6.9	-9.9	-11.1	-11.0
GDEF(%GNPV) *	-0.0	-0.0	0.0	0.1	0.0	0.1	0.0	-0.4	-1.2	-1.8
EXCH(%) **	2.7	5.5	8.3	11.2	6.9	18.9	32.2	37.5	37.2	37.2
CAB(B.US$) ***	0.6	1.2	1.7	2.1	1.4	2.1	1.2	-1.0	-2.7	-2.6
CANADA										
GNP(%)	-0.2	-0.5	-0.9	-1.3	-0.8	-2.4	-3.6	-3.8	-3.4	-3.7
CPI(%)	-0.0	-0.1	-0.2	-0.4	-0.2	-1.5	-3.6	-5.7	-6.3	-5.8
GDEF(%GNPV) *	-0.0	0.1	0.2	0.3	0.1	0.6	0.6	0.1	-0.9	-1.3
EXCH(%) **	1.3	2.6	3.9	5.3	3.3	8.7	14.4	16.7	16.6	16.6
CAB(B.US$) ***	0.2	0.1	-0.2	-0.7	-0.1	-1.8	-3.5	-4.5	-3.6	-4.1
REST OF WORLD										
CAB(B.US$) ***	-	-	-	-	-	-	-	-	-	-

* Government deficit as a percentage of baseline nominal GNP.
** Exchange rate : Bilateral rate against U.S. $ ($/local currency).
*** Local currency units translated into U.S. $ at baseline exchange rates.

EEC Commission
COMPACT Model

See part 1 of this volume for design and detailed description of the simulations. See part 4 for bibliographical references.

Model: EEC
Simulation A: Baseline Path

	1985	1986	1987	1988	1989	1990
UNITED STATES						
GNPV(B.$)	3880.0	4129.0	4426.0	4758.0	5124.0	5518.0
GNP(B.72$)	1652.8	1697.2	1752.0	1806.0	1864.1	1921.3
PGNP(72=100)	234.7	243.3	252.6	263.5	274.9	287.2
CPI(72=100)	261.4	274.8	289.3	304.9	321.4	339.4
WAGES(72=100)	272.7	288.4	306.1	322.9	342.3	361.1
UN(%)	7.2	7.3	7.1	6.6	6.5	6.3
G(B.72$)	325.6	331.1	339.4	347.7	356.9	366.1
C(B.72$)	1056.8	1081.2	1110.9	1144.4	1179.4	1216.7
IFP(B.72$)	253.8	269.2	291.3	300.7	312.0	330.1
II(B.72$)	-	-	-	-	-	-
XGS(B.72$)	152.0	160.9	169.8	179.6	190.2	201.8
MGS(B.72$)	165.7	170.6	176.9	181.8	187.5	191.2
M1(B.$)	579.0	615.0	649.0	692.0	735.0	782.0
RS(%)	10.5	10.6	10.4	10.4	10.5	10.5
RL(%)	12.5	12.1	11.9	12.0	12.1	12.1
GDEF(B.$)	196.2	206.0	220.0	230.0	250.0	260.0
PXGS(72=100)	-	-	-	-	-	-
PMGS(72=100)	372.4	385.5	398.5	418.2	437.2	455.0
EXCH(72=100) *	127.2	125.2	123.2	121.2	119.3	117.5
CAB(B.$)	-141.0	-154.0	-169.0	-191.0	-211.0	-222.0
NON-US OECD						
GNPV(B.$) **	1886.0	2053.0	2218.0	2447.0	2667.0	2914.0
GNP(B.72$) **	1022.0	1076.0	1121.0	1195.0	1259.0	1327.0
PGNP(72=100)	184.5	190.8	197.9	204.8	211.8	219.6
CPI(72=100)	2.0	2.1	2.1	2.2	2.3	2.4
WAGES(72=100)	-	-	-	-	-	-
UN(%)	-	-	-	-	-	-
C(B.72$) **	598.0	626.0	650.0	690.0	725.0	763.0
IFP(B.72$) **	182.0	196.0	208.0	227.0	245.0	265.0
RS(%)	-	-	-	-	-	-
RL(%)	9.4	9.4	9.4	9.3	9.3	9.3
GDEF(B.US$) **	82.0	85.0	87.0	91.0	95.0	99.0
PXGS(72=100)	-	-	-	-	-	-
PMGS(72=100)	191.5	198.6	205.4	212.5	219.8	227.7
EXCH(72=100) ***	76.4	78.1	79.7	81.6	83.4	85.2
CAB(B.US$)	13.9	18.2	19.7	24.4	25.0	26.6

* Exchange rate : (Weighted average of foreign currencies)/U.S. $.
** Local currency units translated into U.S. $ at baseline exchange rates.
*** Exchange rate : U.S. $/(weighted average of non-US OECD currencies).

Model: EEC
Simulation A: Baseline Path

	1985	1986	1987	1988	1989	1990
JAPAN						
GNP(B.72Y)	-	-	-	-	-	-
CPI(72=100)	-	-	-	-	-	-
RS(%)	-	-	-	-	-	-
GDEF(%GNPV) *	-	-	-	-	-	-
EXCH(72=100) **	-	-	-	-	-	-
CAB(B.US$) ***	-	-	-	-	-	-
GERMANY						
GNP(B.72DM)	-	-	-	-	-	-
CPI(72=100)	-	-	-	-	-	-
RS(%)	-	-	-	-	-	-
GDEF(%GNPV) *	-	-	-	-	-	-
EXCH(72=100) **	-	-	-	-	-	-
CAB(B.US$) ***	-	-	-	-	-	-
FRANCE						
GNP(B.72F)	-	-	-	-	-	-
CPI(72=100)	-	-	-	-	-	-
GDEF(%GNPV) *	-	-	-	-	-	-
EXCH(72=100) **	-	-	-	-	-	-
CAB(B.US$) ***	-	-	-	-	-	-
UNITED KINGDOM						
GNP(B.72LB)	-	-	-	-	-	-
CPI(72=100)	-	-	-	-	-	-
GDEF(%GNPV) *	-	-	-	-	-	-
EXCH(72=100) **	-	-	-	-	-	-
CAB(B.US$) ***	-	-	-	-	-	-
ITALY						
GNP(B.72L)	-	-	-	-	-	-
CPI(72=100)	-	-	-	-	-	-
GDEF(%GNPV) *	-	-	-	-	-	-
EXCH(72=100) **	-	-	-	-	-	-
CAB(B.US$) ***	-	-	-	-	-	-
CANADA						
GNP(B.72C$)	-	-	-	-	-	-
CPI(72=100)	-	-	-	-	-	-
GDEF(%GNPV) *	-	-	-	-	-	-
EXCH(72=100) **	-	-	-	-	-	-
CAB(B.US$) ***	-	-	-	-	-	-
REST OF WORLD						
CAB(B.US$) ***	-	-	-	-	-	-

* Government deficit as a percentage of baseline nominal GNP.
** Exchange rate: Bilateral rate against U.S. $ ($/local currency).
*** Local currency units translated into U.S. $ at baseline exchange rates.

Model: EEC
Simulation B: Reduction in U.S. Government Purchases with Foreign Monetary Aggregates Unchanged from Baseline
(Deviation of Shock Path from Baseline Path)

	1985 Q1	1985 Q2	1985 Q3	1985 Q4	1985	1986	1987	1988	1989	1990
UNITED STATES										
GNPV(%)	-	-	-	-	-1.5	-1.7	-2.0	-2.1	-2.1	-2.1
GNP(%)	-	-	-	-	-1.3	-1.2	-1.0	-0.8	-0.6	-0.4
PGNP(%)	-	-	-	-	-0.2	-0.4	-1.0	-1.3	-1.5	-1.7
CPI(%)	-	-	-	-	-0.3	-0.6	-1.1	-1.6	-1.6	-1.8
WAGES(%)	-	-	-	-	-0.2	-0.9	-1.5	-2.1	-2.6	-3.0
UN(% PTS)	-	-	-	-	0.6	0.7	0.8	0.8	0.8	0.8
GNP(B.72$)	-	-	-	-	-22.1	-21.1	-18.4	-15.4	-12.0	-8.6
G(B.72$)	-	-	-	-	-18.7	-18.7	-18.8	-18.9	-18.7	-18.9
C(B.72$)	-	-	-	-	0.0	-4.9	-7.3	-8.6	-9.2	-10.4
IFP(B.72$)	-	-	-	-	-2.9	-3.9	-2.8	-2.6	-2.7	-1.5
II(B.72$)	-	-	-	-	-	-	-	-	-	-
XGS(B.72$)	-	-	-	-	0.4	1.0	1.3	1.3	1.6	1.7
MGS(B.72$)	-	-	-	-	-2.0	-2.7	-2.4	-2.1	-1.8	-1.6
M1(%)	-	-	-	-	0.0	0.0	0.0	0.0	0.0	0.0
RS(% PTS)	-	-	-	-	-1.0	-1.5	-1.7	-1.8	-1.9	-2.1
RL(% PTS)	-	-	-	-	-0.5	-1.0	-1.2	-1.3	-1.5	-1.8
GDEF(B$)	-	-	-	-	-32.3	-31.6	-39.2	-30.2	-26.0	-28.2
PXGS(%)	-	-	-	-	-	-	-	-	-	-
PMGS(%)	-	-	-	-	0.2	0.4	0.2	-0.1	-0.3	-0.4
EXCH(%) *	-	-	-	-	-0.4	-0.6	-0.5	-0.2	-0.4	-0.2
CAB(B$)	-	-	-	-	10.9	11.6	12.8	13.1	12.0	10.9
NON-US OECD										
GNPV(%) **	-	-	-	-	-0.2	-0.4	-0.6	-0.6	-0.7	-0.7
GNP(%) **	-	-	-	-	-0.2	-0.3	-0.3	-0.2	-0.2	-0.1
PGNP(%)	-	-	-	-	0.0	-0.1	-0.3	-0.4	-0.5	-0.6
CPI(%)	-	-	-	-	-0.1	-0.2	-0.4	-0.5	-0.6	-0.6
WAGES(%)	-	-	-	-	-	-	-	-	-	-
UN(% PTS)	-	-	-	-	-	-	-	-	-	-
C(%) **	-	-	-	-	-0.1	-0.2	-0.3	-0.2	-0.2	-0.1
IFP(%) **	-	-	-	-	-0.3	-0.4	-0.5	-0.4	-0.2	-0.1
RS(% PTS)	-	-	-	-	-	-	-	-	-	-
RL(% PTS)	-	-	-	-	-0.1	-0.3	-0.6	-0.7	-0.9	-1.2
GDEF (B.US$) **	-	-	-	-	0.9	2.0	2.3	3.6	5.2	6.1
PXGS(%)	-	-	-	-	-	-	-	-	-	-
PMGS(%)	-	-	-	-	-0.2	-0.5	-0.8	-0.8	-0.9	-0.8
EXCH(%) ***	-	-	-	-	0.5	0.9	0.8	0.5	0.5	0.4
CAB(B.US$) **	-	-	-	-	-4.8	-6.6	-7.9	-9.2	-8.1	-7.7

* Exchange rate : (Weighted average of foreign currencies)/U.S. $.
** Local currency units translated into U.S. $ at baseline exchange rates.
*** Exchange rate : U.S. $/(weighted average of non-US OECD currencies).

Model: EEC
Simulation B: Reduction in U.S. Government Purchases with Foreign Monetary Aggregates Unchanged from Baseline
(Deviation of Shock Path from Baseline Path)

	1985									
	Q1	Q2	Q3	Q4	1985	1986	1987	1988	1989	1990
JAPAN										
GNP(%)	-	-	-	-	-	-	-	-	-	-
CPI(%)	-	-	-	-	-	-	-	-	-	-
RS(% PTS)	-	-	-	-	-	-	-	-	-	-
GDEF(%GNPV) *	-	-	-	-	-	-	-	-	-	-
EXCH(%) **	-	-	-	-	-	-	-	-	-	-
CAB(B.US$) ***	-	-	-	-	-	-	-	-	-	-
GERMANY										
GNP(%)	-	-	-	-	-	-	-	-	-	-
CPI(%)	-	-	-	-	-	-	-	-	-	-
RS(% PTS)	-	-	-	-	-	-	-	-	-	-
GDEF(%GNPV) *	-	-	-	-	-	-	-	-	-	-
EXCH(%) **	-	-	-	-	-	-	-	-	-	-
CAB(B.US$) ***	-	-	-	-	-	-	-	-	-	-
FRANCE										
GNP(%)	-	-	-	-	-	-	-	-	-	-
CPI(%)	-	-	-	-	-	-	-	-	-	-
GDEF(%GNPV) *	-	-	-	-	-	-	-	-	-	-
EXCH(%) **	-	-	-	-	-	-	-	-	-	-
CAB(B.US$) ***	-	-	-	-	-	-	-	-	-	-
UNITED KINGDOM										
GNP(%)	-	-	-	-	-	-	-	-	-	-
CPI(%)	-	-	-	-	-	-	-	-	-	-
GDEF(%GNPV) *	-	-	-	-	-	-	-	-	-	-
EXCH(%) **	-	-	-	-	-	-	-	-	-	-
CAB(B.US$) ***	-	-	-	-	-	-	-	-	-	-
ITALY										
GNP(%)	-	-	-	-	-	-	-	-	-	-
CPI(%)	-	-	-	-	-	-	-	-	-	-
GDEF(%GNPV) *	-	-	-	-	-	-	-	-	-	-
EXCH(%) **	-	-	-	-	-	-	-	-	-	-
CAB(B.US$) ***	-	-	-	-	-	-	-	-	-	-
CANADA										
GNP(%)	-	-	-	-	-	-	-	-	-	-
CPI(%)	-	-	-	-	-	-	-	-	-	-
GDEF(%GNPV) *	-	-	-	-	-	-	-	-	-	-
EXCH(%) **	-	-	-	-	-	-	-	-	-	-
CAB(B.US$) ***	-	-	-	-	-	-	-	-	-	-
REST OF WORLD										
CAB(B.US$) ***	-	-	-	-	-	-	-	-	-	-

* Government deficit as a percentage of baseline nominal GNP.
** Exchange rate : Bilateral rate against U.S. $ ($/local currency).
*** Local currency units translated into U.S. $ at baseline exchange rates.

Model: EEC
Simulation C: Reduction in U.S. Government Purchases with Foreign Short-Term Interest Rates Unchanged from Baseline
(Deviation of Shock Path from Baseline Path)

	1985									
	Q1	Q2	Q3	Q4	1985	1986	1987	1988	1989	1990
UNITED STATES										
GNPV(%)	-	-	-	-	-1.5	-1.7	-2.0	-2.0	-2.0	-2.0
GNP(%)	-	-	-	-	-1.3	-1.2	-1.0	-0.8	-0.6	-0.4
PGNP(%)	-	-	-	-	-0.1	-0.5	-1.0	-1.2	-1.4	-1.5
CPI(%)	-	-	-	-	-0.3	-0.6	-1.2	-1.6	-1.7	-2.0
WAGES(%)	-	-	-	-	-0.2	-0.9	-1.4	-2.1	-2.7	-3.1
UN(% PTS)	-	-	-	-	0.6	0.7	0.7	0.8	0.8	0.8
GNP(B.72$)	-	-	-	-	-22.1	-21.1	-18.3	-15.3	-12.1	-8.6
G(B.72$)	-	-	-	-	-18.7	-18.7	-18.8	-18.6	-18.7	-18.9
C(B.72$)	-	-	-	-	-4.9	-7.2	-8.4	-7.5	-7.7	-7.9
IFP(B.72$)	-	-	-	-	-2.9	-3.9	-2.8	-2.3	-1.7	-1.2
II(B.72$)	-	-	-	-	-	-	-	-	-	-
XGS(B.72$)	-	-	-	-	0.4	1.2	1.6	1.7	2.0	2.2
MGS(B.72$)	-	-	-	-	-2.0	-2.8	-2.5	-2.4	-2.2	-2.0
M1(%)	-	-	-	-	0.0	0.0	0.0	0.0	0.0	0.0
RS(% PTS)	-	-	-	-	-1.0	-1.5	-1.7	-1.8	-2.0	-2.2
RL(% PTS)	-	-	-	-	-0.5	-1.0	-1.2	-1.0	-1.4	-1.7
GDEF(B$)	-	-	-	-	-32.1	-31.3	-29.9	-29.1	-27.5	-28.2
PXGS(%)	-	-	-	-	-	-	-	-	-	-
PMGS(%)	-	-	-	-	0.2	0.4	0.2	0.2	0.1	-0.2
EXCH(%) *	-	-	-	-	-0.5	-1.0	-1.1	-1.2	-1.3	-1.3
CAB(B$)	-	-	-	-	11.0	12.3	13.8	14.6	13.1	12.0
NON-US OECD										
GNPV(%) **	-	-	-	-	-0.2	-0.5	-0.7	-0.8	-0.9	-1.0
GNP(%) **	-	-	-	-	-0.2	-0.4	-0.5	-0.4	-0.4	-0.4
PGNP(%)	-	-	-	-	-0.0	-0.1	-0.2	-0.4	-0.5	-0.6
CPI(%)	-	-	-	-	-0.1	-0.2	-0.3	-0.5	-0.6	-0.8
WAGES(%)	-	-	-	-	-	-	-	-	-	-
UN(% PTS)	-	-	-	-	-	-	-	-	-	-
C(%) **	-	-	-	-	-0.1	-0.3	-0.4	-0.4	-0.3	-0.3
IFP(%) **	-	-	-	-	-0.3	-0.4	-0.6	-0.8	-0.6	-0.4
RS(% PTS)	-	-	-	-	-	-	-	-	-	-
RL(% PTS)	-	-	-	-	0.0	-0.0	-0.1	-0.1	-0.2	-0.3
GDEF (B.US$) **	-	-	-	-	0.4	1.8	3.0	4.4	6.2	8.0
PXGS(%)	-	-	-	-	-	-	-	-	-	-
PMGS(%)	-	-	-	-	-0.2	-0.6	-1.0	-1.2	-1.1	-1.0
EXCH(%) ***	-	-	-	-	0.4	1.2	1.1	1.0	1.0	0.9
CAB(B.US$) **	-	-	-	-	-4.9	-7.2	-8.9	-11.1	-9.6	-8.9

* Exchange rate : (Weighted average of foreign currencies)/U.S. $.
** Local currency units translated into U.S. $ at baseline exchange rates.
*** Exchange rate : U.S. $/(weighted average of non-US OECD currencies).

Model: EEC
Simulation C: Reduction in U.S. Government Purchases with Foreign Short-Term Interest Rates Unchanged from Baseline
(Deviation of Shock Path from Baseline Path)

	1985									
	Q1	Q2	Q3	Q4	1985	1986	1987	1988	1989	1990
JAPAN										
GNP(%)	-	-	-	-	-	-	-	-	-	-
CPI(%)	-	-	-	-	-	-	-	-	-	-
RS(% PTS)	-	-	-	-	-	-	-	-	-	-
GDEF(%GNPV) *	-	-	-	-	-	-	-	-	-	-
EXCH(%) **	-	-	-	-	-	-	-	-	-	-
CAB(B.US$) ***	-	-	-	-	-	-	-	-	-	-
GERMANY										
GNP(%)	-	-	-	-	-	-	-	-	-	-
CPI(%)	-	-	-	-	-	-	-	-	-	-
RS(% PTS)	-	-	-	-	-	-	-	-	-	-
GDEF(%GNPV) *	-	-	-	-	-	-	-	-	-	-
EXCH(%) **	-	-	-	-	-	-	-	-	-	-
CAB(B.US$) ***	-	-	-	-	-	-	-	-	-	-
FRANCE										
GNP(%)	-	-	-	-	-	-	-	-	-	-
CPI(%)	-	-	-	-	-	-	-	-	-	-
GDEF(%GNPV) *	-	-	-	-	-	-	-	-	-	-
EXCH(%) **	-	-	-	-	-	-	-	-	-	-
CAB(B.US$) ***	-	-	-	-	-	-	-	-	-	-
UNITED KINGDOM										
GNP(%)	-	-	-	-	-	-	-	-	-	-
CPI(%)	-	-	-	-	-	-	-	-	-	-
GDEF(%GNPV) *	-	-	-	-	-	-	-	-	-	-
EXCH(%) **	-	-	-	-	-	-	-	-	-	-
CAB(B.US$) ***	-	-	-	-	-	-	-	-	-	-
ITALY										
GNP(%)	-	-	-	-	-	-	-	-	-	-
CPI(%)	-	-	-	-	-	-	-	-	-	-
GDEF(%GNPV) *	-	-	-	-	-	-	-	-	-	-
EXCH(%) **	-	-	-	-	-	-	-	-	-	-
CAB(B.US$) ***	-	-	-	-	-	-	-	-	-	-
CANADA										
GNP(%)	-	-	-	-	-	-	-	-	-	-
CPI(%)	-	-	-	-	-	-	-	-	-	-
GDEF(%GNPV) *	-	-	-	-	-	-	-	-	-	-
EXCH(%) **	-	-	-	-	-	-	-	-	-	-
CAB(B.US$) ***	-	-	-	-	-	-	-	-	-	-
REST OF WORLD										
CAB(B.US$) ***	-	-	-	-	-	-	-	-	-	-

* Government deficit as a percentage of baseline nominal GNP.
** Exchange rate : Bilateral rate against U.S. $ ($/local currency).
*** Local currency units translated into U.S. $ at baseline exchange rates.

Model: EEC
Simulation D: U.S. Monetary Expansion with foreign Monetary Aggregates Unchanged from Baseline
(Deviation of Shock Path from Baseline Path)

	1985									
	Q1	Q2	Q3	Q4	1985	1986	1987	1988	1989	1990
UNITED STATES										
GNPV(%)	-	-	-	-	0.9	2.1	2.5	2.6	2.8	2.8
GNP(%)	-	-	-	-	0.6	1.0	1.0	1.0	0.9	0.8
PGNP(%)	-	-	-	-	0.3	1.1	1.4	1.6	1.9	1.9
CPI(%)	-	-	-	-	0.3	0.8	1.2	1.6	2.0	2.3
WAGES(%)	-	-	-	-	0.2	0.9	1.4	1.8	2.6	3.4
UN(% PTS)	-	-	-	-	-0.4	-0.5	-0.5	-0.6	-0.6	-0.5
GNP(B.72$)	-	-	-	-	9.9	17.3	17.7	17.5	17.0	15.8
G(B.72$)	-	-	-	-	0.0	0.0	0.0	0.0	0.0	0.0
C(B.72$)	-	-	-	-	5.4	9.9	10.0	10.9	9.7	9.2
IFP(B.72$)	-	-	-	-	2.9	6.2	9.9	10.9	9.5	8.5
II(B.72$)	-	-	-	-	-	-	-	-	-	-
XGS(B.72$)	-	-	-	-	0.0	0.3	1.0	0.7	0.5	0.4
MGS(B.72$)	-	-	-	-	1.1	3.5	4.3	5.2	4.6	4.2
M1(%)	-	-	-	-	2.0	4.0	4.0	4.0	4.0	4.0
RS(% PTS)	-	-	-	-	-1.2	-2.4	-2.3	-2.1	-1.6	-1.5
RL(% PTS)	-	-	-	-	-0.4	-1.2	-1.6	-1.8	-1.3	-1.2
GDEF(B$)	-	-	-	-	-4.2	-21.8	-34.2	-47.6	-56.7	-66.2
PXGS(%)	-	-	-	-	-	-	-	-	-	-
PMGS(%)	-	-	-	-	0.8	1.1	1.3	1.5	1.5	1.5
EXCH(%) *	-	-	-	-	-1.9	-4.0	-4.6	-4.5	-4.3	-4.2
CAB(B$)	-	-	-	-	-1.5	-2.8	-3.7	-5.7	-8.9	-9.5
NON-US OECD										
GNPV(%) **	-	-	-	-	0.1	-0.1	-0.1	-0.2	-0.3	-0.5
GNP(%) **	-	-	-	-	0.0	0.2	0.4	0.4	0.3	0.2
PGNP(%)	-	-	-	-	0.0	-0.3	-0.5	-0.6	-0.6	-0.7
CPI(%)	-	-	-	-	-0.1	-0.4	-0.6	-0.7	-0.7	-0.6
WAGES(%)	-	-	-	-	-	-	-	-	-	-
UN(% PTS)	-	-	-	-	-	-	-	-	-	-
C(%) **	-	-	-	-	0.1	0.2	0.2	0.2	0.2	0.1
IFP(%) **	-	-	-	-	0.1	0.3	0.6	0.8	0.8	0.6
RS(% PTS)	-	-	-	-	-	-	-	-	-	-
RL(% PTS)	-	-	-	-	-0.1	-0.5	-0.8	-0.9	-0.9	-1.1
GDEF (B.US$) **	-	-	-	-	-1.9	-3.2	-4.3	-6.0	-7.2	-9.0
PXGS(%)	-	-	-	-	-	-	-	-	-	-
PMGS(%)	-	-	-	-	-0.8	-2.7	-4.8	-5.5	-5.6	-5.1
EXCH(%) ***	-	-	-	-	2.0	4.4	5.3	5.8	5.6	4.7
CAB(B.US$) **	-	-	-	-	0.6	1.2	1.9	2.6	4.9	5.6

* Exchange rate : (Weighted average of foreign currencies)/U.S. $.
** Local currency units translated into U.S. $ at baseline exchange rates.
*** Exchange rate : U.S. $/(weighted average of non-US OECD currencies).

Model: EEC
Simulation D: U.S. Monetary Expansion with Foreign Monetary Aggregates Unchanged from Baseline
(Deviation of Shock Path from Baseline Path)

	1985									
	Q1	Q2	Q3	Q4	1985	1986	1987	1988	1989	1990
JAPAN										
GNP(%)	-	-	-	-	-	-	-	-	-	-
CPI(%)	-	-	-	-	-	-	-	-	-	-
RS(% PTS)	-	-	-	-	-	-	-	-	-	-
GDEF(%GNPV) *	-	-	-	-	-	-	-	-	-	-
EXCH(%) **	-	-	-	-	-	-	-	-	-	-
CAB(B.US$) ***	-	-	-	-	-	-	-	-	-	-
GERMANY										
GNP(%)	-	-	-	-	-	-	-	-	-	-
CPI(%)	-	-	-	-	-	-	-	-	-	-
RS(% PTS)	-	-	-	-	-	-	-	-	-	-
GDEF(%GNPV) *	-	-	-	-	-	-	-	-	-	-
EXCH(%) **	-	-	-	-	-	-	-	-	-	-
CAB(B.US$) ***	-	-	-	-	-	-	-	-	-	-
FRANCE										
GNP(%)	-	-	-	-	-	-	-	-	-	-
CPI(%)	-	-	-	-	-	-	-	-	-	-
GDEF(%GNPV) *	-	-	-	-	-	-	-	-	-	-
EXCH(%) **	-	-	-	-	-	-	-	-	-	-
CAB(B.US$) ***	-	-	-	-	-	-	-	-	-	-
UNITED KINGDOM										
GNP(%)	-	-	-	-	-	-	-	-	-	-
CPI(%)	-	-	-	-	-	-	-	-	-	-
GDEF(%GNPV) *	-	-	-	-	-	-	-	-	-	-
EXCH(%) **	-	-	-	-	-	-	-	-	-	-
CAB(B.US$) ***	-	-	-	-	-	-	-	-	-	-
ITALY										
GNP(%)	-	-	-	-	-	-	-	-	-	-
CPI(%)	-	-	-	-	-	-	-	-	-	-
GDEF(%GNPV) *	-	-	-	-	-	-	-	-	-	-
EXCH(%) **	-	-	-	-	-	-	-	-	-	-
CAB(B.US$) ***	-	-	-	-	-	-	-	-	-	-
CANADA										
GNP(%)	-	-	-	-	-	-	-	-	-	-
CPI(%)	-	-	-	-	-	-	-	-	-	-
GDEF(%GNPV) *	-	-	-	-	-	-	-	-	-	-
EXCH(%) **	-	-	-	-	-	-	-	-	-	-
CAB(B.US$) ***	-	-	-	-	-	-	-	-	-	-
REST OF WORLD										
CAB(B.US$) ***	-	-	-	-	-	-	-	-	-	-

* Government deficit as a percentage of baseline nominal GNP.
** Exchange rate : Bilateral rate against U.S. $ ($/local currency).
*** Local currency units translated into U.S. $ at baseline exchange rates.

Model: EEC
Simulation E: U.S. Monetary Expansion with Foreign Short-Term Interest Rates Unchanged from Baseline
(Deviation of Shock Path from Baseline Path)

	1985									
	Q1	Q2	Q3	Q4	1985	1986	1987	1988	1989	1990
UNITED STATES										
GNPV(%)	-	-	-	-	0.9	1.5	2.2	2.5	2.6	2.6
GNP(%)	-	-	-	-	0.7	0.9	1.2	1.1	0.9	0.7
PGNP(%)	-	-	-	-	0.2	0.6	1.0	1.4	1.7	1.9
CPI(%)	-	-	-	-	0.3	0.7	1.1	1.5	1.9	2.1
WAGES(%)	-	-	-	-	0.2	0.8	1.4	1.7	2.5	3.3
UN(% PTS)	-	-	-	-	-0.4	-0.4	-0.5	-0.5	-0.6	-0.5
GNP(B.72$)	-	-	-	-	11.6	15.3	21.0	19.9	16.8	13.4
G(B.72$)	-	-	-	-	0.0	0.0	0.0	0.0	0.0	0.0
C(B.72$)	-	-	-	-	6.3	10.8	10.0	10.3	9.4	8.5
IFP(B.72$)	-	-	-	-	3.0	7.0	10.8	11.1	9.0	8.3
II(B.72$)	-	-	-	-	-	-	-	-	-	-
XGS(B.72$)	-	-	-	-	0.0	0.3	0.8	0.5	0.4	0.2
MGS(B.72$)	-	-	-	-	1.0	3.4	4.2	4.9	4.3	4.0
M1(%)	-	-	-	-	2.0	4.0	4.0	4.0	4.0	4.0
RS(% PTS)	-	-	-	-	-1.2	-2.4	-2.3	-2.3	-1.7	-1.5
RL(% PTS)	-	-	-	-	-0.4	-1.2	-1.6	-1.8	-1.3	-1.3
GDEF(B$)	-	-	-	-	-4.0	-22.1	-35.2	-46.9	-56.3	-66.1
PXGS(%)	-	-	-	-	-	-	-	-	-	-
PMGS(%)	-	-	-	-	0.8	1.2	1.5	1.8	1.8	2.0
EXCH(%) *	-	-	-	-	-1.9	-4.4	-5.5	-5.0	-4.8	-4.5
CAB(B$)	-	-	-	-	-1.0	-2.5	-3.3	-4.5	-7.0	-8.5
NON-US OECD										
GNPV(%) **	-	-	-	-	0.1	-0.2	-0.3	-0.3	-0.5	-0.6
GNP(%) **	-	-	-	-	0.1	0.1	0.2	0.2	0.1	-0.0
PGNP(%)	-	-	-	-	-0.0	-0.3	-0.5	-0.5	-0.6	-0.6
CPI(%)	-	-	-	-	-0.1	-0.3	-0.5	-0.6	-0.6	-0.5
WAGES(%)	-	-	-	-	-	-	-	-	-	-
UN(% PTS)	-	-	-	-	-	-	-	-	-	-
C(%) **	-	-	-	-	0.1	0.2	0.1	0.1	0.1	0.0
IFP(%) **	-	-	-	-	0.1	0.2	0.3	0.2	0.1	0.1
RS(% PTS)	-	-	-	-	-	-	-	-	-	-
RL(% PTS)	-	-	-	-	0.0	-0.0	-0.1	-0.1	-0.2	-0.3
GDEF (B.US$) **	-	-	-	-	-0.2	-0.9	-2.0	-2.4	-2.6	-3.0
PXGS(%)	-	-	-	-	-	-	-	-	-	-
PMGS(%)	-	-	-	-	-0.9	-3.1	-5.4	-5.8	-6.3	-5.5
EXCH(%) ***	-	-	-	-	2.2	5.4	7.2	6.7	6.6	5.8
CAB(B.US$) **	-	-	-	-	0.5	1.1	1.3	2.1	3.7	4.5

* Exchange rate : (Weighted average of foreign currencies)/U.S. $.
** Local currency units translated into U.S. $ at baseline exchange rates.
*** Exchange rate : U.S. $/(weighted average of non-US OECD currencies).

Model: EEC
Simulation E: U.S. Monetary Expansion with Foreign Short-Term Interest Rates Unchanged from Baseline
(Deviation of Shock Path from Baseline Path)

	1985									
	Q1	Q2	Q3	Q4	1985	1986	1987	1988	1989	1990
JAPAN										
GNP(%)	-	-	-	-	-	-	-	-	-	-
CPI(%)	-	-	-	-	-	-	-	-	-	-
RS(% PTS)	-	-	-	-	-	-	-	-	-	-
GDEF(%GNPV) *	-	-	-	-	-	-	-	-	-	-
EXCH(%) **	-	-	-	-	-	-	-	-	-	-
CAB(B.US$) ***	-	-	-	-	-	-	-	-	-	-
GERMANY										
GNP(%)	-	-	-	-	-	-	-	-	-	-
CPI(%)	-	-	-	-	-	-	-	-	-	-
RS(% PTS)	-	-	-	-	-	-	-	-	-	-
GDEF(%GNPV) *	-	-	-	-	-	-	-	-	-	-
EXCH(%) **	-	-	-	-	-	-	-	-	-	-
CAB(B.US$) ***	-	-	-	-	-	-	-	-	-	-
FRANCE										
GNP(%)	-	-	-	-	-	-	-	-	-	-
CPI(%)	-	-	-	-	-	-	-	-	-	-
GDEF(%GNPV) *	-	-	-	-	-	-	-	-	-	-
EXCH(%) **	-	-	-	-	-	-	-	-	-	-
CAB(B.US$) ***	-	-	-	-	-	-	-	-	-	-
UNITED KINGDOM										
GNP(%)	-	-	-	-	-	-	-	-	-	-
CPI(%)	-	-	-	-	-	-	-	-	-	-
GDEF(%GNPV) *	-	-	-	-	-	-	-	-	-	-
EXCH(%) **	-	-	-	-	-	-	-	-	-	-
CAB(B.US$) ***	-	-	-	-	-	-	-	-	-	-
ITALY										
GNP(%)	-	-	-	-	-	-	-	-	-	-
CPI(%)	-	-	-	-	-	-	-	-	-	-
GDEF(%GNPV) *	-	-	-	-	-	-	-	-	-	-
EXCH(%) **	-	-	-	-	-	-	-	-	-	-
CAB(B.US$) ***	-	-	-	-	-	-	-	-	-	-
CANADA										
GNP(%)	-	-	-	-	-	-	-	-	-	-
CPI(%)	-	-	-	-	-	-	-	-	-	-
GDEF(%GNPV) *	-	-	-	-	-	-	-	-	-	-
EXCH(%) **	-	-	-	-	-	-	-	-	-	-
CAB(B.US$) ***	-	-	-	-	-	-	-	-	-	-
REST OF WORLD										
CAB(B.US$) ***	-	-	-	-	-	-	-	-	-	-

* Government deficit as a percentage of baseline nominal GNP.
** Exchange rate : Bilateral rate against U.S. $ ($/local currency).
*** Local currency units translated into U.S. $ at baseline exchange rates.

Model: EEC
Simulation F: Nonpolicy Exogenous Depreciation of the Dollar
(Deviation of Shock Path from Baseline Path)

	1985 Q1	1985 Q2	1985 Q3	1985 Q4	1985	1986	1987	1988	1989	1990
UNITED STATES										
GNPV(%)	-	-	-	-	0.5	1.1	1.9	2.5	3.5	4.5
GNP(%)	-	-	-	-	0.2	0.4	0.7	0.7	0.6	0.5
PGNP(%)	-	-	-	-	0.3	0.7	1.2	1.8	2.9	4.0
CPI(%)	-	-	-	-	0.5	1.1	1.6	2.2	3.3	4.3
WAGES(%)	-	-	-	-	0.6	1.3	2.0	2.3	3.5	4.6
UN(% PTS)	-	-	-	-	0.0	0.1	-0.2	-0.4	-0.5	-0.6
GNP(B.72$)	-	-	-	-	3.3	6.8	12.3	12.6	11.2	9.6
G(B.72$)	-	-	-	-	0.0	0.0	0.0	0.0	0.0	0.0
C(B.72$)	-	-	-	-	-1.1	-2.7	-1.6	2.2	1.3	0.5
IFP(B.72$)	-	-	-	-	-0.3	0.0	0.6	0.9	1.6	1.1
II(B.72$)	-	-	-	-	-	-	-	-	-	-
XGS(B.72$)	-	-	-	-	2.2	8.2	15.3	18.0	21.1	20.8
MGS(B.72$)	-	-	-	-	-0.0	-0.2	-0.8	-2.6	-3.6	-3.6
M1(%)	-	-	-	-	0.0	0.0	0.0	0.0	0.0	0.0
RS(% PTS)	-	-	-	-	0.2	0.4	0.9	1.3	1.6	2.2
RL(% PTS)	-	-	-	-	0.0	0.2	0.5	0.9	1.2	1.5
GDEF(B$)	-	-	-	-	0.0	1.2	-4.8	-5.2	-4.9	-4.8
PXGS(%)	-	-	-	-	-	-	-	-	-	-
PMGS(%)	-	-	-	-	5.0	9.7	14.9	21.0	22.1	21.4
EXCH(%) *	-	-	-	-	-10.0	-18.1	-24.8	-24.8	-24.8	-24.8
CAB(B$)	-	-	-	-	3.8	14.1	30.5	42.9	36.2	34.9
NON-US OECD										
GNPV(%) **	-	-	-	-	-0.6	-1.6	-2.8	-3.7	-4.0	-4.0
GNP(%) **	-	-	-	-	-0.2	-0.6	-1.0	-1.2	-1.5	-1.4
PGNP(%)	-	-	-	-	-0.4	-1.0	-1.8	-2.6	-2.5	-2.6
CPI(%)	-	-	-	-	-0.5	-1.2	-2.0	-2.5	-3.0	-3.8
WAGES(%)	-	-	-	-	-	-	-	-	-	-
UN(% PTS)	-	-	-	-	-	-	-	-	-	-
C(%) **	-	-	-	-	0.3	0.2	0.2	0.0	-0.3	-0.5
IFP(%) **	-	-	-	-	-0.1	-0.7	-1.8	-1.9	-2.1	-2.5
RS(% PTS)	-	-	-	-	-	-	-	-	-	-
RL(% PTS)	-	-	-	-	0.1	-0.1	-0.4	-1.0	-1.2	-1.3
GDEF (B.US$) **	-	-	-	-	-1.7	-0.1	4.1	7.3	8.1	9.7
PXGS(%)	-	-	-	-	-	-	-	-	-	-
PMGS(%)	-	-	-	-	-5.0	-12.9	-18.7	-19.8	-21.7	-22.8
EXCH(%) ***	-	-	-	-	9.9	20.0	30.0	30.0	30.0	30.0
CAB(B.US$) **	-	-	-	-	-2.7	-13.2	-39.8	-59.7	-53.1	-52.9

* Exchange rate : (Weighted average of foreign currencies)/U.S. $.
** Local currency units translated into U.S. $ at baseline exchange rates.
*** Exchange rate : U.S. $/(weighted average of non-US OECD currencies).

Model: EEC
Simulation F: Nonpolicy Exogenous Depreciation of the Dollar
(Deviation of Shock Path from Baseline Path)

	1985									
	Q1	Q2	Q3	Q4	1985	1986	1987	1988	1989	1990
JAPAN										
GNP(%)	-	-	-	-	-	-	-	-	-	-
CPI(%)	-	-	-	-	-	-	-	-	-	-
RS(% PTS)	-	-	-	-	-	-	-	-	-	-
GDEF(%GNPV) *	-	-	-	-	-	-	-	-	-	-
EXCH(%) **	-	-	-	-	-	-	-	-	-	-
CAB(B.US$) ***	-	-	-	-	-	-	-	-	-	-
GERMANY										
GNP(%)	-	-	-	-	-	-	-	-	-	-
CPI(%)	-	-	-	-	-	-	-	-	-	-
RS(% PTS)	-	-	-	-	-	-	-	-	-	-
GDEF(%GNPV) *	-	-	-	-	-	-	-	-	-	-
EXCH(%) **	-	-	-	-	-	-	-	-	-	-
CAB(B.US$) ***	-	-	-	-	-	-	-	-	-	-
FRANCE										
GNP(%)	-	-	-	-	-	-	-	-	-	-
CPI(%)	-	-	-	-	-	-	-	-	-	-
GDEF(%GNPV) *	-	-	-	-	-	-	-	-	-	-
EXCH(%) **	-	-	-	-	-	-	-	-	-	-
CAB(B.US$) ***	-	-	-	-	-	-	-	-	-	-
UNITED KINGDOM										
GNP(%)	-	-	-	-	-	-	-	-	-	-
CPI(%)	-	-	-	-	-	-	-	-	-	-
GDEF(%GNPV) *	-	-	-	-	-	-	-	-	-	-
EXCH(%) **	-	-	-	-	-	-	-	-	-	-
CAB(B.US$) ***	-	-	-	-	-	-	-	-	-	-
ITALY										
GNP(%)	-	-	-	-	-	-	-	-	-	-
CPI(%)	-	-	-	-	-	-	-	-	-	-
GDEF(%GNPV) *	-	-	-	-	-	-	-	-	-	-
EXCH(%) **	-	-	-	-	-	-	-	-	-	-
CAB(B.US$) ***	-	-	-	-	-	-	-	-	-	-
CANADA										
GNP(%)	-	-	-	-	-	-	-	-	-	-
CPI(%)	-	-	-	-	-	-	-	-	-	-
GDEF(%GNPV) *	-	-	-	-	-	-	-	-	-	-
EXCH(%) **	-	-	-	-	-	-	-	-	-	-
CAB(B.US$) ***	-	-	-	-	-	-	-	-	-	-
REST OF WORLD										
CAB(B.US$) ***	-	-	-	-	-	-	-	-	-	-

* Government deficit as a percentage of baseline nominal GNP.
** Exchange rate : Bilateral rate against U.S. $ ($/local currency).
*** Local currency units translated into U.S. $ at baseline exchange rates.

Model: EEC

Simulation G: Increase in Government Purchases in Non-U.S. OECD Countries with U.S. Policies Unchanged from Baseline

(Deviation of Shock Path from Baseline Path)

	1985									
	Q1	Q2	Q3	Q4	1985	1986	1987	1988	1989	1990
UNITED STATES										
GNPV(%)	-	-	-	-	0.1	0.2	0.3	0.3	0.2	0.3
GNP(%)	-	-	-	-	0.1	0.2	0.2	0.2	0.2	0.1
PGNP(%)	-	-	-	-	0.0	0.0	0.1	0.1	0.0	0.1
CPI(%)	-	-	-	-	0.0	0.1	0.1	0.1	0.2	0.2
WAGES(%)	-	-	-	-	0.0	0.1	0.2	0.2	0.3	0.3
UN(% PTS)	-	-	-	-	0.0	-0.1	-0.2	-0.2	-0.3	-0.3
GNP(B.72$)	-	-	-	-	1.7	3.4	4.0	4.5	3.2	2.7
G(B.72$)	-	-	-	-	0.0	0.0	0.0	0.0	0.0	0.0
C(B.72$)	-	-	-	-	0.1	0.9	1.2	1.6	1.5	1.0
IFP(B.72$)	-	-	-	-	0.1	0.5	0.8	1.0	0.7	0.5
II(B.72$)	-	-	-	-	-	-	-	-	-	-
XGS(B.72$)	-	-	-	-	1.2	1.6	1.8	1.7	1.6	1.3
MGS(B.72$)	-	-	-	-	0.2	0.5	0.6	0.6	0.4	0.4
M1(%)	-	-	-	-	0.0	0.0	0.0	0.0	0.0	0.0
RS(% PTS)	-	-	-	-	0.0	0.0	0.1	0.2	0.1	0.1
RL(% PTS)	-	-	-	-	0.0	0.0	0.0	0.1	0.1	0.1
GDEF(B$)	-	-	-	-	-1.2	-2.1	-4.0	-5.2	-7.6	-7.4
PXGS(%)	-	-	-	-	-	-	-	-	-	-
PMGS(%)	-	-	-	-	0.1	0.3	0.3	0.4	0.4	0.5
EXCH(%) *	-	-	-	-	0.5	0.8	0.9	0.9	1.0	0.9
CAB(B$)	-	-	-	-	1.9	3.0	3.7	3.7	3.7	3.4
NON-US OECD										
GNPV(%) **	-	-	-	-	1.3	1.7	2.2	2.2	2.4	2.5
GNP(%) **	-	-	-	-	1.1	1.3	1.2	1.0	1.0	0.8
PGNP(%)	-	-	-	-	0.2	0.4	0.9	1.1	1.4	1.7
CPI(%)	-	-	-	-	0.4	0.8	1.3	1.5	1.8	2.2
WAGES(%)	-	-	-	-	-	-	-	-	-	-
UN(% PTS)	-	-	-	-	-	-	-	-	-	-
C(%) **	-	-	-	-	0.3	0.4	0.4	0.4	0.3	0.3
IFP(%) **	-	-	-	-	1.0	1.9	1.5	1.0	0.3	-0.1
RS(% PTS)	-	-	-	-	-	-	-	-	-	-
RL(% PTS)	-	-	-	-	0.3	0.4	0.5	1.1	1.6	1.6
GDEF (B.US$) **	-	-	-	-	17.0	15.6	14.9	14.8	17.6	19.4
PXGS(%)	-	-	-	-	-	-	-	-	-	-
PMGS(%)	-	-	-	-	0.4	0.4	0.5	0.6	0.8	1.0
EXCH(%) ***	-	-	-	-	-0.5	-0.6	-0.8	-0.9	-1.0	-1.2
CAB(B.US$) **	-	-	-	-	-5.1	-9.3	-10.6	-11.2	-10.4	-9.8

* Exchange rate : (Weighted average of foreign currencies)/U.S. $.

** Local currency units translated into U.S. $ at baseline exchange rates.

*** Exchange rate : U.S. $/(weighted average of non-US OECD currencies).

Model: EEC
Simulation G: Increase in Government Purchases in Non-U.S. OECD Countries with U.S. Policies Unchanged from Baseline
(Deviation of Shock Path from Baseline Path)

	1985									
	Q1	Q2	Q3	Q4	1985	1986	1987	1988	1989	1990
JAPAN										
GNP(%)	-	-	-	-	-	-	-	-	-	-
CPI(%)	-	-	-	-	-	-	-	-	-	-
RS(% PTS)	-	-	-	-	-	-	-	-	-	-
GDEF(%GNPV) *	-	-	-	-	-	-	-	-	-	-
EXCH(%) **	-	-	-	-	-	-	-	-	-	-
CAB(B.US$) ***	-	-	-	-	-	-	-	-	-	-
GERMANY										
GNP(%)	-	-	-	-	-	-	-	-	-	-
CPI(%)	-	-	-	-	-	-	-	-	-	-
RS(% PTS)	-	-	-	-	-	-	-	-	-	-
GDEF(%GNPV) *	-	-	-	-	-	-	-	-	-	-
EXCH(%) **	-	-	-	-	-	-	-	-	-	-
CAB(B.US$) ***	-	-	-	-	-	-	-	-	-	-
FRANCE										
GNP(%)	-	-	-	-	-	-	-	-	-	-
CPI(%)	-	-	-	-	-	-	-	-	-	-
GDEF(%GNPV) *	-	-	-	-	-	-	-	-	-	-
EXCH(%) **	-	-	-	-	-	-	-	-	-	-
CAB(B.US$) ***	-	-	-	-	-	-	-	-	-	-
UNITED KINGDOM										
GNP(%)	-	-	-	-	-	-	-	-	-	-
CPI(%)	-	-	-	-	-	-	-	-	-	-
GDEF(%GNPV) *	-	-	-	-	-	-	-	-	-	-
EXCH(%) **	-	-	-	-	-	-	-	-	-	-
CAB(B.US$) ***	-	-	-	-	-	-	-	-	-	-
ITALY										
GNP(%)	-	-	-	-	-	-	-	-	-	-
CPI(%)	-	-	-	-	-	-	-	-	-	-
GDEF(%GNPV) *	-	-	-	-	-	-	-	-	-	-
EXCH(%) **	-	-	-	-	-	-	-	-	-	-
CAB(B.US$) ***	-	-	-	-	-	-	-	-	-	-
CANADA										
GNP(%)	-	-	-	-	-	-	-	-	-	-
CPI(%)	-	-	-	-	-	-	-	-	-	-
GDEF(%GNPV) *	-	-	-	-	-	-	-	-	-	-
EXCH(%) **	-	-	-	-	-	-	-	-	-	-
CAB(B.US$) ***	-	-	-	-	-	-	-	-	-	-
REST OF WORLD										
CAB(B.US$) ***	-	-	-	-	-	-	-	-	-	-

* Government deficit as a percentage of baseline nominal GNP.
** Exchange rate : Bilateral rate against U.S. $ ($/local currency).
*** Local currency units translated into U.S. $ at baseline exchange rates.

Model: EEC
Simulation H: Monetary Expansion in Non-U.S. OECD Countries
with U.S. Policies Unchanged from Baseline
(Deviation of Shock Path from Baseline Path)

	1985									
	Q1	Q2	Q3	Q4	1985	1986	1987	1988	1989	1990
UNITED STATES										
GNPV(%)	-	-	-	-	0.0	0.1	0.3	0.3	0.4	0.5
GNP(%)	-	-	-	-	0.0	0.1	0.2	0.3	0.2	0.2
PGNP(%)	-	-	-	-	0.0	0.0	0.1	0.0	0.2	0.3
CPI(%)	-	-	-	-	0.2	0.1	0.1	0.2	0.3	0.3
WAGES(%)	-	-	-	-	0.2	0.1	0.1	0.2	0.3	0.4
UN(% PTS)	-	-	-	-	0.0	0.0	-0.1	-0.2	-0.3	-0.3
GNP(B.72$)	-	-	-	-	0.3	1.5	3.3	5.8	4.7	3.7
G(B.72$)	-	-	-	-	0.0	0.0	0.0	0.0	0.0	0.0
C(B.72$)	-	-	-	-	0.2	0.4	1.0	1.6	1.8	1.6
IFP(B.72$)	-	-	-	-	0.1	0.3	0.5	1.2	1.1	0.8
II(B.72$)	-	-	-	-	-	-	-	-	-	-
XGS(B.72$)	-	-	-	-	0.4	1.6	2.1	2.5	2.4	2.0
MGS(B.72$)	-	-	-	-	0.0	0.1	0.5	0.7	0.6	0.4
M1(%)	-	-	-	-	0.0	0.0	0.0	0.0	0.0	0.0
RS(% PTS)	-	-	-	-	0.0	0.0	0.0	0.1	0.1	0.1
RL(% PTS)	-	-	-	-	0.0	0.0	0.0	0.0	0.1	0.1
GDEF(B$)	-	-	-	-	-1.0	-1.9	-2.5	-4.2	-5.6	-7.3
PXGS(%)	-	-	-	-	-	-	-	-	-	-
PMGS(%)	-	-	-	-	0.2	0.5	0.7	0.6	0.5	0.5
EXCH(%) *	-	-	-	-	0.4	1.0	1.5	1.1	1.0	0.0
CAB(B$)	-	-	-	-	0.5	1.9	3.9	4.1	3.8	3.6
NON-US OECD										
GNPV(%) **	-	-	-	-	0.9	1.8	2.6	3.1	3.2	3.4
GNP(%) **	-	-	-	-	0.4	0.8	1.1	1.1	1.0	0.8
PGNP(%)	-	-	-	-	0.5	1.0	1.5	2.0	2.2	2.5
CPI(%)	-	-	-	-	0.6	1.0	1.8	2.4	2.8	3.0
WAGES(%)	-	-	-	-	-	-	-	-	-	-
UN(% PTS)	-	-	-	-	-	-	-	-	-	-
C(%) **	-	-	-	-	0.3	0.9	1.0	1.0	0.9	0.8
IFP(%) **	-	-	-	-	0.6	2.2	3.6	3.5	2.9	2.0
RS(% PTS)	-	-	-	-	-	-	-	-	-	-
RL(% PTS)	-	-	-	-	-0.4	-1.0	-1.5	-1.6	-1.8	-2.1
GDEF (B.US$) **	-	-	-	-	-1.9	-8.1	-9.0	-14.4	-20.1	-23.0
PXGS(%)	-	-	-	-	-	-	-	-	-	-
PMGS(%)	-	-	-	-	0.1	1.2	1.9	1.5	1.5	1.3
EXCH(%) ***	-	-	-	-	-0.7	-2.3	-3.8	-2.6	-2.4	-2.0
CAB(B.US$) **	-	-	-	-	-1.9	-5.2	-11.1	-11.5	-11.0	-9.9

* Exchange rate : (Weighted average of foreign currencies)/U.S. $.
** Local currency units translated into U.S. $ at baseline exchange rates.
*** Exchange rate : U.S. $/(weighted average of non-US OECD currencies).

Model: EEC
Simulation H: Monetary Expansion in Non-U.S. OECD Countries
with U.S. Policies Unchanged from Baseline
(Deviation of Shock Path from Baseline Path)

	1985									
	Q1	Q2	Q3	Q4	1985	1986	1987	1988	1989	1990
JAPAN										
GNP(%)	-	-	-	-	-	-	-	-	-	-
CPI(%)	-	-	-	-	-	-	-	-	-	-
RS(% PTS)	-	-	-	-	-	-	-	-	-	-
GDEF(%GNPV) *	-	-	-	-	-	-	-	-	-	-
EXCH(%) **	-	-	-	-	-	-	-	-	-	-
CAB(B.US$) ***	-	-	-	-	-	-	-	-	-	-
GERMANY										
GNP(%)	-	-	-	-	-	-	-	-	-	-
CPI(%)	-	-	-	-	-	-	-	-	-	-
RS(% PTS)	-	-	-	-	-	-	-	-	-	-
GDEF(%GNPV) *	-	-	-	-	-	-	-	-	-	-
EXCH(%) **	-	-	-	-	-	-	-	-	-	-
CAB(B.US$) ***	-	-	-	-	-	-	-	-	-	-
FRANCE										
GNP(%)	-	-	-	-	-	-	-	-	-	-
CPI(%)	-	-	-	-	-	-	-	-	-	-
GDEF(%GNPV) *	-	-	-	-	-	-	-	-	-	-
EXCH(%) **	-	-	-	-	-	-	-	-	-	-
CAB(B.US$) ***	-	-	-	-	-	-	-	-	-	-
UNITED KINGDOM										
GNP(%)	-	-	-	-	-	-	-	-	-	-
CPI(%)	-	-	-	-	-	-	-	-	-	-
GDEF(%GNPV) *	-	-	-	-	-	-	-	-	-	-
EXCH(%) **	-	-	-	-	-	-	-	-	-	-
CAB(B.US$) ***	-	-	-	-	-	-	-	-	-	-
ITALY										
GNP(%)	-	-	-	-	-	-	-	-	-	-
CPI(%)	-	-	-	-	-	-	-	-	-	-
GDEF(%GNPV) *	-	-	-	-	-	-	-	-	-	-
EXCH(%) **	-	-	-	-	-	-	-	-	-	-
CAB(B.US$) ***	-	-	-	-	-	-	-	-	-	-
CANADA										
GNP(%)	-	-	-	-	-	-	-	-	-	-
CPI(%)	-	-	-	-	-	-	-	-	-	-
GDEF(%GNPV) *	-	-	-	-	-	-	-	-	-	-
EXCH(%) **	-	-	-	-	-	-	-	-	-	-
CAB(B.US$) ***	-	-	-	-	-	-	-	-	-	-
REST OF WORLD										
CAB(B.US$) ***	-	-	-	-	-	-	-	-	-	-

* Government deficit as a percentage of baseline nominal GNP.
** Exchange rate : Bilateral rate against U.S. $ ($/local currency).
*** Local currency units translated into U.S. $ at baseline exchange rates.

EPA—Japanese Economic Planning Agency World Model

See part 1 of this volume for design and detailed description of the simulations. See part 4 for bibliographical references.

The figures for the ratio of government budget deficits to GNP should be interpreted with caution. For all other models the variable GDEF(%GNPV) is calculated with both the numerator and denominator expressed in local currency. For the Japanese EPA model, however, the government deficits in the numerator are expressed in U.S. dollars.

A correctly run version of simulation H is not available for this model.

Model: EPA
Simulation A: Baseline Path

	1985	1986	1987	1988	1989	1990
UNITED STATES						
GNPV(B.$)	3917.4	4171.4	4446.9	4741.3	5054.1	5387.7
GNP(B.72$)	1688.1	1738.4	1790.6	1844.4	1899.7	1956.7
PGNP(72=100)	232.0	239.9	248.3	257.0	266.0	275.3
CPI(72=100)	227.9	234.9	241.9	249.2	256.7	264.4
WAGES(72=100)	236.3	246.1	254.5	263.1	272.1	281.6
UN(%)	7.5	7.3	7.1	6.9	6.7	6.5
G(B.72$)	319.3	332.2	345.5	359.3	373.7	388.7
C(B.72$)	1095.9	1130.8	1164.7	1199.7	1235.7	1272.8
IFP(B.72$)	276.4	285.0	293.9	303.4	313.5	324.2
II(B.72$)	-4.1	0.0	0.0	0.0	0.0	0.0
XGS(B.72$)	157.0	165.3	174.8	184.9	195.5	206.8
MGS(B.72$)	184.5	196.9	208.3	220.2	232.9	246.3
M1(B.$)	585.2	615.5	643.0	671.0	700.2	730.8
RS(%)	8.0	8.0	8.0	8.0	8.0	8.0
RL(%)	12.3	12.3	12.3	12.3	12.3	12.3
GDEF(B.$)	185.5	207.3	246.2	285.2	328.8	380.5
PXGS(72=100)	253.5	261.7	270.3	280.5	291.4	303.1
PMGS(72=100)	274.8	285.6	297.2	309.5	322.1	336.9
EXCH(72=100) *	135.5	135.5	135.5	135.5	135.5	135.6
CAB(B.$)	-168.0	-198.3	-223.6	-248.9	-274.8	-306.8
NON-US OECD						
GNPV(B.$) **	565.6	604.7	646.4	691.1	738.8	789.2
GNP(B.72$) **	204.1	210.3	216.7	223.3	230.1	236.9
PGNP(72=100)	277.1	287.5	298.3	309.5	321.1	333.1
CPI(72=100)	291.8	303.7	316.0	328.7	342.0	355.9
WAGES(72=100)	397.0	417.2	436.9	456.9	478.4	502.8
UN(%)	6.8	6.6	6.3	6.1	5.7	5.1
C(B.72$) **	117.1	120.1	123.4	126.7	130.2	133.6
IFP(B.72$) **	36.0	37.5	39.2	40.9	42.8	44.7
RS(%)	9.0	9.0	9.0	9.0	9.0	9.0
RL(%)	9.7	9.7	9.7	9.7	9.7	9.7
GDEF(B.US$) **	-	-	-	-	-	-
PXGS(72=100)	83.8	86.9	89.8	92.6	95.9	99.7
PMGS(72=100)	227.8	238.3	247.2	255.7	265.6	277.1
EXCH(72=100) ***	73.8	73.8	73.8	73.8	73.8	73.8
CAB(B.US$)	-	-	-	-	-	-

* Exchange rate : (Weighted average of foreign currencies)/U.S. $.
** Local currency units translated into U.S. $ at baseline exchange rates.
*** Exchange rate : U.S. $/(weighted average of non-US OECD currencies).

Model: EPA
Simulation A: Baseline Path

	1985	1986	1987	1988	1989	1990
JAPAN						
GNP(B.72Y)	160591.4	168039.9	175603.8	183508.9	191767.6	200393.8
CPI(72=100)	233.1	240.1	247.3	254.8	262.4	270.3
RS(%)	6.5	6.5	6.5	6.5	6.5	6.5
GDEF(%GNPV) *	1.6	1.4	1.2	0.9	0.6	0.4
EXCH(72=100) **	115.7	115.6	115.5	115.6	115.6	115.5
CAB(B.US$) ***	41.9	54.2	63.2	85.3	109.3	138.1
GERMANY						
GNP(B.72DM)	1064.7	1093.5	1123.7	1154.5	1186.3	1218.8
CPI(72=100)	178.4	182.3	186.4	190.6	194.8	199.2
RS(%)	6.5	6.5	6.5	6.5	6.5	6.5
GDEF(%GNPV) *	-0.1	-0.1	-0.4	-0.7	-0.9	-1.1
EXCH(72=100) **	103.0	103.0	103.1	103.1	103.2	102.9
CAB(B.US$) ***	3.2	7.1	6.7	3.2	-0.6	-5.4
FRANCE						
GNP(B.72F)	-	-	-	-	-	-
CPI(72=100)	-	-	-	-	-	-
GDEF(%GNPV) *	-	-	-	-	-	-
EXCH(72=100) **	-	-	-	-	-	-
CAB(B.US$) ***	-	-	-	-	-	-
UNITED KINGDOM						
GNP(B.72LB)	77.2	79.3	81.5	83.8	86.1	88.5
CPI(72=100)	422.4	441.9	462.3	483.6	505.9	529.2
GDEF(%GNPV) *	4.1	3.6	3.2	3.0	2.6	2.2
EXCH(72=100) **	50.5	50.5	50.4	50.5	50.5	50.5
CAB(B.US$) ***	0.7	-0.7	1.0	3.2	4.7	5.7
ITALY						
GNP(B.72L)	-	-	-	-	-	-
CPI(72=100)	-	-	-	-	-	-
GDEF(%GNPV) *	-	-	-	-	-	-
EXCH(72=100) **	-	-	-	-	-	-
CAB(B.US$) ***	-	-	-	-	-	-
CANADA						
GNP(B.72C$)	150.6	153.8	157.0	160.3	163.6	167.0
CPI(72=100)	285.5	296.7	308.4	320.5	333.2	346.3
GDEF(%GNPV) *	0.1	0.4	0.5	0.5	0.5	0.6
EXCH(72=100) **	72.6	72.6	72.6	72.6	72.6	72.6
CAB(B.US$) ***	0.5	0.1	0.4	0.0	-0.5	-1.2
REST OF WORLD						
CAB(B.US$) ***	-	-	-	-	-	-

* Government deficit as a percentage of baseline nominal GNP.
** Exchange rate: Bilateral rate against U.S. $ ($/local currency).
*** Local currency units translated into U.S. $ at baseline exchange rates.

Model: EPA
Simulation B: Reduction in U.S. Government Purchases with Foreign Monetary Aggregates Unchanged from Baseline
(Deviation of Shock Path from Baseline Path)

	1985									
	Q1	Q2	Q3	Q4	1985	1986	1987	1988	1989	1990
UNITED STATES										
GNPV(%)	-1.5	-2.3	-2.6	-2.8	-2.3	-3.1	-3.7	-4.4	-5.2	-6.6
GNP(%)	-1.1	-1.6	-1.7	-1.8	-1.6	-1.7	-1.6	-1.6	-1.6	-1.9
PGNP(%)	-0.4	-0.7	-0.8	-1.0	-0.7	-1.4	-2.1	-2.8	-3.7	-4.7
CPI(%)	-0.1	-0.2	-0.4	-0.6	-0.3	-0.9	-1.5	-2.1	-2.8	-3.8
WAGES(%)	-0.2	-0.4	-0.6	-0.8	-0.5	-1.4	-2.2	-3.1	-4.0	-5.2
UN(% PTS)	0.8	1.0	1.0	1.0	0.9	0.9	0.8	0.8	0.8	1.0
GNP(B.72$)	-19.1	-27.4	-29.6	-30.4	-26.6	-29.7	-28.7	-29.0	-30.5	-37.5
G(B.72$)	-16.7	-16.8	-16.9	-17.1	-16.9	-17.4	-17.9	-18.4	-19.0	-19.6
C(B.72$)	-4.5	-8.0	-9.9	-10.9	-8.3	-12.3	-14.3	-16.8	-20.0	-25.8
IFP(B.72$)	-2.2	-3.9	-5.1	-5.9	-4.3	-6.7	-6.9	-6.7	-6.7	-9.1
II(B.72$)	2.9	-1.5	-1.7	-2.0	-0.6	-0.9	0.5	1.2	1.8	1.9
XGS(B.72$)	-2.0	-2.7	-3.0	-3.6	-2.8	-5.4	-8.2	-11.9	-17.0	-25.2
MGS(B.72$)	-3.4	-5.4	-7.1	-9.0	-6.2	-12.9	-18.0	-23.6	-30.5	-40.2
M1(%)	-0.4	-0.4	-0.3	-0.4	-0.4	-0.4	-0.4	-0.4	-0.5	-0.9
RS(% PTS)	-1.1	-1.5	-1.5	-1.7	-1.5	-2.2	-3.0	-3.7	-4.7	-5.9
RL(% PTS)	-0.3	-0.4	-0.5	-0.7	-0.5	-1.2	-2.0	-2.9	-3.7	-4.7
GDEF(B$)	-21.7	-11.3	-7.9	-6.5	-11.8	-11.0	-26.2	-46.0	-68.9	-91.2
PXGS(%)	0.1	0.0	-0.0	-0.1	-0.0	-0.4	-0.7	-0.8	-0.9	-0.8
PMGS(%)	0.6	0.8	0.8	0.8	0.8	1.0	1.4	2.0	2.5	3.3
EXCH(%) *	-0.4	-0.7	-0.9	-1.1	-0.7	-1.9	-3.3	-4.6	-5.8	-7.0
CAB(B$)	2.8	6.0	9.9	14.3	8.3	20.5	26.9	32.2	38.3	46.1
NON-US OECD										
GNPV(%) **	-0.0	-0.1	-0.3	-0.4	-0.2	-0.9	-1.8	-2.7	-3.7	-5.0
GNP(%) **	-0.1	-0.2	-0.3	-0.4	-0.2	-0.9	-1.5	-2.2	-2.8	-3.6
PGNP(%)	0.0	0.0	0.0	0.0	0.0	-0.0	-0.3	-0.6	-0.9	-1.5
CPI(%)	-0.0	-0.0	-0.1	-0.1	-0.1	-0.3	-0.6	-1.0	-1.5	-2.3
WAGES(%)	-0.0	-0.0	-0.1	-0.1	-0.1	-0.4	-0.9	-1.5	-2.3	-3.6
UN(% PTS)	0.0	0.0	0.0	0.0	0.0	0.1	0.2	0.4	0.8	1.2
C(%) **	0.0	-0.0	-0.0	-0.1	-0.0	-0.2	-0.4	-0.7	-1.0	-1.4
IFP(%) **	-0.0	-0.1	-0.2	-0.4	-0.2	-0.8	-1.5	-1.9	-2.3	-2.8
RS(% PTS)	-0.2	-0.2	-0.3	-0.3	-0.2	-0.5	-0.6	-0.7	-0.8	-1.0
RL(% PTS)	-0.1	-0.1	-0.2	-0.2	-0.1	-0.3	-0.5	-0.6	-0.7	-0.8
GDEF (B.US$) **	-	-	-	-	-	-	-	-	-	-
PXGS(%)	-0.1	-0.2	-0.3	-0.5	-0.3	-0.9	-1.8	-2.7	-3.6	-4.7
PMGS(%)	-0.2	-0.3	-0.5	-0.7	-0.4	-1.4	-2.6	-3.7	-4.9	-6.4
EXCH(%) ***	0.4	0.7	0.9	1.1	0.8	1.9	3.4	4.9	6.2	7.5
CAB(B.US$) **	-	-	-	-	-	-	-	-	-	-

* Exchange rate : (Weighted average of foreign currencies)/U.S. $.
** Local currency units translated into U.S. $ at baseline exchange rates.
*** Exchange rate : U.S. $/(weighted average of non-US OECD currencies).

Model: EPA
Simulation B: Reduction in U.S. Government Purchases with Foreign Monetary Aggregates Unchanged from Baseline
(Deviation of Shock Path from Baseline Path)

	1985									
	Q1	Q2	Q3	Q4	1985	1986	1987	1988	1989	1990
JAPAN										
GNP(%)	-0.1	-0.2	-0.3	-0.5	-0.3	-0.9	-1.6	-2.4	-3.4	-4.9
CPI(%)	-0.0	-0.0	-0.1	-0.2	-0.1	-0.4	-0.8	-1.3	-2.0	-2.8
RS(% PTS)	-0.1	-0.1	-0.1	-0.2	-0.1	-0.2	-0.3	-0.4	-0.5	-0.6
GDEF(%GNPV) *	0.0	0.0	0.0	0.0	0.0	0.1	0.1	0.2	0.2	0.3
EXCH(%) **	0.3	0.8	1.1	1.2	0.8	1.7	3.3	5.3	8.0	11.7
CAB(B.US$) ***	-0.3	-0.5	-1.1	-2.3	-1.1	-4.7	-8.3	-13.5	-21.1	-32.9
GERMANY										
GNP(%)	-0.1	-0.3	-0.5	-0.7	-0.4	-1.4	-2.7	-4.0	-5.1	-5.7
CPI(%)	-0.0	-0.0	-0.1	-0.1	-0.1	-0.4	-0.8	-1.4	-2.0	-3.2
RS(% PTS)	-0.0	-0.0	-0.0	-0.1	-0.0	-0.1	-0.2	-0.2	-0.2	-0.2
GDEF(%GNPV) *	0.0	0.0	0.0	0.0	0.0	0.1	0.2	0.3	0.4	0.4
EXCH(%) **	0.8	1.8	2.4	3.3	2.1	6.4	11.1	14.6	15.7	14.3
CAB(B.US$) ***	0.2	0.3	0.1	-0.0	0.1	-0.4	-1.5	-2.9	-4.0	-3.9
FRANCE										
GNP(%)	-	-	-	-	-	-	-	-	-	-
CPI(%)	-	-	-	-	-	-	-	-	-	-
GDEF(%GNPV) *	-	-	-	-	-	-	-	-	-	-
EXCH(%) **	-	-	-	-	-	-	-	-	-	-
CAB(B.US$) ***	-	-	-	-	-	-	-	-	-	-
UNITED KINGDOM										
GNP(%)	-0.1	-0.2	-0.2	-0.3	-0.2	-0.9	-1.7	-2.2	-2.9	-3.7
CPI(%)	-0.0	-0.0	-0.1	-0.1	-0.1	-0.3	-0.9	-1.6	-2.4	-3.5
GDEF(%GNPV) *	-0.0	-0.0	-0.1	-0.1	-0.0	-0.2	-0.2	-0.2	-0.2	-0.2
EXCH(%) **	0.7	0.6	0.6	0.8	0.7	1.7	3.1	4.1	5.6	7.9
CAB(B.US$) ***	-0.4	-0.7	-1.0	-1.4	-0.9	-2.4	-4.6	-8.1	-11.7	-15.3
ITALY										
GNP(%)	-	-	-	-	-	-	-	-	-	-
CPI(%)	-	-	-	-	-	-	-	-	-	-
GDEF(%GNPV) *	-	-	-	-	-	-	-	-	-	-
EXCH(%) **	-	-	-	-	-	-	-	-	-	-
CAB(B.US$) ***	-	-	-	-	-	-	-	-	-	-
CANADA										
GNP(%)	-0.1	-0.2	-0.4	-0.7	-0.4	-1.1	-1.0	-1.2	-1.4	-2.0
CPI(%)	-0.0	-0.1	-0.1	-0.2	-0.1	-0.5	-1.0	-1.7	-2.7	-4.2
GDEF(%GNPV) *	0.0	0.0	0.1	0.2	0.1	0.3	0.2	0.2	0.2	0.3
EXCH(%) **	0.1	0.3	0.4	0.5	0.3	0.4	1.0	2.2	3.6	6.3
CAB(B.US$) ***	-0.2	-0.7	-1.2	-1.6	-0.9	-1.8	-2.6	-4.3	-5.8	-7.4
REST OF WORLD										
CAB(B.US$) ***	-	-	-	-	-	-	-	-	-	-

* Government deficit as a percentage of baseline nominal GNP.
** Exchange rate : Bilateral rate against U.S. $ ($/local currency).
*** Local currency units translated into U.S. $ at baseline exchange rates.

Model: EPA
Simulation C: Reduction in U.S. Government Purchases with Foreign Short-Term Interest Rates Unchanged from Baseline
(Deviation of Shock Path from Baseline Path)

	1985									
	Q1	Q2	Q3	Q4	1985	1986	1987	1988	1989	1990
UNITED STATES										
GNPV(%)	-1.5	-2.3	-2.6	-2.8	-2.3	-3.1	-3.7	-4.3	-5.2	-6.5
GNP(%)	-1.1	-1.6	-1.7	-1.8	-1.6	-1.7	-1.6	-1.6	-1.6	-1.9
PGNP(%)	-0.4	-0.7	-0.8	-1.0	-0.7	-1.4	-2.1	-2.8	-3.6	-4.7
CPI(%)	-0.1	-0.2	-0.4	-0.5	-0.3	-0.9	-1.4	-2.0	-2.7	-3.6
WAGES(%)	-0.2	-0.4	-0.6	-0.8	-0.5	-1.3	-2.2	-3.0	-4.0	-5.1
UN(% PTS)	0.8	1.0	1.0	1.0	0.9	0.9	0.8	0.8	0.8	1.0
GNP(B.72$)	-19.0	-27.3	-29.5	-30.4	-26.5	-29.9	-29.3	-29.4	-30.7	-37.5
G(B.72$)	-16.7	-16.8	-16.9	-17.1	-16.9	-17.4	-17.9	-18.4	-19.0	-19.6
C(B.72$)	-4.5	-8.0	-10.0	-11.0	-8.4	-12.6	-14.6	-17.1	-20.3	-26.1
IFP(B.72$)	-2.2	-3.9	-5.1	-5.9	-4.3	-6.7	-7.0	-6.8	-6.8	-9.1
II(B.72$)	2.8	-1.5	-1.8	-2.0	-0.6	-1.0	0.3	1.1	1.7	1.9
XGS(B.72$)	-1.9	-2.6	-2.9	-3.5	-2.7	-5.4	-8.5	-12.1	-17.0	-25.0
MGS(B.72$)	-3.5	-5.5	-7.2	-9.2	-6.3	-13.2	-18.4	-23.9	-30.7	-40.3
M1(%)	-0.4	-0.4	-0.3	-0.4	-0.4	-0.4	-0.4	-0.4	-0.5	-0.9
RS(% PTS)	-1.1	-1.4	-1.5	-1.6	-1.4	-2.2	-2.9	-3.7	-4.6	-5.8
RL(% PTS)	-0.3	-0.3	-0.5	-0.7	-0.4	-1.2	-2.0	-2.8	-3.7	-4.6
GDEF(B$)	-21.8	-11.3	-7.8	-6.1	-11.8	-10.0	-24.3	-44.0	-66.7	-88.7
PXGS(%)	0.1	0.0	-0.0	-0.1	0.0	-0.4	-0.7	-0.9	-0.9	-0.9
PMGS(%)	0.7	1.0	1.1	1.1	1.0	1.3	1.7	2.2	2.8	3.7
EXCH(%) *	-0.4	-0.8	-1.1	-1.3	-0.9	-2.2	-3.7	-5.1	-6.3	-7.6
CAB(B$)	2.6	5.6	9.5	13.8	7.9	19.5	25.6	30.8	36.8	44.1
NON-US OECD										
GNPV(%) **	-0.0	-0.2	-0.3	-0.5	-0.3	-1.1	-2.2	-3.2	-4.3	-5.7
GNP(%) **	-0.1	-0.2	-0.3	-0.5	-0.3	-1.0	-1.8	-2.5	-3.1	-3.9
PGNP(%)	0.0	0.0	0.0	-0.0	0.0	-0.1	-0.4	-0.7	-1.2	-1.8
CPI(%)	-0.0	-0.0	-0.1	-0.1	-0.1	-0.4	-0.8	-1.3	-1.9	-2.7
WAGES(%)	-0.0	-0.0	-0.1	-0.2	-0.1	-0.5	-1.1	-1.8	-2.7	-4.1
UN(% PTS)	0.0	0.0	0.0	0.0	0.0	0.1	0.3	0.5	0.8	1.3
C(%) **	-0.0	-0.0	-0.1	-0.1	-0.0	-0.2	-0.5	-0.9	-1.2	-1.6
IFP(%) **	-0.0	-0.2	-0.4	-0.6	-0.3	-1.3	-2.3	-2.8	-3.1	-3.6
RS(% PTS)	0.0	0.0	0.0	0.0	0.0	0.0	0.0	0.0	0.0	0.0
RL(% PTS)	-0.0	-0.1	-0.1	-0.1	-0.1	-0.2	-0.3	-0.4	-0.4	-0.4
GDEF (B.US$) **	-	-	-	-	-	-	-	-	-	-
PXGS(%)	-0.1	-0.2	-0.4	-0.5	-0.3	-1.1	-2.0	-3.0	-3.9	-5.1
PMGS(%)	-0.2	-0.4	-0.6	-0.9	-0.5	-1.6	-2.9	-4.2	-5.4	-7.0
EXCH(%) ***	0.4	0.8	1.1	1.3	0.9	2.3	3.9	5.4	6.8	8.3
CAB(B.US$) **	-	-	-	-	-	-	-	-	-	-

* Exchange rate : (Weighted average of foreign currencies)/U.S. $.
** Local currency units translated into U.S. $ at baseline exchange rates.
*** Exchange rate : U.S. $/(weighted average of non-US OECD currencies).

Model: EPA
Simulation C: Reduction in U.S. Government Purchases with Foreign Short-Term Interest Rates Unchanged from Baseline
(Deviation of Shock Path from Baseline Path)

	1985									
	Q1	Q2	Q3	Q4	1985	1986	1987	1988	1989	1990
JAPAN										
GNP(%)	-0.1	-0.2	-0.3	-0.5	-0.3	-0.9	-1.7	-2.6	-3.7	-5.2
CPI(%)	-0.0	-0.1	-0.1	-0.2	-0.1	-0.5	-0.9	-1.5	-2.1	-2.9
RS(% PTS)	0.0	0.0	0.0	0.0	0.0	0.0	0.0	0.0	0.0	0.0
GDEF(%GNPV) *	0.0	0.0	0.0	0.0	0.0	0.1	0.1	0.2	0.2	0.3
EXCH(%) **	0.4	0.9	1.2	1.4	1.0	2.0	3.6	5.8	8.5	12.3
CAB(B.US$) ***	-0.2	-0.4	-1.0	-2.1	-0.9	-4.6	-8.4	-13.9	-21.5	-33.1
GERMANY										
GNP(%)	-0.1	-0.3	-0.5	-0.7	-0.4	-1.5	-2.9	-4.2	-5.2	-5.8
CPI(%)	-0.0	-0.0	-0.1	-0.1	-0.1	-0.4	-0.8	-1.3	-2.0	-3.1
RS(% PTS)	0.0	0.0	0.0	0.0	0.0	0.0	0.0	0.0	0.0	0.0
GDEF(%GNPV) *	0.0	0.0	0.0	0.0	0.0	0.1	0.2	0.3	0.4	0.4
EXCH(%) **	0.8	1.8	2.5	3.3	2.1	6.4	10.8	14.0	15.2	14.1
CAB(B.US$) ***	0.2	0.3	0.0	-0.1	0.1	-0.4	-1.5	-2.7	-3.7	-3.8
FRANCE										
GNP(%)	-	-	-	-	-	-	-	-	-	-
CPI(%)	-	-	-	-	-	-	-	-	-	-
GDEF(%GNPV) *	-	-	-	-	-	-	-	-	-	-
EXCH(%) **	-	-	-	-	-	-	-	-	-	-
CAB(B.US$) ***	-	-	-	-	-	-	-	-	-	-
UNITED KINGDOM										
GNP(%)	-0.1	-0.2	-0.3	-0.5	-0.3	-1.1	-2.0	-2.6	-3.1	-3.9
CPI(%)	-0.0	-0.1	-0.1	-0.2	-0.1	-0.4	-1.2	-2.1	-2.9	-3.9
GDEF(%GNPV) *	-0.0	-0.1	-0.1	-0.1	-0.1	-0.2	-0.3	-0.3	-0.2	-0.2
EXCH(%) **	0.8	0.9	1.0	1.3	1.0	2.4	4.0	5.1	6.3	8.1
CAB(B.US$) ***	-0.3	-0.7	-0.9	-1.1	-0.8	-2.1	-4.5	-8.0	-11.8	-15.5
ITALY										
GNP(%)	-	-	-	-	-	-	-	-	-	-
CPI(%)	-	-	-	-	-	-	-	-	-	-
GDEF(%GNPV) *	-	-	-	-	-	-	-	-	-	-
EXCH(%) **	-	-	-	-	-	-	-	-	-	-
CAB(B.US$) ***	-	-	-	-	-	-	-	-	-	-
CANADA										
GNP(%)	-0.1	-0.3	-0.7	-1.1	-0.6	-1.8	-2.1	-2.4	-3.0	-4.0
CPI(%)	-0.0	-0.1	-0.3	-0.5	-0.2	-1.1	-2.3	-3.6	-5.2	-7.5
GDEF(%GNPV) *	0.0	0.0	0.1	0.2	0.1	0.4	0.5	0.5	0.6	0.7
EXCH(%) **	0.5	1.1	1.5	1.9	1.3	2.8	4.4	6.3	9.0	13.6
CAB(B.US$) ***	0.1	-0.1	-0.5	-0.7	-0.3	-0.0	-0.4	-2.6	-4.5	-5.9
REST OF WORLD										
CAB(B.US$) ***	-	-	-	-	-	-	-	-	-	-

* Government deficit as a percentage of baseline nominal GNP.
** Exchange rate : Bilateral rate against U.S. $ ($/local currency).
*** Local currency units translated into U.S. $ at baseline exchange rates.

Model: EPA
Simulation D: U.S. Monetary Expansion with foreign Monetary Aggregates Unchanged from Baseline
(Deviation of Shock Path from Baseline Path)

	1985									
	Q1	Q2	Q3	Q4	1985	1986	1987	1988	1989	1990
UNITED STATES										
GNPV(%)	0.2	1.2	1.7	2.1	1.3	1.9	1.9	1.4	0.7	-0.2
GNP(%)	0.3	1.1	1.5	1.7	1.2	1.2	0.9	0.4	-0.1	-0.6
PGNP(%)	-0.1	0.1	0.2	0.4	0.1	0.7	1.0	1.0	0.8	0.4
CPI(%)	0.0	0.2	0.4	0.6	0.3	1.0	1.3	1.3	1.1	0.6
WAGES(%)	0.1	0.3	0.5	0.7	0.4	1.2	1.8	2.1	1.9	1.4
UN(% PTS)	-0.2	-0.7	-0.9	-1.0	-0.7	-0.6	-0.4	-0.2	0.1	0.3
GNP(B.72$)	4.8	18.2	25.3	29.5	19.5	20.9	16.7	7.6	-2.7	-11.5
G(B.72$)	0.0	0.0	0.0	0.0	0.0	0.0	0.0	0.0	0.0	0.0
C(B.72$)	2.8	8.8	12.6	14.5	9.7	8.8	5.7	1.0	-4.3	-9.7
IFP(B.72$)	0.4	1.9	2.7	3.2	2.1	1.8	-0.1	-3.3	-7.2	-9.6
II(B.72$)	-0.6	4.7	6.4	7.0	4.4	4.7	2.9	1.7	1.2	1.0
XGS(B.72$)	-5.0	-5.8	-6.1	-7.2	-6.0	-2.9	-4.4	-8.1	-13.4	-20.6
MGS(B.72$)	-7.2	-8.6	-9.7	-12.0	-9.4	-8.5	-12.6	-16.2	-21.0	-27.4
M1(%)	0.6	2.2	3.8	4.9	2.9	4.8	4.8	4.8	4.7	4.7
RS(% PTS)	-2.8	-3.1	-3.3	-3.8	-3.2	-2.2	-2.6	-3.1	-3.9	-4.9
RL(% PTS)	-0.7	-0.7	-1.0	-1.4	-1.0	-1.6	-2.2	-2.7	-3.1	-3.9
GDEF(B$)	-7.2	-28.1	-41.4	-52.4	-32.3	-48.6	-51.3	-48.1	-47.8	-56.1
PXGS(%)	0.6	0.9	1.2	1.6	1.1	1.7	2.2	2.5	2.6	2.6
PMGS(%)	1.9	2.8	3.7	5.0	3.4	5.1	6.3	6.3	5.7	5.1
EXCH(%) *	-1.6	-3.0	-4.1	-5.4	-3.5	-6.4	-7.9	-7.2	-5.4	-3.9
CAB(B$)	2.4	1.4	0.5	-0.1	1.0	-1.6	2.4	4.6	9.6	15.8
NON-US OECD										
GNPV(%) **	-0.1	-0.2	-0.3	-0.3	-0.2	-0.6	-1.3	-1.9	-2.3	-2.7
GNP(%) **	-0.1	-0.2	-0.2	-0.2	-0.2	-0.4	-0.9	-1.3	-1.5	-1.7
PGNP(%)	-0.0	-0.1	-0.1	-0.1	-0.1	-0.2	-0.4	-0.6	-0.8	-0.9
CPI(%)	-0.0	-0.1	-0.2	-0.3	-0.2	-0.5	-0.7	-0.9	-1.1	-1.2
WAGES(%)	-0.0	-0.1	-0.1	-0.2	-0.1	-0.5	-0.9	-1.1	-1.4	-2.0
UN(% PTS)	0.0	0.0	0.0	0.0	0.0	0.0	0.1	0.4	0.6	1.0
C(%) **	0.0	0.0	0.0	0.1	0.0	0.2	0.0	-0.3	-0.7	-1.0
IFP(%) **	-0.1	-0.1	-0.0	0.2	0.0	0.4	-0.1	-0.8	-1.1	-1.1
RS(% PTS)	-0.5	-0.6	-0.7	-0.9	-0.6	-0.6	-0.5	-0.6	-0.6	-0.6
RL(% PTS)	-0.2	-0.3	-0.5	-0.6	-0.4	-0.5	-0.6	-0.5	-0.4	-0.5
GDEF (B.US$) **	-	-	-	-	-	-	-	-	-	-
PXGS(%)	-0.4	-0.8	-1.2	-1.6	-1.0	-1.8	-2.3	-2.3	-1.9	-1.7
PMGS(%)	-0.5	-1.3	-1.9	-2.5	-1.6	-2.9	-3.6	-3.5	-2.8	-2.2
EXCH(%) ***	1.7	3.0	4.2	5.7	3.7	6.9	8.6	7.8	5.7	4.0
CAB(B.US$) **	-	-	-	-	-	-	-	-	-	-

* Exchange rate : (Weighted average of foreign currencies)/U.S. $.
** Local currency units translated into U.S. $ at baseline exchange rates.
*** Exchange rate : U.S. $/(weighted average of non-US OECD currencies).

Model: EPA
Simulation D: U.S. Monetary Expansion with Foreign Monetary Aggregates Unchanged from Baseline
(Deviation of Shock Path from Baseline Path)

	1985									
	Q1	Q2	Q3	Q4	1985	1986	1987	1988	1989	1990
JAPAN										
GNP(%)	-0.1	-0.2	-0.3	-0.4	-0.3	-0.6	-0.9	-1.2	-1.4	-1.4
CPI(%)	-0.1	-0.4	-0.8	-1.3	-0.6	-2.0	-2.7	-3.0	-2.7	-1.6
RS(% PTS)	-0.2	-0.3	-0.4	-0.6	-0.4	-0.4	-0.3	-0.3	-0.2	-0.2
GDEF(%GNPV) *	0.0	0.0	0.1	0.1	0.0	0.0	-0.0	-0.1	-0.0	-0.0
EXCH(%) **	3.2	6.5	9.1	11.7	7.6	11.5	13.1	11.7	7.5	0.9
CAB(B.US$) ***	1.3	3.4	4.3	3.8	3.2	-1.8	-4.6	-8.9	-12.9	-14.7
GERMANY										
GNP(%)	-0.2	-0.5	-0.7	-1.0	-0.6	-1.7	-3.0	-3.8	-4.2	-4.3
CPI(%)	-0.0	-0.1	-0.2	-0.3	-0.1	-0.7	-1.2	-1.5	-1.6	-2.4
RS(% PTS)	-0.0	-0.1	-0.1	-0.2	-0.1	-0.2	-0.3	-0.2	-0.2	-0.2
GDEF(%GNPV) *	-0.0	0.0	0.0	0.0	0.0	0.1	0.1	0.3	0.3	0.3
EXCH(%) **	2.2	4.6	6.5	9.7	5.8	15.3	19.9	16.6	10.7	10.2
CAB(B.US$) ***	0.7	0.9	0.5	0.8	0.8	-0.2	-2.9	-4.3	-3.8	-1.5
FRANCE										
GNP(%)	-	-	-	-	-	-	-	-	-	-
CPI(%)	-	-	-	-	-	-	-	-	-	-
GDEF(%GNPV) *	-	-	-	-	-	-	-	-	-	-
EXCH(%) **	-	-	-	-	-	-	-	-	-	-
CAB(B.US$) ***	-	-	-	-	-	-	-	-	-	-
UNITED KINGDOM										
GNP(%)	-0.1	-0.1	-0.1	-0.1	-0.1	-0.6	-1.4	-1.7	-2.2	-2.8
CPI(%)	-0.0	-0.0	0.0	0.0	0.0	0.0	-0.4	-1.1	-1.9	-3.0
GDEF(%GNPV) *	-0.0	-0.1	-0.0	-0.0	-0.0	-0.1	-0.1	-0.1	-0.1	-0.2
EXCH(%) **	1.3	1.4	2.0	3.3	2.0	5.4	7.7	8.0	8.6	10.5
CAB(B.US$) ***	-0.7	-1.3	-2.0	-2.9	-1.7	-3.9	-5.7	-8.2	-10.2	-12.5
ITALY										
GNP(%)	-	-	-	-	-	-	-	-	-	-
CPI(%)	-	-	-	-	-	-	-	-	-	-
GDEF(%GNPV) *	-	-	-	-	-	-	-	-	-	-
EXCH(%) **	-	-	-	-	-	-	-	-	-	-
CAB(B.US$) ***	-	-	-	-	-	-	-	-	-	-
CANADA										
GNP(%)	0.1	0.4	0.8	1.2	0.6	1.8	1.4	0.7	0.1	-0.5
CPI(%)	0.0	0.1	0.2	0.3	0.1	0.7	0.9	0.5	-0.4	-1.7
GDEF(%GNPV) *	-0.0	-0.1	-0.2	-0.3	-0.1	-0.5	-0.4	-0.2	-0.1	-0.0
EXCH(%) **	0.2	0.3	0.5	0.6	0.4	0.5	1.3	2.8	4.1	6.2
CAB(B.US$) ***	-0.2	-0.5	-1.0	-1.8	-0.9	-4.2	-5.2	-3.6	-3.1	-3.8
REST OF WORLD										
CAB(B.US$) ***	-	-	-	-	-	-	-	-	-	-

* Government deficit as a percentage of baseline nominal GNP.
** Exchange rate : Bilateral rate against U.S. $ ($/local currency).
*** Local currency units translated into U.S. $ at baseline exchange rates.

Model: EPA
Simulation E: U.S. Monetary Expansion with Foreign Short-Term Interest Rates Unchanged from Baseline
(Deviation of Shock Path from Baseline Path)

	1985									
	Q1	Q2	Q3	Q4	1985	1986	1987	1988	1989	1990
UNITED STATES										
GNPV(%)	0.2	1.2	1.7	2.1	1.3	1.9	1.9	1.5	0.7	-0.1
GNP(%)	0.3	1.1	1.5	1.7	1.2	1.2	0.9	0.4	-0.1	-0.6
PGNP(%)	-0.1	0.0	0.2	0.4	0.1	0.7	1.0	1.1	0.9	0.4
CPI(%)	0.1	0.2	0.4	0.7	0.4	1.1	1.4	1.4	1.2	0.7
WAGES(%)	0.1	0.3	0.5	0.7	0.4	1.3	1.9	2.1	1.9	1.5
UN(% PTS)	-0.2	-0.7	-0.9	-1.0	-0.7	-0.6	-0.4	-0.1	0.1	0.3
GNP(B.72$)	5.0	18.6	25.4	29.4	19.6	20.2	15.8	7.1	-2.7	-11.0
G(B.72$)	0.0	0.0	0.0	0.0	0.0	0.0	0.0	0.0	0.0	0.0
C(B.72$)	2.8	8.8	12.3	14.0	9.5	8.2	5.2	0.7	-4.5	-9.7
IFP(B.72$)	0.4	1.9	2.7	3.2	2.1	1.6	-0.3	-3.4	-7.2	-9.4
II(B.72$)	-0.6	4.7	6.3	6.8	4.3	4.5	2.8	1.7	1.2	1.1
XGS(B.72$)	-4.9	-5.5	-5.8	-6.9	-5.8	-3.2	-4.8	-8.2	-13.2	-20.4
MGS(B.72$)	-7.3	-8.7	-9.9	-12.4	-9.6	-9.1	-12.8	-16.3	-21.0	-27.4
M1(%)	0.6	2.2	3.8	4.9	2.9	4.8	4.8	4.8	4.7	4.7
RS(% PTS)	-2.8	-3.0	-3.2	-3.7	-3.2	-2.2	-2.5	-3.1	-3.9	-4.8
RL(% PTS)	-0.7	-0.7	-1.0	-1.4	-0.9	-1.6	-2.2	-2.6	-3.1	-3.8
GDEF(B$)	-7.4	-28.2	-40.9	-51.1	-31.9	-46.2	-48.3	-45.7	-46.0	-54.8
PXGS(%)	0.6	0.9	1.2	1.6	1.1	1.7	2.2	2.4	2.5	2.6
PMGS(%)	2.2	3.3	4.3	5.8	3.9	5.7	6.5	6.4	5.8	5.3
EXCH(%) *	-1.8	-3.3	-4.6	-6.1	-4.0	-7.1	-8.3	-7.5	-5.6	-4.1
CAB(B$)	1.7	0.3	-1.0	-2.0	-0.2	-3.2	0.9	3.7	8.9	14.5
NON-US OECD										
GNPV(%) **	-0.1	-0.3	-0.4	-0.6	-0.4	-1.0	-1.8	-2.4	-2.8	-3.1
GNP(%) **	-0.1	-0.2	-0.3	-0.4	-0.3	-0.6	-1.2	-1.5	-1.8	-2.0
PGNP(%)	-0.0	-0.1	-0.1	-0.2	-0.1	-0.4	-0.6	-0.9	-1.0	-1.2
CPI(%)	-0.0	-0.1	-0.3	-0.4	-0.2	-0.7	-1.0	-1.2	-1.4	-1.5
WAGES(%)	-0.0	-0.1	-0.2	-0.3	-0.2	-0.7	-1.2	-1.5	-1.8	-2.4
UN(% PTS)	0.0	0.0	0.0	0.0	0.0	0.1	0.2	0.4	0.7	1.0
C(%) **	-0.0	-0.0	-0.0	0.0	-0.0	0.1	-0.2	-0.5	-0.9	-1.3
IFP(%) **	-0.1	-0.3	-0.4	-0.4	-0.3	-0.4	-1.0	-1.4	-1.6	-1.6
RS(% PTS)	0.0	0.0	0.0	0.0	0.0	0.0	0.0	0.0	0.0	0.0
RL(% PTS)	-0.1	-0.2	-0.3	-0.4	-0.3	-0.3	-0.3	-0.2	-0.2	-0.2
GDEF (B.US$) **	-	-	-	-	-	-	-	-	-	-
PXGS(%)	-0.5	-0.9	-1.3	-1.8	-1.1	-2.1	-2.6	-2.6	-2.1	-2.0
PMGS(%)	-0.6	-1.4	-2.2	-2.9	-1.8	-3.4	-4.1	-3.9	-3.1	-2.5
EXCH(%) ***	1.9	3.4	4.8	6.5	4.2	7.7	9.1	8.2	6.0	4.2
CAB(B.US$) **	-	-	-	-	-	-	-	-	-	-

* Exchange rate : (Weighted average of foreign currencies)/U.S. $.
** Local currency units translated into U.S. $ at baseline exchange rates.
*** Exchange rate : U.S. $/(weighted average of non-US OECD currencies).

Model: EPA
Simulation E: U.S. Monetary Expansion with Foreign Short-Term Interest Rates Unchanged from Baseline
(Deviation of Shock Path from Baseline Path)

	1985									
	Q1	Q2	Q3	Q4	1985	1986	1987	1988	1989	1990
JAPAN										
GNP(%)	-0.1	-0.3	-0.4	-0.5	-0.3	-0.8	-1.1	-1.4	-1.6	-1.4
CPI(%)	-0.1	-0.4	-0.8	-1.4	-0.7	-2.2	-2.9	-3.1	-2.6	-1.4
RS(% PTS)	0.0	0.0	0.0	0.0	0.0	0.0	0.0	0.0	0.0	0.0
GDEF(%GNPV) *	0.0	0.0	0.1	0.1	0.0	0.0	0.0	-0.0	-0.0	-0.0
EXCH(%) **	3.4	6.8	9.6	12.4	8.1	12.4	13.5	11.7	7.0	0.1
CAB(B.US$) ***	1.4	3.6	4.7	4.3	3.5	-1.7	-5.2	-9.4	-12.9	-14.2
GERMANY										
GNP(%)	-0.2	-0.5	-0.7	-1.0	-0.6	-1.9	-3.2	-4.1	-4.3	-4.3
CPI(%)	-0.0	-0.1	-0.2	-0.3	-0.1	-0.6	-1.2	-1.5	-1.6	-2.4
RS(% PTS)	0.0	0.0	0.0	0.0	0.0	0.0	0.0	0.0	0.0	0.0
GDEF(%GNPV) *	-0.0	0.0	0.0	0.0	0.0	0.1	0.2	0.3	0.4	0.4
EXCH(%) **	2.3	4.7	6.6	9.9	5.9	15.4	19.8	16.4	10.5	10.0
CAB(B.US$) ***	0.7	0.9	0.5	0.8	0.7	-0.1	-2.6	-4.0	-3.7	-1.6
FRANCE										
GNP(%)	-	-	-	-	-	-	-	-	-	-
CPI(%)	-	-	-	-	-	-	-	-	-	-
GDEF(%GNPV) *	-	-	-	-	-	-	-	-	-	-
EXCH(%) **	-	-	-	-	-	-	-	-	-	-
CAB(B.US$) ***	-	-	-	-	-	-	-	-	-	-
UNITED KINGDOM										
GNP(%)	-0.1	-0.2	-0.3	-0.5	-0.3	-0.9	-1.6	-1.9	-2.3	-2.8
CPI(%)	-0.0	-0.1	-0.1	-0.1	-0.1	-0.2	-0.8	-1.4	-2.1	-3.1
GDEF(%GNPV) *	-0.0	-0.1	-0.1	-0.1	-0.1	-0.1	-0.1	-0.1	-0.1	-0.2
EXCH(%) **	1.7	2.0	2.9	4.4	2.7	6.3	8.2	8.4	8.7	10.1
CAB(B.US$) ***	-0.6	-1.1	-1.6	-2.3	-1.4	-3.5	-5.8	-8.4	-10.3	-12.4
ITALY										
GNP(%)	-	-	-	-	-	-	-	-	-	-
CPI(%)	-	-	-	-	-	-	-	-	-	-
GDEF(%GNPV) *	-	-	-	-	-	-	-	-	-	-
EXCH(%) **	-	-	-	-	-	-	-	-	-	-
CAB(B.US$) ***	-	-	-	-	-	-	-	-	-	-
CANADA										
GNP(%)	0.0	0.0	0.1	0.1	0.1	0.2	-0.1	-0.6	-1.4	-2.3
CPI(%)	-0.1	-0.2	-0.3	-0.5	-0.2	-0.7	-1.3	-2.2	-3.5	-5.4
GDEF(%GNPV) *	-0.0	-0.1	-0.1	-0.1	-0.1	-0.1	-0.0	0.1	0.2	0.4
EXCH(%) **	1.5	2.8	3.9	5.1	3.3	4.8	5.7	7.3	9.7	13.2
CAB(B.US$) ***	0.7	1.0	0.9	0.8	0.9	-1.1	-3.0	-3.3	-3.3	-3.4
REST OF WORLD										
CAB(B.US$) ***	-	-	-	-	-	-	-	-	-	-

* Government deficit as a percentage of baseline nominal GNP.
** Exchange rate : Bilateral rate against U.S. $ ($/local currency).
*** Local currency units translated into U.S. $ at baseline exchange rates.

Model: EPA

Simulation F: Nonpolicy Exogenous Depreciation of the Dollar

(Deviation of Shock Path from Baseline Path)

	1985									
	Q1	Q2	Q3	Q4	1985	1986	1987	1988	1989	1990
UNITED STATES										
GNPV(%)	0.0	0.1	0.2	0.3	0.2	0.9	2.0	3.2	4.2	5.1
GNP(%)	0.1	0.2	0.2	0.3	0.2	0.3	0.3	-0.1	-0.4	-0.6
PGNP(%)	-0.1	-0.1	-0.0	0.1	-0.0	0.6	1.7	3.3	4.6	5.7
CPI(%)	0.0	0.2	0.3	0.6	0.3	1.3	2.8	4.4	5.6	6.6
WAGES(%)	0.0	0.1	0.2	0.3	0.1	0.8	2.1	3.5	4.7	5.5
UN(% PTS)	-0.1	-0.1	-0.1	-0.1	-0.1	-0.1	-0.1	0.1	0.3	0.3
GNP(B.72$)	1.6	3.2	4.0	4.3	3.3	4.8	4.5	-2.1	-8.2	-11.1
G(B.72$)	0.0	0.0	0.0	0.0	0.0	0.0	0.0	0.0	0.0	0.0
C(B.72$)	0.3	0.4	-0.1	-1.1	-0.1	-3.3	-6.1	-10.2	-11.5	-12.5
IFP(B.72$)	0.2	0.3	0.4	0.4	0.3	0.4	0.3	-0.5	-0.9	-0.2
II(B.72$)	-0.4	-0.3	-0.6	-1.0	-0.6	-1.8	-3.2	-4.1	-4.5	-4.6
XGS(B.72$)	1.4	2.6	3.8	4.9	3.2	8.0	13.8	18.1	22.5	28.3
MGS(B.72$)	-0.1	-0.2	-0.6	-1.0	-0.5	-1.4	0.3	5.4	13.8	22.1
M1(%)	-0.0	-0.0	-0.1	-0.2	-0.1	-0.5	-0.9	-1.4	-1.7	-2.0
RS(% PTS)	0.1	0.3	0.6	0.8	0.5	1.5	3.0	4.3	5.2	6.2
RL(% PTS)	0.0	0.1	0.2	0.3	0.1	0.7	1.7	2.9	4.1	5.1
GDEF(B$)	-1.9	-2.7	-2.0	-0.4	-1.7	5.7	24.3	62.9	111.8	171.8
PXGS(%)	-0.0	0.1	0.3	0.5	0.2	1.3	2.6	3.9	4.3	4.4
PMGS(%)	1.0	2.1	3.2	4.4	2.7	7.1	11.2	12.2	11.3	10.7
EXCH(%) *	-2.5	-4.9	-7.3	-9.6	-6.1	-15.1	-23.3	-26.1	-26.1	-26.1
CAB(B$)	-1.0	-2.9	-4.3	-5.6	-3.5	-9.6	-22.3	-34.5	-50.8	-67.8
NON-US OECD										
GNPV(%) **	-0.1	-0.3	-0.6	-1.0	-0.5	-2.4	-4.8	-7.0	-8.2	-9.0
GNP(%) **	-0.1	-0.3	-0.6	-0.8	-0.5	-1.6	-3.0	-4.1	-4.6	-4.9
PGNP(%)	0.0	0.0	-0.0	-0.2	-0.0	-0.7	-1.8	-3.0	-3.8	-4.4
CPI(%)	-0.1	-0.2	-0.4	-0.7	-0.3	-1.5	-3.2	-4.7	-5.5	-6.0
WAGES(%)	-0.0	-0.1	-0.3	-0.6	-0.3	-1.6	-3.5	-5.3	-6.6	-7.7
UN(% PTS)	0.0	0.0	0.0	0.1	0.0	0.2	0.4	0.7	1.1	1.6
C(%) **	0.0	-0.0	-0.0	-0.0	-0.0	-0.0	-0.2	-0.5	-1.1	-1.7
IFP(%) **	-0.1	-0.4	-0.7	-1.1	-0.6	-2.3	-4.3	-5.8	-6.6	-7.2
RS(% PTS)	-0.1	-0.1	-0.1	-0.2	-0.1	-0.1	0.2	0.9	1.8	2.6
RL(% PTS)	-0.0	-0.1	-0.2	-0.3	-0.2	-0.3	-0.2	0.3	1.1	1.7
GDEF (B.US$) **	-	-	-	-	-	-	-	-	-	-
PXGS(%)	-0.5	-1.1	-1.7	-2.4	-1.4	-4.1	-6.7	-8.1	-8.2	-8.1
PMGS(%)	-1.0	-2.2	-3.4	-4.6	-2.8	-7.6	-12.2	-14.1	-14.0	-13.9
EXCH(%) ***	2.6	5.1	7.9	10.6	6.5	17.8	30.4	35.4	35.4	35.4
CAB(B.US$) **	-	-	-	-	-	-	-	-	-	-

* Exchange rate : (Weighted average of foreign currencies)/U.S. $.

** Local currency units translated into U.S. $ at baseline exchange rates.

*** Exchange rate : U.S. $/(weighted average of non-US OECD currencies).

Model: EPA
Simulation F: Nonpolicy Exogenous Depreciation of the Dollar
(Deviation of Shock Path from Baseline Path)

	1985									
	Q1	Q2	Q3	Q4	1985	1986	1987	1988	1989	1990
JAPAN										
GNP(%)	-0.1	-0.2	-0.3	-0.4	-0.3	-0.8	-1.5	-2.2	-2.6	-2.9
CPI(%)	-0.1	-0.3	-0.6	-1.0	-0.5	-2.2	-4.4	-6.3	-7.0	-7.1
RS(% PTS)	0.0	-0.0	-0.1	-0.2	-0.1	-0.2	-0.2	-0.1	0.2	0.3
GDEF(%GNPV) *	0.0	0.0	0.0	0.1	0.0	0.0	0.0	-0.1	-0.1	-0.1
EXCH(%) **	2.7	5.4	8.2	11.1	6.8	18.7	32.0	37.2	37.2	37.2
CAB(B.US$) ***	0.8	2.4	4.0	4.8	3.0	4.5	3.8	-0.3	-1.9	1.1
GERMANY										
GNP(%)	-0.2	-0.5	-0.8	-1.1	-0.7	-2.1	-4.2	-6.0	-7.1	-7.6
CPI(%)	-0.0	-0.1	-0.1	-0.2	-0.1	-0.4	-0.8	-1.3	-1.7	-2.9
RS(% PTS)	0.0	0.1	0.2	0.4	0.2	0.7	1.7	3.0	4.5	6.1
GDEF(%GNPV) *	0.0	0.0	0.0	0.0	0.0	0.1	0.3	0.4	0.5	0.6
EXCH(%) **	2.7	5.4	8.2	11.1	6.8	18.7	32.0	37.2	37.2	37.2
CAB(B.US$) ***	0.5	0.5	0.4	0.4	0.4	0.2	0.1	0.3	1.5	4.3
FRANCE										
GNP(%)	-	-	-	-	-	-	-	-	-	-
CPI(%)	-	-	-	-	-	-	-	-	-	-
GDEF(%GNPV) *	-	-	-	-	-	-	-	-	-	-
EXCH(%) **	-	-	-	-	-	-	-	-	-	-
CAB(B.US$) ***	-	-	-	-	-	-	-	-	-	-
UNITED KINGDOM										
GNP(%)	-0.2	-0.6	-1.1	-1.6	-0.9	-2.7	-4.5	-5.5	-5.9	-6.3
CPI(%)	-0.0	-0.2	-0.4	-0.6	-0.3	-1.5	-3.5	-5.4	-6.6	-7.2
GDEF(%GNPV) *	-0.0	-0.2	-0.3	-0.4	-0.2	-0.6	-0.8	-0.5	-0.1	0.3
EXCH(%) **	2.7	5.4	8.2	11.1	6.8	18.7	32.0	37.2	37.2	37.2
CAB(B.US$) ***	-0.3	-0.9	-1.3	-1.6	-1.0	-3.2	-7.2	-11.3	-14.2	-15.2
ITALY										
GNP(%)	-	-	-	-	-	-	-	-	-	-
CPI(%)	-	-	-	-	-	-	-	-	-	-
GDEF(%GNPV) *	-	-	-	-	-	-	-	-	-	-
EXCH(%) **	-	-	-	-	-	-	-	-	-	-
CAB(B.US$) ***	-	-	-	-	-	-	-	-	-	-
CANADA										
GNP(%)	0.0	0.0	-0.1	-0.4	-0.1	-1.2	-2.3	-3.1	-3.3	-3.4
CPI(%)	-0.0	-0.1	-0.3	-0.5	-0.2	-1.3	-2.9	-4.7	-5.8	-6.5
GDEF(%GNPV) *	-0.0	-0.1	-0.0	0.0	-0.0	0.2	0.6	0.9	1.0	1.1
EXCH(%) **	1.3	2.6	3.9	5.2	3.3	8.7	14.4	16.6	16.6	16.6
CAB(B.US$) ***	0.7	0.9	0.9	0.8	0.8	1.4	2.8	2.8	3.3	3.9
REST OF WORLD										
CAB(B.US$) ***	-	-	-	-	-	-	-	-	-	-

* Government deficit as a percentage of baseline nominal GNP.
** Exchange rate : Bilateral rate against U.S. $ ($/local currency).
*** Local currency units translated into U.S. $ at baseline exchange rates.

Model: EPA
Simulation G: Increase in Government Purchases in Non-U.S. OECD Countries with U.S. Policies Unchanged from Baseline
(Deviation of Shock Path from Baseline Path)

	1985									
	Q1	Q2	Q3	Q4	1985	1986	1987	1988	1989	1990
UNITED STATES										
GNPV(%)	0.1	0.1	0.2	0.3	0.2	0.6	0.9	1.1	1.4	1.8
GNP(%)	0.0	0.1	0.2	0.2	0.1	0.3	0.2	0.2	0.1	0.2
PGNP(%)	0.0	0.0	0.1	0.1	0.1	0.3	0.7	1.0	1.2	1.6
CPI(%)	0.0	0.0	0.1	0.1	0.1	0.3	0.7	1.0	1.3	1.8
WAGES(%)	0.0	0.0	0.1	0.1	0.1	0.3	0.6	0.9	1.2	1.7
UN(% PTS)	-0.0	-0.1	-0.1	-0.1	-0.1	-0.1	-0.1	-0.1	-0.1	-0.1
GNP(B.72$)	0.8	1.8	2.8	3.8	2.3	4.6	3.9	2.9	2.5	3.0
G(B.72$)	0.0	0.0	0.0	0.0	0.0	0.0	0.0	0.0	0.0	0.0
C(B.72$)	0.2	0.4	0.6	0.8	0.5	0.7	0.4	0.4	0.1	-0.5
IFP(B.72$)	0.1	0.2	0.4	0.6	0.3	0.8	0.8	0.7	0.6	1.0
II(B.72$)	-0.1	-0.1	-0.1	-0.1	-0.1	-0.2	-0.6	-0.8	-1.1	-1.4
XGS(B.72$)	0.9	1.7	2.6	3.5	2.2	5.1	6.0	6.7	8.7	12.3
MGS(B.72$)	0.3	0.5	0.7	1.0	0.6	1.7	2.7	4.1	5.9	8.3
M1(%)	0.0	0.0	0.0	0.0	0.0	-0.0	-0.1	-0.2	-0.3	-0.5
RS(% PTS)	0.0	0.1	0.2	0.3	0.2	0.6	0.9	1.1	1.5	2.0
RL(% PTS)	0.0	0.0	0.1	0.1	0.1	0.2	0.5	0.8	1.1	1.5
GDEF(B$)	-1.2	-2.5	-4.0	-5.4	-3.3	-6.0	-2.2	4.3	13.6	28.5
PXGS(%)	0.1	0.2	0.3	0.4	0.2	0.7	1.1	1.2	1.3	1.4
PMGS(%)	0.1	0.2	0.3	0.6	0.3	1.1	1.4	1.3	1.8	2.9
EXCH(%) *	-0.0	0.2	0.5	0.6	0.3	0.7	1.2	1.9	1.1	-2.1
CAB(B$)	1.2	2.6	3.8	4.7	3.1	4.7	3.4	1.3	-2.8	-11.1
NON-US OECD										
GNPV(%) **	1.2	1.6	2.0	2.3	1.8	2.8	3.3	3.6	4.2	5.1
GNP(%) **	1.1	1.5	1.8	1.9	1.6	2.3	2.5	2.6	2.5	2.2
PGNP(%)	0.1	0.1	0.2	0.4	0.2	0.5	0.7	1.0	1.7	2.8
CPI(%)	0.1	0.2	0.3	0.4	0.2	0.7	1.0	1.2	1.7	2.5
WAGES(%)	0.1	0.3	0.5	0.7	0.4	1.2	1.7	2.3	3.4	5.1
UN(% PTS)	-0.1	-0.1	-0.2	-0.2	-0.2	-0.3	-0.5	-0.7	-1.0	-0.7
C(%) **	0.2	0.3	0.5	0.6	0.4	0.9	1.1	1.2	1.4	1.7
IFP(%) **	1.8	2.7	3.3	3.6	2.8	4.0	3.8	3.0	2.6	2.4
RS(% PTS)	0.0	0.1	0.2	0.2	0.1	0.3	0.4	0.5	0.5	0.7
RL(% PTS)	0.1	0.1	0.2	0.2	0.2	0.3	0.4	0.4	0.5	0.5
GDEF (B.US$) **	-	-	-	-	-	-	-	-	-	-
PXGS(%)	0.1	0.3	0.5	0.7	0.4	1.0	1.6	2.1	2.4	2.2
PMGS(%)	0.1	0.4	0.7	0.9	0.5	1.4	2.0	2.5	2.8	2.2
EXCH(%) ***	0.0	-0.2	-0.5	-0.6	-0.3	-0.7	-1.2	-1.9	-1.0	2.2
CAB(B.US$) **	-	-	-	-	-	-	-	-	-	-

* Exchange rate : (Weighted average of foreign currencies)/U.S. $.
** Local currency units translated into U.S. $ at baseline exchange rates.
*** Exchange rate : U.S. $/(weighted average of non-US OECD currencies).

Model: EPA
Simulation G: Increase in Government Purchases in Non-U.S. OECD Countries with U.S. Policies Unchanged from Baseline
(Deviation of Shock Path from Baseline Path)

	1985									
	Q1	Q2	Q3	Q4	1985	1986	1987	1988	1989	1990
JAPAN										
GNP(%)	1.0	1.1	1.3	1.5	1.2	2.0	2.5	2.7	2.7	3.1
CPI(%)	0.1	0.2	0.3	0.4	0.2	0.6	0.7	0.5	0.4	0.3
RS(% PTS)	0.0	0.1	0.1	0.1	0.1	0.2	0.1	0.1	0.1	0.2
GDEF(%GNPV) *	0.3	0.3	0.2	0.2	0.3	0.2	0.1	0.1	0.1	0.1
EXCH(%) **	-0.2	-0.4	-0.7	-0.9	-0.5	-0.9	-0.3	0.0	0.0	0.7
CAB(B.US$) ***	-1.7	-2.4	-2.3	-2.0	-2.1	0.7	3.0	3.3	4.8	11.8
GERMANY										
GNP(%)	1.2	1.6	2.0	2.4	1.8	3.0	3.6	3.6	2.9	1.0
CPI(%)	0.0	0.0	0.0	0.0	0.0	0.1	0.5	1.3	2.4	3.9
RS(% PTS)	-0.0	0.0	0.0	0.0	0.0	0.0	0.1	0.1	0.0	-0.1
GDEF(%GNPV) *	0.2	0.2	0.2	0.1	0.2	0.1	0.0	0.0	0.1	0.1
EXCH(%) **	0.5	0.3	-0.1	-0.3	0.1	-1.3	-5.1	-7.2	-0.7	18.8
CAB(B.US$) ***	-4.2	-4.6	-5.0	-5.3	-4.8	-6.1	-6.2	-3.0	-0.5	-5.4
FRANCE										
GNP(%)	-	-	-	-	-	-	-	-	-	-
CPI(%)	-	-	-	-	-	-	-	-	-	-
GDEF(%GNPV) *	-	-	-	-	-	-	-	-	-	-
EXCH(%) **	-	-	-	-	-	-	-	-	-	-
CAB(B.US$) ***	-	-	-	-	-	-	-	-	-	-
UNITED KINGDOM										
GNP(%)	1.2	1.6	1.7	1.7	1.5	1.7	1.8	2.4	3.2	3.8
CPI(%)	0.0	0.1	0.3	0.5	0.2	1.0	1.5	2.0	3.3	5.7
GDEF(%GNPV) *	1.5	1.6	1.6	1.6	1.5	1.5	1.4	1.4	1.7	2.1
EXCH(%) **	-0.1	-1.1	-1.6	-1.7	-1.1	-0.8	-0.8	-2.8	-5.3	-7.6
CAB(B.US$) ***	-1.9	-4.2	-4.8	-4.5	-3.8	-2.8	-0.8	-0.6	-2.1	-4.3
ITALY										
GNP(%)	-	-	-	-	-	-	-	-	-	-
CPI(%)	-	-	-	-	-	-	-	-	-	-
GDEF(%GNPV) *	-	-	-	-	-	-	-	-	-	-
EXCH(%) **	-	-	-	-	-	-	-	-	-	-
CAB(B.US$) ***	-	-	-	-	-	-	-	-	-	-
CANADA										
GNP(%)	1.1	2.0	2.4	2.6	2.1	2.4	2.0	1.9	1.8	1.6
CPI(%)	0.2	0.4	0.6	0.8	0.5	1.2	1.7	2.1	2.5	3.0
GDEF(%GNPV) *	0.5	0.2	0.1	-0.0	0.2	0.0	0.2	0.2	0.3	0.4
EXCH(%) **	0.0	0.0	0.0	0.0	0.0	-0.1	-0.4	-0.7	-1.0	-1.3
CAB(B.US$) ***	0.1	-0.7	-2.0	-3.4	-1.5	-4.9	-3.5	-1.9	-1.1	-0.3
REST OF WORLD										
CAB(B.US$) ***	-	-	-	-	-	-	-	-	-	-

* Government deficit as a percentage of baseline nominal GNP.
** Exchange rate : Bilateral rate against U.S. $ ($/local currency).
*** Local currency units translated into U.S. $ at baseline exchange rates.

LINK Project World Model

See part 1 of this volume for design and detailed description of the simulations. See part 4 for bibliographical references.

Model: LINK
Simulation A: Baseline Path

	1985	1986	1987	1988	1989	1990
UNITED STATES						
GNPV(B.$)	3886.0	4132.0	4482.8	4856.9	5251.2	5690.2
GNP(B.72$)	1678.6	1715.2	1775.4	1840.0	1904.8	1967.6
PGNP(72=100)	231.5	240.9	252.5	263.9	275.6	289.2
CPI(72=100)	227.2	235.9	246.4	257.4	268.2	281.3
WAGES(72=100)	14.1	14.8	15.6	16.5	17.4	18.4
UN(%)	7.3	7.4	7.1	6.7	6.4	6.0
G(B.72$)	314.5	321.1	325.7	333.8	341.4	348.9
C(B.72$)	1104.2	1131.5	1162.1	1198.4	1230.1	1267.7
IFP(B.72$)	282.6	297.3	313.9	324.4	339.5	360.3
II(B.72$)	11.4	2.1	4.3	7.6	8.9	-2.6
XGS(B.72$)	141.5	150.2	161.9	175.7	193.2	211.8
MGS(B.72$)	175.6	187.0	192.5	199.8	208.3	218.5
M1(B.$)	583.5	623.3	672.3	725.1	781.1	840.8
RS(%)	7.6	6.9	6.8	6.5	6.8	6.4
RL(%)	9.9	8.8	8.6	8.6	8.8	8.4
GDEF(B.$)	189.1	191.3	191.4	190.6	168.5	147.9
PXGS(72=100)	266.5	275.6	287.1	302.8	320.4	339.6
PMGS(72=100)	264.4	271.3	282.4	297.3	313.8	332.0
EXCH(72=100) *	125.0	115.7	108.6	106.2	104.2	102.6
CAB(B.$)	-129.6	-148.1	-143.7	-121.6	-101.7	-83.9
NON-US OECD						
GNPV(B.$) **	4520.3	5282.5	6040.1	6623.3	7204.3	7817.4
GNP(B.72$) **	1625.9	1666.9	1713.1	1760.2	1809.6	1859.8
PGNP(72=100)	278.0	316.9	352.6	376.3	398.1	420.3
CPI(72=100)	1875.3	1996.1	2109.9	2240.7	2360.0	2506.4
WAGES(72=100)	-	-	-	-	-	-
UN(%)	-	-	-	-	-	-
C(B.72$) **	901.3	931.7	956.5	980.2	1001.7	1022.4
IFP(B.72$) **	927.2	984.2	1023.4	1060.2	1095.0	1127.1
RS(%)	-	-	-	-	-	-
RL(%)	-	-	-	-	-	-
GDEF(B.US$) **	-	-	-	-	-	-
PXGS(72=100)	255.7	270.4	282.9	294.6	301.9	314.2
PMGS(72=100)	342.0	349.1	357.6	370.2	383.7	400.8
EXCH(72=100) ***	-	-	-	-	-	-
CAB(B.US$)	69.1	70.2	74.6	70.1	56.0	52.3

* Exchange rate : (Weighted average of foreign currencies)/U.S. $.
** Local currency units translated into U.S. $ at baseline exchange rates.
*** Exchange rate : U.S. $/(weighted average of non-US OECD currencies).

Model: LINK
Simulation A: Baseline Path

	1985	1986	1987	1988	1989	1990
JAPAN						
GNP(B.72Y)	232098.7	240764.9	249743.2	258298.4	266746.8	275098.0
CPI(72=100)	1.5	1.6	1.6	1.6	1.7	1.7
RS(%)	6.5	6.3	6.2	6.1	6.3	6.3
GDEF(%GNPV) *	-	-	-	-	-	-
EXCH(72=100) **	0.0	0.0	0.0	0.0	0.0	0.0
CAB(B.US$) ***	45.9	50.9	53.8	59.5	51.8	49.4
GERMANY						
GNP(B.72DM)	938.8	954.7	976.1	997.8	1022.8	1047.6
CPI(72=100)	201.5	206.6	211.4	218.1	226.7	236.5
RS(%)	6.5	6.4	6.1	5.9	5.7	5.6
GDEF(%GNPV) *	1.6	2.0	1.9	1.5	1.3	0.9
EXCH(72=100) **	0.3	0.4	0.4	0.5	0.5	0.5
CAB(B.US$) ***	7.4	6.6	7.3	6.8	4.7	5.0
FRANCE						
GNP(B.72F)	1067.0	1089.9	1109.2	1130.7	1159.1	1187.7
CPI(72=100)	3753.0	3901.4	4051.7	4205.4	4363.7	4519.4
GDEF(%GNPV) *	-	-	-	-	-	-
EXCH(72=100) **	0.1	0.1	0.1	0.1	0.1	0.1
CAB(B.US$) ***	-4.4	-2.8	-0.1	-2.2	-4.5	-7.1
UNITED KINGDOM						
GNP(B.72LB)	105.4	107.6	109.7	111.9	114.3	116.5
CPI(72=100)	2.7	2.8	2.9	3.0	3.1	3.3
GDEF(%GNPV) *	-	-	-	-	-	-
EXCH(72=100) **	1.3	1.4	1.6	1.6	1.6	1.6
CAB(B.US$) ***	-0.0	-2.4	-5.9	-7.6	-10.7	-10.7
ITALY						
GNP(B.72L)	81288.1	82995.3	85710.1	88666.8	91433.6	94365.8
CPI(72=100)	738.9	793.4	845.9	904.6	961.0	1012.2
GDEF(%GNPV) *	-	-	-	-	-	-
EXCH(72=100) **	0.0	0.0	0.0	0.0	0.0	0.0
CAB(B.US$) ***	-8.6	-11.5	-13.4	-13.6	-15.9	-19.5
CANADA						
GNP(B.72C$)	146.4	150.5	155.7	161.2	166.0	170.7
CPI(72=100)	3.0	3.1	3.2	3.4	3.5	3.7
GDEF(%GNPV) *	5.2	5.9	5.9	3.1	-0.3	-3.0
EXCH(72=100) **	0.7	0.8	0.8	0.8	0.8	0.8
CAB(B.US$) ***	1.9	1.2	1.3	0.6	-0.4	-1.9
REST OF WORLD						
CAB(B.US$) ***	51.7	43.3	38.3	36.5	38.4	35.7

* Government deficit as a percentage of baseline nominal GNP.
** Exchange rate: Bilateral rate against U.S. $ ($/local currency).
*** Local currency units translated into U.S. $ at baseline exchange rates.

Model: LINK
Simulation B: Reduction in U.S. Government Purchases with Foreign Monetary Aggregates Unchanged from Baseline
(Deviation of Shock Path from Baseline Path)

	1985									
	Q1	Q2	Q3	Q4	1985	1986	1987	1988	1989	1990
UNITED STATES										
GNPV(%)	-	-	-	-	-1.4	-1.7	-2.0	-2.2	-2.4	-2.6
GNP(%)	-	-	-	-	-1.2	-1.2	-1.0	-0.7	-0.5	-0.3
PGNP(%)	-	-	-	-	-0.2	-0.5	-1.0	-1.5	-2.0	-2.3
CPI(%)	-	-	-	-	-0.1	-0.5	-0.9	-1.4	-1.8	-2.1
WAGES(%)	-	-	-	-	-0.1	-0.5	-1.1	-1.7	-2.3	-2.8
UN(% PTS)	-	-	-	-	0.7	1.0	1.1	0.9	0.7	0.5
GNP(B.72$)	-	-	-	-	-20.9	-20.9	-17.5	-13.0	-9.0	-5.5
G(B.72$)	-	-	-	-	-16.8	-17.2	-17.8	-18.4	-19.0	-19.7
C(B.72$)	-	-	-	-	-2.3	-1.8	0.8	4.7	8.3	11.0
IFP(B.72$)	-	-	-	-	-3.2	-3.4	-2.3	-1.2	-0.1	1.2
II(B.72$)	-	-	-	-	-0.4	-0.7	-0.5	-0.5	-0.6	-0.8
XGS(B.72$)	-	-	-	-	-0.2	-0.2	0.1	0.4	0.9	1.3
MGS(B.72$)	-	-	-	-	-2.0	-2.4	-2.2	-1.8	-1.6	-1.5
M1(%)	-	-	-	-	-0.0	-0.0	-0.0	-0.0	-0.0	-0.0
RS(% PTS)	-	-	-	-	-0.1	-0.2	-0.3	-0.5	-0.6	-0.7
RL(% PTS)	-	-	-	-	-0.1	-0.2	-0.4	-0.5	-0.7	-0.8
GDEF(B$)	-	-	-	-	-19.2	-15.9	-17.3	-22.0	-29.8	-39.6
PXGS(%)	-	-	-	-	-0.0	-0.1	-0.2	-0.3	-0.4	-0.4
PMGS(%)	-	-	-	-	-0.2	-0.3	-0.4	-0.4	-0.3	-0.2
EXCH(%) *	-	-	-	-	0.0	0.1	0.3	0.3	0.2	0.1
CAB(B$)	-	-	-	-	5.0	6.4	6.5	6.0	5.5	5.3
NON-US OECD										
GNPV(%) **	-	-	-	-	-0.1	-0.3	-0.5	-0.6	-0.5	-0.3
GNP(%) **	-	-	-	-	-0.1	-0.1	-0.1	-0.1	-0.1	-0.0
PGNP(%)	-	-	-	-	-0.0	-0.2	-0.4	-0.5	-0.4	-0.3
CPI(%)	-	-	-	-	-0.0	0.0	0.1	0.3	0.5	0.8
WAGES(%)	-	-	-	-	-	-	-	-	-	-
UN(% PTS)	-	-	-	-	-	-	-	-	-	-
C(%) **	-	-	-	-	-0.0	-0.0	-0.0	-0.1	-0.1	-0.1
IFP(%) **	-	-	-	-	-0.1	-0.1	-0.0	-0.0	-0.1	-0.2
RS(% PTS)	-	-	-	-	-	-	-	-	-	-
RL(% PTS)	-	-	-	-	-	-	-	-	-	-
GDEF (B.US$) **	-	-	-	-	-	-	-	-	-	-
PXGS(%)	-	-	-	-	0.0	0.2	0.6	1.0	1.3	1.6
PMGS(%)	-	-	-	-	0.1	0.4	0.9	1.2	1.4	1.4
EXCH(%) ***	-	-	-	-	-	-	-	-	-	-
CAB(B.US$) **	-	-	-	-	-1.8	-1.9	-1.3	-0.1	1.0	2.2

* Exchange rate : (Weighted average of foreign currencies)/U.S. $.
** Local currency units translated into U.S. $ at baseline exchange rates.
*** Exchange rate : U.S. $/(weighted average of non-US OECD currencies).

Model: LINK
Simulation B: Reduction in U.S. Government Purchases with Foreign Monetary Aggregates Unchanged from Baseline
(Deviation of Shock Path from Baseline Path)

	1985 Q1	1985 Q2	1985 Q3	1985 Q4	1985	1986	1987	1988	1989	1990
JAPAN										
GNP(%)	-	-	-	-	-0.1	-0.1	-0.1	-0.1	-0.0	-0.0
CPI(%)	-	-	-	-	-0.0	-0.0	-0.0	-0.0	-0.1	-0.1
RS(% PTS)	-	-	-	-	-0.0	0.0	0.0	-0.0	-0.0	-0.0
GDEF(%GNPV) *	-	-	-	-	-	-	-	-	-	-
EXCH(%) **	-	-	-	-	-0.0	-0.2	-0.3	-0.3	-0.1	0.1
CAB(B.US$) ***	-	-	-	-	-0.7	-0.9	-0.9	-1.0	-1.1	-1.3
GERMANY										
GNP(%)	-	-	-	-	-0.1	-0.1	-0.0	-0.0	-0.1	-0.1
CPI(%)	-	-	-	-	0.0	0.0	0.1	0.1	0.1	0.1
RS(% PTS)	-	-	-	-	-0.1	-0.1	-0.0	-0.0	-0.0	-0.0
GDEF(%GNPV) *	-	-	-	-	0.0	0.0	-0.0	-0.0	-0.0	-0.0
EXCH(%) **	-	-	-	-	-0.1	-0.3	-0.6	-0.7	-0.6	-0.3
CAB(B.US$) ***	-	-	-	-	0.1	0.2	0.3	0.5	0.5	0.4
FRANCE										
GNP(%)	-	-	-	-	-0.0	0.1	0.1	0.1	-0.0	-0.2
CPI(%)	-	-	-	-	0.0	0.0	0.2	0.4	0.7	1.2
GDEF(%GNPV) *	-	-	-	-	-	-	-	-	-	-
EXCH(%) **	-	-	-	-	-0.1	-0.7	-1.5	-2.0	-2.2	-2.3
CAB(B.US$) ***	-	-	-	-	-0.1	-0.3	-0.3	0.3	0.9	1.5
UNITED KINGDOM										
GNP(%)	-	-	-	-	-0.1	-0.1	-0.0	0.0	0.0	0.0
CPI(%)	-	-	-	-	0.0	-0.0	-0.1	-0.0	0.0	0.0
GDEF(%GNPV) *	-	-	-	-	-	-	-	-	-	-
EXCH(%) **	-	-	-	-	-0.0	-0.2	-0.5	-0.6	-0.7	-0.5
CAB(B.US$) ***	-	-	-	-	-0.2	-0.3	-0.3	-0.2	-0.1	0.0
ITALY										
GNP(%)	-	-	-	-	-0.0	-0.0	-0.0	0.0	0.1	0.1
CPI(%)	-	-	-	-	-0.0	0.0	0.0	0.1	0.1	0.1
GDEF(%GNPV) *	-	-	-	-	-	-	-	-	-	-
EXCH(%) **	-	-	-	-	-0.1	-0.2	-0.4	-0.5	-0.5	-0.5
CAB(B.US$) ***	-	-	-	-	-0.1	-0.1	0.0	0.0	0.1	0.2
CANADA										
GNP(%)	-	-	-	-	-0.2	-0.3	-0.3	-0.3	-0.3	-0.1
CPI(%)	-	-	-	-	-0.0	-0.2	-0.3	-0.5	-0.7	-0.9
GDEF(%GNPV) *	-	-	-	-	0.1	0.2	0.2	0.2	0.1	0.0
EXCH(%) **	-	-	-	-	0.0	0.1	0.1	0.2	0.2	0.3
CAB(B.US$) ***	-	-	-	-	-0.5	-0.5	-0.6	-0.5	-0.3	-0.2
REST OF WORLD										
CAB(B.US$) ***	-	-	-	-	-1.6	-2.2	-2.4	-2.6	-2.9	-3.3

* Government deficit as a percentage of baseline nominal GNP.
** Exchange rate : Bilateral rate against U.S. $ ($/local currency).
*** Local currency units translated into U.S. $ at baseline exchange rates.

Model: LINK
Simulation C: Reduction in U.S. Government Purchases with Foreign Short-Term Interest Rates Unchanged from Baseline
(Deviation of Shock Path from Baseline Path)

	1985 Q1	1985 Q2	1985 Q3	1985 Q4	1985	1986	1987	1988	1989	1990
UNITED STATES										
GNPV(%)	-	-	-	-	-1.4	-1.7	-2.0	-2.2	-2.4	-2.6
GNP(%)	-	-	-	-	-1.2	-1.2	-1.0	-0.7	-0.5	-0.3
PGNP(%)	-	-	-	-	-0.2	-0.5	-1.0	-1.5	-2.0	-2.3
CPI(%)	-	-	-	-	-0.1	-0.5	-0.9	-1.4	-1.8	-2.1
WAGES(%)	-	-	-	-	-0.1	-0.5	-1.1	-1.7	-2.3	-2.8
UN(% PTS)	-	-	-	-	0.7	1.0	1.1	0.9	0.7	0.5
GNP(B.72$)	-	-	-	-	-20.9	-20.9	-17.5	-13.0	-9.0	-5.5
G(B.72$)	-	-	-	-	-16.8	-17.2	-17.8	-18.4	-19.0	-19.7
C(B.72$)	-	-	-	-	-2.3	-1.8	0.8	4.7	8.2	11.0
IFP(B.72$)	-	-	-	-	-3.2	-3.4	-2.3	-1.2	-0.1	1.1
II(B.72$)	-	-	-	-	-0.4	-0.7	-0.5	-0.5	-0.6	-0.8
XGS(B.72$)	-	-	-	-	-0.2	-0.2	0.1	0.5	0.9	1.4
MGS(B.72$)	-	-	-	-	-2.0	-2.4	-2.2	-1.9	-1.6	-1.5
M1(%)	-	-	-	-	-0.0	-0.0	-0.0	-0.0	-0.0	-0.0
RS(% PTS)	-	-	-	-	-0.1	-0.2	-0.3	-0.5	-0.6	-0.7
RL(% PTS)	-	-	-	-	-0.1	-0.2	-0.4	-0.5	-0.7	-0.8
GDEF(B$)	-	-	-	-	-19.2	-15.9	-17.4	-22.1	-29.8	-39.7
PXGS(%)	-	-	-	-	-0.0	-0.1	-0.2	-0.3	-0.4	-0.4
PMGS(%)	-	-	-	-	-0.2	-0.3	-0.4	-0.3	-0.3	-0.2
EXCH(%) *	-	-	-	-	0.0	0.1	0.3	0.3	0.3	0.2
CAB(B$)	-	-	-	-	5.1	6.5	6.5	6.1	5.5	5.5
NON-US OECD										
GNPV(%) **	-	-	-	-	-0.1	-0.3	-0.5	-0.6	-0.5	-0.4
GNP(%) **	-	-	-	-	-0.1	-0.1	-0.1	-0.0	-0.0	0.0
PGNP(%)	-	-	-	-	-0.0	-0.2	-0.4	-0.5	-0.5	-0.4
CPI(%)	-	-	-	-	0.0	0.0	0.1	0.3	0.5	0.7
WAGES(%)	-	-	-	-	-	-	-	-	-	-
UN(% PTS)	-	-	-	-	-	-	-	-	-	-
C(%) **	-	-	-	-	-0.0	-0.0	-0.0	-0.1	-0.1	-0.1
IFP(%) **	-	-	-	-	-0.1	-0.1	-0.0	0.0	0.0	0.1
RS(% PTS)	-	-	-	-	-	-	-	-	-	-
RL(% PTS)	-	-	-	-	-	-	-	-	-	-
GDEF (B.US$) **	-	-	-	-	-	-	-	-	-	-
PXGS(%)	-	-	-	-	0.0	0.2	0.7	1.1	1.7	2.2
PMGS(%)	-	-	-	-	0.1	0.4	0.9	1.4	1.8	2.2
EXCH(%) ***	-	-	-	-	-	-	-	-	-	-
CAB(B.US$) **	-	-	-	-	-1.9	-2.2	-1.5	-0.5	0.5	1.5

* Exchange rate : (Weighted average of foreign currencies)/U.S. $.
** Local currency units translated into U.S. $ at baseline exchange rates.
*** Exchange rate : U.S. $/(weighted average of non-US OECD currencies).

Model: LINK
Simulation C: Reduction in U.S. Government Purchases with Foreign Short-Term Interest Rates Unchanged from Baseline
(Deviation of Shock Path from Baseline Path)

	1985									
	Q1	Q2	Q3	Q4	1985	1986	1987	1988	1989	1990
JAPAN										
GNP(%)	-	-	-	-	-0.1	-0.1	-0.1	-0.1	-0.0	-0.0
CPI(%)	-	-	-	-	-0.0	-0.0	-0.0	-0.0	-0.0	-0.1
RS(% PTS)	-	-	-	-	0.0	0.0	0.0	0.0	0.0	0.0
GDEF(%GNPV) *	-	-	-	-	-	-	-	-	-	-
EXCH(%) **	-	-	-	-	-0.0	-0.2	-0.3	-0.3	-0.1	0.1
CAB(B.US$) ***	-	-	-	-	-0.6	-0.9	-0.9	-0.9	-1.0	-1.2
GERMANY										
GNP(%)	-	-	-	-	-0.1	-0.1	0.0	0.0	0.0	0.0
CPI(%)	-	-	-	-	-0.0	0.0	0.1	0.1	0.1	0.1
RS(% PTS)	-	-	-	-	0.0	0.0	0.0	0.0	0.0	0.0
GDEF(%GNPV) *	-	-	-	-	0.0	0.0	0.0	0.0	-0.0	-0.0
EXCH(%) **	-	-	-	-	-0.0	-0.2	-0.6	-0.7	-0.7	-0.5
CAB(B.US$) ***	-	-	-	-	-0.2	-0.4	-0.4	-0.3	-0.4	-0.6
FRANCE										
GNP(%)	-	-	-	-	-0.0	0.1	0.2	0.2	0.2	0.3
CPI(%)	-	-	-	-	0.0	0.0	0.1	0.3	0.6	1.0
GDEF(%GNPV) *	-	-	-	-	-	-	-	-	-	-
EXCH(%) **	-	-	-	-	-0.1	-0.7	-1.6	-2.3	-3.0	-3.6
CAB(B.US$) ***	-	-	-	-	-0.1	-0.3	-0.3	-0.1	0.3	0.5
UNITED KINGDOM										
GNP(%)	-	-	-	-	-0.1	-0.0	0.0	0.0	0.1	0.0
CPI(%)	-	-	-	-	0.0	-0.0	-0.0	0.0	0.0	0.0
GDEF(%GNPV) *	-	-	-	-	-	-	-	-	-	-
EXCH(%) **	-	-	-	-	-0.0	-0.2	-0.5	-0.7	-0.7	-0.5
CAB(B.US$) ***	-	-	-	-	-0.2	-0.3	-0.3	-0.2	-0.0	0.2
ITALY										
GNP(%)	-	-	-	-	-0.0	-0.0	0.0	0.1	0.1	0.2
CPI(%)	-	-	-	-	0.0	0.0	0.0	0.1	0.1	0.1
GDEF(%GNPV) *	-	-	-	-	-	-	-	-	-	-
EXCH(%) **	-	-	-	-	-0.1	-0.2	-0.4	-0.5	-0.5	-0.5
CAB(B.US$) ***	-	-	-	-	-0.1	-0.0	0.1	0.1	0.2	0.3
CANADA										
GNP(%)	-	-	-	-	-0.2	-0.3	-0.4	-0.5	-0.6	-0.4
CPI(%)	-	-	-	-	-0.0	-0.2	-0.3	-0.4	-0.6	-0.7
GDEF(%GNPV) *	-	-	-	-	0.1	0.2	0.2	0.2	0.2	0.1
EXCH(%) **	-	-	-	-	0.0	0.1	0.1	0.1	0.2	0.3
CAB(B.US$) ***	-	-	-	-	-0.5	-0.5	-0.6	-0.6	-0.5	-0.4
REST OF WORLD										
CAB(B.US$) ***	-	-	-	-	-1.6	-2.0	-2.3	-2.4	-2.6	-3.0

* Government deficit as a percentage of baseline nominal GNP.
** Exchange rate : Bilateral rate against U.S. $ ($/local currency).
*** Local currency units translated into U.S. $ at baseline exchange rates.

Model: LINK
Simulation D: U.S. Monetary Expansion with foreign Monetary Aggregates Unchanged from Baseline
(Deviation of Shock Path from Baseline Path)

	1985 Q1	1985 Q2	1985 Q3	1985 Q4	1985	1986	1987	1988	1989	1990
UNITED STATES										
GNPV(%)	-	-	-	-	0.0	0.4	1.0	1.3	1.6	2.1
GNP(%)	-	-	-	-	0.1	1.0	2.1	2.5	2.5	2.4
PGNP(%)	-	-	-	-	-0.1	-0.6	-1.1	-1.2	-0.9	-0.3
CPI(%)	-	-	-	-	-0.1	-0.4	-0.7	-0.8	-0.6	-0.1
WAGES(%)	-	-	-	-	-0.0	-0.3	-0.5	-0.4	0.1	1.0
UN(% PTS)	-	-	-	-	-0.0	-0.4	-1.0	-1.6	-1.7	-1.6
GNP(B.72$)	-	-	-	-	2.3	17.3	37.2	46.7	47.7	47.1
G(B.72$)	-	-	-	-	0.0	0.0	0.0	0.0	0.0	0.0
C(B.72$)	-	-	-	-	1.2	8.0	18.1	26.9	30.5	30.8
IFP(B.72$)	-	-	-	-	1.0	9.5	20.0	21.3	19.3	18.7
II(B.72$)	-	-	-	-	0.1	0.8	1.4	1.6	0.8	0.4
XGS(B.72$)	-	-	-	-	0.2	1.1	2.4	3.4	3.9	3.9
MGS(B.72$)	-	-	-	-	0.3	2.1	4.8	6.5	6.8	6.8
M1(%)	-	-	-	-	2.0	4.0	4.0	4.0	4.0	4.0
RS(% PTS)	-	-	-	-	-0.7	-1.4	-1.3	-1.3	-1.3	-1.3
RL(% PTS)	-	-	-	-	-0.6	-1.5	-1.5	-1.5	-1.6	-1.5
GDEF(B$)	-	-	-	-	-2.1	-15.7	-37.3	-52.6	-62.8	-72.8
PXGS(%)	-	-	-	-	0.0	0.0	0.1	0.3	0.6	1.0
PMGS(%)	-	-	-	-	0.2	0.8	1.3	1.8	2.3	2.7
EXCH(%) *	-	-	-	-	-0.6	-2.3	-3.1	-3.8	-4.6	-5.3
CAB(B$)	-	-	-	-	-0.9	-5.9	-12.6	-17.8	-20.4	-22.3
NON-US OECD										
GNPV(%) **	-	-	-	-	0.6	2.1	2.8	3.5	4.3	5.2
GNP(%) **	-	-	-	-	-0.1	-0.1	0.0	0.1	0.1	0.2
PGNP(%)	-	-	-	-	0.6	2.2	2.8	3.4	4.2	5.0
CPI(%)	-	-	-	-	-0.0	-0.1	-0.3	-0.5	-0.8	-1.2
WAGES(%)	-	-	-	-	-	-	-	-	-	-
UN(% PTS)	-	-	-	-	-	-	-	-	-	-
C(%) **	-	-	-	-	0.0	0.0	0.1	0.1	0.2	0.3
IFP(%) **	-	-	-	-	-0.1	-0.2	-0.1	0.2	0.3	0.4
RS(% PTS)	-	-	-	-	-	-	-	-	-	-
RL(% PTS)	-	-	-	-	-	-	-	-	-	-
GDEF (B.US$) **	-	-	-	-	-	-	-	-	-	-
PXGS(%)	-	-	-	-	-0.1	-0.6	-1.0	-1.5	-2.2	-3.1
PMGS(%)	-	-	-	-	-0.2	-1.0	-1.4	-1.9	-2.7	-3.4
EXCH(%) ***	-	-	-	-	-	-	-	-	-	-
CAB(B.US$) **	-	-	-	-	0.5	1.5	4.0	7.6	10.0	11.5

* Exchange rate : (Weighted average of foreign currencies)/U.S. $.
** Local currency units translated into U.S. $ at baseline exchange rates.
*** Exchange rate : U.S. $/(weighted average of non-US OECD currencies).

Model: LINK
Simulation D: U.S. Monetary Expansion with Foreign Monetary Aggregates Unchanged from Baseline
(Deviation of Shock Path from Baseline Path)

	1985 Q1	1985 Q2	1985 Q3	1985 Q4	1985	1986	1987	1988	1989	1990
JAPAN										
GNP(%)	-	-	-	-	-0.1	-0.2	-0.1	0.1	0.1	0.0
CPI(%)	-	-	-	-	-0.1	-0.4	-0.7	-0.9	-1.1	-1.1
RS(% PTS)	-	-	-	-	-0.0	-0.1	-0.0	-0.0	-0.0	-0.0
GDEF(%GNPV) *	-	-	-	-	-	-	-	-	-	-
EXCH(%) **	-	-	-	-	1.3	4.5	5.7	6.5	7.5	8.3
CAB(B.US$) ***	-	-	-	-	-0.4	-1.4	-0.7	0.6	2.5	4.8
GERMANY										
GNP(%)	-	-	-	-	-0.2	-0.5	-0.5	-0.5	-0.6	-0.7
CPI(%)	-	-	-	-	-0.0	-0.3	-0.6	-0.9	-1.4	-1.9
RS(% PTS)	-	-	-	-	-0.1	-0.2	-0.3	-0.4	-0.6	-0.8
GDEF(%GNPV) *	-	-	-	-	-0.0	-0.0	-0.0	-0.1	-0.1	-0.1
EXCH(%) **	-	-	-	-	0.6	2.3	3.5	4.5	5.8	6.9
CAB(B.US$) ***	-	-	-	-	0.8	0.9	0.4	1.2	1.7	1.8
FRANCE										
GNP(%)	-	-	-	-	-0.0	0.0	0.2	0.3	0.3	0.5
CPI(%)	-	-	-	-	-0.0	-0.1	-0.3	-0.6	-1.0	-1.7
GDEF(%GNPV) *	-	-	-	-	-	-	-	-	-	-
EXCH(%) **	-	-	-	-	0.4	1.7	2.5	3.6	5.1	6.6
CAB(B.US$) ***	-	-	-	-	0.1	0.0	-0.2	-0.1	-0.1	-0.9
UNITED KINGDOM										
GNP(%)	-	-	-	-	0.0	0.1	0.1	0.2	0.2	0.3
CPI(%)	-	-	-	-	-0.0	-0.5	-1.2	-1.9	-2.4	-2.7
GDEF(%GNPV) *	-	-	-	-	-	-	-	-	-	-
EXCH(%) **	-	-	-	-	0.3	1.5	3.1	4.9	7.0	9.1
CAB(B.US$) ***	-	-	-	-	-0.1	-0.1	0.5	1.4	2.3	3.0
ITALY										
GNP(%)	-	-	-	-	0.0	0.1	0.3	0.4	0.5	0.6
CPI(%)	-	-	-	-	0.0	0.1	0.3	0.3	0.4	0.4
GDEF(%GNPV) *	-	-	-	-	-	-	-	-	-	-
EXCH(%) **	-	-	-	-	0.1	0.4	0.6	0.9	1.3	1.7
CAB(B.US$) ***	-	-	-	-	0.0	0.3	0.7	0.9	1.1	1.1
CANADA										
GNP(%)	-	-	-	-	-0.0	-0.0	0.1	0.3	0.4	0.5
CPI(%)	-	-	-	-	-0.1	-0.2	-0.3	-0.3	-0.2	0.1
GDEF(%GNPV) *	-	-	-	-	0.0	0.0	-0.1	-0.1	-0.2	-0.3
EXCH(%) **	-	-	-	-	0.2	0.7	0.9	0.9	0.9	1.0
CAB(B.US$) ***	-	-	-	-	0.1	0.3	0.5	0.9	1.1	1.6
REST OF WORLD										
CAB(B.US$) ***	-	-	-	-	-0.5	0.3	2.6	3.9	4.9	5.4

* Government deficit as a percentage of baseline nominal GNP.
** Exchange rate : Bilateral rate against U.S. $ ($/local currency).
*** Local currency units translated into U.S. $ at baseline exchange rates.

Model: LINK

Simulation E: U.S. Monetary Expansion with Foreign Short-Term Interest Rates Unchanged from Baseline

(Deviation of Shock Path from Baseline Path)

	1985									
	Q1	Q2	Q3	Q4	1985	1986	1987	1988	1989	1990
UNITED STATES										
GNPV(%)	-	-	-	-	0.0	0.4	1.0	1.3	1.6	2.1
GNP(%)	-	-	-	-	0.1	1.0	2.1	2.5	2.5	2.4
PGNP(%)	-	-	-	-	-0.1	-0.6	-1.1	-1.2	-0.9	-0.3
CPI(%)	-	-	-	-	-0.1	-0.4	-0.8	-0.9	-0.6	-0.2
WAGES(%)	-	-	-	-	-0.0	-0.3	-0.5	-0.5	0.0	1.0
UN(% PTS)	-	-	-	-	-0.0	-0.4	-1.0	-1.6	-1.7	-1.6
GNP(B.72$)	-	-	-	-	2.3	17.3	37.1	46.5	47.4	46.5
G(B.72$)	-	-	-	-	0.0	0.0	0.0	0.0	0.0	0.0
C(B.72$)	-	-	-	-	1.2	8.0	18.1	26.9	30.7	31.0
IFP(B.72$)	-	-	-	-	1.0	9.5	20.0	21.3	19.3	18.8
II(B.72$)	-	-	-	-	0.1	0.8	1.5	1.6	0.8	0.4
XGS(B.72$)	-	-	-	-	0.2	1.1	2.3	3.2	3.4	3.1
MGS(B.72$)	-	-	-	-	0.3	2.1	4.9	6.5	6.8	6.8
M1(%)	-	-	-	-	2.0	4.0	4.0	4.0	4.0	4.0
RS(% PTS)	-	-	-	-	-0.7	-1.4	-1.3	-1.3	-1.4	-1.3
RL(% PTS)	-	-	-	-	-0.6	-1.5	-1.5	-1.5	-1.6	-1.5
GDEF(B$)	-	-	-	-	-2.2	-15.8	-37.3	-52.3	-62.3	-71.8
PXGS(%)	-	-	-	-	0.0	-0.0	0.1	0.3	0.6	1.0
PMGS(%)	-	-	-	-	0.2	0.7	1.2	1.6	2.1	2.5
EXCH(%) *	-	-	-	-	-0.6	-2.3	-3.1	-3.8	-4.7	-5.6
CAB(B$)	-	-	-	-	-0.8	-5.7	-12.6	-18.2	-21.4	-24.3
NON-US OECD										
GNPV(%) **	-	-	-	-	0.6	2.0	2.6	3.2	4.1	4.8
GNP(%) **	-	-	-	-	-0.0	-0.0	0.1	0.1	0.1	0.0
PGNP(%)	-	-	-	-	0.6	2.0	2.6	3.1	4.0	4.8
CPI(%)	-	-	-	-	-0.0	-0.1	-0.2	-0.4	-0.7	-1.1
WAGES(%)	-	-	-	-	-	-	-	-	-	-
UN(% PTS)	-	-	-	-	-	-	-	-	-	-
C(%) **	-	-	-	-	0.0	0.0	0.1	0.1	0.2	0.2
IFP(%) **	-	-	-	-	-0.1	-0.2	-0.1	0.1	0.1	0.0
RS(% PTS)	-	-	-	-	-	-	-	-	-	-
RL(% PTS)	-	-	-	-	-	-	-	-	-	-
GDEF (B.US$) **	-	-	-	-	-	-	-	-	-	-
PXGS(%)	-	-	-	-	-0.1	-0.6	-1.1	-1.7	-2.7	-4.0
PMGS(%)	-	-	-	-	-0.3	-1.2	-1.7	-2.5	-3.5	-4.8
EXCH(%) ***	-	-	-	-	-	-	-	-	-	-
CAB(B.US$) **	-	-	-	-	0.2	1.1	4.1	8.2	11.6	14.4

* Exchange rate : (Weighted average of foreign currencies)/U.S. $.

** Local currency units translated into U.S. $ at baseline exchange rates.

*** Exchange rate : U.S. $/(weighted average of non-US OECD currencies).

Model: LINK
Simulation E: U.S. Monetary Expansion with Foreign Short-Term Interest Rates Unchanged from Baseline
(Deviation of Shock Path from Baseline Path)

	1985									
	Q1	Q2	Q3	Q4	1985	1986	1987	1988	1989	1990
JAPAN										
GNP(%)	-	-	-	-	-0.1	-0.2	-0.1	0.0	0.0	-0.0
CPI(%)	-	-	-	-	-0.1	-0.4	-0.7	-1.0	-1.2	-1.2
RS(% PTS)	-	-	-	-	0.0	0.0	0.0	0.0	0.0	0.0
GDEF(%GNPV) *	-	-	-	-	-	-	-	-	-	-
EXCH(%) **	-	-	-	-	1.3	4.7	5.8	6.6	7.6	8.5
CAB(B.US$) ***	-	-	-	-	-0.4	-1.5	-0.9	0.4	2.1	4.1
GERMANY										
GNP(%)	-	-	-	-	-0.1	-0.3	-0.5	-0.7	-1.1	-1.6
CPI(%)	-	-	-	-	-0.1	-0.4	-0.8	-1.3	-2.0	-2.8
RS(% PTS)	-	-	-	-	0.0	0.0	0.0	0.0	0.0	0.0
GDEF(%GNPV) *	-	-	-	-	-0.0	-0.0	-0.0	-0.0	0.0	0.1
EXCH(%) **	-	-	-	-	0.7	2.6	3.9	5.2	7.0	9.1
CAB(B.US$) ***	-	-	-	-	0.2	-0.1	-0.6	-0.2	0.2	0.8
FRANCE										
GNP(%)	-	-	-	-	-0.0	0.0	0.1	0.0	-0.1	-0.3
CPI(%)	-	-	-	-	-0.0	-0.1	-0.3	-0.6	-0.9	-1.5
GDEF(%GNPV) *	-	-	-	-	-	-	-	-	-	-
EXCH(%) **	-	-	-	-	0.5	1.7	2.7	4.1	6.2	8.9
CAB(B.US$) ***	-	-	-	-	0.1	0.3	0.3	0.7	0.9	1.0
UNITED KINGDOM										
GNP(%)	-	-	-	-	0.0	0.1	0.2	0.2	0.3	0.3
CPI(%)	-	-	-	-	-0.1	-0.7	-1.6	-2.2	-2.7	-3.1
GDEF(%GNPV) *	-	-	-	-	-	-	-	-	-	-
EXCH(%) **	-	-	-	-	0.4	1.7	3.3	5.2	7.4	9.8
CAB(B.US$) ***	-	-	-	-	-0.1	0.0	0.6	1.6	2.6	3.3
ITALY										
GNP(%)	-	-	-	-	0.0	0.2	0.4	0.5	0.5	0.5
CPI(%)	-	-	-	-	0.0	0.1	0.2	0.2	0.1	0.2
GDEF(%GNPV) *	-	-	-	-	-	-	-	-	-	-
EXCH(%) **	-	-	-	-	0.1	0.4	0.6	1.0	1.4	1.7
CAB(B.US$) ***	-	-	-	-	0.1	0.4	0.8	0.9	0.9	0.8
CANADA										
GNP(%)	-	-	-	-	-0.0	-0.1	0.0	0.3	0.5	0.6
CPI(%)	-	-	-	-	-0.1	-0.2	-0.3	-0.3	-0.3	-0.1
GDEF(%GNPV) *	-	-	-	-	0.0	0.0	-0.1	-0.1	-0.2	-0.3
EXCH(%) **	-	-	-	-	0.2	0.7	0.9	0.9	1.0	1.0
CAB(B.US$) ***	-	-	-	-	0.1	0.3	0.5	0.9	1.1	1.6
REST OF WORLD										
CAB(B.US$) ***	-	-	-	-	-0.4	0.5	2.6	3.5	3.9	3.5

* Government deficit as a percentage of baseline nominal GNP.
** Exchange rate : Bilateral rate against U.S. $ ($/local currency).
*** Local currency units translated into U.S. $ at baseline exchange rates.

Model: LINK
Simulation F: Nonpolicy Exogenous Depreciation of the Dollar
(Deviation of Shock Path from Baseline Path)

	1985 Q1	1985 Q2	1985 Q3	1985 Q4	1985	1986	1987	1988	1989	1990
UNITED STATES										
GNPV(%)	-	-	-	-	-0.0	0.2	0.4	0.8	0.9	0.9
GNP(%)	-	-	-	-	0.1	0.2	0.2	0.0	-0.3	-0.6
PGNP(%)	-	-	-	-	-0.1	-0.0	0.2	0.7	1.2	1.5
CPI(%)	-	-	-	-	0.1	0.3	0.7	1.2	1.6	1.8
WAGES(%)	-	-	-	-	0.0	0.3	0.6	1.2	1.7	2.1
UN(% PTS)	-	-	-	-	-0.0	-0.2	-0.3	-0.4	-0.3	-0.1
GNP(B.72$)	-	-	-	-	1.1	3.6	4.0	0.8	-6.1	-11.2
G(B.72$)	-	-	-	-	0.0	-0.0	0.0	0.0	0.0	0.0
C(B.72$)	-	-	-	-	-0.3	-1.5	-4.1	-8.2	-12.4	-15.3
IFP(B.72$)	-	-	-	-	0.3	0.8	-0.1	-1.9	-3.8	-4.9
II(B.72$)	-	-	-	-	-0.3	-0.7	-0.9	-0.3	0.4	0.6
XGS(B.72$)	-	-	-	-	0.9	3.6	6.6	7.7	5.6	3.8
MGS(B.72$)	-	-	-	-	-0.5	-1.4	-2.5	-3.4	-4.1	-4.5
M1(%)	-	-	-	-	-0.0	-0.0	-0.0	-0.0	-0.0	-0.0
RS(% PTS)	-	-	-	-	-0.0	0.0	0.1	0.2	0.3	0.3
RL(% PTS)	-	-	-	-	-0.0	0.0	0.1	0.2	0.3	0.3
GDEF(B$)	-	-	-	-	-0.0	-2.6	-6.4	-9.9	-8.5	-5.2
PXGS(%)	-	-	-	-	0.1	0.5	0.7	0.9	0.7	0.6
PMGS(%)	-	-	-	-	2.0	5.1	7.8	8.0	6.7	5.7
EXCH(%) *	-	-	-	-	-5.3	-13.4	-20.8	-23.5	-23.5	-23.6
CAB(B$)	-	-	-	-	-2.7	-3.5	-0.9	5.4	6.7	6.9
NON-US OECD										
GNPV(%) **	-	-	-	-	5.6	14.8	24.2	26.5	24.3	22.5
GNP(%) **	-	-	-	-	-0.5	-1.1	-1.7	-1.8	-2.3	-2.5
PGNP(%)	-	-	-	-	6.1	16.1	26.3	28.8	27.1	25.6
CPI(%)	-	-	-	-	-0.4	-1.8	-4.2	-7.0	-9.3	-11.6
WAGES(%)	-	-	-	-	-	-	-	-	-	-
UN(% PTS)	-	-	-	-	-	-	-	-	-	-
C(%) **	-	-	-	-	0.1	0.2	0.4	0.5	0.5	0.5
IFP(%) **	-	-	-	-	-0.4	-0.9	-0.8	-0.1	-0.3	-0.8
RS(% PTS)	-	-	-	-	-	-	-	-	-	-
RL(% PTS)	-	-	-	-	-	-	-	-	-	-
GDEF (B.US$) **	-	-	-	-	-	-	-	-	-	-
PXGS(%)	-	-	-	-	-2.3	-7.2	-12.6	-16.7	-19.1	-21.1
PMGS(%)	-	-	-	-	-3.5	-10.1	-16.6	-20.4	-20.7	-21.2
EXCH(%) ***	-	-	-	-	-	-	-	-	-	-
CAB(B.US$) **	-	-	-	-	-3.6	-15.5	-29.7	-38.0	-33.0	-31.3

* Exchange rate : (Weighted average of foreign currencies)/U.S. $.
** Local currency units translated into U.S. $ at baseline exchange rates.
*** Exchange rate : U.S. $/(weighted average of non-US OECD currencies).

Model: LINK
Simulation F: Nonpolicy Exogenous Depreciation of the Dollar
(Deviation of Shock Path from Baseline Path)

	1985									
	Q1	Q2	Q3	Q4	1985	1986	1987	1988	1989	1990
JAPAN										
GNP(%)	-	-	-	-	-0.2	-0.6	-0.9	-1.1	-1.3	-1.6
CPI(%)	-	-	-	-	-0.4	-1.4	-2.9	-4.4	-5.5	-6.2
RS(% PTS)	-	-	-	-	-0.1	-0.2	-0.3	-0.2	-0.1	-0.1
GDEF(%GNPV) *	-	-	-	-	-	-	-	-	-	-
EXCH(%) **	-	-	-	-	6.8	18.4	31.8	37.2	37.2	37.2
CAB(B.US$) ***	-	-	-	-	-2.2	-7.2	-13.2	-17.4	-17.6	-20.3
GERMANY										
GNP(%)	-	-	-	-	-1.0	-2.1	-3.2	-3.9	-6.5	-7.0
CPI(%)	-	-	-	-	-0.4	-1.6	-3.7	-6.2	-8.6	-11.1
RS(% PTS)	-	-	-	-	-0.3	-0.9	-1.5	-2.3	-2.9	-2.8
GDEF(%GNPV) *	-	-	-	-	0.0	0.1	0.2	0.3	0.4	0.3
EXCH(%) **	-	-	-	-	6.7	18.4	31.8	37.2	37.2	37.2
CAB(B.US$) ***	-	-	-	-	0.5	-2.0	-3.8	-4.1	4.5	16.8
FRANCE										
GNP(%)	-	-	-	-	-0.3	-0.3	0.2	1.4	1.5	1.3
CPI(%)	-	-	-	-	-0.3	-1.5	-3.8	-6.8	-9.2	-11.6
GDEF(%GNPV) *	-	-	-	-	-	-	-	-	-	-
EXCH(%) **	-	-	-	-	6.7	18.4	31.8	37.2	37.2	37.2
CAB(B.US$) ***	-	-	-	-	0.6	-1.0	-4.1	-9.8	-10.6	-6.9
UNITED KINGDOM										
GNP(%)	-	-	-	-	0.1	0.6	0.9	1.7	2.1	1.7
CPI(%)	-	-	-	-	-2.8	-7.8	-11.7	-12.2	-10.5	-8.3
GDEF(%GNPV) *	-	-	-	-	-	-	-	-	-	-
EXCH(%) **	-	-	-	-	6.7	18.5	31.8	37.2	37.2	37.2
CAB(B.US$) ***	-	-	-	-	-1.4	-0.7	2.9	7.3	7.8	7.0
ITALY										
GNP(%)	-	-	-	-	-0.9	-2.4	-4.8	-6.6	-7.0	-8.1
CPI(%)	-	-	-	-	-0.6	-2.1	-3.9	-5.3	-5.9	-6.6
GDEF(%GNPV) *	-	-	-	-	-	-	-	-	-	-
EXCH(%) **	-	-	-	-	6.8	18.5	31.8	37.2	37.2	37.2
CAB(B.US$) ***	-	-	-	-	-0.2	-2.9	-5.7	-7.9	-9.8	-12.5
CANADA										
GNP(%)	-	-	-	-	-0.4	-1.5	-2.3	-3.1	-2.4	-0.3
CPI(%)	-	-	-	-	-0.8	-2.3	-4.3	-6.2	-7.9	-9.2
GDEF(%GNPV) *	-	-	-	-	0.3	0.6	0.9	1.1	0.8	-0.3
EXCH(%) **	-	-	-	-	3.3	8.5	13.7	15.7	15.7	15.7
CAB(B.US$) ***	-	-	-	-	0.5	0.6	0.8	0.7	1.5	-0.2
REST OF WORLD										
CAB(B.US$) ***	-	-	-	-	1.1	7.2	14.3	20.3	16.8	13.2

* Government deficit as a percentage of baseline nominal GNP.
** Exchange rate : Bilateral rate against U.S. $ ($/local currency).
*** Local currency units translated into U.S. $ at baseline exchange rates.

Model: LINK
Simulation G: Increase in Government Purchases in Non-U.S. OECD Countries with U.S. Policies Unchanged from Baseline
(Deviation of Shock Path from Baseline Path)

	1985 Q1	1985 Q2	1985 Q3	1985 Q4	1985	1986	1987	1988	1989	1990
UNITED STATES										
GNPV(%)	-	-	-	-	0.1	0.2	0.2	0.2	0.2	0.2
GNP(%)	-	-	-	-	0.1	0.2	0.1	0.1	0.1	0.1
PGNP(%)	-	-	-	-	0.0	0.0	0.1	0.1	0.1	0.1
CPI(%)	-	-	-	-	0.0	0.0	0.1	0.1	0.2	0.2
WAGES(%)	-	-	-	-	0.0	0.0	0.1	0.1	0.2	0.2
UN(% PTS)	-	-	-	-	-0.0	-0.0	-0.0	-0.0	-0.0	-0.0
GNP(B.72$)	-	-	-	-	2.2	2.6	2.3	1.9	1.8	1.9
G(B.72$)	-	-	-	-	0.0	0.0	0.0	0.0	0.0	0.0
C(B.72$)	-	-	-	-	0.0	-0.2	-0.7	-1.1	-1.5	-1.7
IFP(B.72$)	-	-	-	-	0.1	-0.0	-0.3	-0.4	-0.3	-0.3
II(B.72$)	-	-	-	-	-0.0	-0.1	-0.1	-0.1	-0.0	-0.0
XGS(B.72$)	-	-	-	-	2.2	3.2	3.5	3.6	3.6	3.8
MGS(B.72$)	-	-	-	-	0.1	0.2	0.2	0.1	0.0	-0.0
M1(%)	-	-	-	-	-0.0	-0.0	-0.0	-0.0	-0.0	-0.0
RS(% PTS)	-	-	-	-	0.0	0.0	0.0	0.0	0.1	0.1
RL(% PTS)	-	-	-	-	0.0	0.1	0.1	0.1	0.1	0.1
GDEF(B$)	-	-	-	-	-2.1	-3.2	-3.5	-3.7	-3.9	-4.3
PXGS(%)	-	-	-	-	0.0	0.1	0.1	0.1	0.2	0.2
PMGS(%)	-	-	-	-	0.2	0.4	0.5	0.6	0.8	0.9
EXCH(%) *	-	-	-	-	-0.1	0.1	0.2	0.4	0.5	0.6
CAB(B$)	-	-	-	-	4.3	6.3	7.5	7.7	7.9	8.6
NON-US OECD										
GNPV(%) **	-	-	-	-	1.4	1.6	1.8	1.9	2.1	2.2
GNP(%) **	-	-	-	-	1.1	1.2	1.3	1.2	1.1	1.1
PGNP(%)	-	-	-	-	0.4	0.4	0.5	0.7	0.9	1.1
CPI(%)	-	-	-	-	0.0	0.1	0.4	0.8	1.2	1.8
WAGES(%)	-	-	-	-	-	-	-	-	-	-
UN(% PTS)	-	-	-	-	-	-	-	-	-	-
C(%) **	-	-	-	-	0.1	0.3	0.5	0.6	0.7	0.8
IFP(%) **	-	-	-	-	1.2	1.7	1.6	1.1	0.8	0.7
RS(% PTS)	-	-	-	-	-	-	-	-	-	-
RL(% PTS)	-	-	-	-	-	-	-	-	-	-
GDEF (B.US$) **	-	-	-	-	-	-	-	-	-	-
PXGS(%)	-	-	-	-	0.1	0.5	0.8	1.1	1.4	1.8
PMGS(%)	-	-	-	-	-0.4	0.1	0.4	0.7	0.9	1.0
EXCH(%) ***	-	-	-	-	-	-	-	-	-	-
CAB(B.US$) **	-	-	-	-	-4.0	-6.1	-6.9	-6.8	-7.0	-8.1

* Exchange rate : (Weighted average of foreign currencies)/U.S. $.
** Local currency units translated into U.S. $ at baseline exchange rates.
*** Exchange rate : U.S. $/(weighted average of non-US OECD currencies).

Model: LINK
Simulation G: Increase in Government Purchases in Non-U.S. OECD Countries with U.S. Policies Unchanged from Baseline
(Deviation of Shock Path from Baseline Path)

	1985									
	Q1	Q2	Q3	Q4	1985	1986	1987	1988	1989	1990
JAPAN										
GNP(%)	-	-	-	-	1.2	1.5	1.6	1.5	1.5	1.5
CPI(%)	-	-	-	-	0.1	0.3	0.7	1.1	1.4	1.5
RS(% PTS)	-	-	-	-	0.0	0.0	0.0	0.0	0.0	0.0
GDEF(%GNPV) *	-	-	-	-	-	-	-	-	-	-
EXCH(%) **	-	-	-	-	-0.1	-0.3	-0.6	-0.8	-1.0	-1.2
CAB(B.US$) ***	-	-	-	-	0.2	0.1	-0.4	-1.2	-2.0	-2.5
GERMANY										
GNP(%)	-	-	-	-	1.0	1.1	1.1	1.1	1.0	0.9
CPI(%)	-	-	-	-	-0.1	-0.0	0.2	0.5	0.9	1.3
RS(% PTS)	-	-	-	-	0.6	0.7	0.8	0.9	1.1	1.4
GDEF(%GNPV) *	-	-	-	-	0.9	0.7	0.7	0.6	0.6	0.7
EXCH(%) **	-	-	-	-	0.7	0.8	0.6	0.4	0.5	0.8
CAB(B.US$) ***	-	-	-	-	-0.5	-0.9	-1.7	-1.6	-2.2	-3.0
FRANCE										
GNP(%)	-	-	-	-	1.0	0.8	0.9	0.8	0.7	0.5
CPI(%)	-	-	-	-	0.0	0.2	0.5	0.9	1.5	2.2
GDEF(%GNPV) *	-	-	-	-	-	-	-	-	-	-
EXCH(%) **	-	-	-	-	0.5	0.1	-0.3	-0.5	-0.7	-0.8
CAB(B.US$) ***	-	-	-	-	-1.5	-1.2	-0.8	-0.5	-0.3	-0.6
UNITED KINGDOM										
GNP(%)	-	-	-	-	1.0	1.3	1.3	0.9	0.6	0.4
CPI(%)	-	-	-	-	0.4	0.1	0.7	1.8	2.5	2.8
GDEF(%GNPV) *	-	-	-	-	-	-	-	-	-	-
EXCH(%) **	-	-	-	-	0.0	-0.4	-1.0	-1.5	-2.0	-2.5
CAB(B.US$) ***	-	-	-	-	-0.4	-1.4	-2.1	-2.3	-2.7	-3.5
ITALY										
GNP(%)	-	-	-	-	1.3	1.7	1.9	1.9	1.9	2.0
CPI(%)	-	-	-	-	0.0	-0.1	-0.1	0.0	0.1	0.2
GDEF(%GNPV) *	-	-	-	-	-	-	-	-	-	-
EXCH(%) **	-	-	-	-	-0.1	-0.2	-0.4	-0.5	-0.6	-0.7
CAB(B.US$) ***	-	-	-	-	-0.5	-1.1	-1.7	-2.1	-2.3	-2.7
CANADA										
GNP(%)	-	-	-	-	1.0	0.9	0.9	0.8	0.7	0.4
CPI(%)	-	-	-	-	-0.0	0.4	0.7	1.0	1.2	1.5
GDEF(%GNPV) *	-	-	-	-	0.7	0.6	0.7	0.9	1.2	1.6
EXCH(%) **	-	-	-	-	-0.0	-0.1	-0.1	-0.2	-0.2	-0.3
CAB(B.US$) ***	-	-	-	-	-1.1	-1.9	-2.3	-3.0	-3.7	-4.5
REST OF WORLD										
CAB(B.US$) ***	-	-	-	-	2.7	4.0	4.5	4.4	4.4	5.0

* Government deficit as a percentage of baseline nominal GNP.
** Exchange rate : Bilateral rate against U.S. $ ($/local currency).
*** Local currency units translated into U.S. $ at baseline exchange rates.

Model: LINK
Simulation H: Monetary Expansion in Non-U.S. OECD Countries
with U.S. Policies Unchanged from Baseline
(Deviation of Shock Path from Baseline Path)

	1985									
	Q1	Q2	Q3	Q4	1985	1986	1987	1988	1989	1990
UNITED STATES										
GNPV(%)	-	-	-	-	0.0	0.1	0.1	0.0	0.0	0.0
GNP(%)	-	-	-	-	0.0	0.1	0.1	0.0	0.0	0.0
PGNP(%)	-	-	-	-	0.0	0.0	-0.0	-0.0	-0.0	-0.0
CPI(%)	-	-	-	-	-0.0	-0.0	-0.1	-0.1	-0.1	-0.0
WAGES(%)	-	-	-	-	-0.0	-0.0	-0.0	-0.1	-0.1	-0.0
UN(% PTS)	-	-	-	-	0.0	0.0	0.0	-0.0	-0.0	-0.0
GNP(B.72$)	-	-	-	-	0.2	0.9	1.1	0.5	0.5	0.9
G(B.72$)	-	-	-	-	0.0	0.0	0.0	0.0	0.0	0.0
C(B.72$)	-	-	-	-	0.1	0.2	0.3	0.4	0.5	0.5
IFP(B.72$)	-	-	-	-	-0.0	-0.0	0.1	0.3	0.4	0.4
II(B.72$)	-	-	-	-	0.0	0.1	0.1	0.0	0.0	0.0
XGS(B.72$)	-	-	-	-	0.3	1.0	1.1	0.2	0.0	0.5
MGS(B.72$)	-	-	-	-	0.1	0.4	0.5	0.5	0.4	0.5
M1(%)	-	-	-	-	-0.0	-0.0	-0.0	-0.0	-0.0	-0.0
RS(% PTS)	-	-	-	-	0.0	0.0	0.0	-0.0	-0.0	0.0
RL(% PTS)	-	-	-	-	0.0	0.0	0.0	-0.0	-0.0	0.0
GDEF(B$)	-	-	-	-	-0.4	-1.2	-1.3	-0.6	-0.7	-1.4
PXGS(%)	-	-	-	-	-0.0	-0.0	-0.1	-0.0	-0.0	-0.0
PMGS(%)	-	-	-	-	-0.3	-0.5	-0.6	-0.5	-0.4	-0.4
EXCH(%) *	-	-	-	-	1.0	2.3	2.7	2.7	2.6	2.5
CAB(B$)	-	-	-	-	1.2	3.5	3.5	1.2	0.5	1.6
NON-US OECD										
GNPV(%) **	-	-	-	-	-0.9	-1.8	-1.9	-1.7	-1.4	-1.2
GNP(%) **	-	-	-	-	0.3	0.8	0.8	0.5	0.5	0.7
PGNP(%)	-	-	-	-	-1.2	-2.5	-2.7	-2.2	-1.9	-1.9
CPI(%)	-	-	-	-	-0.3	-0.6	-0.4	0.1	0.2	-0.2
WAGES(%)	-	-	-	-	-	-	-	-	-	-
UN(% PTS)	-	-	-	-	-	-	-	-	-	-
C(%) **	-	-	-	-	0.0	0.2	0.2	0.2	0.3	0.4
IFP(%) **	-	-	-	-	1.4	3.0	2.8	1.6	1.0	1.4
RS(% PTS)	-	-	-	-	-	-	-	-	-	-
RL(% PTS)	-	-	-	-	-	-	-	-	-	-
GDEF (B.US$) **	-	-	-	-	-	-	-	-	-	-
PXGS(%)	-	-	-	-	1.0	3.3	5.2	5.4	4.4	3.5
PMGS(%)	-	-	-	-	1.6	4.3	5.8	5.6	4.4	3.7
EXCH(%) ***	-	-	-	-	-	-	-	-	-	-
CAB(B.US$) **	-	-	-	-	-0.4	-1.4	-0.5	2.3	1.8	-0.4

* Exchange rate : (Weighted average of foreign currencies)/U.S. $.
** Local currency units translated into U.S. $ at baseline exchange rates.
*** Exchange rate : U.S. $/(weighted average of non-US OECD currencies).

Model: LINK
Simulation H: Monetary Expansion in Non-U.S. OECD Countries
with U.S. Policies Unchanged from Baseline
(Deviation of Shock Path from Baseline Path)

	1985 Q1	1985 Q2	1985 Q3	1985 Q4	1985	1986	1987	1988	1989	1990
JAPAN										
GNP(%)	-	-	-	-	0.2	0.4	0.4	0.4	0.4	0.5
CPI(%)	-	-	-	-	0.2	0.5	0.9	1.2	1.4	1.4
RS(% PTS)	-	-	-	-	-0.7	-1.0	-1.0	-1.0	-1.0	-1.0
GDEF(%GNPV) *	-	-	-	-	-	-	-	-	-	-
EXCH(%) **	-	-	-	-	-1.4	-3.5	-4.3	-4.4	-4.4	-4.4
CAB(B.US$) ***	-	-	-	-	0.7	2.6	3.7	3.7	3.3	2.9
GERMANY										
GNP(%)	-	-	-	-	0.8	1.4	1.2	0.8	0.7	0.8
CPI(%)	-	-	-	-	0.2	0.6	1.1	1.5	1.8	2.0
RS(% PTS)	-	-	-	-	-1.4	-1.5	-0.7	-0.7	-0.5	-0.4
GDEF(%GNPV) *	-	-	-	-	-0.1	-0.2	-0.2	-0.0	0.0	0.0
EXCH(%) **	-	-	-	-	-1.6	-3.3	-3.4	-3.1	-2.8	-2.7
CAB(B.US$) ***	-	-	-	-	0.1	1.4	1.7	0.6	-1.9	-1.0
FRANCE										
GNP(%)	-	-	-	-	0.8	2.5	2.6	1.1	0.7	1.5
CPI(%)	-	-	-	-	-0.4	-0.8	-0.5	0.0	0.1	-0.5
GDEF(%GNPV) *	-	-	-	-	-	-	-	-	-	-
EXCH(%) **	-	-	-	-	-3.0	-7.4	-8.9	-7.6	-5.8	-5.5
CAB(B.US$) ***	-	-	-	-	-1.7	-6.7	-5.3	2.4	4.0	-1.2
UNITED KINGDOM										
GNP(%)	-	-	-	-	0.1	0.2	-0.2	-0.4	-0.5	-0.3
CPI(%)	-	-	-	-	0.1	0.8	1.6	2.5	2.9	2.7
GDEF(%GNPV) *	-	-	-	-	-	-	-	-	-	-
EXCH(%) **	-	-	-	-	-1.6	-2.8	-3.3	-3.6	-3.7	-3.7
CAB(B.US$) ***	-	-	-	-	-0.8	-1.7	-1.2	-1.3	-1.0	-0.8
ITALY										
GNP(%)	-	-	-	-	0.2	0.8	1.3	1.3	1.3	1.4
CPI(%)	-	-	-	-	-0.1	-0.2	-0.2	-0.0	0.0	0.1
GDEF(%GNPV) *	-	-	-	-	-	-	-	-	-	-
EXCH(%) **	-	-	-	-	-0.3	-0.6	-0.8	-0.9	-0.9	-0.9
CAB(B.US$) ***	-	-	-	-	0.1	-0.1	-1.2	-2.3	-2.2	-2.2
CANADA										
GNP(%)	-	-	-	-	0.1	0.5	1.0	1.3	1.5	1.7
CPI(%)	-	-	-	-	-0.1	-0.3	-0.7	-0.9	-1.0	-1.0
GDEF(%GNPV) *	-	-	-	-	-0.0	-0.0	-0.1	-0.2	-0.3	-0.5
EXCH(%) **	-	-	-	-	0.0	0.0	0.0	0.1	0.1	0.1
CAB(B.US$) ***	-	-	-	-	-0.0	-0.0	0.3	0.7	1.6	2.0
REST OF WORLD										
CAB(B.US$) ***	-	-	-	-	0.7	1.7	1.3	-0.5	-0.5	0.7

* Government deficit as a percentage of baseline nominal GNP.
** Exchange rate : Bilateral rate against U.S. $ ($/local currency).
*** Local currency units translated into U.S. $ at baseline exchange rates.

LIVERPOOL Model

See part 1 of this volume for design and detailed description of the simulations. See part 4 for bibliographical references.

The figures for consumption in the tables represent an aggregate of both consumption and investment expenditures. Figures were not available separately for real exports of goods and services and real imports of goods and services; the data on the lines for XGS refer to real *net* exports of goods and services.

Simulation F is not available for this model.

Model: LIVERPL
Simulation A: Baseline Path

	1985	1986	1987	1988	1989	1990
UNITED STATES						
GNPV(B.$)	3907.9	4212.9	4516.6	4844.3	5199.6	5587.0
GNP(B.72$)	1644.6	1718.3	1780.9	1842.1	1905.6	1973.4
PGNP(72=100)	237.6	245.2	253.6	263.0	272.9	283.1
CPI(72=100)	237.3	244.8	253.2	262.6	272.4	282.7
WAGES(72=100)	-	-	-	-	-	-
UN(%)	-	-	-	-	-	-
G(B.72$)	304.7	312.9	321.4	330.0	338.9	348.1
C(B.72$)	1496.2	1533.3	1585.1	1636.9	1697.0	1753.3
IFP(B.72$)	-	-	-	-	-	-
II(B.72$)	-	-	-	-	-	-
XGS(B.72$)	-156.3	-127.9	-125.5	-124.8	-130.4	-128.0
MGS(B.72$)	-	-	-	-	-	-
M1(B.$)	575.3	617.1	661.8	709.8	761.2	816.4
RS(%)	6.2	6.2	6.2	6.5	5.6	5.8
RL(%)	6.1	6.0	5.9	5.8	5.6	6.1
GDEF(B.$)	134.2	111.0	104.2	98.2	89.9	84.3
PXGS(72=100)	-	-	-	-	-	-
PMGS(72=100)	-	-	-	-	-	-
EXCH(72=100) *	101.9	102.7	102.7	102.6	102.4	102.2
CAB(B.$)	-223.4	-153.5	-149.1	-151.4	-176.4	-175.8
NON-US OECD						
GNPV(B.$) **	744.7	784.8	844.3	906.3	972.1	1039.7
GNP(B.72$) **	274.9	278.1	288.4	297.9	307.9	317.8
PGNP(72=100)	270.9	282.2	292.8	304.2	315.8	327.1
CPI(72=100)	266.1	277.2	287.6	298.8	310.2	321.3
WAGES(72=100)	-	-	-	-	-	-
UN(%)	-	-	-	-	-	-
C(B.72$) **	134.8	139.2	146.1	153.6	161.5	169.3
IFP(B.72$) **	-	-	-	-	-	-
RS(%)	6.6	5.8	5.7	6.0	5.3	5.9
RL(%)	-	-	-	-	-	-
GDEF(B.US$) **	-	-	-	-	-	-
PXGS(72=100)	-	-	-	-	-	-
PMGS(72=100)	-	-	-	-	-	-
EXCH(72=100) ***	101.1	100.2	100.4	100.6	100.8	101.1
CAB(B.US$)	28.2	48.2	47.4	58.7	81.1	93.3

* Exchange rate : (Weighted average of foreign currencies)/U.S. $.
** Local currency units translated into U.S. $ at baseline exchange rates.
*** Exchange rate : U.S. $/(weighted average of non-US OECD currencies).

Model: LIVERPL
Simulation A: Baseline Path

	1985	1986	1987	1988	1989	1990
JAPAN						
GNP(B.72Y)	136064.3	142239.8	148660.2	155326.9	162313.8	169595.2
CPI(72=100)	216.0	218.9	222.2	225.9	229.6	232.2
RS(%)	6.7	6.1	5.6	5.6	4.3	4.9
GDEF(%GNPV) *	0.1	0.1	0.1	0.1	0.1	0.1
EXCH(72=100) **	152.5	151.0	151.0	151.8	153.1	155.3
CAB(B.US$) ***	21.2	25.4	30.8	36.9	43.7	49.4
GERMANY						
GNP(B.72DM)	1348.0	1329.6	1369.9	1406.4	1444.5	1479.0
CPI(72=100)	170.1	178.7	185.9	192.9	199.6	207.1
RS(%)	4.2	3.7	3.4	3.8	3.7	4.2
GDEF(%GNPV) *	-0.6	-0.4	-0.4	-0.4	-0.3	-0.2
EXCH(72=100) **	157.7	160.6	165.1	170.0	175.1	179.1
CAB(B.US$) ***	18.2	35.7	41.1	48.0	55.4	65.0
FRANCE						
GNP(B.72F)	1419.1	1433.9	1459.1	1482.3	1506.7	1532.8
CPI(72=100)	337.1	356.3	373.4	393.4	415.5	438.3
GDEF(%GNPV) *	0.1	0.2	0.3	0.3	0.4	0.4
EXCH(72=100) **	75.4	73.9	73.5	72.6	71.5	70.3
CAB(B.US$) ***	-6.5	-5.9	-5.8	-5.8	-5.9	-6.0
UNITED KINGDOM						
GNP(B.72LB)	82.7	83.3	85.6	86.6	87.4	87.7
CPI(72=100)	426.0	441.8	456.2	471.0	487.8	508.2
GDEF(%GNPV) *	-9.2	-5.0	-1.1	-0.2	-0.3	-0.2
EXCH(72=100) **	67.9	67.8	69.0	70.1	71.1	71.4
CAB(B.US$) ***	-11.7	-13.5	-22.3	-24.3	-21.4	-19.3
ITALY						
GNP(B.72L)	113249.5	117440.0	122026.9	126823.4	131935.3	136349.4
CPI(72=100)	555.6	596.6	638.9	682.6	726.7	773.3
GDEF(%GNPV) *	0.0	0.0	0.0	0.0	0.0	0.0
EXCH(72=100) **	36.2	34.4	33.0	31.7	30.6	29.4
CAB(B.US$) ***	-8.0	-5.9	-3.5	-0.9	1.9	-1.2
CANADA						
GNP(B.72C$)	163.9	170.5	180.8	190.0	197.1	205.3
CPI(72=100)	269.8	284.4	301.7	324.7	350.7	371.9
GDEF(%GNPV) *	6.3	6.6	6.5	6.5	6.6	7.3
EXCH(72=100) **	87.3	85.8	85.0	83.1	80.6	79.7
CAB(B.US$) ***	15.1	12.3	7.2	4.8	7.5	5.4
REST OF WORLD						
CAB(B.US$) ***	-	-	-	-	-	-

* Government deficit as a percentage of baseline nominal GNP.
** Exchange rate: Bilateral rate against U.S. $ ($/local currency).
*** Local currency units translated into U.S. $ at baseline exchange rates.

Model: LIVERPL
Simulation B: Reduction in U.S. Government Purchases with Foreign Monetary Aggregates Unchanged from Baseline
(Deviation of Shock Path from Baseline Path)

	1985									
	Q1	Q2	Q3	Q4	1985	1986	1987	1988	1989	1990
UNITED STATES										
GNPV(%)	-	-	-	-	-0.7	-0.7	-0.8	-0.8	-0.8	-0.8
GNP(%)	-	-	-	-	-0.7	-0.6	-0.5	-0.5	-0.5	-0.4
PGNP(%)	-	-	-	-	-0.1	-0.2	-0.2	-0.3	-0.3	-0.3
CPI(%)	-	-	-	-	-0.1	-0.2	-0.2	-0.3	-0.3	-0.3
WAGES(%)	-	-	-	-	-	-	-	-	-	-
UN(% PTS)	-	-	-	-	-	-	-	-	-	-
GNP(B.72$)	-	-	-	-	-10.7	-9.8	-9.3	-9.2	-9.0	-8.8
G(B.72$)	-	-	-	-	-16.4	-17.2	-17.8	-18.4	-19.1	-19.7
C(B.72$)	-	-	-	-	2.5	4.1	5.7	6.7	7.9	8.7
IFP(B.72$)	-	-	-	-	-	-	-	-	-	-
II(B.72$)	-	-	-	-	-	-	-	-	-	-
XGS(B.72$)	-	-	-	-	3.2	3.2	2.8	2.6	2.2	2.3
MGS(B.72$)	-	-	-	-	-	-	-	-	-	-
M1(%)	-	-	-	-	0.0	0.0	0.0	0.0	0.0	0.0
RS(% PTS)	-	-	-	-	-0.3	-0.4	-0.4	-0.5	-0.5	-0.5
RL(% PTS)	-	-	-	-	-0.3	-0.3	-0.3	-0.2	-0.2	-0.2
GDEF(B$)	-	-	-	-	-38.2	-41.8	-46.6	-51.6	-57.1	-64.5
PXGS(%)	-	-	-	-	-	-	-	-	-	-
PMGS(%)	-	-	-	-	-	-	-	-	-	-
EXCH(%) *	-	-	-	-	-0.9	-1.0	-0.9	-0.9	-0.9	-0.8
CAB(B$)	-	-	-	-	6.6	7.0	6.4	6.1	5.4	5.8
NON-US OECD										
GNPV(%) **	-	-	-	-	-0.4	-0.6	-0.7	-0.7	-0.7	-0.7
GNP(%) **	-	-	-	-	0.0	0.0	0.1	0.1	0.1	0.1
PGNP(%)	-	-	-	-	-0.4	-0.6	-0.7	-0.8	-0.8	-0.8
CPI(%)	-	-	-	-	-0.4	-0.6	-0.7	-0.8	-0.8	-0.8
WAGES(%)	-	-	-	-	-	-	-	-	-	-
UN(% PTS)	-	-	-	-	-	-	-	-	-	-
C(%) **	-	-	-	-	0.1	0.2	0.2	0.2	0.2	0.2
IFP(%) **	-	-	-	-	-	-	-	-	-	-
RS(% PTS)	-	-	-	-	-0.1	-0.1	-0.2	-0.3	-0.4	-0.4
RL(% PTS)	-	-	-	-	-	-	-	-	-	-
GDEF (B.US$) **	-	-	-	-	-4.3	-4.5	-6.3	-8.5	-10.5	-14.0
PXGS(%)	-	-	-	-	-	-	-	-	-	-
PMGS(%)	-	-	-	-	-	-	-	-	-	-
EXCH(%) ***	-	-	-	-	1.1	1.2	1.1	1.1	1.1	1.0
CAB(B.US$) **	-	-	-	-	-4.0	-3.4	-3.3	-3.4	-3.3	-3.4

* Exchange rate : (Weighted average of foreign currencies)/U.S. $.
** Local currency units translated into U.S. $ at baseline exchange rates.
*** Exchange rate : U.S. $/(weighted average of non-US OECD currencies).

Model: LIVERPL
Simulation B: Reduction in U.S. Government Purchases with Foreign Monetary Aggregates Unchanged from Baseline
(Deviation of Shock Path from Baseline Path)

	1985									
	Q1	Q2	Q3	Q4	1985	1986	1987	1988	1989	1990
JAPAN										
GNP(%)	-	-	-	-	0.0	0.1	0.2	0.2	0.2	0.2
CPI(%)	-	-	-	-	-0.6	-0.9	-1.1	-1.3	-1.4	-1.5
RS(% PTS)	-	-	-	-	-0.1	-0.1	-0.2	-0.3	-0.4	-0.3
GDEF(%GNPV) *	-	-	-	-	-0.0	-0.0	-0.0	-0.0	-0.0	-0.0
EXCH(%) **	-	-	-	-	1.4	1.6	1.6	1.6	1.7	1.7
CAB(B.US$) ***	-	-	-	-	-1.5	-1.7	-1.9	-2.0	-2.2	-2.4
GERMANY										
GNP(%)	-	-	-	-	0.1	-0.0	-0.0	0.0	0.0	0.0
CPI(%)	-	-	-	-	-0.0	0.1	0.3	0.4	0.6	0.8
RS(% PTS)	-	-	-	-	-0.1	-0.1	-0.2	-0.3	-0.3	-0.3
GDEF(%GNPV) *	-	-	-	-	-0.0	-0.0	-0.0	-0.0	-0.0	-0.0
EXCH(%) **	-	-	-	-	0.5	0.2	-0.1	-0.3	-0.5	-0.7
CAB(B.US$) ***	-	-	-	-	-1.1	-0.4	-0.2	-0.2	0.1	0.4
FRANCE										
GNP(%)	-	-	-	-	-0.1	-0.1	-0.0	0.0	0.0	0.1
CPI(%)	-	-	-	-	-0.3	-0.6	-0.8	-0.9	-1.1	-1.2
GDEF(%GNPV) *	-	-	-	-	0.0	-0.0	-0.0	-0.0	-0.0	-0.0
EXCH(%) **	-	-	-	-	1.0	1.1	1.2	1.3	1.4	1.4
CAB(B.US$) ***	-	-	-	-	-0.5	-0.5	-0.4	-0.4	-0.4	-0.5
UNITED KINGDOM										
GNP(%)	-	-	-	-	0.0	-0.0	-0.0	-0.0	-0.1	-0.1
CPI(%)	-	-	-	-	-0.1	-0.1	-0.1	-0.1	-0.1	-0.1
GDEF(%GNPV) *	-	-	-	-	-0.1	-0.1	-0.1	-0.1	-0.1	-0.0
EXCH(%) **	-	-	-	-	0.6	0.4	0.3	0.2	0.1	0.0
CAB(B.US$) ***	-	-	-	-	-0.3	-0.1	-0.0	0.1	0.1	0.2
ITALY										
GNP(%)	-	-	-	-	0.0	0.1	0.2	0.2	0.2	0.2
CPI(%)	-	-	-	-	-1.1	-1.8	-2.1	-2.1	-1.9	-1.8
GDEF(%GNPV) *	-	-	-	-	-0.0	-0.0	-0.0	-0.0	-0.0	-0.0
EXCH(%) **	-	-	-	-	1.8	2.3	2.5	2.4	2.3	2.1
CAB(B.US$) ***	-	-	-	-	-0.3	-0.4	-0.5	-0.6	-0.6	-0.6
CANADA										
GNP(%)	-	-	-	-	0.1	0.1	0.1	0.1	0.1	0.1
CPI(%)	-	-	-	-	-0.5	-1.0	-1.3	-1.6	-1.7	-1.7
GDEF(%GNPV) *	-	-	-	-	-0.1	-0.1	-0.1	-0.1	-0.2	-0.2
EXCH(%) **	-	-	-	-	1.8	2.1	2.1	2.2	2.2	2.2
CAB(B.US$) ***	-	-	-	-	-0.3	-0.3	-0.3	-0.3	-0.4	-0.5
REST OF WORLD										
CAB(B.US$) ***	-	-	-	-	-	-	-	-	-	-

* Government deficit as a percentage of baseline nominal GNP.
** Exchange rate : Bilateral rate against U.S. $ ($/local currency).
*** Local currency units translated into U.S. $ at baseline exchange rates.

Model: LIVERPL
Simulation C: Reduction in U.S. Government Purchases with Foreign Short-Term Interest Rates Unchanged from Baseline
(Deviation of Shock Path from Baseline Path)

	1985 Q1	1985 Q2	1985 Q3	1985 Q4	1985	1986	1987	1988	1989	1990
UNITED STATES										
GNPV(%)	-	-	-	-	-0.6	-0.4	-0.4	-0.3	-0.2	-0.2
GNP(%)	-	-	-	-	-0.7	-0.7	-0.7	-0.7	-0.7	-0.6
PGNP(%)	-	-	-	-	0.2	0.3	0.4	0.4	0.5	0.4
CPI(%)	-	-	-	-	0.2	0.3	0.4	0.4	0.5	0.4
WAGES(%)	-	-	-	-	-	-	-	-	-	-
UN(% PTS)	-	-	-	-	-	-	-	-	-	-
GNP(B.72$)	-	-	-	-	-12.1	-12.5	-13.0	-13.1	-13.0	-12.4
G(B.72$)	-	-	-	-	-16.4	-17.2	-17.8	-18.4	-19.1	-19.7
C(B.72$)	-	-	-	-	0.6	0.4	0.8	1.7	2.6	4.4
IFP(B.72$)	-	-	-	-	-	-	-	-	-	-
II(B.72$)	-	-	-	-	-	-	-	-	-	-
XGS(B.72$)	-	-	-	-	3.7	4.2	4.1	3.6	3.5	2.9
MGS(B.72$)	-	-	-	-	-	-	-	-	-	-
M1(%)	-	-	-	-	0.0	0.0	0.0	0.0	0.0	0.0
RS(% PTS)	-	-	-	-	-0.2	-0.2	-0.3	-0.3	-0.4	-0.4
RL(% PTS)	-	-	-	-	-0.2	-0.2	-0.2	-0.2	-0.2	-0.2
GDEF(B$)	-	-	-	-	-36.0	-39.7	-44.1	-49.0	-54.3	-61.8
PXGS(%)	-	-	-	-	-	-	-	-	-	-
PMGS(%)	-	-	-	-	-	-	-	-	-	-
EXCH(%) *	-	-	-	-	-1.5	-2.3	-2.7	-2.9	-3.0	-2.9
CAB(B$)	-	-	-	-	6.8	8.2	8.1	7.2	7.0	5.8
NON-US OECD										
GNPV(%) **	-	-	-	-	-0.6	-1.1	-1.5	-1.7	-1.8	-1.9
GNP(%) **	-	-	-	-	0.1	0.0	0.1	0.1	0.1	0.1
PGNP(%)	-	-	-	-	-0.7	-1.1	-1.6	-1.7	-1.9	-2.0
CPI(%)	-	-	-	-	-0.7	-1.1	-1.6	-1.7	-1.9	-2.0
WAGES(%)	-	-	-	-	-	-	-	-	-	-
UN(% PTS)	-	-	-	-	-	-	-	-	-	-
C(%) **	-	-	-	-	0.1	0.2	0.2	0.3	0.3	0.3
IFP(%) **	-	-	-	-	-	-	-	-	-	-
RS(% PTS)	-	-	-	-	-0.0	-0.1	-0.2	-0.2	-0.3	-0.3
RL(% PTS)	-	-	-	-	-	-	-	-	-	-
GDEF (B.US$) **	-	-	-	-	-6.5	-5.6	-7.8	-9.6	-12.3	-14.9
PXGS(%)	-	-	-	-	-	-	-	-	-	-
PMGS(%)	-	-	-	-	-	-	-	-	-	-
EXCH(%) ***	-	-	-	-	1.9	2.5	2.9	3.1	3.2	3.1
CAB(B.US$) **	-	-	-	-	-5.2	-4.1	-4.7	-4.6	-5.5	-5.2

* Exchange rate : (Weighted average of foreign currencies)/U.S. $.
** Local currency units translated into U.S. $ at baseline exchange rates.
*** Exchange rate : U.S. $/(weighted average of non-US OECD currencies).

Model: LIVERPL
Simulation C: Reduction in U.S. Government Purchases with Foreign
Short-Term Interest Rates Unchanged from Baseline
(Deviation of Shock Path from Baseline Path)

	1985									
	Q1	Q2	Q3	Q4	1985	1986	1987	1988	1989	1990
JAPAN										
GNP(%)	-	-	-	-	0.0	0.1	0.1	0.2	0.2	0.2
CPI(%)	-	-	-	-	-0.8	-1.2	-1.6	-1.9	-2.2	-2.3
RS(% PTS)	-	-	-	-	-0.0	-0.1	-0.2	-0.2	-0.3	-0.3
GDEF(%GNPV) *	-	-	-	-	-0.0	-0.0	-0.0	-0.0	-0.0	-0.0
EXCH(%) **	-	-	-	-	2.1	2.6	3.0	3.3	3.5	3.5
CAB(B.US$) ***	-	-	-	-	-1.3	-1.6	-1.9	-2.3	-2.6	-2.9
GERMANY										
GNP(%)	-	-	-	-	0.3	-0.1	-0.0	-0.1	0.0	-0.1
CPI(%)	-	-	-	-	-0.3	-0.5	-0.9	-1.0	-1.2	-1.1
RS(% PTS)	-	-	-	-	0.0	-0.1	-0.2	-0.2	-0.3	-0.3
GDEF(%GNPV) *	-	-	-	-	-0.0	-0.0	-0.0	-0.0	-0.0	-0.0
EXCH(%) **	-	-	-	-	1.5	1.9	2.3	2.3	2.5	2.3
CAB(B.US$) ***	-	-	-	-	-2.2	-0.8	-1.2	-1.0	-1.4	-0.9
FRANCE										
GNP(%)	-	-	-	-	-0.1	-0.1	-0.1	-0.0	-0.0	0.0
CPI(%)	-	-	-	-	-0.4	-0.9	-1.4	-1.6	-1.8	-1.9
GDEF(%GNPV) *	-	-	-	-	0.0	-0.0	-0.0	-0.0	-0.0	-0.0
EXCH(%) **	-	-	-	-	1.7	2.3	2.8	3.0	3.1	3.1
CAB(B.US$) ***	-	-	-	-	-0.6	-0.5	-0.5	-0.4	-0.4	-0.4
UNITED KINGDOM										
GNP(%)	-	-	-	-	0.1	0.0	0.0	0.0	0.0	-0.0
CPI(%)	-	-	-	-	-0.3	-0.7	-1.1	-1.4	-1.7	-1.9
GDEF(%GNPV) *	-	-	-	-	-0.1	-0.1	-0.1	-0.1	-0.1	-0.0
EXCH(%) **	-	-	-	-	1.4	2.0	2.4	2.6	2.9	3.0
CAB(B.US$) ***	-	-	-	-	-0.5	-0.4	-0.1	0.1	0.2	0.3
ITALY										
GNP(%)	-	-	-	-	-0.0	0.1	0.2	0.2	0.2	0.2
CPI(%)	-	-	-	-	-2.3	-3.6	-3.7	-3.6	-3.4	-3.1
GDEF(%GNPV) *	-	-	-	-	-0.0	-0.0	-0.0	-0.0	-0.0	-0.0
EXCH(%) **	-	-	-	-	3.9	4.9	5.1	5.0	4.8	4.3
CAB(B.US$) ***	-	-	-	-	-0.1	-0.4	-0.6	-0.7	-0.8	-0.8
CANADA										
GNP(%)	-	-	-	-	0.2	0.1	0.1	0.1	0.1	0.1
CPI(%)	-	-	-	-	-0.4	-1.1	-1.7	-1.9	-2.1	-2.1
GDEF(%GNPV) *	-	-	-	-	-0.1	-0.1	-0.1	-0.2	-0.2	-0.2
EXCH(%) **	-	-	-	-	1.9	2.7	3.2	3.4	3.5	3.3
CAB(B.US$) ***	-	-	-	-	-0.5	-0.4	-0.3	-0.3	-0.4	-0.5
REST OF WORLD										
CAB(B.US$) ***	-	-	-	-	-	-	-	-	-	-

* Government deficit as a percentage of baseline nominal GNP.
** Exchange rate : Bilateral rate against U.S. $ ($/local currency).
*** Local currency units translated into U.S. $ at baseline exchange rates.

Model: LIVERPL
Simulation D: U.S. Monetary Expansion with foreign Monetary Aggregates Unchanged from Baseline
(Deviation of Shock Path from Baseline Path)

	1985 Q1	1985 Q2	1985 Q3	1985 Q4	1985	1986	1987	1988	1989	1990
UNITED STATES										
GNPV(%)	-	-	-	-	2.3	3.9	3.8	4.0	4.1	4.3
GNP(%)	-	-	-	-	0.6	0.1	-0.1	-0.2	-0.2	-0.2
PGNP(%)	-	-	-	-	1.8	3.7	3.9	4.1	4.4	4.5
CPI(%)	-	-	-	-	1.8	3.7	3.9	4.1	4.4	4.5
WAGES(%)	-	-	-	-	-	-	-	-	-	-
UN(% PTS)	-	-	-	-	-	-	-	-	-	-
GNP(B.72$)	-	-	-	-	9.3	2.5	-1.3	-3.2	-4.1	-4.5
G(B.72$)	-	-	-	-	0.0	0.0	0.0	0.0	0.0	0.0
C(B.72$)	-	-	-	-	10.1	4.9	-0.1	-2.7	-4.0	-4.5
IFP(B.72$)	-	-	-	-	-	-	-	-	-	-
II(B.72$)	-	-	-	-	-	-	-	-	-	-
XGS(B.72$)	-	-	-	-	-0.8	-2.4	-1.1	-0.6	-0.1	0.0
MGS(B.72$)	-	-	-	-	-	-	-	-	-	-
M1(%)	-	-	-	-	2.0	4.1	4.1	4.1	4.1	4.1
RS(% PTS)	-	-	-	-	0.4	-0.3	-0.1	-0.1	-0.0	-0.0
RL(% PTS)	-	-	-	-	0.1	-0.0	0.0	0.0	0.1	0.0
GDEF(B$)	-	-	-	-	-0.7	0.7	1.0	1.7	1.9	1.1
PXGS(%)	-	-	-	-	-	-	-	-	-	-
PMGS(%)	-	-	-	-	-	-	-	-	-	-
EXCH(%) *	-	-	-	-	-2.2	-3.9	-4.0	-4.1	-4.3	-4.4
CAB(B$)	-	-	-	-	-6.9	-13.0	-9.7	-8.6	-8.8	-8.5
NON-US OECD										
GNPV(%) **	-	-	-	-	-0.0	-0.1	0.0	0.0	0.1	0.1
GNP(%) **	-	-	-	-	0.1	-0.0	-0.0	-0.0	-0.0	-0.0
PGNP(%)	-	-	-	-	-0.1	-0.0	0.0	0.1	0.1	0.1
CPI(%)	-	-	-	-	-0.1	-0.0	0.0	0.1	0.1	0.1
WAGES(%)	-	-	-	-	-	-	-	-	-	-
UN(% PTS)	-	-	-	-	-	-	-	-	-	-
C(%) **	-	-	-	-	0.0	0.0	0.0	0.0	0.0	-0.0
IFP(%) **	-	-	-	-	-	-	-	-	-	-
RS(% PTS)	-	-	-	-	-0.1	-0.1	-0.0	-0.0	-0.0	-0.0
RL(% PTS)	-	-	-	-	-	-	-	-	-	-
GDEF (B.US$) **	-	-	-	-	-2.9	-2.8	-4.2	-5.3	-6.6	-8.1
PXGS(%)	-	-	-	-	-	-	-	-	-	-
PMGS(%)	-	-	-	-	-	-	-	-	-	-
EXCH(%) ***	-	-	-	-	2.4	4.2	4.2	4.4	4.5	4.6
CAB(B.US$) **	-	-	-	-	-0.8	0.1	-0.1	-0.3	-0.2	-0.1

* Exchange rate : (Weighted average of foreign currencies)/U.S. $.
** Local currency units translated into U.S. $ at baseline exchange rates.
*** Exchange rate : U.S. $/(weighted average of non-US OECD currencies).

Model: LIVERPL
Simulation D: U.S. Monetary Expansion with Foreign Monetary Aggregates Unchanged from Baseline
(Deviation of Shock Path from Baseline Path)

	1985									
	Q1	Q2	Q3	Q4	1985	1986	1987	1988	1989	1990
JAPAN										
GNP(%)	-	-	-	-	0.0	0.0	0.0	0.0	0.0	0.0
CPI(%)	-	-	-	-	-0.2	-0.1	-0.0	0.0	0.0	0.1
RS(% PTS)	-	-	-	-	-0.2	-0.1	-0.0	-0.0	-0.0	-0.0
GDEF(%GNPV) *	-	-	-	-	-0.0	-0.0	-0.0	0.0	0.0	0.0
EXCH(%) **	-	-	-	-	2.4	4.3	4.3	4.4	4.6	4.6
CAB(B.US$) ***	-	-	-	-	-0.5	-0.4	-0.3	-0.2	-0.1	-0.1
GERMANY										
GNP(%)	-	-	-	-	0.2	-0.1	-0.1	-0.1	-0.0	-0.0
CPI(%)	-	-	-	-	-0.2	-0.1	-0.1	-0.1	-0.1	-0.1
RS(% PTS)	-	-	-	-	-0.1	0.0	0.0	0.0	0.0	0.0
GDEF(%GNPV) *	-	-	-	-	-0.0	0.0	0.0	0.0	0.0	0.0
EXCH(%) **	-	-	-	-	2.6	4.4	4.4	4.6	4.8	4.9
CAB(B.US$) ***	-	-	-	-	-0.5	0.3	0.0	-0.1	-0.1	-0.1
FRANCE										
GNP(%)	-	-	-	-	0.1	-0.0	-0.0	-0.0	-0.0	-0.0
CPI(%)	-	-	-	-	-0.1	-0.1	-0.1	-0.0	-0.0	0.0
GDEF(%GNPV) *	-	-	-	-	-0.0	0.0	0.0	0.0	0.0	-0.0
EXCH(%) **	-	-	-	-	2.4	4.3	4.3	4.5	4.7	4.7
CAB(B.US$) ***	-	-	-	-	0.0	-0.0	-0.0	-0.1	-0.0	-0.0
UNITED KINGDOM										
GNP(%)	-	-	-	-	0.1	-0.0	-0.0	-0.0	-0.0	-0.0
CPI(%)	-	-	-	-	-0.1	-0.0	-0.0	-0.0	-0.0	-0.0
GDEF(%GNPV) *	-	-	-	-	-0.0	0.0	0.0	0.0	0.0	0.0
EXCH(%) **	-	-	-	-	2.4	4.2	4.3	4.5	4.6	4.7
CAB(B.US$) ***	-	-	-	-	-0.1	0.1	0.1	-0.0	-0.0	-0.0
ITALY										
GNP(%)	-	-	-	-	0.1	0.1	0.0	0.0	0.0	0.0
CPI(%)	-	-	-	-	-0.4	-0.5	-0.4	-0.4	-0.3	-0.2
GDEF(%GNPV) *	-	-	-	-	-0.0	-0.0	-0.0	-0.0	-0.0	-0.0
EXCH(%) **	-	-	-	-	2.7	4.6	4.7	4.8	4.9	4.9
CAB(B.US$) ***	-	-	-	-	0.2	0.0	-0.0	-0.0	-0.0	0.0
CANADA										
GNP(%)	-	-	-	-	0.0	0.0	0.0	0.0	-0.0	-0.0
CPI(%)	-	-	-	-	-0.1	-0.1	0.0	0.1	0.1	0.1
GDEF(%GNPV) *	-	-	-	-	-0.0	-0.0	0.0	0.0	0.0	0.0
EXCH(%) **	-	-	-	-	2.5	4.3	4.3	4.4	4.5	4.6
CAB(B.US$) ***	-	-	-	-	0.1	0.1	0.1	0.1	0.1	0.1
REST OF WORLD										
CAB(B.US$) ***	-	-	-	-	-	-	-	-	-	-

* Government deficit as a percentage of baseline nominal GNP.
** Exchange rate : Bilateral rate against U.S. $ ($/local currency).
*** Local currency units translated into U.S. $ at baseline exchange rates.

Model: LIVERPL
Simulation E: U.S. Monetary Expansion with Foreign Short-Term Interest Rates Unchanged from Baseline
(Deviation of Shock Path from Baseline Path)

	1985 Q1	1985 Q2	1985 Q3	1985 Q4	1985	1986	1987	1988	1989	1990
UNITED STATES										
GNPV(%)	-	-	-	-	2.4	3.9	3.8	3.9	4.1	4.2
GNP(%)	-	-	-	-	0.6	0.2	0.0	-0.1	-0.1	-0.1
PGNP(%)	-	-	-	-	1.8	3.7	3.8	4.0	4.2	4.3
CPI(%)	-	-	-	-	1.8	3.7	3.8	4.0	4.2	4.3
WAGES(%)	-	-	-	-	-	-	-	-	-	-
UN(% PTS)	-	-	-	-	-	-	-	-	-	-
GNP(B.72$)	-	-	-	-	9.8	3.9	0.4	-1.3	-2.2	-2.5
G(B.72$)	-	-	-	-	0.0	0.0	0.0	0.0	0.0	0.0
C(B.72$)	-	-	-	-	10.4	6.1	1.3	-0.9	-2.1	-2.6
IFP(B.72$)	-	-	-	-	-	-	-	-	-	-
II(B.72$)	-	-	-	-	-	-	-	-	-	-
XGS(B.72$)	-	-	-	-	-0.6	-2.2	-0.9	-0.4	-0.1	0.1
MGS(B.72$)	-	-	-	-	-	-	-	-	-	-
M1(%)	-	-	-	-	2.0	4.1	4.1	4.1	4.1	4.1
RS(% PTS)	-	-	-	-	0.4	-0.3	-0.2	-0.1	-0.1	-0.0
RL(% PTS)	-	-	-	-	0.1	-0.0	0.0	0.0	0.1	0.0
GDEF(B$)	-	-	-	-	-0.9	0.1	0.2	0.7	0.9	0.0
PXGS(%)	-	-	-	-	-	-	-	-	-	-
PMGS(%)	-	-	-	-	-	-	-	-	-	-
EXCH(%) *	-	-	-	-	-2.2	-3.8	-3.9	-3.9	-4.1	-4.2
CAB(B$)	-	-	-	-	-6.3	-12.3	-8.9	-7.8	-8.2	-7.7
NON-US OECD										
GNPV(%) **	-	-	-	-	-0.1	-0.1	-0.1	-0.1	-0.1	-0.1
GNP(%) **	-	-	-	-	0.1	-0.0	-0.0	-0.0	-0.0	-0.0
PGNP(%)	-	-	-	-	-0.2	-0.1	-0.1	-0.0	-0.1	-0.1
CPI(%)	-	-	-	-	-0.2	-0.1	-0.1	-0.0	-0.1	-0.1
WAGES(%)	-	-	-	-	-	-	-	-	-	-
UN(% PTS)	-	-	-	-	-	-	-	-	-	-
C(%) **	-	-	-	-	0.0	0.0	0.0	-0.0	-0.0	-0.0
IFP(%) **	-	-	-	-	-	-	-	-	-	-
RS(% PTS)	-	-	-	-	-0.0	-0.0	-0.1	-0.0	-0.0	-0.0
RL(% PTS)	-	-	-	-	-	-	-	-	-	-
GDEF (B.US$) **	-	-	-	-	-1.8	-0.3	-0.5	0.1	-0.4	-0.2
PXGS(%)	-	-	-	-	-	-	-	-	-	-
PMGS(%)	-	-	-	-	-	-	-	-	-	-
EXCH(%) ***	-	-	-	-	2.5	4.1	4.3	4.3	4.5	4.5
CAB(B.US$) **	-	-	-	-	-1.0	-0.7	-1.2	-0.5	-0.9	-0.5

* Exchange rate : (Weighted average of foreign currencies)/U.S. $.
** Local currency units translated into U.S. $ at baseline exchange rates.
*** Exchange rate : U.S. $/(weighted average of non-US OECD currencies).

Model: LIVERPL
Simulation E: U.S. Monetary Expansion with Foreign Short-Term Interest Rates Unchanged from Baseline
(Deviation of Shock Path from Baseline Path)

	1985									
	Q1	Q2	Q3	Q4	1985	1986	1987	1988	1989	1990
JAPAN										
GNP(%)	-	-	-	-	0.0	-0.0	-0.0	-0.0	-0.0	-0.0
CPI(%)	-	-	-	-	-0.3	-0.2	-0.2	-0.1	-0.1	-0.1
RS(% PTS)	-	-	-	-	-0.1	-0.0	-0.0	-0.0	-0.0	-0.0
GDEF(%GNPV) *	-	-	-	-	-0.0	-0.0	-0.0	-0.0	-0.0	-0.0
EXCH(%) **	-	-	-	-	2.6	4.3	4.3	4.4	4.5	4.5
CAB(B.US$) ***	-	-	-	-	-0.5	-0.5	-0.4	-0.3	-0.2	-0.2
GERMANY										
GNP(%)	-	-	-	-	0.2	-0.1	-0.1	-0.1	-0.0	-0.1
CPI(%)	-	-	-	-	-0.2	-0.1	-0.3	-0.2	-0.3	-0.3
RS(% PTS)	-	-	-	-	0.0	-0.0	-0.0	-0.0	-0.1	-0.1
GDEF(%GNPV) *	-	-	-	-	-0.0	0.0	0.0	0.0	-0.0	0.0
EXCH(%) **	-	-	-	-	2.5	4.2	4.5	4.5	4.8	4.8
CAB(B.US$) ***	-	-	-	-	-0.5	0.0	-0.4	0.0	-0.4	-0.1
FRANCE										
GNP(%)	-	-	-	-	0.0	-0.1	-0.1	-0.1	-0.0	-0.0
CPI(%)	-	-	-	-	-0.2	-0.1	-0.2	-0.1	-0.0	-0.0
GDEF(%GNPV) *	-	-	-	-	-0.0	0.0	0.0	0.0	0.0	0.0
EXCH(%) **	-	-	-	-	2.5	4.2	4.3	4.4	4.5	4.5
CAB(B.US$) ***	-	-	-	-	-0.1	-0.1	-0.2	-0.2	-0.2	-0.1
UNITED KINGDOM										
GNP(%)	-	-	-	-	0.1	-0.0	-0.0	-0.0	-0.0	-0.0
CPI(%)	-	-	-	-	-0.1	-0.1	-0.3	-0.3	-0.4	-0.6
GDEF(%GNPV) *	-	-	-	-	-0.0	-0.0	-0.0	-0.0	-0.0	-0.0
EXCH(%) **	-	-	-	-	2.4	4.2	4.4	4.6	4.8	5.1
CAB(B.US$) ***	-	-	-	-	-0.1	-0.0	-0.1	-0.0	-0.1	-0.0
ITALY										
GNP(%)	-	-	-	-	0.1	0.0	0.0	0.0	0.0	0.0
CPI(%)	-	-	-	-	-0.7	-0.5	-0.4	-0.3	-0.3	-0.3
GDEF(%GNPV) *	-	-	-	-	-0.0	-0.0	-0.0	-0.0	-0.0	-0.0
EXCH(%) **	-	-	-	-	3.0	4.5	4.5	4.5	4.7	4.7
CAB(B.US$) ***	-	-	-	-	0.1	-0.0	-0.1	-0.1	-0.1	-0.0
CANADA										
GNP(%)	-	-	-	-	0.0	0.0	0.0	-0.0	-0.0	-0.0
CPI(%)	-	-	-	-	-0.1	-0.1	-0.1	0.1	0.1	0.1
GDEF(%GNPV) *	-	-	-	-	-0.0	-0.0	-0.0	0.0	0.0	0.0
EXCH(%) **	-	-	-	-	2.4	4.2	4.2	4.2	4.3	4.4
CAB(B.US$) ***	-	-	-	-	0.1	0.0	-0.0	0.0	0.0	0.1
REST OF WORLD										
CAB(B.US$) ***	-	-	-	-	-	-	-	-	-	-

* Government deficit as a percentage of baseline nominal GNP.
** Exchange rate : Bilateral rate against U.S. $ ($/local currency).
*** Local currency units translated into U.S. $ at baseline exchange rates.

Model: LIVERPL
Simulation G: Increase in Government Purchases in Non-U.S. OECD Countries with U.S. Policies Unchanged from Baseline
(Deviation of Shock Path from Baseline Path)

	1985									
	Q1	Q2	Q3	Q4	1985	1986	1987	1988	1989	1990
UNITED STATES										
GNPV(%)	-	-	-	-	1.7	2.6	3.5	4.1	4.6	4.8
GNP(%)	-	-	-	-	0.1	-0.5	-0.7	-1.0	-1.1	-1.4
PGNP(%)	-	-	-	-	1.6	3.1	4.3	5.2	5.8	6.3
CPI(%)	-	-	-	-	1.6	3.1	4.3	5.2	5.8	6.3
WAGES(%)	-	-	-	-	-	-	-	-	-	-
UN(% PTS)	-	-	-	-	-	-	-	-	-	-
GNP(B.72$)	-	-	-	-	2.1	-8.1	-13.3	-17.6	-21.5	-28.2
G(B.72$)	-	-	-	-	0.0	0.0	0.0	0.0	0.0	0.0
C(B.72$)	-	-	-	-	-9.4	-15.4	-22.8	-29.2	-35.5	-44.4
IFP(B.72$)	-	-	-	-	-	-	-	-	-	-
II(B.72$)	-	-	-	-	-	-	-	-	-	-
XGS(B.72$)	-	-	-	-	11.4	7.2	9.5	11.6	14.0	16.2
MGS(B.72$)	-	-	-	-	-	-	-	-	-	-
M1(%)	-	-	-	-	0.0	0.0	0.0	0.0	0.0	0.0
RS(% PTS)	-	-	-	-	0.9	0.8	0.8	0.8	1.0	0.8
RL(% PTS)	-	-	-	-	0.9	0.9	0.9	0.8	0.8	0.8
GDEF(B$)	-	-	-	-	12.9	14.1	17.7	21.6	25.7	32.5
PXGS(%)	-	-	-	-	-	-	-	-	-	-
PMGS(%)	-	-	-	-	-	-	-	-	-	-
EXCH(%) *	-	-	-	-	-2.1	-3.2	-4.4	-5.4	-6.2	-7.0
CAB(B$)	-	-	-	-	23.0	11.9	16.9	22.2	27.8	34.2
NON-US OECD										
GNPV(%) **	-	-	-	-	1.3	1.1	1.2	1.1	0.9	0.8
GNP(%) **	-	-	-	-	0.9	0.3	0.4	0.4	0.4	0.5
PGNP(%)	-	-	-	-	0.4	0.8	0.8	0.6	0.4	0.4
CPI(%)	-	-	-	-	0.4	0.8	0.8	0.6	0.4	0.4
WAGES(%)	-	-	-	-	-	-	-	-	-	-
UN(% PTS)	-	-	-	-	-	-	-	-	-	-
C(%) **	-	-	-	-	-0.1	-0.2	-0.2	-0.1	-0.0	0.0
IFP(%) **	-	-	-	-	-	-	-	-	-	-
RS(% PTS)	-	-	-	-	0.3	0.0	-0.0	0.0	0.2	0.8
RL(% PTS)	-	-	-	-	-	-	-	-	-	-
GDEF (B.US$) **	-	-	-	-	47.1	55.5	62.7	71.6	81.5	96.0
PXGS(%)	-	-	-	-	-	-	-	-	-	-
PMGS(%)	-	-	-	-	-	-	-	-	-	-
EXCH(%) ***	-	-	-	-	2.0	3.3	4.6	5.7	6.7	7.6
CAB(B.US$) **	-	-	-	-	-22.4	-17.2	-22.6	-27.2	-31.9	-37.4

* Exchange rate : (Weighted average of foreign currencies)/U.S. $.
** Local currency units translated into U.S. $ at baseline exchange rates.
*** Exchange rate : U.S. $/(weighted average of non-US OECD currencies).

Model: LIVERPL
Simulation G: Increase in Government Purchases in Non-U.S. OECD Countries with U.S. Policies Unchanged from Baseline
(Deviation of Shock Path from Baseline Path)

	1985 Q1	1985 Q2	1985 Q3	1985 Q4	1985	1986	1987	1988	1989	1990
JAPAN										
GNP(%)	-	-	-	-	0.6	0.4	0.3	0.3	0.3	0.3
CPI(%)	-	-	-	-	1.8	2.3	2.6	2.7	2.8	3.1
RS(% PTS)	-	-	-	-	0.2	0.1	0.2	0.3	0.5	0.3
GDEF(%GNPV) *	-	-	-	-	0.0	0.0	0.0	0.0	0.0	0.0
EXCH(%) **	-	-	-	-	-0.4	0.8	1.9	2.8	3.5	4.0
CAB(B.US$) ***	-	-	-	-	-0.6	-1.2	-1.9	-2.7	-3.8	-4.2
GERMANY										
GNP(%)	-	-	-	-	1.9	-1.0	-0.2	0.1	0.3	0.6
CPI(%)	-	-	-	-	-2.7	-2.4	-3.3	-4.4	-5.6	-6.9
RS(% PTS)	-	-	-	-	0.6	-0.2	-0.5	-0.6	-0.7	1.6
GDEF(%GNPV) *	-	-	-	-	0.3	0.6	0.6	0.6	0.6	0.7
EXCH(%) **	-	-	-	-	8.0	9.3	11.3	13.4	15.6	18.1
CAB(B.US$) ***	-	-	-	-	-15.0	-7.4	-10.2	-12.4	-14.8	-19.0
FRANCE										
GNP(%)	-	-	-	-	1.6	1.5	1.3	1.1	0.8	0.6
CPI(%)	-	-	-	-	0.4	1.0	1.4	1.6	1.8	2.0
GDEF(%GNPV) *	-	-	-	-	0.1	0.1	0.1	0.1	0.2	0.2
EXCH(%) **	-	-	-	-	1.9	3.1	4.0	4.7	5.3	5.8
CAB(B.US$) ***	-	-	-	-	-2.1	-2.2	-2.6	-2.8	-3.0	-3.1
UNITED KINGDOM										
GNP(%)	-	-	-	-	0.6	0.5	0.7	0.8	0.9	0.9
CPI(%)	-	-	-	-	-0.3	-0.6	-0.8	-0.9	-0.9	-0.4
GDEF(%GNPV) *	-	-	-	-	1.5	1.7	1.7	1.7	1.6	1.6
EXCH(%) **	-	-	-	-	3.1	5.0	6.4	7.5	8.3	8.9
CAB(B.US$) ***	-	-	-	-	-4.0	-4.5	-5.2	-6.0	-6.5	-6.7
ITALY										
GNP(%)	-	-	-	-	0.5	0.2	0.2	0.1	0.0	0.0
CPI(%)	-	-	-	-	1.1	1.5	1.4	1.1	0.8	0.8
GDEF(%GNPV) *	-	-	-	-	0.0	0.0	0.0	0.0	0.0	0.0
EXCH(%) **	-	-	-	-	1.1	2.5	3.8	5.0	6.0	6.7
CAB(B.US$) ***	-	-	-	-	-0.6	-0.9	-1.1	-1.4	-1.8	-2.2
CANADA										
GNP(%)	-	-	-	-	0.4	0.5	0.7	0.7	0.6	0.6
CPI(%)	-	-	-	-	1.7	2.8	3.4	3.8	3.9	4.2
GDEF(%GNPV) *	-	-	-	-	1.0	1.1	1.1	1.2	1.2	1.3
EXCH(%) **	-	-	-	-	-2.5	-1.2	-0.1	0.9	1.8	2.6
CAB(B.US$) ***	-	-	-	-	-0.1	-0.9	-1.5	-2.0	-2.1	-2.3
REST OF WORLD										
CAB(B.US$) ***	-	-	-	-	-	-	-	-	-	-

* Government deficit as a percentage of baseline nominal GNP.
** Exchange rate : Bilateral rate against U.S. $ ($/local currency).
*** Local currency units translated into U.S. $ at baseline exchange rates.

Model: LIVERPL
Simulation H: Monetary Expansion in Non-U.S. OECD Countries
with U.S. Policies Unchanged from Baseline
(Deviation of Shock Path from Baseline Path)

	1985									
	Q1	Q2	Q3	Q4	1985	1986	1987	1988	1989	1990
UNITED STATES										
GNPV(%)	-	-	-	-	-0.7	-1.8	-2.3	-2.4	-2.3	-2.1
GNP(%)	-	-	-	-	1.5	1.6	1.5	1.3	1.1	0.9
PGNP(%)	-	-	-	-	-2.2	-3.4	-3.8	-3.7	-3.4	-3.1
CPI(%)	-	-	-	-	-2.2	-3.4	-3.8	-3.7	-3.4	-3.1
WAGES(%)	-	-	-	-	-	-	-	-	-	-
UN(% PTS)	-	-	-	-	-	-	-	-	-	-
GNP(B.72$)	-	-	-	-	24.9	27.5	26.7	24.6	21.8	18.6
G(B.72$)	-	-	-	-	0.0	0.0	0.0	0.0	0.0	0.0
C(B.72$)	-	-	-	-	30.5	34.9	34.0	31.9	29.1	25.7
IFP(B.72$)	-	-	-	-	-	-	-	-	-	-
II(B.72$)	-	-	-	-	-	-	-	-	-	-
XGS(B.72$)	-	-	-	-	-5.6	-7.4	-7.2	-7.3	-7.3	-7.1
MGS(B.72$)	-	-	-	-	-	-	-	-	-	-
M1(%)	-	-	-	-	0.0	0.0	0.0	0.0	0.0	0.0
RS(% PTS)	-	-	-	-	-1.5	-1.1	-0.8	-0.5	-0.4	-0.2
RL(% PTS)	-	-	-	-	-0.7	-0.5	-0.3	-0.1	-0.0	-0.1
GDEF(B$)	-	-	-	-	-21.8	-17.2	-16.4	-15.7	-15.2	-16.1
PXGS(%)	-	-	-	-	-	-	-	-	-	-
PMGS(%)	-	-	-	-	-	-	-	-	-	-
EXCH(%) *	-	-	-	-	5.8	8.1	8.2	8.0	7.5	7.1
CAB(B$)	-	-	-	-	-2.6	-8.2	-8.4	-9.8	-10.5	-11.8
NON-US OECD										
GNPV(%) **	-	-	-	-	1.8	3.2	3.2	3.3	3.4	3.5
GNP(%) **	-	-	-	-	0.4	0.4	0.4	0.3	0.3	0.3
PGNP(%)	-	-	-	-	1.4	2.8	2.8	3.0	3.1	3.2
CPI(%)	-	-	-	-	1.4	2.8	2.8	3.0	3.1	3.2
WAGES(%)	-	-	-	-	-	-	-	-	-	-
UN(% PTS)	-	-	-	-	-	-	-	-	-	-
C(%) **	-	-	-	-	0.1	0.2	0.2	0.2	0.1	0.1
IFP(%) **	-	-	-	-	-	-	-	-	-	-
RS(% PTS)	-	-	-	-	0.3	-0.9	-0.8	-0.8	-0.7	-0.6
RL(% PTS)	-	-	-	-	-	-	-	-	-	-
GDEF (B.US$) **	-	-	-	-	-2.9	-3.2	-3.8	-2.8	-1.8	-2.2
PXGS(%)	-	-	-	-	-	-	-	-	-	-
PMGS(%)	-	-	-	-	-	-	-	-	-	-
EXCH(%) ***	-	-	-	-	-6.6	-8.4	-8.3	-8.0	-7.6	-7.1
CAB(B.US$) **	-	-	-	-	6.1	7.1	6.9	7.9	9.0	9.5

* Exchange rate : (Weighted average of foreign currencies)/U.S. $.
** Local currency units translated into U.S. $ at baseline exchange rates.
*** Exchange rate : U.S. $/(weighted average of non-US OECD currencies).

Model: LIVERPL
Simulation H: Monetary Expansion in Non-U.S. OECD Countries
with U.S. Policies Unchanged from Baseline
(Deviation of Shock Path from Baseline Path)

	1985									
	Q1	Q2	Q3	Q4	1985	1986	1987	1988	1989	1990
JAPAN										
GNP(%)	-	-	-	-	0.4	0.4	0.4	0.3	0.3	0.3
CPI(%)	-	-	-	-	1.0	2.0	2.0	2.1	2.3	2.2
RS(% PTS)	-	-	-	-	0.2	-0.6	-0.5	-0.6	-0.6	-0.4
GDEF(%GNPV) *	-	-	-	-	-0.0	0.0	0.0	0.0	0.0	0.0
EXCH(%) **	-	-	-	-	-5.7	-7.2	-7.2	-6.9	-6.5	-6.0
CAB(B.US$) ***	-	-	-	-	-0.3	0.0	0.3	0.8	1.3	1.5
GERMANY										
GNP(%)	-	-	-	-	0.7	0.6	0.7	0.5	0.4	0.4
CPI(%)	-	-	-	-	2.0	4.4	4.6	5.0	5.2	5.5
RS(% PTS)	-	-	-	-	0.8	-0.9	-0.8	-0.7	-0.7	-0.5
GDEF(%GNPV) *	-	-	-	-	-0.1	-0.1	-0.1	-0.1	-0.1	-0.1
EXCH(%) **	-	-	-	-	-7.7	-10.3	-10.3	-10.1	-9.7	-9.3
CAB(B.US$) ***	-	-	-	-	2.9	4.1	3.9	4.6	5.1	5.8
FRANCE										
GNP(%)	-	-	-	-	0.7	0.5	0.6	0.5	0.4	0.4
CPI(%)	-	-	-	-	1.1	2.2	1.9	1.8	2.0	2.1
GDEF(%GNPV) *	-	-	-	-	-0.0	-0.0	-0.0	-0.0	-0.0	-0.0
EXCH(%) **	-	-	-	-	-6.2	-7.8	-7.4	-7.0	-6.5	-6.1
CAB(B.US$) ***	-	-	-	-	1.4	1.5	1.2	1.1	0.9	0.7
UNITED KINGDOM										
GNP(%)	-	-	-	-	-0.2	-0.1	-0.1	-0.1	-0.1	-0.1
CPI(%)	-	-	-	-	2.4	4.0	4.4	4.5	4.5	4.5
GDEF(%GNPV) *	-	-	-	-	-0.3	-0.5	-0.3	-0.2	-0.2	-0.1
EXCH(%) **	-	-	-	-	-8.9	-10.7	-10.8	-10.4	-9.8	-9.1
CAB(B.US$) ***	-	-	-	-	2.0	1.2	0.7	0.6	0.5	0.5
ITALY										
GNP(%)	-	-	-	-	0.3	0.2	0.1	0.1	0.1	0.1
CPI(%)	-	-	-	-	2.5	4.8	4.7	4.7	4.7	4.7
GDEF(%GNPV) *	-	-	-	-	0.0	0.0	0.0	0.0	0.0	0.0
EXCH(%) **	-	-	-	-	-7.0	-9.3	-9.3	-8.9	-8.5	-8.0
CAB(B.US$) ***	-	-	-	-	-0.0	0.3	0.6	0.8	1.0	0.8
CANADA										
GNP(%)	-	-	-	-	0.2	0.3	0.2	0.2	0.2	0.2
CPI(%)	-	-	-	-	0.4	1.2	1.1	1.3	1.7	1.9
GDEF(%GNPV) *	-	-	-	-	-0.1	-0.1	-0.0	-0.0	-0.0	-0.0
EXCH(%) **	-	-	-	-	-5.4	-6.6	-6.5	-6.3	-6.0	-5.7
CAB(B.US$) ***	-	-	-	-	0.1	0.0	0.2	0.2	0.2	0.1
REST OF WORLD										
CAB(B.US$) ***	-	-	-	-	-	-	-	-	-	-

* Government deficit as a percentage of baseline nominal GNP.
** Exchange rate : Bilateral rate against U.S. $ ($/local currency).
*** Local currency units translated into U.S. $ at baseline exchange rates.

MCM—Multicountry Model of Federal Reserve Board Staff

See part 1 of this volume for design and detailed description of the simulations. See part 4 for bibliographical references.

Model: MCM
Simulation A: Baseline Path

	1985	1986	1987	1988	1989	1990
UNITED STATES						
GNPV(B.$)	3912.5	4169.0	4444.3	4737.9	5050.8	5384.4
GNP(B.72$)	1690.3	1740.8	1793.0	1846.8	1902.2	1959.2
PGNP(72=100)	234.4	242.6	251.1	259.9	268.9	278.4
CPI(72=100)	260.2	268.3	276.4	284.7	293.2	302.0
WAGES(72=100)	269.5	282.3	295.5	310.3	325.3	339.5
UN(%)	6.7	6.4	6.1	5.9	5.8	5.7
G(B.72$)	351.7	365.9	380.6	395.8	411.6	428.1
C(B.72$)	1073.4	1108.0	1141.2	1175.4	1210.7	1247.0
IFP(B.72$)	273.4	281.7	289.8	298.5	307.7	317.5
II(B.72$)	13.7	13.7	13.7	13.7	13.7	13.7
XGS(B.72$)	151.3	159.2	167.2	175.5	184.3	193.5
MGS(B.72$)	170.3	182.4	194.2	206.9	220.3	234.6
M1(B.$)	579.5	601.3	630.8	670.0	714.3	761.3
RS(%)	8.7	8.7	8.7	8.7	8.7	8.7
RL(%)	12.1	12.1	12.1	12.1	12.1	12.1
GDEF(B.$)	151.0	162.5	180.6	179.7	173.6	166.4
PXGS(72=100)	287.2	297.2	307.6	318.3	329.5	341.0
PMGS(72=100)	354.7	354.4	367.4	376.4	384.7	393.2
EXCH(72=100) *	113.8	113.8	113.8	113.8	113.8	113.8
CAB(B.$)	-104.7	-123.4	-143.4	-163.7	-186.6	-212.6
NON-US OECD						
GNPV(B.$) **	9763.9	10381.6	11033.2	11725.6	12461.4	13243.5
GNP(B.72$) **	4260.4	4409.6	4559.7	4714.9	4875.4	5041.3
PGNP(72=100)	229.2	235.4	242.0	248.7	255.6	262.7
CPI(72=100)	262.5	270.8	279.3	288.1	297.2	306.6
WAGES(72=100)	339.9	348.3	357.5	367.2	377.1	387.0
UN(%)	5.8	5.9	5.8	5.8	5.8	5.8
C(B.72$) **	2370.5	2442.3	2518.2	2596.5	2677.2	2760.5
IFP(B.72$) **	691.8	726.4	762.0	799.7	839.7	882.2
RS(%)	7.5	7.5	7.5	7.5	7.5	7.5
RL(%)	8.4	8.4	8.4	8.4	8.4	8.4
GDEF(B.US$) **	49.9	36.2	17.0	-3.9	-27.6	-53.9
PXGS(72=100)	238.8	245.3	252.1	259.1	266.3	273.7
PMGS(72=100)	361.4	367.4	376.1	385.9	396.1	406.5
EXCH(72=100) ***	87.9	87.9	87.9	87.9	87.9	87.9
CAB(B.US$)	37.8	50.2	63.0	77.5	93.9	112.5

* Exchange rate : (Weighted average of foreign currencies)/U.S. $.

** Local currency units translated into U.S. $ at baseline exchange rates.

*** Exchange rate : U.S. $/(weighted average of non-US OECD currencies).

Model: MCM
Simulation A: Baseline Path

	1985	1986	1987	1988	1989	1990
JAPAN						
GNP(B.72Y)	161301.5	168883.3	176482.0	184422.8	192721.4	201393.5
CPI(72=100)	252.4	259.9	267.7	275.7	284.0	292.5
RS(%)	6.1	6.1	6.1	6.1	6.1	6.1
GDEF(%GNPV) *	0.9	-0.1	-0.9	-1.8	-2.6	-3.5
EXCH(72=100) **	117.7	117.7	117.7	117.7	117.7	117.7
CAB(B.US$) ***	27.8	36.5	46.3	57.3	69.8	83.9
GERMANY						
GNP(B.72DM)	1073.9	1102.0	1132.4	1163.5	1195.5	1228.4
CPI(72=100)	181.0	185.0	189.1	193.4	197.8	202.2
RS(%)	6.2	6.2	6.2	6.2	6.2	6.2
GDEF(%GNPV) *	1.4	0.1	-1.5	-2.9	-4.4	-5.9
EXCH(72=100) **	98.0	98.0	98.0	98.0	98.0	98.0
CAB(B.US$) ***	19.7	25.7	32.9	41.2	50.5	61.1
FRANCE						
GNP(B.72F)	-	-	-	-	-	-
CPI(72=100)	-	-	-	-	-	-
GDEF(%GNPV) *	-	-	-	-	-	-
EXCH(72=100) **	-	-	-	-	-	-
CAB(B.US$) ***	-	-	-	-	-	-
UNITED KINGDOM						
GNP(B.72LB)	69.9	72.0	74.0	76.0	78.1	80.2
CPI(72=100)	444.6	465.5	486.5	508.4	531.3	555.2
GDEF(%GNPV) *	-1.4	-1.5	-2.3	-3.3	-4.4	-5.5
EXCH(72=100) **	44.6	44.6	44.6	44.6	44.6	44.6
CAB(B.US$) ***	-11.1	-13.6	-17.2	-21.2	-25.8	-31.0
ITALY						
GNP(B.72L)	-	-	-	-	-	-
CPI(72=100)	-	-	-	-	-	-
GDEF(%GNPV) *	-	-	-	-	-	-
EXCH(72=100) **	-	-	-	-	-	-
CAB(B.US$) ***	-	-	-	-	-	-
CANADA						
GNP(B.72C$)	151.6	154.8	157.9	161.1	164.3	167.6
CPI(72=100)	292.4	303.0	313.6	324.6	336.0	347.7
GDEF(%GNPV) *	10.7	11.7	12.6	13.6	14.8	16.1
EXCH(72=100) **	73.2	73.2	73.2	73.2	73.2	73.2
CAB(B.US$) ***	1.4	1.6	1.0	0.3	-0.5	-1.5
REST OF WORLD						
CAB(B.US$) ***	-	-	-	-	-	-

* Government deficit as a percentage of baseline nominal GNP.
** Exchange rate: Bilateral rate against U.S. $ ($/local currency).
*** Local currency units translated into U.S. $ at baseline exchange rates.

Model: MCM
Simulation B: Reduction in U.S. Government Purchases with Foreign Monetary Aggregates Unchanged from Baseline
(Deviation of Shock Path from Baseline Path)

	1985									
	Q1	Q2	Q3	Q4	1985	1986	1987	1988	1989	1990
UNITED STATES										
GNPV(%)	-1.3	-1.5	-1.8	-2.1	-1.7	-2.4	-2.5	-2.6	-2.7	-2.7
GNP(%)	-1.3	-1.4	-1.7	-1.8	-1.6	-1.8	-1.4	-0.9	-0.5	-0.1
PGNP(%)	0.0	-0.0	-0.1	-0.3	-0.1	-0.6	-1.1	-1.6	-2.2	-2.6
CPI(%)	-0.0	-0.0	-0.1	-0.2	-0.1	-0.4	-0.9	-1.4	-1.9	-2.3
WAGES(%)	-0.3	-0.4	-0.5	-0.6	-0.5	-1.2	-1.9	-2.7	-3.4	-3.9
UN(% PTS)	0.5	0.8	1.0	1.1	0.8	1.0	0.7	0.5	0.3	0.1
GNP(B.72$)	-21.0	-24.4	-28.8	-31.5	-26.4	-32.0	-25.7	-17.3	-9.9	-1.1
G(B.72$)	-16.7	-16.8	-17.0	-17.1	-16.9	-17.4	-17.9	-18.5	-19.0	-19.6
C(B.72$)	-4.9	-7.8	-11.6	-14.3	-9.6	-16.8	-16.3	-14.0	-12.2	-9.7
IFP(B.72$)	-2.2	-3.5	-4.9	-5.9	-4.1	-5.5	-1.8	1.4	3.6	6.2
II(B.72$)	0.0	0.0	0.0	0.0	0.0	0.0	0.0	0.0	0.0	0.0
XGS(B.72$)	-1.3	-2.3	-3.2	-4.3	-2.8	-5.0	-4.2	-2.6	-1.1	0.8
MGS(B.72$)	-4.1	-6.0	-8.0	-10.1	-7.0	-12.7	-14.5	-16.3	-18.8	-21.1
M1(%)	0.0	0.0	0.0	0.0	0.0	0.0	0.0	0.0	0.0	0.0
RS(% PTS)	-0.7	-0.8	-1.1	-1.5	-1.0	-1.7	-2.0	-2.2	-2.4	-2.5
RL(% PTS)	-0.1	-0.2	-0.3	-0.5	-0.3	-0.9	-1.4	-1.7	-1.9	-2.1
GDEF(B$)	-20.4	-16.4	-12.5	-10.5	-14.9	-13.4	-26.6	-43.2	-60.0	-79.4
PXGS(%)	0.0	-0.1	-0.1	-0.3	-0.1	-0.5	-1.0	-1.6	-2.1	-2.6
PMGS(%)	0.1	0.2	0.3	0.3	0.2	0.4	0.5	0.4	0.4	0.3
EXCH(%) *	-1.3	-1.3	-1.9	-2.3	-1.7	-2.8	-3.2	-3.5	-3.7	-3.9
CAB(B$)	7.2	8.8	11.0	12.6	9.9	16.5	23.3	31.1	41.3	53.5
NON-US OECD										
GNPV(%) **	-0.1	-0.2	-0.3	-0.4	-0.2	-0.7	-1.1	-1.3	-1.6	-1.8
GNP(%) **	-0.2	-0.2	-0.4	-0.5	-0.3	-0.7	-0.9	-0.9	-1.0	-1.0
PGNP(%)	0.1	0.0	0.1	0.1	0.1	-0.0	-0.2	-0.4	-0.6	-0.9
CPI(%)	-0.1	-0.1	-0.2	-0.2	-0.2	-0.4	-0.6	-0.7	-1.0	-1.2
WAGES(%)	0.0	0.0	0.0	-0.0	0.0	-0.1	-0.2	-0.5	-0.7	-1.1
UN(% PTS)	0.0	0.0	0.0	0.1	0.0	0.1	0.2	0.3	0.3	0.3
C(%) **	0.1	0.1	0.1	0.1	0.1	0.1	0.0	0.0	0.0	0.1
IFP(%) **	-0.0	-0.1	-0.1	-0.2	-0.1	-0.5	-0.7	-0.6	-0.3	-0.2
RS(% PTS)	-0.2	-0.2	-0.2	-0.3	-0.2	-0.4	-0.5	-0.5	-0.6	-0.7
RL(% PTS)	-0.0	-0.1	-0.1	-0.1	-0.1	-0.2	-0.3	-0.3	-0.4	-0.4
GDEF (B.US$) **	1.2	1.8	2.4	3.0	2.1	5.0	6.1	5.7	4.8	3.6
PXGS(%)	0.0	-0.2	-0.2	-0.3	-0.2	-0.5	-0.7	-1.0	-1.4	-1.8
PMGS(%)	-1.1	-1.2	-1.7	-2.1	-1.5	-2.6	-3.1	-3.4	-3.8	-4.1
EXCH(%) ***	1.3	1.4	1.9	2.4	1.8	2.9	3.3	3.6	3.8	4.1
CAB(B.US$) **	-0.5	-3.2	-3.9	-5.4	-3.2	-8.9	-12.2	-14.5	-17.5	-20.6

* Exchange rate : (Weighted average of foreign currencies)/U.S. $.
** Local currency units translated into U.S. $ at baseline exchange rates.
*** Exchange rate : U.S. $/(weighted average of non-US OECD currencies).

Model: MCM
Simulation B: Reduction in U.S. Government Purchases with Foreign Monetary Aggregates Unchanged from Baseline
(Deviation of Shock Path from Baseline Path)

	1985									
	Q1	Q2	Q3	Q4	1985	1986	1987	1988	1989	1990
JAPAN										
GNP(%)	-0.2	-0.3	-0.5	-0.7	-0.4	-1.1	-1.4	-1.4	-1.4	-1.5
CPI(%)	-0.1	-0.1	-0.1	-0.1	-0.1	-0.2	-0.2	-0.3	-0.5	-0.6
RS(% PTS)	-0.1	-0.1	-0.1	-0.2	-0.1	-0.3	-0.4	-0.3	-0.3	-0.4
GDEF(%GNPV) *	0.0	0.0	0.1	0.1	0.0	0.2	0.2	0.3	0.3	0.3
EXCH(%) **	1.6	1.6	2.2	2.7	2.0	2.8	3.0	3.3	3.7	4.0
CAB(B.US$) ***	0.0	-1.2	-1.7	-2.5	-1.3	-4.9	-6.9	-8.2	-10.2	-12.3
GERMANY										
GNP(%)	-0.1	-0.1	-0.2	-0.2	-0.2	-0.4	-0.6	-0.7	-0.8	-0.7
CPI(%)	-0.1	-0.2	-0.2	-0.3	-0.2	-0.5	-0.7	-0.9	-1.2	-1.5
RS(% PTS)	-0.3	-0.3	-0.4	-0.6	-0.4	-0.5	-0.5	-0.6	-0.8	-1.0
GDEF(%GNPV) *	-0.0	-0.0	0.0	0.0	-0.0	0.1	0.2	0.3	0.4	0.5
EXCH(%) **	0.9	1.1	1.5	2.0	1.4	2.8	3.4	3.6	3.6	3.5
CAB(B.US$) ***	0.1	-0.1	-0.3	-0.3	-0.2	-0.8	-1.5	-2.4	-3.2	-4.3
FRANCE										
GNP(%)	-	-	-	-	-	-	-	-	-	-
CPI(%)	-	-	-	-	-	-	-	-	-	-
GDEF(%GNPV) *	-	-	-	-	-	-	-	-	-	-
EXCH(%) **	-	-	-	-	-	-	-	-	-	-
CAB(B.US$) ***	-	-	-	-	-	-	-	-	-	-
UNITED KINGDOM										
GNP(%)	-0.0	-0.1	-0.1	-0.1	-0.1	-0.2	-0.3	-0.3	-0.3	-0.3
CPI(%)	-0.1	-0.1	-0.1	-0.1	-0.1	-0.2	-0.2	-0.3	-0.4	-0.6
GDEF(%GNPV) *	0.1	0.1	0.2	0.2	0.2	0.3	0.3	0.2	0.2	0.1
EXCH(%) **	1.5	1.2	1.6	2.0	1.6	2.9	3.6	4.0	4.3	4.6
CAB(B.US$) ***	-0.0	-1.0	-1.2	-1.6	-1.0	-2.2	-3.0	-3.4	-3.6	-3.8
ITALY										
GNP(%)	-	-	-	-	-	-	-	-	-	-
CPI(%)	-	-	-	-	-	-	-	-	-	-
GDEF(%GNPV) *	-	-	-	-	-	-	-	-	-	-
EXCH(%) **	-	-	-	-	-	-	-	-	-	-
CAB(B.US$) ***	-	-	-	-	-	-	-	-	-	-
CANADA										
GNP(%)	-0.3	-0.4	-0.6	-0.8	-0.5	-1.0	-1.1	-0.9	-0.7	-0.5
CPI(%)	-0.2	-0.3	-0.6	-0.8	-0.5	-1.2	-1.8	-2.4	-3.1	-3.7
GDEF(%GNPV) *	0.0	0.1	0.1	0.0	0.1	0.0	-0.1	-0.4	-0.7	-1.1
EXCH(%) **	1.2	1.1	2.4	2.7	1.9	3.5	3.9	4.1	4.3	4.6
CAB(B.US$) ***	-0.6	-0.9	-0.6	-1.0	-0.8	-1.0	-0.8	-0.5	-0.4	-0.2
REST OF WORLD										
CAB(B.US$) ***	-	-	-	-	-	-	-	-	-	-

* Government deficit as a percentage of baseline nominal GNP.
** Exchange rate : Bilateral rate against U.S. $ ($/local currency).
*** Local currency units translated into U.S. $ at baseline exchange rates.

Model: MCM
Simulation C: Reduction in U.S. Government Purchases with Foreign Short-Term Interest Rates Unchanged from Baseline
(Deviation of Shock Path from Baseline Path)

	1985									
	Q1	Q2	Q3	Q4	1985	1986	1987	1988	1989	1990
UNITED STATES										
GNPV(%)	-1.3	-1.5	-1.8	-2.1	-1.7	-2.4	-2.6	-2.8	-3.2	-3.5
GNP(%)	-1.3	-1.5	-1.7	-1.9	-1.6	-1.9	-1.6	-1.1	-0.9	-0.5
PGNP(%)	-0.0	-0.0	-0.1	-0.3	-0.1	-0.6	-1.1	-1.7	-2.3	-3.0
CPI(%)	-0.0	-0.0	-0.1	-0.2	-0.1	-0.4	-0.9	-1.4	-2.0	-2.5
WAGES(%)	-0.3	-0.4	-0.5	-0.6	-0.5	-1.2	-2.0	-2.8	-3.7	-4.5
UN(% PTS)	0.5	0.8	1.0	1.1	0.8	1.0	0.8	0.6	0.5	0.4
GNP(B.72$)	-21.0	-24.6	-29.0	-31.9	-26.6	-33.0	-27.9	-21.2	-16.2	-10.4
G(B.72$)	-16.7	-16.8	-17.0	-17.1	-16.9	-17.4	-17.9	-18.5	-19.0	-19.6
C(B.72$)	-4.9	-7.9	-11.8	-14.7	-9.8	-17.5	-17.7	-16.4	-16.0	-15.5
IFP(B.72$)	-2.2	-3.6	-5.0	-6.0	-4.2	-5.8	-2.3	0.6	2.4	4.6
II(B.72$)	0.0	0.0	0.0	0.0	0.0	0.0	0.0	0.0	0.0	0.0
XGS(B.72$)	-1.3	-2.4	-3.4	-4.5	-2.9	-5.5	-5.5	-5.1	-5.5	-6.4
MGS(B.72$)	-4.1	-6.1	-8.1	-10.3	-7.2	-13.3	-15.6	-18.1	-22.0	-26.5
M1(%)	0.0	0.0	0.0	0.0	0.0	0.0	0.0	0.0	0.0	0.0
RS(% PTS)	-0.7	-0.8	-1.1	-1.5	-1.0	-1.7	-2.0	-2.3	-2.7	-3.1
RL(% PTS)	-0.1	-0.2	-0.3	-0.5	-0.3	-0.9	-1.5	-1.8	-2.1	-2.4
GDEF(B$)	-20.4	-16.1	-12.1	-9.8	-14.6	-11.9	-23.6	-38.2	-52.2	-68.0
PXGS(%)	0.0	-0.0	-0.1	-0.2	-0.1	-0.4	-1.0	-1.6	-2.1	-2.7
PMGS(%)	0.1	0.3	0.3	0.4	0.3	0.6	0.7	0.7	0.7	0.6
EXCH(%) *	-1.6	-1.6	-2.3	-3.0	-2.1	-3.8	-4.7	-5.5	-6.5	-7.9
CAB(B$)	7.2	8.3	10.5	11.9	9.5	15.2	20.8	26.6	33.9	42.2
NON-US OECD										
GNPV(%) **	-0.1	-0.2	-0.3	-0.5	-0.3	-0.9	-1.6	-2.2	-3.0	-3.9
GNP(%) **	-0.2	-0.3	-0.4	-0.5	-0.3	-0.9	-1.3	-1.7	-2.0	-2.3
PGNP(%)	0.1	0.0	0.1	0.0	0.1	-0.0	-0.3	-0.6	-1.0	-1.6
CPI(%)	-0.1	-0.2	-0.3	-0.4	-0.2	-0.5	-0.9	-1.3	-1.8	-2.5
WAGES(%)	0.0	0.0	-0.0	-0.0	-0.0	-0.1	-0.3	-0.7	-1.3	-2.0
UN(% PTS)	0.0	0.0	0.1	0.1	0.0	0.2	0.3	0.4	0.5	0.6
C(%) **	0.0	0.1	0.1	0.1	0.1	0.0	-0.1	-0.3	-0.5	-0.6
IFP(%) **	-0.0	-0.1	-0.2	-0.3	-0.2	-0.8	-1.6	-1.9	-2.1	-2.5
RS(% PTS)	0.0	0.0	0.0	0.0	0.0	-0.0	0.0	0.0	0.0	0.0
RL(% PTS)	-0.0	-0.0	-0.0	-0.0	-0.0	-0.0	-0.0	-0.0	-0.0	-0.0
GDEF (B.US$) **	1.4	2.3	3.0	4.2	2.7	8.1	13.0	17.6	22.9	30.7
PXGS(%)	0.0	-0.2	-0.2	-0.3	-0.2	-0.5	-0.9	-1.4	-2.0	-2.7
PMGS(%)	-1.3	-1.4	-2.0	-2.6	-1.8	-3.4	-4.3	-5.1	-6.3	-7.6
EXCH(%) ***	1.6	1.7	2.3	3.1	2.2	4.0	4.9	5.8	7.0	8.6
CAB(B.US$) **	0.4	-2.6	-3.3	-4.3	-2.4	-8.1	-12.1	-15.1	-19.0	-24.5

* Exchange rate : (Weighted average of foreign currencies)/U.S. $.
** Local currency units translated into U.S. $ at baseline exchange rates.
*** Exchange rate : U.S. $/(weighted average of non-US OECD currencies).

Model: MCM
Simulation C: Reduction in U.S. Government Purchases with Foreign Short-Term Interest Rates Unchanged from Baseline
(Deviation of Shock Path from Baseline Path)

	1985									
	Q1	Q2	Q3	Q4	1985	1986	1987	1988	1989	1990
JAPAN										
GNP(%)	-0.2	-0.3	-0.5	-0.7	-0.5	-1.3	-1.9	-2.3	-2.6	-3.0
CPI(%)	-0.1	-0.1	-0.1	-0.1	-0.1	-0.2	-0.3	-0.5	-0.7	-1.0
RS(% PTS)	0.0	0.0	-0.0	0.0	0.0	-0.0	-0.0	0.0	0.0	0.0
GDEF(%GNPV) *	0.0	0.0	0.1	0.1	0.0	0.2	0.4	0.5	0.6	0.7
EXCH(%) **	1.7	1.8	2.4	3.1	2.2	3.7	4.2	4.7	5.6	6.6
CAB(B.US$) ***	0.0	-1.1	-1.7	-2.5	-1.3	-5.0	-7.7	-9.3	-11.6	-14.7
GERMANY										
GNP(%)	-0.1	-0.2	-0.3	-0.3	-0.2	-0.6	-0.9	-1.1	-1.3	-1.4
CPI(%)	-0.2	-0.3	-0.4	-0.6	-0.4	-0.8	-1.1	-1.4	-1.9	-2.5
RS(% PTS)	0.0	0.0	0.0	-0.0	0.0	-0.0	0.0	0.0	0.0	0.0
GDEF(%GNPV) *	-0.1	0.0	0.0	0.0	-0.0	0.2	0.4	0.6	0.7	0.9
EXCH(%) **	1.7	1.9	2.7	3.5	2.5	4.6	5.5	6.2	7.2	8.7
CAB(B.US$) ***	0.9	0.0	0.1	0.1	0.3	-0.5	-1.5	-2.5	-3.4	-4.9
FRANCE										
GNP(%)	-	-	-	-	-	-	-	-	-	-
CPI(%)	-	-	-	-	-	-	-	-	-	-
GDEF(%GNPV) *	-	-	-	-	-	-	-	-	-	-
EXCH(%) **	-	-	-	-	-	-	-	-	-	-
CAB(B.US$) ***	-	-	-	-	-	-	-	-	-	-
UNITED KINGDOM										
GNP(%)	0.0	0.0	0.1	0.1	0.0	0.1	-0.0	-0.1	-0.0	0.0
CPI(%)	-0.0	-0.0	-0.0	-0.0	-0.0	-0.1	-0.2	-0.3	-0.3	-0.4
GDEF(%GNPV) *	0.1	0.1	0.1	0.2	0.1	0.2	0.2	0.2	0.2	0.2
EXCH(%) **	1.0	0.6	1.0	1.3	1.0	2.4	3.3	3.7	4.0	4.4
CAB(B.US$) ***	-0.4	-1.1	-1.2	-1.6	-1.1	-2.0	-2.9	-3.6	-4.1	-4.7
ITALY										
GNP(%)	-	-	-	-	-	-	-	-	-	-
CPI(%)	-	-	-	-	-	-	-	-	-	-
GDEF(%GNPV) *	-	-	-	-	-	-	-	-	-	-
EXCH(%) **	-	-	-	-	-	-	-	-	-	-
CAB(B.US$) ***	-	-	-	-	-	-	-	-	-	-
CANADA										
GNP(%)	-0.4	-0.6	-0.9	-1.2	-0.8	-1.8	-2.5	-3.2	-4.2	-5.7
CPI(%)	-0.4	-0.7	-0.9	-1.3	-0.8	-2.1	-3.5	-5.3	-7.9	-11.2
GDEF(%GNPV) *	0.0	0.1	0.1	0.1	0.1	0.3	0.4	0.4	0.3	0.3
EXCH(%) **	2.1	2.6	3.6	4.8	3.3	6.5	9.1	12.3	17.1	23.9
CAB(B.US$) ***	-0.1	-0.4	-0.5	-0.4	-0.3	-0.5	-0.1	0.2	0.2	-0.2
REST OF WORLD										
CAB(B.US$) ***	-	-	-	-	-	-	-	-	-	-

* Government deficit as a percentage of baseline nominal GNP.
** Exchange rate : Bilateral rate against U.S. $ ($/local currency).
*** Local currency units translated into U.S. $ at baseline exchange rates.

Model: MCM
Simulation D: U.S. Monetary Expansion with foreign Monetary Aggregates Unchanged from Baseline
(Deviation of Shock Path from Baseline Path)

	1985									
	Q1	Q2	Q3	Q4	1985	1986	1987	1988	1989	1990
UNITED STATES										
GNPV(%)	-0.0	0.1	0.4	1.2	0.4	1.8	2.9	3.4	3.5	3.7
GNP(%)	0.0	0.2	0.4	1.1	0.4	1.5	2.2	2.0	1.4	0.9
PGNP(%)	-0.0	-0.0	-0.0	0.1	0.0	0.3	0.8	1.4	2.1	2.7
CPI(%)	0.0	0.1	0.2	0.3	0.1	0.4	0.8	1.4	2.1	2.6
WAGES(%)	-0.0	0.0	0.1	0.2	0.1	0.6	1.4	2.4	3.3	4.1
UN(% PTS)	0.0	-0.0	-0.1	-0.4	-0.1	-0.8	-1.1	-0.9	-0.6	-0.3
GNP(B.72$)	0.0	3.0	7.4	18.2	7.1	26.2	39.0	36.2	26.9	17.9
G(B.72$)	0.0	0.0	0.0	0.0	0.0	0.0	0.0	0.0	0.0	0.0
C(B.72$)	-0.3	2.2	4.7	12.8	4.8	11.8	17.2	15.4	9.7	3.8
IFP(B.72$)	-0.1	0.7	2.4	7.0	2.5	14.4	21.8	21.2	17.3	14.0
II(B.72$)	0.0	0.0	0.0	0.0	0.0	0.0	0.0	0.0	0.0	0.0
XGS(B.72$)	-1.2	-4.0	-9.8	-8.9	-6.0	-5.2	-0.9	0.6	0.5	0.2
MGS(B.72$)	-1.7	-4.2	-10.0	-7.3	-5.8	-5.3	-0.9	0.9	0.6	0.1
M1(%)	0.5	1.5	3.5	4.0	2.4	4.0	4.0	4.0	4.0	4.0
RS(% PTS)	-1.2	-2.3	-4.8	-2.1	-2.6	-2.2	-1.4	-0.9	-0.8	-0.6
RL(% PTS)	-0.1	-0.4	-1.0	-1.2	-0.7	-1.5	-1.5	-1.0	-0.7	-0.5
GDEF(B$)	-1.0	-5.3	-13.2	-23.8	-10.8	-36.5	-55.1	-56.4	-48.1	-39.3
PXGS(%)	0.2	0.4	1.0	0.7	0.6	1.1	1.6	2.3	3.0	3.6
PMGS(%)	0.2	0.6	1.1	1.4	0.8	1.1	1.1	1.2	1.2	1.2
EXCH(%) *	-2.6	-4.7	-9.5	-3.1	-5.0	-6.0	-6.0	-6.3	-6.6	-6.9
CAB(B$)	-0.0	-2.8	-5.1	-8.6	-4.1	-3.1	-1.9	-1.8	0.3	2.4
NON-US OECD										
GNPV(%) **	0.1	0.1	0.1	-0.5	-0.0	-0.6	-0.9	-1.0	-1.3	-1.6
GNP(%) **	-0.0	-0.1	-0.3	-0.3	-0.2	-0.7	-0.8	-0.8	-0.9	-1.1
PGNP(%)	0.1	0.2	0.4	-0.2	0.1	0.1	-0.1	-0.2	-0.3	-0.5
CPI(%)	-0.2	-0.4	-0.8	-0.4	-0.4	-0.6	-0.7	-0.7	-0.9	-1.1
WAGES(%)	0.0	0.0	0.1	0.1	0.1	0.0	-0.1	-0.3	-0.5	-0.7
UN(% PTS)	0.0	0.0	0.0	0.0	0.0	0.1	0.2	0.2	0.3	0.3
C(%) **	0.1	0.3	0.6	0.5	0.4	0.5	0.4	0.3	0.3	0.3
IFP(%) **	0.0	0.1	0.2	0.3	0.1	-0.1	-0.4	-0.2	-0.2	-0.2
RS(% PTS)	-0.2	-0.3	-0.7	-0.4	-0.4	-0.5	-0.4	-0.4	-0.5	-0.7
RL(% PTS)	-0.0	-0.1	-0.2	-0.2	-0.1	-0.3	-0.3	-0.3	-0.3	-0.4
GDEF (B.US$) **	0.3	0.8	-0.4	0.8	0.3	3.4	3.2	1.9	1.6	1.4
PXGS(%)	0.1	-0.2	-0.4	-1.3	-0.5	-0.6	-0.6	-0.7	-0.9	-1.1
PMGS(%)	-2.2	-4.0	-8.1	-2.5	-4.2	-5.0	-4.8	-5.0	-5.2	-5.3
EXCH(%) ***	2.7	4.9	10.5	3.2	5.3	6.4	6.4	6.7	7.1	7.4
CAB(B.US$) **	6.5	7.8	14.3	-9.8	4.7	-3.5	-3.3	-4.7	-9.3	-14.2

* Exchange rate : (Weighted average of foreign currencies)/U.S. $.
** Local currency units translated into U.S. $ at baseline exchange rates.
*** Exchange rate : U.S. $/(weighted average of non-US OECD currencies).

Model: MCM
Simulation D: U.S. Monetary Expansion with Foreign Monetary Aggregates Unchanged from Baseline
(Deviation of Shock Path from Baseline Path)

	1985									
	Q1	Q2	Q3	Q4	1985	1986	1987	1988	1989	1990
JAPAN										
GNP(%)	-0.1	-0.3	-0.7	-0.7	-0.5	-1.4	-1.4	-1.3	-1.5	-1.8
CPI(%)	-0.1	-0.2	-0.4	-0.1	-0.2	-0.2	-0.3	-0.4	-0.5	-0.6
RS(% PTS)	-0.0	-0.1	-0.2	-0.2	-0.1	-0.4	-0.3	-0.2	-0.3	-0.4
GDEF(%GNPV) *	-0.1	-0.1	-0.1	0.1	-0.0	0.2	0.2	0.2	0.2	0.3
EXCH(%) **	3.0	5.7	11.9	3.7	6.1	5.9	5.6	6.4	7.0	7.3
CAB(B.US$) ***	2.4	2.5	3.5	-6.4	0.5	-6.2	-6.2	-7.0	-9.8	-12.2
GERMANY										
GNP(%)	0.1	0.2	0.3	0.2	0.2	0.0	-0.3	-0.6	-0.8	-0.9
CPI(%)	-0.2	-0.4	-0.9	-0.7	-0.6	-0.9	-1.0	-1.0	-1.2	-1.4
RS(% PTS)	-0.5	-0.9	-1.9	-0.5	-1.0	-0.7	-0.5	-0.5	-0.7	-0.9
GDEF(%GNPV) *	-0.1	-0.3	-0.6	-0.3	-0.3	-0.3	-0.1	-0.0	0.1	0.2
EXCH(%) **	1.6	3.3	7.0	3.4	3.8	5.8	6.3	6.4	6.6	6.8
CAB(B.US$) ***	1.3	2.3	3.9	-0.3	1.8	0.8	0.3	-0.1	-0.7	-1.8
FRANCE										
GNP(%)	-	-	-	-	-	-	-	-	-	-
CPI(%)	-	-	-	-	-	-	-	-	-	-
GDEF(%GNPV) *	-	-	-	-	-	-	-	-	-	-
EXCH(%) **	-	-	-	-	-	-	-	-	-	-
CAB(B.US$) ***	-	-	-	-	-	-	-	-	-	-
UNITED KINGDOM										
GNP(%)	0.1	0.1	0.3	-0.2	0.1	-0.1	-0.1	-0.1	-0.0	0.0
CPI(%)	-0.2	-0.2	-0.5	-0.0	-0.2	-0.4	-0.4	-0.5	-0.6	-0.8
GDEF(%GNPV) *	0.2	0.4	0.8	0.3	0.4	0.5	0.5	0.4	0.4	0.3
EXCH(%) **	2.7	4.7	9.9	2.1	4.8	7.5	7.8	7.9	8.1	8.5
CAB(B.US$) ***	1.1	1.1	2.4	-1.9	0.7	0.5	1.0	1.1	0.5	-0.2
ITALY										
GNP(%)	-	-	-	-	-	-	-	-	-	-
CPI(%)	-	-	-	-	-	-	-	-	-	-
GDEF(%GNPV) *	-	-	-	-	-	-	-	-	-	-
EXCH(%) **	-	-	-	-	-	-	-	-	-	-
CAB(B.US$) ***	-	-	-	-	-	-	-	-	-	-
CANADA										
GNP(%)	-0.1	-0.3	-0.8	-0.3	-0.4	-0.7	-0.6	-0.6	-0.7	-0.9
CPI(%)	-0.6	-1.2	-2.7	-1.3	-1.5	-2.0	-1.9	-2.0	-2.2	-2.5
GDEF(%GNPV) *	-0.3	-0.4	-0.9	-0.3	-0.5	-0.5	-0.6	-0.6	-0.7	-0.7
EXCH(%) **	3.6	5.9	14.4	2.7	6.7	8.1	7.2	6.8	7.0	7.1
CAB(B.US$) ***	1.7	1.9	4.5	-1.3	1.7	1.5	1.7	1.3	0.6	-0.0
REST OF WORLD										
CAB(B.US$) ***	-	-	-	-	-	-	-	-	-	-

* Government deficit as a percentage of baseline nominal GNP.
** Exchange rate : Bilateral rate against U.S. $ ($/local currency).
*** Local currency units translated into U.S. $ at baseline exchange rates.

Model: MCM
Simulation E: U.S. Monetary Expansion with Foreign Short-Term Interest Rates Unchanged from Baseline
(Deviation of Shock Path from Baseline Path)

	1985 Q1	1985 Q2	1985 Q3	1985 Q4	1985	1986	1987	1988	1989	1990
UNITED STATES										
GNPV(%)	-0.0	0.1	0.4	1.1	0.4	1.8	2.9	3.3	3.3	3.2
GNP(%)	0.0	0.2	0.4	1.0	0.4	1.5	2.1	1.9	1.2	0.7
PGNP(%)	-0.0	-0.0	-0.0	0.1	-0.0	0.3	0.8	1.4	2.0	2.6
CPI(%)	0.0	0.1	0.2	0.3	0.1	0.5	0.9	1.5	2.1	2.6
WAGES(%)	-0.0	0.0	0.1	0.2	0.1	0.6	1.4	2.3	3.2	3.8
UN(% PTS)	0.0	-0.0	-0.1	-0.4	-0.1	-0.8	-1.0	-0.8	-0.5	-0.1
GNP(B.72$)	0.1	3.1	7.5	17.7	7.1	26.0	38.2	34.5	23.6	12.8
G(B.72$)	0.0	0.0	0.0	0.0	0.0	0.0	0.0	0.0	0.0	0.0
C(B.72$)	-0.3	2.1	4.6	12.4	4.7	11.2	16.4	14.2	7.7	0.5
IFP(B.72$)	-0.1	0.7	2.4	6.9	2.5	14.1	21.4	20.6	16.4	12.9
II(B.72$)	0.0	0.0	0.0	0.0	0.0	0.0	0.0	0.0	0.0	0.0
XGS(B.72$)	-1.2	-4.0	-9.6	-9.2	-6.0	-5.2	-1.1	-0.4	-1.6	-3.6
MGS(B.72$)	-1.7	-4.3	-10.2	-7.7	-5.9	-5.9	-1.5	0.0	-1.1	-3.0
M1(%)	0.5	1.5	3.5	4.0	2.4	4.0	4.0	4.0	4.0	4.0
RS(% PTS)	-1.2	-2.3	-4.8	-2.1	-2.6	-2.1	-1.4	-1.0	-0.9	-0.9
RL(% PTS)	-0.1	-0.4	-1.0	-1.2	-0.7	-1.5	-1.5	-1.1	-0.7	-0.6
GDEF(B$)	-1.1	-5.2	-13.0	-22.9	-10.5	-35.4	-53.4	-53.4	-42.9	-31.3
PXGS(%)	0.2	0.5	1.1	0.8	0.6	1.2	1.7	2.3	3.0	3.6
PMGS(%)	0.2	0.6	1.3	1.6	0.9	1.4	1.4	1.4	1.4	1.5
EXCH(%) *	-2.7	-5.0	-10.2	-4.0	-5.5	-7.3	-7.3	-7.8	-8.7	-9.8
CAB(B$)	0.0	-3.0	-5.4	-9.8	-4.5	-3.6	-2.8	-4.2	-4.1	-4.8
NON-US OECD										
GNPV(%) **	0.1	0.1	0.1	-0.6	-0.1	-0.8	-1.4	-1.8	-2.3	-3.1
GNP(%) **	0.0	-0.1	-0.3	-0.4	-0.2	-0.9	-1.3	-1.4	-1.7	-2.1
PGNP(%)	0.1	0.1	0.3	-0.2	0.1	0.1	-0.1	-0.4	-0.6	-1.0
CPI(%)	-0.2	-0.5	-1.0	-0.6	-0.6	-0.8	-0.9	-1.1	-1.5	-2.0
WAGES(%)	0.0	0.0	0.1	0.0	0.0	-0.0	-0.2	-0.5	-0.9	-1.4
UN(% PTS)	0.0	0.0	0.0	0.1	0.0	0.2	0.3	0.4	0.4	0.5
C(%) **	0.1	0.3	0.6	0.5	0.4	0.5	0.2	-0.0	-0.1	-0.2
IFP(%) **	0.0	0.1	0.1	0.2	0.1	-0.6	-1.3	-1.3	-1.4	-1.8
RS(% PTS)	0.0	0.0	0.0	0.0	0.0	-0.0	0.0	0.0	0.0	0.0
RL(% PTS)	-0.0	-0.0	-0.1	-0.1	-0.0	-0.0	-0.0	-0.0	-0.0	-0.0
GDEF (B.US$) **	0.2	0.7	-0.8	3.9	1.0	6.8	10.0	11.6	14.9	21.0
PXGS(%)	0.1	-0.2	-0.3	-1.2	-0.4	-0.6	-0.7	-1.0	-1.3	-1.8
PMGS(%)	-2.3	-4.2	-8.5	-3.2	-4.6	-6.0	-5.9	-6.2	-7.0	-7.9
EXCH(%) ***	2.8	5.3	11.3	4.2	5.9	7.9	7.8	8.4	9.6	10.9
CAB(B.US$) **	6.9	8.8	16.0	-9.2	5.6	-2.8	-4.5	-5.9	-10.7	-17.2

* Exchange rate : (Weighted average of foreign currencies)/U.S. $.
** Local currency units translated into U.S. $ at baseline exchange rates.
*** Exchange rate : U.S. $/(weighted average of non-US OECD currencies).

Model: MCM
Simulation E: U.S. Monetary Expansion with Foreign Short-Term Interest Rates Unchanged from Baseline
(Deviation of Shock Path from Baseline Path)

	1985									
	Q1	Q2	Q3	Q4	1985	1986	1987	1988	1989	1990
JAPAN										
GNP(%)	-0.1	-0.3	-0.8	-0.7	-0.5	-1.6	-2.0	-2.1	-2.5	-3.0
CPI(%)	-0.1	-0.2	-0.4	-0.1	-0.2	-0.2	-0.3	-0.5	-0.7	-0.9
RS(% PTS)	0.0	0.0	-0.0	0.0	0.0	-0.0	-0.0	0.0	0.0	0.0
GDEF(%GNPV) *	-0.1	-0.1	-0.1	0.1	-0.0	0.2	0.4	0.4	0.5	0.6
EXCH(%) **	2.9	5.7	12.0	4.2	6.2	6.9	6.7	7.5	8.5	9.5
CAB(B.US$) ***	2.2	2.5	3.6	-5.9	0.6	-6.3	-7.1	-7.6	-10.1	-13.4
GERMANY										
GNP(%)	0.1	0.0	0.0	-0.3	-0.0	-0.5	-0.9	-1.1	-1.2	-1.4
CPI(%)	-0.4	-0.8	-1.7	-1.0	-1.0	-1.3	-1.4	-1.6	-2.1	-2.6
RS(% PTS)	0.0	0.0	0.0	-0.0	0.0	-0.0	0.0	0.0	0.0	0.0
GDEF(%GNPV) *	-0.2	-0.3	-0.6	0.1	-0.2	-0.1	0.2	0.3	0.5	0.6
EXCH(%) **	3.0	5.8	12.4	5.0	6.5	8.8	8.6	8.9	10.1	11.5
CAB(B.US$) ***	2.5	3.2	6.2	-3.0	2.2	0.7	-0.4	-0.8	-1.6	-3.1
FRANCE										
GNP(%)	-	-	-	-	-	-	-	-	-	-
CPI(%)	-	-	-	-	-	-	-	-	-	-
GDEF(%GNPV) *	-	-	-	-	-	-	-	-	-	-
EXCH(%) **	-	-	-	-	-	-	-	-	-	-
CAB(B.US$) ***	-	-	-	-	-	-	-	-	-	-
UNITED KINGDOM										
GNP(%)	0.2	0.3	0.8	0.3	0.4	0.2	-0.0	-0.1	-0.0	0.0
CPI(%)	-0.1	-0.1	-0.2	-0.0	-0.1	-0.4	-0.4	-0.5	-0.5	-0.6
GDEF(%GNPV) *	0.2	0.3	0.6	0.1	0.3	0.5	0.5	0.5	0.5	0.6
EXCH(%) **	1.7	2.7	6.3	1.5	3.1	7.7	8.3	8.3	8.5	8.8
CAB(B.US$) ***	0.6	0.6	1.6	-0.6	0.5	1.0	1.1	0.8	0.1	-0.7
ITALY										
GNP(%)	-	-	-	-	-	-	-	-	-	-
CPI(%)	-	-	-	-	-	-	-	-	-	-
GDEF(%GNPV) *	-	-	-	-	-	-	-	-	-	-
EXCH(%) **	-	-	-	-	-	-	-	-	-	-
CAB(B.US$) ***	-	-	-	-	-	-	-	-	-	-
CANADA										
GNP(%)	-0.1	-0.4	-1.0	-0.9	-0.6	-1.2	-1.4	-1.8	-2.7	-4.0
CPI(%)	-0.6	-1.4	-2.9	-2.1	-1.8	-2.4	-2.8	-3.5	-4.9	-7.0
GDEF(%GNPV) *	-0.3	-0.5	-0.9	-0.3	-0.5	-0.4	-0.3	-0.2	-0.1	0.2
EXCH(%) **	3.5	7.2	15.3	6.8	8.2	9.9	9.7	11.2	14.1	18.5
CAB(B.US$) ***	1.6	2.6	4.6	0.4	2.3	1.7	1.9	1.6	0.9	-0.0
REST OF WORLD										
CAB(B.US$) ***	-	-	-	-	-	-	-	-	-	-

* Government deficit as a percentage of baseline nominal GNP.
** Exchange rate : Bilateral rate against U.S. $ ($/local currency).
*** Local currency units translated into U.S. $ at baseline exchange rates.

Model: MCM
Simulation F: Nonpolicy Exogenous Depreciation of the Dollar
(Deviation of Shock Path from Baseline Path)

	1985									
	Q1	Q2	Q3	Q4	1985	1986	1987	1988	1989	1990
UNITED STATES										
GNPV(%)	0.0	0.0	0.1	0.1	0.1	0.4	1.2	2.0	2.7	2.8
GNP(%)	0.1	0.1	0.1	0.1	0.1	0.3	0.7	1.1	1.2	0.9
PGNP(%)	-0.0	-0.0	-0.0	0.0	-0.0	0.1	0.5	0.9	1.4	2.0
CPI(%)	0.0	0.1	0.2	0.3	0.1	0.6	1.1	1.6	2.0	2.5
WAGES(%)	0.0	0.0	0.0	0.0	0.0	0.1	0.5	1.1	1.9	2.6
UN(% PTS)	-0.0	-0.0	-0.0	-0.0	-0.0	-0.1	-0.4	-0.6	-0.6	-0.5
GNP(B.72$)	0.9	1.3	1.5	1.9	1.4	5.1	12.7	20.0	22.6	16.9
G(B.72$)	0.0	0.0	0.0	0.0	0.0	0.0	0.0	0.0	0.0	0.0
C(B.72$)	0.0	-0.3	-1.1	-1.9	-0.8	-3.1	-2.8	-0.0	3.8	3.9
IFP(B.72$)	0.0	-0.0	-0.3	-0.6	-0.2	-1.2	-2.0	-3.0	-4.8	-8.4
II(B.72$)	0.0	0.0	0.0	0.0	0.0	0.0	0.0	0.0	0.0	0.0
XGS(B.72$)	0.7	1.1	1.6	2.3	1.4	5.6	13.4	20.8	26.0	27.0
MGS(B.72$)	-0.1	-0.6	-1.2	-2.0	-1.0	-3.8	-4.1	-2.3	2.3	5.6
M1(%)	0.0	0.0	0.0	0.0	0.0	0.0	0.0	0.0	0.0	0.0
RS(% PTS)	0.1	0.2	0.3	0.4	0.2	0.7	1.5	2.2	2.8	3.1
RL(% PTS)	0.0	0.0	0.1	0.1	0.1	0.3	0.8	1.4	1.9	2.4
GDEF(B$)	-0.3	0.2	0.9	1.8	0.6	2.4	0.8	-0.7	1.8	15.1
PXGS(%)	0.2	0.5	0.8	1.1	0.6	1.8	3.0	3.7	4.0	4.4
PMGS(%)	0.2	0.6	1.1	1.6	0.9	2.7	4.6	5.4	5.1	4.7
EXCH(%) *	-2.4	-4.8	-7.2	-9.4	-6.0	-14.8	-22.9	-25.7	-25.7	-25.7
CAB(B$)	0.3	-0.7	-0.9	-0.6	-0.5	3.1	12.1	21.6	25.3	21.3
NON-US OECD										
GNPV(%) **	0.2	0.1	-0.0	-0.3	-0.0	-1.1	-3.0	-5.3	-6.8	-7.8
GNP(%) **	0.0	-0.1	-0.3	-0.5	-0.2	-1.4	-3.1	-4.8	-5.5	-5.6
PGNP(%)	0.1	0.2	0.2	0.3	0.2	0.3	0.2	-0.4	-1.3	-2.4
CPI(%)	-0.2	-0.4	-0.6	-0.8	-0.5	-1.4	-2.5	-3.3	-3.9	-4.8
WAGES(%)	0.0	0.0	0.1	0.1	0.1	0.1	-0.1	-0.7	-1.8	-3.2
UN(% PTS)	-0.0	0.0	0.0	0.1	0.0	0.2	0.7	1.2	1.5	1.5
C(%) **	0.2	0.3	0.5	0.7	0.4	1.0	1.4	1.1	0.7	0.6
IFP(%) **	0.0	0.1	0.2	0.3	0.2	0.0	-1.1	-2.2	-2.6	-2.0
RS(% PTS)	-0.3	-0.6	-0.9	-1.4	-0.8	-1.8	-2.8	-2.9	-3.1	-2.9
RL(% PTS)	-0.1	-0.1	-0.2	-0.4	-0.2	-0.6	-1.1	-1.5	-1.7	-1.7
GDEF (B.US$) **	-0.3	0.3	-0.3	0.7	0.1	5.8	13.0	25.1	29.3	25.7
PXGS(%)	0.1	-0.1	-0.4	-0.7	-0.3	-1.4	-2.8	-4.2	-5.1	-6.2
PMGS(%)	-2.1	-4.1	-6.0	-7.9	-5.0	-12.6	-19.6	-22.1	-22.2	-22.3
EXCH(%) ***	2.5	5.1	7.7	10.4	6.4	17.5	29.8	34.6	34.6	34.6
CAB(B.US$) **	5.9	7.4	6.9	4.2	6.1	-3.3	-19.9	-48.6	-66.5	-80.8

* Exchange rate : (Weighted average of foreign currencies)/U.S. $.
** Local currency units translated into U.S. $ at baseline exchange rates.
*** Exchange rate : U.S. $/(weighted average of non-US OECD currencies).

Model: MCM
Simulation F: Nonpolicy Exogenous Depreciation of the Dollar
(Deviation of Shock Path from Baseline Path)

	1985									
	Q1	Q2	Q3	Q4	1985	1986	1987	1988	1989	1990
JAPAN										
GNP(%)	-0.1	-0.3	-0.6	-1.0	-0.5	-2.5	-5.2	-7.3	-8.0	-7.9
CPI(%)	-0.1	-0.2	-0.3	-0.3	-0.2	-0.6	-1.3	-1.8	-2.3	-2.8
RS(% PTS)	-0.0	-0.1	-0.2	-0.3	-0.1	-0.7	-1.4	-1.8	-1.7	-1.5
GDEF(%GNPV) *	-0.1	-0.1	-0.1	-0.0	-0.0	0.2	0.6	1.1	1.3	1.4
EXCH(%) **	2.7	5.4	8.2	11.1	6.9	18.7	31.9	37.2	37.2	37.2
CAB(B.US$) ***	2.1	2.5	1.7	-0.4	1.5	-6.9	-20.7	-37.3	-46.5	-53.4
GERMANY										
GNP(%)	0.1	0.1	0.0	-0.1	0.0	-0.7	-1.9	-3.9	-5.3	-5.7
CPI(%)	-0.3	-0.8	-1.3	-1.7	-1.0	-2.9	-4.9	-6.2	-7.2	-8.6
RS(% PTS)	-1.0	-1.6	-2.3	-3.1	-2.0	-3.3	-4.2	-3.9	-4.3	-3.9
GDEF(%GNPV) *	-0.2	-0.4	-0.5	-0.6	-0.4	-0.5	-0.3	0.7	1.8	2.5
EXCH(%) **	2.7	5.4	8.2	11.1	6.9	18.7	31.9	37.2	37.2	37.2
CAB(B.US$) ***	2.0	2.3	2.2	1.7	2.1	1.0	-0.9	-8.1	-13.1	-17.6
FRANCE										
GNP(%)	-	-	-	-	-	-	-	-	-	-
CPI(%)	-	-	-	-	-	-	-	-	-	-
GDEF(%GNPV) *	-	-	-	-	-	-	-	-	-	-
EXCH(%) **	-	-	-	-	-	-	-	-	-	-
CAB(B.US$) ***	-	-	-	-	-	-	-	-	-	-
UNITED KINGDOM										
GNP(%)	0.1	0.2	0.1	-0.0	0.1	-0.2	-0.7	-1.3	-1.3	-1.1
CPI(%)	-0.1	-0.3	-0.4	-0.5	-0.3	-0.9	-1.4	-1.8	-2.1	-2.6
GDEF(%GNPV) *	0.2	0.5	0.7	1.0	0.6	1.4	1.9	2.0	1.8	1.5
EXCH(%) **	2.7	5.4	8.2	11.1	6.9	18.7	31.9	37.2	37.2	37.2
CAB(B.US$) ***	1.1	1.6	1.8	1.8	1.6	1.6	1.0	-2.1	-4.3	-6.0
ITALY										
GNP(%)	-	-	-	-	-	-	-	-	-	-
CPI(%)	-	-	-	-	-	-	-	-	-	-
GDEF(%GNPV) *	-	-	-	-	-	-	-	-	-	-
EXCH(%) **	-	-	-	-	-	-	-	-	-	-
CAB(B.US$) ***	-	-	-	-	-	-	-	-	-	-
CANADA										
GNP(%)	-0.0	-0.1	-0.3	-0.5	-0.2	-1.1	-2.3	-3.4	-3.9	-4.1
CPI(%)	-0.2	-0.4	-0.7	-0.9	-0.6	-1.7	-3.0	-4.0	-5.1	-6.5
GDEF(%GNPV) *	-0.1	-0.2	-0.2	-0.3	-0.2	-0.3	-0.4	-0.4	-0.5	-1.0
EXCH(%) **	1.3	2.6	3.9	5.3	3.3	8.7	14.4	16.6	16.6	16.6
CAB(B.US$) ***	0.6	1.0	1.2	1.1	1.0	1.0	0.6	-1.2	-2.6	-3.7
REST OF WORLD										
CAB(B.US$) ***	-	-	-	-	-	-	-	-	-	-

* Government deficit as a percentage of baseline nominal GNP.
** Exchange rate : Bilateral rate against U.S. $ ($/local currency).
*** Local currency units translated into U.S. $ at baseline exchange rates.

Model: MCM
Simulation G: Increase in Government Purchases in Non-U.S. OECD Countries with U.S. Policies Unchanged from Baseline
(Deviation of Shock Path from Baseline Path)

	1985									
	Q1	Q2	Q3	Q4	1985	1986	1987	1988	1989	1990
UNITED STATES										
GNPV(%)	0.2	0.3	0.4	0.5	0.3	0.6	0.7	0.7	0.7	0.7
GNP(%)	0.2	0.3	0.3	0.4	0.3	0.5	0.4	0.2	0.1	0.0
PGNP(%)	0.0	0.0	0.1	0.1	0.0	0.2	0.3	0.5	0.6	0.7
CPI(%)	0.0	0.0	0.1	0.1	0.0	0.2	0.3	0.4	0.6	0.7
WAGES(%)	0.0	0.1	0.1	0.1	0.1	0.3	0.5	0.7	0.9	1.0
UN(% PTS)	-0.1	-0.1	-0.2	-0.2	-0.1	-0.2	-0.2	-0.1	-0.1	-0.0
GNP(B.72$)	3.3	4.4	5.6	6.6	5.0	8.0	7.0	4.4	2.3	0.2
G(B.72$)	0.0	0.0	0.0	0.0	0.0	0.0	0.0	0.0	0.0	0.0
C(B.72$)	0.8	1.2	1.9	2.6	1.6	3.5	3.5	2.5	1.4	0.3
IFP(B.72$)	0.3	0.6	0.9	1.1	0.7	1.2	0.4	-0.9	-1.8	-2.8
II(B.72$)	0.0	0.0	0.0	0.0	0.0	0.0	0.0	0.0	0.0	0.0
XGS(B.72$)	2.7	2.9	3.4	3.9	3.2	4.9	5.3	5.0	4.9	4.8
MGS(B.72$)	0.5	0.3	0.6	0.9	0.6	1.6	2.2	2.2	2.2	2.2
M1(%)	0.0	0.0	0.0	0.0	0.0	0.0	0.0	0.0	0.0	0.0
RS(% PTS)	0.1	0.2	0.3	0.3	0.2	0.5	0.6	0.6	0.7	0.8
RL(% PTS)	0.0	0.0	0.1	0.1	0.1	0.2	0.4	0.5	0.6	0.6
GDEF(B$)	-2.9	-4.1	-5.6	-6.7	-4.8	-8.0	-6.3	-2.3	1.7	6.2
PXGS(%)	0.2	0.4	0.5	0.5	0.4	0.6	0.7	0.8	0.9	1.0
PMGS(%)	0.1	0.2	0.2	0.1	0.1	0.2	0.2	0.3	0.4	0.5
EXCH(%) *	-1.0	-0.7	-0.6	-0.4	-0.7	-0.3	0.3	0.6	0.8	1.0
CAB(B$)	4.9	5.6	6.6	7.1	6.0	7.9	7.6	6.7	5.6	4.0
NON-US OECD										
GNPV(%) **	1.0	1.2	1.3	1.5	1.3	1.8	2.0	2.2	2.6	3.0
GNP(%) **	1.0	1.1	1.2	1.3	1.1	1.4	1.3	1.2	1.1	1.1
PGNP(%)	0.1	0.1	0.1	0.2	0.1	0.4	0.7	1.0	1.4	1.9
CPI(%)	-0.1	-0.0	0.1	0.1	0.0	0.3	0.6	0.9	1.2	1.6
WAGES(%)	0.0	0.1	0.1	0.2	0.1	0.4	0.8	1.3	1.8	2.3
UN(% PTS)	-0.0	-0.1	-0.2	-0.3	-0.2	-0.3	-0.3	-0.3	-0.3	-0.3
C(%) **	0.2	0.4	0.5	0.6	0.4	0.7	0.7	0.6	0.6	0.6
IFP(%) **	0.2	0.6	1.1	1.5	0.9	1.8	1.4	0.8	0.5	0.3
RS(% PTS)	0.4	0.5	0.5	0.5	0.5	0.6	0.6	0.7	0.9	1.0
RL(% PTS)	0.1	0.1	0.2	0.2	0.2	0.3	0.4	0.5	0.5	0.6
GDEF (B.US$) **	18.5	17.4	16.1	16.3	17.1	16.3	18.9	22.3	25.9	30.0
PXGS(%)	0.0	-0.0	0.0	0.1	0.0	0.4	0.8	1.2	1.7	2.2
PMGS(%)	-0.8	-0.5	-0.4	-0.2	-0.5	-0.1	0.5	0.9	1.2	1.5
EXCH(%) ***	1.0	0.7	0.6	0.4	0.7	0.3	-0.3	-0.6	-0.8	-1.0
CAB(B.US$) **	-2.0	-4.5	-5.8	-6.6	-4.7	-7.2	-7.1	-5.8	-4.6	-3.4

* Exchange rate : (Weighted average of foreign currencies)/U.S. $.
** Local currency units translated into U.S. $ at baseline exchange rates.
*** Exchange rate : U.S. $/(weighted average of non-US OECD currencies).

Model: MCM
Simulation G: Increase in Government Purchases in Non-U.S. OECD Countries with U.S. Policies Unchanged from Baseline
(Deviation of Shock Path from Baseline Path)

	1985									
	Q1	Q2	Q3	Q4	1985	1986	1987	1988	1989	1990
JAPAN										
GNP(%)	1.0	1.2	1.3	1.4	1.2	1.5	1.5	1.4	1.4	1.5
CPI(%)	-0.0	0.1	0.1	0.2	0.1	0.4	0.6	0.8	0.9	1.0
RS(% PTS)	0.5	0.5	0.6	0.7	0.6	0.8	0.7	0.5	0.5	0.5
GDEF(%GNPV) *	0.8	0.8	0.7	0.7	0.8	0.7	0.8	0.8	0.8	0.8
EXCH(%) **	1.1	0.9	0.9	0.8	0.9	0.5	-0.3	-0.8	-1.0	-1.3
CAB(B.US$) ***	-0.4	-1.5	-2.0	-2.8	-1.7	-3.5	-3.2	-2.2	-1.6	-1.1
GERMANY										
GNP(%)	1.0	1.2	1.4	1.5	1.3	1.7	1.5	1.3	1.1	0.9
CPI(%)	0.0	0.0	0.1	0.1	0.1	0.3	0.7	1.1	1.6	2.2
RS(% PTS)	0.1	0.2	0.2	0.2	0.2	0.3	0.5	0.9	1.2	1.6
GDEF(%GNPV) *	0.6	0.4	0.3	0.3	0.4	0.2	0.2	0.3	0.2	0.2
EXCH(%) **	0.0	-0.1	-0.1	-0.3	-0.1	-0.4	-0.7	-0.7	-0.6	-0.6
CAB(B.US$) ***	-1.7	-1.5	-2.1	-2.3	-1.9	-2.5	-2.5	-1.8	-1.1	-0.2
FRANCE										
GNP(%)	-	-	-	-	-	-	-	-	-	-
CPI(%)	-	-	-	-	-	-	-	-	-	-
GDEF(%GNPV) *	-	-	-	-	-	-	-	-	-	-
EXCH(%) **	-	-	-	-	-	-	-	-	-	-
CAB(B.US$) ***	-	-	-	-	-	-	-	-	-	-
UNITED KINGDOM										
GNP(%)	0.9	0.8	0.7	0.7	0.8	0.8	0.8	0.8	0.7	0.7
CPI(%)	-0.1	-0.1	-0.0	0.0	-0.0	0.0	0.1	0.3	0.6	1.0
GDEF(%GNPV) *	1.1	1.0	1.0	1.0	1.0	1.0	1.0	1.1	1.2	1.4
EXCH(%) **	1.8	1.2	0.8	0.3	1.0	0.7	0.2	-0.0	-0.6	-1.1
CAB(B.US$) ***	-0.2	-1.0	-0.8	-0.7	-0.7	-0.3	-0.2	-0.5	-0.6	-0.7
ITALY										
GNP(%)	-	-	-	-	-	-	-	-	-	-
CPI(%)	-	-	-	-	-	-	-	-	-	-
GDEF(%GNPV) *	-	-	-	-	-	-	-	-	-	-
EXCH(%) **	-	-	-	-	-	-	-	-	-	-
CAB(B.US$) ***	-	-	-	-	-	-	-	-	-	-
CANADA										
GNP(%)	0.7	0.9	1.0	1.1	0.9	1.2	1.2	1.1	0.9	0.7
CPI(%)	-0.3	-0.2	0.1	0.1	-0.1	0.4	1.0	1.8	2.6	3.5
GDEF(%GNPV) *	0.5	0.5	0.5	0.5	0.5	0.5	0.7	1.0	1.4	1.9
EXCH(%) **	1.8	1.3	0.6	0.8	1.1	0.6	0.1	-0.2	-0.5	-0.8
CAB(B.US$) ***	0.3	-0.5	-0.9	-0.7	-0.5	-0.9	-1.2	-1.3	-1.4	-1.4
REST OF WORLD										
CAB(B.US$) ***	-	-	-	-	-	-	-	-	-	-

* Government deficit as a percentage of baseline nominal GNP.
** Exchange rate : Bilateral rate against U.S. $ ($/local currency).
*** Local currency units translated into U.S. $ at baseline exchange rates.

Model: MCM
Simulation H: Monetary Expansion in Non-U.S. OECD Countries
with U.S. Policies Unchanged from Baseline
(Deviation of Shock Path from Baseline Path)

	1985 Q1	1985 Q2	1985 Q3	1985 Q4	1985	1986	1987	1988	1989	1990
UNITED STATES										
GNPV(%)	-0.0	0.0	0.0	0.0	0.0	-0.0	-0.0	0.1	0.1	0.0
GNP(%)	-0.0	-0.0	-0.0	0.1	0.0	0.0	0.0	0.1	0.1	-0.0
PGNP(%)	0.0	0.0	0.0	-0.0	0.0	-0.1	-0.1	-0.0	0.0	0.0
CPI(%)	-0.0	-0.1	-0.2	-0.3	-0.1	-0.2	-0.2	-0.1	-0.1	-0.0
WAGES(%)	-0.0	0.0	0.0	0.0	0.0	-0.0	-0.0	-0.0	0.0	0.1
UN(% PTS)	0.0	0.0	0.0	-0.0	-0.0	-0.0	-0.0	-0.1	-0.1	0.0
GNP(B.72$)	-0.5	-0.4	-0.2	1.6	0.1	0.6	0.5	2.1	1.8	-0.1
G(B.72$)	0.0	0.0	0.0	0.0	0.0	0.0	0.0	0.0	0.0	0.0
C(B.72$)	0.0	0.5	1.4	2.8	1.2	2.8	1.5	1.6	1.5	0.2
IFP(B.72$)	-0.0	0.1	0.4	1.0	0.4	1.2	1.1	1.3	1.2	0.5
II(B.72$)	0.0	0.0	0.0	0.0	0.0	0.0	0.0	0.0	0.0	0.0
XGS(B.72$)	-0.4	-0.4	-0.5	0.1	-0.3	-0.8	-0.9	0.2	0.4	-0.3
MGS(B.72$)	0.1	0.6	1.6	2.3	1.1	2.6	1.1	1.1	1.2	0.6
M1(%)	0.0	0.0	0.0	0.0	0.0	0.0	0.0	0.0	0.0	0.0
RS(% PTS)	-0.0	-0.1	-0.3	-0.3	-0.2	-0.2	-0.1	-0.0	0.0	0.0
RL(% PTS)	-0.0	-0.0	-0.0	-0.1	-0.0	-0.1	-0.1	-0.1	-0.0	0.0
GDEF(B$)	0.1	-0.8	-2.4	-4.6	-1.9	-4.2	-3.5	-5.5	-5.0	-2.2
PXGS(%)	-0.2	-0.4	-0.8	-0.7	-0.5	-0.5	-0.1	-0.0	-0.1	-0.2
PMGS(%)	-0.1	-0.5	-1.0	-1.5	-0.8	-1.2	-0.7	-0.5	-0.4	-0.3
EXCH(%) *	1.9	4.0	8.1	5.2	4.8	5.7	4.0	4.1	4.3	4.6
CAB(B$)	0.0	1.7	3.4	4.3	2.4	0.1	0.1	2.9	1.9	0.5
NON-US OECD										
GNPV(%) **	-0.1	-0.0	0.2	0.7	0.2	1.5	2.6	3.0	3.1	3.2
GNP(%) **	0.0	0.1	0.4	0.8	0.3	1.5	2.3	2.2	1.8	1.5
PGNP(%)	-0.1	-0.1	-0.3	-0.0	-0.1	-0.0	0.3	0.7	1.2	1.7
CPI(%)	0.2	0.4	0.8	0.6	0.5	0.6	0.7	1.1	1.5	2.0
WAGES(%)	-0.0	-0.0	-0.0	-0.0	-0.0	0.1	0.4	1.0	1.6	2.2
UN(% PTS)	-0.0	-0.0	-0.0	-0.1	-0.0	-0.3	-0.5	-0.6	-0.5	-0.4
C(%) **	-0.1	-0.1	-0.2	-0.0	-0.1	0.6	1.6	1.8	1.6	1.3
IFP(%) **	0.0	0.0	0.3	0.7	0.3	2.4	4.0	3.8	2.5	1.3
RS(% PTS)	-0.7	-1.7	-3.9	-3.7	-2.5	-2.1	-1.1	-0.7	-0.5	-0.3
RL(% PTS)	-0.2	-0.5	-1.1	-1.1	-0.7	-1.2	-1.0	-0.6	-0.3	-0.2
GDEF (B.US$) **	-1.0	-2.7	-5.0	-7.9	-4.1	-17.7	-27.4	-29.3	-27.2	-24.4
PXGS(%)	-0.1	-0.0	0.0	0.2	0.0	0.4	0.6	1.0	1.6	2.1
PMGS(%)	1.6	3.2	6.5	4.1	3.9	4.7	3.4	3.5	3.8	4.1
EXCH(%) ***	-1.9	-3.8	-7.5	-4.9	-4.5	-5.4	-3.8	-3.9	-4.2	-4.4
CAB(B.US$) **	-5.1	-7.4	-13.7	2.3	-6.0	3.5	6.0	3.3	5.0	8.0

* Exchange rate : (Weighted average of foreign currencies)/U.S. $.
** Local currency units translated into U.S. $ at baseline exchange rates.
*** Exchange rate : U.S. $/(weighted average of non-US OECD currencies).

Model: MCM
Simulation H: Monetary Expansion in Non-U.S. OECD Countries
with U.S. Policies Unchanged from Baseline
(Deviation of Shock Path from Baseline Path)

	1985									
	Q1	Q2	Q3	Q4	1985	1986	1987	1988	1989	1990
JAPAN										
GNP(%)	0.0	0.2	0.5	0.8	0.4	1.9	3.1	3.0	2.5	2.0
CPI(%)	0.0	0.1	0.2	0.1	0.1	0.2	0.4	0.7	1.0	1.2
RS(% PTS)	-0.4	-1.2	-2.3	-2.4	-1.6	-1.7	-0.6	-0.2	-0.0	-0.0
GDEF(%GNPV) *	0.0	0.0	-0.0	-0.2	-0.0	-0.5	-0.9	-0.9	-0.8	-0.6
EXCH(%) **	-1.1	-2.6	-4.7	-3.9	-3.1	-4.4	-2.6	-2.2	-2.6	-2.7
CAB(B.US$) ***	-0.7	-1.2	-0.9	0.6	-0.6	3.1	2.3	-1.2	-1.4	0.1
GERMANY										
GNP(%)	-0.0	0.1	0.3	0.9	0.3	1.6	2.2	1.9	1.3	0.9
CPI(%)	0.3	0.9	1.9	1.9	1.2	1.5	1.4	1.7	2.3	2.9
RS(% PTS)	-0.9	-2.2	-4.9	-4.8	-3.2	-2.8	-1.6	-1.2	-1.0	-0.7
GDEF(%GNPV) *	0.1	0.2	0.3	-0.2	0.1	-0.8	-1.4	-1.4	-1.3	-1.3
EXCH(%) **	-2.4	-5.5	-11.7	-10.5	-7.5	-9.1	-6.8	-6.2	-6.4	-6.6
CAB(B.US$) ***	-2.2	-3.9	-7.7	-1.7	-3.8	0.7	3.6	4.0	5.3	7.2
FRANCE										
GNP(%)	-	-	-	-	-	-	-	-	-	-
CPI(%)	-	-	-	-	-	-	-	-	-	-
GDEF(%GNPV) *	-	-	-	-	-	-	-	-	-	-
EXCH(%) **	-	-	-	-	-	-	-	-	-	-
CAB(B.US$) ***	-	-	-	-	-	-	-	-	-	-
UNITED KINGDOM										
GNP(%)	-0.1	-0.1	-0.0	0.6	0.1	0.7	0.8	1.2	1.3	1.2
CPI(%)	0.2	0.2	0.3	-0.1	0.1	0.1	0.1	0.3	0.5	0.8
GDEF(%GNPV) *	-0.3	-0.5	-1.0	-0.8	-0.6	-1.0	-1.0	-1.3	-1.5	-1.6
EXCH(%) **	-2.7	-4.4	-7.2	-1.8	-4.0	-3.8	-2.5	-4.2	-3.8	-4.2
CAB(B.US$) ***	-1.1	-0.9	-1.3	1.8	-0.4	-0.2	0.2	0.4	0.7	-0.1
ITALY										
GNP(%)	-	-	-	-	-	-	-	-	-	-
CPI(%)	-	-	-	-	-	-	-	-	-	-
GDEF(%GNPV) *	-	-	-	-	-	-	-	-	-	-
EXCH(%) **	-	-	-	-	-	-	-	-	-	-
CAB(B.US$) ***	-	-	-	-	-	-	-	-	-	-
CANADA										
GNP(%)	0.2	0.5	1.4	0.7	0.7	1.4	1.7	1.7	1.6	1.3
CPI(%)	0.4	0.8	1.8	0.6	0.9	0.9	1.6	2.5	3.6	4.8
GDEF(%GNPV) *	0.1	0.0	-0.0	-0.5	-0.1	-0.6	-0.7	-0.6	-0.3	0.1
EXCH(%) **	-2.2	-3.6	-8.5	-0.7	-3.7	-3.1	-3.8	-4.5	-5.2	-5.6
CAB(B.US$) ***	-1.2	-1.5	-3.8	1.7	-1.2	-0.1	-0.1	0.1	0.4	0.8
REST OF WORLD										
CAB(B.US$) ***	-	-	-	-	-	-	-	-	-	-

* Government deficit as a percentage of baseline nominal GNP.
** Exchange rate : Bilateral rate against U.S. $ ($/local currency).
*** Local currency units translated into U.S. $ at baseline exchange rates.

MINIMODR—Haas/Masson Simulation Model

See part 1 of this volume for design and detailed description of the simulations. See part 4 for bibliographical references.

Figures for exports of goods and services (XGS) exclude investment income receipts, and figures for imports of goods and services (MGS) exclude investment income payments.

The version of MINIMOD used for these simulations was the one incorporating rational (model-consistent) expectations.

Model: MINIMODR
Simulation A: Baseline Path

	1985	1986	1987	1988	1989	1990
UNITED STATES						
GNPV(B.$)	3913.0	4169.0	4444.7	4737.3	5050.6	5384.9
GNP(B.72$)	1690.3	1740.8	1793.0	1846.8	1902.2	1959.2
PGNP(72=100)	231.5	239.5	247.9	256.5	265.5	274.8
CPI(72=100)	233.3	241.4	249.8	258.5	267.6	277.0
WAGES(72=100)	-	-	-	-	-	-
UN(%)	-	-	-	-	-	-
G(B.72$)	351.7	365.9	380.6	395.8	411.6	428.1
C(B.72$)	1073.4	1108.0	1141.2	1175.4	1210.7	1247.0
IFP(B.72$)	273.4	280.7	287.5	294.7	302.2	310.1
II(B.72$)	-	-	-	-	-	-
XGS(B.72$)	108.2	113.6	119.2	125.0	131.1	137.5
MGS(B.72$)	137.0	146.8	156.4	166.6	177.5	189.2
M1(B.$)	582.2	612.0	644.5	689.9	748.2	811.5
RS(%)	8.4	8.4	8.4	8.4	8.4	8.4
RL(%)	12.0	12.0	12.0	12.0	12.0	12.0
GDEF(B.$)	158.7	168.0	187.2	197.3	194.3	189.6
PXGS(72=100)	231.5	239.5	247.9	256.5	265.5	274.8
PMGS(72=100)	166.0	170.1	174.3	178.7	183.1	187.7
EXCH(72=100) *	125.3	125.3	125.3	125.3	125.3	125.3
CAB(B.$)	-86.3	-93.3	-100.0	-107.1	-114.5	-122.4
NON-US OECD						
GNPV(B.$) **	5200.8	5518.5	5855.7	6211.8	6590.1	6991.4
GNP(B.72$) **	2500.0	2589.4	2680.1	2774.0	2871.1	2971.7
PGNP(72=100)	208.0	213.1	218.5	223.9	229.5	235.2
CPI(72=100)	220.8	226.3	231.9	237.7	243.7	249.8
WAGES(72=100)	-	-	-	-	-	-
UN(%)	-	-	-	-	-	-
C(B.72$) **	1361.2	1401.9	1444.7	1488.9	1534.4	1581.3
IFP(B.72$) **	740.8	740.5	743.1	749.8	760.0	773.1
RS(%)	7.2	7.2	7.2	7.2	7.2	7.2
RL(%)	8.2	8.2	8.2	8.2	8.2	8.2
GDEF(B.US$) **	58.5	52.5	51.6	49.3	45.5	40.6
PXGS(72=100)	208.0	213.1	218.5	223.9	229.5	235.2
PMGS(72=100)	290.1	300.1	310.6	321.4	332.7	344.4
EXCH(72=100) ***	79.8	79.8	79.8	79.8	79.8	79.8
CAB(B.US$)	50.9	55.1	59.0	63.2	67.6	72.2

* Exchange rate : (Weighted average of foreign currencies)/U.S. $.
** Local currency units translated into U.S. $ at baseline exchange rates.
*** Exchange rate : U.S. $/(weighted average of non-US OECD currencies).

Model: MINIMODR
Simulation A: Baseline Path

	1985	1986	1987	1988	1989	1990
JAPAN						
GNP(B.72Y)	-	-	-	-	-	-
CPI(72=100)	-	-	-	-	-	-
RS(%)	-	-	-	-	-	-
GDEF(%GNPV) *	-	-	-	-	-	-
EXCH(72=100) **	-	-	-	-	-	-
CAB(B.US$) ***	-	-	-	-	-	-
GERMANY						
GNP(B.72DM)	-	-	-	-	-	-
CPI(72=100)	-	-	-	-	-	-
RS(%)	-	-	-	-	-	-
GDEF(%GNPV) *	-	-	-	-	-	-
EXCH(72=100) **	-	-	-	-	-	-
CAB(B.US$) ***	-	-	-	-	-	-
FRANCE						
GNP(B.72F)	-	-	-	-	-	-
CPI(72=100)	-	-	-	-	-	-
GDEF(%GNPV) *	-	-	-	-	-	-
EXCH(72=100) **	-	-	-	-	-	-
CAB(B.US$) ***	-	-	-	-	-	-
UNITED KINGDOM						
GNP(B.72LB)	-	-	-	-	-	-
CPI(72=100)	-	-	-	-	-	-
GDEF(%GNPV) *	-	-	-	-	-	-
EXCH(72=100) **	-	-	-	-	-	-
CAB(B.US$) ***	-	-	-	-	-	-
ITALY						
GNP(B.72L)	-	-	-	-	-	-
CPI(72=100)	-	-	-	-	-	-
GDEF(%GNPV) *	-	-	-	-	-	-
EXCH(72=100) **	-	-	-	-	-	-
CAB(B.US$) ***	-	-	-	-	-	-
CANADA						
GNP(B.72C$)	-	-	-	-	-	-
CPI(72=100)	-	-	-	-	-	-
GDEF(%GNPV) *	-	-	-	-	-	-
EXCH(72=100) **	-	-	-	-	-	-
CAB(B.US$) ***	-	-	-	-	-	-
REST OF WORLD						
CAB(B.US$) ***	35.4	38.3	41.0	43.9	47.0	50.2

* Government deficit as a percentage of baseline nominal GNP.
** Exchange rate: Bilateral rate against U.S. $ ($/local currency).
*** Local currency units translated into U.S. $ at baseline exchange rates.

Model: MINIMODR
Simulation B: Reduction in U.S. Government Purchases with Foreign Monetary Aggregates Unchanged from Baseline
(Deviation of Shock Path from Baseline Path)

	1985									
	Q1	Q2	Q3	Q4	1985	1986	1987	1988	1989	1990
UNITED STATES										
GNPV(%)	-1.1	-1.3	-1.3	-1.4	-1.3	-1.5	-1.7	-1.9	-2.1	-2.3
GNP(%)	-1.1	-1.1	-1.1	-1.1	-1.1	-1.0	-0.8	-0.6	-0.4	-0.2
PGNP(%)	-0.0	-0.1	-0.2	-0.3	-0.2	-0.5	-0.9	-1.3	-1.8	-2.2
CPI(%)	0.1	-0.0	-0.1	-0.1	-0.0	-0.3	-0.7	-1.1	-1.5	-1.9
WAGES(%)	-	-	-	-	-	-	-	-	-	-
UN(% PTS)	-	-	-	-	-	-	-	-	-	-
GNP(B.72$)	-18.2	-19.2	-19.0	-18.4	-18.7	-16.6	-13.5	-10.2	-6.7	-3.4
G(B.72$)	-16.7	-16.8	-17.0	-17.1	-16.9	-17.4	-17.9	-18.5	-19.0	-19.6
C(B.72$)	-3.2	-5.0	-5.7	-5.8	-4.9	-5.7	-5.0	-3.9	-2.9	-2.0
IFP(B.72$)	-0.6	-0.7	-0.7	-0.6	-0.7	-0.0	0.8	1.7	2.5	3.1
II(B.72$)	-	-	-	-	-	-	-	-	-	-
XGS(B.72$)	0.0	0.2	0.3	0.4	0.2	0.8	1.3	1.9	2.6	3.3
MGS(B.72$)	-2.3	-3.1	-3.8	-4.3	-3.4	-5.1	-5.7	-6.1	-6.5	-6.9
M1(%)	0.0	0.0	0.0	0.0	0.0	0.0	0.0	0.0	0.0	0.0
RS(% PTS)	-0.6	-1.1	-1.0	-1.0	-0.9	-1.1	-1.3	-1.5	-1.6	-1.8
RL(% PTS)	-0.1	-0.1	-0.1	-0.1	-0.1	-0.1	-0.2	-0.2	-0.2	-0.2
GDEF(B$)	-27.2	-19.1	-19.9	-19.2	-21.3	-22.0	-26.0	-30.2	-34.7	-39.5
PXGS(%)	-0.0	-0.1	-0.2	-0.3	-0.2	-0.5	-0.9	-1.3	-1.8	-2.2
PMGS(%)	0.9	1.0	1.0	1.0	1.0	1.0	0.9	0.9	0.8	0.6
EXCH(%) *	-0.9	-1.0	-1.0	-1.0	-1.0	-1.0	-1.1	-1.1	-1.2	-1.1
CAB(B$)	1.8	3.1	4.8	6.0	3.9	8.5	11.8	15.3	19.7	25.1
NON-US OECD										
GNPV(%) **	-0.1	-0.1	-0.2	-0.2	-0.1	-0.3	-0.5	-0.6	-0.8	-1.0
GNP(%) **	-0.1	-0.1	-0.2	-0.2	-0.1	-0.3	-0.3	-0.4	-0.4	-0.5
PGNP(%)	-0.0	-0.0	-0.0	-0.0	-0.0	-0.1	-0.2	-0.3	-0.4	-0.5
CPI(%)	-0.0	-0.1	-0.1	-0.1	-0.1	-0.1	-0.2	-0.3	-0.4	-0.6
WAGES(%)	-	-	-	-	-	-	-	-	-	-
UN(% PTS)	-	-	-	-	-	-	-	-	-	-
C(%) **	0.0	-0.0	-0.0	-0.0	-0.0	-0.1	-0.1	-0.1	-0.2	-0.2
IFP(%) **	0.0	0.0	0.0	0.0	0.0	0.0	0.0	0.1	0.2	0.3
RS(% PTS)	-0.1	-0.1	-0.1	-0.1	-0.1	-0.2	-0.3	-0.4	-0.5	-0.6
RL(% PTS)	-0.0	-0.0	-0.0	-0.0	-0.0	-0.0	-0.0	-0.0	-0.0	-0.0
GDEF (B.US$) **	-0.1	-0.0	0.8	1.2	0.5	1.9	3.1	4.3	5.8	7.6
PXGS(%)	-0.0	-0.0	-0.0	-0.0	-0.0	-0.1	-0.2	-0.3	-0.4	-0.5
PMGS(%)	-1.0	-1.2	-1.2	-1.3	-1.2	-1.5	-2.0	-2.5	-2.9	-3.3
EXCH(%) ***	0.9	1.0	1.0	1.0	1.0	1.1	1.1	1.1	1.2	1.2
CAB(B.US$) **	-1.5	-2.3	-3.3	-4.0	-2.8	-5.5	-7.5	-9.7	-12.3	-15.5

* Exchange rate : (Weighted average of foreign currencies)/U.S. $.
** Local currency units translated into U.S. $ at baseline exchange rates.
*** Exchange rate : U.S. $/(weighted average of non-US OECD currencies).

Model: MINIMODR
Simulation B: Reduction in U.S. Government Purchases with Foreign Monetary Aggregates Unchanged from Baseline
(Deviation of Shock Path from Baseline Path)

	1985									
	Q1	Q2	Q3	Q4	1985	1986	1987	1988	1989	1990
JAPAN										
GNP(%)	-	-	-	-	-	-	-	-	-	-
CPI(%)	-	-	-	-	-	-	-	-	-	-
RS(% PTS)	-	-	-	-	-	-	-	-	-	-
GDEF(%GNPV) *	-	-	-	-	-	-	-	-	-	-
EXCH(%) **	-	-	-	-	-	-	-	-	-	-
CAB(B.US$) ***	-	-	-	-	-	-	-	-	-	-
GERMANY										
GNP(%)	-	-	-	-	-	-	-	-	-	-
CPI(%)	-	-	-	-	-	-	-	-	-	-
RS(% PTS)	-	-	-	-	-	-	-	-	-	-
GDEF(%GNPV) *	-	-	-	-	-	-	-	-	-	-
EXCH(%) **	-	-	-	-	-	-	-	-	-	-
CAB(B.US$) ***	-	-	-	-	-	-	-	-	-	-
FRANCE										
GNP(%)	-	-	-	-	-	-	-	-	-	-
CPI(%)	-	-	-	-	-	-	-	-	-	-
GDEF(%GNPV) *	-	-	-	-	-	-	-	-	-	-
EXCH(%) **	-	-	-	-	-	-	-	-	-	-
CAB(B.US$) ***	-	-	-	-	-	-	-	-	-	-
UNITED KINGDOM										
GNP(%)	-	-	-	-	-	-	-	-	-	-
CPI(%)	-	-	-	-	-	-	-	-	-	-
GDEF(%GNPV) *	-	-	-	-	-	-	-	-	-	-
EXCH(%) **	-	-	-	-	-	-	-	-	-	-
CAB(B.US$) ***	-	-	-	-	-	-	-	-	-	-
ITALY										
GNP(%)	-	-	-	-	-	-	-	-	-	-
CPI(%)	-	-	-	-	-	-	-	-	-	-
GDEF(%GNPV) *	-	-	-	-	-	-	-	-	-	-
EXCH(%) **	-	-	-	-	-	-	-	-	-	-
CAB(B.US$) ***	-	-	-	-	-	-	-	-	-	-
CANADA										
GNP(%)	-	-	-	-	-	-	-	-	-	-
CPI(%)	-	-	-	-	-	-	-	-	-	-
GDEF(%GNPV) *	-	-	-	-	-	-	-	-	-	-
EXCH(%) **	-	-	-	-	-	-	-	-	-	-
CAB(B.US$) ***	-	-	-	-	-	-	-	-	-	-
REST OF WORLD										
CAB(B.US$) ***	-1.1	-1.6	-2.3	-2.8	-2.0	-3.9	-5.2	-6.7	-8.5	-10.8

* Government deficit as a percentage of baseline nominal GNP.
** Exchange rate : Bilateral rate against U.S. $ ($/local currency).
*** Local currency units translated into U.S. $ at baseline exchange rates.

Model: MINIMODR
Simulation C: Reduction in U.S. Government Purchases with Foreign Short-Term Interest Rates Unchanged from Baseline
(Deviation of Shock Path from Baseline Path)

	1985 Q1	1985 Q2	1985 Q3	1985 Q4	1985	1986	1987	1988	1989	1990
UNITED STATES										
GNPV(%)	-1.1	-1.3	-1.3	-1.4	-1.3	-1.4	-1.6	-1.8	-2.1	-2.3
GNP(%)	-1.1	-1.1	-1.1	-1.1	-1.1	-1.0	-0.7	-0.5	-0.3	-0.2
PGNP(%)	-0.0	-0.1	-0.2	-0.3	-0.2	-0.5	-0.9	-1.3	-1.7	-2.1
CPI(%)	0.1	0.0	-0.1	-0.1	-0.0	-0.3	-0.6	-1.0	-1.4	-1.8
WAGES(%)	-	-	-	-	-	-	-	-	-	-
UN(% PTS)	-	-	-	-	-	-	-	-	-	-
GNP(B.72$)	-18.3	-19.2	-19.0	-18.3	-18.7	-16.5	-13.4	-10.1	-6.6	-3.3
G(B.72$)	-16.7	-16.8	-17.0	-17.1	-16.9	-17.4	-17.9	-18.5	-19.0	-19.6
C(B.72$)	-3.3	-5.0	-5.7	-5.9	-5.0	-5.8	-5.1	-4.1	-3.1	-2.3
IFP(B.72$)	-0.6	-0.8	-0.8	-0.6	-0.7	-0.1	0.8	1.6	2.4	3.0
II(B.72$)	-	-	-	-	-	-	-	-	-	-
XGS(B.72$)	0.0	0.2	0.3	0.5	0.2	0.8	1.4	2.0	2.7	3.5
MGS(B.72$)	-2.3	-3.1	-3.9	-4.4	-3.4	-5.2	-5.9	-6.4	-6.9	-7.4
M1(%)	0.0	0.0	0.0	0.0	0.0	0.0	0.0	0.0	0.0	0.0
RS(% PTS)	-0.6	-1.1	-0.9	-1.0	-0.9	-1.1	-1.2	-1.4	-1.6	-1.7
RL(% PTS)	-0.1	-0.1	-0.1	-0.1	-0.1	-0.1	-0.2	-0.2	-0.2	-0.2
GDEF(B$)	-27.0	-18.8	-19.8	-19.0	-21.2	-21.8	-25.8	-30.0	-34.5	-39.3
PXGS(%)	-0.0	-0.1	-0.2	-0.3	-0.2	-0.5	-0.9	-1.3	-1.7	-2.1
PMGS(%)	1.1	1.2	1.1	1.2	1.1	1.2	1.2	1.2	1.2	1.1
EXCH(%) *	-1.0	-1.2	-1.2	-1.2	-1.1	-1.3	-1.4	-1.5	-1.6	-1.6
CAB(B$)	1.6	2.9	4.6	5.8	3.7	8.3	11.6	15.1	19.4	24.8
NON-US OECD										
GNPV(%) **	-0.1	-0.1	-0.2	-0.3	-0.2	-0.4	-0.6	-0.9	-1.1	-1.4
GNP(%) **	-0.1	-0.1	-0.2	-0.2	-0.1	-0.3	-0.5	-0.6	-0.7	-0.8
PGNP(%)	-0.0	-0.0	-0.0	-0.0	-0.0	-0.1	-0.2	-0.3	-0.4	-0.6
CPI(%)	-0.1	-0.1	-0.1	-0.1	-0.1	-0.1	-0.2	-0.4	-0.5	-0.7
WAGES(%)	-	-	-	-	-	-	-	-	-	-
UN(% PTS)	-	-	-	-	-	-	-	-	-	-
C(%) **	0.0	-0.0	-0.0	-0.0	-0.0	-0.1	-0.1	-0.2	-0.2	-0.2
IFP(%) **	-0.0	-0.0	-0.1	-0.1	-0.0	-0.2	-0.4	-0.5	-0.6	-0.7
RS(% PTS)	0.0	0.0	0.0	0.0	0.0	0.0	0.0	0.0	0.0	0.0
RL(% PTS)	-0.0	-0.0	-0.0	-0.0	-0.0	-0.0	-0.0	-0.0	-0.0	-0.0
GDEF (B.US$) **	-0.2	0.7	1.5	2.1	1.0	3.7	6.3	9.2	12.6	16.5
PXGS(%)	-0.0	-0.0	-0.0	-0.0	-0.0	-0.1	-0.2	-0.3	-0.4	-0.6
PMGS(%)	-1.1	-1.3	-1.4	-1.5	-1.3	-1.8	-2.3	-2.8	-3.3	-3.7
EXCH(%) ***	1.1	1.2	1.2	1.2	1.2	1.3	1.4	1.5	1.6	1.7
CAB(B.US$) **	-1.4	-2.3	-3.3	-4.0	-2.8	-5.6	-7.6	-9.7	-12.3	-15.6

* Exchange rate : (Weighted average of foreign currencies)/U.S. $.
** Local currency units translated into U.S. $ at baseline exchange rates.
*** Exchange rate : U.S. $/(weighted average of non-US OECD currencies).

Model: MINIMODR
Simulation C: Reduction in U.S. Government Purchases with Foreign Short-Term Interest Rates Unchanged from Baseline
(Deviation of Shock Path from Baseline Path)

	1985									
	Q1	Q2	Q3	Q4	1985	1986	1987	1988	1989	1990
JAPAN										
GNP(%)	-	-	-	-	-	-	-	-	-	-
CPI(%)	-	-	-	-	-	-	-	-	-	-
RS(% PTS)	-	-	-	-	-	-	-	-	-	-
GDEF(%GNPV) *	-	-	-	-	-	-	-	-	-	-
EXCH(%) **	-	-	-	-	-	-	-	-	-	-
CAB(B.US$) ***	-	-	-	-	-	-	-	-	-	-
GERMANY										
GNP(%)	-	-	-	-	-	-	-	-	-	-
CPI(%)	-	-	-	-	-	-	-	-	-	-
RS(% PTS)	-	-	-	-	-	-	-	-	-	-
GDEF(%GNPV) *	-	-	-	-	-	-	-	-	-	-
EXCH(%) **	-	-	-	-	-	-	-	-	-	-
CAB(B.US$) ***	-	-	-	-	-	-	-	-	-	-
FRANCE										
GNP(%)	-	-	-	-	-	-	-	-	-	-
CPI(%)	-	-	-	-	-	-	-	-	-	-
GDEF(%GNPV) *	-	-	-	-	-	-	-	-	-	-
EXCH(%) **	-	-	-	-	-	-	-	-	-	-
CAB(B.US$) ***	-	-	-	-	-	-	-	-	-	-
UNITED KINGDOM										
GNP(%)	-	-	-	-	-	-	-	-	-	-
CPI(%)	-	-	-	-	-	-	-	-	-	-
GDEF(%GNPV) *	-	-	-	-	-	-	-	-	-	-
EXCH(%) **	-	-	-	-	-	-	-	-	-	-
CAB(B.US$) ***	-	-	-	-	-	-	-	-	-	-
ITALY										
GNP(%)	-	-	-	-	-	-	-	-	-	-
CPI(%)	-	-	-	-	-	-	-	-	-	-
GDEF(%GNPV) *	-	-	-	-	-	-	-	-	-	-
EXCH(%) **	-	-	-	-	-	-	-	-	-	-
CAB(B.US$) ***	-	-	-	-	-	-	-	-	-	-
CANADA										
GNP(%)	-	-	-	-	-	-	-	-	-	-
CPI(%)	-	-	-	-	-	-	-	-	-	-
GDEF(%GNPV) *	-	-	-	-	-	-	-	-	-	-
EXCH(%) **	-	-	-	-	-	-	-	-	-	-
CAB(B.US$) ***	-	-	-	-	-	-	-	-	-	-
REST OF WORLD										
CAB(B.US$) ***	-1.0	-1.6	-2.3	-2.8	-1.9	-3.9	-5.3	-6.8	-8.6	-10.8

* Government deficit as a percentage of baseline nominal GNP.
** Exchange rate : Bilateral rate against U.S. $ ($/local currency).
*** Local currency units translated into U.S. $ at baseline exchange rates.

Model: MINIMODR
Simulation D: U.S. Monetary Expansion with foreign Monetary Aggregates Unchanged from Baseline
(Deviation of Shock Path from Baseline Path)

	1985 Q1	1985 Q2	1985 Q3	1985 Q4	1985	1986	1987	1988	1989	1990
UNITED STATES										
GNPV(%)	0.3	0.6	0.9	1.1	0.7	1.4	1.8	2.0	2.3	2.4
GNP(%)	0.3	0.5	0.7	0.9	0.6	1.0	1.0	1.0	0.9	0.8
PGNP(%)	0.0	0.1	0.1	0.2	0.1	0.4	0.7	1.1	1.4	1.6
CPI(%)	0.4	0.5	0.5	0.6	0.5	0.8	1.1	1.4	1.7	1.9
WAGES(%)	-	-	-	-	-	-	-	-	-	-
UN(% PTS)	-	-	-	-	-	-	-	-	-	-
GNP(B.72$)	4.4	8.6	12.6	15.8	10.3	18.0	18.4	17.7	16.6	15.2
G(B.72$)	0.0	0.0	0.0	0.0	0.0	0.0	0.0	0.0	0.0	0.0
C(B.72$)	-1.1	-0.7	-0.0	1.0	-0.2	1.6	1.2	0.1	-1.0	-2.1
IFP(B.72$)	5.0	8.0	9.1	9.5	7.9	8.6	7.7	6.8	6.0	4.9
II(B.72$)	-	-	-	-	-	-	-	-	-	-
XGS(B.72$)	0.2	1.1	2.0	2.7	1.5	4.0	5.3	5.9	6.1	6.0
MGS(B.72$)	-0.1	-0.3	-1.4	-2.1	-1.0	-3.0	-3.0	-3.0	-3.0	-3.1
M1(%)	0.5	1.5	2.5	3.5	2.0	4.0	4.0	4.0	4.0	4.0
RS(% PTS)	-0.1	-2.3	-2.3	-3.1	-1.9	-1.8	-1.4	-1.2	-1.1	-1.0
RL(% PTS)	-0.3	-0.3	-0.3	-0.3	-0.3	-0.3	-0.2	-0.2	-0.2	-0.2
GDEF(B$)	2.6	-1.8	-16.6	-19.2	-8.7	-26.3	-31.3	-36.4	-41.3	-46.2
PXGS(%)	0.0	0.1	0.1	0.2	0.1	0.4	0.7	1.1	1.4	1.6
PMGS(%)	6.5	7.0	6.9	6.7	6.8	6.1	5.8	5.6	5.3	5.0
EXCH(%) *	-6.1	-6.6	-6.4	-6.3	-6.3	-5.7	-5.5	-5.3	-5.1	-4.8
CAB(B$)	-13.3	-12.6	-7.9	-4.2	-9.5	2.8	7.9	12.2	15.8	19.4
NON-US OECD										
GNPV(%) **	0.1	0.1	-0.0	-0.1	0.0	-0.2	-0.3	-0.4	-0.4	-0.5
GNP(%) **	0.1	0.1	-0.0	-0.1	0.0	-0.2	-0.3	-0.4	-0.4	-0.4
PGNP(%)	-0.0	-0.0	-0.0	0.0	0.0	0.0	0.0	0.0	-0.0	-0.1
CPI(%)	-0.3	-0.3	-0.3	-0.2	-0.3	-0.2	-0.1	-0.1	-0.1	-0.2
WAGES(%)	-	-	-	-	-	-	-	-	-	-
UN(% PTS)	-	-	-	-	-	-	-	-	-	-
C(%) **	0.2	0.1	0.1	0.1	0.1	0.0	-0.1	-0.1	-0.2	-0.2
IFP(%) **	0.0	0.1	0.1	0.2	0.1	0.2	0.1	0.1	0.1	0.2
RS(% PTS)	-0.5	-0.1	-0.1	-0.1	-0.2	-0.1	-0.2	-0.2	-0.3	-0.3
RL(% PTS)	-0.0	-0.0	-0.0	-0.0	-0.0	-0.0	-0.0	-0.0	-0.0	-0.0
GDEF (B.US$) **	-5.5	-6.0	-2.7	-1.9	-4.0	-0.4	1.2	2.5	3.8	4.9
PXGS(%)	-0.0	-0.0	-0.0	0.0	0.0	0.0	0.0	0.0	-0.0	-0.1
PMGS(%)	-6.0	-6.5	-6.3	-6.1	-6.2	-5.4	-4.8	-4.2	-3.8	-3.3
EXCH(%) ***	6.5	7.0	6.9	6.7	6.8	6.1	5.8	5.5	5.3	5.1
CAB(B.US$) **	4.4	3.7	1.0	-1.0	2.0	-4.7	-7.6	-10.1	-12.3	-14.4

* Exchange rate : (Weighted average of foreign currencies)/U.S. $.
** Local currency units translated into U.S. $ at baseline exchange rates.
*** Exchange rate : U.S. $/(weighted average of non-US OECD currencies).

Model: MINIMODR
Simulation D: U.S. Monetary Expansion with Foreign Monetary Aggregates Unchanged from Baseline
(Deviation of Shock Path from Baseline Path)

	1985									
	Q1	Q2	Q3	Q4	1985	1986	1987	1988	1989	1990
JAPAN										
GNP(%)	-	-	-	-	-	-	-	-	-	-
CPI(%)	-	-	-	-	-	-	-	-	-	-
RS(% PTS)	-	-	-	-	-	-	-	-	-	-
GDEF(%GNPV) *	-	-	-	-	-	-	-	-	-	-
EXCH(%) **	-	-	-	-	-	-	-	-	-	-
CAB(B.US$) ***	-	-	-	-	-	-	-	-	-	-
GERMANY										
GNP(%)	-	-	-	-	-	-	-	-	-	-
CPI(%)	-	-	-	-	-	-	-	-	-	-
RS(% PTS)	-	-	-	-	-	-	-	-	-	-
GDEF(%GNPV) *	-	-	-	-	-	-	-	-	-	-
EXCH(%) **	-	-	-	-	-	-	-	-	-	-
CAB(B.US$) ***	-	-	-	-	-	-	-	-	-	-
FRANCE										
GNP(%)	-	-	-	-	-	-	-	-	-	-
CPI(%)	-	-	-	-	-	-	-	-	-	-
GDEF(%GNPV) *	-	-	-	-	-	-	-	-	-	-
EXCH(%) **	-	-	-	-	-	-	-	-	-	-
CAB(B.US$) ***	-	-	-	-	-	-	-	-	-	-
UNITED KINGDOM										
GNP(%)	-	-	-	-	-	-	-	-	-	-
CPI(%)	-	-	-	-	-	-	-	-	-	-
GDEF(%GNPV) *	-	-	-	-	-	-	-	-	-	-
EXCH(%) **	-	-	-	-	-	-	-	-	-	-
CAB(B.US$) ***	-	-	-	-	-	-	-	-	-	-
ITALY										
GNP(%)	-	-	-	-	-	-	-	-	-	-
CPI(%)	-	-	-	-	-	-	-	-	-	-
GDEF(%GNPV) *	-	-	-	-	-	-	-	-	-	-
EXCH(%) **	-	-	-	-	-	-	-	-	-	-
CAB(B.US$) ***	-	-	-	-	-	-	-	-	-	-
CANADA										
GNP(%)	-	-	-	-	-	-	-	-	-	-
CPI(%)	-	-	-	-	-	-	-	-	-	-
GDEF(%GNPV) *	-	-	-	-	-	-	-	-	-	-
EXCH(%) **	-	-	-	-	-	-	-	-	-	-
CAB(B.US$) ***	-	-	-	-	-	-	-	-	-	-
REST OF WORLD										
CAB(B.US$) ***	3.0	2.6	0.7	-0.7	1.4	-3.3	-5.3	-7.0	-8.5	-10.0

* Government deficit as a percentage of baseline nominal GNP.
** Exchange rate : Bilateral rate against U.S. $ ($/local currency).
*** Local currency units translated into U.S. $ at baseline exchange rates.

Model: MINIMODR
Simulation E: U.S. Monetary Expansion with Foreign Short-Term Interest Rates Unchanged from Baseline
(Deviation of Shock Path from Baseline Path)

	1985 Q1	1985 Q2	1985 Q3	1985 Q4	1985	1986	1987	1988	1989	1990
UNITED STATES										
GNPV(%)	0.3	0.6	0.9	1.1	0.7	1.4	1.8	2.1	2.3	2.5
GNP(%)	0.3	0.5	0.7	0.9	0.6	1.0	1.0	1.0	0.9	0.8
PGNP(%)	0.0	0.1	0.1	0.2	0.1	0.4	0.7	1.1	1.4	1.7
CPI(%)	0.4	0.5	0.5	0.6	0.5	0.8	1.1	1.4	1.7	2.0
WAGES(%)	-	-	-	-	-	-	-	-	-	-
UN(% PTS)	-	-	-	-	-	-	-	-	-	-
GNP(B.72$)	4.3	8.6	12.7	15.8	10.3	18.1	18.6	17.8	16.7	15.2
G(B.72$)	0.0	0.0	0.0	0.0	0.0	0.0	0.0	0.0	0.0	0.0
C(B.72$)	-1.1	-0.8	-0.1	0.9	-0.3	1.5	1.1	-0.0	-1.2	-2.4
IFP(B.72$)	5.0	7.9	9.0	9.5	7.9	8.5	7.7	6.7	5.9	4.8
II(B.72$)	-	-	-	-	-	-	-	-	-	-
XGS(B.72$)	0.2	1.1	2.0	2.8	1.5	4.1	5.4	6.0	6.2	6.2
MGS(B.72$)	-0.2	-0.4	-1.5	-2.3	-1.1	-3.2	-3.2	-3.3	-3.4	-3.5
M1(%)	0.5	1.5	2.5	3.5	2.0	4.0	4.0	4.0	4.0	4.0
RS(% PTS)	-0.1	-2.3	-2.2	-3.1	-1.9	-1.7	-1.4	-1.2	-1.0	-1.0
RL(% PTS)	-0.3	-0.3	-0.3	-0.3	-0.3	-0.3	-0.2	-0.2	-0.2	-0.2
GDEF(B$)	2.9	-1.4	-16.6	-19.0	-8.5	-26.2	-31.1	-36.2	-41.1	-46.0
PXGS(%)	0.0	0.1	0.1	0.2	0.1	0.4	0.7	1.1	1.4	1.7
PMGS(%)	6.7	7.2	7.1	6.9	7.0	6.4	6.1	5.9	5.7	5.3
EXCH(%) *	-6.3	-6.7	-6.6	-6.5	-6.5	-6.0	-5.7	-5.6	-5.4	-5.2
CAB(B$)	-13.8	-12.9	-8.0	-4.4	-9.8	2.6	7.8	12.0	15.6	19.2
NON-US OECD										
GNPV(%) **	0.1	0.1	-0.0	-0.1	-0.0	-0.3	-0.4	-0.6	-0.8	-0.9
GNP(%) **	0.1	0.1	-0.0	-0.1	-0.0	-0.3	-0.4	-0.6	-0.7	-0.7
PGNP(%)	-0.0	-0.0	-0.0	0.0	0.0	0.0	0.0	-0.0	-0.1	-0.2
CPI(%)	-0.3	-0.3	-0.3	-0.2	-0.3	-0.2	-0.2	-0.2	-0.2	-0.3
WAGES(%)	-	-	-	-	-	-	-	-	-	-
UN(% PTS)	-	-	-	-	-	-	-	-	-	-
C(%) **	0.2	0.2	0.2	0.1	0.2	0.0	-0.1	-0.2	-0.2	-0.3
IFP(%) **	0.0	0.0	0.0	0.0	0.0	-0.1	-0.3	-0.5	-0.6	-0.7
RS(% PTS)	0.0	0.0	0.0	0.0	0.0	0.0	0.0	0.0	0.0	0.0
RL(% PTS)	-0.0	-0.0	-0.0	-0.0	-0.0	-0.0	-0.0	-0.0	-0.0	-0.0
GDEF (B.US$) **	-5.6	-3.4	-1.9	-0.8	-2.9	1.4	4.2	6.9	9.6	12.1
PXGS(%)	-0.0	-0.0	-0.0	0.0	0.0	0.0	0.0	-0.0	-0.1	-0.2
PMGS(%)	-6.3	-6.7	-6.5	-6.3	-6.4	-5.6	-5.0	-4.5	-4.1	-3.6
EXCH(%) ***	6.7	7.2	7.1	6.9	7.0	6.3	6.1	5.9	5.8	5.5
CAB(B.US$) **	4.5	3.7	1.0	-1.0	2.1	-4.7	-7.7	-10.2	-12.4	-14.5

* Exchange rate : (Weighted average of foreign currencies)/U.S. $.
** Local currency units translated into U.S. $ at baseline exchange rates.
*** Exchange rate : U.S. $/(weighted average of non-US OECD currencies).

Model: MINIMODR
Simulation E: U.S. Monetary Expansion with Foreign Short-Term Interest Rates Unchanged from Baseline
(Deviation of Shock Path from Baseline Path)

	1985									
	Q1	Q2	Q3	Q4	1985	1986	1987	1988	1989	1990
JAPAN										
GNP(%)	-	-	-	-	-	-	-	-	-	-
CPI(%)	-	-	-	-	-	-	-	-	-	-
RS(% PTS)	-	-	-	-	-	-	-	-	-	-
GDEF(%GNPV) *	-	-	-	-	-	-	-	-	-	-
EXCH(%) **	-	-	-	-	-	-	-	-	-	-
CAB(B.US$) ***	-	-	-	-	-	-	-	-	-	-
GERMANY										
GNP(%)	-	-	-	-	-	-	-	-	-	-
CPI(%)	-	-	-	-	-	-	-	-	-	-
RS(% PTS)	-	-	-	-	-	-	-	-	-	-
GDEF(%GNPV) *	-	-	-	-	-	-	-	-	-	-
EXCH(%) **	-	-	-	-	-	-	-	-	-	-
CAB(B.US$) ***	-	-	-	-	-	-	-	-	-	-
FRANCE										
GNP(%)	-	-	-	-	-	-	-	-	-	-
CPI(%)	-	-	-	-	-	-	-	-	-	-
GDEF(%GNPV) *	-	-	-	-	-	-	-	-	-	-
EXCH(%) **	-	-	-	-	-	-	-	-	-	-
CAB(B.US$) ***	-	-	-	-	-	-	-	-	-	-
UNITED KINGDOM										
GNP(%)	-	-	-	-	-	-	-	-	-	-
CPI(%)	-	-	-	-	-	-	-	-	-	-
GDEF(%GNPV) *	-	-	-	-	-	-	-	-	-	-
EXCH(%) **	-	-	-	-	-	-	-	-	-	-
CAB(B.US$) ***	-	-	-	-	-	-	-	-	-	-
ITALY										
GNP(%)	-	-	-	-	-	-	-	-	-	-
CPI(%)	-	-	-	-	-	-	-	-	-	-
GDEF(%GNPV) *	-	-	-	-	-	-	-	-	-	-
EXCH(%) **	-	-	-	-	-	-	-	-	-	-
CAB(B.US$) ***	-	-	-	-	-	-	-	-	-	-
CANADA										
GNP(%)	-	-	-	-	-	-	-	-	-	-
CPI(%)	-	-	-	-	-	-	-	-	-	-
GDEF(%GNPV) *	-	-	-	-	-	-	-	-	-	-
EXCH(%) **	-	-	-	-	-	-	-	-	-	-
CAB(B.US$) ***	-	-	-	-	-	-	-	-	-	-
REST OF WORLD										
CAB(B.US$) ***	3.1	2.6	0.7	-0.7	1.4	-3.3	-5.4	-7.1	-8.6	-10.1

* Government deficit as a percentage of baseline nominal GNP.
** Exchange rate : Bilateral rate against U.S. $ ($/local currency).
*** Local currency units translated into U.S. $ at baseline exchange rates.

Model: MINIMODR
Simulation F: Nonpolicy Exogenous Depreciation of the Dollar
(Deviation of Shock Path from Baseline Path)

	1985 Q1	1985 Q2	1985 Q3	1985 Q4	1985	1986	1987	1988	1989	1990
UNITED STATES										
GNPV(%)	-0.7	-1.1	-1.4	-1.6	-1.2	-1.4	-0.5	1.2	3.2	5.6
GNP(%)	-0.8	-1.1	-1.4	-1.6	-1.2	-1.8	-1.7	-1.3	-0.8	-0.2
PGNP(%)	0.0	-0.0	0.0	0.1	0.0	0.4	1.3	2.6	4.1	5.8
CPI(%)	0.1	0.3	0.4	0.6	0.4	1.3	2.8	4.2	5.7	7.3
WAGES(%)	-	-	-	-	-	-	-	-	-	-
UN(% PTS)	-	-	-	-	-	-	-	-	-	-
GNP(B.72$)	-12.6	-19.2	-24.6	-28.0	-21.1	-31.2	-31.3	-24.5	-15.6	-4.6
G(B.72$)	0.0	0.0	0.0	0.0	0.0	0.0	0.0	0.0	0.0	0.0
C(B.72$)	-2.6	-5.2	-10.4	-14.5	-8.2	-21.7	-30.5	-34.5	-33.5	-28.9
IFP(B.72$)	-10.7	-15.9	-19.4	-22.3	-17.1	-28.3	-36.3	-40.3	-39.2	-33.7
II(B.72$)	-	-	-	-	-	-	-	-	-	-
XGS(B.72$)	-0.7	-0.1	0.8	1.8	0.4	5.5	13.1	21.3	26.3	28.3
MGS(B.72$)	-1.5	-2.0	-4.4	-6.9	-3.7	-13.4	-23.0	-29.9	-31.6	-30.2
M1(%)	0.0	0.0	0.0	0.0	0.0	0.0	0.0	0.0	0.0	0.0
RS(% PTS)	-0.1	-0.5	-0.4	-0.4	-0.4	0.1	1.5	2.8	4.4	6.2
RL(% PTS)	0.6	0.7	0.8	0.9	0.8	1.2	1.7	2.0	2.1	1.9
GDEF(B$)	8.9	21.4	29.0	37.2	24.1	48.0	59.5	54.5	42.7	26.9
PXGS(%)	0.0	-0.0	0.0	0.1	0.0	0.4	1.3	2.6	4.1	5.8
PMGS(%)	2.0	4.0	6.0	8.0	5.0	13.2	21.8	24.6	24.0	23.6
EXCH(%) *	-2.0	-3.9	-5.8	-7.6	-4.8	-12.1	-18.8	-21.2	-21.2	-21.2
CAB(B$)	-3.5	-5.7	-4.2	-2.0	-3.8	7.0	24.7	54.8	77.4	87.4
NON-US OECD										
GNPV(%) **	0.1	0.3	0.3	0.4	0.3	0.4	-0.0	-0.7	-1.5	-2.2
GNP(%) **	0.1	0.3	0.5	0.6	0.4	0.9	1.2	1.1	0.9	0.4
PGNP(%)	-0.0	-0.1	-0.1	-0.2	-0.1	-0.6	-1.2	-1.9	-2.3	-2.6
CPI(%)	-0.1	-0.3	-0.4	-0.6	-0.3	-1.0	-1.9	-2.5	-2.9	-3.1
WAGES(%)	-	-	-	-	-	-	-	-	-	-
UN(% PTS)	-	-	-	-	-	-	-	-	-	-
C(%) **	0.1	0.2	0.3	0.4	0.2	0.7	1.0	1.2	1.0	0.8
IFP(%) **	0.2	1.0	1.7	2.3	1.3	4.1	6.3	7.5	7.4	6.3
RS(% PTS)	-0.2	-0.2	-0.2	-0.3	-0.2	-0.4	-0.8	-1.0	-1.3	-1.5
RL(% PTS)	-0.2	-0.2	-0.3	-0.3	-0.2	-0.3	-0.4	-0.4	-0.3	-0.3
GDEF (B.US$) **	-2.5	-6.9	-8.9	-10.7	-7.2	-15.2	-18.8	-17.4	-9.7	0.2
PXGS(%)	-0.0	-0.1	-0.1	-0.2	-0.1	-0.6	-1.2	-1.9	-2.3	-2.6
PMGS(%)	-2.0	-3.9	-5.8	-7.6	-4.8	-11.8	-17.8	-19.2	-18.0	-16.7
EXCH(%) ***	2.0	4.1	6.2	8.3	5.1	13.8	23.3	27.0	27.0	27.0
CAB(B.US$) **	1.0	1.3	-0.7	-3.0	-0.3	-10.3	-22.9	-38.9	-50.3	-55.9

* Exchange rate : (Weighted average of foreign currencies)/U.S. $.
** Local currency units translated into U.S. $ at baseline exchange rates.
*** Exchange rate : U.S. $/(weighted average of non-US OECD currencies).

Model: MINIMODR
Simulation F: Nonpolicy Exogenous Depreciation of the Dollar
(Deviation of Shock Path from Baseline Path)

	1985									
	Q1	Q2	Q3	Q4	1985	1986	1987	1988	1989	1990
JAPAN										
GNP(%)	-	-	-	-	-	-	-	-	-	-
CPI(%)	-	-	-	-	-	-	-	-	-	-
RS(% PTS)	-	-	-	-	-	-	-	-	-	-
GDEF(%GNPV) *	-	-	-	-	-	-	-	-	-	-
EXCH(%) **	-	-	-	-	-	-	-	-	-	-
CAB(B.US$) ***	-	-	-	-	-	-	-	-	-	-
GERMANY										
GNP(%)	-	-	-	-	-	-	-	-	-	-
CPI(%)	-	-	-	-	-	-	-	-	-	-
RS(% PTS)	-	-	-	-	-	-	-	-	-	-
GDEF(%GNPV) *	-	-	-	-	-	-	-	-	-	-
EXCH(%) **	-	-	-	-	-	-	-	-	-	-
CAB(B.US$) ***	-	-	-	-	-	-	-	-	-	-
FRANCE										
GNP(%)	-	-	-	-	-	-	-	-	-	-
CPI(%)	-	-	-	-	-	-	-	-	-	-
GDEF(%GNPV) *	-	-	-	-	-	-	-	-	-	-
EXCH(%) **	-	-	-	-	-	-	-	-	-	-
CAB(B.US$) ***	-	-	-	-	-	-	-	-	-	-
UNITED KINGDOM										
GNP(%)	-	-	-	-	-	-	-	-	-	-
CPI(%)	-	-	-	-	-	-	-	-	-	-
GDEF(%GNPV) *	-	-	-	-	-	-	-	-	-	-
EXCH(%) **	-	-	-	-	-	-	-	-	-	-
CAB(B.US$) ***	-	-	-	-	-	-	-	-	-	-
ITALY										
GNP(%)	-	-	-	-	-	-	-	-	-	-
CPI(%)	-	-	-	-	-	-	-	-	-	-
GDEF(%GNPV) *	-	-	-	-	-	-	-	-	-	-
EXCH(%) **	-	-	-	-	-	-	-	-	-	-
CAB(B.US$) ***	-	-	-	-	-	-	-	-	-	-
CANADA										
GNP(%)	-	-	-	-	-	-	-	-	-	-
CPI(%)	-	-	-	-	-	-	-	-	-	-
GDEF(%GNPV) *	-	-	-	-	-	-	-	-	-	-
EXCH(%) **	-	-	-	-	-	-	-	-	-	-
CAB(B.US$) ***	-	-	-	-	-	-	-	-	-	-
REST OF WORLD										
CAB(B.US$) ***	0.7	0.9	-0.5	-2.1	-0.2	-7.2	-15.9	-27.0	-35.0	-38.9

* Government deficit as a percentage of baseline nominal GNP.
** Exchange rate : Bilateral rate against U.S. $ ($/local currency).
*** Local currency units translated into U.S. $ at baseline exchange rates.

Model: MINIMODR
Simulation G: Increase in Government Purchases in Non-U.S. OECD Countries with U.S. Policies Unchanged from Baseline
(Deviation of Shock Path from Baseline Path)

	1985 Q1	1985 Q2	1985 Q3	1985 Q4	1985	1986	1987	1988	1989	1990
UNITED STATES										
GNPV(%)	0.1	0.1	0.1	0.1	0.1	0.2	0.4	0.5	0.7	0.9
GNP(%)	0.1	0.1	0.1	0.1	0.1	0.1	0.1	0.2	0.2	0.2
PGNP(%)	0.0	0.0	0.0	0.0	0.0	0.1	0.2	0.4	0.5	0.7
CPI(%)	0.0	0.1	0.1	0.1	0.1	0.2	0.3	0.5	0.7	0.9
WAGES(%)	-	-	-	-	-	-	-	-	-	-
UN(% PTS)	-	-	-	-	-	-	-	-	-	-
GNP(B.72$)	0.9	1.1	1.4	1.6	1.2	2.1	2.6	2.8	3.0	3.0
G(B.72$)	0.0	0.0	0.0	0.0	0.0	0.0	0.0	0.0	0.0	0.0
C(B.72$)	-0.0	0.1	0.0	0.0	0.0	-0.0	-0.2	-0.5	-0.8	-1.2
IFP(B.72$)	-0.1	-0.2	-0.2	-0.2	-0.2	-0.3	-0.5	-0.7	-1.0	-1.3
II(B.72$)	-	-	-	-	-	-	-	-	-	-
XGS(B.72$)	0.9	1.1	1.3	1.5	1.2	1.8	2.4	2.9	3.4	3.9
MGS(B.72$)	-0.1	-0.1	-0.3	-0.4	-0.2	-0.6	-1.0	-1.4	-1.9	-2.5
M1(%)	0.0	0.0	0.0	0.0	0.0	0.0	0.0	0.0	0.0	0.0
RS(% PTS)	0.1	0.1	0.2	0.2	0.1	0.3	0.4	0.6	0.7	0.9
RL(% PTS)	0.0	0.0	0.0	0.0	0.0	0.0	0.0	0.1	0.1	0.1
GDEF(B$)	-0.1	-0.1	-0.7	-0.8	-0.4	-1.3	-1.9	-2.3	-2.7	-3.0
PXGS(%)	0.0	0.0	0.0	0.0	0.0	0.1	0.2	0.4	0.5	0.7
PMGS(%)	0.5	0.6	0.7	0.8	0.7	1.0	1.4	1.9	2.3	2.7
EXCH(%) *	-0.4	-0.5	-0.5	-0.6	-0.5	-0.6	-0.7	-0.8	-0.8	-0.8
CAB(B$)	1.2	1.4	1.9	2.3	1.7	3.2	4.2	5.0	5.6	6.0
NON-US OECD										
GNPV(%) **	1.2	1.4	1.5	1.7	1.4	2.0	2.4	2.7	3.1	3.4
GNP(%) **	1.1	1.3	1.4	1.5	1.3	1.6	1.7	1.6	1.5	1.4
PGNP(%)	0.1	0.1	0.1	0.2	0.1	0.4	0.7	1.1	1.5	1.9
CPI(%)	-0.0	0.0	0.0	0.1	0.0	0.2	0.5	0.9	1.2	1.7
WAGES(%)	-	-	-	-	-	-	-	-	-	-
UN(% PTS)	-	-	-	-	-	-	-	-	-	-
C(%) **	0.3	0.5	0.6	0.8	0.5	0.9	1.0	1.1	1.1	1.1
IFP(%) **	0.0	0.2	0.3	0.4	0.2	0.6	0.7	0.6	0.4	0.1
RS(% PTS)	0.4	0.6	0.7	0.7	0.6	0.9	1.1	1.3	1.4	1.6
RL(% PTS)	0.0	0.1	0.1	0.1	0.1	0.1	0.1	0.1	0.1	0.1
GDEF (B.US$) **	18.1	18.1	17.6	17.2	17.7	16.9	17.3	18.5	20.0	21.7
PXGS(%)	0.1	0.1	0.1	0.2	0.1	0.4	0.7	1.1	1.5	1.9
PMGS(%)	-0.4	-0.5	-0.5	-0.5	-0.5	-0.5	-0.5	-0.4	-0.2	-0.0
EXCH(%) ***	0.4	0.5	0.6	0.6	0.5	0.6	0.7	0.8	0.8	0.8
CAB(B.US$) **	-0.9	-1.1	-1.4	-1.7	-1.3	-2.2	-2.9	-3.4	-3.8	-4.1

* Exchange rate : (Weighted average of foreign currencies)/U.S. $.
** Local currency units translated into U.S. $ at baseline exchange rates.
*** Exchange rate : U.S. $/(weighted average of non-US OECD currencies).

Model: MINIMODR
Simulation G: Increase in Government Purchases in Non-U.S. OECD Countries with U.S. Policies Unchanged from Baseline
(Deviation of Shock Path from Baseline Path)

	1985									
	Q1	Q2	Q3	Q4	1985	1986	1987	1988	1989	1990
JAPAN										
GNP(%)	-	-	-	-	-	-	-	-	-	-
CPI(%)	-	-	-	-	-	-	-	-	-	-
RS(% PTS)	-	-	-	-	-	-	-	-	-	-
GDEF(%GNPV) *	-	-	-	-	-	-	-	-	-	-
EXCH(%) **	-	-	-	-	-	-	-	-	-	-
CAB(B.US$) ***	-	-	-	-	-	-	-	-	-	-
GERMANY										
GNP(%)	-	-	-	-	-	-	-	-	-	-
CPI(%)	-	-	-	-	-	-	-	-	-	-
RS(% PTS)	-	-	-	-	-	-	-	-	-	-
GDEF(%GNPV) *	-	-	-	-	-	-	-	-	-	-
EXCH(%) **	-	-	-	-	-	-	-	-	-	-
CAB(B.US$) ***	-	-	-	-	-	-	-	-	-	-
FRANCE										
GNP(%)	-	-	-	-	-	-	-	-	-	-
CPI(%)	-	-	-	-	-	-	-	-	-	-
GDEF(%GNPV) *	-	-	-	-	-	-	-	-	-	-
EXCH(%) **	-	-	-	-	-	-	-	-	-	-
CAB(B.US$) ***	-	-	-	-	-	-	-	-	-	-
UNITED KINGDOM										
GNP(%)	-	-	-	-	-	-	-	-	-	-
CPI(%)	-	-	-	-	-	-	-	-	-	-
GDEF(%GNPV) *	-	-	-	-	-	-	-	-	-	-
EXCH(%) **	-	-	-	-	-	-	-	-	-	-
CAB(B.US$) ***	-	-	-	-	-	-	-	-	-	-
ITALY										
GNP(%)	-	-	-	-	-	-	-	-	-	-
CPI(%)	-	-	-	-	-	-	-	-	-	-
GDEF(%GNPV) *	-	-	-	-	-	-	-	-	-	-
EXCH(%) **	-	-	-	-	-	-	-	-	-	-
CAB(B.US$) ***	-	-	-	-	-	-	-	-	-	-
CANADA										
GNP(%)	-	-	-	-	-	-	-	-	-	-
CPI(%)	-	-	-	-	-	-	-	-	-	-
GDEF(%GNPV) *	-	-	-	-	-	-	-	-	-	-
EXCH(%) **	-	-	-	-	-	-	-	-	-	-
CAB(B.US$) ***	-	-	-	-	-	-	-	-	-	-
REST OF WORLD										
CAB(B.US$) ***	-0.6	-0.8	-1.0	-1.2	-0.9	-1.5	-2.0	-2.4	-2.6	-2.8

* Government deficit as a percentage of baseline nominal GNP.
** Exchange rate : Bilateral rate against U.S. $ ($/local currency).
*** Local currency units translated into U.S. $ at baseline exchange rates.

Model: MINIMODR
Simulation H: Monetary Expansion in Non-U.S. OECD Countries
with U.S. Policies Unchanged from Baseline
(Deviation of Shock Path from Baseline Path)

	1985 Q1	Q2	Q3	Q4	1985	1986	1987	1988	1989	1990
UNITED STATES										
GNPV(%)	0.1	0.0	-0.1	-0.2	-0.0	-0.4	-0.6	-0.7	-0.9	-1.0
GNP(%)	0.1	0.0	-0.0	-0.1	-0.0	-0.3	-0.3	-0.3	-0.3	-0.2
PGNP(%)	-0.0	-0.0	-0.0	-0.1	-0.0	-0.1	-0.3	-0.4	-0.6	-0.8
CPI(%)	-0.3	-0.4	-0.4	-0.4	-0.4	-0.5	-0.6	-0.7	-0.9	-1.1
WAGES(%)	-	-	-	-	-	-	-	-	-	-
UN(% PTS)	-	-	-	-	-	-	-	-	-	-
GNP(B.72$)	1.7	0.7	-0.7	-2.3	-0.2	-4.7	-5.6	-5.5	-4.8	-3.8
G(B.72$)	0.0	0.0	0.0	0.0	0.0	0.0	0.0	0.0	0.0	0.0
C(B.72$)	1.7	1.8	2.3	2.2	2.0	1.7	1.2	1.2	1.4	1.6
IFP(B.72$)	0.9	0.8	0.8	0.7	0.8	0.4	0.4	0.7	0.9	1.3
II(B.72$)	-	-	-	-	-	-	-	-	-	-
XGS(B.72$)	-0.1	-0.7	-1.4	-1.9	-1.0	-2.8	-3.6	-4.1	-4.2	-4.3
MGS(B.72$)	0.8	1.4	2.6	3.6	2.1	4.5	4.5	4.3	4.3	4.2
M1(%)	0.0	0.0	0.0	0.0	0.0	0.0	0.0	0.0	0.0	0.0
RS(% PTS)	-0.8	-0.1	-0.5	-0.5	-0.5	-0.6	-0.8	-0.9	-1.0	-1.1
RL(% PTS)	-0.0	-0.0	-0.0	-0.1	-0.0	-0.1	-0.1	-0.1	-0.1	-0.1
GDEF(B$)	-5.0	-9.4	-3.7	-4.3	-5.6	-0.2	1.7	2.4	2.6	2.6
PXGS(%)	-0.0	-0.0	-0.0	-0.1	-0.0	-0.1	-0.3	-0.4	-0.6	-0.8
PMGS(%)	-5.0	-5.5	-5.4	-5.3	-5.3	-4.7	-4.4	-4.2	-4.0	-3.8
EXCH(%) *	5.3	5.8	5.8	5.6	5.6	5.0	4.8	4.6	4.5	4.4
CAB(B$)	9.4	8.8	5.5	2.9	6.6	-1.4	-3.3	-4.0	-4.2	-3.8
NON-US OECD										
GNPV(%) **	0.0	0.2	0.4	0.5	0.3	0.8	1.2	1.4	1.5	1.6
GNP(%) **	0.0	0.2	0.3	0.5	0.2	0.8	1.1	1.2	1.2	1.1
PGNP(%)	0.0	0.0	0.0	0.0	0.0	0.1	0.1	0.2	0.3	0.5
CPI(%)	0.2	0.2	0.2	0.2	0.2	0.2	0.2	0.3	0.4	0.5
WAGES(%)	-	-	-	-	-	-	-	-	-	-
UN(% PTS)	-	-	-	-	-	-	-	-	-	-
C(%) **	-0.1	-0.1	-0.2	-0.2	-0.2	-0.1	0.1	0.2	0.2	0.2
IFP(%) **	0.1	0.6	1.1	1.4	0.8	2.2	2.8	3.1	3.2	3.2
RS(% PTS)	-0.5	-1.9	-2.4	-2.9	-1.9	-1.8	-1.5	-1.4	-1.4	-1.3
RL(% PTS)	-0.1	-0.2	-0.2	-0.2	-0.2	-0.1	-0.1	-0.1	-0.1	-0.1
GDEF (B.US$) **	3.9	-2.3	-12.6	-16.7	-6.9	-19.9	-22.7	-26.0	-28.7	-31.0
PXGS(%)	0.0	0.0	0.0	0.0	0.0	0.1	0.1	0.2	0.3	0.5
PMGS(%)	5.2	5.8	5.7	5.5	5.6	4.8	4.5	4.2	3.9	3.6
EXCH(%) ***	-5.0	-5.5	-5.5	-5.3	-5.3	-4.8	-4.5	-4.4	-4.3	-4.2
CAB(B.US$) **	-3.2	-2.6	-0.5	1.2	-1.3	3.6	4.8	5.4	5.7	5.6

* Exchange rate : (Weighted average of foreign currencies)/U.S. $.
** Local currency units translated into U.S. $ at baseline exchange rates.
*** Exchange rate : U.S. $/(weighted average of non-US OECD currencies).

Model: MINIMODR
Simulation H: Monetary Expansion in Non-U.S. OECD Countries with U.S. Policies Unchanged from Baseline
(Deviation of Shock Path from Baseline Path)

	1985									
	Q1	Q2	Q3	Q4	1985	1986	1987	1988	1989	1990
JAPAN										
GNP(%)	-	-	-	-	-	-	-	-	-	-
CPI(%)	-	-	-	-	-	-	-	-	-	-
RS(% PTS)	-	-	-	-	-	-	-	-	-	-
GDEF(%GNPV) *	-	-	-	-	-	-	-	-	-	-
EXCH(%) **	-	-	-	-	-	-	-	-	-	-
CAB(B.US$) ***	-	-	-	-	-	-	-	-	-	-
GERMANY										
GNP(%)	-	-	-	-	-	-	-	-	-	-
CPI(%)	-	-	-	-	-	-	-	-	-	-
RS(% PTS)	-	-	-	-	-	-	-	-	-	-
GDEF(%GNPV) *	-	-	-	-	-	-	-	-	-	-
EXCH(%) **	-	-	-	-	-	-	-	-	-	-
CAB(B.US$) ***	-	-	-	-	-	-	-	-	-	-
FRANCE										
GNP(%)	-	-	-	-	-	-	-	-	-	-
CPI(%)	-	-	-	-	-	-	-	-	-	-
GDEF(%GNPV) *	-	-	-	-	-	-	-	-	-	-
EXCH(%) **	-	-	-	-	-	-	-	-	-	-
CAB(B.US$) ***	-	-	-	-	-	-	-	-	-	-
UNITED KINGDOM										
GNP(%)	-	-	-	-	-	-	-	-	-	-
CPI(%)	-	-	-	-	-	-	-	-	-	-
GDEF(%GNPV) *	-	-	-	-	-	-	-	-	-	-
EXCH(%) **	-	-	-	-	-	-	-	-	-	-
CAB(B.US$) ***	-	-	-	-	-	-	-	-	-	-
ITALY										
GNP(%)	-	-	-	-	-	-	-	-	-	-
CPI(%)	-	-	-	-	-	-	-	-	-	-
GDEF(%GNPV) *	-	-	-	-	-	-	-	-	-	-
EXCH(%) **	-	-	-	-	-	-	-	-	-	-
CAB(B.US$) ***	-	-	-	-	-	-	-	-	-	-
CANADA										
GNP(%)	-	-	-	-	-	-	-	-	-	-
CPI(%)	-	-	-	-	-	-	-	-	-	-
GDEF(%GNPV) *	-	-	-	-	-	-	-	-	-	-
EXCH(%) **	-	-	-	-	-	-	-	-	-	-
CAB(B.US$) ***	-	-	-	-	-	-	-	-	-	-
REST OF WORLD										
CAB(B.US$) ***	-2.2	-1.8	-0.3	0.8	-0.9	2.5	3.4	3.8	3.9	3.9

* Government deficit as a percentage of baseline nominal GNP.
** Exchange rate : Bilateral rate against U.S. $ ($/local currency).
*** Local currency units translated into U.S. $ at baseline exchange rates.

MSG—McKibbin/Sachs Global Simulation Model (McKibb)

See part 1 of this volume for design and detailed description of the simulations. See part 4 for bibliographical references.

The figures for consumption in the tables represent an aggregate of both consumption and investment expenditures.

Model: MCKIBB
Simulation A: Baseline Path

	1985	1986	1987	1988	1989	1990
UNITED STATES						
GNPV(B.$)	3899.2	4129.3	4375.5	4630.1	4900.2	5190.9
GNP(B.72$)	1689.4	1741.9	1796.0	1848.0	1901.4	1956.4
PGNP(72=100)	230.8	237.1	243.6	250.5	257.7	265.3
CPI(72=100)	256.8	263.9	271.3	279.1	287.2	295.8
WAGES(72=100)	237.6	244.0	250.8	257.9	265.3	273.1
UN(%)	7.4	7.3	7.3	7.3	7.4	7.4
G(B.72$)	318.3	337.5	360.3	378.8	396.0	411.8
C(B.72$)	1394.8	1430.9	1466.5	1501.9	1538.2	1575.5
IFP(B.72$)	-	-	-	-	-	-
II(B.72$)	-	-	-	-	-	-
XGS(B.72$)	148.5	150.4	150.9	153.3	157.6	163.8
MGS(B.72$)	165.0	169.5	174.3	178.7	183.1	187.4
M1(B.$)	566.7	580.3	594.7	610.2	626.1	643.0
RS(%)	7.2	6.7	7.1	7.2	7.4	7.6
RL(%)	11.6	11.8	12.0	12.1	12.3	12.5
GDEF(B.$)	131.3	138.7	156.9	168.9	177.3	182.3
PXGS(72=100)	-	-	-	-	-	-
PMGS(72=100)	279.2	288.1	297.4	307.3	317.5	328.4
EXCH(72=100) *	120.8	120.3	119.4	117.6	115.0	111.4
CAB(B.$)	-113.3	-122.8	-142.9	-158.5	-170.2	-178.6
NON-US OECD						
GNPV(B.$) **	5346.5	5717.0	5995.9	6284.1	6560.0	6819.6
GNP(B.72$) **	1925.1	1996.3	2035.6	2092.0	2160.6	2241.9
PGNP(72=100)	-	-	-	-	-	-
CPI(72=100)	263.8	271.1	277.9	282.9	285.7	286.5
WAGES(72=100)	262.8	270.2	277.1	282.1	285.0	285.8
UN(%)	8.5	8.5	9.0	9.3	9.4	9.4
C(B.72$) **	1254.3	1302.7	1332.3	1370.2	1413.4	1462.5
IFP(B.72$) **	-	-	-	-	-	-
RS(%)	6.7	6.0	5.7	5.1	4.6	4.3
RL(%)	-	-	-	-	-	-
GDEF(B.US$) **	215.8	223.9	232.9	237.9	241.2	242.8
PXGS(72=100)	-	-	-	-	-	-
PMGS(72=100)	346.4	355.2	363.5	369.2	372.1	372.4
EXCH(72=100) ***	82.8	83.1	83.7	85.0	87.0	89.7
CAB(B.US$)	51.3	30.3	23.1	18.1	20.3	31.2

* Exchange rate : (Weighted average of foreign currencies)/U.S. $.
** Local currency units translated into U.S. $ at baseline exchange rates.
*** Exchange rate : U.S. $/(weighted average of non-US OECD currencies).

Model: MCKIBB
Simulation A: Baseline Path

	1985	1986	1987	1988	1989	1990
JAPAN						
GNP(B.72Y)	158204.1	163647.7	167423.7	172193.0	177759.5	184175.3
CPI(72=100)	243.8	248.0	251.8	254.8	257.0	258.7
RS(%)	5.6	4.8	4.7	4.5	4.4	4.5
GDEF(%GNPV) *	2.3	2.3	2.3	2.3	2.3	2.3
EXCH(72=100) **	131.2	133.2	135.4	138.3	141.7	145.6
CAB(B.US$) ***	34.6	30.6	29.1	29.1	31.7	37.4
GERMANY						
GNP(B.72DM)	-	-	-	-	-	-
CPI(72=100)	-	-	-	-	-	-
RS(%)	-	-	-	-	-	-
GDEF(%GNPV) *	-	-	-	-	-	-
EXCH(72=100) **	-	-	-	-	-	-
CAB(B.US$) ***	-	-	-	-	-	-
FRANCE						
GNP(B.72F)	-	-	-	-	-	-
CPI(72=100)	-	-	-	-	-	-
GDEF(%GNPV) *	-	-	-	-	-	-
EXCH(72=100) **	-	-	-	-	-	-
CAB(B.US$) ***	-	-	-	-	-	-
UNITED KINGDOM						
GNP(B.72LB)	-	-	-	-	-	-
CPI(72=100)	-	-	-	-	-	-
GDEF(%GNPV) *	-	-	-	-	-	-
EXCH(72=100) **	-	-	-	-	-	-
CAB(B.US$) ***	-	-	-	-	-	-
ITALY						
GNP(B.72L)	-	-	-	-	-	-
CPI(72=100)	-	-	-	-	-	-
GDEF(%GNPV) *	-	-	-	-	-	-
EXCH(72=100) **	-	-	-	-	-	-
CAB(B.US$) ***	-	-	-	-	-	-
CANADA						
GNP(B.72C$)	-	-	-	-	-	-
CPI(72=100)	-	-	-	-	-	-
GDEF(%GNPV) *	-	-	-	-	-	-
EXCH(72=100) **	-	-	-	-	-	-
CAB(B.US$) ***	-	-	-	-	-	-
REST OF WORLD						
CAB(B.US$) ***	-43.5	-19.1	1.8	15.3	17.4	6.9

* Government deficit as a percentage of baseline nominal GNP.
** Exchange rate: Bilateral rate against U.S. $ ($/local currency).
*** Local currency units translated into U.S. $ at baseline exchange rates.

Model: MCKIBB
Simulation B: Reduction in U.S. Government Purchases with Foreign Monetary Aggregates Unchanged from Baseline
(Deviation of Shock Path from Baseline Path)

	1985 Q1	Q2	Q3	Q4	1985	1986	1987	1988	1989	1990
UNITED STATES										
GNPV(%)	-	-	-	-	-0.8	-0.9	-1.1	-1.4	-1.9	-2.4
GNP(%)	-	-	-	-	-0.8	-0.9	-0.8	-0.7	-0.6	-0.6
PGNP(%)	-	-	-	-	0.0	-0.1	-0.3	-0.7	-1.2	-1.8
CPI(%)	-	-	-	-	0.2	0.1	-0.1	-0.5	-1.0	-1.6
WAGES(%)	-	-	-	-	0.0	-0.1	-0.4	-0.7	-1.2	-1.8
UN(% PTS)	-	-	-	-	0.3	0.3	0.3	0.3	0.2	0.2
GNP(B.72$)	-	-	-	-	-13.7	-14.9	-14.0	-13.0	-11.8	-10.8
G(B.72$)	-	-	-	-	-17.7	-18.3	-18.8	-19.3	-20.0	-20.5
C(B.72$)	-	-	-	-	-3.1	-3.8	-3.1	-2.2	-1.0	0.2
IFP(B.72$)	-	-	-	-	-	-	-	-	-	-
II(B.72$)	-	-	-	-	-	-	-	-	-	-
XGS(B.72$)	-	-	-	-	4.1	4.0	4.7	5.3	5.9	6.2
MGS(B.72$)	-	-	-	-	-3.1	-3.0	-3.1	-3.2	-3.3	-3.3
M1(%)	-	-	-	-	0.0	0.0	0.0	0.0	0.0	0.0
RS(% PTS)	-	-	-	-	-0.7	-0.9	-1.4	-1.9	-2.5	-3.2
RL(% PTS)	-	-	-	-	-2.6	-2.8	-2.9	-2.9	-2.9	-3.0
GDEF(B$)	-	-	-	-	-29.5	-33.5	-41.3	-50.6	-62.4	-76.6
PXGS(%)	-	-	-	-	-	-	-	-	-	-
PMGS(%)	-	-	-	-	3.1	2.6	2.5	2.3	1.9	1.4
EXCH(%) *	-	-	-	-	-3.3	-3.2	-3.4	-3.6	-3.7	-3.5
CAB(B$)	-	-	-	-	19.4	21.6	28.4	36.8	47.1	59.3
NON-US OECD										
GNPV(%) **	-	-	-	-	-0.6	-0.7	-0.9	-1.2	-1.6	-1.9
GNP(%) **	-	-	-	-	-0.6	-0.3	-0.2	-0.1	-0.1	-0.0
PGNP(%)	-	-	-	-	-	-	-	-	-	-
CPI(%)	-	-	-	-	-0.2	-0.5	-0.8	-1.2	-1.6	-2.0
WAGES(%)	-	-	-	-	0.0	-0.4	-0.7	-1.1	-1.4	-1.8
UN(% PTS)	-	-	-	-	0.2	0.1	0.1	0.0	0.0	0.0
C(%) **	-	-	-	-	-0.4	0.1	0.2	0.4	0.5	0.6
IFP(%) **	-	-	-	-	-	-	-	-	-	-
RS(% PTS)	-	-	-	-	-0.5	-1.0	-1.4	-1.7	-2.1	-2.6
RL(% PTS)	-	-	-	-	-	-	-	-	-	-
GDEF (B.US$) **	-	-	-	-	28.8	23.7	7.1	-7.5	-23.1	-39.7
PXGS(%)	-	-	-	-	-	-	-	-	-	-
PMGS(%)	-	-	-	-	-1.6	-1.7	-2.1	-2.6	-3.0	-3.5
EXCH(%) ***	-	-	-	-	3.4	3.4	3.6	3.8	3.8	3.8
CAB(B.US$) **	-	-	-	-	-21.0	-22.7	-29.2	-36.9	-47.0	-59.5

* Exchange rate : (Weighted average of foreign currencies)/U.S. $.
** Local currency units translated into U.S. $ at baseline exchange rates.
*** Exchange rate : U.S. $/(weighted average of non-US OECD currencies).

Model: MCKIBB
Simulation B: Reduction in U.S. Government Purchases with Foreign Monetary Aggregates Unchanged from Baseline
(Deviation of Shock Path from Baseline Path)

	1985									
	Q1	Q2	Q3	Q4	1985	1986	1987	1988	1989	1990
JAPAN										
GNP(%)	-	-	-	-	-0.5	-0.3	-0.2	-0.1	-0.1	-0.1
CPI(%)	-	-	-	-	-0.1	-0.4	-0.7	-1.0	-1.3	-1.6
RS(% PTS)	-	-	-	-	-0.5	-0.9	-1.2	-1.5	-1.8	-2.2
GDEF(%GNPV) *	-	-	-	-	0.4	0.4	0.2	0.0	-0.1	-0.3
EXCH(%) **	-	-	-	-	3.2	2.9	3.1	3.2	3.1	2.9
CAB(B.US$) ***	-	-	-	-	-4.8	-5.0	-6.8	-9.1	-12.3	-16.5
GERMANY										
GNP(%)	-	-	-	-	-	-	-	-	-	-
CPI(%)	-	-	-	-	-	-	-	-	-	-
RS(% PTS)	-	-	-	-	-	-	-	-	-	-
GDEF(%GNPV) *	-	-	-	-	-	-	-	-	-	-
EXCH(%) **	-	-	-	-	-	-	-	-	-	-
CAB(B.US$) ***	-	-	-	-	-	-	-	-	-	-
FRANCE										
GNP(%)	-	-	-	-	-	-	-	-	-	-
CPI(%)	-	-	-	-	-	-	-	-	-	-
GDEF(%GNPV) *	-	-	-	-	-	-	-	-	-	-
EXCH(%) **	-	-	-	-	-	-	-	-	-	-
CAB(B.US$) ***	-	-	-	-	-	-	-	-	-	-
UNITED KINGDOM										
GNP(%)	-	-	-	-	-	-	-	-	-	-
CPI(%)	-	-	-	-	-	-	-	-	-	-
GDEF(%GNPV) *	-	-	-	-	-	-	-	-	-	-
EXCH(%) **	-	-	-	-	-	-	-	-	-	-
CAB(B.US$) ***	-	-	-	-	-	-	-	-	-	-
ITALY										
GNP(%)	-	-	-	-	-	-	-	-	-	-
CPI(%)	-	-	-	-	-	-	-	-	-	-
GDEF(%GNPV) *	-	-	-	-	-	-	-	-	-	-
EXCH(%) **	-	-	-	-	-	-	-	-	-	-
CAB(B.US$) ***	-	-	-	-	-	-	-	-	-	-
CANADA										
GNP(%)	-	-	-	-	-	-	-	-	-	-
CPI(%)	-	-	-	-	-	-	-	-	-	-
GDEF(%GNPV) *	-	-	-	-	-	-	-	-	-	-
EXCH(%) **	-	-	-	-	-	-	-	-	-	-
CAB(B.US$) ***	-	-	-	-	-	-	-	-	-	-
REST OF WORLD										
CAB(B.US$) ***	-	-	-	-	1.7	1.3	1.1	1.1	1.5	2.7

* Government deficit as a percentage of baseline nominal GNP.
** Exchange rate : Bilateral rate against U.S. $ ($/local currency).
*** Local currency units translated into U.S. $ at baseline exchange rates.

Model: MCKIBB
Simulation C: Reduction in U.S. Government Purchases with Foreign Short-Term Interest Rates Unchanged from Baseline
(Deviation of Shock Path from Baseline Path)

	1985									
	Q1	Q2	Q3	Q4	1985	1986	1987	1988	1989	1990
UNITED STATES										
GNPV(%)	-	-	-	-	-0.1	0.1	0.3	0.2	-0.1	-0.7
GNP(%)	-	-	-	-	-0.1	-0.5	-0.6	-0.8	-1.0	-1.1
PGNP(%)	-	-	-	-	0.0	0.6	0.9	1.0	0.9	0.4
CPI(%)	-	-	-	-	0.6	1.1	1.4	1.4	1.1	0.6
WAGES(%)	-	-	-	-	0.0	0.6	0.9	1.0	0.9	0.4
UN(% PTS)	-	-	-	-	0.0	0.2	0.2	0.3	0.3	0.4
GNP(B.72$)	-	-	-	-	-1.1	-8.2	-11.4	-15.3	-18.8	-22.1
G(B.72$)	-	-	-	-	-17.7	-18.3	-18.8	-19.3	-20.0	-20.5
C(B.72$)	-	-	-	-	1.0	-4.3	-6.1	-7.8	-8.6	-8.7
IFP(B.72$)	-	-	-	-	-	-	-	-	-	-
II(B.72$)	-	-	-	-	-	-	-	-	-	-
XGS(B.72$)	-	-	-	-	10.9	9.5	8.6	7.2	5.4	3.2
MGS(B.72$)	-	-	-	-	-4.8	-4.8	-4.7	-4.6	-4.4	-4.0
M1(%)	-	-	-	-	0.0	0.0	0.0	0.0	0.0	0.0
RS(% PTS)	-	-	-	-	-0.1	0.9	0.8	0.5	-0.1	-1.1
RL(% PTS)	-	-	-	-	-2.4	-2.6	-2.8	-3.0	-3.3	-3.5
GDEF(B$)	-	-	-	-	-39.6	-35.7	-37.5	-38.6	-40.7	-43.5
PXGS(%)	-	-	-	-	-	-	-	-	-	-
PMGS(%)	-	-	-	-	8.4	7.6	7.2	6.3	5.1	3.6
EXCH(%) *	-	-	-	-	-8.6	-8.6	-9.0	-9.4	-9.7	-9.8
CAB(B$)	-	-	-	-	39.2	31.9	32.7	32.7	33.9	37.2
NON-US OECD										
GNPV(%) **	-	-	-	-	-2.0	-2.8	-3.7	-4.6	-5.6	-6.6
GNP(%) **	-	-	-	-	-2.0	-1.6	-1.4	-1.2	-1.1	-1.2
PGNP(%)	-	-	-	-	-	-	-	-	-	-
CPI(%)	-	-	-	-	-0.4	-1.4	-2.5	-3.9	-5.3	-6.8
WAGES(%)	-	-	-	-	0.0	-1.1	-2.3	-3.7	-5.1	-6.6
UN(% PTS)	-	-	-	-	0.7	0.5	0.4	0.2	0.1	0.1
C(%) **	-	-	-	-	-1.9	-1.7	-1.6	-1.5	-1.5	-1.6
IFP(%) **	-	-	-	-	-	-	-	-	-	-
RS(% PTS)	-	-	-	-	0.0	0.0	0.0	0.0	0.0	0.0
RL(% PTS)	-	-	-	-	-	-	-	-	-	-
GDEF (B.US$) **	-	-	-	-	66.9	61.2	42.2	27.8	17.9	13.7
PXGS(%)	-	-	-	-	-	-	-	-	-	-
PMGS(%)	-	-	-	-	-4.1	-4.2	-4.7	-5.4	-6.3	-7.5
EXCH(%) ***	-	-	-	-	9.3	9.5	10.0	10.4	10.7	10.9
CAB(B.US$) **	-	-	-	-	-41.4	-28.3	-26.1	-25.5	-30.0	-39.7

* Exchange rate : (Weighted average of foreign currencies)/U.S. $.
** Local currency units translated into U.S. $ at baseline exchange rates.
*** Exchange rate : U.S. $/(weighted average of non-US OECD currencies).

Model: MCKIBB
Simulation C: Reduction in U.S. Government Purchases with Foreign Short-Term Interest Rates Unchanged from Baseline
(Deviation of Shock Path from Baseline Path)

	1985 Q1	1985 Q2	1985 Q3	1985 Q4	1985	1986	1987	1988	1989	1990
JAPAN										
GNP(%)	-	-	-	-	-1.5	-1.7	-2.3	-2.8	-3.1	-2.9
CPI(%)	-	-	-	-	-0.2	-1.2	-2.7	-4.9	-7.7	-10.9
RS(% PTS)	-	-	-	-	0.0	0.0	0.0	0.0	0.0	0.0
GDEF(%GNPV) *	-	-	-	-	0.7	0.8	0.8	0.8	0.7	0.5
EXCH(%) **	-	-	-	-	8.2	10.0	13.5	17.1	19.9	21.3
CAB(B.US$) ***	-	-	-	-	-8.8	-8.5	-13.6	-19.3	-24.3	-26.9
GERMANY										
GNP(%)	-	-	-	-	-	-	-	-	-	-
CPI(%)	-	-	-	-	-	-	-	-	-	-
RS(% PTS)	-	-	-	-	-	-	-	-	-	-
GDEF(%GNPV) *	-	-	-	-	-	-	-	-	-	-
EXCH(%) **	-	-	-	-	-	-	-	-	-	-
CAB(B.US$) ***	-	-	-	-	-	-	-	-	-	-
FRANCE										
GNP(%)	-	-	-	-	-	-	-	-	-	-
CPI(%)	-	-	-	-	-	-	-	-	-	-
GDEF(%GNPV) *	-	-	-	-	-	-	-	-	-	-
EXCH(%) **	-	-	-	-	-	-	-	-	-	-
CAB(B.US$) ***	-	-	-	-	-	-	-	-	-	-
UNITED KINGDOM										
GNP(%)	-	-	-	-	-	-	-	-	-	-
CPI(%)	-	-	-	-	-	-	-	-	-	-
GDEF(%GNPV) *	-	-	-	-	-	-	-	-	-	-
EXCH(%) **	-	-	-	-	-	-	-	-	-	-
CAB(B.US$) ***	-	-	-	-	-	-	-	-	-	-
ITALY										
GNP(%)	-	-	-	-	-	-	-	-	-	-
CPI(%)	-	-	-	-	-	-	-	-	-	-
GDEF(%GNPV) *	-	-	-	-	-	-	-	-	-	-
EXCH(%) **	-	-	-	-	-	-	-	-	-	-
CAB(B.US$) ***	-	-	-	-	-	-	-	-	-	-
CANADA										
GNP(%)	-	-	-	-	-	-	-	-	-	-
CPI(%)	-	-	-	-	-	-	-	-	-	-
GDEF(%GNPV) *	-	-	-	-	-	-	-	-	-	-
EXCH(%) **	-	-	-	-	-	-	-	-	-	-
CAB(B.US$) ***	-	-	-	-	-	-	-	-	-	-
REST OF WORLD										
CAB(B.US$) ***	-	-	-	-	2.2	-4.2	-7.8	-8.5	-5.1	1.9

* Government deficit as a percentage of baseline nominal GNP.
** Exchange rate : Bilateral rate against U.S. $ ($/local currency).
*** Local currency units translated into U.S. $ at baseline exchange rates.

Model: MCKIBB
Simulation D: U.S. Monetary Expansion with foreign Monetary Aggregates Unchanged from Baseline
(Deviation of Shock Path from Baseline Path)

	1985 Q1	1985 Q2	1985 Q3	1985 Q4	1985	1986	1987	1988	1989	1990
UNITED STATES										
GNPV(%)	-	-	-	-	2.5	1.8	2.4	2.7	3.0	3.3
GNP(%)	-	-	-	-	2.5	0.3	0.3	-0.0	-0.2	-0.4
PGNP(%)	-	-	-	-	0.0	1.5	2.1	2.8	3.3	3.7
CPI(%)	-	-	-	-	0.5	1.5	2.1	2.7	3.1	3.5
WAGES(%)	-	-	-	-	0.0	1.5	2.1	2.8	3.2	3.7
UN(% PTS)	-	-	-	-	-1.0	-0.1	-0.1	0.0	0.0	0.1
GNP(B.72$)	-	-	-	-	43.0	5.0	5.0	-0.5	-3.9	-7.1
G(B.72$)	-	-	-	-	0.0	0.0	0.0	0.0	0.0	0.0
C(B.72$)	-	-	-	-	33.5	5.2	5.2	0.9	-2.2	-5.0
IFP(B.72$)	-	-	-	-	-	-	-	-	-	-
II(B.72$)	-	-	-	-	-	-	-	-	-	-
XGS(B.72$)	-	-	-	-	9.5	0.3	0.3	-0.8	-1.3	-1.8
MGS(B.72$)	-	-	-	-	-0.1	0.5	0.6	0.6	0.4	0.3
M1(%)	-	-	-	-	4.1	4.1	4.1	4.1	4.1	4.1
RS(% PTS)	-	-	-	-	-6.7	-0.8	-1.2	-0.7	-0.5	-0.3
RL(% PTS)	-	-	-	-	-0.5	-0.1	0.0	0.1	0.2	0.2
GDEF(B$)	-	-	-	-	-56.2	-20.0	-25.3	-21.2	-18.7	-15.7
PXGS(%)	-	-	-	-	-	-	-	-	-	-
PMGS(%)	-	-	-	-	7.1	1.3	1.9	1.6	1.9	2.1
EXCH(%) *	-	-	-	-	-7.2	-2.0	-2.6	-2.3	-2.4	-2.4
CAB(B$)	-	-	-	-	58.7	2.6	7.3	1.1	-2.0	-4.8
NON-US OECD										
GNPV(%) **	-	-	-	-	-1.2	-0.3	-0.5	-0.4	-0.4	-0.3
GNP(%) **	-	-	-	-	-1.2	0.4	0.3	0.4	0.4	0.3
PGNP(%)	-	-	-	-	-	-	-	-	-	-
CPI(%)	-	-	-	-	-0.3	-0.7	-0.8	-0.8	-0.7	-0.5
WAGES(%)	-	-	-	-	0.0	-0.7	-0.8	-0.9	-0.7	-0.6
UN(% PTS)	-	-	-	-	0.4	-0.1	0.0	-0.1	-0.1	-0.1
C(%) **	-	-	-	-	-0.8	0.7	0.3	0.4	0.3	0.2
IFP(%) **	-	-	-	-	-	-	-	-	-	-
RS(% PTS)	-	-	-	-	-1.0	-1.2	-0.8	-0.6	-0.4	-0.2
RL(% PTS)	-	-	-	-	-	-	-	-	-	-
GDEF (B.US$) **	-	-	-	-	43.2	-0.4	-6.2	-19.2	-24.9	-27.9
PXGS(%)	-	-	-	-	-	-	-	-	-	-
PMGS(%)	-	-	-	-	-3.4	-0.6	-0.7	-0.3	-0.0	0.2
EXCH(%) ***	-	-	-	-	7.7	2.0	2.6	2.4	2.4	2.6
CAB(B.US$) **	-	-	-	-	-70.3	-4.4	-9.6	-1.9	1.3	4.0

* Exchange rate : (Weighted average of foreign currencies)/U.S. $.
** Local currency units translated into U.S. $ at baseline exchange rates.
*** Exchange rate : U.S. $/(weighted average of non-US OECD currencies).

Model: MCKIBB
Simulation D: U.S. Monetary Expansion with Foreign Monetary Aggregates Unchanged from Baseline
(Deviation of Shock Path from Baseline Path)

	1985									
	Q1	Q2	Q3	Q4	1985	1986	1987	1988	1989	1990
JAPAN										
GNP(%)	-	-	-	-	-1.1	0.4	0.2	0.4	0.4	0.3
CPI(%)	-	-	-	-	-0.3	-0.7	-0.7	-0.7	-0.6	-0.4
RS(% PTS)	-	-	-	-	-1.0	-1.2	-0.7	-0.6	-0.3	-0.1
GDEF(%GNPV) *	-	-	-	-	0.5	0.1	0.0	-0.1	-0.1	-0.2
EXCH(%) **	-	-	-	-	7.7	1.9	2.5	2.2	2.4	2.5
CAB(B.US$) ***	-	-	-	-	-18.3	0.3	-2.0	0.3	1.2	2.0
GERMANY										
GNP(%)	-	-	-	-	-	-	-	-	-	-
CPI(%)	-	-	-	-	-	-	-	-	-	-
RS(% PTS)	-	-	-	-	-	-	-	-	-	-
GDEF(%GNPV) *	-	-	-	-	-	-	-	-	-	-
EXCH(%) **	-	-	-	-	-	-	-	-	-	-
CAB(B.US$) ***	-	-	-	-	-	-	-	-	-	-
FRANCE										
GNP(%)	-	-	-	-	-	-	-	-	-	-
CPI(%)	-	-	-	-	-	-	-	-	-	-
GDEF(%GNPV) *	-	-	-	-	-	-	-	-	-	-
EXCH(%) **	-	-	-	-	-	-	-	-	-	-
CAB(B.US$) ***	-	-	-	-	-	-	-	-	-	-
UNITED KINGDOM										
GNP(%)	-	-	-	-	-	-	-	-	-	-
CPI(%)	-	-	-	-	-	-	-	-	-	-
GDEF(%GNPV) *	-	-	-	-	-	-	-	-	-	-
EXCH(%) **	-	-	-	-	-	-	-	-	-	-
CAB(B.US$) ***	-	-	-	-	-	-	-	-	-	-
ITALY										
GNP(%)	-	-	-	-	-	-	-	-	-	-
CPI(%)	-	-	-	-	-	-	-	-	-	-
GDEF(%GNPV) *	-	-	-	-	-	-	-	-	-	-
EXCH(%) **	-	-	-	-	-	-	-	-	-	-
CAB(B.US$) ***	-	-	-	-	-	-	-	-	-	-
CANADA										
GNP(%)	-	-	-	-	-	-	-	-	-	-
CPI(%)	-	-	-	-	-	-	-	-	-	-
GDEF(%GNPV) *	-	-	-	-	-	-	-	-	-	-
EXCH(%) **	-	-	-	-	-	-	-	-	-	-
CAB(B.US$) ***	-	-	-	-	-	-	-	-	-	-
REST OF WORLD										
CAB(B.US$) ***	-	-	-	-	11.6	0.2	-0.3	-2.6	-3.6	-4.4

* Government deficit as a percentage of baseline nominal GNP.
** Exchange rate : Bilateral rate against U.S. $ ($/local currency).
*** Local currency units translated into U.S. $ at baseline exchange rates.

Model: MCKIBB
Simulation E: U.S. Monetary Expansion with Foreign Short-Term Interest Rates Unchanged from Baseline
(Deviation of Shock Path from Baseline Path)

	1985									
	Q1	Q2	Q3	Q4	1985	1986	1987	1988	1989	1990
UNITED STATES										
GNPV(%)	-	-	-	-	2.9	2.2	2.9	3.3	3.7	4.2
GNP(%)	-	-	-	-	2.9	0.3	0.3	-0.0	-0.2	-0.2
PGNP(%)	-	-	-	-	0.0	1.8	2.6	3.4	3.9	4.4
CPI(%)	-	-	-	-	0.7	1.9	2.6	3.2	3.8	4.3
WAGES(%)	-	-	-	-	0.0	1.8	2.6	3.3	3.9	4.4
UN(% PTS)	-	-	-	-	-1.2	-0.1	-0.1	0.0	0.0	0.1
GNP(B.72$)	-	-	-	-	49.3	5.8	4.5	-0.6	-2.9	-3.9
G(B.72$)	-	-	-	-	0.0	0.0	0.0	0.0	0.0	0.0
C(B.72$)	-	-	-	-	35.9	5.0	5.2	1.8	-0.1	-1.6
IFP(B.72$)	-	-	-	-	-	-	-	-	-	-
II(B.72$)	-	-	-	-	-	-	-	-	-	-
XGS(B.72$)	-	-	-	-	12.6	0.8	-0.3	-1.7	-2.1	-1.9
MGS(B.72$)	-	-	-	-	-0.9	0.1	0.5	0.7	0.7	0.5
M1(%)	-	-	-	-	4.1	4.1	4.1	4.1	4.1	4.1
RS(% PTS)	-	-	-	-	-6.4	0.0	-0.5	0.0	0.3	0.7
RL(% PTS)	-	-	-	-	1.5	2.1	2.2	2.4	2.6	2.7
GDEF(B$)	-	-	-	-	-43.0	1.0	0.7	6.7	9.8	11.6
PXGS(%)	-	-	-	-	-	-	-	-	-	-
PMGS(%)	-	-	-	-	9.8	2.7	2.5	2.1	2.4	3.1
EXCH(%) *	-	-	-	-	-9.9	-3.7	-3.6	-3.4	-3.9	-4.7
CAB(B$)	-	-	-	-	68.1	1.7	2.4	-5.8	-10.5	-14.0
NON-US OECD										
GNPV(%) **	-	-	-	-	-2.2	-1.5	-1.4	-1.0	-0.3	0.5
GNP(%) **	-	-	-	-	-2.2	-0.3	0.1	0.5	0.6	0.5
PGNP(%)	-	-	-	-	-	-	-	-	-	-
CPI(%)	-	-	-	-	-0.5	-1.2	-1.7	-2.0	-2.2	-2.2
WAGES(%)	-	-	-	-	0.0	-1.2	-1.7	-2.1	-2.3	-2.3
UN(% PTS)	-	-	-	-	0.7	0.0	-0.2	-0.4	-0.4	-0.4
C(%) **	-	-	-	-	-2.2	-0.6	-0.2	0.1	0.2	0.1
IFP(%) **	-	-	-	-	-	-	-	-	-	-
RS(% PTS)	-	-	-	-	0.0	0.0	0.0	0.0	0.0	0.0
RL(% PTS)	-	-	-	-	-	-	-	-	-	-
GDEF (B.US$) **	-	-	-	-	72.4	21.2	-1.4	-20.4	-29.4	-28.5
PXGS(%)	-	-	-	-	-	-	-	-	-	-
PMGS(%)	-	-	-	-	-4.6	-1.2	-0.9	-0.5	-0.6	-1.0
EXCH(%) ***	-	-	-	-	10.9	3.9	3.8	3.5	4.0	5.0
CAB(B.US$) **	-	-	-	-	-79.9	-1.1	-1.6	7.5	11.3	13.4

* Exchange rate : (Weighted average of foreign currencies)/U.S. $.
** Local currency units translated into U.S. $ at baseline exchange rates.
*** Exchange rate : U.S. $/(weighted average of non-US OECD currencies).

Model: MCKIBB
Simulation E: U.S. Monetary Expansion with Foreign Short-Term Interest Rates Unchanged from Baseline
(Deviation of Shock Path from Baseline Path)

	1985									
	Q1	Q2	Q3	Q4	1985	1986	1987	1988	1989	1990
JAPAN										
GNP(%)	-	-	-	-	-2.0	-1.2	-1.8	-2.2	-2.3	-1.8
CPI(%)	-	-	-	-	-0.4	-1.5	-2.9	-5.0	-7.4	-10.0
RS(% PTS)	-	-	-	-	0.0	0.0	0.0	0.0	0.0	0.0
GDEF(%GNPV) *	-	-	-	-	0.8	0.6	0.7	0.6	0.5	0.2
EXCH(%) **	-	-	-	-	11.1	6.8	10.6	14.2	17.4	19.4
CAB(B.US$) ***	-	-	-	-	-22.0	-5.3	-12.7	-15.6	-16.3	-11.9
GERMANY										
GNP(%)	-	-	-	-	-	-	-	-	-	-
CPI(%)	-	-	-	-	-	-	-	-	-	-
RS(% PTS)	-	-	-	-	-	-	-	-	-	-
GDEF(%GNPV) *	-	-	-	-	-	-	-	-	-	-
EXCH(%) **	-	-	-	-	-	-	-	-	-	-
CAB(B.US$) ***	-	-	-	-	-	-	-	-	-	-
FRANCE										
GNP(%)	-	-	-	-	-	-	-	-	-	-
CPI(%)	-	-	-	-	-	-	-	-	-	-
GDEF(%GNPV) *	-	-	-	-	-	-	-	-	-	-
EXCH(%) **	-	-	-	-	-	-	-	-	-	-
CAB(B.US$) ***	-	-	-	-	-	-	-	-	-	-
UNITED KINGDOM										
GNP(%)	-	-	-	-	-	-	-	-	-	-
CPI(%)	-	-	-	-	-	-	-	-	-	-
GDEF(%GNPV) *	-	-	-	-	-	-	-	-	-	-
EXCH(%) **	-	-	-	-	-	-	-	-	-	-
CAB(B.US$) ***	-	-	-	-	-	-	-	-	-	-
ITALY										
GNP(%)	-	-	-	-	-	-	-	-	-	-
CPI(%)	-	-	-	-	-	-	-	-	-	-
GDEF(%GNPV) *	-	-	-	-	-	-	-	-	-	-
EXCH(%) **	-	-	-	-	-	-	-	-	-	-
CAB(B.US$) ***	-	-	-	-	-	-	-	-	-	-
CANADA										
GNP(%)	-	-	-	-	-	-	-	-	-	-
CPI(%)	-	-	-	-	-	-	-	-	-	-
GDEF(%GNPV) *	-	-	-	-	-	-	-	-	-	-
EXCH(%) **	-	-	-	-	-	-	-	-	-	-
CAB(B.US$) ***	-	-	-	-	-	-	-	-	-	-
REST OF WORLD										
CAB(B.US$) ***	-	-	-	-	11.9	-2.7	-4.0	-5.8	-6.0	-5.7

* Government deficit as a percentage of baseline nominal GNP.
** Exchange rate : Bilateral rate against U.S. $ ($/local currency).
*** Local currency units translated into U.S. $ at baseline exchange rates.

Model: MCKIBB
Simulation F: Nonpolicy Exogenous Depreciation of the Dollar
(Deviation of Shock Path from Baseline Path)

	1985									
	Q1	Q2	Q3	Q4	1985	1986	1987	1988	1989	1990
UNITED STATES										
GNPV(%)	-	-	-	-	1.6	3.4	5.7	7.0	8.6	9.9
GNP(%)	-	-	-	-	1.6	2.0	2.2	0.7	0.1	-0.4
PGNP(%)	-	-	-	-	0.0	1.3	3.6	6.5	8.7	10.6
CPI(%)	-	-	-	-	0.7	2.5	4.9	7.3	9.3	11.0
WAGES(%)	-	-	-	-	0.0	1.4	3.5	6.5	8.7	10.6
UN(% PTS)	-	-	-	-	-0.7	-0.9	-1.0	-0.3	-0.1	0.1
GNP(B.72$)	-	-	-	-	27.0	35.5	40.2	13.0	1.4	-7.8
G(B.72$)	-	-	-	-	0.0	0.0	0.0	0.0	0.0	0.0
C(B.72$)	-	-	-	-	9.3	6.6	2.2	-14.1	-20.0	-24.5
IFP(B.72$)	-	-	-	-	-	-	-	-	-	-
II(B.72$)	-	-	-	-	-	-	-	-	-	-
XGS(B.72$)	-	-	-	-	14.6	23.5	30.7	21.4	16.4	12.1
MGS(B.72$)	-	-	-	-	-3.3	-5.6	-7.5	-5.8	-5.1	-4.8
M1(%)	-	-	-	-	0.0	0.0	0.0	0.0	0.0	0.0
RS(% PTS)	-	-	-	-	1.4	4.9	8.5	11.3	12.3	13.6
RL(% PTS)	-	-	-	-	1.9	3.7	5.4	5.1	4.6	3.9
GDEF(B$)	-	-	-	-	-24.8	-23.6	-12.0	39.9	82.4	133.1
PXGS(%)	-	-	-	-	-	-	-	-	-	-
PMGS(%)	-	-	-	-	10.2	16.2	21.5	16.9	16.1	16.4
EXCH(%) *	-	-	-	-	-10.2	-17.5	-24.8	-21.7	-21.7	-22.4
CAB(B$)	-	-	-	-	40.9	53.0	59.1	13.0	-15.6	-50.1
NON-US OECD										
GNPV(%) **	-	-	-	-	-1.5	-2.4	-3.4	-3.2	-3.7	-4.1
GNP(%) **	-	-	-	-	-1.5	-1.4	-1.1	0.8	1.3	1.3
PGNP(%)	-	-	-	-	-	-	-	-	-	-
CPI(%)	-	-	-	-	-0.5	-1.6	-3.2	-4.6	-5.4	-5.9
WAGES(%)	-	-	-	-	0.0	-1.0	-2.4	-4.1	-5.1	-5.6
UN(% PTS)	-	-	-	-	0.5	0.5	0.4	-0.2	-0.3	-0.3
C(%) **	-	-	-	-	-1.0	-0.3	0.5	2.4	2.9	3.0
IFP(%) **	-	-	-	-	-	-	-	-	-	-
RS(% PTS)	-	-	-	-	-1.3	-3.4	-5.4	-6.0	-5.8	-5.7
RL(% PTS)	-	-	-	-	-	-	-	-	-	-
GDEF (B.US$) **	-	-	-	-	51.0	58.0	41.7	-45.3	-100.9	-141.8
PXGS(%)	-	-	-	-	-	-	-	-	-	-
PMGS(%)	-	-	-	-	-4.7	-7.9	-10.9	-9.2	-8.7	-8.4
EXCH(%) ***	-	-	-	-	11.2	19.1	26.8	22.9	22.5	23.0
CAB(B.US$) **	-	-	-	-	-41.8	-42.6	-34.2	26.0	49.7	67.1

* Exchange rate : (Weighted average of foreign currencies)/U.S. $.
** Local currency units translated into U.S. $ at baseline exchange rates.
*** Exchange rate : U.S. $/(weighted average of non-US OECD currencies).

Model: MCKIBB
Simulation F: Nonpolicy Exogenous Depreciation of the Dollar
(Deviation of Shock Path from Baseline Path)

	1985									
	Q1	Q2	Q3	Q4	1985	1986	1987	1988	1989	1990
JAPAN										
GNP(%)	-	-	-	-	-1.4	-1.4	-1.2	0.6	1.0	1.1
CPI(%)	-	-	-	-	-0.4	-1.5	-3.0	-4.4	-5.3	-5.9
RS(% PTS)	-	-	-	-	-1.3	-3.4	-5.3	-6.0	-5.9	-6.1
GDEF(%GNPV) *	-	-	-	-	0.6	0.8	0.7	-0.2	-0.8	-1.2
EXCH(%) **	-	-	-	-	11.2	18.7	26.0	22.3	22.4	23.2
CAB(B.US$) ***	-	-	-	-	-9.5	-6.0	0.7	21.0	31.0	40.6
GERMANY										
GNP(%)	-	-	-	-	-	-	-	-	-	-
CPI(%)	-	-	-	-	-	-	-	-	-	-
RS(% PTS)	-	-	-	-	-	-	-	-	-	-
GDEF(%GNPV) *	-	-	-	-	-	-	-	-	-	-
EXCH(%) **	-	-	-	-	-	-	-	-	-	-
CAB(B.US$) ***	-	-	-	-	-	-	-	-	-	-
FRANCE										
GNP(%)	-	-	-	-	-	-	-	-	-	-
CPI(%)	-	-	-	-	-	-	-	-	-	-
GDEF(%GNPV) *	-	-	-	-	-	-	-	-	-	-
EXCH(%) **	-	-	-	-	-	-	-	-	-	-
CAB(B.US$) ***	-	-	-	-	-	-	-	-	-	-
UNITED KINGDOM										
GNP(%)	-	-	-	-	-	-	-	-	-	-
CPI(%)	-	-	-	-	-	-	-	-	-	-
GDEF(%GNPV) *	-	-	-	-	-	-	-	-	-	-
EXCH(%) **	-	-	-	-	-	-	-	-	-	-
CAB(B.US$) ***	-	-	-	-	-	-	-	-	-	-
ITALY										
GNP(%)	-	-	-	-	-	-	-	-	-	-
CPI(%)	-	-	-	-	-	-	-	-	-	-
GDEF(%GNPV) *	-	-	-	-	-	-	-	-	-	-
EXCH(%) **	-	-	-	-	-	-	-	-	-	-
CAB(B.US$) ***	-	-	-	-	-	-	-	-	-	-
CANADA										
GNP(%)	-	-	-	-	-	-	-	-	-	-
CPI(%)	-	-	-	-	-	-	-	-	-	-
GDEF(%GNPV) *	-	-	-	-	-	-	-	-	-	-
EXCH(%) **	-	-	-	-	-	-	-	-	-	-
CAB(B.US$) ***	-	-	-	-	-	-	-	-	-	-
REST OF WORLD										
CAB(B.US$) ***	-	-	-	-	1.0	-11.8	-29.1	-47.0	-45.5	-31.6

* Government deficit as a percentage of baseline nominal GNP.
** Exchange rate : Bilateral rate against U.S. $ ($/local currency).
*** Local currency units translated into U.S. $ at baseline exchange rates.

Model: MCKIBB
Simulation G: Increase in Government Purchases in Non-U.S. OECD Countries with U.S. Policies Unchanged from Baseline
(Deviation of Shock Path from Baseline Path)

	1985									
	Q1	Q2	Q3	Q4	1985	1986	1987	1988	1989	1990
UNITED STATES										
GNPV(%)	-	-	-	-	0.5	0.8	1.2	1.6	2.1	2.6
GNP(%)	-	-	-	-	0.5	0.4	0.4	0.3	0.2	0.1
PGNP(%)	-	-	-	-	0.0	0.4	0.9	1.4	1.9	2.5
CPI(%)	-	-	-	-	0.2	0.6	1.0	1.5	2.1	2.7
WAGES(%)	-	-	-	-	0.0	0.4	0.8	1.4	1.9	2.5
UN(% PTS)	-	-	-	-	-0.2	-0.1	-0.2	-0.1	-0.1	-0.1
GNP(B.72$)	-	-	-	-	8.9	6.4	6.4	5.5	4.4	2.9
G(B.72$)	-	-	-	-	0.0	0.0	0.0	0.0	0.0	0.0
C(B.72$)	-	-	-	-	2.4	0.0	-0.6	-1.7	-2.9	-4.2
IFP(B.72$)	-	-	-	-	-	-	-	-	-	-
II(B.72$)	-	-	-	-	-	-	-	-	-	-
XGS(B.72$)	-	-	-	-	5.6	5.3	5.8	5.9	5.8	5.4
MGS(B.72$)	-	-	-	-	-1.0	-1.0	-1.1	-1.3	-1.5	-1.6
M1(%)	-	-	-	-	0.0	0.0	0.0	0.0	0.0	0.0
RS(% PTS)	-	-	-	-	0.4	1.3	1.7	2.3	2.9	3.5
RL(% PTS)	-	-	-	-	1.4	1.4	1.3	1.3	1.2	1.0
GDEF(B$)	-	-	-	-	-8.1	-3.1	0.1	6.4	15.3	27.7
PXGS(%)	-	-	-	-	-	-	-	-	-	-
PMGS(%)	-	-	-	-	2.9	2.8	3.3	3.9	4.6	5.2
EXCH(%) *	-	-	-	-	-3.1	-2.7	-2.8	-2.7	-2.7	-2.4
CAB(B$)	-	-	-	-	14.8	10.5	9.7	6.5	0.9	-7.4
NON-US OECD										
GNPV(%) **	-	-	-	-	0.9	1.3	1.7	2.2	2.8	3.5
GNP(%) **	-	-	-	-	0.9	1.1	1.1	1.0	0.8	0.6
PGNP(%)	-	-	-	-	-	-	-	-	-	-
CPI(%)	-	-	-	-	-0.2	0.1	0.5	1.1	1.9	2.8
WAGES(%)	-	-	-	-	0.0	0.2	0.6	1.2	2.0	2.9
UN(% PTS)	-	-	-	-	-0.2	-0.3	-0.3	-0.3	-0.2	-0.2
C(%) **	-	-	-	-	0.3	0.4	0.3	0.1	-0.2	-0.4
IFP(%) **	-	-	-	-	-	-	-	-	-	-
RS(% PTS)	-	-	-	-	0.9	1.4	2.1	2.9	3.7	4.7
RL(% PTS)	-	-	-	-	-	-	-	-	-	-
GDEF (B.US$) **	-	-	-	-	65.9	80.3	87.7	106.1	132.9	168.1
PXGS(%)	-	-	-	-	-	-	-	-	-	-
PMGS(%)	-	-	-	-	-1.4	-1.0	-0.6	0.0	0.8	1.6
EXCH(%) ***	-	-	-	-	3.1	2.9	3.0	2.8	2.8	2.6
CAB(B.US$) **	-	-	-	-	-14.6	-5.3	-1.5	3.0	7.3	12.4

* Exchange rate : (Weighted average of foreign currencies)/U.S. $.
** Local currency units translated into U.S. $ at baseline exchange rates.
*** Exchange rate : U.S. $/(weighted average of non-US OECD currencies).

Model: MCKIBB
Simulation G: Increase in Government Purchases in Non-U.S. OECD Countries with U.S. Policies Unchanged from Baseline
(Deviation of Shock Path from Baseline Path)

	1985 Q1	1985 Q2	1985 Q3	1985 Q4	1985	1986	1987	1988	1989	1990
JAPAN										
GNP(%)	-	-	-	-	0.9	1.0	1.0	0.9	0.7	0.6
CPI(%)	-	-	-	-	-0.1	0.1	0.6	1.2	2.0	2.9
RS(% PTS)	-	-	-	-	0.7	1.4	2.2	3.0	3.9	4.8
GDEF(%GNPV) *	-	-	-	-	1.0	1.2	1.3	1.5	1.7	2.1
EXCH(%) **	-	-	-	-	3.1	2.8	3.0	3.0	2.9	2.8
CAB(B.US$) ***	-	-	-	-	-3.3	-0.7	0.5	2.0	3.5	5.5
GERMANY										
GNP(%)	-	-	-	-	-	-	-	-	-	-
CPI(%)	-	-	-	-	-	-	-	-	-	-
RS(% PTS)	-	-	-	-	-	-	-	-	-	-
GDEF(%GNPV) *	-	-	-	-	-	-	-	-	-	-
EXCH(%) **	-	-	-	-	-	-	-	-	-	-
CAB(B.US$) ***	-	-	-	-	-	-	-	-	-	-
FRANCE										
GNP(%)	-	-	-	-	-	-	-	-	-	-
CPI(%)	-	-	-	-	-	-	-	-	-	-
GDEF(%GNPV) *	-	-	-	-	-	-	-	-	-	-
EXCH(%) **	-	-	-	-	-	-	-	-	-	-
CAB(B.US$) ***	-	-	-	-	-	-	-	-	-	-
UNITED KINGDOM										
GNP(%)	-	-	-	-	-	-	-	-	-	-
CPI(%)	-	-	-	-	-	-	-	-	-	-
GDEF(%GNPV) *	-	-	-	-	-	-	-	-	-	-
EXCH(%) **	-	-	-	-	-	-	-	-	-	-
CAB(B.US$) ***	-	-	-	-	-	-	-	-	-	-
ITALY										
GNP(%)	-	-	-	-	-	-	-	-	-	-
CPI(%)	-	-	-	-	-	-	-	-	-	-
GDEF(%GNPV) *	-	-	-	-	-	-	-	-	-	-
EXCH(%) **	-	-	-	-	-	-	-	-	-	-
CAB(B.US$) ***	-	-	-	-	-	-	-	-	-	-
CANADA										
GNP(%)	-	-	-	-	-	-	-	-	-	-
CPI(%)	-	-	-	-	-	-	-	-	-	-
GDEF(%GNPV) *	-	-	-	-	-	-	-	-	-	-
EXCH(%) **	-	-	-	-	-	-	-	-	-	-
CAB(B.US$) ***	-	-	-	-	-	-	-	-	-	-
REST OF WORLD										
CAB(B.US$) ***	-	-	-	-	-0.2	-5.5	-9.3	-11.2	-10.7	-8.6

* Government deficit as a percentage of baseline nominal GNP.
** Exchange rate : Bilateral rate against U.S. $ ($/local currency).
*** Local currency units translated into U.S. $ at baseline exchange rates.

Model: MCKIBB
Simulation H: Monetary Expansion in Non-U.S. OECD Countries
with U.S. Policies Unchanged from Baseline
(Deviation of Shock Path from Baseline Path)

	1985 Q1	1985 Q2	1985 Q3	1985 Q4	1985	1986	1987	1988	1989	1990
UNITED STATES										
GNPV(%)	-	-	-	-	-0.7	-0.4	-0.4	-0.3	-0.1	0.1
GNP(%)	-	-	-	-	-0.7	0.3	0.2	0.3	0.3	0.2
PGNP(%)	-	-	-	-	0.0	-0.7	-0.6	-0.6	-0.3	-0.1
CPI(%)	-	-	-	-	-0.4	-0.6	-0.6	-0.5	-0.2	0.0
WAGES(%)	-	-	-	-	0.0	-0.7	-0.6	-0.6	-0.4	-0.1
UN(% PTS)	-	-	-	-	0.2	-0.1	-0.1	-0.1	-0.1	-0.1
GNP(B.72$)	-	-	-	-	-11.6	5.9	3.9	5.8	5.4	4.3
G(B.72$)	-	-	-	-	0.0	0.0	0.0	0.0	0.0	0.0
C(B.72$)	-	-	-	-	-5.1	4.6	2.3	3.0	2.2	1.1
IFP(B.72$)	-	-	-	-	-	-	-	-	-	-
II(B.72$)	-	-	-	-	-	-	-	-	-	-
XGS(B.72$)	-	-	-	-	-4.4	1.3	1.4	2.4	2.6	2.5
MGS(B.72$)	-	-	-	-	2.0	0.1	-0.1	-0.4	-0.6	-0.7
M1(%)	-	-	-	-	0.0	0.0	0.0	0.0	0.0	0.0
RS(% PTS)	-	-	-	-	-0.6	-1.2	-0.4	-0.3	0.1	0.4
RL(% PTS)	-	-	-	-	0.1	0.1	0.2	0.3	0.3	0.2
GDEF(B$)	-	-	-	-	10.9	-10.4	-8.0	-11.3	-10.9	-9.0
PXGS(%)	-	-	-	-	-	-	-	-	-	-
PMGS(%)	-	-	-	-	-5.5	0.1	0.1	0.9	1.2	1.5
EXCH(%) *	-	-	-	-	6.5	1.4	2.3	2.2	2.4	2.9
CAB(B$)	-	-	-	-	-15.3	12.0	6.7	10.5	9.4	7.2
NON-US OECD										
GNPV(%) **	-	-	-	-	3.9	1.8	2.6	3.0	3.4	3.8
GNP(%) **	-	-	-	-	3.9	0.2	0.2	-0.2	-0.5	-0.7
PGNP(%)	-	-	-	-	-	-	-	-	-	-
CPI(%)	-	-	-	-	0.2	1.5	2.4	3.1	3.8	4.4
WAGES(%)	-	-	-	-	0.0	1.6	2.4	3.2	3.9	4.5
UN(% PTS)	-	-	-	-	-1.1	0.0	0.0	0.1	0.2	0.2
C(%) **	-	-	-	-	5.8	0.5	0.5	-0.2	-0.6	-1.0
IFP(%) **	-	-	-	-	-	-	-	-	-	-
RS(% PTS)	-	-	-	-	-6.7	-0.7	-0.8	-0.2	0.1	0.4
RL(% PTS)	-	-	-	-	-	-	-	-	-	-
GDEF (B.US$) **	-	-	-	-	-119.7	-13.1	-30.9	-22.2	-17.0	-10.5
PXGS(%)	-	-	-	-	-	-	-	-	-	-
PMGS(%)	-	-	-	-	2.9	1.2	2.0	2.5	3.1	3.7
EXCH(%) ***	-	-	-	-	-6.0	-1.4	-2.2	-2.1	-2.4	-2.7
CAB(B.US$) **	-	-	-	-	15.6	-15.9	-7.9	-9.5	-5.9	-1.9

* Exchange rate : (Weighted average of foreign currencies)/U.S. $.
** Local currency units translated into U.S. $ at baseline exchange rates.
*** Exchange rate : U.S. $/(weighted average of non-US OECD currencies).

Model: MCKIBB
Simulation H: Monetary Expansion in Non-U.S. OECD Countries
with U.S. Policies Unchanged from Baseline
(Deviation of Shock Path from Baseline Path)

	1985									
	Q1	Q2	Q3	Q4	1985	1986	1987	1988	1989	1990
JAPAN										
GNP(%)	-	-	-	-	3.4	0.2	0.2	-0.1	-0.3	-0.5
CPI(%)	-	-	-	-	0.2	1.6	2.3	3.1	3.7	4.3
RS(% PTS)	-	-	-	-	-5.9	-0.7	-0.9	-0.3	0.0	0.3
GDEF(%GNPV) *	-	-	-	-	-1.2	-0.1	-0.3	-0.2	-0.1	-0.1
EXCH(%) **	-	-	-	-	-6.3	-1.4	-2.2	-2.0	-2.3	-2.5
CAB(B.US$) ***	-	-	-	-	7.6	-4.5	-1.6	-2.5	-1.5	-0.2
GERMANY										
GNP(%)	-	-	-	-	-	-	-	-	-	-
CPI(%)	-	-	-	-	-	-	-	-	-	-
RS(% PTS)	-	-	-	-	-	-	-	-	-	-
GDEF(%GNPV) *	-	-	-	-	-	-	-	-	-	-
EXCH(%) **	-	-	-	-	-	-	-	-	-	-
CAB(B.US$) ***	-	-	-	-	-	-	-	-	-	-
FRANCE										
GNP(%)	-	-	-	-	-	-	-	-	-	-
CPI(%)	-	-	-	-	-	-	-	-	-	-
GDEF(%GNPV) *	-	-	-	-	-	-	-	-	-	-
EXCH(%) **	-	-	-	-	-	-	-	-	-	-
CAB(B.US$) ***	-	-	-	-	-	-	-	-	-	-
UNITED KINGDOM										
GNP(%)	-	-	-	-	-	-	-	-	-	-
CPI(%)	-	-	-	-	-	-	-	-	-	-
GDEF(%GNPV) *	-	-	-	-	-	-	-	-	-	-
EXCH(%) **	-	-	-	-	-	-	-	-	-	-
CAB(B.US$) ***	-	-	-	-	-	-	-	-	-	-
ITALY										
GNP(%)	-	-	-	-	-	-	-	-	-	-
CPI(%)	-	-	-	-	-	-	-	-	-	-
GDEF(%GNPV) *	-	-	-	-	-	-	-	-	-	-
EXCH(%) **	-	-	-	-	-	-	-	-	-	-
CAB(B.US$) ***	-	-	-	-	-	-	-	-	-	-
CANADA										
GNP(%)	-	-	-	-	-	-	-	-	-	-
CPI(%)	-	-	-	-	-	-	-	-	-	-
GDEF(%GNPV) *	-	-	-	-	-	-	-	-	-	-
EXCH(%) **	-	-	-	-	-	-	-	-	-	-
CAB(B.US$) ***	-	-	-	-	-	-	-	-	-	-
REST OF WORLD										
CAB(B.US$) ***	-	-	-	-	-0.3	4.8	1.9	-0.2	-3.0	-5.2

* Government deficit as a percentage of baseline nominal GNP.
** Exchange rate : Bilateral rate against U.S. $ ($/local currency).
*** Local currency units translated into U.S. $ at baseline exchange rates.

OECD INTERLINK Model

See part 1 of this volume for design and detailed description of the simulations. See part 4 for bibliographical references.

The figures in the tables for the nominal GNP (GNPV) and the GNP deflator (PGNP) of the non-U.S. OECD region are incorrect because of errors in weighting.

Model: OECD
Simulation A: Baseline Path

	1985	1986	1987	1988	1989	1990
UNITED STATES						
GNPV(B.$)	3913.9	4158.8	4429.8	4720.9	5032.4	5365.4
GNP(B.72$)	1677.1	1723.9	1778.2	1834.7	1893.6	1954.6
PGNP(72=100)	231.4	239.2	247.0	255.1	263.5	272.1
CPI(72=100)	227.7	235.4	243.2	251.2	259.6	268.2
WAGES(72=100)	326.4	339.2	352.8	367.0	381.7	397.0
UN(%)	7.2	7.3	7.4	7.5	7.7	7.8
G(B.72$)	317.5	327.3	337.4	347.7	358.3	369.3
C(B.72$)	1099.0	1131.8	1164.1	1197.5	1232.0	1267.4
IFP(B.72$)	281.9	293.5	308.6	324.7	341.7	359.6
II(B.72$)	19.5	18.1	16.6	15.1	13.8	12.5
XGS(B.72$)	149.0	154.1	158.5	162.9	167.4	172.1
MGS(B.72$)	175.3	186.0	191.6	197.4	203.3	209.4
M1(B.$)	581.3	624.2	670.2	719.6	772.7	829.7
RS(%)	8.6	9.0	9.0	9.0	9.0	9.0
RL(%)	12.5	12.4	12.3	12.2	12.1	12.0
GDEF(B.$)	146.0	158.4	175.4	196.4	221.0	249.4
PXGS(72=100)	251.3	257.2	263.7	270.3	277.0	284.0
PMGS(72=100)	260.7	267.1	274.5	282.1	289.9	297.9
EXCH(72=100) *	147.4	146.6	146.6	146.6	146.6	146.6
CAB(B.$)	-119.7	-145.3	-144.4	-142.8	-140.8	-138.0
NON-US OECD						
GNPV(B.$) **	4412.9	4745.8	5059.9	5400.1	5766.4	6161.1
GNP(B.72$) **	2175.0	2238.9	2303.5	2371.6	2442.7	2517.2
PGNP(72=100)	202.9	212.0	219.6	227.7	236.0	244.7
CPI(72=100)	269.2	282.6	296.2	310.5	325.5	341.2
WAGES(72=100)	354.8	378.7	403.7	430.4	458.9	489.3
UN(%)	9.7	9.8	9.9	10.0	10.1	10.2
C(B.72$) **	-	-	-	-	-	-
IFP(B.72$) **	-	-	-	-	-	-
RS(%)	10.6	10.4	10.4	10.5	10.5	10.5
RL(%)	11.5	11.1	10.8	10.6	10.4	10.2
GDEF(B.US$) **	143.5	136.4	125.9	109.4	82.2	34.1
PXGS(72=100)	244.9	253.8	262.8	272.2	281.8	291.8
PMGS(72=100)	332.2	344.3	358.0	372.1	386.8	402.1
EXCH(72=100) ***	87.1	87.6	87.2	86.8	86.4	86.0
CAB(B.US$)	47.7	71.4	95.2	122.1	152.0	185.3

* Exchange rate : (Weighted average of foreign currencies)/U.S. $.
** Local currency units translated into U.S. $ at baseline exchange rates.
*** Exchange rate : U.S. $/(weighted average of non-US OECD currencies).

Model: OECD
Simulation A: Baseline Path

	1985	1986	1987	1988	1989	1990
JAPAN						
GNP(B.72Y)	159016.4	166043.6	173132.8	180692.3	188666.2	197078.8
CPI(72=100)	251.0	257.0	263.1	269.4	275.9	282.5
RS(%)	6.1	6.1	6.1	6.1	6.1	6.1
GDEF(%GNPV) *	1.4	0.5	-0.2	-0.9	-1.6	-2.3
EXCH(72=100) **	118.9	119.4	119.4	119.4	119.4	119.4
CAB(B.US$) ***	39.3	48.1	57.5	68.4	80.7	94.5
GERMANY						
GNP(B.72DM)	1079.3	1109.0	1142.7	1178.3	1215.7	1254.9
CPI(72=100)	181.3	185.6	190.2	194.9	199.7	204.7
RS(%)	6.2	6.2	6.2	6.2	6.2	6.2
GDEF(%GNPV) *	1.5	1.3	1.4	1.5	1.5	1.6
EXCH(72=100) **	101.1	102.1	102.1	102.1	102.1	102.1
CAB(B.US$) ***	12.2	18.5	23.9	30.5	38.0	46.7
FRANCE						
GNP(B.72F)	1183.5	1206.8	1229.3	1253.1	1277.6	1302.9
CPI(72=100)	3.8	4.0	4.2	4.3	4.5	4.7
GDEF(%GNPV) *	3.2	3.4	3.5	3.6	3.7	3.7
EXCH(72=100) **	0.1	0.1	0.1	0.1	0.1	0.1
CAB(B.US$) ***	0.5	2.8	5.0	7.4	10.1	12.9
UNITED KINGDOM						
GNP(B.72LB)	70.5	72.2	73.8	75.5	77.3	79.1
CPI(72=100)	439.5	461.6	483.4	506.6	530.8	556.2
GDEF(%GNPV) *	3.6	2.9	2.1	1.5	0.8	0.2
EXCH(72=100) **	48.6	49.8	49.8	49.8	49.8	49.8
CAB(B.US$) ***	1.2	1.7	2.3	2.6	3.0	3.2
ITALY						
GNP(B.72L)	89113.5	90774.1	92185.0	93630.0	95103.7	96607.1
CPI(72=100)	7.6	8.1	8.7	9.4	10.0	10.8
GDEF(%GNPV) *	13.1	13.1	12.4	10.5	6.7	-0.6
EXCH(72=100) **	0.0	0.0	0.0	0.0	0.0	0.0
CAB(B.US$) ***	-4.5	-4.1	-5.2	-6.4	-7.7	-9.3
CANADA						
GNP(B.72C$)	151.7	156.6	161.7	167.1	172.7	178.6
CPI(72=100)	289.6	300.1	311.5	323.2	335.3	347.9
GDEF(%GNPV) *	6.0	5.5	4.9	4.4	3.9	3.3
EXCH(72=100) **	73.5	73.3	73.3	73.3	73.3	73.3
CAB(B.US$) ***	1.6	2.5	4.0	5.6	7.5	9.5
REST OF WORLD						
CAB(B.US$) ***	-24.5	-30.2	-32.4	-34.2	-33.8	-29.6

* Government deficit as a percentage of baseline nominal GNP.
** Exchange rate: Bilateral rate against U.S. $ ($/local currency).
*** Local currency units translated into U.S. $ at baseline exchange rates.

Model: OECD
Simulation B: Reduction in U.S. Government Purchases with Foreign Monetary Aggregates Unchanged from Baseline
(Deviation of Shock Path from Baseline Path)

	1985 Q1	1985 Q2	1985 Q3	1985 Q4	1985	1986	1987	1988	1989	1990
UNITED STATES										
GNPV(%)	-	-	-	-	-1.7	-1.8	-1.8	-2.2	-2.5	-2.7
GNP(%)	-	-	-	-	-1.5	-1.1	-0.6	-0.5	-0.3	0.0
PGNP(%)	-	-	-	-	-0.2	-0.7	-1.2	-1.7	-2.2	-2.7
CPI(%)	-	-	-	-	-0.1	-0.6	-1.1	-1.6	-2.1	-2.6
WAGES(%)	-	-	-	-	-0.4	-1.2	-1.9	-2.6	-3.2	-3.8
UN(% PTS)	-	-	-	-	0.8	0.8	0.6	0.4	0.3	0.1
GNP(B.72$)	-	-	-	-	-25.8	-18.7	-11.3	-9.4	-5.2	0.8
G(B.72$)	-	-	-	-	-16.9	-17.4	-17.9	-18.5	-19.1	-19.7
C(B.72$)	-	-	-	-	-5.9	-6.7	-3.8	-3.0	-1.7	0.7
IFP(B.72$)	-	-	-	-	-2.1	0.7	1.8	1.5	2.9	5.3
II(B.72$)	-	-	-	-	-6.8	-0.9	2.9	4.5	6.5	8.3
XGS(B.72$)	-	-	-	-	-0.9	-1.0	-0.7	-0.5	-0.3	0.1
MGS(B.72$)	-	-	-	-	-6.6	-6.5	-6.2	-6.5	-6.4	-6.1
M1(%)	-	-	-	-	0.0	0.0	0.0	0.0	0.0	0.0
RS(% PTS)	-	-	-	-	-1.0	-1.7	-1.7	-1.9	-2.2	-2.3
RL(% PTS)	-	-	-	-	-0.3	-0.8	-1.2	-1.5	-1.7	-2.0
GDEF(B$)	-	-	-	-	-29.4	-34.4	-53.6	-77.6	-104.8	-138.9
PXGS(%)	-	-	-	-	-0.2	-0.5	-0.8	-1.3	-1.9	-2.5
PMGS(%)	-	-	-	-	0.0	-0.1	-0.5	-1.0	-1.6	-2.2
EXCH(%) *	-	-	-	-	-0.2	-0.4	-0.1	0.3	0.6	1.0
CAB(B$)	-	-	-	-	14.9	14.2	15.5	18.0	19.3	20.6
NON-US OECD										
GNPV(%) **	-	-	-	-	-0.4	-0.7	-0.8	-0.8	-0.9	-0.8
GNP(%) **	-	-	-	-	-0.4	-0.4	-0.3	-0.2	-0.1	0.1
PGNP(%)	-	-	-	-	-0.1	-0.3	-0.5	-0.6	-0.8	-0.9
CPI(%)	-	-	-	-	-0.1	-0.3	-0.5	-0.7	-0.9	-1.1
WAGES(%)	-	-	-	-	-0.1	-0.4	-0.7	-0.9	-1.1	-1.3
UN(% PTS)	-	-	-	-	0.1	0.1	0.1	0.1	0.1	-0.0
C(%) **	-	-	-	-	-	-	-	-	-	-
IFP(%) **	-	-	-	-	-	-	-	-	-	-
RS(% PTS)	-	-	-	-	-0.4	-0.7	-0.9	-1.0	-1.1	-1.2
RL(% PTS)	-	-	-	-	-0.1	-0.3	-0.4	-0.5	-0.7	-0.8
GDEF (B.US$) **	-	-	-	-	3.5	6.9	7.2	6.0	4.5	2.0
PXGS(%)	-	-	-	-	-0.1	-0.3	-0.5	-0.6	-0.8	-1.1
PMGS(%)	-	-	-	-	-0.2	-0.4	-0.5	-0.6	-0.8	-1.1
EXCH(%) ***	-	-	-	-	0.2	0.3	-0.1	-0.5	-1.0	-1.4
CAB(B.US$) **	-	-	-	-	-9.0	-11.4	-12.9	-14.6	-15.6	-16.8

* Exchange rate : (Weighted average of foreign currencies)/U.S. $.
** Local currency units translated into U.S. $ at baseline exchange rates.
*** Exchange rate : U.S. $/(weighted average of non-US OECD currencies).

Model: OECD
Simulation B: Reduction in U.S. Government Purchases with Foreign Monetary Aggregates Unchanged from Baseline
(Deviation of Shock Path from Baseline Path)

	1985									
	Q1	Q2	Q3	Q4	1985	1986	1987	1988	1989	1990
JAPAN										
GNP(%)	-	-	-	-	-0.6	-0.6	-0.4	-0.4	-0.3	-0.1
CPI(%)	-	-	-	-	-0.1	-0.3	-0.5	-0.6	-0.8	-1.1
RS(% PTS)	-	-	-	-	-0.5	-0.8	-0.8	-0.8	-0.9	-1.0
GDEF(%GNPV) *	-	-	-	-	0.1	0.1	0.2	0.2	0.2	0.2
EXCH(%) **	-	-	-	-	0.0	0.0	-0.3	-0.6	-1.0	-1.3
CAB(B.US$) ***	-	-	-	-	-3.4	-3.9	-4.4	-5.1	-5.3	-5.4
GERMANY										
GNP(%)	-	-	-	-	-0.3	-0.4	-0.3	-0.2	-0.0	0.2
CPI(%)	-	-	-	-	-0.1	-0.2	-0.4	-0.5	-0.7	-0.9
RS(% PTS)	-	-	-	-	-0.7	-1.1	-1.0	-0.9	-0.9	-0.8
GDEF(%GNPV) *	-	-	-	-	0.1	0.1	0.1	0.1	0.0	-0.1
EXCH(%) **	-	-	-	-	0.0	-0.0	-0.4	-0.7	-0.9	-1.1
CAB(B.US$) ***	-	-	-	-	-1.4	-1.9	-1.9	-2.1	-2.3	-2.4
FRANCE										
GNP(%)	-	-	-	-	-0.3	-0.4	-0.3	-0.3	-0.2	0.0
CPI(%)	-	-	-	-	-0.1	-0.2	-0.4	-0.6	-0.8	-1.0
GDEF(%GNPV) *	-	-	-	-	0.1	0.1	0.1	0.1	0.0	-0.1
EXCH(%) **	-	-	-	-	0.3	0.5	0.2	-0.1	-0.4	-0.7
CAB(B.US$) ***	-	-	-	-	-0.7	-1.0	-1.3	-1.5	-1.6	-1.6
UNITED KINGDOM										
GNP(%)	-	-	-	-	-0.2	-0.2	-0.2	-0.2	-0.0	0.2
CPI(%)	-	-	-	-	-0.1	-0.4	-0.6	-0.9	-1.3	-1.6
GDEF(%GNPV) *	-	-	-	-	0.0	0.1	0.1	0.1	0.1	0.0
EXCH(%) **	-	-	-	-	0.3	0.7	0.4	0.0	-0.3	-0.6
CAB(B.US$) ***	-	-	-	-	-0.6	-0.8	-1.2	-1.6	-1.9	-2.2
ITALY										
GNP(%)	-	-	-	-	-0.2	-0.3	-0.3	-0.2	-0.0	0.2
CPI(%)	-	-	-	-	-0.0	-0.3	-0.7	-1.1	-1.6	-2.1
GDEF(%GNPV) *	-	-	-	-	0.1	0.1	0.1	0.1	0.1	0.0
EXCH(%) **	-	-	-	-	0.4	0.8	0.8	0.6	0.6	0.5
CAB(B.US$) ***	-	-	-	-	-0.3	-0.4	-0.6	-0.8	-0.9	-1.1
CANADA										
GNP(%)	-	-	-	-	-0.7	-0.6	-0.5	-0.6	-0.6	-0.5
CPI(%)	-	-	-	-	-0.2	-0.7	-1.1	-1.4	-1.9	-2.4
GDEF(%GNPV) *	-	-	-	-	0.2	0.2	0.1	0.1	0.0	-0.1
EXCH(%) **	-	-	-	-	0.3	0.8	0.8	0.7	0.6	0.5
CAB(B.US$) ***	-	-	-	-	-1.2	-1.5	-1.6	-1.6	-1.7	-1.9
REST OF WORLD										
CAB(B.US$) ***	-	-	-	-	-5.0	-1.7	-0.6	-0.7	-0.2	1.0

* Government deficit as a percentage of baseline nominal GNP.
** Exchange rate : Bilateral rate against U.S. $ ($/local currency).
*** Local currency units translated into U.S. $ at baseline exchange rates.

Model: OECD
Simulation C: Reduction in U.S. Government Purchases with Foreign
Short-Term Interest Rates Unchanged from Baseline
(Deviation of Shock Path from Baseline Path)

	1985 Q1	1985 Q2	1985 Q3	1985 Q4	1985	1986	1987	1988	1989	1990
UNITED STATES										
GNPV(%)	-	-	-	-	-1.5	-1.7	-1.8	-2.1	-2.3	-2.5
GNP(%)	-	-	-	-	-1.3	-1.0	-0.7	-0.5	-0.2	0.1
PGNP(%)	-	-	-	-	-0.2	-0.6	-1.1	-1.6	-2.1	-2.6
CPI(%)	-	-	-	-	-0.1	-0.5	-1.0	-1.4	-1.9	-2.4
WAGES(%)	-	-	-	-	-0.4	-1.1	-1.7	-2.4	-3.0	-3.5
UN(% PTS)	-	-	-	-	0.8	0.8	0.6	0.4	0.2	0.0
GNP(B.72$)	-	-	-	-	-22.6	-17.6	-12.8	-9.3	-4.3	1.9
G(B.72$)	-	-	-	-	-16.9	-17.4	-17.9	-18.5	-19.1	-19.7
C(B.72$)	-	-	-	-	-5.3	-6.3	-4.3	-3.4	-1.9	0.5
IFP(B.72$)	-	-	-	-	-0.6	1.2	1.2	1.6	3.4	5.8
II(B.72$)	-	-	-	-	-5.4	-1.2	1.6	3.7	5.8	7.5
XGS(B.72$)	-	-	-	-	-0.9	-0.9	-0.7	-0.6	-0.4	-0.2
MGS(B.72$)	-	-	-	-	-6.3	-6.9	-7.3	-7.7	-7.9	-8.0
M1(%)	-	-	-	-	0.3	0.3	0.2	0.2	0.2	0.3
RS(% PTS)	-	-	-	-	-1.5	-1.5	-1.7	-2.0	-2.2	-2.5
RL(% PTS)	-	-	-	-	-0.5	-0.9	-1.2	-1.5	-1.8	-2.0
GDEF(B$)	-	-	-	-	-34.1	-37.2	-54.3	-78.1	-106.6	-142.2
PXGS(%)	-	-	-	-	-0.1	-0.3	-0.5	-0.9	-1.4	-1.9
PMGS(%)	-	-	-	-	0.5	0.5	0.4	0.1	-0.3	-0.7
EXCH(%) *	-	-	-	-	-0.8	-1.1	-1.2	-1.2	-1.2	-1.2
CAB(B$)	-	-	-	-	12.8	13.0	14.8	16.6	17.8	18.7
NON-US OECD										
GNPV(%) **	-	-	-	-	-0.6	-1.0	-1.4	-1.7	-2.0	-2.3
GNP(%) **	-	-	-	-	-0.4	-0.7	-0.8	-0.9	-1.0	-1.0
PGNP(%)	-	-	-	-	-0.1	-0.3	-0.6	-0.8	-1.0	-1.3
CPI(%)	-	-	-	-	-0.1	-0.3	-0.5	-0.8	-1.0	-1.3
WAGES(%)	-	-	-	-	-0.1	-0.4	-0.8	-1.1	-1.5	-1.8
UN(% PTS)	-	-	-	-	0.1	0.2	0.3	0.3	0.4	0.4
C(%) **	-	-	-	-	-	-	-	-	-	-
IFP(%) **	-	-	-	-	-	-	-	-	-	-
RS(% PTS)	-	-	-	-	0.0	0.0	0.0	0.0	0.0	0.0
RL(% PTS)	-	-	-	-	0.0	-0.0	-0.0	-0.0	-0.0	-0.0
GDEF (B.US$) **	-	-	-	-	5.7	13.6	21.5	29.3	38.0	47.7
PXGS(%)	-	-	-	-	-0.2	-0.4	-0.6	-0.8	-1.2	-1.6
PMGS(%)	-	-	-	-	-0.4	-0.6	-0.7	-0.9	-1.3	-1.7
EXCH(%) ***	-	-	-	-	0.8	1.1	1.1	1.0	1.0	0.9
CAB(B.US$) **	-	-	-	-	-7.5	-10.4	-12.6	-14.4	-16.1	-18.0

* Exchange rate : (Weighted average of foreign currencies)/U.S. $.
** Local currency units translated into U.S. $ at baseline exchange rates.
*** Exchange rate : U.S. $/(weighted average of non-US OECD currencies).

Model: OECD
Simulation C: Reduction in U.S. Government Purchases with Foreign Short-Term Interest Rates Unchanged from Baseline
(Deviation of Shock Path from Baseline Path)

	1985									
	Q1	Q2	Q3	Q4	1985	1986	1987	1988	1989	1990
JAPAN										
GNP(%)	-	-	-	-	-0.7	-1.1	-1.3	-1.4	-1.5	-1.4
CPI(%)	-	-	-	-	-0.1	-0.3	-0.4	-0.5	-0.7	-0.8
RS(% PTS)	-	-	-	-	0.0	0.0	0.0	0.0	0.0	0.0
GDEF(%GNPV) *	-	-	-	-	0.1	0.3	0.5	0.6	0.8	0.9
EXCH(%) **	-	-	-	-	0.7	0.8	0.7	0.6	0.4	0.2
CAB(B.US$) ***	-	-	-	-	-2.9	-3.6	-4.3	-5.1	-5.6	-6.2
GERMANY										
GNP(%)	-	-	-	-	-0.4	-0.7	-0.9	-1.1	-1.3	-1.4
CPI(%)	-	-	-	-	-0.1	-0.3	-0.6	-0.8	-0.9	-1.1
RS(% PTS)	-	-	-	-	0.0	0.0	0.0	0.0	0.0	0.0
GDEF(%GNPV) *	-	-	-	-	0.1	0.4	0.6	0.8	1.0	1.2
EXCH(%) **	-	-	-	-	0.8	1.1	1.2	1.1	1.0	0.8
CAB(B.US$) ***	-	-	-	-	-1.0	-1.5	-1.9	-2.3	-2.5	-2.6
FRANCE										
GNP(%)	-	-	-	-	-0.3	-0.5	-0.6	-0.7	-0.8	-0.7
CPI(%)	-	-	-	-	-0.0	-0.2	-0.3	-0.3	-0.4	-0.4
GDEF(%GNPV) *	-	-	-	-	0.1	0.2	0.4	0.5	0.6	0.7
EXCH(%) **	-	-	-	-	0.8	1.0	0.9	0.7	0.5	0.2
CAB(B.US$) ***	-	-	-	-	-0.7	-1.0	-1.3	-1.4	-1.6	-1.7
UNITED KINGDOM										
GNP(%)	-	-	-	-	-0.2	-0.4	-0.5	-0.5	-0.5	-0.5
CPI(%)	-	-	-	-	-0.1	-0.3	-0.5	-0.8	-1.1	-1.5
GDEF(%GNPV) *	-	-	-	-	0.1	0.2	0.3	0.4	0.6	0.7
EXCH(%) **	-	-	-	-	0.8	1.1	1.1	1.1	1.2	1.3
CAB(B.US$) ***	-	-	-	-	-0.5	-0.8	-1.0	-1.2	-1.4	-1.7
ITALY										
GNP(%)	-	-	-	-	-0.2	-0.4	-0.4	-0.5	-0.5	-0.5
CPI(%)	-	-	-	-	-0.0	-0.2	-0.5	-0.8	-1.1	-1.4
GDEF(%GNPV) *	-	-	-	-	0.1	0.2	0.3	0.4	0.4	0.5
EXCH(%) **	-	-	-	-	0.8	1.2	1.2	1.2	1.2	1.2
CAB(B.US$) ***	-	-	-	-	-0.3	-0.4	-0.5	-0.6	-0.6	-0.6
CANADA										
GNP(%)	-	-	-	-	-0.8	-0.8	-0.9	-1.1	-1.2	-1.4
CPI(%)	-	-	-	-	-0.2	-0.7	-1.1	-1.5	-1.9	-2.3
GDEF(%GNPV) *	-	-	-	-	0.3	0.4	0.6	0.7	0.9	1.1
EXCH(%) **	-	-	-	-	0.8	1.4	1.6	1.8	2.0	2.2
CAB(B.US$) ***	-	-	-	-	-0.9	-1.3	-1.3	-1.3	-1.4	-1.4
REST OF WORLD										
CAB(B.US$) ***	-	-	-	-	-4.8	-2.8	-2.2	-2.4	-2.1	-1.4

* Government deficit as a percentage of baseline nominal GNP.
** Exchange rate : Bilateral rate against U.S. $ ($/local currency).
*** Local currency units translated into U.S. $ at baseline exchange rates.

Model: OECD
Simulation D: U.S. Monetary Expansion with foreign Monetary Aggregates Unchanged from Baseline
(Deviation of Shock Path from Baseline Path)

	1985 Q1	1985 Q2	1985 Q3	1985 Q4	1985	1986	1987	1988	1989	1990
UNITED STATES										
GNPV(%)	-	-	-	-	1.0	2.0	1.4	1.4	1.9	2.2
GNP(%)	-	-	-	-	1.0	1.6	0.4	0.2	0.4	0.5
PGNP(%)	-	-	-	-	-0.0	0.4	1.0	1.3	1.5	1.8
CPI(%)	-	-	-	-	0.1	0.7	1.1	1.4	1.6	1.8
WAGES(%)	-	-	-	-	0.3	1.2	1.9	2.3	2.6	3.0
UN(% PTS)	-	-	-	-	-0.6	-1.1	-0.4	-0.1	-0.1	-0.0
GNP(B.72$)	-	-	-	-	17.4	27.6	6.7	2.9	8.5	8.9
G(B.72$)	-	-	-	-	0.0	0.0	0.0	0.0	0.0	0.0
C(B.72$)	-	-	-	-	2.7	7.4	4.1	2.6	4.8	5.7
IFP(B.72$)	-	-	-	-	7.3	11.0	1.3	0.5	3.6	3.9
II(B.72$)	-	-	-	-	8.5	9.4	-1.0	-2.0	-0.7	-1.4
XGS(B.72$)	-	-	-	-	0.8	2.2	1.6	0.8	0.6	0.6
MGS(B.72$)	-	-	-	-	1.8	2.1	-0.7	-1.1	-0.3	-0.3
M1(%)	-	-	-	-	2.0	4.0	4.0	4.0	4.0	4.0
RS(% PTS)	-	-	-	-	-3.6	-0.8	-0.3	-0.9	-0.7	-0.5
RL(% PTS)	-	-	-	-	-1.0	-1.5	-0.9	-0.8	-0.8	-0.7
GDEF(B$)	-	-	-	-	-28.7	-52.7	-49.7	-48.4	-59.9	-76.8
PXGS(%)	-	-	-	-	0.4	1.2	1.7	1.8	2.1	2.4
PMGS(%)	-	-	-	-	1.6	2.4	2.1	2.3	2.5	2.8
EXCH(%) *	-	-	-	-	-2.0	-2.6	-2.1	-2.4	-2.6	-2.7
CAB(B$)	-	-	-	-	-9.3	-8.4	1.8	-0.1	-3.4	-3.6
NON-US OECD										
GNPV(%) **	-	-	-	-	-0.1	-0.0	-0.1	-0.2	-0.1	-0.1
GNP(%) **	-	-	-	-	0.1	0.3	0.0	-0.0	0.1	0.1
PGNP(%)	-	-	-	-	-0.2	-0.3	-0.2	-0.2	-0.2	-0.2
CPI(%)	-	-	-	-	-0.1	-0.1	-0.0	-0.0	-0.0	0.0
WAGES(%)	-	-	-	-	-0.0	-0.0	-0.0	0.0	0.0	0.1
UN(% PTS)	-	-	-	-	-0.0	-0.1	-0.1	-0.0	-0.0	-0.0
C(%) **	-	-	-	-	-	-	-	-	-	-
IFP(%) **	-	-	-	-	-	-	-	-	-	-
RS(% PTS)	-	-	-	-	-0.2	-0.1	-0.2	-0.3	-0.3	-0.2
RL(% PTS)	-	-	-	-	-0.0	-0.1	-0.1	-0.2	-0.2	-0.2
GDEF (B.US$) **	-	-	-	-	1.6	-1.6	-2.5	-0.1	-1.1	-4.0
PXGS(%)	-	-	-	-	-0.2	-0.2	0.0	0.0	0.0	0.1
PMGS(%)	-	-	-	-	-0.6	-0.4	-0.1	-0.1	-0.1	0.0
EXCH(%) ***	-	-	-	-	2.2	2.9	2.3	2.6	2.8	2.9
CAB(B.US$) **	-	-	-	-	4.7	3.1	-1.9	-2.0	-1.0	-1.1

* Exchange rate : (Weighted average of foreign currencies)/U.S. $.
** Local currency units translated into U.S. $ at baseline exchange rates.
*** Exchange rate : U.S. $/(weighted average of non-US OECD currencies).

Model: OECD
Simulation D: U.S. Monetary Expansion with Foreign Monetary Aggregates Unchanged from Baseline
(Deviation of Shock Path from Baseline Path)

	1985 Q1	1985 Q2	1985 Q3	1985 Q4	1985	1986	1987	1988	1989	1990
JAPAN										
GNP(%)	-	-	-	-	0.2	0.2	-0.1	-0.2	-0.1	-0.1
CPI(%)	-	-	-	-	-0.1	-0.2	-0.1	-0.2	-0.3	-0.3
RS(% PTS)	-	-	-	-	0.1	0.1	-0.1	-0.3	-0.3	-0.3
GDEF(%GNPV) *	-	-	-	-	-0.0	-0.1	-0.0	0.0	0.0	0.0
EXCH(%) **	-	-	-	-	2.2	3.1	2.6	2.9	3.2	3.5
CAB(B.US$) ***	-	-	-	-	1.4	0.8	-1.3	-1.4	-1.1	-1.5
GERMANY										
GNP(%)	-	-	-	-	0.1	0.3	-0.0	-0.1	0.0	0.1
CPI(%)	-	-	-	-	-0.0	-0.2	-0.3	-0.4	-0.5	-0.5
RS(% PTS)	-	-	-	-	0.4	0.1	-0.4	-0.7	-0.5	-0.3
GDEF(%GNPV) *	-	-	-	-	-0.0	-0.1	-0.1	-0.0	-0.0	-0.1
EXCH(%) **	-	-	-	-	2.3	3.1	2.6	2.9	3.2	3.6
CAB(B.US$) ***	-	-	-	-	1.3	1.2	-0.4	-0.6	-0.1	0.0
FRANCE										
GNP(%)	-	-	-	-	0.1	0.2	0.0	-0.1	-0.0	-0.0
CPI(%)	-	-	-	-	-0.1	-0.2	-0.1	-0.1	-0.1	-0.1
GDEF(%GNPV) *	-	-	-	-	-0.0	-0.1	-0.1	-0.0	-0.0	-0.0
EXCH(%) **	-	-	-	-	2.2	2.7	2.2	2.6	2.8	2.9
CAB(B.US$) ***	-	-	-	-	0.4	0.1	-0.1	-0.1	-0.2	-0.2
UNITED KINGDOM										
GNP(%)	-	-	-	-	0.1	0.2	-0.0	-0.0	0.0	0.1
CPI(%)	-	-	-	-	-0.2	-0.3	-0.2	-0.2	-0.2	-0.1
GDEF(%GNPV) *	-	-	-	-	-0.0	-0.1	-0.1	-0.0	-0.0	-0.1
EXCH(%) **	-	-	-	-	2.3	3.0	2.2	2.5	2.7	2.8
CAB(B.US$) ***	-	-	-	-	0.5	0.1	-0.3	-0.0	0.1	0.1
ITALY										
GNP(%)	-	-	-	-	0.0	0.1	0.1	0.0	0.0	0.1
CPI(%)	-	-	-	-	-0.0	-0.2	-0.2	-0.2	-0.2	-0.2
GDEF(%GNPV) *	-	-	-	-	-0.0	-0.0	-0.0	-0.0	-0.0	-0.1
EXCH(%) **	-	-	-	-	2.2	2.8	2.3	2.6	2.8	2.8
CAB(B.US$) ***	-	-	-	-	0.3	0.0	-0.2	-0.1	-0.1	-0.2
CANADA										
GNP(%)	-	-	-	-	0.3	0.3	-0.3	-0.1	0.1	0.0
CPI(%)	-	-	-	-	-0.3	-0.5	-0.3	-0.3	-0.4	-0.3
GDEF(%GNPV) *	-	-	-	-	-0.1	-0.3	-0.1	-0.0	-0.1	-0.2
EXCH(%) **	-	-	-	-	2.2	2.8	2.2	2.6	2.8	2.9
CAB(B.US$) ***	-	-	-	-	0.7	0.1	-0.0	0.0	-0.0	0.1
REST OF WORLD										
CAB(B.US$) ***	-	-	-	-	2.8	1.1	-2.8	-1.7	-0.2	-0.3

* Government deficit as a percentage of baseline nominal GNP.
** Exchange rate : Bilateral rate against U.S. $ ($/local currency).
*** Local currency units translated into U.S. $ at baseline exchange rates.

Model: OECD
Simulation E: U.S. Monetary Expansion with Foreign Short-Term Interest Rates Unchanged from Baseline
(Deviation of Shock Path from Baseline Path)

	1985 Q1	1985 Q2	1985 Q3	1985 Q4	1985	1986	1987	1988	1989	1990
UNITED STATES										
GNPV(%)	-	-	-	-	1.0	2.0	1.4	1.4	1.9	2.2
GNP(%)	-	-	-	-	1.0	1.6	0.4	0.1	0.4	0.4
PGNP(%)	-	-	-	-	-0.0	0.4	1.0	1.3	1.5	1.8
CPI(%)	-	-	-	-	0.1	0.7	1.2	1.4	1.6	1.9
WAGES(%)	-	-	-	-	0.3	1.2	1.9	2.3	2.7	3.0
UN(% PTS)	-	-	-	-	-0.6	-1.1	-0.4	-0.1	-0.1	-0.0
GNP(B.72$)	-	-	-	-	17.5	27.5	6.5	2.6	8.0	8.4
G(B.72$)	-	-	-	-	0.0	0.0	0.0	0.0	0.0	0.0
C(B.72$)	-	-	-	-	2.7	7.4	4.0	2.3	4.5	5.3
IFP(B.72$)	-	-	-	-	7.3	11.0	1.3	0.4	3.4	3.6
II(B.72$)	-	-	-	-	8.5	9.3	-1.1	-2.2	-1.1	-1.9
XGS(B.72$)	-	-	-	-	0.8	2.2	1.6	0.8	0.6	0.6
MGS(B.72$)	-	-	-	-	1.8	2.1	-0.9	-1.3	-0.8	-0.9
M1(%)	-	-	-	-	2.0	4.0	4.0	4.0	4.0	4.0
RS(% PTS)	-	-	-	-	-3.6	-0.8	-0.3	-0.9	-0.7	-0.4
RL(% PTS)	-	-	-	-	-1.0	-1.5	-0.9	-0.8	-0.8	-0.7
GDEF(B$)	-	-	-	-	-28.7	-52.6	-49.4	-47.9	-58.8	-75.3
PXGS(%)	-	-	-	-	0.4	1.3	1.7	1.9	2.2	2.6
PMGS(%)	-	-	-	-	1.6	2.5	2.2	2.6	2.9	3.2
EXCH(%) *	-	-	-	-	-2.1	-2.8	-2.4	-2.8	-3.2	-3.4
CAB(B$)	-	-	-	-	-9.4	-8.5	1.7	-0.6	-3.8	-3.7
NON-US OECD										
GNPV(%) **	-	-	-	-	-0.1	-0.2	-0.3	-0.5	-0.6	-0.7
GNP(%) **	-	-	-	-	0.1	0.2	-0.1	-0.2	-0.2	-0.2
PGNP(%)	-	-	-	-	-0.2	-0.4	-0.3	-0.3	-0.4	-0.5
CPI(%)	-	-	-	-	-0.1	-0.2	-0.1	-0.1	-0.2	-0.2
WAGES(%)	-	-	-	-	-0.0	-0.1	-0.0	-0.1	-0.1	-0.2
UN(% PTS)	-	-	-	-	-0.0	-0.1	-0.0	0.0	0.1	0.1
C(%) **	-	-	-	-	-	-	-	-	-	-
IFP(%) **	-	-	-	-	-	-	-	-	-	-
RS(% PTS)	-	-	-	-	0.0	0.0	0.0	0.0	0.0	0.0
RL(% PTS)	-	-	-	-	0.0	-0.0	0.0	0.0	0.0	0.0
GDEF (B.US$) **	-	-	-	-	1.5	-1.0	-0.4	4.3	5.6	5.3
PXGS(%)	-	-	-	-	-0.3	-0.3	-0.1	-0.2	-0.2	-0.2
PMGS(%)	-	-	-	-	-0.6	-0.5	-0.2	-0.3	-0.3	-0.2
EXCH(%) ***	-	-	-	-	2.3	3.1	2.6	3.1	3.5	3.8
CAB(B.US$) **	-	-	-	-	4.8	3.2	-1.9	-2.0	-1.7	-2.8

* Exchange rate : (Weighted average of foreign currencies)/U.S. $.
** Local currency units translated into U.S. $ at baseline exchange rates.
*** Exchange rate : U.S. $/(weighted average of non-US OECD currencies).

Model: OECD
Simulation E: U.S. Monetary Expansion with Foreign Short-Term Interest Rates Unchanged from Baseline
(Deviation of Shock Path from Baseline Path)

	1985									
	Q1	Q2	Q3	Q4	1985	1986	1987	1988	1989	1990
JAPAN										
GNP(%)	-	-	-	-	0.2	0.3	-0.1	-0.3	-0.3	-0.3
CPI(%)	-	-	-	-	-0.1	-0.1	-0.1	-0.1	-0.2	-0.3
RS(% PTS)	-	-	-	-	0.0	0.0	0.0	0.0	0.0	0.0
GDEF(%GNPV) *	-	-	-	-	-0.0	-0.1	-0.1	0.0	0.1	0.1
EXCH(%) **	-	-	-	-	2.2	3.0	2.5	3.0	3.4	3.9
CAB(B.US$) ***	-	-	-	-	1.3	0.8	-1.1	-1.1	-1.0	-1.5
GERMANY										
GNP(%)	-	-	-	-	0.2	0.3	0.0	-0.2	-0.2	-0.3
CPI(%)	-	-	-	-	-0.0	-0.1	-0.1	-0.2	-0.4	-0.5
RS(% PTS)	-	-	-	-	0.0	0.0	0.0	0.0	0.0	0.0
GDEF(%GNPV) *	-	-	-	-	-0.1	-0.2	-0.1	0.0	0.1	0.1
EXCH(%) **	-	-	-	-	2.1	2.8	2.5	3.1	3.6	4.1
CAB(B.US$) ***	-	-	-	-	1.0	0.9	-0.2	-0.2	0.0	-0.2
FRANCE										
GNP(%)	-	-	-	-	0.1	0.2	-0.0	-0.1	-0.1	-0.1
CPI(%)	-	-	-	-	-0.1	-0.2	-0.1	-0.0	-0.0	0.0
GDEF(%GNPV) *	-	-	-	-	-0.0	-0.1	-0.1	0.0	0.0	0.0
EXCH(%) **	-	-	-	-	2.2	2.8	2.3	2.6	2.9	3.0
CAB(B.US$) ***	-	-	-	-	0.4	0.2	-0.2	-0.2	-0.1	-0.2
UNITED KINGDOM										
GNP(%)	-	-	-	-	0.1	0.2	-0.0	-0.1	-0.0	-0.0
CPI(%)	-	-	-	-	-0.2	-0.1	-0.1	-0.1	-0.1	0.0
GDEF(%GNPV) *	-	-	-	-	-0.0	-0.1	-0.1	0.0	0.0	0.0
EXCH(%) **	-	-	-	-	2.3	2.9	2.3	2.6	2.9	3.0
CAB(B.US$) ***	-	-	-	-	0.4	0.1	-0.2	0.0	0.1	0.1
ITALY										
GNP(%)	-	-	-	-	0.0	0.1	0.1	0.0	0.0	0.0
CPI(%)	-	-	-	-	-0.0	-0.1	-0.2	-0.1	-0.0	0.1
GDEF(%GNPV) *	-	-	-	-	-0.0	-0.0	-0.0	-0.0	-0.0	-0.1
EXCH(%) **	-	-	-	-	2.2	2.8	2.2	2.6	2.8	2.8
CAB(B.US$) ***	-	-	-	-	0.3	0.0	-0.2	-0.2	-0.1	-0.2
CANADA										
GNP(%)	-	-	-	-	0.3	0.2	-0.3	-0.2	-0.0	-0.0
CPI(%)	-	-	-	-	-0.3	-0.5	-0.3	-0.3	-0.4	-0.3
GDEF(%GNPV) *	-	-	-	-	-0.1	-0.3	-0.1	0.1	-0.0	-0.1
EXCH(%) **	-	-	-	-	2.2	2.9	2.3	2.7	3.0	3.0
CAB(B.US$) ***	-	-	-	-	0.7	0.2	0.0	0.1	0.1	0.2
REST OF WORLD										
CAB(B.US$) ***	-	-	-	-	2.8	0.9	-3.1	-2.3	-0.9	-1.1

* Government deficit as a percentage of baseline nominal GNP.
** Exchange rate : Bilateral rate against U.S. $ ($/local currency).
*** Local currency units translated into U.S. $ at baseline exchange rates.

Model: OECD
Simulation F: Nonpolicy Exogenous Depreciation of the Dollar
(Deviation of Shock Path from Baseline Path)

	1985									
	Q1	Q2	Q3	Q4	1985	1986	1987	1988	1989	1990
UNITED STATES										
GNPV(%)	-	-	-	-	-0.1	-0.2	0.0	1.0	2.3	3.3
GNP(%)	-	-	-	-	0.0	-0.4	-0.8	-0.7	0.0	0.6
PGNP(%)	-	-	-	-	-0.2	0.2	0.8	1.7	2.2	2.7
CPI(%)	-	-	-	-	0.3	1.2	2.1	2.9	3.2	3.6
WAGES(%)	-	-	-	-	0.2	0.7	1.4	2.2	3.1	4.1
UN(% PTS)	-	-	-	-	-0.2	-0.2	-0.2	-0.2	-0.5	-0.7
GNP(B.72$)	-	-	-	-	0.8	-7.1	-13.6	-13.4	0.4	11.6
G(B.72$)	-	-	-	-	0.0	0.0	0.0	0.0	0.0	0.0
C(B.72$)	-	-	-	-	-2.0	-8.7	-15.5	-17.8	-13.7	-9.5
IFP(B.72$)	-	-	-	-	0.2	-4.2	-9.6	-12.7	-9.3	-5.9
II(B.72$)	-	-	-	-	-0.6	-8.7	-18.1	-24.4	-21.4	-17.8
XGS(B.72$)	-	-	-	-	1.3	5.1	10.5	14.9	16.2	15.7
MGS(B.72$)	-	-	-	-	-1.9	-9.4	-19.1	-26.5	-28.7	-29.1
M1(%)	-	-	-	-	0.0	0.0	0.0	0.0	0.0	0.0
RS(% PTS)	-	-	-	-	-0.3	0.8	1.5	2.4	1.9	2.4
RL(% PTS)	-	-	-	-	-0.1	0.2	0.6	1.3	1.6	1.9
GDEF(B$)	-	-	-	-	-2.4	11.8	35.0	60.1	61.8	65.0
PXGS(%)	-	-	-	-	1.3	4.2	7.5	9.5	9.8	9.8
PMGS(%)	-	-	-	-	5.9	14.6	23.7	25.9	24.7	23.4
EXCH(%) *	-	-	-	-	-6.7	-14.8	-22.1	-23.9	-23.9	-23.9
CAB(B$)	-	-	-	-	-14.6	-16.2	-2.8	32.7	49.7	54.4
NON-US OECD										
GNPV(%) **	-	-	-	-	-0.2	-1.4	-3.3	-5.3	-6.7	-7.4
GNP(%) **	-	-	-	-	-0.1	-0.5	-1.2	-1.8	-1.8	-1.2
PGNP(%)	-	-	-	-	-0.1	-0.9	-2.1	-3.6	-5.0	-6.2
CPI(%)	-	-	-	-	-0.4	-1.5	-3.0	-4.7	-6.1	-7.4
WAGES(%)	-	-	-	-	-0.3	-1.1	-2.6	-4.4	-6.0	-7.3
UN(% PTS)	-	-	-	-	0.0	0.1	0.2	0.3	0.3	0.1
C(%) **	-	-	-	-	-	-	-	-	-	-
IFP(%) **	-	-	-	-	-	-	-	-	-	-
RS(% PTS)	-	-	-	-	-0.0	-0.9	-2.3	-4.1	-5.3	-5.8
RL(% PTS)	-	-	-	-	-0.0	-0.3	-0.9	-1.8	-2.6	-3.3
GDEF (B.US$) **	-	-	-	-	11.3	26.0	47.1	58.2	58.4	39.1
PXGS(%)	-	-	-	-	-1.2	-2.9	-5.0	-6.4	-7.7	-9.1
PMGS(%)	-	-	-	-	-2.4	-5.2	-8.0	-9.1	-10.0	-11.1
EXCH(%) ***	-	-	-	-	9.1	21.9	36.3	40.1	40.1	40.1
CAB(B.US$) **	-	-	-	-	7.1	-2.5	-23.7	-56.2	-74.9	-87.6

* Exchange rate : (Weighted average of foreign currencies)/U.S. $.
** Local currency units translated into U.S. $ at baseline exchange rates.
*** Exchange rate : U.S. $/(weighted average of non-US OECD currencies).

Model: OECD
Simulation F: Nonpolicy Exogenous Depreciation of the Dollar
(Deviation of Shock Path from Baseline Path)

	1985									
	Q1	Q2	Q3	Q4	1985	1986	1987	1988	1989	1990
JAPAN										
GNP(%)	-	-	-	-	-0.2	-0.9	-2.0	-2.9	-2.9	-2.4
CPI(%)	-	-	-	-	-0.3	-1.1	-2.3	-3.6	-4.9	-6.2
RS(% PTS)	-	-	-	-	-0.3	-1.4	-3.2	-5.0	-6.2	-6.9
GDEF(%GNPV) *	-	-	-	-	-0.0	0.0	0.2	0.5	0.8	0.9
EXCH(%) **	-	-	-	-	8.5	20.5	33.9	37.4	37.4	37.4
CAB(B.US$) ***	-	-	-	-	0.4	-5.0	-14.1	-25.3	-31.6	-35.4
GERMANY										
GNP(%)	-	-	-	-	0.0	-0.1	-0.7	-1.1	-1.0	-0.0
CPI(%)	-	-	-	-	-0.2	-1.1	-2.7	-4.8	-6.7	-8.3
RS(% PTS)	-	-	-	-	0.3	-1.5	-4.5	-8.4	-10.1	-9.9
GDEF(%GNPV) *	-	-	-	-	0.0	-0.1	-0.1	-0.3	-0.6	-1.3
EXCH(%) **	-	-	-	-	8.6	20.6	34.0	37.5	37.5	37.5
CAB(B.US$) ***	-	-	-	-	2.3	1.8	-1.6	-8.4	-12.8	-14.8
FRANCE										
GNP(%)	-	-	-	-	0.0	-0.1	-0.5	-0.9	-1.0	-0.7
CPI(%)	-	-	-	-	-0.3	-1.3	-2.5	-3.8	-4.6	-5.3
GDEF(%GNPV) *	-	-	-	-	-0.0	-0.2	-0.4	-0.5	-0.5	-0.7
EXCH(%) **	-	-	-	-	8.6	20.5	33.9	37.4	37.4	37.4
CAB(B.US$) ***	-	-	-	-	0.5	-1.0	-3.6	-7.1	-8.9	-9.9
UNITED KINGDOM										
GNP(%)	-	-	-	-	0.1	0.1	-0.1	-0.3	-0.3	0.3
CPI(%)	-	-	-	-	-0.7	-1.9	-3.5	-5.0	-6.5	-7.9
GDEF(%GNPV) *	-	-	-	-	-0.0	-0.1	-0.2	-0.2	-0.2	-0.2
EXCH(%) **	-	-	-	-	8.6	20.4	33.8	37.3	37.3	37.3
CAB(B.US$) ***	-	-	-	-	0.6	-0.4	-2.4	-5.6	-7.5	-8.9
ITALY										
GNP(%)	-	-	-	-	-0.1	-0.5	-0.7	-0.7	-0.0	0.9
CPI(%)	-	-	-	-	-0.2	-1.0	-2.7	-4.9	-7.2	-9.0
GDEF(%GNPV) *	-	-	-	-	0.0	0.1	0.2	0.1	-0.0	-0.2
EXCH(%) **	-	-	-	-	8.8	21.0	34.4	38.0	38.0	38.0
CAB(B.US$) ***	-	-	-	-	0.7	0.4	-0.6	-2.4	-3.0	-3.9
CANADA										
GNP(%)	-	-	-	-	-0.1	-0.7	-1.4	-1.9	-2.0	-2.0
CPI(%)	-	-	-	-	-0.2	-0.3	-0.4	-0.4	-0.6	-1.0
GDEF(%GNPV) *	-	-	-	-	0.0	0.1	0.3	0.4	0.5	0.4
EXCH(%) **	-	-	-	-	4.1	9.6	15.4	16.9	16.9	16.9
CAB(B.US$) ***	-	-	-	-	1.2	1.4	1.7	0.9	1.1	1.0
REST OF WORLD										
CAB(B.US$) ***	-	-	-	-	0.3	-6.3	-14.4	-20.9	-17.2	-11.9

* Government deficit as a percentage of baseline nominal GNP.
** Exchange rate : Bilateral rate against U.S. $ ($/local currency).
*** Local currency units translated into U.S. $ at baseline exchange rates.

Model: OECD
Simulation G: Increase in Government Purchases in Non-U.S. OECD Countries with U.S. Policies Unchanged from Baseline
(Deviation of Shock Path from Baseline Path)

	1985									
	Q1	Q2	Q3	Q4	1985	1986	1987	1988	1989	1990
UNITED STATES										
GNPV(%)	-	-	-	-	0.2	0.2	0.2	0.3	0.4	0.4
GNP(%)	-	-	-	-	0.1	0.1	0.0	0.0	-0.0	-0.1
PGNP(%)	-	-	-	-	0.0	0.1	0.2	0.3	0.4	0.5
CPI(%)	-	-	-	-	0.1	0.2	0.3	0.4	0.5	0.6
WAGES(%)	-	-	-	-	0.1	0.2	0.3	0.5	0.6	0.7
UN(% PTS)	-	-	-	-	-0.1	-0.1	-0.1	-0.1	-0.1	-0.0
GNP(B.72$)	-	-	-	-	2.5	1.8	0.6	0.5	-0.3	-1.9
G(B.72$)	-	-	-	-	0.0	0.0	0.0	0.0	0.0	0.0
C(B.72$)	-	-	-	-	0.3	-0.1	-0.8	-1.0	-1.2	-1.7
IFP(B.72$)	-	-	-	-	0.2	-0.4	-0.9	-0.9	-1.2	-1.8
II(B.72$)	-	-	-	-	0.4	-0.7	-1.8	-2.4	-2.9	-3.3
XGS(B.72$)	-	-	-	-	1.9	2.7	3.0	3.0	2.7	2.1
MGS(B.72$)	-	-	-	-	0.3	-0.3	-1.1	-1.7	-2.3	-2.9
M1(%)	-	-	-	-	0.0	0.0	0.0	0.0	0.0	0.0
RS(% PTS)	-	-	-	-	0.1	0.3	0.3	0.3	0.4	0.4
RL(% PTS)	-	-	-	-	0.0	0.1	0.2	0.2	0.3	0.3
GDEF(B$)	-	-	-	-	-2.0	-2.2	-0.7	1.3	4.0	8.4
PXGS(%)	-	-	-	-	0.2	0.5	0.6	0.7	0.8	1.0
PMGS(%)	-	-	-	-	0.6	1.2	1.6	1.9	2.1	2.2
EXCH(%) *	-	-	-	-	-0.5	-0.6	-0.3	0.1	0.7	1.3
CAB(B$)	-	-	-	-	2.1	3.3	4.4	5.2	5.4	5.0
NON-US OECD										
GNPV(%) **	-	-	-	-	1.5	2.2	2.6	3.1	3.4	3.7
GNP(%) **	-	-	-	-	1.4	1.5	1.3	1.0	0.7	0.2
PGNP(%)	-	-	-	-	0.1	0.7	1.3	2.0	2.8	3.5
CPI(%)	-	-	-	-	0.2	0.7	1.4	2.1	2.9	3.6
WAGES(%)	-	-	-	-	0.3	1.1	1.9	2.8	3.6	4.2
UN(% PTS)	-	-	-	-	-0.3	-0.5	-0.6	-0.5	-0.4	-0.2
C(%) **	-	-	-	-	-	-	-	-	-	-
IFP(%) **	-	-	-	-	-	-	-	-	-	-
RS(% PTS)	-	-	-	-	1.4	1.9	2.0	2.1	2.3	2.4
RL(% PTS)	-	-	-	-	0.5	0.8	1.0	1.3	1.5	1.7
GDEF (B.US$) **	-	-	-	-	41.5	37.7	44.1	59.8	80.0	105.5
PXGS(%)	-	-	-	-	0.0	0.5	1.3	2.1	3.0	3.8
PMGS(%)	-	-	-	-	-0.0	0.4	1.0	1.7	2.4	3.2
EXCH(%) ***	-	-	-	-	0.7	0.9	0.6	0.1	-0.5	-1.1
CAB(B.US$) **	-	-	-	-	-7.3	-6.9	-6.6	-6.2	-4.8	-1.7

* Exchange rate : (Weighted average of foreign currencies)/U.S. $.
** Local currency units translated into U.S. $ at baseline exchange rates.
*** Exchange rate : U.S. $/(weighted average of non-US OECD currencies).

Model: OECD
Simulation G: Increase in Government Purchases in Non-U.S. OECD Countries with U.S. Policies Unchanged from Baseline
(Deviation of Shock Path from Baseline Path)

	1985									
	Q1	Q2	Q3	Q4	1985	1986	1987	1988	1989	1990
JAPAN										
GNP(%)	-	-	-	-	1.4	1.4	1.0	0.8	0.5	0.1
CPI(%)	-	-	-	-	0.1	0.6	1.0	1.5	2.0	2.6
RS(% PTS)	-	-	-	-	1.4	1.9	2.0	2.1	2.2	2.3
GDEF(%GNPV) *	-	-	-	-	1.0	1.0	1.1	1.3	1.4	1.6
EXCH(%) **	-	-	-	-	0.7	1.1	1.0	0.6	0.1	-0.5
CAB(B.US$) ***	-	-	-	-	-1.2	-1.0	-0.7	-0.3	-0.1	-0.1
GERMANY										
GNP(%)	-	-	-	-	1.5	1.6	1.2	0.6	0.1	-0.4
CPI(%)	-	-	-	-	0.1	0.4	0.5	0.7	1.0	1.5
RS(% PTS)	-	-	-	-	3.3	3.8	2.8	2.0	1.7	1.5
GDEF(%GNPV) *	-	-	-	-	0.8	0.6	0.7	1.1	1.6	2.1
EXCH(%) **	-	-	-	-	1.7	2.9	3.0	2.5	1.8	1.0
CAB(B.US$) ***	-	-	-	-	1.2	1.6	0.2	-0.9	-0.7	-0.3
FRANCE										
GNP(%)	-	-	-	-	1.5	1.7	1.4	1.0	0.6	-0.0
CPI(%)	-	-	-	-	0.0	0.5	1.0	1.4	2.0	2.6
GDEF(%GNPV) *	-	-	-	-	1.1	1.0	1.2	1.7	2.3	3.1
EXCH(%) **	-	-	-	-	0.4	0.7	0.7	0.4	0.1	-0.4
CAB(B.US$) ***	-	-	-	-	-1.0	-0.9	-0.4	-0.2	-0.3	-0.6
UNITED KINGDOM										
GNP(%)	-	-	-	-	1.0	1.1	1.0	0.7	0.3	-0.3
CPI(%)	-	-	-	-	0.0	0.7	1.5	2.4	3.1	3.6
GDEF(%GNPV) *	-	-	-	-	0.9	0.8	1.0	1.4	1.9	2.6
EXCH(%) **	-	-	-	-	0.7	0.8	0.5	0.3	0.2	0.2
CAB(B.US$) ***	-	-	-	-	-1.0	-1.2	-0.6	0.1	0.6	0.9
ITALY										
GNP(%)	-	-	-	-	1.1	1.3	1.2	0.7	0.1	-0.5
CPI(%)	-	-	-	-	0.1	0.7	1.9	3.4	5.0	6.3
GDEF(%GNPV) *	-	-	-	-	1.1	1.1	1.1	1.5	1.9	2.4
EXCH(%) **	-	-	-	-	0.1	-0.1	-0.7	-1.5	-2.4	-3.2
CAB(B.US$) ***	-	-	-	-	-1.0	-1.3	-1.2	-0.9	-0.5	0.1
CANADA										
GNP(%)	-	-	-	-	1.1	1.0	0.9	0.9	0.8	0.6
CPI(%)	-	-	-	-	0.2	0.8	1.5	2.1	2.8	3.6
GDEF(%GNPV) *	-	-	-	-	1.1	1.3	1.7	2.2	2.8	3.7
EXCH(%) **	-	-	-	-	-0.0	-0.4	-0.9	-1.3	-1.7	-2.2
CAB(B.US$) ***	-	-	-	-	-0.9	-0.8	-0.7	-0.7	-0.8	-0.8
REST OF WORLD										
CAB(B.US$) ***	-	-	-	-	5.4	2.5	0.4	-0.4	-1.2	-2.4

* Government deficit as a percentage of baseline nominal GNP.
** Exchange rate : Bilateral rate against U.S. $ ($/local currency).
*** Local currency units translated into U.S. $ at baseline exchange rates.

Model: OECD
Simulation H: Monetary Expansion in Non-U.S. OECD Countries
with U.S. Policies Unchanged from Baseline
(Deviation of Shock Path from Baseline Path)

	1985 Q1	1985 Q2	1985 Q3	1985 Q4	1985	1986	1987	1988	1989	1990
UNITED STATES										
GNPV(%)	-	-	-	-	0.1	0.1	0.0	-0.0	-0.1	-0.1
GNP(%)	-	-	-	-	0.0	0.1	0.1	0.0	-0.0	-0.0
PGNP(%)	-	-	-	-	0.0	-0.0	-0.1	-0.1	-0.1	-0.1
CPI(%)	-	-	-	-	-0.0	-0.1	-0.1	-0.1	-0.1	-0.1
WAGES(%)	-	-	-	-	-0.0	-0.0	-0.1	-0.1	-0.1	-0.1
UN(% PTS)	-	-	-	-	-0.0	-0.0	-0.0	0.0	0.0	0.0
GNP(B.72$)	-	-	-	-	0.8	2.5	2.0	0.2	-0.2	-0.1
G(B.72$)	-	-	-	-	0.0	0.0	0.0	0.0	0.0	0.0
C(B.72$)	-	-	-	-	0.5	1.7	1.5	0.8	0.5	0.5
IFP(B.72$)	-	-	-	-	0.0	0.8	1.1	0.4	0.2	0.3
II(B.72$)	-	-	-	-	0.3	1.6	1.7	0.9	0.6	0.4
XGS(B.72$)	-	-	-	-	0.5	0.1	-0.2	-0.1	0.2	0.4
MGS(B.72$)	-	-	-	-	0.5	1.7	2.2	1.9	1.7	1.6
M1(%)	-	-	-	-	0.0	0.0	0.0	0.0	0.0	0.0
RS(% PTS)	-	-	-	-	0.1	-0.2	-0.0	-0.0	-0.0	-0.0
RL(% PTS)	-	-	-	-	0.0	-0.0	-0.0	-0.0	-0.0	-0.0
GDEF(B$)	-	-	-	-	-0.1	-3.9	-5.6	-3.9	-3.3	-3.9
PXGS(%)	-	-	-	-	-0.2	-0.5	-0.5	-0.5	-0.4	-0.3
PMGS(%)	-	-	-	-	-1.0	-1.6	-1.3	-1.1	-0.9	-0.8
EXCH(%) *	-	-	-	-	1.2	2.1	2.2	2.3	2.5	2.7
CAB(B$)	-	-	-	-	4.0	2.3	-1.4	-1.4	-0.7	-0.3
NON-US OECD										
GNPV(%) **	-	-	-	-	0.6	1.2	1.5	1.7	2.0	2.2
GNP(%) **	-	-	-	-	0.5	0.8	0.9	0.8	0.8	0.7
PGNP(%)	-	-	-	-	0.1	0.3	0.6	0.9	1.2	1.5
CPI(%)	-	-	-	-	0.0	0.3	0.5	0.8	1.1	1.4
WAGES(%)	-	-	-	-	0.1	0.4	0.8	1.2	1.6	2.0
UN(% PTS)	-	-	-	-	-0.1	-0.3	-0.4	-0.4	-0.4	-0.4
C(%) **	-	-	-	-	-	-	-	-	-	-
IFP(%) **	-	-	-	-	-	-	-	-	-	-
RS(% PTS)	-	-	-	-	-2.2	-1.3	-0.5	-0.4	-0.3	-0.2
RL(% PTS)	-	-	-	-	-0.7	-0.7	-0.6	-0.5	-0.5	-0.4
GDEF (B.US$) **	-	-	-	-	-13.3	-26.7	-35.8	-43.9	-51.6	-58.2
PXGS(%)	-	-	-	-	0.1	0.3	0.6	0.9	1.2	1.6
PMGS(%)	-	-	-	-	0.4	0.6	0.8	1.0	1.4	1.8
EXCH(%) ***	-	-	-	-	-1.3	-2.1	-2.0	-2.0	-2.2	-2.4
CAB(B.US$) **	-	-	-	-	-4.3	-1.6	2.5	3.3	3.6	4.6

* Exchange rate : (Weighted average of foreign currencies)/U.S. $.
** Local currency units translated into U.S. $ at baseline exchange rates.
*** Exchange rate : U.S. $/(weighted average of non-US OECD currencies).

Model: OECD
Simulation H: Monetary Expansion in Non-U.S. OECD Countries
with U.S. Policies Unchanged from Baseline
(Deviation of Shock Path from Baseline Path)

	1985 Q1	1985 Q2	1985 Q3	1985 Q4	1985	1986	1987	1988	1989	1990
JAPAN										
GNP(%)	-	-	-	-	0.9	1.6	1.5	1.3	1.2	1.0
CPI(%)	-	-	-	-	0.1	0.4	0.8	1.2	1.7	2.1
RS(% PTS)	-	-	-	-	-2.3	-1.4	-0.5	-0.4	-0.2	-0.0
GDEF(%GNPV) *	-	-	-	-	-0.2	-0.6	-0.8	-0.9	-0.9	-1.0
EXCH(%) **	-	-	-	-	-1.4	-2.4	-2.4	-2.7	-3.1	-3.6
CAB(B.US$) ***	-	-	-	-	-1.2	-0.7	0.8	1.6	2.6	3.9
GERMANY										
GNP(%)	-	-	-	-	0.7	1.1	1.3	1.3	1.1	1.0
CPI(%)	-	-	-	-	0.1	0.8	1.3	1.4	1.4	1.5
RS(% PTS)	-	-	-	-	-4.6	-1.6	0.1	0.1	-0.2	-0.2
GDEF(%GNPV) *	-	-	-	-	-0.5	-0.9	-1.1	-1.4	-1.6	-1.6
EXCH(%) **	-	-	-	-	-2.5	-3.6	-2.9	-2.5	-2.5	-2.6
CAB(B.US$) ***	-	-	-	-	-2.0	-0.5	1.8	1.9	1.1	1.1
FRANCE										
GNP(%)	-	-	-	-	0.7	1.1	1.2	1.2	1.2	1.1
CPI(%)	-	-	-	-	0.1	0.5	0.9	1.1	1.2	1.3
GDEF(%GNPV) *	-	-	-	-	-0.6	-0.9	-1.1	-1.3	-1.5	-1.7
EXCH(%) **	-	-	-	-	-1.8	-2.9	-2.7	-2.6	-2.6	-2.7
CAB(B.US$) ***	-	-	-	-	-0.9	-0.5	-0.0	-0.0	-0.0	-0.1
UNITED KINGDOM										
GNP(%)	-	-	-	-	0.2	0.3	0.3	0.3	0.3	0.2
CPI(%)	-	-	-	-	-0.0	0.0	0.2	0.4	0.6	0.9
GDEF(%GNPV) *	-	-	-	-	-0.2	-0.4	-0.5	-0.6	-0.6	-0.8
EXCH(%) **	-	-	-	-	-0.8	-1.2	-1.2	-1.3	-1.5	-1.7
CAB(B.US$) ***	-	-	-	-	-0.1	-0.2	-0.1	0.1	0.4	0.6
ITALY										
GNP(%)	-	-	-	-	0.2	0.4	0.7	0.7	0.6	0.4
CPI(%)	-	-	-	-	-0.0	-0.1	0.1	0.6	1.3	2.2
GDEF(%GNPV) *	-	-	-	-	-0.1	-0.4	-0.7	-0.9	-1.1	-1.1
EXCH(%) **	-	-	-	-	-0.7	-1.3	-1.6	-1.9	-2.3	-2.7
CAB(B.US$) ***	-	-	-	-	0.0	-0.4	-0.6	-0.7	-0.6	-0.4
CANADA										
GNP(%)	-	-	-	-	0.7	0.6	0.7	0.8	0.9	0.9
CPI(%)	-	-	-	-	0.2	0.9	1.6	2.2	2.9	3.6
GDEF(%GNPV) *	-	-	-	-	-0.7	-1.0	-1.1	-1.4	-1.7	-1.9
EXCH(%) **	-	-	-	-	-1.3	-2.6	-3.1	-3.6	-4.1	-4.5
CAB(B.US$) ***	-	-	-	-	-1.2	-0.2	0.3	0.2	0.2	0.2
REST OF WORLD										
CAB(B.US$) ***	-	-	-	-	1.4	2.5	1.8	1.3	1.1	0.8

* Government deficit as a percentage of baseline nominal GNP.
** Exchange rate : Bilateral rate against U.S. $ ($/local currency).
*** Local currency units translated into U.S. $ at baseline exchange rates.

TAYLOR Multicountry Model

See part 1 of this voume for design and detailed description of the simulations. See part 4 for bibliographical references.

Figures were not available for the consumer price index for any of the countries or regions. Data shown on the lines for CPI pertain to GNP deflators.

Model: TAYLOR
Simulation A: Baseline Path

	1985	1986	1987	1988	1989	1990
UNITED STATES						
GNPV(B.$)	3919.0	4176.0	4451.8	4745.8	5059.1	5392.8
GNP(B.72$)	1691.7	1742.1	1794.4	1848.2	1903.7	1960.7
PGNP(72=100)	231.7	239.7	248.1	256.8	265.7	275.0
CPI(72=100)	-	-	-	-	-	-
WAGES(72=100)	249.6	258.2	267.3	276.6	286.3	296.3
UN(%)	-	-	-	-	-	-
G(B.72$)	317.7	330.6	343.8	357.5	371.8	386.7
C(B.72$)	1095.8	1131.1	1165.0	1200.0	1236.0	1273.0
IFP(B.72$)	279.3	288.9	298.3	308.2	318.7	329.8
II(B.72$)	-	-	-	-	-	-
XGS(B.72$)	152.3	160.2	168.2	176.6	185.4	194.7
MGS(B.72$)	169.3	181.4	193.2	205.7	219.1	233.3
M1(B.$)	582.2	619.7	660.0	702.9	748.6	797.2
RS(%)	7.8	7.7	7.7	7.7	7.7	7.7
RL(%)	12.3	12.3	12.3	12.3	12.3	12.3
GDEF(B.$)	-	-	-	-	-	-
PXGS(72=100)	255.7	264.6	273.9	283.4	293.4	303.6
PMGS(72=100)	270.2	279.5	289.3	299.4	309.9	320.7
EXCH(72=100) *	135.3	135.3	135.3	135.3	135.3	135.3
CAB(B.$)	-	-	-	-	-	-
NON-US OECD						
GNPV(B.$) **	615.0	658.0	703.1	751.3	802.8	857.6
GNP(B.72$) **	224.8	231.8	238.9	246.1	253.6	261.2
PGNP(72=100)	273.6	283.8	294.3	305.2	316.6	328.3
CPI(72=100)	273.6	283.8	294.3	305.2	316.6	328.3
WAGES(72=100)	391.7	406.4	421.5	437.1	453.3	470.0
UN(%)	-	-	-	-	-	-
C(B.72$) **	125.7	129.0	132.5	136.1	139.8	143.6
IFP(B.72$) **	45.4	47.6	49.8	52.1	54.5	57.1
RS(%)	8.2	8.2	8.2	8.2	8.2	8.2
RL(%)	8.7	8.7	8.7	8.7	8.7	8.7
GDEF(B.US$) **	-	-	-	-	-	-
PXGS(72=100)	255.7	265.3	275.1	285.4	295.9	306.9
PMGS(72=100)	342.0	354.8	367.9	381.6	395.7	410.4
EXCH(72=100) ***	73.9	73.9	73.9	73.9	73.9	73.9
CAB(B.US$)	-	-	-	-	-	-

* Exchange rate : (Weighted average of foreign currencies)/U.S. $.
** Local currency units translated into U.S. $ at baseline exchange rates.
*** Exchange rate : U.S. $/(weighted average of non-US OECD currencies).

Model: TAYLOR
Simulation A: Baseline Path

	1985	1986	1987	1988	1989	1990
JAPAN						
GNP(B.72Y)	162291.4	169924.1	177571.1	185555.9	193893.2	202599.0
CPI(72=100)	193.2	197.1	201.0	205.1	209.2	213.3
RS(%)	6.4	6.4	6.4	6.4	6.4	6.4
GDEF(%GNPV) *	-	-	-	-	-	-
EXCH(72=100) **	119.9	119.9	119.9	119.9	119.9	119.9
CAB(B.US$) ***	-	-	-	-	-	-
GERMANY						
GNP(B.72DM)	1055.0	1082.7	1112.5	1143.1	1174.5	1206.7
CPI(72=100)	172.0	175.7	179.7	183.7	187.9	192.1
RS(%)	5.6	5.6	5.6	5.6	5.6	5.6
GDEF(%GNPV) *	-	-	-	-	-	-
EXCH(72=100) **	100.3	100.3	100.3	100.2	100.2	100.2
CAB(B.US$) ***	-	-	-	-	-	-
FRANCE						
GNP(B.72F)	1335.9	1363.7	1390.9	1418.8	1447.2	1476.0
CPI(72=100)	346.0	365.9	386.0	407.2	429.6	453.2
GDEF(%GNPV) *	-	-	-	-	-	-
EXCH(72=100) **	52.2	52.1	52.1	52.1	52.1	52.1
CAB(B.US$) ***	-	-	-	-	-	-
UNITED KINGDOM						
GNP(B.72LB)	80.7	83.1	85.4	87.7	90.2	92.6
CPI(72=100)	428.9	448.2	468.4	489.6	511.7	534.6
GDEF(%GNPV) *	-	-	-	-	-	-
EXCH(72=100) **	47.3	47.3	47.3	47.3	47.3	47.2
CAB(B.US$) ***	-	-	-	-	-	-
ITALY						
GNP(B.72L)	100838.4	102949.1	105008.1	107108.4	109250.1	111432.8
CPI(72=100)	668.5	722.2	778.2	838.5	903.4	973.4
GDEF(%GNPV) *	-	-	-	-	-	-
EXCH(72=100) **	30.0	30.0	30.0	30.0	30.0	30.0
CAB(B.US$) ***	-	-	-	-	-	-
CANADA						
GNP(B.72C$)	152.0	155.2	158.3	161.5	164.7	168.0
CPI(72=100)	293.9	304.9	317.1	329.8	343.0	356.7
GDEF(%GNPV) *	-	-	-	-	-	-
EXCH(72=100) **	74.6	74.6	74.6	74.6	74.6	74.6
CAB(B.US$) ***	-	-	-	-	-	-
REST OF WORLD						
CAB(B.US$) ***	-	-	-	-	-	-

* Government deficit as a percentage of baseline nominal GNP.
** Exchange rate: Bilateral rate against U.S. $ ($/local currency).
*** Local currency units translated into U.S. $ at baseline exchange rates.

Model: TAYLOR

Simulation B: Reduction in U.S. Government Purchases with Foreign Monetary Aggregates Unchanged from Baseline

(Deviation of Shock Path from Baseline Path)

	1985									
	Q1	Q2	Q3	Q4	1985	1986	1987	1988	1989	1990
UNITED STATES										
GNPV(%)	-1.3	-2.4	-2.2	-1.4	-1.8	-1.1	-1.4	-1.6	-1.7	-2.0
GNP(%)	-1.3	-2.2	-2.0	-1.0	-1.6	-0.6	-0.6	-0.7	-0.6	-0.7
PGNP(%)	-0.0	-0.1	-0.2	-0.3	-0.2	-0.5	-0.8	-0.9	-1.1	-1.3
CPI(%)	-	-	-	-	-	-	-	-	-	-
WAGES(%)	-0.6	-1.2	-1.7	-2.2	-1.4	-2.0	-2.1	-2.2	-2.4	-2.6
UN(% PTS)	-	-	-	-	-	-	-	-	-	-
GNP(B.72$)	-21.3	-37.8	-34.3	-17.2	-27.7	-9.9	-11.2	-13.1	-11.9	-12.9
G(B.72$)	-16.7	-16.9	-17.0	-17.1	-16.9	-17.4	-17.9	-18.5	-19.0	-19.6
C(B.72$)	-7.9	-13.2	-10.9	-3.9	-9.0	-1.2	-1.6	-2.5	-2.2	-2.6
IFP(B.72$)	-0.1	-9.6	-11.2	-5.4	-6.6	-0.4	-2.0	-2.4	-1.6	-2.0
II(B.72$)	-	-	-	-	-	-	-	-	-	-
XGS(B.72$)	0.1	0.3	0.4	0.7	0.4	1.4	2.1	2.3	2.3	2.3
MGS(B.72$)	-3.3	-7.4	-9.2	-8.0	-7.0	-6.3	-7.6	-8.1	-8.2	-8.7
M1(%)	0.0	0.0	0.0	0.0	0.0	0.0	0.0	0.0	0.0	0.0
RS(% PTS)	-0.3	-0.5	-0.5	-0.3	-0.4	-0.3	-0.3	-0.3	-0.4	-0.4
RL(% PTS)	-0.4	-0.4	-0.4	-0.3	-0.4	-0.4	-0.4	-0.4	-0.5	-0.5
GDEF(B$)	-	-	-	-	-	-	-	-	-	-
PXGS(%)	-0.0	-0.1	-0.2	-0.4	-0.2	-0.6	-0.8	-1.0	-1.2	-1.4
PMGS(%)	0.7	1.3	1.7	2.0	1.4	2.5	2.7	2.5	2.2	1.8
EXCH(%) *	-5.2	-4.9	-4.6	-4.2	-4.7	-4.0	-3.7	-3.5	-3.4	-3.3
CAB(B$)	-	-	-	-	-	-	-	-	-	-
NON-US OECD										
GNPV(%) **	-0.1	-0.3	-0.5	-0.6	-0.4	-0.9	-1.4	-1.9	-2.4	-2.8
GNP(%) **	-0.1	-0.3	-0.4	-0.4	-0.3	-0.4	-0.6	-0.6	-0.6	-0.6
PGNP(%)	-0.0	-0.1	-0.1	-0.2	-0.1	-0.4	-0.9	-1.3	-1.8	-2.2
CPI(%)	-0.0	-0.1	-0.1	-0.2	-0.1	-0.4	-0.9	-1.3	-1.8	-2.2
WAGES(%)	-0.1	-0.4	-0.6	-0.9	-0.5	-1.3	-2.0	-2.5	-3.0	-3.3
UN(% PTS)	-	-	-	-	-	-	-	-	-	-
C(%) **	-0.0	-0.1	-0.1	-0.2	-0.1	-0.2	-0.4	-0.4	-0.5	-0.5
IFP(%) **	0.0	-0.1	-0.2	-0.3	-0.1	-0.3	-0.5	-0.5	-0.4	-0.3
RS(% PTS)	-0.0	-0.1	-0.2	-0.2	-0.1	-0.2	-0.3	-0.3	-0.4	-0.4
RL(% PTS)	-0.2	-0.2	-0.3	-0.3	-0.3	-0.3	-0.4	-0.4	-0.4	-0.5
GDEF (B.US$) **	-	-	-	-	-	-	-	-	-	-
PXGS(%)	-0.0	-0.1	-0.1	-0.2	-0.1	-0.4	-0.7	-1.0	-1.4	-1.7
PMGS(%)	-0.2	-0.4	-0.5	-0.7	-0.5	-1.0	-1.3	-1.6	-1.9	-2.3
EXCH(%) ***	5.5	5.2	4.8	4.4	5.0	4.2	3.8	3.6	3.5	3.4
CAB(B.US$) **	-	-	-	-	-	-	-	-	-	-

* Exchange rate : (Weighted average of foreign currencies)/U.S. $.

** Local currency units translated into U.S. $ at baseline exchange rates.

*** Exchange rate : U.S. $/(weighted average of non-US OECD currencies).

Model: TAYLOR
Simulation B: Reduction in U.S. Government Purchases with Foreign Monetary Aggregates Unchanged from Baseline
(Deviation of Shock Path from Baseline Path)

	1985									
	Q1	Q2	Q3	Q4	1985	1986	1987	1988	1989	1990
JAPAN										
GNP(%)	-0.1	-0.2	-0.4	-0.5	-0.3	-0.8	-1.2	-1.4	-1.4	-1.3
CPI(%)	-0.0	-0.1	-0.1	-0.2	-0.1	-0.6	-1.3	-2.1	-3.0	-3.7
RS(% PTS)	-0.0	-0.0	-0.1	-0.1	-0.0	-0.1	-0.2	-0.3	-0.4	-0.4
GDEF(%GNPV) *	-	-	-	-	-	-	-	-	-	-
EXCH(%) **	7.1	6.8	6.3	5.8	6.5	5.4	4.8	4.6	4.6	4.6
CAB(B.US$) ***	-	-	-	-	-	-	-	-	-	-
GERMANY										
GNP(%)	-0.0	-0.2	-0.3	-0.2	-0.2	-0.1	-0.1	-0.1	-0.1	-0.0
CPI(%)	-0.0	-0.0	-0.1	-0.1	-0.0	-0.2	-0.3	-0.4	-0.6	-0.7
RS(% PTS)	-0.0	-0.1	-0.2	-0.2	-0.1	-0.2	-0.2	-0.3	-0.3	-0.3
GDEF(%GNPV) *	-	-	-	-	-	-	-	-	-	-
EXCH(%) **	4.5	4.2	3.9	3.6	4.1	3.4	3.0	2.7	2.5	2.2
CAB(B.US$) ***	-	-	-	-	-	-	-	-	-	-
FRANCE										
GNP(%)	-0.1	-0.3	-0.5	-0.4	-0.3	-0.1	-0.2	-0.2	-0.2	-0.2
CPI(%)	-0.0	-0.0	-0.1	-0.1	-0.1	-0.2	-0.3	-0.4	-0.6	-0.7
GDEF(%GNPV) *	-	-	-	-	-	-	-	-	-	-
EXCH(%) **	3.2	3.0	2.6	2.4	2.8	2.4	2.0	1.8	1.4	1.1
CAB(B.US$) ***	-	-	-	-	-	-	-	-	-	-
UNITED KINGDOM										
GNP(%)	-0.1	-0.3	-0.4	-0.3	-0.3	-0.2	-0.3	-0.2	-0.2	-0.2
CPI(%)	-0.0	-0.1	-0.2	-0.3	-0.2	-0.7	-1.2	-1.6	-2.1	-2.4
GDEF(%GNPV) *	-	-	-	-	-	-	-	-	-	-
EXCH(%) **	4.9	4.7	4.4	4.1	4.5	3.9	3.6	3.6	3.6	3.6
CAB(B.US$) ***	-	-	-	-	-	-	-	-	-	-
ITALY										
GNP(%)	-0.1	-0.2	-0.3	-0.3	-0.2	-0.2	-0.3	-0.2	-0.2	-0.2
CPI(%)	-0.0	-0.1	-0.1	-0.2	-0.1	-0.4	-0.7	-1.1	-1.4	-1.7
GDEF(%GNPV) *	-	-	-	-	-	-	-	-	-	-
EXCH(%) **	5.9	5.7	5.3	4.9	5.4	4.7	4.3	4.2	4.1	4.0
CAB(B.US$) ***	-	-	-	-	-	-	-	-	-	-
CANADA										
GNP(%)	-0.2	-0.4	-0.7	-0.8	-0.5	-0.7	-0.8	-0.9	-0.9	-0.9
CPI(%)	-0.0	-0.1	-0.2	-0.3	-0.2	-0.7	-1.2	-1.9	-2.5	-3.1
GDEF(%GNPV) *	-	-	-	-	-	-	-	-	-	-
EXCH(%) **	6.1	5.9	5.5	5.2	5.7	5.1	5.0	5.1	5.2	5.4
CAB(B.US$) ***	-	-	-	-	-	-	-	-	-	-
REST OF WORLD										
CAB(B.US$) ***	-	-	-	-	-	-	-	-	-	-

* Government deficit as a percentage of baseline nominal GNP.
** Exchange rate : Bilateral rate against U.S. $ ($/local currency).
*** Local currency units translated into U.S. $ at baseline exchange rates.

Model: TAYLOR
Simulation C: Reduction in U.S. Government Purchases with Foreign Short-Term Interest Rates Unchanged from Baseline
(Deviation of Shock Path from Baseline Path)

	1985									
	Q1	Q2	Q3	Q4	1985	1986	1987	1988	1989	1990
UNITED STATES										
GNPV(%)	-1.2	-2.2	-2.0	-1.0	-1.6	-0.5	-0.2	-0.0	0.1	-0.0
GNP(%)	-1.2	-2.1	-1.9	-0.9	-1.5	-0.4	-0.4	-0.5	-0.5	-0.7
PGNP(%)	-0.0	-0.0	-0.1	-0.1	-0.1	-0.0	0.2	0.5	0.6	0.6
CPI(%)	-	-	-	-	-	-	-	-	-	-
WAGES(%)	-0.5	-1.0	-1.4	-1.7	-1.2	-1.2	-0.7	-0.5	-0.5	-0.7
UN(% PTS)	-	-	-	-	-	-	-	-	-	-
GNP(B.72$)	-20.5	-35.9	-32.0	-15.3	-25.9	-7.7	-7.2	-9.2	-9.8	-13.0
G(B.72$)	-16.7	-16.9	-17.0	-17.1	-16.9	-17.4	-17.9	-18.5	-19.0	-19.6
C(B.72$)	-7.4	-12.4	-10.0	-3.1	-8.2	-0.4	-0.5	-1.7	-2.2	-3.2
IFP(B.72$)	0.1	-9.0	-10.2	-4.4	-5.9	0.4	-0.8	-1.5	-1.5	-2.6
II(B.72$)	-	-	-	-	-	-	-	-	-	-
XGS(B.72$)	-0.3	-0.8	-1.2	-1.4	-0.9	-0.8	1.3	2.9	2.9	1.9
MGS(B.72$)	-3.7	-8.3	-10.5	-9.8	-8.1	-8.8	-9.8	-9.8	-10.0	-10.8
M1(%)	0.0	0.0	0.0	0.0	0.0	0.0	0.0	0.0	0.0	0.0
RS(% PTS)	-0.2	-0.4	-0.4	-0.2	-0.3	-0.1	-0.0	0.0	0.0	-0.0
RL(% PTS)	-0.1	-0.1	-0.1	-0.1	-0.1	-0.0	-0.0	-0.1	-0.1	-0.2
GDEF(B$)	-	-	-	-	-	-	-	-	-	-
PXGS(%)	-0.0	-0.0	-0.1	-0.1	-0.1	-0.0	0.2	0.5	0.7	0.7
PMGS(%)	1.6	3.0	4.0	4.8	3.4	5.9	6.4	6.3	5.9	5.5
EXCH(%) *	-10.5	-10.3	-9.9	-9.6	-10.1	-9.3	-9.0	-9.1	-9.3	-9.4
CAB(B$)	-	-	-	-	-	-	-	-	-	-
NON-US OECD										
GNPV(%) **	-0.8	-1.5	-2.2	-2.7	-1.8	-3.4	-4.1	-4.6	-5.5	-6.4
GNP(%) **	-0.7	-1.3	-1.7	-1.9	-1.4	-1.8	-1.3	-1.1	-1.1	-1.3
PGNP(%)	-0.1	-0.2	-0.5	-0.8	-0.4	-1.7	-2.8	-3.6	-4.4	-5.2
CPI(%)	-0.1	-0.2	-0.5	-0.8	-0.4	-1.7	-2.8	-3.6	-4.4	-5.2
WAGES(%)	-0.7	-1.6	-2.6	-3.8	-2.2	-4.8	-5.3	-5.7	-6.6	-7.5
UN(% PTS)	-	-	-	-	-	-	-	-	-	-
C(%) **	-0.3	-0.6	-0.9	-1.2	-0.7	-1.5	-1.3	-1.1	-1.0	-1.1
IFP(%) **	-0.7	-1.6	-2.5	-3.2	-2.0	-3.6	-2.9	-2.1	-2.0	-2.2
RS(% PTS)	-0.0	-0.0	-0.0	-0.0	-0.0	-0.0	-0.0	-0.0	-0.0	0.0
RL(% PTS)	0.0	0.0	0.0	0.0	0.0	0.0	0.0	0.0	0.0	0.0
GDEF (B.US$) **	-	-	-	-	-	-	-	-	-	-
PXGS(%)	-0.1	-0.2	-0.5	-0.8	-0.4	-1.5	-2.5	-3.1	-3.7	-4.4
PMGS(%)	-0.3	-0.7	-0.9	-1.2	-0.8	-1.8	-2.7	-3.5	-4.1	-4.7
EXCH(%) ***	11.8	11.5	11.0	10.6	11.2	10.3	9.9	10.1	10.3	10.3
CAB(B.US$) **	-	-	-	-	-	-	-	-	-	-

* Exchange rate : (Weighted average of foreign currencies)/U.S. $.
** Local currency units translated into U.S. $ at baseline exchange rates.
*** Exchange rate : U.S. $/(weighted average of non-US OECD currencies).

Model: TAYLOR
Simulation C: Reduction in U.S. Government Purchases with Foreign Short-Term Interest Rates Unchanged from Baseline
(Deviation of Shock Path from Baseline Path)

	1985									
	Q1	Q2	Q3	Q4	1985	1986	1987	1988	1989	1990
JAPAN										
GNP(%)	-0.2	-0.5	-0.9	-1.2	-0.7	-1.8	-2.3	-2.3	-2.2	-2.2
CPI(%)	-0.0	-0.1	-0.2	-0.4	-0.2	-1.1	-2.4	-3.8	-5.1	-6.3
RS(% PTS)	-0.0	-0.0	-0.0	-0.0	-0.0	-0.0	-0.0	-0.0	0.0	0.0
GDEF(%GNPV) *	-	-	-	-	-	-	-	-	-	-
EXCH(%) **	11.8	11.5	11.0	10.6	11.2	10.3	9.9	10.0	10.2	10.3
CAB(B.US$) ***	-	-	-	-	-	-	-	-	-	-
GERMANY										
GNP(%)	-2.4	-3.6	-4.3	-4.4	-3.7	-3.3	-0.8	0.2	-0.2	-0.8
CPI(%)	-0.2	-0.5	-1.0	-1.7	-0.8	-3.1	-4.2	-4.2	-4.1	-4.5
RS(% PTS)	-0.0	-0.0	-0.0	-0.0	-0.0	-0.0	-0.0	-0.0	-0.0	0.0
GDEF(%GNPV) *	-	-	-	-	-	-	-	-	-	-
EXCH(%) **	11.8	11.5	11.0	10.6	11.2	10.3	9.9	10.1	10.3	10.3
CAB(B.US$) ***	-	-	-	-	-	-	-	-	-	-
FRANCE										
GNP(%)	-0.4	-0.9	-1.4	-1.6	-1.1	-1.2	-0.7	-0.6	-0.7	-0.8
CPI(%)	-0.1	-0.2	-0.4	-0.7	-0.4	-1.5	-2.3	-3.0	-3.6	-4.4
GDEF(%GNPV) *	-	-	-	-	-	-	-	-	-	-
EXCH(%) **	11.8	11.5	11.0	10.6	11.2	10.3	9.9	10.1	10.3	10.3
CAB(B.US$) ***	-	-	-	-	-	-	-	-	-	-
UNITED KINGDOM										
GNP(%)	-0.5	-0.8	-1.1	-1.1	-0.9	-1.0	-0.7	-0.5	-0.5	-0.5
CPI(%)	-0.1	-0.3	-0.6	-1.1	-0.5	-2.1	-3.5	-4.5	-5.3	-6.1
GDEF(%GNPV) *	-	-	-	-	-	-	-	-	-	-
EXCH(%) **	11.8	11.6	11.1	10.6	11.3	10.3	10.0	10.1	10.4	10.5
CAB(B.US$) ***	-	-	-	-	-	-	-	-	-	-
ITALY										
GNP(%)	-0.2	-0.4	-0.6	-0.7	-0.5	-0.7	-0.6	-0.4	-0.4	-0.4
CPI(%)	-0.0	-0.1	-0.2	-0.3	-0.2	-0.8	-1.5	-2.1	-2.7	-3.3
GDEF(%GNPV) *	-	-	-	-	-	-	-	-	-	-
EXCH(%) **	11.8	11.5	11.0	10.6	11.2	10.3	9.9	10.0	10.2	10.3
CAB(B.US$) ***	-	-	-	-	-	-	-	-	-	-
CANADA										
GNP(%)	-0.4	-1.1	-1.7	-2.0	-1.3	-2.0	-1.9	-1.9	-2.0	-2.1
CPI(%)	-0.1	-0.2	-0.3	-0.6	-0.3	-1.2	-2.2	-3.1	-4.0	-4.9
GDEF(%GNPV) *	-	-	-	-	-	-	-	-	-	-
EXCH(%) **	11.8	11.5	11.0	10.6	11.2	10.3	9.9	10.0	10.2	10.3
CAB(B.US$) ***	-	-	-	-	-	-	-	-	-	-
REST OF WORLD										
CAB(B.US$) ***	-	-	-	-	-	-	-	-	-	-

* Government deficit as a percentage of baseline nominal GNP.
** Exchange rate : Bilateral rate against U.S. $ ($/local currency).
*** Local currency units translated into U.S. $ at baseline exchange rates.

Model: TAYLOR

Simulation D: U.S. Monetary Expansion with foreign Monetary Aggregates Unchanged from Baseline

(Deviation of Shock Path from Baseline Path)

	1985									
	Q1	Q2	Q3	Q4	1985	1986	1987	1988	1989	1990
UNITED STATES										
GNPV(%)	0.6	1.4	1.7	1.7	1.4	1.8	2.4	2.8	2.9	3.0
GNP(%)	0.6	1.2	1.3	1.1	1.0	0.6	0.5	0.3	0.2	0.1
PGNP(%)	0.1	0.2	0.4	0.6	0.3	1.2	1.9	2.4	2.7	2.9
CPI(%)	-	-	-	-	-	-	-	-	-	-
WAGES(%)	0.5	1.0	1.6	2.2	1.3	2.6	2.9	3.0	3.1	3.2
UN(% PTS)	-	-	-	-	-	-	-	-	-	-
GNP(B.72$)	9.4	19.7	22.8	18.1	17.5	11.0	9.2	6.1	3.4	2.4
G(B.72$)	0.0	0.0	0.0	0.0	0.0	0.0	0.0	0.0	0.0	0.0
C(B.72$)	4.8	8.3	8.8	6.4	7.1	2.9	1.7	0.8	0.2	0.3
IFP(B.72$)	2.5	7.3	9.6	8.4	6.9	4.8	4.7	3.5	2.5	2.2
II(B.72$)	-	-	-	-	-	-	-	-	-	-
XGS(B.72$)	0.3	0.8	1.2	1.6	1.0	1.9	1.5	0.8	0.3	-0.1
MGS(B.72$)	0.6	1.8	2.4	1.9	1.7	0.1	0.2	0.1	0.2	0.5
M1(%)	0.5	1.5	2.5	3.5	2.0	4.0	4.0	4.0	4.0	4.0
RS(% PTS)	-0.2	-0.5	-0.6	-0.8	-0.5	-0.4	-0.2	-0.2	-0.2	-0.2
RL(% PTS)	-0.3	-0.4	-0.3	-0.3	-0.3	-0.2	-0.2	-0.2	-0.2	-0.2
GDEF(B$)	-	-	-	-	-	-	-	-	-	-
PXGS(%)	0.1	0.2	0.4	0.7	0.4	1.3	2.1	2.7	3.0	3.2
PMGS(%)	1.1	2.0	2.8	3.3	2.3	3.8	3.9	3.8	3.5	3.3
EXCH(%) *	-7.5	-7.3	-6.8	-6.2	-7.0	-4.9	-4.2	-4.0	-3.9	-3.9
CAB(B$)	-	-	-	-	-	-	-	-	-	-
NON-US OECD										
GNPV(%) **	-0.0	-0.0	-0.0	-0.1	-0.0	-0.4	-0.7	-1.0	-1.1	-1.2
GNP(%) **	0.0	0.0	0.0	-0.0	0.0	-0.2	-0.3	-0.3	-0.2	-0.2
PGNP(%)	-0.0	-0.0	-0.1	-0.1	-0.0	-0.2	-0.5	-0.7	-0.9	-1.0
CPI(%)	-0.0	-0.0	-0.1	-0.1	-0.0	-0.2	-0.5	-0.7	-0.9	-1.0
WAGES(%)	-0.0	-0.0	-0.1	-0.2	-0.1	-0.5	-0.9	-1.2	-1.3	-1.3
UN(% PTS)	-	-	-	-	-	-	-	-	-	-
C(%) **	0.0	0.0	0.0	0.0	0.0	-0.1	-0.1	-0.2	-0.2	-0.2
IFP(%) **	-0.0	-0.0	-0.0	-0.0	-0.0	-0.1	-0.2	-0.3	-0.2	-0.1
RS(% PTS)	0.0	0.0	0.0	-0.0	-0.0	-0.1	-0.1	-0.2	-0.2	-0.2
RL(% PTS)	-0.1	-0.1	-0.1	-0.1	-0.1	-0.1	-0.1	-0.2	-0.1	-0.1
GDEF (B.US$) **	-	-	-	-	-	-	-	-	-	-
PXGS(%)	-0.0	-0.0	-0.0	-0.1	-0.0	-0.2	-0.4	-0.6	-0.7	-0.8
PMGS(%)	-0.2	-0.5	-0.6	-0.8	-0.5	-0.9	-1.0	-1.0	-1.0	-1.0
EXCH(%) ***	8.1	7.9	7.3	6.7	7.5	5.2	4.4	4.2	4.1	4.0
CAB(B.US$) **	-	-	-	-	-	-	-	-	-	-

* Exchange rate : (Weighted average of foreign currencies)/U.S. $.

** Local currency units translated into U.S. $ at baseline exchange rates.

*** Exchange rate : U.S. $/(weighted average of non-US OECD currencies).

Model: TAYLOR
Simulation D: U.S. Monetary Expansion with Foreign Monetary Aggregates Unchanged from Baseline
(Deviation of Shock Path from Baseline Path)

	1985									
	Q1	Q2	Q3	Q4	1985	1986	1987	1988	1989	1990
JAPAN										
GNP(%)	-0.0	-0.0	-0.0	-0.1	-0.0	-0.3	-0.5	-0.7	-0.6	-0.5
CPI(%)	-0.0	-0.0	-0.0	-0.1	-0.0	-0.2	-0.6	-1.0	-1.4	-1.6
RS(% PTS)	-0.0	-0.0	-0.0	-0.0	-0.0	-0.1	-0.1	-0.1	-0.2	-0.2
GDEF(%GNPV) *	-	-	-	-	-	-	-	-	-	-
EXCH(%) **	8.7	8.5	7.9	7.3	8.1	5.7	4.8	4.3	4.2	4.1
CAB(B.US$) ***	-	-	-	-	-	-	-	-	-	-
GERMANY										
GNP(%)	0.0	0.1	0.1	0.0	0.1	-0.1	-0.1	-0.1	-0.0	0.0
CPI(%)	-0.0	-0.0	-0.0	-0.0	-0.0	-0.1	-0.2	-0.3	-0.3	-0.4
RS(% PTS)	0.0	0.0	0.0	0.0	0.0	-0.1	-0.2	-0.2	-0.2	-0.1
GDEF(%GNPV) *	-	-	-	-	-	-	-	-	-	-
EXCH(%) **	7.7	7.4	6.8	6.1	7.0	4.6	3.9	3.8	3.8	3.8
CAB(B.US$) ***	-	-	-	-	-	-	-	-	-	-
FRANCE										
GNP(%)	0.0	0.1	0.2	0.1	0.1	-0.1	-0.1	-0.1	-0.0	-0.0
CPI(%)	0.0	0.0	0.0	0.0	0.0	-0.0	-0.2	-0.2	-0.3	-0.3
GDEF(%GNPV) *	-	-	-	-	-	-	-	-	-	-
EXCH(%) **	7.4	7.1	6.5	5.8	6.7	4.3	3.6	3.4	3.4	3.4
CAB(B.US$) ***	-	-	-	-	-	-	-	-	-	-
UNITED KINGDOM										
GNP(%)	-0.0	0.0	0.0	-0.0	-0.0	-0.1	-0.1	-0.1	-0.1	0.0
CPI(%)	-0.0	-0.1	-0.1	-0.2	-0.1	-0.4	-0.7	-0.9	-1.1	-1.1
GDEF(%GNPV) *	-	-	-	-	-	-	-	-	-	-
EXCH(%) **	7.9	7.7	7.2	6.6	7.3	5.2	4.6	4.4	4.4	4.3
CAB(B.US$) ***	-	-	-	-	-	-	-	-	-	-
ITALY										
GNP(%)	0.0	0.0	0.0	0.0	0.0	-0.0	-0.0	-0.0	-0.0	0.0
CPI(%)	-0.0	-0.0	-0.1	-0.1	-0.1	-0.2	-0.4	-0.6	-0.8	-0.9
GDEF(%GNPV) *	-	-	-	-	-	-	-	-	-	-
EXCH(%) **	8.6	8.3	7.8	7.1	8.0	5.6	4.8	4.5	4.4	4.3
CAB(B.US$) ***	-	-	-	-	-	-	-	-	-	-
CANADA										
GNP(%)	-0.0	-0.1	-0.1	-0.2	-0.1	-0.3	-0.3	-0.3	-0.3	-0.2
CPI(%)	-0.0	-0.1	-0.1	-0.2	-0.1	-0.5	-0.8	-1.1	-1.3	-1.5
GDEF(%GNPV) *	-	-	-	-	-	-	-	-	-	-
EXCH(%) **	8.2	8.0	7.5	6.9	7.6	5.6	5.1	4.9	4.9	4.8
CAB(B.US$) ***	-	-	-	-	-	-	-	-	-	-
REST OF WORLD										
CAB(B.US$) ***	-	-	-	-	-	-	-	-	-	-

* Government deficit as a percentage of baseline nominal GNP.
** Exchange rate : Bilateral rate against U.S. $ ($/local currency).
*** Local currency units translated into U.S. $ at baseline exchange rates.

Model: TAYLOR
Simulation E: U.S. Monetary Expansion with Foreign Short-Term Interest Rates Unchanged from Baseline
(Deviation of Shock Path from Baseline Path)

	1985 Q1	1985 Q2	1985 Q3	1985 Q4	1985	1986	1987	1988	1989	1990
UNITED STATES										
GNPV(%)	0.7	1.4	1.8	1.8	1.4	2.1	2.9	3.4	3.6	3.7
GNP(%)	0.6	1.2	1.4	1.1	1.1	0.7	0.6	0.4	0.2	0.1
PGNP(%)	0.1	0.2	0.4	0.7	0.4	1.4	2.3	2.9	3.3	3.6
CPI(%)	-	-	-	-	-	-	-	-	-	-
WAGES(%)	0.5	1.1	1.7	2.4	1.4	2.9	3.4	3.7	3.8	3.8
UN(% PTS)	-	-	-	-	-	-	-	-	-	-
GNP(B.72$)	9.7	20.3	23.5	18.7	18.0	11.8	10.8	7.7	4.1	2.1
G(B.72$)	0.0	0.0	0.0	0.0	0.0	0.0	0.0	0.0	0.0	0.0
C(B.72$)	5.0	8.6	9.1	6.6	7.3	3.2	2.2	1.1	0.1	-0.1
IFP(B.72$)	2.5	7.5	10.0	8.7	7.2	5.1	5.2	3.9	2.5	1.9
II(B.72$)	-	-	-	-	-	-	-	-	-	-
XGS(B.72$)	0.1	0.3	0.6	0.8	0.4	1.0	1.2	1.2	0.7	-0.1
MGS(B.72$)	0.5	1.5	1.9	1.2	1.3	-0.8	-0.6	-0.5	-0.3	-0.1
M1(%)	0.5	1.5	2.5	3.5	2.0	4.0	4.0	4.0	4.0	4.0
RS(% PTS)	-0.2	-0.5	-0.6	-0.7	-0.5	-0.3	-0.1	-0.0	-0.0	-0.0
RL(% PTS)	-0.3	-0.3	-0.3	-0.2	-0.3	-0.1	-0.1	-0.1	-0.1	-0.1
GDEF(B$)	-	-	-	-	-	-	-	-	-	-
PXGS(%)	0.1	0.3	0.5	0.8	0.4	1.5	2.5	3.2	3.7	4.0
PMGS(%)	1.4	2.6	3.6	4.3	3.0	5.0	5.3	5.0	4.7	4.4
EXCH(%) *	-9.3	-9.1	-8.7	-8.1	-8.8	-6.9	-6.2	-5.8	-5.7	-5.6
CAB(B$)	-	-	-	-	-	-	-	-	-	-
NON-US OECD										
GNPV(%) **	-0.3	-0.5	-0.7	-0.9	-0.6	-1.4	-1.7	-1.9	-2.1	-2.2
GNP(%) **	-0.2	-0.4	-0.5	-0.6	-0.4	-0.7	-0.5	-0.4	-0.3	-0.3
PGNP(%)	-	-	-	-	-	-	-	-	-	-
CPI(%)	-0.0	-0.1	-0.2	-0.3	-0.2	-0.7	-1.2	-1.5	-1.7	-1.9
WAGES(%)	-0.2	-0.5	-0.9	-1.3	-0.7	-1.9	-2.2	-2.2	-2.4	-2.5
UN(% PTS)	-	-	-	-	-	-	-	-	-	-
C(%) **	-0.1	-0.2	-0.3	-0.4	-0.2	-0.5	-0.5	-0.4	-0.3	-0.3
IFP(%) **	-0.3	-0.6	-0.9	-1.1	-0.8	-1.4	-1.1	-0.7	-0.6	-0.5
RS(% PTS)	-0.0	-0.0	-0.0	-0.0	-0.0	-0.0	-0.0	-0.0	-0.0	0.0
RL(% PTS)	0.0	0.0	0.0	0.0	0.0	0.0	0.0	0.0	0.0	0.0
GDEF (B.US$) **	-	-	-	-	-	-	-	-	-	-
PXGS(%)	-0.0	-0.1	-0.2	-0.3	-0.2	-0.6	-1.0	-1.3	-1.5	-1.6
PMGS(%)	-0.3	-0.5	-0.8	-0.9	-0.6	-1.2	-1.5	-1.7	-1.7	-1.8
EXCH(%) ***	10.3	10.0	9.5	8.9	9.7	7.4	6.6	6.2	6.0	5.9
CAB(B.US$) **	-	-	-	-	-	-	-	-	-	-

* Exchange rate : (Weighted average of foreign currencies)/U.S. $.
** Local currency units translated into U.S. $ at baseline exchange rates.
*** Exchange rate : U.S. $/(weighted average of non-US OECD currencies).

Model: TAYLOR
Simulation E: U.S. Monetary Expansion with Foreign Short-Term Interest Rates Unchanged from Baseline
(Deviation of Shock Path from Baseline Path)

	1985									
	Q1	Q2	Q3	Q4	1985	1986	1987	1988	1989	1990
JAPAN										
GNP(%)	-0.1	-0.1	-0.2	-0.3	-0.2	-0.6	-0.9	-1.0	-0.8	-0.7
CPI(%)	-0.0	-0.0	-0.1	-0.2	-0.1	-0.4	-1.0	-1.6	-2.1	-2.5
RS(% PTS)	-0.0	-0.0	-0.0	-0.0	-0.0	-0.0	-0.0	-0.0	0.0	0.0
GDEF(%GNPV) *	-	-	-	-	-	-	-	-	-	-
EXCH(%) **	10.3	10.1	9.5	8.9	9.7	7.4	6.6	6.2	6.0	5.9
CAB(B.US$) ***	-	-	-	-	-	-	-	-	-	-
GERMANY										
GNP(%)	-0.9	-1.3	-1.5	-1.6	-1.3	-1.3	-0.3	0.2	0.2	-0.1
CPI(%)	-0.1	-0.2	-0.4	-0.6	-0.3	-1.2	-1.7	-1.7	-1.5	-1.5
RS(% PTS)	-0.0	-0.0	-0.0	-0.0	-0.0	-0.0	-0.0	-0.0	-0.0	0.0
GDEF(%GNPV) *	-	-	-	-	-	-	-	-	-	-
EXCH(%) **	10.3	10.0	9.5	8.9	9.7	7.4	6.6	6.2	6.0	5.9
CAB(B.US$) ***	-	-	-	-	-	-	-	-	-	-
FRANCE										
GNP(%)	-0.1	-0.1	-0.2	-0.3	-0.2	-0.5	-0.3	-0.2	-0.2	-0.2
CPI(%)	-0.0	-0.1	-0.1	-0.2	-0.1	-0.5	-0.9	-1.2	-1.4	-1.6
GDEF(%GNPV) *	-	-	-	-	-	-	-	-	-	-
EXCH(%) **	10.3	10.0	9.5	8.8	9.6	7.4	6.6	6.2	6.1	5.9
CAB(B.US$) ***	-	-	-	-	-	-	-	-	-	-
UNITED KINGDOM										
GNP(%)	-0.1	-0.2	-0.3	-0.3	-0.2	-0.4	-0.2	-0.1	-0.1	-0.1
CPI(%)	-0.0	-0.1	-0.3	-0.5	-0.2	-0.9	-1.5	-1.8	-2.0	-2.1
GDEF(%GNPV) *	-	-	-	-	-	-	-	-	-	-
EXCH(%) **	10.3	10.1	9.5	8.9	9.7	7.4	6.6	6.3	6.2	6.0
CAB(B.US$) ***	-	-	-	-	-	-	-	-	-	-
ITALY										
GNP(%)	-0.0	-0.1	-0.1	-0.1	-0.1	-0.2	-0.2	-0.1	-0.0	-0.0
CPI(%)	-0.0	-0.1	-0.1	-0.2	-0.1	-0.4	-0.7	-0.9	-1.1	-1.3
GDEF(%GNPV) *	-	-	-	-	-	-	-	-	-	-
EXCH(%) **	10.3	10.0	9.5	8.9	9.7	7.4	6.6	6.2	6.0	5.9
CAB(B.US$) ***	-	-	-	-	-	-	-	-	-	-
CANADA										
GNP(%)	-0.1	-0.3	-0.5	-0.7	-0.4	-0.8	-0.7	-0.6	-0.5	-0.5
CPI(%)	-0.0	-0.1	-0.2	-0.3	-0.2	-0.7	-1.2	-1.5	-1.8	-1.9
GDEF(%GNPV) *	-	-	-	-	-	-	-	-	-	-
EXCH(%) **	10.3	10.0	9.5	8.9	9.6	7.4	6.6	6.2	6.0	5.9
CAB(B.US$) ***	-	-	-	-	-	-	-	-	-	-
REST OF WORLD										
CAB(B.US$) ***	-	-	-	-	-	-	-	-	-	-

* Government deficit as a percentage of baseline nominal GNP.
** Exchange rate : Bilateral rate against U.S. $ ($/local currency).
*** Local currency units translated into U.S. $ at baseline exchange rates.

Model: TAYLOR
Simulation F: Nonpolicy Exogenous Depreciation of the Dollar
(Deviation of Shock Path from Baseline Path)

	1985 Q1	1985 Q2	1985 Q3	1985 Q4	1985	1986	1987	1988	1989	1990
UNITED STATES										
GNPV(%)	-0.1	-0.0	0.4	1.0	0.3	2.6	5.8	9.5	12.7	15.2
GNP(%)	-0.1	-0.1	0.2	0.6	0.1	1.2	1.9	2.2	1.9	1.4
PGNP(%)	0.0	0.1	0.2	0.4	0.2	1.4	3.8	7.1	10.6	13.6
CPI(%)	-	-	-	-	-	-	-	-	-	-
WAGES(%)	0.2	0.5	1.0	1.8	0.9	3.9	7.8	11.7	14.6	16.6
UN(% PTS)	-	-	-	-	-	-	-	-	-	-
GNP(B.72$)	-2.4	-2.1	2.9	10.2	2.1	20.6	35.0	40.2	35.2	26.8
G(B.72$)	0.0	0.0	0.0	0.0	0.0	0.0	0.0	0.0	0.0	0.0
C(B.72$)	-1.2	-0.8	1.4	4.2	0.9	7.5	10.9	10.2	6.6	3.4
IFP(B.72$)	-1.0	-1.8	-0.7	1.8	-0.4	5.5	9.4	10.2	7.8	4.6
II(B.72$)	-	-	-	-	-	-	-	-	-	-
XGS(B.72$)	0.2	0.6	1.1	1.8	0.9	4.0	7.8	11.1	11.8	10.6
MGS(B.72$)	-0.5	-1.1	-1.2	-0.9	-1.0	-1.3	-3.7	-7.0	-9.0	-9.7
M1(%)	0.0	0.0	0.0	0.0	0.0	0.0	0.0	0.0	0.0	0.0
RS(% PTS)	-0.0	0.0	0.2	0.3	0.1	0.7	1.5	2.3	2.8	3.2
RL(% PTS)	1.2	1.3	1.4	1.6	1.4	1.9	2.4	2.7	2.8	2.8
GDEF(B$)	-	-	-	-	-	-	-	-	-	-
PXGS(%)	0.0	0.1	0.2	0.5	0.2	1.5	4.2	7.9	11.8	15.1
PMGS(%)	0.4	1.0	2.0	3.2	1.7	7.2	15.4	23.2	27.2	28.7
EXCH(%) *	-2.4	-4.8	-7.2	-9.4	-6.0	-14.8	-22.9	-25.7	-25.7	-25.7
CAB(B$)	-	-	-	-	-	-	-	-	-	-
NON-US OECD										
GNPV(%) **	0.1	0.2	0.2	0.2	0.2	-0.0	-1.0	-2.5	-4.1	-5.5
GNP(%) **	0.1	0.1	0.2	0.2	0.2	0.1	-0.4	-0.9	-1.3	-1.4
PGNP(%)	0.0	0.0	0.0	0.0	0.0	-0.1	-0.6	-1.6	-2.8	-4.1
CPI(%)	0.0	0.0	0.0	0.0	0.0	-0.1	-0.6	-1.6	-2.8	-4.1
WAGES(%)	0.1	0.1	0.2	0.2	0.1	-0.1	-1.4	-3.3	-5.2	-6.8
UN(% PTS)	-	-	-	-	-	-	-	-	-	-
C(%) **	0.0	0.1	0.1	0.2	0.1	0.2	-0.1	-0.5	-0.8	-1.1
IFP(%) **	0.1	0.3	0.4	0.5	0.3	0.6	0.3	-0.1	-0.3	-0.2
RS(% PTS)	0.1	0.1	0.1	0.2	0.1	0.1	-0.3	-0.7	-1.1	-1.4
RL(% PTS)	-0.3	-0.3	-0.4	-0.4	-0.3	-0.6	-0.9	-1.1	-1.3	-1.3
GDEF (B.US$) **	-	-	-	-	-	-	-	-	-	-
PXGS(%)	0.0	0.0	0.0	0.0	0.0	-0.1	-0.5	-1.3	-2.3	-3.3
PMGS(%)	-0.1	-0.2	-0.4	-0.7	-0.3	-1.4	-3.0	-4.6	-5.6	-6.3
EXCH(%) ***	2.5	5.1	7.7	10.4	6.4	17.5	29.8	34.6	34.6	34.6
CAB(B.US$) **	-	-	-	-	-	-	-	-	-	-

* Exchange rate : (Weighted average of foreign currencies)/U.S. $.
** Local currency units translated into U.S. $ at baseline exchange rates.
*** Exchange rate : U.S. $/(weighted average of non-US OECD currencies).

Model: TAYLOR
Simulation F: Nonpolicy Exogenous Depreciation of the Dollar
(Deviation of Shock Path from Baseline Path)

	1985 Q1	1985 Q2	1985 Q3	1985 Q4	1985	1986	1987	1988	1989	1990
JAPAN										
GNP(%)	0.0	0.0	0.0	0.0	0.0	-0.2	-0.9	-1.9	-2.9	-3.5
CPI(%)	-0.0	-0.0	-0.0	-0.0	-0.0	-0.2	-0.8	-2.0	-3.8	-5.9
RS(% PTS)	-0.0	-0.0	-0.0	-0.0	-0.0	-0.1	-0.2	-0.4	-0.6	-0.8
GDEF(%GNPV) *	-	-	-	-	-	-	-	-	-	-
EXCH(%) **	2.7	5.4	8.2	11.1	6.9	18.7	31.9	37.2	37.2	37.2
CAB(B.US$) ***	-	-	-	-	-	-	-	-	-	-
GERMANY										
GNP(%)	0.5	0.6	0.7	0.7	0.6	0.5	-0.3	-0.9	-0.9	-0.7
CPI(%)	0.0	0.1	0.1	0.2	0.1	0.3	-0.0	-1.0	-2.2	-3.2
RS(% PTS)	0.3	0.4	0.5	0.6	0.5	0.4	-0.3	-1.1	-1.7	-2.1
GDEF(%GNPV) *	-	-	-	-	-	-	-	-	-	-
EXCH(%) **	2.7	5.4	8.2	11.1	6.9	18.7	31.9	37.2	37.2	37.2
CAB(B.US$) ***	-	-	-	-	-	-	-	-	-	-
FRANCE										
GNP(%)	0.0	0.1	0.1	0.1	0.1	0.1	-0.4	-0.8	-1.0	-0.9
CPI(%)	0.0	0.0	0.0	0.0	0.0	-0.1	-0.6	-1.7	-3.0	-4.3
GDEF(%GNPV) *	-	-	-	-	-	-	-	-	-	-
EXCH(%) **	2.7	5.4	8.2	11.1	6.9	18.7	31.9	37.2	37.2	37.2
CAB(B.US$) ***	-	-	-	-	-	-	-	-	-	-
UNITED KINGDOM										
GNP(%)	0.0	-0.0	-0.0	-0.0	-0.0	-0.2	-0.4	-0.6	-0.6	-0.5
CPI(%)	-0.0	-0.0	-0.1	-0.2	-0.1	-0.7	-1.9	-3.6	-5.3	-6.6
GDEF(%GNPV) *	-	-	-	-	-	-	-	-	-	-
EXCH(%) **	2.7	5.4	8.2	11.1	6.9	18.7	31.9	37.2	37.2	37.2
CAB(B.US$) ***	-	-	-	-	-	-	-	-	-	-
ITALY										
GNP(%)	0.0	0.0	0.0	0.0	0.0	0.0	-0.1	-0.2	-0.3	-0.3
CPI(%)	-0.0	-0.0	-0.0	-0.1	-0.0	-0.3	-0.8	-1.7	-2.7	-3.8
GDEF(%GNPV) *	-	-	-	-	-	-	-	-	-	-
EXCH(%) **	2.7	5.4	8.2	11.1	6.9	18.7	31.9	37.2	37.2	37.2
CAB(B.US$) ***	-	-	-	-	-	-	-	-	-	-
CANADA										
GNP(%)	0.0	0.1	0.2	0.3	0.2	0.7	1.1	1.3	1.2	0.9
CPI(%)	0.0	0.0	0.1	0.2	0.1	0.5	1.4	2.6	3.8	4.8
GDEF(%GNPV) *	-	-	-	-	-	-	-	-	-	-
EXCH(%) **	1.3	2.6	3.9	5.3	3.3	8.7	14.4	16.6	16.6	16.6
CAB(B.US$) ***	-	-	-	-	-	-	-	-	-	-
REST OF WORLD										
CAB(B.US$) ***	-	-	-	-	-	-	-	-	-	-

* Government deficit as a percentage of baseline nominal GNP.
** Exchange rate : Bilateral rate against U.S. $ ($/local currency).
*** Local currency units translated into U.S. $ at baseline exchange rates.

Model: TAYLOR
Simulation G: Increase in Government Purchases in Non-U.S. OECD Countries with U.S. Policies Unchanged from Baseline
(Deviation of Shock Path from Baseline Path)

	1985									
	Q1	Q2	Q3	Q4	1985	1986	1987	1988	1989	1990
UNITED STATES										
GNPV(%)	0.2	0.6	1.0	1.2	0.7	1.4	2.1	2.5	2.9	3.4
GNP(%)	0.2	0.5	0.7	0.8	0.5	0.6	0.5	0.4	0.3	0.3
PGNP(%)	0.0	0.1	0.3	0.4	0.2	0.9	1.5	2.1	2.6	3.1
CPI(%)	-	-	-	-	-	-	-	-	-	-
WAGES(%)	0.3	0.6	1.1	1.5	0.9	2.0	2.6	2.9	3.3	3.7
UN(% PTS)	-	-	-	-	-	-	-	-	-	-
GNP(B.72$)	3.0	8.0	12.0	13.0	9.0	10.1	9.3	7.3	6.0	5.7
G(B.72$)	0.0	0.0	0.0	0.0	0.0	0.0	0.0	0.0	0.0	0.0
C(B.72$)	1.3	3.1	4.4	4.4	3.3	2.7	1.8	1.0	0.7	0.8
IFP(B.72$)	0.3	1.8	3.3	3.8	2.3	2.3	1.9	1.0	0.4	0.1
II(B.72$)	-	-	-	-	-	-	-	-	-	-
XGS(B.72$)	1.0	2.2	3.3	4.2	2.7	5.2	5.7	5.6	5.3	5.2
MGS(B.72$)	-0.0	0.3	0.8	1.0	0.5	0.4	0.1	-0.2	-0.3	-0.4
M1(%)	0.0	0.0	0.0	0.0	0.0	0.0	0.0	0.0	0.0	0.0
RS(% PTS)	0.1	0.2	0.3	0.3	0.2	0.4	0.5	0.6	0.6	0.7
RL(% PTS)	0.4	0.5	0.5	0.5	0.5	0.6	0.6	0.7	0.8	0.8
GDEF(B$)	-	-	-	-	-	-	-	-	-	-
PXGS(%)	0.0	0.1	0.3	0.5	0.2	1.0	1.7	2.3	2.9	3.4
PMGS(%)	0.7	1.3	1.8	2.2	1.5	2.9	3.5	3.9	4.3	4.7
EXCH(%) *	-4.0	-3.8	-3.5	-3.3	-3.6	-2.6	-1.9	-1.5	-1.3	-1.2
CAB(B$)	-	-	-	-	-	-	-	-	-	-
NON-US OECD										
GNPV(%) **	1.1	1.6	1.9	2.3	1.7	2.8	3.6	4.3	4.9	5.5
GNP(%) **	1.0	1.4	1.6	1.7	1.4	1.6	1.5	1.4	1.3	1.2
PGNP(%)	0.1	0.2	0.3	0.6	0.3	1.2	2.1	2.9	3.6	4.2
CPI(%)	0.1	0.2	0.3	0.6	0.3	1.2	2.1	2.9	3.6	4.2
WAGES(%)	0.6	1.4	2.4	3.4	2.0	4.3	5.2	5.8	6.3	6.8
UN(% PTS)	-	-	-	-	-	-	-	-	-	-
C(%) **	0.2	0.4	0.6	0.8	0.5	1.0	1.1	1.1	1.0	1.0
IFP(%) **	0.0	0.7	1.0	1.2	0.7	1.3	1.3	1.1	0.8	0.6
RS(% PTS)	0.3	0.4	0.5	0.6	0.5	0.6	0.6	0.7	0.7	0.8
RL(% PTS)	0.6	0.6	0.6	0.7	0.6	0.7	0.7	0.8	0.8	0.9
GDEF (B.US$) **	-	-	-	-	-	-	-	-	-	-
PXGS(%)	0.0	0.1	0.3	0.5	0.2	0.9	1.6	2.1	2.6	3.1
PMGS(%)	-0.0	-0.1	-0.1	-0.0	-0.1	0.1	0.4	0.9	1.4	2.0
EXCH(%) ***	4.1	3.9	3.6	3.4	3.8	2.7	2.0	1.5	1.3	1.2
CAB(B.US$) **	-	-	-	-	-	-	-	-	-	-

* Exchange rate : (Weighted average of foreign currencies)/U.S. $.
** Local currency units translated into U.S. $ at baseline exchange rates.
*** Exchange rate : U.S. $/(weighted average of non-US OECD currencies).

Model: TAYLOR
Simulation G: Increase in Government Purchases in Non-U.S. OECD Countries with U.S. Policies Unchanged from Baseline
(Deviation of Shock Path from Baseline Path)

	1985									
	Q1	Q2	Q3	Q4	1985	1986	1987	1988	1989	1990
JAPAN										
GNP(%)	1.2	1.8	2.1	2.5	1.9	3.0	3.2	3.0	2.6	2.3
CPI(%)	0.1	0.2	0.5	0.8	0.4	1.9	3.7	5.5	7.1	8.4
RS(% PTS)	0.1	0.1	0.2	0.3	0.2	0.4	0.6	0.7	0.7	0.8
GDEF(%GNPV) *	-	-	-	-	-	-	-	-	-	-
EXCH(%) **	-0.4	-0.4	-0.3	-0.3	-0.3	-0.3	-0.6	-1.0	-1.4	-1.7
CAB(B.US$) ***	-	-	-	-	-	-	-	-	-	-
GERMANY										
GNP(%)	0.7	0.9	0.9	0.9	0.9	0.6	0.3	0.2	0.1	0.2
CPI(%)	0.0	0.1	0.2	0.3	0.2	0.6	0.8	0.9	1.0	1.1
RS(% PTS)	0.5	0.6	0.7	0.8	0.7	0.7	0.6	0.5	0.6	0.6
GDEF(%GNPV) *	-	-	-	-	-	-	-	-	-	-
EXCH(%) **	5.7	5.4	4.8	4.4	5.0	3.2	2.2	2.1	2.3	2.6
CAB(B.US$) ***	-	-	-	-	-	-	-	-	-	-
FRANCE										
GNP(%)	1.1	1.6	1.8	1.6	1.5	0.8	0.4	0.5	0.5	0.5
CPI(%)	0.1	0.2	0.3	0.6	0.3	0.9	1.0	1.0	1.1	1.1
GDEF(%GNPV) *	-	-	-	-	-	-	-	-	-	-
EXCH(%) **	10.1	9.7	9.1	8.4	9.3	7.0	5.5	4.8	4.7	4.9
CAB(B.US$) ***	-	-	-	-	-	-	-	-	-	-
UNITED KINGDOM										
GNP(%)	1.1	1.2	1.2	1.2	1.2	1.0	0.9	0.8	0.8	0.8
CPI(%)	0.1	0.2	0.4	0.7	0.4	1.4	2.2	2.8	3.4	4.0
GDEF(%GNPV) *	-	-	-	-	-	-	-	-	-	-
EXCH(%) **	7.0	6.7	6.4	6.1	6.5	5.3	4.6	4.1	3.7	3.4
CAB(B.US$) ***	-	-	-	-	-	-	-	-	-	-
ITALY										
GNP(%)	0.8	0.9	1.0	1.0	0.9	1.1	1.0	0.9	0.9	0.8
CPI(%)	0.0	0.1	0.2	0.3	0.1	0.6	1.1	1.5	2.0	2.4
GDEF(%GNPV) *	-	-	-	-	-	-	-	-	-	-
EXCH(%) **	4.3	4.0	3.8	3.6	3.9	3.1	2.4	1.9	1.6	1.3
CAB(B.US$) ***	-	-	-	-	-	-	-	-	-	-
CANADA										
GNP(%)	1.1	1.9	2.2	2.2	1.8	2.0	2.0	2.1	2.1	2.1
CPI(%)	0.1	0.2	0.3	0.5	0.2	1.0	1.9	2.8	3.7	4.6
GDEF(%GNPV) *	-	-	-	-	-	-	-	-	-	-
EXCH(%) **	1.7	1.5	1.2	0.9	1.3	0.4	-0.3	-0.8	-1.3	-1.7
CAB(B.US$) ***	-	-	-	-	-	-	-	-	-	-
REST OF WORLD										
CAB(B.US$) ***	-	-	-	-	-	-	-	-	-	-

* Government deficit as a percentage of baseline nominal GNP.
** Exchange rate : Bilateral rate against U.S. $ ($/local currency).
*** Local currency units translated into U.S. $ at baseline exchange rates.

Model: TAYLOR
Simulation H: Monetary Expansion in Non-U.S. OECD Countries
with U.S. Policies Unchanged from Baseline
(Deviation of Shock Path from Baseline Path)

	1985 Q1	1985 Q2	1985 Q3	1985 Q4	1985	1986	1987	1988	1989	1990
UNITED STATES										
GNPV(%)	-0.1	-0.3	-0.4	-0.5	-0.3	-0.6	-0.8	-1.0	-1.1	-1.1
GNP(%)	-0.1	-0.2	-0.3	-0.2	-0.2	-0.1	-0.1	-0.1	-0.0	0.0
PGNP(%)	-0.0	-0.1	-0.2	-0.2	-0.1	-0.5	-0.7	-0.9	-1.1	-1.1
CPI(%)	-	-	-	-	-	-	-	-	-	-
WAGES(%)	-0.1	-0.3	-0.4	-0.6	-0.3	-0.7	-0.9	-1.1	-1.1	-1.1
UN(% PTS)	-	-	-	-	-	-	-	-	-	-
GNP(B.72$)	-1.5	-3.6	-4.6	-4.0	-3.4	-2.2	-1.7	-1.1	-0.4	0.1
G(B.72$)	0.0	0.0	0.0	0.0	0.0	0.0	0.0	0.0	0.0	0.0
C(B.72$)	-0.8	-1.5	-1.7	-1.4	-1.3	-0.5	-0.2	0.0	0.2	0.3
IFP(B.72$)	-0.3	-1.1	-1.6	-1.5	-1.1	-0.7	-0.5	-0.1	0.3	0.5
II(B.72$)	-	-	-	-	-	-	-	-	-	-
XGS(B.72$)	0.1	0.2	0.4	0.5	0.3	0.7	0.5	0.1	-0.2	-0.3
MGS(B.72$)	0.3	0.5	0.7	1.0	0.6	1.7	1.6	1.3	1.0	0.8
M1(%)	0.0	0.0	0.0	0.0	0.0	0.0	0.0	0.0	0.0	0.0
RS(% PTS)	-0.0	-0.1	-0.1	-0.1	-0.1	-0.2	-0.2	-0.2	-0.2	-0.2
RL(% PTS)	-0.2	-0.2	-0.2	-0.2	-0.2	-0.2	-0.2	-0.2	-0.2	-0.2
GDEF(B$)	-	-	-	-	-	-	-	-	-	-
PXGS(%)	-0.0	-0.1	-0.2	-0.3	-0.1	-0.5	-0.8	-1.0	-1.2	-1.3
PMGS(%)	-0.8	-1.4	-1.9	-2.2	-1.6	-2.4	-2.3	-2.1	-1.9	-1.7
EXCH(%) *	5.7	5.6	5.1	4.6	5.3	3.7	3.4	3.3	3.3	3.3
CAB(B$)	-	-	-	-	-	-	-	-	-	-
NON-US OECD										
GNPV(%) **	0.3	0.6	0.9	1.1	0.7	1.6	1.8	1.8	1.8	1.7
GNP(%) **	0.3	0.5	0.7	0.8	0.6	0.8	0.6	0.3	0.1	0.0
PGNP(%)	0.0	0.1	0.2	0.4	0.2	0.7	1.3	1.5	1.7	1.7
CPI(%)	0.0	0.1	0.2	0.4	0.2	0.7	1.3	1.5	1.7	1.7
WAGES(%)	0.3	0.7	1.1	1.7	0.9	2.2	2.3	2.1	1.9	1.8
UN(% PTS)	-	-	-	-	-	-	-	-	-	-
C(%) **	0.1	0.2	0.4	0.5	0.3	0.7	0.7	0.5	0.3	0.2
IFP(%) **	0.4	0.8	1.2	1.5	1.0	1.8	1.5	1.0	0.6	0.4
RS(% PTS)	-0.1	-0.5	-0.6	-0.7	-0.5	-0.3	-0.2	-0.2	-0.3	-0.3
RL(% PTS)	-0.3	-0.3	-0.3	-0.3	-0.3	-0.2	-0.2	-0.3	-0.3	-0.3
GDEF (B.US$) **	-	-	-	-	-	-	-	-	-	-
PXGS(%)	0.0	0.1	0.2	0.3	0.2	0.7	1.2	1.4	1.6	1.6
PMGS(%)	0.1	0.3	0.4	0.4	0.3	0.6	0.8	1.1	1.3	1.4
EXCH(%) ***	-5.4	-5.3	-4.9	-4.4	-5.0	-3.5	-3.2	-3.2	-3.2	-3.2
CAB(B.US$) **	-	-	-	-	-	-	-	-	-	-

* Exchange rate : (Weighted average of foreign currencies)/U.S. $.
** Local currency units translated into U.S. $ at baseline exchange rates.
*** Exchange rate : U.S. $/(weighted average of non-US OECD currencies).

Model: TAYLOR
Simulation H: Monetary Expansion in Non-U.S. OECD Countries
with U.S. Policies Unchanged from Baseline
(Deviation of Shock Path from Baseline Path)

	1985 Q1	1985 Q2	1985 Q3	1985 Q4	1985	1986	1987	1988	1989	1990
JAPAN										
GNP(%)	0.1	0.2	0.3	0.4	0.3	0.5	0.5	0.2	0.0	-0.1
CPI(%)	0.0	0.0	0.1	0.1	0.1	0.3	0.5	0.6	0.6	0.5
RS(% PTS)	-0.4	-0.8	-0.8	-0.9	-0.7	-0.3	-0.2	-0.2	-0.2	-0.3
GDEF(%GNPV) *	-	-	-	-	-	-	-	-	-	-
EXCH(%) **	-4.3	-4.0	-3.3	-2.6	-3.6	-1.6	-1.4	-1.6	-1.7	-1.7
CAB(B.US$) ***	-	-	-	-	-	-	-	-	-	-
GERMANY										
GNP(%)	1.0	1.5	1.8	2.0	1.5	1.8	1.1	0.5	0.2	0.2
CPI(%)	0.1	0.2	0.4	0.7	0.3	1.5	2.4	2.8	3.0	3.1
RS(% PTS)	0.4	0.2	0.1	-0.1	0.1	0.1	0.0	-0.2	-0.3	-0.3
GDEF(%GNPV) *	-	-	-	-	-	-	-	-	-	-
EXCH(%) **	-2.8	-3.2	-3.4	-3.6	-3.3	-3.9	-4.9	-5.4	-5.4	-5.1
CAB(B.US$) ***	-	-	-	-	-	-	-	-	-	-
FRANCE										
GNP(%)	0.2	0.5	0.8	1.0	0.6	1.1	0.7	0.4	0.2	0.1
CPI(%)	0.1	0.2	0.4	0.6	0.3	1.4	2.4	3.0	3.2	3.3
GDEF(%GNPV) *	-	-	-	-	-	-	-	-	-	-
EXCH(%) **	-10.9	-10.7	-10.2	-9.4	-10.3	-7.2	-5.2	-4.3	-4.2	-4.4
CAB(B.US$) ***	-	-	-	-	-	-	-	-	-	-
UNITED KINGDOM										
GNP(%)	0.2	0.3	0.4	0.4	0.3	0.4	0.3	0.1	0.1	0.1
CPI(%)	0.0	0.1	0.2	0.4	0.2	0.7	1.2	1.4	1.6	1.7
GDEF(%GNPV) *	-	-	-	-	-	-	-	-	-	-
EXCH(%) **	-4.7	-4.6	-4.2	-3.8	-4.3	-3.0	-2.9	-2.8	-2.8	-2.7
CAB(B.US$) ***	-	-	-	-	-	-	-	-	-	-
ITALY										
GNP(%)	0.1	0.2	0.2	0.3	0.2	0.4	0.3	0.2	0.1	-0.0
CPI(%)	0.0	0.1	0.2	0.3	0.1	0.6	1.2	1.6	2.0	2.2
GDEF(%GNPV) *	-	-	-	-	-	-	-	-	-	-
EXCH(%) **	-7.8	-7.6	-7.2	-6.7	-7.3	-5.6	-5.1	-4.9	-4.7	-4.6
CAB(B.US$) ***	-	-	-	-	-	-	-	-	-	-
CANADA										
GNP(%)	0.1	0.2	0.3	0.3	0.2	0.3	0.2	0.2	0.2	0.2
CPI(%)	-0.0	-0.0	-0.0	-0.1	-0.0	-0.2	-0.3	-0.4	-0.5	-0.6
GDEF(%GNPV) *	-	-	-	-	-	-	-	-	-	-
EXCH(%) **	-2.8	-2.6	-2.1	-1.7	-2.3	-1.0	-0.8	-0.7	-0.6	-0.5
CAB(B.US$) ***	-	-	-	-	-	-	-	-	-	-
REST OF WORLD										
CAB(B.US$) ***	-	-	-	-	-	-	-	-	-	-

* Government deficit as a percentage of baseline nominal GNP.
** Exchange rate : Bilateral rate against U.S. $ ($/local currency).
*** Local currency units translated into U.S. $ at baseline exchange rates.

VAR—Minneapolis World Vector Autoregression Model

See part 1 of this volume for design and detailed description of the simulations. See part 4 for bibliographical references.

Figures were not available for the consumer price index for any of the countries or regions. Data shown on the lines for CPI pertain to GNP deflators.

Model: VAR
Simulation A: Baseline Path

	1985	1986	1987	1988	1989	1990
UNITED STATES						
GNPV(B.$)	3944.5	4204.0	4480.9	4776.0	5091.2	5424.5
GNP(B.72$)	1689.8	1740.3	1792.4	1846.3	1901.6	1958.6
PGNP(72=100)	233.4	241.5	249.9	258.6	267.6	276.9
CPI(72=100)	-	-	-	-	-	-
WAGES(72=100)	238.3	245.3	253.3	262.4	272.7	283.6
UN(%)	7.3	7.4	7.4	7.5	7.5	7.5
G(B.72$)	318.2	331.1	344.4	358.2	372.5	387.3
C(B.72$)	1398.8	1439.7	1480.5	1522.3	1565.3	1609.3
IFP(B.72$)	-	-	-	-	-	-
II(B.72$)	-	-	-	-	-	-
XGS(B.72$)	157.7	167.0	176.7	187.0	197.8	209.1
MGS(B.72$)	184.9	197.4	209.2	221.2	233.9	247.1
M1(B.$)	582.4	609.5	637.8	665.4	688.7	708.9
RS(%)	8.5	8.5	8.5	8.5	8.5	8.5
RL(%)	-	-	-	-	-	-
GDEF(B.$)	192.2	194.5	196.8	200.6	217.5	230.4
PXGS(72=100)	-	-	-	-	-	-
PMGS(72=100)	258.3	265.3	271.8	278.8	285.6	293.2
EXCH(72=100) *	138.4	138.4	138.5	138.5	138.3	138.3
CAB(B.$)	-108.3	-115.7	-118.7	-122.0	-126.7	-133.9
NON-US OECD						
GNPV(B.$) **	1090.4	1131.4	1171.6	1214.3	1259.1	1305.8
GNP(B.72$) **	360.0	361.7	362.3	363.1	364.1	365.3
PGNP(72=100)	240.1	247.5	255.2	263.3	271.6	280.2
CPI(72=100)	-	-	-	-	-	-
WAGES(72=100)	-	-	-	-	-	-
UN(%)	-	-	-	-	-	-
C(B.72$) **	-	-	-	-	-	-
IFP(B.72$) **	-	-	-	-	-	-
RS(%)	6.2	6.2	6.2	6.2	6.2	6.2
RL(%)	-	-	-	-	-	-
GDEF(B.US$) **	-	-	-	-	-	-
PXGS(72=100)	-	-	-	-	-	-
PMGS(72=100)	-	-	-	-	-	-
EXCH(72=100) ***	72.3	72.2	72.2	72.2	72.3	72.3
CAB(B.US$)	109.6	167.7	213.2	220.3	189.9	191.7

* Exchange rate : (Weighted average of foreign currencies)/U.S. $.
** Local currency units translated into U.S. $ at baseline exchange rates.
*** Exchange rate : U.S. $/(weighted average of non-US OECD currencies).

Model: VAR
Simulation A: Baseline Path

	1985	1986	1987	1988	1989	1990
JAPAN						
GNP(B.72Y)	64261.0	65265.4	66262.9	67342.4	68424.9	69491.9
CPI(72=100)	247.3	254.4	261.8	269.5	277.4	285.6
RS(%)	5.0	5.0	5.0	5.0	5.0	5.0
GDEF(%GNPV) *	-	-	-	-	-	-
EXCH(72=100) **	118.0	118.0	118.0	118.0	118.0	118.0
CAB(B.US$) ***	54.0	82.2	104.5	107.7	92.1	92.7
GERMANY						
GNP(B.72DM)	-	-	-	-	-	-
CPI(72=100)	-	-	-	-	-	-
RS(%)	-	-	-	-	-	-
GDEF(%GNPV) *	-	-	-	-	-	-
EXCH(72=100) **	-	-	-	-	-	-
CAB(B.US$) ***	-	-	-	-	-	-
FRANCE						
GNP(B.72F)	-	-	-	-	-	-
CPI(72=100)	-	-	-	-	-	-
GDEF(%GNPV) *	-	-	-	-	-	-
EXCH(72=100) **	-	-	-	-	-	-
CAB(B.US$) ***	-	-	-	-	-	-
UNITED KINGDOM						
GNP(B.72LB)	-	-	-	-	-	-
CPI(72=100)	-	-	-	-	-	-
GDEF(%GNPV) *	-	-	-	-	-	-
EXCH(72=100) **	-	-	-	-	-	-
CAB(B.US$) ***	-	-	-	-	-	-
ITALY						
GNP(B.72L)	-	-	-	-	-	-
CPI(72=100)	-	-	-	-	-	-
GDEF(%GNPV) *	-	-	-	-	-	-
EXCH(72=100) **	-	-	-	-	-	-
CAB(B.US$) ***	-	-	-	-	-	-
CANADA						
GNP(B.72C$)	-	-	-	-	-	-
CPI(72=100)	-	-	-	-	-	-
GDEF(%GNPV) *	-	-	-	-	-	-
EXCH(72=100) **	-	-	-	-	-	-
CAB(B.US$) ***	-	-	-	-	-	-
REST OF WORLD						
CAB(B.US$) ***	-	-	-	-	-	-

* Government deficit as a percentage of baseline nominal GNP.
** Exchange rate: Bilateral rate against U.S. $ ($/local currency).
*** Local currency units translated into U.S. $ at baseline exchange rates.

Model: VAR
Simulation B: Reduction in U.S. Government Purchases with Foreign Monetary Aggregates Unchanged from Baseline
(Deviation of Shock Path from Baseline Path)

	1985									
	Q1	Q2	Q3	Q4	1985	1986	1987	1988	1989	1990
UNITED STATES										
GNPV(%)	0.0	0.2	0.3	0.6	0.3	0.6	0.4	0.4	0.4	0.4
GNP(%)	0.0	-0.0	-0.1	-0.1	-0.0	-0.4	-0.6	-0.7	-0.7	-0.7
PGNP(%)	0.0	0.2	0.4	0.7	0.3	0.9	1.1	1.1	1.1	1.1
CPI(%)	-	-	-	-	-	-	-	-	-	-
WAGES(%)	0.0	0.1	0.3	0.4	0.2	0.6	0.7	0.7	0.7	0.7
UN(% PTS)	0.0	0.0	0.0	0.0	0.0	0.1	0.2	0.3	0.3	0.3
GNP(B.72$)	0.0	-0.0	-1.2	-1.8	-0.8	-6.2	-11.4	-13.0	-14.0	-14.2
G(B.72$)	-16.8	-16.5	-15.8	-15.2	-16.1	-14.7	-15.1	-15.4	-15.8	-16.4
C(B.72$)	16.8	16.5	13.0	8.9	13.8	0.5	-6.8	-8.9	-9.9	-9.9
IFP(B.72$)	-	-	-	-	-	-	-	-	-	-
II(B.72$)	-	-	-	-	-	-	-	-	-	-
XGS(B.72$)	0.0	1.5	1.5	1.8	1.2	1.7	1.3	1.1	1.0	1.0
MGS(B.72$)	0.0	1.6	-0.2	-2.6	-0.3	-6.3	-9.1	-10.1	-10.7	-11.1
M1(%)	0.0	-0.0	-0.0	-0.1	-0.0	0.0	0.0	-0.0	-0.0	0.0
RS(% PTS)	-0.0	-0.0	-0.1	-0.2	-0.1	-0.1	-0.1	-0.0	-0.0	-0.0
RL(% PTS)	-	-	-	-	-	-	-	-	-	-
GDEF(B$)	-16.7	-14.0	-10.0	-9.1	-12.4	-8.0	-6.1	-5.2	-4.7	-4.8
PXGS(%)	-	-	-	-	-	-	-	-	-	-
PMGS(%)	0.0	0.5	1.3	1.9	0.9	2.5	2.9	2.9	2.8	2.8
EXCH(%) *	-0.1	-0.3	-0.5	-0.8	-0.4	-1.2	-1.1	-1.0	-0.9	-1.0
CAB(B$)	0.0	-1.5	-2.3	-1.3	-1.3	0.5	1.9	2.3	2.4	2.3
NON-US OECD										
GNPV(%) **	0.0	0.0	0.0	0.0	0.0	0.0	-0.0	-0.0	-0.0	-0.0
GNP(%) **	0.0	0.0	0.0	0.0	0.0	0.0	-0.0	-0.0	-0.0	-0.0
PGNP(%)	0.0	0.0	0.0	0.0	0.0	0.0	0.0	0.0	-0.0	-0.0
CPI(%)	-	-	-	-	-	-	-	-	-	-
WAGES(%)	-	-	-	-	-	-	-	-	-	-
UN(% PTS)	-	-	-	-	-	-	-	-	-	-
C(%) **	-	-	-	-	-	-	-	-	-	-
IFP(%) **	-	-	-	-	-	-	-	-	-	-
RS(% PTS)	0.0	0.0	0.0	0.0	0.0	0.0	0.0	0.0	0.0	0.0
RL(% PTS)	-	-	-	-	-	-	-	-	-	-
GDEF (B.US$) **	-	-	-	-	-	-	-	-	-	-
PXGS(%)	-	-	-	-	-	-	-	-	-	-
PMGS(%)	-	-	-	-	-	-	-	-	-	-
EXCH(%) ***	0.1	0.3	0.5	0.8	0.4	1.2	1.1	1.0	0.9	1.0
CAB(B.US$) **	0.0	-0.0	-0.0	0.0	-0.0	0.2	-0.0	-0.1	-0.1	-0.1

* Exchange rate : (Weighted average of foreign currencies)/U.S. $.
** Local currency units translated into U.S. $ at baseline exchange rates.
*** Exchange rate : U.S. $/(weighted average of non-US OECD currencies).

Model: VAR
Simulation B: Reduction in U.S. Government Purchases with Foreign Monetary Aggregates Unchanged from Baseline
(Deviation of Shock Path from Baseline Path)

	1985									
	Q1	Q2	Q3	Q4	1985	1986	1987	1988	1989	1990
JAPAN										
GNP(%)	0.0	0.0	0.0	0.0	0.0	0.0	0.0	0.0	0.0	0.0
CPI(%)	0.0	0.0	-0.0	-0.0	-0.0	-0.0	-0.0	-0.0	-0.0	-0.0
RS(% PTS)	0.0	0.0	0.0	0.1	0.0	0.0	0.0	0.0	0.0	0.0
GDEF(%GNPV) *	-	-	-	-	-	-	-	-	-	-
EXCH(%) **	0.1	0.2	0.3	0.5	0.3	0.8	0.7	0.6	0.6	0.6
CAB(B.US$) ***	0.0	-0.0	-0.0	0.0	0.0	0.2	0.1	0.1	0.0	0.1
GERMANY										
GNP(%)	-	-	-	-	-	-	-	-	-	-
CPI(%)	-	-	-	-	-	-	-	-	-	-
RS(% PTS)	-	-	-	-	-	-	-	-	-	-
GDEF(%GNPV) *	-	-	-	-	-	-	-	-	-	-
EXCH(%) **	-	-	-	-	-	-	-	-	-	-
CAB(B.US$) ***	-	-	-	-	-	-	-	-	-	-
FRANCE										
GNP(%)	-	-	-	-	-	-	-	-	-	-
CPI(%)	-	-	-	-	-	-	-	-	-	-
GDEF(%GNPV) *	-	-	-	-	-	-	-	-	-	-
EXCH(%) **	-	-	-	-	-	-	-	-	-	-
CAB(B.US$) ***	-	-	-	-	-	-	-	-	-	-
UNITED KINGDOM										
GNP(%)	-	-	-	-	-	-	-	-	-	-
CPI(%)	-	-	-	-	-	-	-	-	-	-
GDEF(%GNPV) *	-	-	-	-	-	-	-	-	-	-
EXCH(%) **	-	-	-	-	-	-	-	-	-	-
CAB(B.US$) ***	-	-	-	-	-	-	-	-	-	-
ITALY										
GNP(%)	-	-	-	-	-	-	-	-	-	-
CPI(%)	-	-	-	-	-	-	-	-	-	-
GDEF(%GNPV) *	-	-	-	-	-	-	-	-	-	-
EXCH(%) **	-	-	-	-	-	-	-	-	-	-
CAB(B.US$) ***	-	-	-	-	-	-	-	-	-	-
CANADA										
GNP(%)	-	-	-	-	-	-	-	-	-	-
CPI(%)	-	-	-	-	-	-	-	-	-	-
GDEF(%GNPV) *	-	-	-	-	-	-	-	-	-	-
EXCH(%) **	-	-	-	-	-	-	-	-	-	-
CAB(B.US$) ***	-	-	-	-	-	-	-	-	-	-
REST OF WORLD										
CAB(B.US$) ***	-	-	-	-	-	-	-	-	-	-

* Government deficit as a percentage of baseline nominal GNP.
** Exchange rate : Bilateral rate against U.S. $ ($/local currency).
*** Local currency units translated into U.S. $ at baseline exchange rates.

Model: VAR
Simulation C: Reduction in U.S. Government Purchases with Foreign Short-Term Interest Rates Unchanged from Baseline
(Deviation of Shock Path from Baseline Path)

	1985									
	Q1	Q2	Q3	Q4	1985	1986	1987	1988	1989	1990
UNITED STATES										
GNPV(%)	0.0	0.2	0.4	0.6	0.3	0.6	0.4	0.4	0.4	0.4
GNP(%)	0.0	0.0	-0.1	-0.1	-0.0	-0.3	-0.6	-0.7	-0.7	-0.7
PGNP(%)	0.0	0.2	0.4	0.7	0.3	0.9	1.1	1.1	1.1	1.1
CPI(%)	-	-	-	-	-	-	-	-	-	-
WAGES(%)	0.0	0.1	0.3	0.4	0.2	0.6	0.7	0.7	0.7	0.7
UN(% PTS)	0.0	-0.0	0.0	0.0	0.0	0.1	0.2	0.3	0.3	0.3
GNP(B.72$)	0.0	0.1	-0.9	-1.4	-0.6	-6.1	-11.3	-13.0	-13.7	-14.1
G(B.72$)	-16.8	-16.5	-15.8	-15.2	-16.1	-14.8	-15.1	-15.4	-15.8	-16.5
C(B.72$)	16.8	16.6	13.3	9.4	14.0	0.7	-6.5	-8.6	-9.5	-9.7
IFP(B.72$)	-	-	-	-	-	-	-	-	-	-
II(B.72$)	-	-	-	-	-	-	-	-	-	-
XGS(B.72$)	0.0	1.5	1.5	1.9	1.2	1.7	1.3	1.1	1.0	1.0
MGS(B.72$)	0.0	1.6	-0.1	-2.5	-0.3	-6.2	-8.9	-9.9	-10.5	-11.0
M1(%)	0.0	0.0	-0.0	-0.0	-0.0	0.0	0.0	-0.0	0.0	-0.0
RS(% PTS)	-0.0	-0.1	-0.1	-0.2	-0.1	-0.1	-0.1	-0.1	-0.0	-0.0
RL(% PTS)	-	-	-	-	-	-	-	-	-	-
GDEF(B$)	-16.7	-14.0	-10.2	-9.3	-12.5	-8.1	-6.1	-5.2	-4.8	-4.8
PXGS(%)	-	-	-	-	-	-	-	-	-	-
PMGS(%)	0.0	0.5	1.2	1.9	0.9	2.5	2.8	2.8	2.8	2.8
EXCH(%) *	-0.1	-0.4	-0.6	-0.8	-0.5	-1.1	-1.0	-1.0	-0.9	-1.0
CAB(B$)	0.0	-1.5	-2.3	-1.4	-1.3	0.4	1.8	2.2	2.3	2.3
NON-US OECD										
GNPV(%) **	0.0	0.0	0.0	0.0	0.0	0.0	0.0	-0.0	-0.0	-0.0
GNP(%) **	0.0	0.0	0.0	0.0	0.0	0.0	-0.0	-0.0	-0.0	-0.0
PGNP(%)	0.0	-0.0	0.0	0.0	0.0	0.0	0.0	-0.0	-0.0	-0.0
CPI(%)	-	-	-	-	-	-	-	-	-	-
WAGES(%)	-	-	-	-	-	-	-	-	-	-
UN(% PTS)	-	-	-	-	-	-	-	-	-	-
C(%) **	-	-	-	-	-	-	-	-	-	-
IFP(%) **	-	-	-	-	-	-	-	-	-	-
RS(% PTS)	0.0	0.0	0.0	0.0	0.0	0.0	-0.0	-0.0	0.0	0.0
RL(% PTS)	-	-	-	-	-	-	-	-	-	-
GDEF (B.US$) **	-	-	-	-	-	-	-	-	-	-
PXGS(%)	-	-	-	-	-	-	-	-	-	-
PMGS(%)	-	-	-	-	-	-	-	-	-	-
EXCH(%) ***	0.1	0.4	0.6	0.8	0.5	1.1	1.0	1.0	1.0	1.0
CAB(B.US$) **	0.0	0.0	0.1	0.1	0.0	0.2	0.0	-0.1	-0.1	-0.1

* Exchange rate : (Weighted average of foreign currencies)/U.S. $.
** Local currency units translated into U.S. $ at baseline exchange rates.
*** Exchange rate : U.S. $/(weighted average of non-US OECD currencies).

Model: VAR
Simulation C: Reduction in U.S. Government Purchases with Foreign Short-Term Interest Rates Unchanged from Baseline
(Deviation of Shock Path from Baseline Path)

	1985									
	Q1	Q2	Q3	Q4	1985	1986	1987	1988	1989	1990
JAPAN										
GNP(%)	0.0	0.0	0.0	0.0	0.0	0.0	0.0	0.0	0.0	0.0
CPI(%)	0.0	-0.0	-0.0	-0.0	-0.0	-0.0	-0.0	-0.0	-0.0	-0.0
RS(% PTS)	0.0	0.0	0.0	0.0	0.0	0.0	-0.0	0.0	-0.0	-0.0
GDEF(%GNPV) *	-	-	-	-	-	-	-	-	-	-
EXCH(%) **	0.1	0.2	0.4	0.5	0.3	0.7	0.7	0.6	0.6	0.6
CAB(B.US$) ***	0.0	0.0	0.1	0.1	0.0	0.2	0.1	0.1	0.0	0.0
GERMANY										
GNP(%)	-	-	-	-	-	-	-	-	-	-
CPI(%)	-	-	-	-	-	-	-	-	-	-
RS(% PTS)	-	-	-	-	-	-	-	-	-	-
GDEF(%GNPV) *	-	-	-	-	-	-	-	-	-	-
EXCH(%) **	-	-	-	-	-	-	-	-	-	-
CAB(B.US$) ***	-	-	-	-	-	-	-	-	-	-
FRANCE										
GNP(%)	-	-	-	-	-	-	-	-	-	-
CPI(%)	-	-	-	-	-	-	-	-	-	-
GDEF(%GNPV) *	-	-	-	-	-	-	-	-	-	-
EXCH(%) **	-	-	-	-	-	-	-	-	-	-
CAB(B.US$) ***	-	-	-	-	-	-	-	-	-	-
UNITED KINGDOM										
GNP(%)	-	-	-	-	-	-	-	-	-	-
CPI(%)	-	-	-	-	-	-	-	-	-	-
GDEF(%GNPV) *	-	-	-	-	-	-	-	-	-	-
EXCH(%) **	-	-	-	-	-	-	-	-	-	-
CAB(B.US$) ***	-	-	-	-	-	-	-	-	-	-
ITALY										
GNP(%)	-	-	-	-	-	-	-	-	-	-
CPI(%)	-	-	-	-	-	-	-	-	-	-
GDEF(%GNPV) *	-	-	-	-	-	-	-	-	-	-
EXCH(%) **	-	-	-	-	-	-	-	-	-	-
CAB(B.US$) ***	-	-	-	-	-	-	-	-	-	-
CANADA										
GNP(%)	-	-	-	-	-	-	-	-	-	-
CPI(%)	-	-	-	-	-	-	-	-	-	-
GDEF(%GNPV) *	-	-	-	-	-	-	-	-	-	-
EXCH(%) **	-	-	-	-	-	-	-	-	-	-
CAB(B.US$) ***	-	-	-	-	-	-	-	-	-	-
REST OF WORLD										
CAB(B.US$) ***	-	-	-	-	-	-	-	-	-	-

* Government deficit as a percentage of baseline nominal GNP.
** Exchange rate : Bilateral rate against U.S. $ ($/local currency).
*** Local currency units translated into U.S. $ at baseline exchange rates.

Model: VAR
Simulation D: U.S. Monetary Expansion with foreign Monetary Aggregates Unchanged from Baseline
(Deviation of Shock Path from Baseline Path)

	1985 Q1	1985 Q2	1985 Q3	1985 Q4	1985	1986	1987	1988	1989	1990
UNITED STATES										
GNPV(%)	0.0	0.2	0.7	1.4	0.6	3.5	4.0	3.7	3.7	3.7
GNP(%)	0.0	0.2	0.7	1.4	0.6	3.0	2.9	2.3	2.4	2.3
PGNP(%)	0.0	-0.0	0.0	0.1	0.0	0.4	1.1	1.3	1.4	1.4
CPI(%)	-	-	-	-	-	-	-	-	-	-
WAGES(%)	0.0	0.0	0.1	0.3	0.1	0.8	1.4	1.5	1.5	1.5
UN(% PTS)	0.0	-0.1	-0.2	-0.5	-0.2	-1.4	-1.5	-1.1	-1.2	-1.2
GNP(B.72$)	0.0	3.4	11.6	23.1	9.5	52.8	52.4	43.3	44.9	45.7
G(B.72$)	0.0	-0.0	0.1	0.3	0.1	2.0	3.4	4.3	4.7	5.1
C(B.72$)	0.0	3.3	10.8	21.2	8.8	45.0	33.8	20.9	21.6	20.9
IFP(B.72$)	-	-	-	-	-	-	-	-	-	-
II(B.72$)	-	-	-	-	-	-	-	-	-	-
XGS(B.72$)	0.0	-0.0	0.6	1.8	0.6	5.8	8.9	7.7	8.2	8.6
MGS(B.72$)	0.0	-0.2	-0.1	0.2	-0.0	0.1	-6.2	-10.4	-10.4	-11.1
M1(%)	0.2	0.8	1.5	2.4	1.2	4.0	4.0	4.0	4.0	4.0
RS(% PTS)	-1.1	-1.7	-1.9	-2.4	-1.8	-1.9	-1.1	-1.2	-1.2	-1.1
RL(% PTS)	-	-	-	-	-	-	-	-	-	-
GDEF(B$)	0.0	-0.6	-3.6	-8.6	-3.2	-22.4	-24.5	-18.8	-18.2	-17.6
PXGS(%)	-	-	-	-	-	-	-	-	-	-
PMGS(%)	0.0	0.1	0.4	1.1	0.4	3.6	6.2	6.0	5.8	5.7
EXCH(%) *	-2.8	-6.4	-10.9	-15.7	-8.9	-22.9	-22.6	-23.6	-24.2	-25.1
CAB(B$)	0.0	0.7	1.9	2.9	1.4	4.9	7.1	9.6	10.4	10.7
NON-US OECD										
GNPV(%) **	0.0	0.0	0.1	0.1	0.1	0.5	0.6	0.4	0.4	0.4
GNP(%) **	0.0	0.0	0.1	0.1	0.0	0.4	0.4	0.3	0.4	0.5
PGNP(%)	0.0	-0.0	0.0	0.0	0.0	0.1	0.1	0.1	0.0	-0.0
CPI(%)	-	-	-	-	-	-	-	-	-	-
WAGES(%)	-	-	-	-	-	-	-	-	-	-
UN(% PTS)	-	-	-	-	-	-	-	-	-	-
C(%) **	-	-	-	-	-	-	-	-	-	-
IFP(%) **	-	-	-	-	-	-	-	-	-	-
RS(% PTS)	0.3	0.6	0.7	0.7	0.6	0.3	0.5	0.4	0.4	0.4
RL(% PTS)	-	-	-	-	-	-	-	-	-	-
GDEF (B.US$) **	-	-	-	-	-	-	-	-	-	-
PXGS(%)	-	-	-	-	-	-	-	-	-	-
PMGS(%)	-	-	-	-	-	-	-	-	-	-
EXCH(%) ***	2.9	6.8	12.2	18.6	10.1	29.7	29.1	30.9	31.9	33.5
CAB(B.US$) **	0.0	0.6	1.6	2.8	1.2	5.1	2.9	2.6	2.6	2.6

* Exchange rate : (Weighted average of foreign currencies)/U.S. $.
** Local currency units translated into U.S. $ at baseline exchange rates.
*** Exchange rate : U.S. $/(weighted average of non-US OECD currencies).

Model: VAR
Simulation D: U.S. Monetary Expansion with Foreign Monetary Aggregates Unchanged from Baseline
(Deviation of Shock Path from Baseline Path)

	1985									
	Q1	Q2	Q3	Q4	1985	1986	1987	1988	1989	1990
JAPAN										
GNP(%)	0.0	0.0	0.1	0.2	0.1	0.6	0.5	0.3	0.5	0.7
CPI(%)	0.0	-0.0	-0.0	-0.0	-0.0	-0.0	0.2	0.1	-0.1	-0.2
RS(% PTS)	0.2	0.3	0.4	0.5	0.4	0.4	0.4	0.4	0.2	0.2
GDEF(%GNPV) *	-	-	-	-	-	-	-	-	-	-
EXCH(%) **	1.8	4.2	7.1	10.2	5.8	14.9	14.4	15.1	15.3	15.8
CAB(B.US$) ***	0.0	0.5	1.5	2.6	1.1	4.7	1.9	1.9	1.9	1.8
GERMANY										
GNP(%)	-	-	-	-	-	-	-	-	-	-
CPI(%)	-	-	-	-	-	-	-	-	-	-
RS(% PTS)	-	-	-	-	-	-	-	-	-	-
GDEF(%GNPV) *	-	-	-	-	-	-	-	-	-	-
EXCH(%) **	-	-	-	-	-	-	-	-	-	-
CAB(B.US$) ***	-	-	-	-	-	-	-	-	-	-
FRANCE										
GNP(%)	-	-	-	-	-	-	-	-	-	-
CPI(%)	-	-	-	-	-	-	-	-	-	-
GDEF(%GNPV) *	-	-	-	-	-	-	-	-	-	-
EXCH(%) **	-	-	-	-	-	-	-	-	-	-
CAB(B.US$) ***	-	-	-	-	-	-	-	-	-	-
UNITED KINGDOM										
GNP(%)	-	-	-	-	-	-	-	-	-	-
CPI(%)	-	-	-	-	-	-	-	-	-	-
GDEF(%GNPV) *	-	-	-	-	-	-	-	-	-	-
EXCH(%) **	-	-	-	-	-	-	-	-	-	-
CAB(B.US$) ***	-	-	-	-	-	-	-	-	-	-
ITALY										
GNP(%)	-	-	-	-	-	-	-	-	-	-
CPI(%)	-	-	-	-	-	-	-	-	-	-
GDEF(%GNPV) *	-	-	-	-	-	-	-	-	-	-
EXCH(%) **	-	-	-	-	-	-	-	-	-	-
CAB(B.US$) ***	-	-	-	-	-	-	-	-	-	-
CANADA										
GNP(%)	-	-	-	-	-	-	-	-	-	-
CPI(%)	-	-	-	-	-	-	-	-	-	-
GDEF(%GNPV) *	-	-	-	-	-	-	-	-	-	-
EXCH(%) **	-	-	-	-	-	-	-	-	-	-
CAB(B.US$) ***	-	-	-	-	-	-	-	-	-	-
REST OF WORLD										
CAB(B.US$) ***	-	-	-	-	-	-	-	-	-	-

* Government deficit as a percentage of baseline nominal GNP.
** Exchange rate : Bilateral rate against U.S. $ ($/local currency).
*** Local currency units translated into U.S. $ at baseline exchange rates.

Model: VAR
Simulation E: U.S. Monetary Expansion with Foreign Short-Term Interest Rates Unchanged from Baseline
(Deviation of Shock Path from Baseline Path)

	1985 Q1	Q2	Q3	Q4	1985	1986	1987	1988	1989	1990
UNITED STATES										
GNPV(%)	0.0	0.2	0.8	1.6	0.7	3.6	4.0	3.6	3.8	3.7
GNP(%)	0.0	0.2	0.8	1.6	0.7	3.2	3.0	2.4	2.6	2.5
PGNP(%)	0.0	-0.0	-0.0	0.0	-0.0	0.3	1.0	1.1	1.2	1.3
CPI(%)	-	-	-	-	-	-	-	-	-	-
WAGES(%)	0.0	0.0	0.2	0.3	0.1	0.8	1.4	1.4	1.5	1.5
UN(% PTS)	0.0	-0.1	-0.3	-0.6	-0.2	-1.4	-1.5	-1.2	-1.3	-1.2
GNP(B.72$)	0.0	4.1	13.9	27.3	11.3	56.1	53.6	45.1	49.4	48.4
G(B.72$)	0.0	-0.1	-0.1	0.0	-0.0	0.9	3.7	4.5	4.2	4.7
C(B.72$)	0.0	4.1	13.8	26.8	11.2	51.0	36.4	24.5	28.6	25.5
IFP(B.72$)	-	-	-	-	-	-	-	-	-	-
II(B.72$)	-	-	-	-	-	-	-	-	-	-
XGS(B.72$)	0.0	-0.1	0.7	2.1	0.7	6.4	9.0	7.9	8.8	9.3
MGS(B.72$)	0.0	-0.2	0.5	1.7	0.5	2.3	-4.4	-8.1	-7.7	-9.0
M1(%)	0.3	0.9	1.7	2.6	1.4	4.0	4.0	4.0	4.1	3.9
RS(% PTS)	-1.3	-2.0	-2.2	-2.5	-2.0	-1.8	-1.1	-1.3	-1.2	-1.1
RL(% PTS)	-	-	-	-	-	-	-	-	-	-
GDEF(B$)	0.0	-1.1	-5.1	-11.5	-4.4	-25.4	-24.8	-19.5	-20.5	-19.2
PXGS(%)	-	-	-	-	-	-	-	-	-	-
PMGS(%)	0.0	0.0	0.2	0.7	0.2	3.1	5.5	5.2	5.2	5.2
EXCH(%) *	-2.6	-6.1	-10.8	-15.7	-8.8	-22.1	-22.3	-23.6	-24.7	-25.5
CAB(B$)	0.0	0.6	1.4	2.0	1.0	3.2	6.0	8.9	9.4	10.0
NON-US OECD										
GNPV(%) **	0.0	0.0	0.1	0.2	0.1	0.5	0.7	0.6	0.5	0.5
GNP(%) **	0.0	0.0	0.1	0.2	0.1	0.5	0.6	0.5	0.6	0.7
PGNP(%)	0.0	-0.0	-0.0	-0.0	-0.0	0.0	0.1	0.0	-0.1	-0.1
CPI(%)	-	-	-	-	-	-	-	-	-	-
WAGES(%)	-	-	-	-	-	-	-	-	-	-
UN(% PTS)	-	-	-	-	-	-	-	-	-	-
C(%) **	-	-	-	-	-	-	-	-	-	-
IFP(%) **	-	-	-	-	-	-	-	-	-	-
RS(% PTS)	0.0	0.0	0.0	0.0	0.0	-0.1	0.1	0.0	0.0	0.0
RL(% PTS)	-	-	-	-	-	-	-	-	-	-
GDEF (B.US$) **	-	-	-	-	-	-	-	-	-	-
PXGS(%)	-	-	-	-	-	-	-	-	-	-
PMGS(%)	-	-	-	-	-	-	-	-	-	-
EXCH(%) ***	2.7	6.5	12.0	18.7	10.0	28.3	28.6	31.0	32.8	34.3
CAB(B.US$) **	0.0	0.8	2.4	4.0	1.8	5.6	3.0	3.1	3.3	2.9

* Exchange rate : (Weighted average of foreign currencies)/U.S. $.
** Local currency units translated into U.S. $ at baseline exchange rates.
*** Exchange rate : U.S. $/(weighted average of non-US OECD currencies).

Model: VAR
Simulation E: U.S. Monetary Expansion with Foreign Short-Term Interest Rates Unchanged from Baseline
(Deviation of Shock Path from Baseline Path)

	1985									
	Q1	Q2	Q3	Q4	1985	1986	1987	1988	1989	1990
JAPAN										
GNP(%)	0.0	0.1	0.2	0.4	0.1	0.7	0.7	0.7	0.8	1.0
CPI(%)	0.0	-0.0	-0.1	-0.1	-0.1	-0.0	0.2	0.0	-0.2	-0.4
RS(% PTS)	0.0	0.0	0.0	0.0	0.0	-0.1	0.1	0.1	-0.0	-0.0
GDEF(%GNPV) *	-	-	-	-	-	-	-	-	-	-
EXCH(%) **	1.7	4.0	7.1	10.3	5.8	14.4	14.2	15.0	15.6	16.1
CAB(B.US$) ***	0.0	0.7	2.2	3.7	1.6	4.7	2.0	2.2	2.3	1.9
GERMANY										
GNP(%)	-	-	-	-	-	-	-	-	-	-
CPI(%)	-	-	-	-	-	-	-	-	-	-
RS(% PTS)	-	-	-	-	-	-	-	-	-	-
GDEF(%GNPV) *	-	-	-	-	-	-	-	-	-	-
EXCH(%) **	-	-	-	-	-	-	-	-	-	-
CAB(B.US$) ***	-	-	-	-	-	-	-	-	-	-
FRANCE										
GNP(%)	-	-	-	-	-	-	-	-	-	-
CPI(%)	-	-	-	-	-	-	-	-	-	-
GDEF(%GNPV) *	-	-	-	-	-	-	-	-	-	-
EXCH(%) **	-	-	-	-	-	-	-	-	-	-
CAB(B.US$) ***	-	-	-	-	-	-	-	-	-	-
UNITED KINGDOM										
GNP(%)	-	-	-	-	-	-	-	-	-	-
CPI(%)	-	-	-	-	-	-	-	-	-	-
GDEF(%GNPV) *	-	-	-	-	-	-	-	-	-	-
EXCH(%) **	-	-	-	-	-	-	-	-	-	-
CAB(B.US$) ***	-	-	-	-	-	-	-	-	-	-
ITALY										
GNP(%)	-	-	-	-	-	-	-	-	-	-
CPI(%)	-	-	-	-	-	-	-	-	-	-
GDEF(%GNPV) *	-	-	-	-	-	-	-	-	-	-
EXCH(%) **	-	-	-	-	-	-	-	-	-	-
CAB(B.US$) ***	-	-	-	-	-	-	-	-	-	-
CANADA										
GNP(%)	-	-	-	-	-	-	-	-	-	-
CPI(%)	-	-	-	-	-	-	-	-	-	-
GDEF(%GNPV) *	-	-	-	-	-	-	-	-	-	-
EXCH(%) **	-	-	-	-	-	-	-	-	-	-
CAB(B.US$) ***	-	-	-	-	-	-	-	-	-	-
REST OF WORLD										
CAB(B.US$) ***	-	-	-	-	-	-	-	-	-	-

* Government deficit as a percentage of baseline nominal GNP.
** Exchange rate : Bilateral rate against U.S. $ ($/local currency).
*** Local currency units translated into U.S. $ at baseline exchange rates.

Model: VAR
Simulation F: Nonpolicy Exogenous Depreciation of the Dollar
(Deviation of Shock Path from Baseline Path)

	1985 Q1	1985 Q2	1985 Q3	1985 Q4	1985	1986	1987	1988	1989	1990
UNITED STATES										
GNPV(%)	0.0	0.0	0.1	0.2	0.1	0.5	1.1	1.0	1.8	1.2
GNP(%)	0.0	0.0	0.1	0.2	0.1	0.4	0.8	0.5	1.1	0.4
PGNP(%)	0.0	-0.0	-0.0	-0.0	-0.0	0.0	0.3	0.6	0.6	0.8
CPI(%)	-	-	-	-	-	-	-	-	-	-
WAGES(%)	0.0	0.0	0.0	0.0	0.0	0.1	0.4	0.6	0.8	0.9
UN(% PTS)	0.0	-0.0	-0.0	-0.1	-0.0	-0.2	-0.3	-0.1	-0.5	-0.1
GNP(B.72$)	0.0	0.4	1.6	3.4	1.3	7.8	14.7	8.5	21.8	8.0
G(B.72$)	0.0	-0.0	-0.1	-0.1	-0.0	0.2	-0.7	1.1	1.5	2.9
C(B.72$)	0.0	0.2	1.0	1.8	0.7	2.1	2.6	-12.7	-5.0	-26.1
IFP(B.72$)	-	-	-	-	-	-	-	-	-	-
II(B.72$)	-	-	-	-	-	-	-	-	-	-
XGS(B.72$)	0.0	0.0	0.2	0.6	0.2	1.7	4.2	4.4	6.9	6.2
MGS(B.72$)	0.0	-0.1	-0.5	-1.0	-0.4	-3.8	-8.7	-15.7	-18.4	-25.0
M1(%)	-0.0	-0.0	-0.0	-0.1	-0.0	0.0	-0.0	0.0	0.3	-0.3
RS(% PTS)	0.0	0.0	0.2	0.4	0.2	0.2	0.9	0.2	1.1	1.1
RL(% PTS)	-	-	-	-	-	-	-	-	-	-
GDEF(B$)	0.0	-0.4	-1.5	-2.9	-1.2	-5.9	-12.0	-8.1	-16.2	-10.0
PXGS(%)	-	-	-	-	-	-	-	-	-	-
PMGS(%)	0.0	0.0	0.1	0.3	0.1	1.4	3.4	4.4	6.0	6.5
EXCH(%) *	-1.2	-3.7	-6.3	-8.8	-5.0	-14.6	-19.7	-25.2	-27.9	-28.1
CAB(B$)	0.0	0.3	1.0	1.8	0.8	4.4	8.1	12.1	14.3	15.8
NON-US OECD										
GNPV(%) **	0.0	0.0	0.0	0.0	0.0	0.1	0.1	0.0	0.2	0.1
GNP(%) **	0.0	-0.0	0.0	-0.0	-0.0	-0.1	-0.2	-0.4	-0.5	-0.6
PGNP(%)	0.0	0.0	0.0	0.0	0.0	0.2	0.3	0.4	0.5	0.7
CPI(%)	-	-	-	-	-	-	-	-	-	-
WAGES(%)	-	-	-	-	-	-	-	-	-	-
UN(% PTS)	-	-	-	-	-	-	-	-	-	-
C(%) **	-	-	-	-	-	-	-	-	-	-
IFP(%) **	-	-	-	-	-	-	-	-	-	-
RS(% PTS)	-0.0	-0.1	-0.1	-0.1	-0.1	-0.1	-0.1	-0.2	-0.3	0.0
RL(% PTS)	-	-	-	-	-	-	-	-	-	-
GDEF (B.US$) **	-	-	-	-	-	-	-	-	-	-
PXGS(%)	-	-	-	-	-	-	-	-	-	-
PMGS(%)	-	-	-	-	-	-	-	-	-	-
EXCH(%) ***	1.3	3.9	6.7	9.6	5.4	17.2	24.5	34.0	38.8	39.2
CAB(B.US$) **	0.0	0.0	0.1	0.2	0.1	0.0	0.3	-0.5	0.9	-0.9

* Exchange rate : (Weighted average of foreign currencies)/U.S. $.
** Local currency units translated into U.S. $ at baseline exchange rates.
*** Exchange rate : U.S. $/(weighted average of non-US OECD currencies).

Model: VAR
Simulation F: Nonpolicy Exogenous Depreciation of the Dollar
(Deviation of Shock Path from Baseline Path)

	1985									
	Q1	Q2	Q3	Q4	1985	1986	1987	1988	1989	1990
JAPAN										
GNP(%)	0.0	-0.0	-0.0	-0.0	-0.0	-0.3	-0.6	-0.8	-1.0	-1.4
CPI(%)	0.0	0.0	0.0	0.1	0.0	0.3	0.7	0.8	1.2	1.5
RS(% PTS)	-0.1	-0.3	-0.4	-0.4	-0.3	-0.5	-0.7	-0.9	-1.0	-0.9
GDEF(%GNPV) *	-	-	-	-	-	-	-	-	-	-
EXCH(%) **	0.8	2.4	4.0	5.6	3.2	9.4	12.5	16.1	17.9	18.0
CAB(B.US$) ***	0.0	0.0	0.1	0.2	0.1	-0.0	0.1	-0.5	0.6	-0.9
GERMANY										
GNP(%)	-	-	-	-	-	-	-	-	-	-
CPI(%)	-	-	-	-	-	-	-	-	-	-
RS(% PTS)	-	-	-	-	-	-	-	-	-	-
GDEF(%GNPV) *	-	-	-	-	-	-	-	-	-	-
EXCH(%) **	-	-	-	-	-	-	-	-	-	-
CAB(B.US$) ***	-	-	-	-	-	-	-	-	-	-
FRANCE										
GNP(%)	-	-	-	-	-	-	-	-	-	-
CPI(%)	-	-	-	-	-	-	-	-	-	-
GDEF(%GNPV) *	-	-	-	-	-	-	-	-	-	-
EXCH(%) **	-	-	-	-	-	-	-	-	-	-
CAB(B.US$) ***	-	-	-	-	-	-	-	-	-	-
UNITED KINGDOM										
GNP(%)	-	-	-	-	-	-	-	-	-	-
CPI(%)	-	-	-	-	-	-	-	-	-	-
GDEF(%GNPV) *	-	-	-	-	-	-	-	-	-	-
EXCH(%) **	-	-	-	-	-	-	-	-	-	-
CAB(B.US$) ***	-	-	-	-	-	-	-	-	-	-
ITALY										
GNP(%)	-	-	-	-	-	-	-	-	-	-
CPI(%)	-	-	-	-	-	-	-	-	-	-
GDEF(%GNPV) *	-	-	-	-	-	-	-	-	-	-
EXCH(%) **	-	-	-	-	-	-	-	-	-	-
CAB(B.US$) ***	-	-	-	-	-	-	-	-	-	-
CANADA										
GNP(%)	-	-	-	-	-	-	-	-	-	-
CPI(%)	-	-	-	-	-	-	-	-	-	-
GDEF(%GNPV) *	-	-	-	-	-	-	-	-	-	-
EXCH(%) **	-	-	-	-	-	-	-	-	-	-
CAB(B.US$) ***	-	-	-	-	-	-	-	-	-	-
REST OF WORLD										
CAB(B.US$) ***	-	-	-	-	-	-	-	-	-	-

* Government deficit as a percentage of baseline nominal GNP.
** Exchange rate : Bilateral rate against U.S. $ ($/local currency).
*** Local currency units translated into U.S. $ at baseline exchange rates.

Model: VAR
Simulation G: Increase in Government Purchases in Non-U.S. OECD Countries with U.S. Policies Unchanged from Baseline
(Deviation of Shock Path from Baseline Path)

	1985									
	Q1	Q2	Q3	Q4	1985	1986	1987	1988	1989	1990
UNITED STATES										
GNPV(%)	0.0	0.0	0.2	0.3	0.1	0.1	-0.2	-0.0	-0.1	-0.1
GNP(%)	0.0	0.1	0.2	0.5	0.2	0.3	-0.1	0.2	0.2	0.2
PGNP(%)	0.0	-0.0	-0.1	-0.1	-0.1	-0.1	-0.2	-0.2	-0.3	-0.3
CPI(%)	-	-	-	-	-	-	-	-	-	-
WAGES(%)	0.0	0.0	0.0	0.1	0.0	-0.0	-0.1	-0.2	-0.2	-0.2
UN(% PTS)	0.0	-0.0	-0.1	-0.2	-0.1	-0.1	0.1	-0.1	-0.0	-0.1
GNP(B.72$)	0.0	0.9	4.0	7.9	3.2	4.8	-0.9	3.9	3.0	4.4
G(B.72$)	0.0	-0.1	-0.3	-0.4	-0.2	-1.2	-1.0	-1.1	-1.3	-1.3
C(B.72$)	0.0	1.2	5.1	10.2	4.1	8.9	4.1	10.8	10.5	12.6
IFP(B.72$)	-	-	-	-	-	-	-	-	-	-
II(B.72$)	-	-	-	-	-	-	-	-	-	-
XGS(B.72$)	0.0	-0.1	0.2	0.8	0.2	1.0	-0.4	0.3	0.2	0.5
MGS(B.72$)	0.0	0.1	1.0	2.6	0.9	3.9	3.6	6.1	6.4	7.3
M1(%)	0.1	0.2	0.4	0.5	0.3	-0.0	0.0	-0.0	-0.0	0.0
RS(% PTS)	-0.3	-0.6	-0.5	-0.1	-0.4	0.2	-0.3	-0.1	-0.2	-0.1
RL(% PTS)	-	-	-	-	-	-	-	-	-	-
GDEF(B$)	0.0	-0.6	-2.2	-4.6	-1.9	-3.6	0.7	-1.5	-1.0	-1.4
PXGS(%)	-	-	-	-	-	-	-	-	-	-
PMGS(%)	0.0	-0.1	-0.4	-0.7	-0.3	-0.8	-1.5	-1.7	-1.8	-1.9
EXCH(%) *	0.4	0.1	-0.2	-0.2	0.0	2.4	2.6	2.6	2.4	2.2
CAB(B$)	0.0	-0.3	-0.6	-1.2	-0.5	-2.6	-2.3	-3.2	-3.0	-3.2
NON-US OECD										
GNPV(%) **	0.0	0.2	0.3	0.3	0.2	0.3	0.4	0.5	0.5	0.5
GNP(%) **	0.0	0.2	0.5	0.5	0.3	0.5	0.6	0.7	0.8	0.8
PGNP(%)	0.0	-0.1	-0.2	-0.3	-0.1	-0.3	-0.3	-0.3	-0.3	-0.3
CPI(%)	-	-	-	-	-	-	-	-	-	-
WAGES(%)	-	-	-	-	-	-	-	-	-	-
UN(% PTS)	-	-	-	-	-	-	-	-	-	-
C(%) **	-	-	-	-	-	-	-	-	-	-
IFP(%) **	-	-	-	-	-	-	-	-	-	-
RS(% PTS)	-0.4	-0.8	-1.1	-1.1	-0.9	-0.3	-0.5	-0.5	-0.5	-0.5
RL(% PTS)	-	-	-	-	-	-	-	-	-	-
GDEF (B.US$) **	-	-	-	-	-	-	-	-	-	-
PXGS(%)	-	-	-	-	-	-	-	-	-	-
PMGS(%)	-	-	-	-	-	-	-	-	-	-
EXCH(%) ***	-0.4	-0.1	0.2	0.2	-0.0	-2.4	-2.5	-2.5	-2.3	-2.2
CAB(B.US$) **	0.0	1.0	-0.0	1.2	0.5	1.7	0.3	1.1	0.9	1.0

* Exchange rate : (Weighted average of foreign currencies)/U.S. $.
** Local currency units translated into U.S. $ at baseline exchange rates.
*** Exchange rate : U.S. $/(weighted average of non-US OECD currencies).

Model: VAR
Simulation G: Increase in Government Purchases in Non-U.S. OECD Countries with U.S. Policies Unchanged from Baseline
(Deviation of Shock Path from Baseline Path)

	1985									
	Q1	Q2	Q3	Q4	1985	1986	1987	1988	1989	1990
JAPAN										
GNP(%)	0.0	0.6	0.8	1.0	0.6	1.1	1.3	1.5	1.6	1.7
CPI(%)	0.0	-0.1	-0.3	-0.4	-0.2	-0.5	-0.6	-0.7	-0.8	-0.9
RS(% PTS)	-0.4	-0.8	-1.0	-1.4	-0.9	-1.6	-1.6	-1.7	-1.8	-1.8
GDEF(%GNPV) *	-	-	-	-	-	-	-	-	-	-
EXCH(%) **	-0.2	-0.0	0.2	0.2	0.0	-1.7	-1.8	-1.8	-1.7	-1.6
CAB(B.US$) ***	0.0	0.9	2.2	3.3	1.6	1.1	0.8	1.1	1.0	0.9
GERMANY										
GNP(%)	-	-	-	-	-	-	-	-	-	-
CPI(%)	-	-	-	-	-	-	-	-	-	-
RS(% PTS)	-	-	-	-	-	-	-	-	-	-
GDEF(%GNPV) *	-	-	-	-	-	-	-	-	-	-
EXCH(%) **	-	-	-	-	-	-	-	-	-	-
CAB(B.US$) ***	-	-	-	-	-	-	-	-	-	-
FRANCE										
GNP(%)	-	-	-	-	-	-	-	-	-	-
CPI(%)	-	-	-	-	-	-	-	-	-	-
GDEF(%GNPV) *	-	-	-	-	-	-	-	-	-	-
EXCH(%) **	-	-	-	-	-	-	-	-	-	-
CAB(B.US$) ***	-	-	-	-	-	-	-	-	-	-
UNITED KINGDOM										
GNP(%)	-	-	-	-	-	-	-	-	-	-
CPI(%)	-	-	-	-	-	-	-	-	-	-
GDEF(%GNPV) *	-	-	-	-	-	-	-	-	-	-
EXCH(%) **	-	-	-	-	-	-	-	-	-	-
CAB(B.US$) ***	-	-	-	-	-	-	-	-	-	-
ITALY										
GNP(%)	-	-	-	-	-	-	-	-	-	-
CPI(%)	-	-	-	-	-	-	-	-	-	-
GDEF(%GNPV) *	-	-	-	-	-	-	-	-	-	-
EXCH(%) **	-	-	-	-	-	-	-	-	-	-
CAB(B.US$) ***	-	-	-	-	-	-	-	-	-	-
CANADA										
GNP(%)	-	-	-	-	-	-	-	-	-	-
CPI(%)	-	-	-	-	-	-	-	-	-	-
GDEF(%GNPV) *	-	-	-	-	-	-	-	-	-	-
EXCH(%) **	-	-	-	-	-	-	-	-	-	-
CAB(B.US$) ***	-	-	-	-	-	-	-	-	-	-
REST OF WORLD										
CAB(B.US$) ***	-	-	-	-	-	-	-	-	-	-

* Government deficit as a percentage of baseline nominal GNP.
** Exchange rate : Bilateral rate against U.S. $ ($/local currency).
*** Local currency units translated into U.S. $ at baseline exchange rates.

Model: VAR
Simulation H: Monetary Expansion in Non-U.S. OECD Countries
with U.S. Policies Unchanged from Baseline
(Deviation of Shock Path from Baseline Path)

	1985 Q1	1985 Q2	1985 Q3	1985 Q4	1985	1986	1987	1988	1989	1990
UNITED STATES										
GNPV(%)	0.0	0.2	0.7	1.2	0.5	0.5	-0.5	0.3	-0.0	0.3
GNP(%)	0.0	0.3	1.0	1.7	0.7	1.2	0.5	1.4	1.2	1.5
PGNP(%)	0.0	-0.1	-0.3	-0.5	-0.2	-0.7	-1.0	-1.2	-1.2	-1.2
CPI(%)	-	-	-	-	-	-	-	-	-	-
WAGES(%)	0.0	0.1	0.2	0.3	0.1	-0.0	-0.5	-0.6	-0.7	-0.7
UN(% PTS)	0.0	-0.1	-0.3	-0.6	-0.2	-0.6	-0.1	-0.6	-0.4	-0.6
GNP(B.72$)	0.0	4.7	16.3	29.4	12.6	21.4	8.2	26.6	22.2	30.3
G(B.72$)	0.0	-0.4	-1.0	-1.7	-0.8	-4.1	-4.2	-4.9	-4.7	-5.1
C(B.72$)	0.0	5.5	19.8	36.7	15.5	35.5	26.2	49.6	45.0	55.1
IFP(B.72$)	-	-	-	-	-	-	-	-	-	-
II(B.72$)	-	-	-	-	-	-	-	-	-	-
XGS(B.72$)	0.0	-0.3	0.7	2.6	0.7	3.9	0.9	3.9	3.9	5.3
MGS(B.72$)	0.0	0.1	3.2	8.2	2.9	13.9	14.7	22.0	21.9	25.1
M1(%)	0.3	0.8	1.4	1.5	1.0	-0.0	0.0	-0.0	-0.1	0.1
RS(% PTS)	-1.4	-2.1	-1.4	-0.1	-1.2	0.6	-0.9	-0.1	-0.4	-0.4
RL(% PTS)	-	-	-	-	-	-	-	-	-	-
GDEF(B$)	0.0	-2.8	-9.9	-19.5	-8.1	-18.7	-7.6	-16.0	-13.1	-15.6
PXGS(%)	-	-	-	-	-	-	-	-	-	-
PMGS(%)	0.0	-0.4	-1.2	-2.0	-0.9	-3.0	-5.2	-5.4	-5.9	-6.0
EXCH(%) *	0.3	-0.2	-1.3	-1.1	-0.6	5.9	3.8	2.4	0.5	-2.0
CAB(B$)	0.0	-0.5	-1.9	-4.6	-1.8	-10.0	-9.0	-11.2	-9.7	-9.2
NON-US OECD										
GNPV(%) **	0.0	-0.1	-0.0	0.1	0.0	0.4	0.7	0.9	0.9	0.9
GNP(%) **	0.0	0.0	0.1	0.4	0.1	0.7	1.0	1.4	1.5	1.7
PGNP(%)	0.0	-0.1	-0.2	-0.4	-0.2	-0.5	-0.5	-0.7	-0.8	-1.0
CPI(%)	-	-	-	-	-	-	-	-	-	-
WAGES(%)	-	-	-	-	-	-	-	-	-	-
UN(% PTS)	-	-	-	-	-	-	-	-	-	-
C(%) **	-	-	-	-	-	-	-	-	-	-
IFP(%) **	-	-	-	-	-	-	-	-	-	-
RS(% PTS)	-1.5	-3.2	-4.5	-4.9	-3.5	-3.2	-3.5	-3.5	-3.5	-3.6
RL(% PTS)	-	-	-	-	-	-	-	-	-	-
GDEF (B.US$) **	-	-	-	-	-	-	-	-	-	-
PXGS(%)	-	-	-	-	-	-	-	-	-	-
PMGS(%)	-	-	-	-	-	-	-	-	-	-
EXCH(%) ***	-0.3	0.2	1.4	1.1	0.6	-5.5	-3.6	-2.3	-0.5	2.1
CAB(B.US$) **	0.0	1.4	4.7	8.1	3.6	5.2	2.4	4.0	3.0	3.4

* Exchange rate : (Weighted average of foreign currencies)/U.S. $.
** Local currency units translated into U.S. $ at baseline exchange rates.
*** Exchange rate : U.S. $/(weighted average of non-US OECD currencies).

Model: VAR
Simulation H: Monetary Expansion in Non-U.S. OECD Countries
with U.S. Policies Unchanged from Baseline
(Deviation of Shock Path from Baseline Path)

	1985 Q1	Q2	Q3	Q4	1985	1986	1987	1988	1989	1990
JAPAN										
GNP(%)	0.0	0.1	0.4	0.8	0.3	0.9	1.7	2.2	2.6	2.9
CPI(%)	0.0	-0.1	-0.2	-0.3	-0.1	-0.1	-0.3	-0.7	-1.0	-1.4
RS(% PTS)	-0.7	-1.3	-2.1	-2.8	-1.7	-3.1	-3.0	-3.3	-3.4	-3.6
GDEF(%GNPV) *	-	-	-	-	-	-	-	-	-	-
EXCH(%) **	-0.1	0.5	1.3	1.1	0.7	-3.9	-2.5	-1.8	-0.7	0.7
CAB(B.US$) ***	0.0	1.3	4.3	7.0	3.2	1.9	1.1	1.8	1.1	1.3
GERMANY										
GNP(%)	-	-	-	-	-	-	-	-	-	-
CPI(%)	-	-	-	-	-	-	-	-	-	-
RS(% PTS)	-	-	-	-	-	-	-	-	-	-
GDEF(%GNPV) *	-	-	-	-	-	-	-	-	-	-
EXCH(%) **	-	-	-	-	-	-	-	-	-	-
CAB(B.US$) ***	-	-	-	-	-	-	-	-	-	-
FRANCE										
GNP(%)	-	-	-	-	-	-	-	-	-	-
CPI(%)	-	-	-	-	-	-	-	-	-	-
GDEF(%GNPV) *	-	-	-	-	-	-	-	-	-	-
EXCH(%) **	-	-	-	-	-	-	-	-	-	-
CAB(B.US$) ***	-	-	-	-	-	-	-	-	-	-
UNITED KINGDOM										
GNP(%)	-	-	-	-	-	-	-	-	-	-
CPI(%)	-	-	-	-	-	-	-	-	-	-
GDEF(%GNPV) *	-	-	-	-	-	-	-	-	-	-
EXCH(%) **	-	-	-	-	-	-	-	-	-	-
CAB(B.US$) ***	-	-	-	-	-	-	-	-	-	-
ITALY										
GNP(%)	-	-	-	-	-	-	-	-	-	-
CPI(%)	-	-	-	-	-	-	-	-	-	-
GDEF(%GNPV) *	-	-	-	-	-	-	-	-	-	-
EXCH(%) **	-	-	-	-	-	-	-	-	-	-
CAB(B.US$) ***	-	-	-	-	-	-	-	-	-	-
CANADA										
GNP(%)	-	-	-	-	-	-	-	-	-	-
CPI(%)	-	-	-	-	-	-	-	-	-	-
GDEF(%GNPV) *	-	-	-	-	-	-	-	-	-	-
EXCH(%) **	-	-	-	-	-	-	-	-	-	-
CAB(B.US$) ***	-	-	-	-	-	-	-	-	-	-
REST OF WORLD										
CAB(B.US$) ***	-	-	-	-	-	-	-	-	-	-

* Government deficit as a percentage of baseline nominal GNP.
** Exchange rate : Bilateral rate against U.S. $ ($/local currency).
*** Local currency units translated into U.S. $ at baseline exchange rates.

WHARTON—World Model of Wharton Econometrics Associates

See part 1 of this volume for design and detailed description of the simulations. See part 4 for bibliographical references.

Figures for the non-U.S. OECD region shown in simulation A were not based to 1972 = 100 (contrary to the standardized labels shown for the rows).

Model: WHARTON
Simulation A: Baseline Path

	1985	1986	1987	1988	1989	1990
UNITED STATES						
GNPV(B.$)	3856.7	4123.4	4447.8	4804.5	5206.6	5489.0
GNP(B.72$)	1663.0	1709.3	1766.3	1819.0	1876.0	1876.0
PGNP(72=100)	231.9	241.2	251.8	264.1	277.5	292.6
CPI(72=100)	257.2	266.2	277.8	292.7	308.5	324.3
WAGES(72=100)	250.9	263.3	274.6	290.9	310.7	334.1
UN(%)	7.3	7.4	7.2	7.2	7.1	8.1
G(B.72$)	314.7	321.0	326.0	334.3	342.6	351.2
C(B.72$)	1106.5	1135.4	1166.7	1197.3	1231.5	1245.3
IFP(B.72$)	280.8	295.2	310.5	319.5	327.6	310.5
II(B.72$)	9.7	11.5	12.5	11.5	11.5	-1.4
XGS(B.72$)	104.3	107.8	113.6	120.9	128.7	136.6
MGS(B.72$)	154.7	162.8	164.5	165.9	167.6	165.2
M1(B.$)	611.1	650.5	686.2	721.2	754.2	795.4
RS(%)	7.7	6.3	7.0	8.8	9.6	10.4
RL(%)	12.1	11.0	11.2	11.3	11.4	11.7
GDEF(B.$)	136.4	147.1	138.2	132.0	124.9	155.9
PXGS(72=100)	260.3	270.6	283.3	296.2	310.0	323.7
PMGS(72=100)	261.8	269.0	282.3	293.6	306.5	316.4
EXCH(72=100) *	138.9	125.5	120.2	115.0	113.8	114.5
CAB(B.$)	-133.2	-147.9	-144.3	-132.5	-126.0	-96.4
NON-US OECD						
GNPV(B.$) **	782.0	841.5	905.6	974.6	1045.5	1117.1
GNP(B.72$) **	244.0	249.6	256.3	263.5	270.7	276.7
PGNP(72=100)	320.5	337.1	353.4	369.9	386.2	403.8
CPI(72=100)	420.6	442.0	463.1	484.3	505.5	528.3
WAGES(72=100)	258.3	275.9	293.8	312.7	331.8	352.2
UN(%)	7.5	7.6	7.6	7.6	7.5	7.4
C(B.72$) **	133.8	136.9	140.4	144.3	148.1	151.3
IFP(B.72$) **	48.2	49.9	52.1	54.4	56.6	58.4
RS(%)	9.6	8.3	7.9	7.9	7.8	7.9
RL(%)	10.8	9.9	9.2	9.2	9.2	9.2
GDEF(B.US$) **	181.0	194.8	189.3	200.2	199.9	203.3
PXGS(72=100)	374.8	374.7	379.5	388.3	398.8	412.7
PMGS(72=100)	505.0	494.5	498.3	508.0	521.4	544.8
EXCH(72=100) ***	72.0	79.7	83.2	87.0	87.9	87.3
CAB(B.US$)	68.1	86.1	86.5	83.9	79.0	54.4

* Exchange rate : (Weighted average of foreign currencies)/U.S. $.
** Local currency units translated into U.S. $ at baseline exchange rates.
*** Exchange rate : U.S. $/(weighted average of non-US OECD currencies).

Model: WHARTON
Simulation A: Baseline Path

	1985	1986	1987	1988	1989	1990
JAPAN						
GNP(B.72Y)	159252.3	164070.9	168381.3	173558.3	179013.1	183888.3
CPI(72=100)	244.3	249.9	256.9	262.8	267.3	273.0
RS(%)	6.2	5.3	5.5	5.9	6.1	6.6
GDEF(%GNPV) *	2.3	2.6	2.1	2.0	1.9	1.9
EXCH(72=100) **	131.4	143.8	151.7	168.0	177.9	175.8
CAB(B.US$) ***	52.8	58.3	55.6	53.6	50.7	39.1
GERMANY						
GNP(B.72DM)	1064.9	1085.9	1111.5	1139.8	1166.3	1188.7
CPI(72=100)	179.0	182.3	185.8	189.4	193.7	198.1
RS(%)	4.8	4.2	4.1	3.8	3.7	3.7
GDEF(%GNPV) *	1.8	1.8	1.3	1.2	0.9	0.5
EXCH(72=100) **	116.1	139.0	153.2	163.5	171.8	179.8
CAB(B.US$) ***	14.0	22.8	23.1	22.8	21.7	16.9
FRANCE						
GNP(B.72F)	1324.9	1351.2	1382.6	1417.5	1454.5	1485.9
CPI(72=100)	355.3	373.3	388.3	407.5	426.0	447.2
GDEF(%GNPV) *	2.9	2.9	2.8	2.5	2.4	2.1
EXCH(72=100) **	60.3	69.9	71.8	73.8	74.2	73.3
CAB(B.US$) ***	0.5	2.7	3.4	2.9	2.1	0.5
UNITED KINGDOM						
GNP(B.72LB)	80.4	81.6	83.6	85.3	87.1	88.6
CPI(72=100)	436.2	457.0	478.6	500.3	523.8	550.0
GDEF(%GNPV) *	2.7	2.4	2.3	2.3	2.1	2.2
EXCH(72=100) **	57.7	61.9	64.8	66.5	61.6	60.2
CAB(B.US$) ***	4.2	5.0	2.7	2.7	-0.1	-4.3
ITALY						
GNP(B.72L)	101.4	103.4	106.4	109.5	112.9	116.1
CPI(72=100)	626.0	675.2	728.0	784.0	844.5	908.2
GDEF(%GNPV) *	13.9	12.4	12.2	11.9	11.2	10.6
EXCH(72=100) **	30.9	30.3	28.5	27.2	25.7	24.4
CAB(B.US$) ***	-6.1	-4.9	-5.9	-7.5	-6.7	-7.2
CANADA						
GNP(B.72C$)	159.1	163.5	169.2	173.9	178.1	179.1
CPI(72=100)	287.4	299.4	312.5	326.5	340.7	354.6
GDEF(%GNPV) *	4.9	3.7	3.1	2.5	2.2	2.7
EXCH(72=100) **	73.1	73.8	74.1	75.8	77.6	77.4
CAB(B.US$) ***	0.8	0.2	0.7	-0.6	-1.0	-3.6
REST OF WORLD						
CAB(B.US$) ***	-39.6	-41.0	-49.1	-53.1	-60.1	-66.8

* Government deficit as a percentage of baseline nominal GNP.
** Exchange rate: Bilateral rate against U.S. $ ($/local currency).
*** Local currency units translated into U.S. $ at baseline exchange rates.

Model: WHARTON
Simulation B: Reduction in U.S. Government Purchases with Foreign Monetary Aggregates Unchanged from Baseline
(Deviation of Shock Path from Baseline Path)

	1985									
	Q1	Q2	Q3	Q4	1985	1986	1987	1988	1989	1990
UNITED STATES										
GNPV(%)	-	-	-	-	-1.6	-1.8	-2.1	-2.2	-2.2	-2.4
GNP(%)	-	-	-	-	-1.7	-1.4	-1.4	-1.4	-1.4	-1.6
PGNP(%)	-	-	-	-	0.1	-0.4	-0.7	-0.8	-0.8	-0.8
CPI(%)	-	-	-	-	0.2	-0.3	-0.6	-0.8	-0.8	-0.8
WAGES(%)	-	-	-	-	-0.5	-0.7	-1.1	-1.3	-1.4	-1.4
UN(% PTS)	-	-	-	-	0.5	0.7	0.7	0.7	0.7	0.8
GNP(B.72$)	-	-	-	-	-28.0	-23.3	-24.6	-25.3	-26.9	-30.7
G(B.72$)	-	-	-	-	-15.7	-16.1	-16.7	-17.2	-17.7	-17.7
C(B.72$)	-	-	-	-	-12.8	-10.8	-12.1	-12.8	-13.4	-15.2
IFP(B.72$)	-	-	-	-	-5.3	-3.3	-2.2	-0.5	0.9	1.2
II(B.72$)	-	-	-	-	0.0	0.0	0.0	0.0	0.0	0.0
XGS(B.72$)	-	-	-	-	-0.7	-0.8	-1.3	-1.8	-2.3	-2.8
MGS(B.72$)	-	-	-	-	-4.7	-5.3	-5.3	-4.9	-4.2	-3.2
M1(%)	-	-	-	-	0.0	0.0	0.0	0.0	0.0	0.0
RS(% PTS)	-	-	-	-	-1.0	-1.1	-1.4	-1.6	-1.7	-1.9
RL(% PTS)	-	-	-	-	-0.5	-0.9	-1.3	-1.7	-1.9	-2.2
GDEF(B$)	-	-	-	-	-16.0	-17.9	-18.0	-19.3	-20.2	-19.5
PXGS(%)	-	-	-	-	0.0	-0.4	-0.9	-1.2	-1.4	-1.9
PMGS(%)	-	-	-	-	-0.5	-1.0	-1.8	-2.5	-3.1	-4.0
EXCH(%) *	-	-	-	-	0.8	2.1	3.5	5.5	7.4	9.4
CAB(B$)	-	-	-	-	12.2	15.4	16.8	16.7	15.6	13.5
NON-US OECD										
GNPV(%) **	-	-	-	-	-0.2	-0.0	0.0	0.2	0.5	0.8
GNP(%) **	-	-	-	-	-0.3	-0.2	-0.2	-0.1	0.1	0.2
PGNP(%)	-	-	-	-	0.1	0.1	0.2	0.3	0.4	0.6
CPI(%)	-	-	-	-	0.1	0.1	0.2	0.3	0.5	0.6
WAGES(%)	-	-	-	-	-0.0	-0.0	-0.0	0.1	0.2	0.4
UN(% PTS)	-	-	-	-	0.0	0.0	0.0	0.0	0.0	0.0
C(%) **	-	-	-	-	-0.2	-0.1	-0.2	-0.1	-0.1	0.0
IFP(%) **	-	-	-	-	-0.3	-0.0	-0.0	0.1	0.2	0.3
RS(% PTS)	-	-	-	-	-0.6	-0.6	-0.7	-0.7	-0.7	-0.7
RL(% PTS)	-	-	-	-	-0.2	-0.3	-0.5	-0.5	-0.6	-0.6
GDEF (B.US$) **	-	-	-	-	4.0	2.7	3.7	2.6	0.1	-2.2
PXGS(%)	-	-	-	-	0.1	0.6	1.0	1.8	2.6	3.4
PMGS(%)	-	-	-	-	0.2	0.9	1.5	2.5	3.7	4.5
EXCH(%) ***	-	-	-	-	-0.8	-2.0	-3.4	-5.2	-6.9	-8.6
CAB(B.US$) **	-	-	-	-	-6.7	-5.3	-7.2	-5.7	-2.5	0.1

* Exchange rate : (Weighted average of foreign currencies)/U.S. $.
** Local currency units translated into U.S. $ at baseline exchange rates.
*** Exchange rate : U.S. $/(weighted average of non-US OECD currencies).

Model: WHARTON
Simulation B: Reduction in U.S. Government Purchases with Foreign Monetary Aggregates Unchanged from Baseline
(Deviation of Shock Path from Baseline Path)

	1985									
	Q1	Q2	Q3	Q4	1985	1986	1987	1988	1989	1990
JAPAN										
GNP(%)	-	-	-	-	-0.4	-0.2	-0.0	0.4	0.9	1.4
CPI(%)	-	-	-	-	0.1	0.3	0.6	1.1	1.7	2.6
RS(% PTS)	-	-	-	-	-0.0	0.1	0.3	0.5	0.8	1.2
GDEF(%GNPV) *	-	-	-	-	0.1	0.0	0.0	-0.1	-0.1	-0.3
EXCH(%) **	-	-	-	-	-1.8	-4.9	-9.0	-13.0	-17.3	-21.9
CAB(B.US$) ***	-	-	-	-	-2.2	-1.4	-0.3	2.2	5.9	9.6
GERMANY										
GNP(%)	-	-	-	-	-0.2	-0.0	-0.3	-0.3	-0.2	-0.3
CPI(%)	-	-	-	-	0.0	-0.0	-0.0	-0.1	-0.1	-0.1
RS(% PTS)	-	-	-	-	-0.8	-0.9	-1.1	-1.2	-1.2	-1.3
GDEF(%GNPV) *	-	-	-	-	0.1	0.0	0.1	0.1	0.1	0.1
EXCH(%) **	-	-	-	-	-0.4	-1.0	-1.5	-2.5	-3.1	-3.6
CAB(B.US$) ***	-	-	-	-	-0.7	-0.3	-1.0	-1.1	-1.3	-1.4
FRANCE										
GNP(%)	-	-	-	-	-0.2	-0.1	-0.1	-0.1	0.1	0.2
CPI(%)	-	-	-	-	0.1	0.1	-0.1	-0.1	-0.2	-0.4
GDEF(%GNPV) *	-	-	-	-	0.0	0.0	0.0	0.0	0.0	0.0
EXCH(%) **	-	-	-	-	-0.6	-0.7	-1.2	-2.3	-3.1	-3.7
CAB(B.US$) ***	-	-	-	-	-0.5	-0.5	-0.9	-1.2	-1.3	-1.3
UNITED KINGDOM										
GNP(%)	-	-	-	-	-0.1	0.0	0.0	0.0	0.1	0.1
CPI(%)	-	-	-	-	0.0	-0.0	-0.1	-0.1	-0.1	-0.1
GDEF(%GNPV) *	-	-	-	-	0.0	0.0	0.0	0.0	0.0	0.0
EXCH(%) **	-	-	-	-	-0.2	-0.9	-1.2	-2.0	-2.7	-3.0
CAB(B.US$) ***	-	-	-	-	-0.6	-0.6	-1.0	-1.2	-1.3	-1.5
ITALY										
GNP(%)	-	-	-	-	-0.2	-0.2	-0.2	-0.2	-0.2	-0.2
CPI(%)	-	-	-	-	0.1	0.1	0.1	0.0	0.0	-0.1
GDEF(%GNPV) *	-	-	-	-	0.0	0.0	0.0	0.0	0.0	0.0
EXCH(%) **	-	-	-	-	-0.4	-1.2	-1.4	-2.4	-2.9	-3.2
CAB(B.US$) ***	-	-	-	-	-0.4	-0.3	-0.5	-0.7	-0.8	-0.7
CANADA										
GNP(%)	-	-	-	-	-1.1	-0.8	-0.6	-0.3	0.0	0.4
CPI(%)	-	-	-	-	0.2	0.2	0.2	0.2	0.2	0.2
GDEF(%GNPV) *	-	-	-	-	0.3	0.3	0.3	0.2	0.1	0.0
EXCH(%) **	-	-	-	-	-0.8	-1.9	-2.9	-3.7	-4.3	-4.9
CAB(B.US$) ***	-	-	-	-	-1.1	-1.1	-1.4	-1.4	-1.3	-1.5
REST OF WORLD										
CAB(B.US$) ***	-	-	-	-	-5.2	-2.8	-4.3	-3.0	-1.3	-0.1

* Government deficit as a percentage of baseline nominal GNP.
** Exchange rate : Bilateral rate against U.S. $ ($/local currency).
*** Local currency units translated into U.S. $ at baseline exchange rates.

Model: WHARTON
Simulation C: Reduction in U.S. Government Purchases with Foreign Short-Term Interest Rates Unchanged from Baseline
(Deviation of Shock Path from Baseline Path)

	1985									
	Q1	Q2	Q3	Q4	1985	1986	1987	1988	1989	1990
UNITED STATES										
GNPV(%)	-	-	-	-	-1.6	-1.8	-2.1	-2.2	-2.2	-2.4
GNP(%)	-	-	-	-	-1.7	-1.4	-1.4	-1.4	-1.4	-1.6
PGNP(%)	-	-	-	-	0.1	-0.4	-0.7	-0.8	-0.8	-0.8
CPI(%)	-	-	-	-	0.2	-0.3	-0.6	-0.8	-0.8	-0.8
WAGES(%)	-	-	-	-	-0.5	-0.7	-1.1	-1.3	-1.4	-1.4
UN(% PTS)	-	-	-	-	0.5	0.7	0.7	0.7	0.7	0.8
GNP(B.72$)	-	-	-	-	-28.1	-23.4	-24.7	-25.4	-26.9	-30.6
G(B.72$)	-	-	-	-	-15.7	-16.1	-16.7	-17.2	-17.7	-17.7
C(B.72$)	-	-	-	-	-12.9	-10.9	-12.2	-12.8	-13.5	-15.3
IFP(B.72$)	-	-	-	-	-5.3	-3.3	-2.2	-0.5	0.9	1.2
II(B.72$)	-	-	-	-	0.0	0.0	-0.0	-0.0	0.0	0.0
XGS(B.72$)	-	-	-	-	-0.7	-0.8	-1.4	-1.9	-2.4	-2.9
MGS(B.72$)	-	-	-	-	-4.7	-5.3	-5.3	-4.9	-4.3	-3.4
M1(%)	-	-	-	-	0.0	0.0	0.0	0.0	0.0	0.0
RS(% PTS)	-	-	-	-	-1.0	-1.2	-1.4	-1.6	-1.7	-1.9
RL(% PTS)	-	-	-	-	-0.5	-1.0	-1.3	-1.7	-1.9	-2.2
GDEF(B$)	-	-	-	-	-15.9	-17.8	-17.8	-19.2	-20.1	-19.4
PXGS(%)	-	-	-	-	0.0	-0.4	-0.9	-1.2	-1.4	-1.8
PMGS(%)	-	-	-	-	-0.5	-1.0	-1.8	-2.5	-3.1	-3.9
EXCH(%) *	-	-	-	-	0.9	2.1	3.5	5.4	7.3	9.4
CAB(B$)	-	-	-	-	12.2	15.3	16.6	16.5	15.4	13.3
NON-US OECD										
GNPV(%) **	-	-	-	-	-0.2	-0.1	-0.0	0.2	0.4	0.7
GNP(%) **	-	-	-	-	-0.3	-0.2	-0.3	-0.2	-0.0	0.1
PGNP(%)	-	-	-	-	0.1	0.1	0.2	0.3	0.4	0.6
CPI(%)	-	-	-	-	0.1	0.1	0.2	0.3	0.5	0.6
WAGES(%)	-	-	-	-	-0.0	-0.0	-0.0	0.0	0.2	0.4
UN(% PTS)	-	-	-	-	0.0	0.0	0.1	0.1	0.1	0.1
C(%) **	-	-	-	-	-0.2	-0.2	-0.2	-0.2	-0.1	-0.1
IFP(%) **	-	-	-	-	-0.4	-0.2	-0.2	-0.1	0.0	0.1
RS(% PTS)	-	-	-	-	0.0	0.0	0.0	0.0	0.0	0.0
RL(% PTS)	-	-	-	-	-0.0	-0.1	-0.1	-0.2	-0.2	-0.2
GDEF (B.US$) **	-	-	-	-	4.4	3.3	4.7	3.9	1.7	-0.5
PXGS(%)	-	-	-	-	0.1	0.7	1.1	1.8	2.7	3.5
PMGS(%)	-	-	-	-	0.2	1.0	1.5	2.5	3.7	4.6
EXCH(%) ***	-	-	-	-	-0.9	-2.1	-3.4	-5.2	-6.8	-8.6
CAB(B.US$) **	-	-	-	-	-6.8	-5.1	-6.9	-5.4	-2.2	0.4

* Exchange rate : (Weighted average of foreign currencies)/U.S. $.
** Local currency units translated into U.S. $ at baseline exchange rates.
*** Exchange rate : U.S. $/(weighted average of non-US OECD currencies).

Model: WHARTON
Simulation C: Reduction in U.S. Government Purchases with Foreign Short-Term Interest Rates Unchanged from Baseline
(Deviation of Shock Path from Baseline Path)

	1985									
	Q1	Q2	Q3	Q4	1985	1986	1987	1988	1989	1990
JAPAN										
GNP(%)	-	-	-	-	-0.4	-0.2	0.0	0.5	1.0	1.6
CPI(%)	-	-	-	-	0.1	0.3	0.6	1.1	1.8	2.7
RS(% PTS)	-	-	-	-	0.0	0.0	0.0	0.0	0.0	0.0
GDEF(%GNPV) *	-	-	-	-	0.1	0.0	0.0	-0.1	-0.2	-0.3
EXCH(%) **	-	-	-	-	-1.9	-5.1	-9.3	-13.3	-17.8	-22.7
CAB(B.US$) ***	-	-	-	-	-2.2	-1.4	-0.4	2.1	5.9	9.7
GERMANY										
GNP(%)	-	-	-	-	-0.3	-0.1	-0.3	-0.4	-0.3	-0.4
CPI(%)	-	-	-	-	0.0	-0.0	-0.0	-0.1	-0.1	-0.2
RS(% PTS)	-	-	-	-	0.0	0.0	0.0	0.0	0.0	0.0
GDEF(%GNPV) *	-	-	-	-	0.1	0.0	0.1	0.1	0.1	0.1
EXCH(%) **	-	-	-	-	-0.5	-1.0	-1.4	-2.2	-2.8	-3.3
CAB(B.US$) ***	-	-	-	-	-0.7	-0.3	-1.0	-1.1	-1.3	-1.4
FRANCE										
GNP(%)	-	-	-	-	-0.2	-0.1	-0.3	-0.3	-0.2	-0.2
CPI(%)	-	-	-	-	0.2	0.1	0.0	-0.1	-0.2	-0.3
GDEF(%GNPV) *	-	-	-	-	0.0	0.0	0.1	0.1	0.1	0.1
EXCH(%) **	-	-	-	-	-0.7	-0.8	-1.0	-2.1	-2.7	-3.0
CAB(B.US$) ***	-	-	-	-	-0.5	-0.4	-0.8	-1.0	-1.1	-1.0
UNITED KINGDOM										
GNP(%)	-	-	-	-	-0.1	-0.0	0.0	0.0	0.0	0.1
CPI(%)	-	-	-	-	0.0	-0.0	-0.1	-0.1	-0.1	-0.2
GDEF(%GNPV) *	-	-	-	-	0.0	0.0	0.0	0.0	0.0	0.0
EXCH(%) **	-	-	-	-	-0.3	-0.9	-1.1	-1.8	-2.4	-2.8
CAB(B.US$) ***	-	-	-	-	-0.6	-0.6	-1.1	-1.3	-1.4	-1.6
ITALY										
GNP(%)	-	-	-	-	-0.2	-0.2	-0.3	-0.4	-0.4	-0.5
CPI(%)	-	-	-	-	0.1	0.2	0.1	0.1	0.0	-0.1
GDEF(%GNPV) *	-	-	-	-	0.1	0.0	0.1	0.1	0.1	0.1
EXCH(%) **	-	-	-	-	-0.6	-1.2	-1.3	-2.1	-2.5	-2.7
CAB(B.US$) ***	-	-	-	-	-0.4	-0.3	-0.4	-0.6	-0.7	-0.6
CANADA										
GNP(%)	-	-	-	-	-1.1	-0.9	-0.8	-0.5	-0.1	0.2
CPI(%)	-	-	-	-	0.3	0.2	0.2	0.1	0.2	0.2
GDEF(%GNPV) *	-	-	-	-	0.4	0.3	0.3	0.2	0.1	0.1
EXCH(%) **	-	-	-	-	-0.8	-1.9	-2.8	-3.5	-4.1	-4.6
CAB(B.US$) ***	-	-	-	-	-1.1	-1.1	-1.3	-1.3	-1.2	-1.4
REST OF WORLD										
CAB(B.US$) ***	-	-	-	-	-5.5	-3.3	-5.1	-4.2	-2.9	-2.1

* Government deficit as a percentage of baseline nominal GNP.
** Exchange rate : Bilateral rate against U.S. $ ($/local currency).
*** Local currency units translated into U.S. $ at baseline exchange rates.

Model: WHARTON
Simulation D: U.S. Monetary Expansion with foreign Monetary Aggregates Unchanged from Baseline
(Deviation of Shock Path from Baseline Path)

	1985 Q1	1985 Q2	1985 Q3	1985 Q4	1985	1986	1987	1988	1989	1990
UNITED STATES										
GNPV(%)	-	-	-	-	0.3	0.7	1.0	1.2	1.3	1.4
GNP(%)	-	-	-	-	0.4	0.7	0.8	0.9	0.9	1.0
PGNP(%)	-	-	-	-	-0.0	0.1	0.2	0.3	0.4	0.4
CPI(%)	-	-	-	-	-0.0	0.0	0.2	0.3	0.4	0.4
WAGES(%)	-	-	-	-	0.1	0.3	0.4	0.6	0.7	0.8
UN(% PTS)	-	-	-	-	-0.1	-0.3	-0.4	-0.4	-0.4	-0.5
GNP(B.72$)	-	-	-	-	6.0	11.8	13.6	15.5	16.8	17.9
G(B.72$)	-	-	-	-	0.0	0.0	-0.0	-0.0	0.0	0.0
C(B.72$)	-	-	-	-	2.5	4.8	5.5	6.3	6.8	7.5
IFP(B.72$)	-	-	-	-	4.8	9.0	10.8	11.9	12.5	12.0
II(B.72$)	-	-	-	-	0.0	0.0	-0.0	-0.0	0.0	0.0
XGS(B.72$)	-	-	-	-	0.0	0.9	1.1	1.6	2.1	2.7
MGS(B.72$)	-	-	-	-	1.1	2.2	2.9	3.4	3.6	3.5
M1(%)	-	-	-	-	4.0	4.0	4.0	4.0	4.0	4.0
RS(% PTS)	-	-	-	-	-2.2	-2.1	-2.1	-2.1	-2.2	-2.2
RL(% PTS)	-	-	-	-	-1.0	-1.6	-2.0	-2.3	-2.5	-2.7
GDEF(B$)	-	-	-	-	-3.9	-8.4	-10.7	-12.8	-14.6	-15.1
PXGS(%)	-	-	-	-	-0.0	0.0	0.1	0.2	0.3	0.4
PMGS(%)	-	-	-	-	0.1	0.4	0.6	0.9	1.1	1.4
EXCH(%) *	-	-	-	-	-0.1	-1.0	-2.0	-2.8	-3.8	-5.3
CAB(B$)	-	-	-	-	-2.9	-5.1	-7.5	-8.7	-9.1	-8.0
NON-US OECD										
GNPV(%) **	-	-	-	-	0.1	0.3	0.2	0.1	0.0	-0.1
GNP(%) **	-	-	-	-	0.1	0.4	0.4	0.4	0.4	0.3
PGNP(%)	-	-	-	-	-0.0	-0.2	-0.2	-0.2	-0.3	-0.5
CPI(%)	-	-	-	-	-0.0	-0.1	-0.2	-0.2	-0.3	-0.5
WAGES(%)	-	-	-	-	0.0	0.1	0.1	0.1	0.1	-0.0
UN(% PTS)	-	-	-	-	-0.0	-0.1	-0.1	-0.1	-0.1	-0.1
C(%) **	-	-	-	-	0.1	0.3	0.3	0.3	0.3	0.4
IFP(%) **	-	-	-	-	0.4	0.9	0.9	1.0	1.0	1.0
RS(% PTS)	-	-	-	-	-1.3	-1.3	-1.3	-1.4	-1.5	-1.7
RL(% PTS)	-	-	-	-	-0.5	-0.7	-0.9	-1.0	-1.1	-1.1
GDEF (B.US$) **	-	-	-	-	-1.5	-6.7	-6.6	-7.6	-8.0	-8.3
PXGS(%)	-	-	-	-	-0.1	-0.3	-0.8	-1.4	-1.9	-2.8
PMGS(%)	-	-	-	-	-0.1	-0.4	-1.1	-1.9	-2.7	-3.7
EXCH(%) ***	-	-	-	-	0.1	1.0	2.1	2.9	4.0	5.6
CAB(B.US$) **	-	-	-	-	0.0	5.3	2.8	2.5	1.9	1.6

* Exchange rate : (Weighted average of foreign currencies)/U.S. $.
** Local currency units translated into U.S. $ at baseline exchange rates.
*** Exchange rate : U.S. $/(weighted average of non-US OECD currencies).

Model: WHARTON
Simulation D: U.S. Monetary Expansion with Foreign Monetary Aggregates Unchanged from Baseline
(Deviation of Shock Path from Baseline Path)

	1985 Q1	1985 Q2	1985 Q3	1985 Q4	1985	1986	1987	1988	1989	1990
JAPAN										
GNP(%)	-	-	-	-	0.1	0.3	0.1	-0.1	-0.4	-0.9
CPI(%)	-	-	-	-	-0.0	-0.2	-0.4	-0.7	-1.2	-1.9
RS(% PTS)	-	-	-	-	0.0	-0.0	-0.1	-0.3	-0.5	-0.8
GDEF(%GNPV) *	-	-	-	-	-0.0	-0.1	-0.0	-0.0	0.0	0.1
EXCH(%) **	-	-	-	-	0.3	2.2	5.1	8.5	12.7	18.1
CAB(B.US$) ***	-	-	-	-	0.4	2.0	1.0	0.3	-1.2	-2.6
GERMANY										
GNP(%)	-	-	-	-	0.1	0.5	0.4	0.4	0.4	0.5
CPI(%)	-	-	-	-	-0.0	-0.0	0.1	0.1	0.2	0.2
RS(% PTS)	-	-	-	-	-1.8	-1.7	-1.7	-1.8	-1.9	-2.0
GDEF(%GNPV) *	-	-	-	-	-0.0	-0.2	-0.2	-0.2	-0.2	-0.2
EXCH(%) **	-	-	-	-	0.1	0.4	0.9	1.0	1.2	1.9
CAB(B.US$) ***	-	-	-	-	0.0	1.2	0.9	1.2	1.6	2.1
FRANCE										
GNP(%)	-	-	-	-	0.1	0.4	0.3	0.3	0.3	0.4
CPI(%)	-	-	-	-	-0.0	-0.3	-0.5	-0.5	-0.5	-0.6
GDEF(%GNPV) *	-	-	-	-	-0.0	-0.1	-0.1	-0.1	-0.1	-0.1
EXCH(%) **	-	-	-	-	0.1	1.5	2.2	2.3	2.3	3.0
CAB(B.US$) ***	-	-	-	-	0.0	0.6	0.3	0.2	0.2	0.4
UNITED KINGDOM										
GNP(%)	-	-	-	-	0.2	0.4	0.4	0.4	0.4	0.4
CPI(%)	-	-	-	-	-0.0	0.0	0.2	0.4	0.6	0.8
GDEF(%GNPV) *	-	-	-	-	-0.1	-0.1	-0.1	-0.1	-0.1	-0.1
EXCH(%) **	-	-	-	-	-0.0	0.2	0.3	-0.0	-0.3	-0.3
CAB(B.US$) ***	-	-	-	-	-0.3	-0.3	-0.8	-0.9	-0.9	-1.1
ITALY										
GNP(%)	-	-	-	-	0.1	0.4	0.6	0.7	0.9	1.0
CPI(%)	-	-	-	-	-0.0	-0.2	-0.3	-0.3	-0.2	-0.2
GDEF(%GNPV) *	-	-	-	-	-0.0	-0.1	-0.1	-0.2	-0.2	-0.3
EXCH(%) **	-	-	-	-	0.1	0.6	1.2	1.1	0.9	1.2
CAB(B.US$) ***	-	-	-	-	-0.0	0.3	0.2	0.3	0.3	0.5
CANADA										
GNP(%)	-	-	-	-	0.3	0.8	0.8	0.9	0.9	0.8
CPI(%)	-	-	-	-	-0.1	-0.2	-0.1	-0.1	-0.1	-0.1
GDEF(%GNPV) *	-	-	-	-	-0.1	-0.3	-0.3	-0.3	-0.3	-0.3
EXCH(%) **	-	-	-	-	0.1	0.4	0.8	1.2	1.5	1.9
CAB(B.US$) ***	-	-	-	-	0.1	0.4	0.3	0.3	0.3	0.3
REST OF WORLD										
CAB(B.US$) ***	-	-	-	-	0.9	4.9	3.6	4.3	4.7	4.6

* Government deficit as a percentage of baseline nominal GNP.
** Exchange rate : Bilateral rate against U.S. $ ($/local currency).
*** Local currency units translated into U.S. $ at baseline exchange rates.

Model: WHARTON

Simulation E: U.S. Monetary Expansion with Foreign Short-Term Interest Rates Unchanged from Baseline

(Deviation of Shock Path from Baseline Path)

	1985									
	Q1	Q2	Q3	Q4	1985	1986	1987	1988	1989	1990
UNITED STATES										
GNPV(%)	-	-	-	-	0.3	0.7	1.0	1.2	1.3	1.4
GNP(%)	-	-	-	-	0.4	0.7	0.8	0.9	0.9	1.0
PGNP(%)	-	-	-	-	-0.0	0.0	0.2	0.3	0.4	0.4
CPI(%)	-	-	-	-	-0.0	0.0	0.2	0.3	0.4	0.5
WAGES(%)	-	-	-	-	0.1	0.3	0.4	0.6	0.7	0.8
UN(% PTS)	-	-	-	-	-0.1	-0.3	-0.3	-0.4	-0.4	-0.5
GNP(B.72$)	-	-	-	-	6.0	11.7	13.6	15.7	17.2	18.4
G(B.72$)	-	-	-	-	0.0	0.0	0.0	0.0	0.0	0.0
C(B.72$)	-	-	-	-	2.5	4.8	5.4	6.3	6.9	7.6
IFP(B.72$)	-	-	-	-	4.8	8.9	10.8	12.0	12.6	12.1
II(B.72$)	-	-	-	-	0.0	0.0	-0.0	-0.0	0.0	0.0
XGS(B.72$)	-	-	-	-	0.0	0.8	1.0	1.5	2.0	2.5
MGS(B.72$)	-	-	-	-	1.1	2.1	2.7	3.1	3.3	3.2
M1(%)	-	-	-	-	4.0	4.0	4.0	4.0	4.0	4.0
RS(% PTS)	-	-	-	-	-2.2	-2.1	-2.1	-2.1	-2.2	-2.2
RL(% PTS)	-	-	-	-	-1.0	-1.6	-2.0	-2.3	-2.5	-2.7
GDEF(B$)	-	-	-	-	-3.9	-8.3	-10.6	-12.8	-14.7	-15.3
PXGS(%)	-	-	-	-	-0.0	0.0	0.1	0.2	0.3	0.4
PMGS(%)	-	-	-	-	0.1	0.4	0.7	1.0	1.2	1.5
EXCH(%) *	-	-	-	-	-0.1	-1.1	-2.2	-3.1	-4.1	-5.7
CAB(B$)	-	-	-	-	-2.9	-5.3	-7.7	-9.0	-9.3	-8.3
NON-US OECD										
GNPV(%) **	-	-	-	-	0.1	0.2	0.1	-0.0	-0.2	-0.4
GNP(%) **	-	-	-	-	0.1	0.3	0.2	0.2	0.1	0.1
PGNP(%)	-	-	-	-	-0.0	-0.1	-0.1	-0.2	-0.3	-0.5
CPI(%)	-	-	-	-	-0.0	-0.1	-0.2	-0.2	-0.4	-0.6
WAGES(%)	-	-	-	-	0.0	0.1	0.1	0.0	-0.0	-0.2
UN(% PTS)	-	-	-	-	-0.0	-0.0	-0.1	-0.1	-0.1	-0.1
C(%) **	-	-	-	-	0.0	0.2	0.2	0.2	0.2	0.2
IFP(%) **	-	-	-	-	0.2	0.6	0.5	0.5	0.5	0.5
RS(% PTS)	-	-	-	-	0.0	0.0	0.0	0.0	0.0	0.0
RL(% PTS)	-	-	-	-	-0.1	-0.2	-0.2	-0.2	-0.2	-0.2
GDEF (B.US$) **	-	-	-	-	-1.0	-5.3	-4.4	-4.7	-4.2	-3.8
PXGS(%)	-	-	-	-	-0.1	-0.3	-0.8	-1.4	-2.0	-2.8
PMGS(%)	-	-	-	-	-0.1	-0.4	-1.2	-2.0	-2.8	-3.8
EXCH(%) ***	-	-	-	-	0.1	1.1	2.3	3.2	4.3	6.0
CAB(B.US$) **	-	-	-	-	0.5	5.7	3.3	3.1	2.4	2.1

* Exchange rate : (Weighted average of foreign currencies)/U.S. $.

** Local currency units translated into U.S. $ at baseline exchange rates.

*** Exchange rate : U.S. $/(weighted average of non-US OECD currencies).

Model: WHARTON
Simulation E: U.S. Monetary Expansion with Foreign Short-Term Interest Rates Unchanged from Baseline
(Deviation of Shock Path from Baseline Path)

	1985 Q1	1985 Q2	1985 Q3	1985 Q4	1985	1986	1987	1988	1989	1990
JAPAN										
GNP(%)	-	-	-	-	0.1	0.3	0.1	-0.2	-0.5	-0.9
CPI(%)	-	-	-	-	-0.0	-0.2	-0.4	-0.7	-1.1	-1.8
RS(% PTS)	-	-	-	-	0.0	0.0	0.0	0.0	0.0	0.0
GDEF(%GNPV) *	-	-	-	-	-0.0	-0.1	-0.0	0.0	0.0	0.1
EXCH(%) **	-	-	-	-	0.3	2.2	5.0	8.2	12.4	17.5
CAB(B.US$) ***	-	-	-	-	0.4	1.9	0.9	0.2	-1.3	-2.6
GERMANY										
GNP(%)	-	-	-	-	0.0	0.4	0.2	0.2	0.2	0.2
CPI(%)	-	-	-	-	-0.0	-0.0	0.1	0.1	0.1	0.1
RS(% PTS)	-	-	-	-	0.0	0.0	0.0	0.0	0.0	0.0
GDEF(%GNPV) *	-	-	-	-	-0.0	-0.2	-0.1	-0.1	-0.1	-0.1
EXCH(%) **	-	-	-	-	0.1	0.6	1.2	1.5	1.8	2.6
CAB(B.US$) ***	-	-	-	-	0.1	1.3	0.9	1.3	1.6	2.1
FRANCE										
GNP(%)	-	-	-	-	0.0	0.2	0.0	-0.1	-0.1	-0.2
CPI(%)	-	-	-	-	-0.0	-0.3	-0.3	-0.4	-0.4	-0.5
GDEF(%GNPV) *	-	-	-	-	-0.0	-0.0	-0.0	-0.0	-0.0	-0.0
EXCH(%) **	-	-	-	-	0.1	1.6	2.6	2.9	3.3	4.3
CAB(B.US$) ***	-	-	-	-	0.1	0.7	0.5	0.5	0.6	0.8
UNITED KINGDOM										
GNP(%)	-	-	-	-	0.2	0.4	0.3	0.3	0.3	0.4
CPI(%)	-	-	-	-	-0.0	0.0	0.2	0.4	0.6	0.7
GDEF(%GNPV) *	-	-	-	-	-0.1	-0.1	-0.1	-0.1	-0.1	-0.0
EXCH(%) **	-	-	-	-	-0.0	0.2	0.4	0.2	0.0	0.2
CAB(B.US$) ***	-	-	-	-	-0.3	-0.4	-0.8	-1.0	-1.1	-1.3
ITALY										
GNP(%)	-	-	-	-	0.1	0.3	0.4	0.5	0.6	0.7
CPI(%)	-	-	-	-	-0.0	-0.1	-0.2	-0.3	-0.3	-0.2
GDEF(%GNPV) *	-	-	-	-	-0.0	-0.1	-0.1	-0.1	-0.2	-0.2
EXCH(%) **	-	-	-	-	0.1	0.8	1.5	1.6	1.6	2.1
CAB(B.US$) ***	-	-	-	-	0.0	0.4	0.3	0.4	0.5	0.6
CANADA										
GNP(%)	-	-	-	-	0.2	0.6	0.5	0.5	0.5	0.3
CPI(%)	-	-	-	-	-0.1	-0.1	-0.1	-0.1	-0.2	-0.2
GDEF(%GNPV) *	-	-	-	-	-0.1	-0.2	-0.2	-0.2	-0.1	-0.1
EXCH(%) **	-	-	-	-	0.1	0.6	1.1	1.6	2.1	2.6
CAB(B.US$) ***	-	-	-	-	0.2	0.6	0.6	0.6	0.6	0.6
REST OF WORLD										
CAB(B.US$) ***	-	-	-	-	0.9	4.0	2.3	2.3	2.0	1.1

* Government deficit as a percentage of baseline nominal GNP.
** Exchange rate : Bilateral rate against U.S. $ ($/local currency).
*** Local currency units translated into U.S. $ at baseline exchange rates.

Model: WHARTON
Simulation F: Nonpolicy Exogenous Depreciation of the Dollar
(Deviation of Shock Path from Baseline Path)

	1985									
	Q1	Q2	Q3	Q4	1985	1986	1987	1988	1989	1990
UNITED STATES										
GNPV(%)	-	-	-	-	0.3	1.0	2.0	2.8	3.2	3.3
GNP(%)	-	-	-	-	0.5	1.5	2.6	3.3	3.3	3.2
PGNP(%)	-	-	-	-	-0.2	-0.5	-0.6	-0.4	-0.1	0.1
CPI(%)	-	-	-	-	0.1	0.4	0.6	0.9	1.0	1.2
WAGES(%)	-	-	-	-	0.2	0.7	1.3	1.8	2.1	2.2
UN(% PTS)	-	-	-	-	-0.1	-0.3	-0.7	-1.0	-1.1	-1.1
GNP(B.72$)	-	-	-	-	8.3	26.1	46.1	59.2	61.4	59.2
G(B.72$)	-	-	-	-	0.0	0.0	0.0	0.0	0.0	0.0
C(B.72$)	-	-	-	-	1.3	6.0	12.2	17.9	20.3	21.2
IFP(B.72$)	-	-	-	-	1.2	4.0	7.0	8.7	8.0	6.2
II(B.72$)	-	-	-	-	0.0	0.0	-0.0	-0.0	-0.0	0.0
XGS(B.72$)	-	-	-	-	0.9	4.1	8.4	12.1	13.5	13.5
MGS(B.72$)	-	-	-	-	-2.6	-6.2	-9.0	-9.5	-8.7	-8.2
M1(%)	-	-	-	-	0.0	0.0	0.0	0.0	0.0	0.0
RS(% PTS)	-	-	-	-	0.2	0.6	1.3	1.9	2.3	2.4
RL(% PTS)	-	-	-	-	0.1	0.2	0.5	0.9	1.3	1.6
GDEF(B$)	-	-	-	-	-3.4	-13.2	-27.8	-42.2	-50.7	-50.4
PXGS(%)	-	-	-	-	1.2	1.9	2.2	1.6	0.9	1.0
PMGS(%)	-	-	-	-	3.4	8.0	11.7	12.1	10.2	9.7
EXCH(%) *	-	-	-	-	-10.1	-19.2	-27.4	-27.4	-27.4	-27.4
CAB(B$)	-	-	-	-	-1.0	-0.1	5.4	14.8	23.0	25.9
NON-US OECD										
GNPV(%) **	-	-	-	-	-0.3	-1.4	-3.3	-5.0	-6.4	-7.3
GNP(%) **	-	-	-	-	-0.3	-0.9	-2.0	-2.8	-3.3	-3.6
PGNP(%)	-	-	-	-	-0.0	-0.5	-1.3	-2.3	-3.1	-3.8
CPI(%)	-	-	-	-	-0.1	-0.8	-1.8	-2.9	-3.8	-4.5
WAGES(%)	-	-	-	-	-0.1	-0.7	-1.9	-3.4	-4.9	-6.2
UN(% PTS)	-	-	-	-	0.0	0.1	0.3	0.5	0.7	0.8
C(%) **	-	-	-	-	-0.1	-0.3	-0.8	-1.3	-1.8	-2.3
IFP(%) **	-	-	-	-	-0.3	-0.8	-1.8	-2.5	-3.0	-3.2
RS(% PTS)	-	-	-	-	0.0	0.1	0.1	0.1	0.2	0.2
RL(% PTS)	-	-	-	-	0.0	0.0	0.1	0.2	0.2	0.3
GDEF (B.US$) **	-	-	-	-	3.8	11.7	27.9	41.9	51.2	55.9
PXGS(%)	-	-	-	-	-0.9	-4.1	-8.0	-10.9	-12.2	-12.7
PMGS(%)	-	-	-	-	-1.3	-5.6	-10.7	-14.3	-15.6	-15.9
EXCH(%) ***	-	-	-	-	11.3	23.8	37.7	37.7	37.7	37.7
CAB(B.US$) **	-	-	-	-	-2.9	-8.0	-22.3	-33.4	-38.3	-35.3

* Exchange rate : (Weighted average of foreign currencies)/U.S. $.
** Local currency units translated into U.S. $ at baseline exchange rates.
*** Exchange rate : U.S. $/(weighted average of non-US OECD currencies).

Model: WHARTON
Simulation F: Nonpolicy Exogenous Depreciation of the Dollar
(Deviation of Shock Path from Baseline Path)

	1985 Q1	1985 Q2	1985 Q3	1985 Q4	1985	1986	1987	1988	1989	1990
JAPAN										
GNP(%)	-	-	-	-	-0.2	-0.5	-1.2	-1.6	-1.9	-2.0
CPI(%)	-	-	-	-	-0.1	-0.7	-1.7	-2.8	-3.7	-4.4
RS(% PTS)	-	-	-	-	-0.1	-0.5	-0.9	-1.2	-1.4	-1.6
GDEF(%GNPV) *	-	-	-	-	0.1	0.2	0.3	0.3	0.3	0.4
EXCH(%) **	-	-	-	-	11.1	23.5	37.2	37.2	37.2	37.2
CAB(B.US$) ***	-	-	-	-	-2.5	-5.6	-9.9	-11.4	-11.7	-11.5
GERMANY										
GNP(%)	-	-	-	-	-0.2	-0.9	-2.3	-3.5	-4.3	-4.5
CPI(%)	-	-	-	-	-0.1	-0.3	-0.6	-1.1	-1.6	-2.1
RS(% PTS)	-	-	-	-	0.1	0.4	0.7	0.9	0.9	0.8
GDEF(%GNPV) *	-	-	-	-	0.0	0.1	0.4	0.7	0.8	0.9
EXCH(%) **	-	-	-	-	11.1	23.5	37.2	37.2	37.2	37.2
CAB(B.US$) ***	-	-	-	-	0.1	1.0	0.3	-0.0	-0.1	0.5
FRANCE										
GNP(%)	-	-	-	-	-0.2	-0.8	-1.8	-2.8	-3.5	-3.8
CPI(%)	-	-	-	-	-0.0	-0.5	-1.0	-1.7	-2.5	-3.4
GDEF(%GNPV) *	-	-	-	-	0.0	0.1	0.2	0.3	0.5	0.6
EXCH(%) **	-	-	-	-	11.1	23.5	37.2	37.2	37.2	37.2
CAB(B.US$) ***	-	-	-	-	-0.1	-0.5	-2.0	-3.9	-4.8	-4.8
UNITED KINGDOM										
GNP(%)	-	-	-	-	-0.4	-0.9	-1.7	-2.1	-2.3	-2.3
CPI(%)	-	-	-	-	-0.1	-0.8	-2.2	-3.7	-5.1	-6.1
GDEF(%GNPV) *	-	-	-	-	0.1	0.2	0.4	0.5	0.5	0.5
EXCH(%) **	-	-	-	-	11.1	23.5	37.2	37.2	37.2	37.2
CAB(B.US$) ***	-	-	-	-	-0.2	-0.4	-0.6	-0.7	-0.2	1.1
ITALY										
GNP(%)	-	-	-	-	-0.0	-0.4	-1.4	-2.5	-3.4	-3.9
CPI(%)	-	-	-	-	-0.2	-0.8	-1.6	-2.1	-2.1	-2.1
GDEF(%GNPV) *	-	-	-	-	0.0	0.0	0.1	0.3	0.5	0.6
EXCH(%) **	-	-	-	-	11.1	23.5	37.2	37.2	37.2	37.2
CAB(B.US$) ***	-	-	-	-	0.2	0.8	0.8	0.6	-0.1	-0.4
CANADA										
GNP(%)	-	-	-	-	-1.0	-2.2	-3.5	-3.9	-3.9	-4.0
CPI(%)	-	-	-	-	0.2	-0.1	-0.7	-1.6	-2.1	-2.3
GDEF(%GNPV) *	-	-	-	-	0.2	0.6	1.1	1.3	1.3	1.2
EXCH(%) **	-	-	-	-	5.3	10.8	16.6	16.6	16.6	16.6
CAB(B.US$) ***	-	-	-	-	-0.2	-1.3	-2.9	-4.1	-4.5	-3.9
REST OF WORLD										
CAB(B.US$) ***	-	-	-	-	-2.7	-7.3	-12.0	-10.4	-8.5	-10.8

* Government deficit as a percentage of baseline nominal GNP.
** Exchange rate : Bilateral rate against U.S. $ ($/local currency).
*** Local currency units translated into U.S. $ at baseline exchange rates.

Model: WHARTON
Simulation G: Increase in Government Purchases in Non-U.S. OECD Countries with U.S. Policies Unchanged from Baseline
(Deviation of Shock Path from Baseline Path)

	1985									
	Q1	Q2	Q3	Q4	1985	1986	1987	1988	1989	1990
UNITED STATES										
GNPV(%)	-	-	-	-	0.2	0.2	0.1	0.0	-0.1	-0.2
GNP(%)	-	-	-	-	0.1	0.0	-0.1	-0.2	-0.3	-0.4
PGNP(%)	-	-	-	-	0.0	0.1	0.2	0.2	0.2	0.2
CPI(%)	-	-	-	-	-0.1	-0.0	-0.0	-0.0	-0.0	-0.1
WAGES(%)	-	-	-	-	0.0	0.0	-0.0	-0.0	-0.1	-0.2
UN(% PTS)	-	-	-	-	-0.1	-0.1	-0.0	-0.0	0.0	0.1
GNP(B.72$)	-	-	-	-	2.2	0.8	-1.7	-3.6	-6.3	-8.3
G(B.72$)	-	-	-	-	0.0	0.0	-0.0	-0.0	0.0	0.0
C(B.72$)	-	-	-	-	1.6	1.3	0.4	-0.1	-0.9	-1.5
IFP(B.72$)	-	-	-	-	0.7	0.5	-0.1	-0.5	-1.1	-1.3
II(B.72$)	-	-	-	-	0.0	0.0	-0.0	-0.0	0.0	0.0
XGS(B.72$)	-	-	-	-	1.9	2.5	2.5	2.7	2.8	3.3
MGS(B.72$)	-	-	-	-	1.4	2.4	3.0	3.7	4.5	5.4
M1(%)	-	-	-	-	0.0	0.0	0.0	0.0	0.0	0.0
RS(% PTS)	-	-	-	-	0.1	0.1	0.1	0.0	-0.0	-0.1
RL(% PTS)	-	-	-	-	0.0	0.0	0.0	0.0	0.0	-0.0
GDEF(B$)	-	-	-	-	-2.4	-2.7	-1.6	-0.4	1.4	2.7
PXGS(%)	-	-	-	-	-0.2	-0.3	-0.3	-0.4	-0.5	-0.9
PMGS(%)	-	-	-	-	-0.8	-1.2	-1.5	-1.7	-2.1	-2.7
EXCH(%) *	-	-	-	-	1.2	2.4	3.4	5.1	7.0	7.3
CAB(B$)	-	-	-	-	3.7	4.7	4.3	4.3	4.2	3.9
NON-US OECD										
GNPV(%) **	-	-	-	-	1.7	2.5	3.2	4.1	5.0	5.7
GNP(%) **	-	-	-	-	2.6	3.2	3.2	3.5	3.8	4.1
PGNP(%)	-	-	-	-	-0.8	-0.7	-0.0	0.6	1.1	1.5
CPI(%)	-	-	-	-	-1.0	-0.8	-0.1	0.5	1.2	1.6
WAGES(%)	-	-	-	-	0.3	0.7	1.6	2.6	3.7	4.7
UN(% PTS)	-	-	-	-	-0.2	-0.4	-0.6	-0.8	-0.9	-1.0
C(%) **	-	-	-	-	1.7	2.2	2.4	2.7	3.0	3.4
IFP(%) **	-	-	-	-	3.0	3.4	3.3	3.3	3.4	3.6
RS(% PTS)	-	-	-	-	0.6	0.8	0.9	1.1	1.3	1.4
RL(% PTS)	-	-	-	-	0.1	0.3	0.5	0.6	0.7	0.8
GDEF (B.US$) **	-	-	-	-	23.9	17.7	14.8	13.9	12.1	9.5
PXGS(%)	-	-	-	-	-0.7	-0.4	0.2	0.9	1.7	1.8
PMGS(%)	-	-	-	-	-0.3	0.3	1.0	1.8	2.9	2.9
EXCH(%) ***	-	-	-	-	-1.2	-2.4	-3.3	-4.8	-6.6	-6.8
CAB(B.US$) **	-	-	-	-	-8.9	-5.5	-7.0	-7.2	-7.9	-9.2

* Exchange rate : (Weighted average of foreign currencies)/U.S. $.
** Local currency units translated into U.S. $ at baseline exchange rates.
*** Exchange rate : U.S. $/(weighted average of non-US OECD currencies).

Model: WHARTON
Simulation G: Increase in Government Purchases in Non-U.S. OECD Countries with U.S. Policies Unchanged from Baseline
(Deviation of Shock Path from Baseline Path)

	1985 Q1	1985 Q2	1985 Q3	1985 Q4	1985	1986	1987	1988	1989	1990
JAPAN										
GNP(%)	-	-	-	-	2.7	3.0	2.8	2.8	2.8	2.8
CPI(%)	-	-	-	-	-1.2	-1.3	-1.0	-0.6	-0.2	0.1
RS(% PTS)	-	-	-	-	0.6	0.7	0.7	0.8	0.8	0.9
GDEF(%GNPV) *	-	-	-	-	0.8	0.7	0.7	0.6	0.6	0.5
EXCH(%) **	-	-	-	-	-0.6	-1.1	-1.5	-1.6	-1.5	-0.2
CAB(B.US$) ***	-	-	-	-	-1.4	0.6	1.3	2.7	3.5	4.5
GERMANY										
GNP(%)	-	-	-	-	2.4	3.5	3.8	4.3	4.9	5.5
CPI(%)	-	-	-	-	-0.5	0.1	0.9	1.5	2.0	2.4
RS(% PTS)	-	-	-	-	0.8	1.3	1.8	2.4	2.9	3.4
GDEF(%GNPV) *	-	-	-	-	0.3	-0.0	-0.2	-0.2	-0.3	-0.3
EXCH(%) **	-	-	-	-	-2.3	-4.5	-6.3	-9.0	-12.0	-13.6
CAB(B.US$) ***	-	-	-	-	-2.5	-2.7	-4.0	-5.4	-6.6	-7.8
FRANCE										
GNP(%)	-	-	-	-	2.8	3.2	3.1	3.1	3.4	3.7
CPI(%)	-	-	-	-	-1.9	-2.3	-1.8	-0.9	0.1	0.9
GDEF(%GNPV) *	-	-	-	-	0.5	0.4	0.2	0.1	0.1	-0.0
EXCH(%) **	-	-	-	-	-0.6	-0.8	-1.5	-3.6	-6.1	-6.9
CAB(B.US$) ***	-	-	-	-	-0.4	0.2	0.2	0.2	0.1	0.3
UNITED KINGDOM										
GNP(%)	-	-	-	-	1.7	1.6	1.5	1.5	1.6	1.8
CPI(%)	-	-	-	-	-0.6	0.0	1.0	1.8	2.6	3.1
GDEF(%GNPV) *	-	-	-	-	0.6	0.5	0.4	0.4	0.5	0.5
EXCH(%) **	-	-	-	-	-1.2	-2.9	-4.1	-6.0	-8.6	-9.4
CAB(B.US$) ***	-	-	-	-	-1.7	-2.3	-3.2	-3.8	-4.5	-5.7
ITALY										
GNP(%)	-	-	-	-	2.3	3.1	3.4	3.7	4.0	4.4
CPI(%)	-	-	-	-	-0.9	-1.1	-0.8	-0.4	0.1	0.3
GDEF(%GNPV) *	-	-	-	-	0.4	0.3	0.1	0.0	-0.1	-0.2
EXCH(%) **	-	-	-	-	-1.4	-2.7	-3.1	-4.8	-6.5	-6.5
CAB(B.US$) ***	-	-	-	-	-0.5	-0.5	-0.5	-0.3	-0.2	0.5
CANADA										
GNP(%)	-	-	-	-	2.2	2.5	2.6	2.9	3.1	3.3
CPI(%)	-	-	-	-	-0.4	-0.1	0.3	0.5	0.6	0.5
GDEF(%GNPV) *	-	-	-	-	0.3	0.2	0.2	0.2	0.1	0.1
EXCH(%) **	-	-	-	-	-0.7	-1.6	-2.4	-3.0	-3.5	-3.5
CAB(B.US$) ***	-	-	-	-	-1.2	-1.0	-1.2	-1.1	-0.9	-1.0
REST OF WORLD										
CAB(B.US$) ***	-	-	-	-	8.3	12.4	12.2	14.2	17.1	19.5

* Government deficit as a percentage of baseline nominal GNP.
** Exchange rate : Bilateral rate against U.S. $ ($/local currency).
*** Local currency units translated into U.S. $ at baseline exchange rates.

Model: WHARTON
Simulation H: Monetary Expansion in Non-U.S. OECD Countries
with U.S. Policies Unchanged from Baseline
(Deviation of Shock Path from Baseline Path)

	1985									
	Q1	Q2	Q3	Q4	1985	1986	1987	1988	1989	1990
UNITED STATES										
GNPV(%)	-	-	-	-	0.0	0.0	0.0	0.0	0.0	-0.0
GNP(%)	-	-	-	-	0.0	0.0	0.0	-0.0	-0.0	-0.0
PGNP(%)	-	-	-	-	0.0	-0.0	0.0	0.0	0.0	0.0
CPI(%)	-	-	-	-	0.0	0.0	0.0	0.0	0.0	0.0
WAGES(%)	-	-	-	-	0.0	0.0	0.0	0.0	0.0	0.0
UN(% PTS)	-	-	-	-	-0.0	-0.0	-0.0	-0.0	0.0	0.0
GNP(B.72$)	-	-	-	-	0.0	0.9	0.1	-0.1	-0.1	-0.2
G(B.72$)	-	-	-	-	0.0	0.0	0.0	0.0	0.0	0.0
C(B.72$)	-	-	-	-	0.0	0.3	-0.0	-0.1	-0.1	-0.1
IFP(B.72$)	-	-	-	-	0.0	0.2	0.0	-0.0	-0.1	-0.1
II(B.72$)	-	-	-	-	0.0	0.0	-0.0	-0.0	0.0	0.0
XGS(B.72$)	-	-	-	-	0.0	0.3	0.1	0.1	0.1	0.1
MGS(B.72$)	-	-	-	-	0.0	0.0	0.0	0.0	0.1	0.1
M1(%)	-	-	-	-	0.0	0.0	0.0	0.0	0.0	0.0
RS(% PTS)	-	-	-	-	0.0	0.0	0.0	0.0	0.0	-0.0
RL(% PTS)	-	-	-	-	0.0	0.0	0.0	0.0	0.0	0.0
GDEF(B$)	-	-	-	-	-0.0	-0.7	-0.3	-0.2	-0.2	-0.1
PXGS(%)	-	-	-	-	-0.0	-0.0	0.0	0.0	-0.0	-0.0
PMGS(%)	-	-	-	-	-0.0	0.1	0.0	-0.0	-0.0	-0.0
EXCH(%) *	-	-	-	-	-0.0	-0.2	-0.1	0.0	0.1	0.1
CAB(B$)	-	-	-	-	0.0	0.5	0.2	0.2	0.3	0.2
NON-US OECD										
GNPV(%) **	-	-	-	-	0.0	0.1	0.1	0.1	0.1	0.1
GNP(%) **	-	-	-	-	0.0	0.2	0.1	0.1	0.1	0.1
PGNP(%)	-	-	-	-	-0.0	-0.1	0.0	0.0	0.0	0.0
CPI(%)	-	-	-	-	-0.0	-0.1	-0.0	0.0	0.0	0.0
WAGES(%)	-	-	-	-	0.0	0.0	0.0	0.1	0.1	0.1
UN(% PTS)	-	-	-	-	-0.0	-0.0	-0.0	-0.0	-0.0	-0.0
C(%) **	-	-	-	-	0.0	0.1	0.1	0.0	0.1	0.1
IFP(%) **	-	-	-	-	0.1	0.3	0.2	0.2	0.2	0.3
RS(% PTS)	-	-	-	-	-0.9	-0.8	-0.8	-0.8	-0.8	-0.7
RL(% PTS)	-	-	-	-	-0.3	-0.4	-0.4	-0.4	-0.4	-0.5
GDEF (B.US$) **	-	-	-	-	-0.4	-2.8	-1.0	-1.1	-1.5	-1.7
PXGS(%)	-	-	-	-	-0.0	-0.0	-0.1	-0.0	-0.0	0.0
PMGS(%)	-	-	-	-	-0.0	0.0	-0.1	-0.1	0.0	0.0
EXCH(%) ***	-	-	-	-	0.0	0.2	0.1	-0.0	-0.1	-0.1
CAB(B.US$) **	-	-	-	-	-0.2	2.6	-0.7	-0.9	-0.4	-0.4

* Exchange rate : (Weighted average of foreign currencies)/U.S. $.
** Local currency units translated into U.S. $ at baseline exchange rates.
*** Exchange rate : U.S. $/(weighted average of non-US OECD currencies).

Model: WHARTON
Simulation H: Monetary Expansion in Non-U.S. OECD Countries with U.S. Policies Unchanged from Baseline
(Deviation of Shock Path from Baseline Path)

	1985									
	Q1	Q2	Q3	Q4	1985	1986	1987	1988	1989	1990
JAPAN										
GNP(%)	-	-	-	-	0.1	0.3	0.1	0.1	0.1	0.1
CPI(%)	-	-	-	-	-0.0	-0.1	-0.1	-0.1	-0.0	-0.0
RS(% PTS)	-	-	-	-	-1.3	-1.3	-1.4	-1.4	-1.4	-1.4
GDEF(%GNPV) *	-	-	-	-	-0.0	-0.0	-0.0	-0.0	-0.0	-0.0
EXCH(%) **	-	-	-	-	-0.0	0.3	0.3	0.1	0.1	0.1
CAB(B.US$) ***	-	-	-	-	-0.1	0.6	-0.4	-0.4	-0.2	-0.1
GERMANY										
GNP(%)	-	-	-	-	0.0	0.3	0.1	0.1	0.1	0.1
CPI(%)	-	-	-	-	-0.0	-0.0	0.1	0.1	0.1	0.1
RS(% PTS)	-	-	-	-	-0.7	-0.6	-0.6	-0.5	-0.5	-0.5
GDEF(%GNPV) *	-	-	-	-	-0.0	-0.1	-0.0	-0.0	-0.0	-0.0
EXCH(%) **	-	-	-	-	0.0	-0.0	-0.1	-0.2	-0.3	-0.2
CAB(B.US$) ***	-	-	-	-	-0.0	0.6	-0.1	-0.1	0.1	0.1
FRANCE										
GNP(%)	-	-	-	-	0.0	0.1	-0.0	-0.1	-0.0	0.0
CPI(%)	-	-	-	-	-0.0	-0.1	-0.1	-0.1	-0.1	-0.1
GDEF(%GNPV) *	-	-	-	-	-0.0	-0.0	-0.0	-0.0	-0.0	-0.0
EXCH(%) **	-	-	-	-	0.1	0.7	0.7	0.4	0.3	0.3
CAB(B.US$) ***	-	-	-	-	-0.0	0.3	-0.1	-0.3	-0.3	-0.3
UNITED KINGDOM										
GNP(%)	-	-	-	-	0.0	0.1	0.0	0.0	0.0	0.0
CPI(%)	-	-	-	-	-0.0	0.0	0.1	0.1	0.1	0.1
GDEF(%GNPV) *	-	-	-	-	-0.0	-0.0	-0.0	-0.0	-0.0	-0.0
EXCH(%) **	-	-	-	-	0.0	-0.0	-0.1	-0.2	-0.2	-0.2
CAB(B.US$) ***	-	-	-	-	0.0	0.2	-0.0	0.0	0.0	0.0
ITALY										
GNP(%)	-	-	-	-	0.1	0.2	0.2	0.2	0.3	0.4
CPI(%)	-	-	-	-	-0.0	-0.0	-0.0	-0.0	0.0	0.1
GDEF(%GNPV) *	-	-	-	-	-0.0	-0.1	-0.0	-0.1	-0.1	-0.1
EXCH(%) **	-	-	-	-	0.0	-0.0	-0.0	-0.3	-0.5	-0.6
CAB(B.US$) ***	-	-	-	-	-0.0	0.1	-0.2	-0.3	-0.4	-0.5
CANADA										
GNP(%)	-	-	-	-	0.0	0.1	-0.0	0.0	0.0	0.0
CPI(%)	-	-	-	-	-0.0	-0.0	0.0	0.0	-0.0	-0.0
GDEF(%GNPV) *	-	-	-	-	-0.0	-0.0	0.0	0.0	-0.0	-0.0
EXCH(%) **	-	-	-	-	0.0	0.0	-0.0	-0.0	-0.0	-0.0
CAB(B.US$) ***	-	-	-	-	0.0	0.1	-0.0	0.0	0.0	0.0
REST OF WORLD										
CAB(B.US$) ***	-	-	-	-	0.1	1.9	-0.1	-0.1	0.2	0.3

* Government deficit as a percentage of baseline nominal GNP.
** Exchange rate : Bilateral rate against U.S. $ ($/local currency).
*** Local currency units translated into U.S. $ at baseline exchange rates.

PART FOUR

Bibliographical References for Participating Models

Selected General References for Multicountry Models

Ball, R. J., ed. *The International Linkage of National Economic Models.* Amsterdam: North-Holland, 1973.

De Bever, L., and others. "Dynamic Properties of Four Canadian Macroeconomic Models: A Collaborative Research Project." *Canadian Journal of Economics* 12 (1979): 133–94.

de Grauwe, P., and T. Peters, eds. *Exchange Rates in Multicountry Econometric Models.* New York: St. Martin's Press, 1983.

Fair, R. C. "On Modeling the Economic Linkages among Countries." In *International Economic Policy: Theory and Evidence,* edited by R. Dornbusch and J. Frenkel, 209–39. Baltimore: Johns Hopkins University Press, 1979.

———. "Estimated Output, Price, Interest Rate, and Exchange Rate Linkages among Countries." *Journal of Political Economy* 90 (1982): 507–35.

Helliwell, J. F., and C. I. Higgins. "Macroeconomic Adjustment Processes." *European Economic Review* 7 (1976): 221–38.

Helliwell, J. F., and T. Padmore. "Empirical Studies of Macroeconomic Interdependence." In *Handbook of International Economics,* edited by R. W. Jones and P. B. Kenen, vol. 2. Amsterdam: North-Holland, 1984.

Hickman, B. G., ed. *Global International Economic Models.* Amsterdam: North-Holland, 1983.

Laffargue, J.-P. "Une methode d'évaluation interne des modeles multinationaux." *Annales de l'INSEE* 57 (1985): 119–44.

Larsen, F., J. Llewellyn, and S. Potter. "International Economic Linkages." *OECD Economic Studies* 1 (Autumn 1983): 43–91.

Sawyer, J. A., ed. *Modelling the International Transmission Mechanism.* Amsterdam: North-Holland, 1978.

Stevens, G., R. Berner, P. Clark, E. Hernandez-Cata, H. Howe, and S. Kwack. *The U.S. Economy in an International World: A Multicountry Model.* Washington, D.C.: Board of Governors of the Federal Reserve System, 1984.

DRI International Model

Brinner, R. "The 1985 DRI Model: Overview." In *Data Resources Review of the U.S. Economy,* 18–32. Lexington, Mass.: Data Resources/McGraw-Hill, September 1985.

Eckstein, O. *The DRI Model of the U.S. Economy.* New York: McGraw-Hill, 1983.

Frankcom, M. "Properties of the 1984A Version of the European Model." In *Data Resources European Review,* 65–72. London: Data Resources/McGraw-Hill, April 1984.

Gault, N. "Notes on the DRI Simulations." Memorandum prepared for the Brookings Conference on Empirical Macroeconomics for Interdependent Economies. Lexington, Mass.: Data Resources/McGraw-Hill, March 1986.

———. "The Current Account Block in the DRI Model of the U.S. Economy." Brookings Discussion Paper in International Economics 59-A. Washington, D.C.: Brookings, March 1987.

Johnson, S. "The International Sector." In *Data Resources Review of the U.S. Economy,* 26–36. Lexington, Mass.: Data Resources/McGraw-Hill, December 1985.

Napier, R. "The DRI/NIKKEI Japan Macroeconomic Model." In *Data Resources Japanese Economic Review,* 75–90. Lexington, Mass.: Data Resources/McGraw-Hill, Winter 1982.

Vasic, G. D., and A. Redhead. "Overview of the DRI Model of the Canadian Economy." Toronto: Data Resources/McGraw-Hill, 1983.

EEC Commission COMPACT Model

Dramais, A. "COMPACT-Prototype of a Macro Model for the European Community in the World Economy." Discussion Paper 27, 113–66. Commission of the European Communities, Directorate-General for Economic and Financial Affairs, March 1986.

Klein, L. R., and K. Marwah. "A Model of Foreign Exchange Markets: Endogenizing Capital Flows and Exchange Rates." *Zeitschrift für Nationaloekonomie,* supp. 3 (1983): 61–95.

Wymer, C. "Report on the Use of Macroeconomic Models in DG II" (unpublished memorandum). Brussels: Commission of the European Communities, Directorate-General II, May 1982.

EPA—Japanese Economic Planning Agency World Model

Amano, A., E. Kurihara, and L. Samuelson. "Trade Linkage Sub-Models in the EPA World Economic Model." *Economic Bulletin* 19. Tokyo: Economic Planning Agency (EPA), Economic Research Institute (ERI), 1980.

Amano, A., A. Marayama, and M. Yoshitomi. "A Three Country Linkage Model." EPA World Econometric Model Discussion Paper 9. Tokyo: EPA, ERI, September 1981.

———. "EPA World Economic Model," vol. 1: "Model Structure." EPA World Econometric Model Discussion Paper 11. Tokyo: EPA, ERI, March 1982.

———. "EPA World Economic Model," vol. 2: "Simulation Tests." EPA World Econometric Model Discussion Paper 11. Tokyo: EPA, ERI, March 1982.

Amano, A., A. Sadahiro, and T. Sasaki. "Structure and Application of the EPA World Economic Model." Discussion Paper 22. Tokyo: EPA, ERI, August 1981.

Amano, A., N. Yasuhara, F. Hida, and M. Akaike. "Exchange Rate Determination in the EMS: An Econometric Model." Discussion Paper 23. Tokyo: EPA, ERI, March 1983.

Amano, A., T. Kagawa, and M. Yoshitomi. "1982–83 World Economic Forecasts and Policy Simulations." EPA World Econometric Model Discussion Paper 15. Tokyo: EPA, ERI, January 1983.

Butlin, M. W. "The Financial Sector, Financial Sector Linkage and Multiplier Properties of the Economic Model of the Australian Economy." Discussion Paper 34. Tokyo: EPA, ERI, April 1985.

Cockerline, J. "A Model of the Canadian Financial and Capital Account Sectors." Discussion Paper 29. Tokyo: EPA, ERI, March 1984.

Economic Planning Agency, Economic Model Analysis Section, Planning Bureau. *Multi-Sectoral Economic Models for Medium and Long Term Analysis*. Summary of the Seventh Report of the Committee for Econometric Model Analysis.

Economic Planning Agency. *Study of International Policy Coordination in 1986–87*. A Policy Simulation Exercise with the EPA World Economic Model. November 1985.

Economic Planning Agency, World Economic Model Group. "The EPA World Economic Model: An Overview." Discussion Paper 37. Tokyo: EPA, ERI, February 1986.

The Group of the Economic Planning Agency World Model. *A Study on Economic Policy Coordination with Specific Reference to the U.S. and Japan*. Tokyo: EPA, March 1986.

———. *Proceedings of the EPA International Symposium on Economic Interdependence Under Flexible Exchange Rates and the EPA World Economic Model of February 1984*. Part 1: Papers; part 2: Discussions. (M. Yoshitomi, chief economist.) Tokyo: EPA, 1984.

The Group of the EPA World Model and General Management Unit. *Proceedings of the EPA International Symposium on International Policy Coordination of March 1986*. (Y. Tsuruoka, chief economist.) Tokyo: EPA, 1986.

Helkie, W. L. "An Investigation of Alternative Equations for the U.S. Sector of the EPA World Model," and "A Method of Integrating the Oil Market into the EPA World Model." Discussion Paper 33. Tokyo: EPA, ERI, December 1984.

Holtham, G. H. "Consistent Modelling of Exchange Rates: Some Suggestions for Revising Exchange-Rate Determination in the EPA World Economic Model." Discussion Paper 39. Tokyo: EPA, ERI, December 1986.

Lewis, G. R. "The EPA and UK Treasury Macroeconomic Models of the UK Economy: Some Preliminary Comparisons." EPA World Econometric Model Discussion Paper 13. Tokyo: EPA, ERI, December 1982.

Samuelson, L., and E. Kurihara, "OECD Trade Linkage Methods Applied to the EPA World Econometric Model." *Economic Bulletin* 18. Tokyo: EPA, ERI, 1980.

Saville, I. D. "A Simple Aggregated Model of the UK Financial System." Discussion Paper 31. Tokyo: EPA, ERI, April 1984.

Shin, H., M. Yoshitomi, T. Sakuma, J. Kim, and K. Sakaguchi. "Korea: Econometric Model for Short-Term Prediction." EPA World Econometric Model Discussion Paper 12. Tokyo: EPA, ERI, June 1982.

Toyoda, T., J.-I. Itoh, and A. Nagahashi. "France: Econometric Model for Short-Term Prediction." EPA World Econometric Model Discussion Paper 10. Tokyo: EPA, ERI, January 1982.

Yashiro, N., and EPA Model Group. "Exchange Rate Adjustment and Macroeconomic Policy Coordination (Based on a Simulation by the Third Version of the Economic Planning Agency World Economic Model)." Discussion Paper 41. Tokyo: EPA, ERI, February 1987.

Yashiro, N., Y. Utsonomiya, and M. Nakasuka. "Simulation Results by EPA World Economic Model for the Brookings Workshop on U.S. Current Account Imbalance." Brookings Discussion Papers in International Economics 59-A. Washington, D.C.: Brookings, March 1987.

Yoshitomi, Masaru, and others. "EPA World Economic Model," vol. 1: "Model Properties and Multiplier Analysis"; vol. 2: "Model Structure";

vol. 3: "Multiplier Analysis (Detailed)." EPA World Econometric Model Discussion Paper 16. Tokyo: EPA, ERI, July 1984.

LINK Project World Model

Ball, R. J., ed. *The International Linkage of National Economic Models*. Amsterdam: North-Holland, 1973.

Beaumont, Paul, I. Prucha, and V. Filatov. "Performance of the LINK System: 1970 versus 1975 Base Year Trade Share Matrix." *Empirical Economics* 4 (1979): 11–42.

Bollino, C. A., and L. R. Klein. "World Recovery Strategies in the 80's: Is World Recovery Synonymous to LDC Recovery?" *Journal of Policy Modeling* 6, 2 (1984): 175–207.

Bollino, C. A., A. Onishi, P. Pauly, C. E. Petersen, and S. Shishido. "Global Impact of Oil Price Reductions and Official Development Assistance: Medium-Term Comparative Simulations with Alternative Global Econometric Models." *The Developing Economies* 22 (1984): 3–26.

de Grauwe, P., and T. Peters, eds. *Exchange Rates in Multicountry Econometric Models*. New York: St. Martin's Press, 1983.

Hickman, B. G. "Exchange Rates in Project LINK." In *Exchange Rates in Multicountry Econometric Models,* edited by P. de Grauwe and T. Peters. London: Macmillan, 1983.

———. "International Transmission of Economic Fluctuations and Inflation." In *International Aspects of Stabilization Policies,* edited by A. Ando, R. Herring, and R. Marston. Boston: Federal Reserve Bank of Boston, 1974.

———. "Project LINK and Multicountry Modelling." In *A History of Macro-Economic Model-Building,* edited by R. G. Bodkin, L. R. Klein, and K. Marwah. Forthcoming.

———. "Project LINK in 1972: Retrospect and Prospect." In *Modelling the Economy,* edited by G. A. Renton. London: Heinemann, 1975.

Hickman, B. G., and V. Filatov. "A Decomposition of International Income Multipliers." In *Global Econometrics: Essays in Honor of Lawrence R. Klein,* edited by F. G. Adams and B. G. Hickman. Cambridge, Mass.: MIT Press, 1983.

Hickman, B. G., and L. R. Klein. "A Decade of Research by Project Link." *Social Science Research Council Items* 33, 3–4 (1979): 49–56.

———. "Recent Developments in Project LINK." *Social Science Research Council Items* 39, 1–2 (1985): 7–11.

———. "Wage-Price Behavior in the National Models of Project LINK." *American Economic Review* 74 (May 1984, *Papers and Proceedings, 1983):* 150–54.

Hickman, B. G., and S. Schleicher. "The Interdependence of National Economies and the Synchronization of Economic Fluctuations: Evidence from the LINK Project." *Weltwirtschaftsliches Archiv* 114 (1978): 642–708.

Johnson, K. N., and L. R. Klein. "LINK Model Simulations of International Trade: An Evaluation of the Effects of Currency Realignment." *Journal of Finance, Papers and Proceedings* 29 (1974): 617–30.

———. "Stability in the International Economy: The LINK Experience." In *International Aspects of Stabilization Policies,* edited by A. Ando, R. Herring, and R. Marston. Boston: Federal Reserve Bank of Boston, 1974.

Klein, L. R. "Empirical Aspects of Protectionism: LINK Results." *Journal of Policy Modeling* 4, 2 (1982): 175–89.

———. "Project LINK: Entering a New Phase." *Social Science Research Council Items* 27 (1973): 13–16.

Klein, L. R., C. A. Bollino, and S. Fardoust. "Industrial Policy in the World Economy: Medium Term Simulations." *Journal of Policy Modeling* 4, 2 (1982): 174–89.

Klein, L. R., C. Moriguchi, and A. van Peeterssen. "The LINK Model of World Trade with Applications to 1972–73." In *International Trade and Finance,* edited by P. Kenen, 453–83. New York: Cambridge University Press, 1975.

Klein, L. R., P. Pauly, and P. Voisin. "The World Economy—A Global Model." *Perspectives in Computing* 2 (May 1982): 4–17.

Klein, L. R., and A. van Peetersson. "Forecasting World Trade within Project LINK." In *The International Linkage of National Economic Models,* edited by R. J. Ball, 429–63. Amsterdam: North-Holland, 1973.

Pauly, P. "Multi-Country Econometric Models: The State of the Art." Forthcoming.

Pauly, R., and C. E. Petersen. "Exchange Rate Responses in the LINK System." *European Economic Review* 30, 1 (1986): 149–70.

Sawyer, J. A., ed. *Modelling the International Transmission Mechanism*. Amsterdam: North-Holland, 1979.

Waelbroeck, J. L., ed. *The Models of Project LINK.* Amsterdam: North-Holland, 1976.

LIVERPOOL Model

Minford, A. P. L. "The Effects of American Policies—A New Classical Interpretation." In *International Economic Policy Coordination,* edited by W. H. Buiter and R. C. Marston, 84–130. Cambridge: Cambridge University Press, 1985.

Minford, A. P. L., P.-R. Agenor, and E. Nowell. "A New Classical Econometric Model of the World Economy." In *Economic Modelling.* Forthcoming.

Minford, A. P. L., C. Ioannidis, and S. Marwaha. "Rational Expectations in a Multilateral Macro Model." In *Exchange Rates in Multi-Country Econometric Models,* edited by P. de Grauwe and T. Peters, 239–66. New York: St. Martin's Press, 1983.

Minford, A. P. L., S. Marwaha, K. G. P. Matthews, and A. Sprague. "The Liverpool Macroeconomic Model of the United Kingdom." *Economic Modelling* 1 (1984): 24–62.

MCM—Multicountry Model of Federal Reserve Board Staff

Edison, H. J. "The U.K. Sector of the Federal Reserve's Multicountry Model: The Effects of Monetary and Fiscal Policies." *The Manchester School,* December 1986.

Edison, H. J., J. R. Marquez, and R. W. Tryon. "The Structure and Properties of the FRB Multicountry Model." International Finance Discussion Papers 293. Washington, D.C.: Board of Governors of the Federal Reserve System, 1986.

Edison, H. J., and R. Tryon. "An Empirical Analysis of Policy Coordination in the United States, Japan and Europe." International Finance Discussion Papers 286. Washington, D.C.: Board of Governors of the Federal Reserve System, 1986.

Haas, R. "MCM Intervention Functions." Federal Reserve Board memorandum, January 1981.

Haas, R., and S. A. Symansky. "Assessing Dynamic Properties of the MCM: A Simulation Approach." International Finance Discussion Paper 214. Washington, D.C.: Board of Governors of the Federal Reserve System, 1984.

Helkie, W. "A Forecasting Model for the U.S. Merchandise Trade Balance." International Finance Discussion Papers. Washington, D.C.: Board of Governors of the Federal Reserve System. Forthcoming.

———. "Simulations of the Federal Reserve U.S. Current Account Model." Brookings Discussion Papers in International Economics 59-B. Washington, D.C.: Brookings, March 1987.

Helkie, W., and P. Hooper. "The U.S. External Deficit in the 1980's: An Empirical Analysis." Brookings Discussion Papers in International Economics 56. Washington, D.C.: Brookings, March 1987. Published in *External Deficits and the Dollar: The Pit and the Pendulum,* edited by R. Bryant, G. Holtham, and P. Hooper. Washington, D.C.: Brookings, 1987.

Hooper, P. "International Repercussions of the U.S. Budget Deficit." International Finance Discussion Papers 246. Washington, D.C.: Board of Governors of the Federal Reserve System, 1984.

———. "Exchange Rate Simulation Properties of the MCM." *European Economic Review* 30 (1986): 121–98.

Hooper, P., R. Haas, S. Symansky, and L. Stekler. "Alternative Approaches to General Equilibrium Modeling of Exchange Rates and Capital Flows: The MCM Experience." In *Capital Flows and Exchange Rate Determination,* edited by L. Klein and W. Kreller, 29–60. Wien: Springer-Verlag, 1983.

Hooper, P., and R. Tryon. "Macroeconomic and Exchange Rate Effects of an Oil Price Shock under Alternative OPEC Investment Scenarios." In *Proceedings of the Fifth Pacific Basin Central Bank Economists' Conference: Supply Side Shocks, the Balance of Payments and Monetary Policy,* edited by K. Clinton. Ottawa: Bank of Canada, 1982.

Howe, H., E. Hernandez-Cata, G. Stevens, R. Berner, P. Clark, and S. Y. Kwack. "Assessing International Interdependence with a Multi-Country Model." *Journal of Econometrics* 15 (1981): 65–92.

Stevens, G., R. Berner, P. Clark, E. Hernandez-Cata, H. Howe, and S. Kwack. *The U.S. Economy in an International World: A Multicountry Model.* Washington, D.C.: Board of Governors of the Federal Reserve System, 1984.

Symansky, S., and R. Haas. "Alternative Financial Strategies: The Results of Some Policy Simulations with the Multi-Country Model." International Finance Discussion Paper 235. Washington, D.C.: Board of Governors of the Federal Reserve System, 1983.

MINIMOD—Haas/Masson Simulation Model

Haas, R. D., and P. R. Masson, "MINIMOD: Specification and Simulation Results." *Staff Papers* 33 (December 1986): 722–67. Washington, D.C.: International Monetary Fund.

Masson, P. R. "The Dynamics of a Two-Country Minimodel under Rational Expectations." Working Paper WP/86/2. Washington, D.C.: International Monetary Fund. Forthcoming in *Annales d'Economie et de Statistique*. INSEE, Paris.

MSG—McKibbin/Sachs Global Simulation Model

Ishii, N., W. McKibbin, and J. Sachs. "Macroeconomic Interdependence of Japan and the U.S.: Some Simulation Results." NBER Working Paper 1637. Cambridge, Mass.: National Bureau of Economic Research, June 1985. Revised as "The Economic Policy Mix, Policy Cooperation, and Protectionism: Some Aspects of Macroeconomic Interdependence among the United States, Japan, and Other OECD Countries." *Journal of Policy Modeling* 7, 4 (1985): 533–72.

McKibbin, W., and J. Sachs. "Comparing the Global Performance of Alternative Exchange Arrangements." NBER Working Paper 2024. Cambridge, Mass.: National Bureau of Economic Research, 1986. Also available as Brookings Discussion Paper in International Economics 49. Washington, D.C.: Brookings, August 1986.

———. "Coordination of Monetary and Fiscal Policies in the OECD." NBER Working Paper 1800. In *International Aspects of Fiscal Policies*, edited by J. Frenkel. Forthcoming.

———. "The MSG Model." Unpublished memorandum submitted at the March 1986 Brookings conference on Empirical Macroeconomics for Interdependent Economies. Harvard University Department of Economics, February 1986.

Sachs, J. "The Case for More Managed Exchange Rates." In *The U.S. Dollar-Recent Developments, Outlook, and Policy Options*. The Federal Reserve Bank of Kansas City, 1985.

———. "The Dollar and the Policy Mix, 1985." *Brookings Papers on Economic Activity* 1 (1985): 117–85.

Sachs, J., and W. McKibbin. "Macroeconomic Policies in the OECD and LDC External Adjustment." NBER Working Paper 1534. In *International Capital Flow and the Developing Countries*, edited by F. Colaco and S. van Wijnbergen. Forthcoming.

OECD INTERLINK Model

Model Structure and Research Contributing to the INTERLINK Model

Adams, F. G., H. Eguchi, and F. Meyer-zu-Schlochtern. "An Econometric Analysis of International Trade." Paris: OECD, 1969.

Blundell-Wignall, A., M. Rondoni, and H. Ziegelschmidt. "The Demand for Money and Velocity in Major OECD Countries." OECD, Economics and Statistics Department Working Paper 13. February 1984.

Coe, D. T. "Nominal Wages, the NAIRU and Wage Flexibility." *OECD Economic Studies* 5 (Autumn 1985), 87–126.

Coe, D. T., and F. Gagliardi. "Nominal Wage Determination in Ten OECD Economies." OECD, Economics and Statistics Department Working Paper 19. March 1985.

Helliwell, J., P. Sturm, P. Jarrett, and C. Salou. "Aggregate Supply in INTERLINK." OECD, Economics and Statistics Department Working Paper 26. November 1985.

———. "The Supply Side in OECD's Macroeconomic Model." *OECD Economic Studies* 6 (Spring 1986): 75–131.

Holtham, G. "Multinational Modelling of Financial Linkages and Exchange Rates." *OECD Economic Studies* 2 (Spring 1984): 51–92.

Holtham, G., and H. Kato. "Wealth and Inflation Effects in the Aggregate Consumption Function." OECD, Economics and Statistics Department Working Paper 35. July 1986.

Holtham, G., T. Saavalainen, P. Saunders, and H. Sutch. "Commodity Prices in INTERLINK." OECD, Economics and Statistics Department Working Paper 27. November 1985.

Llewellyn, G. E. J., and P. Richardson. "Representing Recent Policy Concerns in INTERLINK." *OECD Economic Studies* 5 (Autumn 1985): 169–80.

Llewellyn, G. E. J., L. W. Samuelson, and S. J. Potter. *Economic Forecasting and Policy*. London: Routledge and Keegan Paul, 1985.

Masson, P., and P. Richardson. "Exchange Rate Expectations and Current Balances in the OECD INTERLINK System." Reprinted in *Interna-*

tional Macroeconomic Modelling for Policy Decisions, edited by P. Artus and O. Guvenen. Boston: Nijhoff, 1986.

Meyer-zu-Schlochtern, F., and A. Yajima. "OECD Trade Model: 1970 Version." *OECD Ėconomic Outlook, Occasional Studies*. December 1970.

OECD. "The OECD International Linkage Model." *OECD Economic Outlook, Occasional Studies*. January 1979.

Richardson, P. "Tracking the U.S. External Deficit, 1980–1986: Experience with the OECD INTERLINK Model." Brookings Discussion Papers in International Economics 59-B. Washington, D.C.: Brookings, March 1987.

Samuelson, L. W. "A New Model of World Trade." *OECD Occasional Economic Studies*. December 1973.

Samuelson, L., and E. Kurihara. "OECD Trade Linkage Methods Applied to the EPA World Econometric Model." *Economic Bulletin* 18. Tokyo: Economic Planning Agency, Economic Research Institute, 1980.

INTERLINK-Related Simulation Studies

Blundell-Wignall, A., M. Rondoni, H. Ziegelschmidt, and J. Morgan. "Monetary Policy in the OECD INTERLINK Model." OECD, Economics and Statistics Department Working Paper 16. September 1984.

Larsen, F., and G. E. J. Llewellyn. "Simulated Macroeconomic Effects of a Large Fall in Oil Prices." OECD, Economics and Statistics Department Working Paper 8. June 1983.

Larsen, F., G. E. J. Llewellyn, and S. J. Potter. "International Economic Linkages." *OECD Economic Studies* 1 (Autumn 1983): 43–91.

Masson, P., A. Blundell-Wignall, and P. Richardson. "Domestic and International Effects of Government Spending under Rational Expectations." *OECD Economic Studies* 3 (Autumn 1984): 177–90.

Muller, P., and R. Price. "Structural Budget Deficits and Fiscal Stance." OECD, Economics and Statistics Department Working Paper 14. July 1984.

OECD. "Fiscal Policy Simulations with the OECD International Linkage Model. *OECD Economic Outlook, Occasional Studies*. July 1980.

———. "Effects of Hypothetical Exchange Rate Changes." Technical Annex to *OECD Economic Outlook* 30 (December 1981).

———. "Possible Effects of a Reduction in Energy Prices in the OECD Economy." Technical Annex to *OECD Economic Outlook* 31 (July 1982).

———. "Effects of Hypothetical Exchange Rate Changes." Technical Annex to *OECD Economic Outlook* 32 (December 1982).

———. Technical Notes to *OECD Economic Survey of Germany*. July 1984.

———. *OECD INTERLINK System, Operations Manual*. December 1984.

———. "Growth and Imbalances." *OECD Economic Outlook* 37 (June 1985).

———. "A Ready Reckoner of a Hypothetical Change of Energy Prices in the OECD Economy." Technical Annex to *OECD Economic Outlook* 39 (May 1986).

———. Technical Notes to *OECD Economic Survey of Canada*. July 1986.

TAYLOR Multicountry Model

Carlozzi, N., and J. B. Taylor. "International Capital Mobility and the Coordination of Monetary Policy Rules." In *Exchange Rate Management under Uncertainty,* edited by J. Bandhari. Cambridge, Mass.: MIT Press, 1985.

Dagli, C. A., and J. B. Taylor. "Estimation and Solution of Linear Rational Expectations Models Using a Polynomial Matrix Factorization." *Journal of Economic Dynamics and Control* 8 (1985): 341–48.

Taylor, J. B. "Estimation and Control of a Macroeconomic Model with Rational Expectations." *Econometrica* 47 (1979): 1267–87.

———. "An Econometric Business Cycle Model with Rational Expectations: Some Estimation Results." Unpublished working paper. Stanford University, 1979.

———. "An Econometric Business Cycle Model with Rational Expectations: Policy Evaluation Results." Unpublished working paper. Stanford University, 1979.

———. "New Econometric Techniques for Stochastic Models of Macroeconomic Fluctuations." In *Handbook of Econometrics,* edited by M. Intriligator and Z. Griliches. Amsterdam: North-Holland. Forthcoming.

———. "The Treatment of Expectations in Large Multicountry Econometric Models." In *Empirical Macroeconomics for Interdependent Economies,* vol. 1 of this publication.

———. *International Monetary Rules: A Rational Expectations Econometric Evaluation* (tentative title). Manuscript in preparation.

Taylor, J. B., with Tamim Bayoumi. "Simulations of the Current Account in a Multicountry Rational Expectations Econometric Model." In Brookings Discussion Papers in International Economics 59-A. Washington, D.C.: Brookings, March 1987.

VAR—Minneapolis World Vector Autoregression Model

Doan, T., R. Litterman, and C. Sims. "Forecasting and Conditional Projections Using Realistic Prior Distributions." *Econometric Reviews* 3, 1 (1984): 1–100.

Sims, C. "Are Forecasting Models Usable for Policy Analysis?" *Quarterly Review* 10 (Winter 1986): 2–16. Minneapolis, Minnesota: Federal Reserve Bank of Minneapolis.

———. "Identifying Policy Effects." In *Empirical Macroeconomics for Interdependent Economies,* vol. 1 of this publication.

Sims, C., and R. Litterman. "The Minneapolis World VAR." Memorandum. September 24, 1985.

WHARTON—World Model of Wharton Econometrics Associates

Ball, R. J. "The Economic Models of Project LINK." In *The International Linkage of National Economic Models*. Amsterdam: North-Holland, 1973, 65–107.

Gana, J. L., B. G. Hickman, L. J. Lau, and L. R. Jacobson. "Alternative Approaches to Linkage of National Econometric Models." In *Modelling the International Transmission Mechanism,* edited by J. A. Sawyer, 9–57. Amsterdam: North-Holland, 1978.

Green, J., and H. Howe. "Results from the WEFA World Model." Brookings Discussion Papers in International Economics 59-B. Washington, D.C.: Brookings, March 1987.

Hickman, B. G., and L. J. Lau. "Elasticities of Substitution and Export Demands in a World Trade Model." *European Economic Review* 4 (1973): 347–80.

Holbrook, R. S. "A Practical Method for Controlling a Large Non-Linear Stochastic System." *Annals of Economic and Social Measurement* 3 (January 1974): 155–76.

Johnson, K. N. "Balance of Payments Equilibrium and Equilibrating Exchange Rates in a World Econometric Model." Ph.D. dissertation, University of Pennsylvania, 1978.

Taplin, G. B. "A Model of World Trade." In *The International Linkage of National Economic Models,* edited by R. J. Ball, 177–223. Amsterdam: North-Holland, 1973.

UNCTAD Staff. "Regional Models of Developing Countries." In *The Models of Project LINK,* edited by J. L. Waelbroeck. Amsterdam: North-Holland, 1976.